Advance Praise for *Business Component Factory*

Probably the most confusing term in the IT industry today is **components**. *Like many terms in the field, it has been used and abused to refer to dozens of different, overlapping concepts. This is unfortunate, primarily because for the first time we have a term that can apply to the software nirvana of construction from (perhaps off-the-shelf) parts, without any reference to the underlying implementation technology such as objects. Herzum and Sims do an admirable job of differentiating the different component concepts, allowing this clearly-written book to focus on the construction of business systems by non-software practitioners, out of business component parts developed separately (and perhaps for a commodity component marketplace). This is the future of software systems, and this book is a practical, giant step in that direction.*

—Richard Mark Soley, Ph.D
Chairman and CEO, OMG

Finally, a book that takes you from component design all the way down to the middleware on which they are deployed. It's an important contribution to the nascent server-side component discipline written by practitioners for practitioners.

—Robert Orfali
Author of *Client/Server Survival Guide, 3E* and *Client/Server Programming with Java and CORBA, 2E*

With the ever-increasing push for component software there is consequential need for methods. Herzum and Sims limit the software component concept to what they call business components: intentionally coarse-grained components that directly map to business concepts. By proceeding to unfold an end-to-end approach to component software development, their book should be very useful for anyone considering the daunting task of adopting component software on an enterprise scale.

—Clemens Szyperski
Microsoft Research and author of the award-winning book
Component Software—Beyond Object-Oriented Programming
(from Addison-Wesley)

Herzum and Sims have made important contributions to the software industry through sharing their experience building enterprise systems with the OMG and the annual OOPSLA Business Object Component Workshop. In this latest book, they provide a groundbreaking view of the most recent concepts on component architecture, implementation, and deployment for software development teams. Recommended.

—Jeff Sutherland
CTO, IDX Systems Corp.
Chair, OOPSLA Business Object Component Workshop

The authors take their years of experience to provide a well thought out recipe for building large-scale distributed systems. You will come away from this book with an understanding of how to design and construct software in the large.

—Cory Casanave
President, Data Access Technologies

12 JAN 05

Dear Ralph,

nice to meet you.
I hope we will find ways
to collaborate

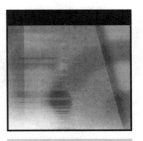

Business Component Factory
A Comprehensive Overview of Component-Based
Development for the Enterprise

Peter Herzum
Oliver Sims

(signature)

Wiley Computer Publishing

John Wiley & Sons, Inc.
NEW YORK · CHICHESTER · WEINHEIM · BRISBANE · SINGAPORE · TORONTO

Publisher: Robert Ipsen

Editor: Theresa Hudson

Assistant Editor: Kathryn Malm

Managing Editor: Brian Snapp

Text Design & Composition: NK Graphics, Inc.

Designations used by companies to distinguish their products are often claimed as trademarks. In all instances where John Wiley & Sons, Inc., is aware of a claim, the product names appear in initial capital or ALL CAPITAL LETTERS. Readers, however, should contact the appropriate companies for more complete information regarding trademarks and registration.

This book is printed on acid-free paper. ∞

Published by John Wiley & Sons, Inc.

Published simultaneously in Canada.

This publication is designed to provide accurate and authoritative information in regard to the subject matter covered. It is sold with the understanding that the publisher is not engaged in professional services. If professional advice or other expert assistance is required, the services of a competent professional person should be sought.

Library of Congress Cataloging-in-Publication Data:
Herzum, Peter, 1963–
    Business component factory : a comprehensive overview of
component-based development for the enterprise / by Peter Herzum and
Oliver Sims.
       p.   cm.
    "Wiley Computer Publishing."
    ISBN 0-471-32760-3 (cloth : alk. paper)
    1. Component software.   2. Object-oriented programming (Computer
science)   3. Business—Data processing.   I. Sims. Oliver. 1943–   .
II. Title.
QA76.76.C66H47   1999
658.4'038'02855117—dc21
                                                        99-43064
                                                          CIP

Printed in the United States of America.

10 9 8 7 6 5 4 3

OMG Press Advisory Board

OMG Press Books in Print

(For complete information about current and upcoming titles, go to *www.wiley.com/compbooks/omg/*)

Building Business Objects by Peter Eeles and Oliver Sims, ISBN: 0471-191760.

Business Component Factory: A Comprehensive Overview of Component-Based Development for the Enterprise by Peter Herzum and Oliver Sims, ISBN: 0471-327603.

Business Modeling with UML: Business Patterns at Work by Hans-Erik Eriksson and Magnus Penker, ISBN: 0471-295515.

CORBA 3 Fundamentals and Programming, 2nd Edition by Jon Siegel, ISBN: 0471-295183.

CORBA Design Patterns by Thomas J. Mowbray and Raphael C. Malveau, ISBN: 0471-158828.

Developing C++ Applications with UML by Michael Sandberg, ISBN: 0471-38304X.

Enterprise Application Integration with CORBA: Component and Web-Based Solutions by Ron Zahavi, ISBN: 0471-327204.

The Essential CORBA: Systems Integration Using Distributed Objects by Thomas J. Mowbray and Ron Zahavi, ISBN: 0471-106119.

Instant CORBA by Robert Orfali, Dan Harkey and Jeri Edwards, ISBN: 0471-183334.

Integrating CORBA and COM Applications by Michael Rosen and David Curtis, ISBN: 0471-198277.

Java Programming with CORBA, 2nd Edition by Andreas Vogel and Keith Duddy, ISBN: 0471-247650.

Mastering XMI: Java Programming with the XMI Toolkit, XML and UML by Stephen Brodsky and Tim Grose, ISBN: 0471-384291.

The Object Technology Casebook: Lessons from Award-Winning Business Applications by Paul Harmon and William Morrisey, ISBN: 0471-147176.

The Object Technology Revolution by Michael Guttman and Jason Matthews, ISBN: 0471-606790.

Programming with Enterprise JavaBeans, JTS and OTS: Building Distributed Transactions with Java and C++ by Andreas Vogel and Madhavan Rangarao, ISBN: 0471-319724.

Programming with Java IDL by Geoffrey Lewis, Steven Barber, and Ellen Siegel, ISBN: 0471-247979.

UML Toolkit by Hans-Erik Eriksson and Magnus Penker, ISBN: 0471-191612.

About the OMG

The Object Management Group (OMG) was chartered to create and foster a component-based software marketplace through the standardization and promotion of object-oriented software. To achieve this goal, the OMG specifies open standards for every aspect of distributed object computing from analysis and design, through infrastructure, to application objects and components.

The well-established CORBA (Common Object Request Broker Architecture) standardizes a platform- and programming-language-independent distributed object computing environment. It is based on OMG/ISO Interface Definition Language (OMG IDL) and the Internet Inter-ORB Protocol (IIOP). Now recognized as a mature technology, CORBA is represented on the marketplace by well over 70 ORBs (Object Request Brokers) plus hundreds of other products. Although most of these ORBs are tuned for general use, others are specialized for real-time or embedded applications, or built into transaction processing systems where they provide scalability, high throughput and reliability. Of the thousands of live, mission-critical CORBA applications in use today around the world, over 300 are documented on the OMG's success-story Web pages at www.corba.org.

CORBA 3, the OMG's latest release, adds a Component Model, quality-of-service control, a messaging invocation model, and tightened integration with the Internet, Enterprise Java Beans and the Java programming language. Widely anticipated by the industry, CORBA 3 keeps this established architecture in the forefront of distributed computing, as will a new OMG specification integrating CORBA with XML. Well-known for its ability to integrate legacy systems into your network, along with the wide variety of heterogeneous hardware and software on the market today, CORBA enters the new millennium prepared to integrate the technologies on the horizon.

Augmenting this core infrastructure are the CORBAservices which standardize naming and directory services, event handling, transaction processing, security, and other functions. Building on this firm foundation, OMG Domain Facilities standardize common objects throughout the supply and service chains in industries such as Telecommunications, Healthcare, Manufacturing, Transportation, Finance/Insurance, Electronic Commerce, Life Science, and Utilities.

The OMG standards extend beyond programming. OMG Specifications for analysis and design include the Unified Modeling Language (UML), the repository standard Meta-Object Facility (MOF), and XML-based Metadata Interchange (XMI). The UML is a result of fusing the concepts of the world's most prominent methodologists. Adopted as an OMG specification in 1997, it represents a collection of best engineering practices that have proven successful in the modeling of large and complex systems and is a well-defined, widely-accepted response to these business needs. The MOF is OMG's standard for metamodeling and metadata repositories. Fully integrated with UML, it uses the UML notation to describe repository metamodels. Extending this work, the XMI standard enables the exchange of objects defined using UML and the MOF. XMI can generate XML Data Type Definitions for any service specification that includes a normative, MOF-based metamodel.

In summary, the OMG provides the computing industry with an open, vendor-neutral, proven process for establishing and promoting standards. OMG makes all of its specifications available without charge from its Web site, www.omg .org. With over a decade of standard-making and consensus-building experience, OMG now counts about 800 companies as members. Delegates from these companies convene at week-long meetings held five times each year at varying sites around the world, to advance OMG technologies. The OMG welcomes guests to their meetings; for an invitation, send your email request to info@omg.org.

Membership in the OMG is open to end users, government organizations, academia, and technology vendors. For more information on the OMG, contact OMG headquarters by phone at 508-820-4300, by fax at 508-820-4303, by email at info@omg.org, or on the Web at www.omg.org.

Dedication

To Simona, my love, and to Solveig and Viveka, for the joy and meaning you bring to my life.

—P.H.

To David and Richard for lending their Dad, and to my wife Heather for most everything else.

—O.S.

Contents

About the Authors

Peter Herzum is internationally recognized as a pioneer of component-based development for large distributed systems, and has participated as consultant, methodologist, lead architect, and senior manager to many large-scale developments using components and object technology. In 1992, after extensive object-oriented experience, Peter started exploring the technical, architectural, methodological, and organizational challenges of enterprise-level component development, which later became the *business component approach*. He has also trained and mentored many organizations around the world in all aspects of cost-effective development of quality software. A frequent speaker at conferences across the world, and active member of the OMG, Peter is Chief Technology Officer and co-founder of Vayda & Herzum (www.vaydaherzum.com).

Oliver Sims is Director of Enterprise Component Programs with Genesis Development Corporation, and is widely recognized as a leader in the design and implementation of distributed business object and component systems. For a number of years he was Principal Architect on advanced component-based enterprise software, and prior to that worked as a Systems Consultant on large-scale business systems. Oliver has served on the OMG Architecture Board, and has been active in the OMG Business Object Domain Task Force since 1994. Author of *Business Objects* and co-author of *Building Business Objects*, he has many published articles to his credit. During his career, Oliver has accumulated significant practical experience across the industry, from some of the first distributed systems in the mid 1970s, through large transaction-based mainframe systems, to client-server and distributed component systems. About ten years ago Oliver originated the *cooperative business object* concept, which through innovative middleware and its use in operational business systems, first proved the synergy between distributed objects and component software.

Preface

Cost-effective software manufacturing is no longer a dream. Already a few organizations have been able to set up their software development to produce quality software cost-effectively and in a repeatable way, using a component-based approach. There is today a confluence of business drivers, technology, development processes, standards, and architectural maturity such that the dream of industrialized software production, which has been a goal of our industry for so long, may at last be achieved.

This book tries to capture and describe the principles, concepts, and practice of mastering the complexities of large-scale software development using components. It is now clear that cost-effective software manufacturing is not only a matter of technology, although, of course, technology is a necessary enabler. Neither is it only a matter of methodology or development process; these are only part of the puzzle. Rather, it requires all aspects of software development to be addressed with a coordinated and integrated set of concepts, architectures, methodology, and more. We call this integrated set of elements an "approach" to software development. This book presents a complete component-based approach, the *business component approach*, applying and extending component thinking to all aspects of development, deployment, run-time, and evolution, and it focuses on large-scale distributed business systems where high rates of change are the norm.

The business component approach is, we believe, the first approach entirely focused on components across the whole development lifecycle and set of architectural viewpoints. It is largely based on a new, holistic, and perhaps revolutionary core concept that we call the *business component*, and that addresses distribution realities, dependency reduction, and autonomous development and deployment in a single multifaceted software construct. The approach includes a conceptual framework that brings component thinking into the world of scalable systems and that makes sense of the different component granularities. It also includes a methodology that goes beyond current object-oriented methodologies to provide the concepts and thinking required to address the real challenges of component-based development for the enterprise.

Using the business component approach, this book describes how a blueprint for a *business component factory* can be created—a development capability able to produce software with the quality, speed, and flexibility needed to match business needs. In addition, the book provides a source of guidelines, practical tips, and architectural patterns that will help the reader understand and shorten the development cycle, and it assists in putting into perspective the various component technologies and development approaches existing today.

Why Should You Read This Book?

So what's different about this book? Well, first of all, *this book is entirely about components*. It is about the conceptual framework, development process, architectures, and practical tips needed to build components, and to assemble systems and federations of systems using components. Second, this book is about building large-scale business systems; not user interfaces only, nor embedded systems or real-time systems. It focuses on business systems for the enterprise. Third, this book is architecture-centric. At one time, some may have thought that a good methodology and process were all that really mattered. Certainly today, if forced to make a choice between a good methodology and a good architecture, we would always choose a good architecture. Of course, a repeatable process could be set up without a good architecture, and poor systems would be able to be built—over and over again.

This is not a marketing book. Building large distributed systems is complex, perhaps more complex than it should be. And component technology is still leading edge. We won't tell you that component-based development will solve all development problems. On the contrary, we'll point out the challenges, risks, and costs of adopting and using components. But we'll also suggest ways to meet the challenges and reduce the risks and costs. Many of the concepts and guidelines presented are a source of golden rules, tips, and tricks for any practitioner in the distributed system field.

Neither is this book another treatise on object-oriented development. We believe that object-oriented development is but one of many factors required to build component-based systems. But we'll talk about how object orientation is important in building components, and how object-oriented principles are applied throughout the development lifecycle in the context of the overall component-based approach.

Finally, this book is not focused on a specific technology. Rather, it describes the principles required by any large component-based business system development and explores how to think about such a development in order to preserve investments across the rapidly changing technologies. From experience, we know that the concepts presented can be implemented on all the major component technologies on the market today.

Who Is This Book For?

This book is, first of all, for anyone involved in, or learning about, or interested in the application of component thinking to business software development, and in the underlying architectures, processes, design techniques, and patterns that are necessary to support the coming revolution in software productivity.

But it is also important for those interested in cost-effective software manufacturing and in building business solutions today.

It is particularly important for the following people:

- Anyone about to embark on a component-based development and who would like an insight into what's ahead. Or anyone currently analyzing a domain with the intention of a component implementation. While you don't learn from a book, you may learn with a book. If you intend to build a business component system, this book may help in organizing your thoughts and confirming your intuitions.

- Software analysts, architects, designers, and software engineers, who will find a conceptual framework, architectural principles, design patterns, and suggestions for methodology that apply from requirements through build to the run-time. You will also find that the business component approach is not an all-or-nothing proposition. Different parts of the book can be applied as appropriate, and even if adopted partially can still lead to substantial cost-savings.

- Software engineers, who will find the discussion of the required business component virtual machine of interest because this outlines, from a top-down viewpoint, what is required to provide functional developers with the software technology transparencies needed.

- Managers, nontechnical professionals, and consultants who need an overview of how components can be applied end-to-end. In particular, you should read Chapter 1, "Component-Based Development," and Chapter 2, "The Business Component Approach."

- Computer science students and graduates interested in understanding the problem of building large-scale distributed systems wholly based on component thinking will find this book a highly useful repository of concepts, viewpoints, and patterns. They will also find that the concepts presented are independent of any specific commercially available component middleware.

- Tools and middleware vendors, who might consider this book as a contribution to their requirement definition work for future versions of tools and/or middleware.

In summary, we hope that this book has something for everyone involved or interested in component-based development.

What This Book Covers

The book assumes a basic understanding of both the main principles of software engineering and of the main concepts of the object-oriented approach. It is organized into three parts: the conceptual framework, setting up the business component factory, and software manufacturing.

Part One: Conceptual Framework. Chapters 1 through 6 describe the concepts used in reaching the goal of high-productivity manufacturing of rapidly evolving distributed component-based systems. This part is organized according to the various levels of component granularity, from smallest to largest, and it presents the concepts required to assemble systems and federations of components.

Part Two: Component Factory Set-up. Chapters 7 through 10 describe how, using the concepts described in the first part, the factory itself can be built—that is, an efficient manufacturing capability for the various granularities of components. This part of the book is organized along the lines of the architectural viewpoints presented in Chapter 2.

Part Three: Manufacturing Component-Based Software. Chapters 11 through 13 describe the main modeling and design considerations for component-based systems and, in the concluding chapter, briefly discuss some of the main considerations for a transition to component-based development.

Finally, there are two appendices, the first covering the naming conventions used in the book, the second providing a glossary of terms used. Throughout the book, both the more detailed technical discussions and the authors' flights of opinion are placed in sidebars.

How This Book Came About

Both authors were separately involved in developing business systems using object-oriented technologies in the 1980s. Object-oriented approaches seemed so powerful, but after a while it became clear that something was missing. The expected gain in productivity, high levels of reuse, and ability to master complex development somehow did not materialize.

In search of more productive ways of developing systems, Peter, together with many excellent colleagues, started around 1992 to work on components and methodologies for large-scale component-based development. This involved architecting, designing, and developing what was probably the first component factory, which included a home-grown technical infrastructure for large component-based systems and the creation of a methodology tailored to the needs of this kind of development. It also included the development and deployment of large-scale systems using this methodology and technical infrastructure. He first defined the business component concept and a first version of the business component approach in 1994, and he successfully applied it to large-scale software development. In 1995, he started to capture many of the concepts for a future book.

Oliver first met object technology not through languages, but through trying to ease the lot of the application programmer in the early days of distributed systems with PC front-ends. Indeed, his first use of object-oriented thinking was in creating real pluggable components for PCs in the late 1980s. Having been involved in distributed systems since the mid-1970s, his next step was to consider the distributed business system as a whole, which led to his development of the four-tier and distribution domains concepts. Following this came a period of technical development that produced one of the first "business object" commercially available component infrastructures, running on multiple platforms, supporting both object-oriented and procedural languages, and giving pluggable binary component capability to large-grained business objects.

In 1996, Systems Software Associates (the Chicago-based ERP software producer) initiated a project, in which both authors were involved, to build a truly revolutionary software component capability for its flagship product, BPCS. The project, through the sponsorship and vision of Riz Shakir and the leadership of Wojtek Kosaczynski, brought together a world-class team, which embarked on building nothing less than a business component factory. This experience, with the contributions from the great team working on the project, permitted to the authors to refine, mature, and improve the business component approach to its current form.

Early in 1998, we decided to write a book centered on the component factory and its enabling concepts. This book is the result. It not only expresses our belief in the coming component revolution, but also, we hope, will contribute in some way towards that revolution.

Acknowledgments

In producing this book, and in developing the concepts it presents, we must first thank our wives and families. They have loyally supported us as we slaved over keyboards on sunny weekends, when we should have been with our wives, or playing with the kids, or participating in other family activities. Thank you, Simona and Heather, and thank you, Solveig, Viveka, David, and Richard.

Many of our colleagues and friends have made important contributions to the concepts presented in this book, and our debt to them is immense. Some of them may not realize how much they have helped because the comprehensive approach that this book aims to present derives very much from numerous discussions in many circumstances—a thoughtful comment is later recollected and provides an insight to the solution of a problem. To the extent that this book contains any errors, however, we claim them for our own.

From the many who have contributed, it is perhaps invidious to name some and not others. Nevertheless, for the major part they played in realizing, in advanced software, many of the concepts expressed in this book, we would especially like to thank Peter Eeles, Neil Howe, Don Kavanagh, Wojtek Kozaczynski, Phil Longden, Boris Lublinsky, Riz Shakir, Steve Terepin, Dan Tkach, and Rick Williams. And for their many insightful comments on early drafts of the book, we are indebted to Robert Mickley and Jeff Sutherland.

In addition, for their direct and indirect contributions and teachings, Peter would like to thank Jean-Claude Bourut, Rich Burns, Ludovic Champenois, Stefano Crespi-Reghizzi, Alberto Dapra, Carlo Ghezzi, Charles Haley, Hans Gyllstrom, Francesco Maderna, Radouane Oudhriri, Paul-Eric Stern, Ed Stover, and Tom Vayda. For their many insights, freely shared at OMG and other places, Oliver would like to thank Martin Anderson, Cory Casanave, Fred Cummins, Dave Frankel, Steve McConnell, Kevin Tyson, and Dave Zenie.

A Personal Note from Oliver Sims

When I first met Peter Herzum, my thinking on the nature of distributed components (DCs) was reasonably advanced (at that time I called them "cooperative business objects"). My colleagues and I understood well that a DC was a pluggable component that realized a business concept, that there were different kinds of DCs at the different distribution tiers, and the four tiers themselves were defined and had been tested. By that time, we had also had considerable experience producing middleware that provided the required level of abstraction for functional programmers, had supported and built DCs in a range of languages (both OO and procedural, compiled and interpreted), and had seen our technology proved in operational systems.

Although I knew that more—much more—was needed beyond the technology alone, neither I nor anyone I had met had a really good understanding of the required methodology, development processes, and project management techniques for scalable development that aimed to map business concepts isomorphically to independently deployable, larger-grained software components. Peter made a major contribution to those things, but he also provided two other things, perhaps even more important. First, while I knew that somehow there had to be a link between a real-world business concept and a component that executed at run-time, the thinking at the time was incomplete, especially regarding development processes. There was a crucial missing link. Peter had the answer to the missing link—a single coherent concept that gathered up not only physical distribution, architectural viewpoints, and development lifecycle factors, but also provided for project management approaches, and at the same time strengthened the mapping between a single business concept at requirements time and a single independent deliverable at deployment. This concept—the business component—is at the core of this book. It gives its name to a whole new approach to developing distributed business systems large and small—the business component approach. Second, the approach to leveraging the power of business components to place software production on an industrialized basis was Peter's.

So this book is to a considerable extent the result of Peter's groundbreaking work not only in conceiving the core business component concept, but also on expanding it into a full and coherent approach to revolutionizing software productivity through a business component factory. At the same time the approach charts a path to the future of commodity software components—at the level of granularity that will interest end users. In working with Peter on this book, I hope I have contributed something to the conceptual whole. However, when business component factories are commonplace, and software development organizations routinely assist rapid business evolution and change instead of being on the critical path, then I have no doubt that part of that future will be seen as being due to Peter's contribution.

For More Information

We have tried to put together a comprehensive overview of the most important aspects of component-based development for the enterprise. While it is certain to evolve and improve, we see the business component approach as being relatively mature, and we hope it may help you and your organization toward a quantum leap to more cost-effective software manufacturing. In preparing the book, many things had to be left out, including a deal of technological detail. A Web site—**www.ComponentFactory.org**—has been set up at which we plan to include further information about business component concepts and practice, links to other useful sites, and information about relevant conference sessions and publications.

Conceptual Framework

Part One provides the conceptual framework for the *business component approach*. The business component approach is the overall mindset and philosophy behind the business component factory, and it is based on a particular concept of component—the *business component*. The conceptual framework consists of the main concepts and viewpoints required for developing software components at industrial and enterprise levels. These concepts do not replace current distributed system thinking, but rather add to that thinking in such a way as to provide a single synergistic conceptual framework—a new mindset.

The first two chapters lay an introductory foundation. After this, chapters are organized by the levels of granularity of components and related software artifacts. These levels of granularity together correspond to one of the five dimensions of the business component approach. A "dimension" is our term for a particular combination of patterns and viewpoints that we find indispensable, as we will see in the course of the book.

Part One is structured as follows:

Chapter 1: Component-Based Development. This chapter presents what is usually meant in the industry and what we mean by component-based development. Of course, we cannot discuss component-based development without first dealing with the concept of a software component.

Chapter 2: The Business Component Approach. This chapter provides an overview of the main concepts and viewpoints of the business component approach. It introduces the main conceptual dimensions and architectural viewpoints required for component-based development for the enterprise, as well as providing a high-level description of the development process.

Chapter 3: The Distributed Component. This chapter explains in detail the distributed component concept, which is the software component concept to which most practitioners refer today when discussing software components for the enterprise.

Chapter 4: The Business Component. This chapter explains in detail the business component concept. This is a powerful software component concept that supports the whole development lifecycle and covers all the architectural viewpoints. It is the core concept of the business component approach and gives it its name.

Chapter 5: The Business Component System. This chapter presents concepts, considerations, and principles concerning business systems that are modeled, designed, and implemented using business components. It also introduces the concept of a *system-level component*—that is, a whole system considered as a single software component.

Chapter 6: The Federation of System-Level Components. This chapter addresses the main concepts required to discuss a federation of systems and/or system-level components. By federation, we mean a set of information systems, usually developed by different software producers, that are required to work together.

The conceptual framework presented in Part One is illustrated by examples that use a particular architectural style, in which all components are managers of objects but do not represent instances of concepts. We call this the *type-based* or *service-based* architectural style. An example is an *Order* component that manages all the sales orders in a business system. With the type-based style, individual orders cannot be directly addressed through the network. Aside from making for shorter examples (!), this style maps well to today's component technologies; in addition, we believe it will be more familiar to those of you who may not be immersed in the depths of object orientation. Of course, this is not the only style possible, and both this and other architectural styles, including the *instance-based* style, are discussed and compared in Part Two, Chapter 9, where we discuss application architecture.

Component-Based Development

This chapter sets the scene for why moving to component-based development is essential. Component-based development is, by far, the most promising way of controlling the soaring complexity and cost of business information systems. It is also the best way to architect, design, implement, and deploy scalable systems that provide the flexibility and agility required by today's enterprise environment. The chapter is structured into three sections, which address the following:

- What we mean by the term *component*—what it is, and what it is not
- What we mean by *component-based development*, and briefly how the industry evolved into components and the main benefits of this approach
- How we believe component-based development will evolve and mature

In the process of describing what we mean by components and component-based development, we also describe our goal—where we want to get to—our vision and our dream. It is a vision for the next wave of computing in the business software industry with two major facets:

1. A world of software as components that are indeed easy to swap, mix-and-match, plug and play *at the enterprise level*, a world where enterprise-level components can be bought and installed over the Internet or off-the-shelf.

2. Enabling the next industrial revolution where software is a commodity, rather than a major expense in the budget and a perennial item on the critical path of business evolution.

We do believe that enterprise-level software will become an off-the-shelf commodity that can easily be integrated and interworked with other similar commodities, forever changing the way we build and assemble, market and sell, and deploy and evolve software. But for this revolution to happen, we still have a long journey ahead of us, with one over-reaching final objective: a dramatic reduction of the cost of producing viable software.

What Is a Component?

In the software industry, the term "component" is used in many different ways. For example, it is applied to user-interface components implemented as ActiveXs or JavaBeans, to major infrastructure items such as database management systems, and to any software artifact that can be reused.

In this book, we use the term "software component," often omitting the "software" qualifier, to mean a self-contained piece of software with a well-defined interface or set of interfaces. We imply a clear run-time and deployment-time connotation; that is, the component has interfaces that are accessible at run-time, and at some point in its development lifecycle, the component can be independently delivered and installed. We also require a component to be easily combined and composed with other components to provide useful functionality: It is generally only through collaboration with other components that an individual component achieves its usefulness.

Components are things that can be plugged into a system. If they are to be plugged in, however, then there must be something for them to be plugged into. The challenge of software components is not only figuring out how to design and build a self-contained and useful piece of software with a clean interface, but also ensuring that there are software sockets into which a compatible component fits when it's deployed. Consider a kettle as a component of a kitchen. It isn't a useful component, though, if it works on 500 volts and has a five-pin plug. Or how about a spark plug that slides into the engine block and is bolted on tight? This is not much use when my engine block has a threaded spark-plug socket and no bolt sockets! Of course, I can always reengineer my engine block or build my own voltage stepper and adapter for the kettle, but this would be quite impractical. In other words, the technical context into which a component plugs is as important as the interfaces it provides. This context—the socket—includes both the technical infrastructure and other components required in order for the component to operate correctly.

An often-ignored but important factor in thinking about components is the user of a component. For example, a computer chip that's useful to a board manufacturer would not be of much use to us—we couldn't slot it into a PC's bus! We can do this, however, with a board. It's the same with software. A given component is designed to be used by a person with a specific (but seldom specified) set of skills. Some components are intended to be used by developers, others by end users.

In summary, we can state four essential characteristics of a software component model: the component, the component socket, the ability of components to cooperate with other components, and the user of the component.

1. A component is a self-contained software construct that has a defined use, has a run-time interface, can be autonomously deployed, and is built with foreknowledge of a specific component socket.

2. A component socket is software that provides a well-defined and well-known run-time interface to a supporting infrastructure into which the component will fit. A design-time interface alone is necessary but not sufficient because it does not exist in the run-time unless it's implemented by some piece of software, that is, by the infrastructure.

3. A component is built for composition and collaboration with other components.

4. A component socket and the corresponding components are designed for use by a person with a defined set of skills and tools.

As a corollary to this last point, we also observe two further points:

- The component user may not have the skills and/or tools necessary to create the component. This means that there is a hierarchy of component-ware, such that one person's end product is a component for someone else.

- The person who creates a component will not normally create the socket—the infrastructure—into which it fits.

The previous description conforms to the slowly evolving consensus in the industry. For example, the Workshop on Component-Oriented Programming at ECOOP'96 defined a software component as "a unit of composition with contractually specified interfaces and explicit context dependencies only. A software component can be deployed independently and is subject to composition by third parties." Again, Szyperski describes a component as being "what is actually deployed—as an isolatable part of the system" [Szyperski 1998, p. 10]. And, of course, Microsoft's COM, Enterprise Java Beans, and the OMG developments [OMG 1999], are all generally supportive of this particular view of the nature of components.

The industry today, however, is still focused on the component as a single pluggable software module. While very necessary, this technology by itself is not at all sufficient to address the many challenges of enterprise development. It is at the enterprise level that most of the complexities of software development arise. What is needed is to build on the component concepts described previously to address the kinds of components that are instrumental in drastically reducing the costs of the software development of large-scale distributed business systems. This is the kind of component that we are interested in discussing in this book. Generally speaking, we refer to these components as *enterprise components*, meaning components that are used to build enterprise-wide systems. Enterprise components have the following four characteristics in addition to the essential characteristics presented earlier:

1. They *address the enterprise challenges*. Such components are explicitly conceived to address the challenges inherent in enterprise-level distributed systems, which include aspects such as concurrency, security, transaction management, database access, and many others.

2. They have what we call *network-addressable interfaces*, meaning interfaces that can be invoked over a network and that are addressable at run-time from anywhere in the system or indeed the world. Such components plug in to a well-defined socket, and they are intended to be easily used or reused at run-time by other software artifacts to create a software system.

3. They are of *medium to very large granularity*. We will discuss various aspects of granularity throughout the book, but it is important to clarify right from the beginning that the software components we discuss in this book are of medium to very large granularity. Too small a granularity increases the complexity of developing and managing large applications. As a rough guideline, each component in the middle of our granularity taxonomy (introduced in Chapter 2, "The Business Component Approach") corresponds to a subject in the application domain served by perhaps 10 to 20 relational database tables. If the component is implemented using an object-oriented language, it may contain from 5 to 200 business-meaningful classes implementing the business logic and the business rules of the component.

4. They *isomorphically represent a business concept*. These components are not arbitrary lump of codes, but they do represent appropriate business concepts in the information system. While this is not always an absolute requirement, it is certainly a very strong principle for the kinds of components we are interested in dealing with in this book.

This is not to say that other types of components are not useful. In development, we will use any technique, any trick or tool, and any level of reuse that allows us to speed up software development, regardless of where it comes from. But the particular category of software components just described is the most useful in addressing the issues of large-scale software development.

Our particular usage of the term "component" at this stage may seem a little skeletal, and we will put flesh on the concept in the course of Part 1. Meanwhile, to avoid possible early misconceptions, it is worth stating the kinds of things that we exclude from our realm of interest in terms of components, and they include the following:

- **A business model.** This does not mean that a business model should not be reused or that it would not be useful to import a business model from one modeling tool into the modeling tool of another vendor. Nor does it mean that component thinking is not useful when applied to business modeling, as we will see in Chapter 11, "Component-Based Business Modeling." It simply means that we do not consider a business model per se to be a component and that not all reusable artifacts are components.

- **A language class.** By this we mean a class defined in a normal object-oriented programming language such as C++. A language class is not a component because it does not have a run-time interface that is network addressable. To the casual observer languages such as Java may appear to make the boundary between components and noncomponents fuzzier, but this is not so—certainly not from a granularity perspective. Analogies abound in other industries—for example, the computer hardware industry. Many years ago a transistor was considered a component. Today, however, no one would dream of building a computer using transistors, but rather only with medium-grained components such as chips and with larger-grained components such as boards. Transistors are like language classes. We don't use language classes to assemble enterprise systems. Rather, we use software components of several granularities.

- **User interface components,** such as JavaBeans, ActiveX controls, or for those of you who are old enough, OpenDoc parts. Technically speaking, these are components. But they are generally of small granularity, and they do not go very far in helping us resolve the enterprise-level problem. In particular, these kinds of components do not significantly reduce the costs of developing enterprise-level systems and hence, in spite of their utility in user-interface technology, are of little interest to us here.

- **A legacy system** accessible through wrappers that provide network addressable interfaces. This is not deemed to be a component unless it satisfies all our characteristics for components. For example, to be considered a component, the wrapped legacy system must be built for composition and collaboration, must comply with an architecture and infrastructure that address the various enterprise challenges, and should be isomorphic with a business concept. This does not mean that a wrapped legacy system is not per se an extremely useful thing; it just means that we do not consider a wrapped legacy system as a component simply because it has a network-addressable interface.

Having discussed what a component is not, here are two things that *are* considered valid components. They reflect what various people in the software industry tend to think about when discussing components for the enterprise.

1. Developers and information system designers often think about components that they can use to build their own server-based information system. For example, if building an invoice management system, there would be considerable interest in preexisting components such as one that managed currencies or another that managed addresses. We call these *enterprise distributed components*, meaning components for the enterprise distributed system. These are discussed in detail in Chapter 3, "The Distributed Component."

2. End users, business analysts, and marketers usually think about large chunks of systems as being components. For example, a payroll system or an invoice management system, with properly defined interfaces and satisfying all the above characteristics, can be considered as components. We call these *system-level components*. These will be discussed in detail in Chapter 5, "The Business Component System," and Chapter 6, "The Federation of System-Level Components."

These two levels of component granularity are illustrated in Figure 1.1. We will revisit these and other component categories in Chapter 2, and in more detail in later chapters. Also, the various architectural and design assumptions

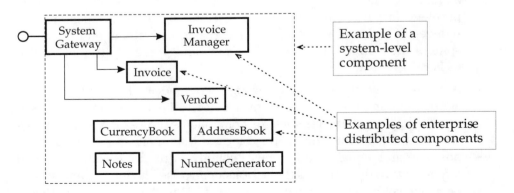

Figure 1.1   System-level components and enterprise distributed components.

reflected in the figure are explained in Chapter 9, "Application Architecture," and Chapter 12, "Component-Based Design."

What Is Component-Based Development?

Some practitioners[1] define component-based development (CBD) as an approach in which all artifacts—including executable code, interface specifications, architectures, business models, and scaling from complete applications and systems down to individual components—can be built by assembling, adapting, and "wiring" together existing components into a variety of configurations.

This definition addresses an important aspect of component-based development (CBD), namely the ability to build systems by assembly of preexisting components. On the other hand, in order to be able to assemble components, these components must first exist. As much as we would like to claim the opposite, at present there is no market selling enterprise components ready for assembly, aside, perhaps, from a few specific market niches. Still, many organizations claim that they are building software using a component-based approach, and our whole industry is apparently in a CBD adoption frenzy. What do they mean, and why are they doing it, since what they are *not* doing is simply to assemble preexisting components? Our preferred definition follows:

> Component-based development is a software development approach where all aspects and phases of the development lifecycle, including requirements analysis, architecture, design, construction, testing, deployment, the supporting technical infrastructure, and also the project management, are based on components.

This definition explicitly declares component-based development to consist of building software using component-based thinking to the extent that the whole software development is component-centered. CBD is extremely beneficial not only when the components are already available for assembly, but also if these components have to be built as part of the project. Indeed, thinking of an information system in component terms, even if these components do not already exist, is the best way to master the complexities of large-scale distributed system development today.

In the following section, we first present a brief history of how the software industry has evolved into component-based development, providing a sidebar on some of the characteristics of the object-oriented approach (an important predecessor of component-based development). Second, we derive the requirements that CBD must fulfill if it is to play the part we firmly believe it will in transforming the efficiency and cost base of the software manufacturing industry. Finally some of the main benefits of CBD are presented.

Brief Historical Perspective

Figure 1.2 illustrates the typical maturity phases of an organization as it has approached today's concept of CBD. This is a highly stylized evolution description, and it does not pretend to reflect the actual evolution of any particular organization.

Initially an organization may use traditional development. By *traditional development* we mean software development using a set of mature and stable technologies that have been around for more than 10 years and sometimes more than 20 years, which often include mainframe-based technologies, structured analysis and development techniques, and languages such as Cobol and RPG. Systems built using this approach are often deployed on mainframes and minis and feature mainframe-based or other nonrelational database systems.

Feeling the heat of the competition, or simply looking for ways to improve its software development, the organization may then move into object-oriented approaches. This usually means at least adopting an object-oriented methodology and object-oriented languages. For the purpose of this discussion, we characterize the object-oriented approach as follows: The *object-oriented approach* uses classes and objects as the main constructs from analysis to implementation. It normally involves using an object-oriented language such as C++ or Java that provides (build-time) encapsulation, inheritance and polymorphism, and the ability for objects to invoke each other within the same address space. This last point is an important constraint when it comes to distributed systems. As Orfali nicely expresses it, "objects only live within a single program. The outside world doesn't know about these objects." [Orfali 1996]. This approach is further explored in the sidebar, "The Object-Oriented Approach."

Over time, the organization will often start to deal with heterogeneous operating systems and try to resolve the challenges of merging an object-oriented

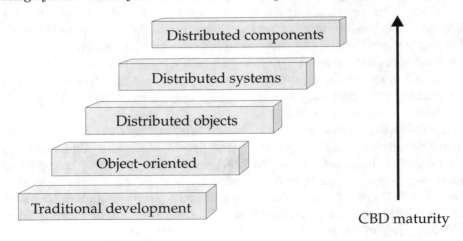

Figure 1.2   CBD maturity phases.

THE OBJECT-ORIENTED APPROACH

The object-oriented approach is a mature approach: It is supported by mature languages and technologies, it has a common standardized modeling language, UML,[2] it is relatively easy to find people with some form of background in object-oriented principles and techniques, and it is possible to buy hundreds of books on the subject. It has been and for many aspects still is an approach to software development of tremendous importance.

The object-oriented approach allows functional designers/developers to focus attention on units that are fairly stable—the classes and objects of the system—which match business concepts and directly represent them in the information system. It provides powerful abstraction mechanisms, including encapsulation of behavior, structure, and polymorphism, all of which enhance modeling capability and support continuity from modeling through to implementation.

On the other hand, an expert is often required to extend or modify an object-oriented application, or even to reuse part of an object-oriented framework; this is also true for simply reusing a single class built using an object-oriented programming language. The object-oriented approach allows for what we call *development-time reuse*, meaning that compared to previous approaches, it enhances developer's ability to build software that reuses pieces designed and coded by other developers. But this level of reuse has clearly fallen short of addressing the needs of large-scale development.

All in all, the object-oriented approach has facilitated mastery of fairly large-scale projects, but it has been mainly limited to the use of one technology on one platform. It has not really developed technologies and models for interoperability, but rather has been mostly focused on the development of one single system. Nor has it, per se, resolved the multiplatform problem—that is, the portability problem. In the 80s, neither interoperability nor portability was a major issue. The need for open systems was already there, but the technology to resolve the issues wasn't. This made it difficult to address portability and interoperability—so much so that in most cases the developers just did not bother.

Also as a consequence, the object-oriented approach has done very little to resolve the problem of legacy systems: To a large extent, either you totally rewrote your system using object-oriented techniques, or you were stuck with your legacy system. There was very little possibility of a partial adoption of object-oriented techniques.

The biggest reason for these shortcomings is that the object-oriented approach changed the way applications were *built*, but it did not change the *nature* of the applications themselves. This is illustrated in Figure 1.3. Before the birth of object-oriented technologies the end user would receive a monolithic application built, say, using COBOL. When developed using object-oriented technologies, the end user would still receive a monolithic application, only this time built, say, using C++. Either way, it was a monolithic application—the end user had no way to tell how the application was implemented; nor did it make any real difference to him or her. The object-oriented approach is at the service of the functional developer, not the end user. It addresses an important but limited aspect—design and development—of the whole software manufacturing cycle. For example, it does not address in any way deployment aspects, nor does it begin to address plug and play.

Indeed, there are many aspects of enterprise system development that the object-oriented approach does not directly address. For example, database modeling is often considered to be external to the object-oriented approach. At most, data is something to which an object-oriented model needs to map. In fact, even today, it is fairly common to find people that declare themselves to be object-oriented experts but who have never designed a database. As such, they are missing a critical part of the development of business systems.

view of the world with various practical challenges such as the needs of portable and interoperable systems. This may lead the organization to expand into distributed object technologies. For the purpose of this discussion, we characterize the distributed object approach as follows: The *distributed object approach* extends the object-oriented approach with the ability to call objects across address space boundaries, typically using an object request broker[3] capability. The vision of the distributed object approach was of thousands or even millions of distributed objects working together across networks and enterprises.

After spending some time trying to model and build applications using distributed object thinking, the organization discovers that a number of crucial architectural and design principles (which we address in Chapter 9 and Chap-

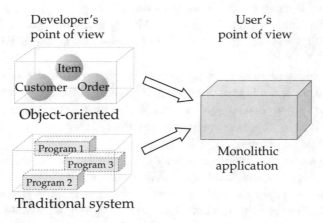

Figure 1.3   Object-oriented application.

ter 12) are required for distributed systems. These principles prevent a system from becoming an unmanageable and nonmaintainable collection of millions of small distributed objects, and they constitute the foundation of the distributed system approach.

By *distributed system approach* we mean a development approach for building systems that are distributed, often are multitier, and generally use a set of technologies that have been around for less than 10 years—including distributed system technologies such as object request brokers, modern transaction processing monitors, relational and object-oriented database management systems, Internet and e-commerce technologies, and graphical user interfaces. Modern distributed systems are required to be accessible from the Internet, to be open to other systems to support e-commerce, to generally satisfy an ever-growing number of new functional and extra-functional requirements, and to cope with a growing number of new and often unstable, bleeding-edge technologies.

Many companies today claim to be doing component-based development when what they are really doing is distributed system development, or using some kind of distributed object technology. While this can, of course, deliver significant benefits, such as allowing the technical bridging of heterogeneous systems, the use of, for example, CORBA[4] per se does not automatically imply component-based development, any more than using C++ guarantees object-oriented development.

The essence of the distributed system approach is that the realities of distribution are taken into account, following appropriate principles. Each system is typically built as a monolith, wrapped perhaps with some interfacing code, so that from outside, it is impossible to see whether these systems (consisting of varying numbers of individual application units) are old wrapped legacy systems. And now the organization realizes that things within these separate isolated systems need to talk to each other. It is in resolving *this* problem—the point-to-point connectivity of otherwise isolated distributed systems—that much of the value of distributed object technology lies. The focus of development moves then to the interoperability of distributed systems and to the techniques and approaches required to address these systems.

But the problem of how to decrease development costs still persists. It is slightly addressed by using object-oriented techniques but not enough to make a big difference. At this point, struggling to reap the desired benefits, often the organization realizes that something else is required; hence the current interest in component technologies and the adoption by some leading-edge organizations of the *distributed component approach*. This uses current build-time and run-time technologies such as Enterprise Java Beans to attempt to reduce cost and development time for distributed systems. It becomes apparent that what is needed is something that addresses both the challenge of distributed systems interoperability and the challenge of how to build individual systems that can be treated as atomic units and can easily be made to cooperate with each other. This leads the organization to an intuition about the power of component technology, and it starts to build systems using distributed components and system-level components. Often, however, this is glued on to an essentially object-oriented methodology development mindset, and while it is clear that use of component technology brings advantages, the lack of a unified approach does not deliver the expected productivity improvements. For this, a further maturity phase not shown in Figure 1.2 is needed—one that unifies through component thinking the entire development lifecycle. The next chapter introduces this crucial additional maturity level, the "business component approach."

The maturity phases just discussed as applying to a typical individual organization also reflect what has happened in the software industry. This is illustrated in Figure 1.4, in which some of the sets of technologies that have become important in the same timeframes are also shown. In this figure, each phase is split into three maturity levels, where B is the bleeding edge, L is the leading edge, and M is mature. We characterize these maturity levels as follows: *Bleeding edge* is a phase in which a few visionary organizations start to work out certain concepts and apply them, having to create new technologies from scratch or use existing technologies in a very unusual way. For example, before creating the C++ language, Stroustrup [Stroustrup 1994] was using the C language with an object-oriented mindset. Because of the high risks involved, it is only visionary organizations that adopt a bleeding-edge technology. *Leading edge* is a phase in which there is industry support for a new technology, but the right way to use this technology is still known to only a few organizations. Still, it is possible in this phase to find niche consultants to help an organization in the transition. *Mature* is the phase in which the knowledge of a new approach is largely available and the supporting technologies are stable.

In the 70s, structured programming and various levels of modularization started. The first structured methodologies were defined. We consider the Ada programming language to be the conceptual turning point and the summit of structured programming, even if, of course, languages like COBOL and RPG have been immensely more successful.

Starting in the 80s, over a period of more than 10 years, the theory and practice of the object-oriented approach evolved. Expanding on the modularization concepts and abstract data types introduced in the 70s, first a few languages such as Smalltalk, C++, and later Eiffel, and then a set of modeling techniques, which became known as object-oriented analysis and design, were born. During the 80s, the object-oriented approach was expanded to a theory that covered most of the aspects of software development, including testing and project management.

In the 90s, the industry started to introduce technologies for distributed objects such as CORBA object request brokers, and the belief was that everything should be a distributed object. In reality, the largest successes came from

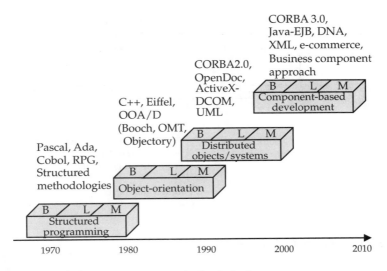

Figure 1.4 The evolution to components in the industry.

large projects using CORBA as a middleware for interoperability between whole systems rather than for large numbers of distributed objects.

Only recently have the software technology underpinnings for component-based development of enterprise systems started to become available. For example, it is only in 1999 that CORBA has been extended to truly deal with components [OMG 1999], and at the time of writing, implementations of this standard are not expected until 2000. CORBA 1.0 was about distributed objects, and it was not yet fully mature to really deal with large-scale systems. CORBA 2.0 permitted large-scale systems to easily talk to each other. With CORBA 3.0 the OMG announced that components are to be added to the picture. A similar evolution has occurred for other component-based models, such as the evolution from Java classes to Enterprise Java Beans.

The component-based approach will probably mature over the first 10 years of the millennium, in a rapid merging with Internet technologies and e-commerce. Right now, CBD is in the leading-edge phase. Indeed, there are now a number of technologies appropriate for, and people with experience in, the application of CBD. There is not industry-wide experience and support. Based on our definition of component-based development, and as far as we know, the approach defined in this book is the first to be truly component-based, and unlike many current leading methodologies, it is *centered* on components.

Figure 1.5 shows another point of view of how component-based development has unfolded over the past 10 years and where we expect it to be within the next 5. In the figure, "SLC" is system-level component and "EDC" is enterprise distributed component, as presented in Figure 1.1.

Shortly after 1990, visionary organizations started to apply component-based

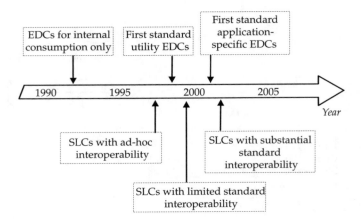

Figure 1.5   Evolution of CBD usage.

thinking to their internal software development. For these organizations, the development of EDCs was a way to master the complexity of large-scale software development. In 1998 the first standard for a "utility" or general-purpose EDC component was presented to the OMG,[5] and we expect that the first application-specific standard EDC will be defined after the year 2001. We also believe that widespread commercial availability of individual EDCs will not happen before 2001.

Similarly, the mid 90s saw SLCs with proprietary and ad hoc interoperability solutions between components within them. It is only in 1999 that technical interoperability protocols such as XML[6] and the first standards based on this technology have started to become widely available. We believe that standard interoperability protocols covering all aspects of SLC-to-SLC communication will start to be available in 2002.

There is a general expectation shared by many in the industry that after the millennium, the market for component-based products and services is going to explode. This is based on the observation that by then the appropriate technologies will be widely available, the architectural understanding of how to use these technologies for large-scale development will have matured, it will be relatively easy to hire experienced professionals and, most importantly, the funding and focus of most organizations will not be tied up in the Y2K problem.

Requirements on Software Manufacturing

Before jumping into the benefits of CBD, let us define the main requirements for modern software manufacturing. Indeed, it is educational here to compare the immaturity of the software industry to other more mature industries.

Characteristics of a Mature Industry

What are the signs of a mature industry? Well, let us point out four of the more important characteristics:

Build-to-order. The manufacturing process is based on *assembly of predefined parts* to provide customized products according to the specific wishes of a customer *within a predefined product framework*. For example, it is today possible to choose the exact configuration of a PC, and the exact trimming of your car, but within a set of predefined choices.

Third-party parts market. In a mature industry, often a thriving third-party *parts market* exists, where all the parts are built to well-defined specifications and architectures. There are companies that focus on building high-quality or low-cost parts, rather than products. For example, any large car manufacturing company produces only a fraction of the parts of its engines and of its cars.

Maintenance by part substitution. When a part breaks, it is cheaper and easier to substitute the whole part rather than fix the issue. Even if as consumers we hate it, it is cheaper to substitute a whole PC motherboard than trying to fix a specific integrated circuit on the existing motherboard. Very few people today know how to replace a component in a motherboard. It is much easier and more cost-effective to throw the whole part away and replace it with a new one. This is true for a car repair or for the repair of an answering machine.

Supply chain. The costs of manufacturing are only a small part compared to the overall costs of the supply chain. Successful businesses are able to reduce the costs of the whole supply chain, including manufacturing but also covering aspects such as distribution.

These four characteristics can be applied to a component-based software industry as follows. *Build-to-order* would require that there is a predefined catalog of components that can be easily assembled to satisfy particular user requests. Each component would have specific characteristics and address specific user requirements. There may also be prebuilt solutions, in which a user can swap one or more parts (components) for better ones. This would require predefined *component frameworks*.

Third-party parts markets would require that industry standard and well-known protocols for interactions between components, as well as standard component specifications, exist and are publicly available. But it would also require a segmentation of the market into solution providers and component providers, and the availability of component-based solutions for which the component providers can deliver individual parts.

Maintenance by part substitution would require that it is easy to identify the source of an issue and easy to replace the affected component with a new version—quite possibly from a different provider. Among other things, this requires that it is possible to prove that two components provide equivalent interfaces and functionality as far as the affected solution is concerned (this capability is also required for a third-party parts market).

Finally, addressing the whole *supply chain* requires that the cost of software manufacturing is understood to be only a part of the whole software supply chain. In a mature software industry, developing software should be a small part of the overall cost, which includes marketing, selling, delivering, and supporting software. Any approach that successfully supports the industrialization of software manufacturing will need to address in a consistent way not only software development but also the deployment, distribution, marketing, and selling of the software.

Requirements for CBD

Now a major objective of any mature industry is to set up efficient production capabilities. For software, we call such an efficient software production capability a *software factory*. Based on the characteristics of a mature component-based software industry, we can derive the following requirements for an *agile factory for software components*:

- It must *cut manufacturing costs* of software development by dramatically reducing the costs of developing, deploying, customizing, and evolving large-scale, high-performance and scalable systems. In other words, it must address not merely the analysis-design-development lifecycle, but the whole *life* of the software product.

- It must be able to respond quickly to changes in *business requirements* on one hand and *technology changes* on the other. It must be able to respond in a *build-to-order* way to the different requirements of a vertical domain or of a specific customer. It must deliver *highly customizable* and *configurable* products and processes.

- It must support building software that is simultaneously *highly modularized* and also *highly integrated*. This seems a contradiction in terms, but it is not: It simply states that software components must have boundaries that are very well defined and at the same time belong to a well-specified architecture.

- *Standards* must exist to govern both the technical and functional aspects of component specification and interaction.

Assuming that these requirements are met and an effective factory exists, the benefits of component-based development in such a factory can be stated.

Benefits

So why should an organization consider adopting a component-based approach? What are the benefits? To some extent, the answer to these questions is the subject of this whole book. Here we give a brief overview of the main advantages of a properly adopted component-based approach. We will see in Chapter 2 that these advantages apply in particular to a specific way of thinking about component-based development—the *business component approach*.

CBD builds on the past. We consider CBD to be a very comprehensive approach to software manufacturing. It covers all aspects of software development, from conceiving and building individual components to the cost-effective assembly of components into systems and federation of systems and the evolution of these systems and federations. As an approach, CBD builds on all the most successful techniques, principles, and best practices of the past to give a theory and practice of software development that addresses large-scale software manufacturing and supports its industrialization. CBD not only retains all the advantages of all the preceding approaches, including the object-oriented and distributed object approaches, but also resolves their limitations.

CBD masters development complexity. Today, leading-edge organizations adopting CBD mainly use this approach in large-scale system development as a way to master project complexity and risks, with its architecture-centric and reuse-centric approach. For example, even if used only to support the complex business modeling activity, CBD offers (see Chapter 11) an excellent way to partition a business domain. Tomorrow, CBD will master the complexities inherent in assembling large-scale systems from components, as opposed to building them.

CBD changes the nature of the information system. Perhaps most important of all due to its far-reaching implications, the *nature* of software—the nature of what an application is—changes radically. As illustrated in Figure 1.6, it changes to the point where the whole concept of what an application *is* needs redefinition (compare this figure with Figure 1.3). Components become highly visible at run-time, and this affects the way software is built, assembled, deployed, tested, evolved, marketed, and sold. Component-based development is not only a development approach but also a deployment approach, and this leads to a new way to market and buy software solutions.

CBD enables autonomous development of parts. Structuring the information system in terms of a set of quasi-autonomous deployment units supports new and challenging opportunities for high levels of concurrent

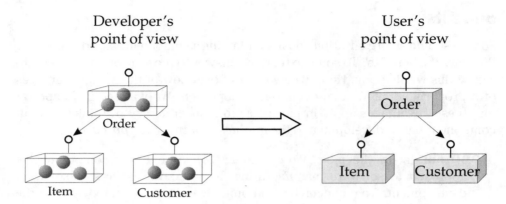

Figure 1.6 Component-based information system.

development, testing, and deployment. The challenges arise from the various architectural layers and concepts required to truly enable concurrent development of autonomous components. Of course, any new development approach creates new challenges, and this is true for CBD as well. These challenges, and many of the solutions to these challenges, are discussed in this book.

CBD masters deployment complexity. Organizing the whole development process around components is a powerful mechanism for reducing the complexity and costs of all phases of development. Such a reduction is particularly noticeable in system evolution, since many system changes or corrections affect only a single component. Indeed, it is not uncommon for a system built using traditional approaches to have a small modification go through a cycle such as that illustrated in Figure 1.7: A modification request may conceptually affect only one module, but implementation of the modification usually ends up impacting several modules. Furthermore, in many cases the whole application needs to be redeployed.

Using a component-based approach, the same cycle becomes as illustrated in Figure 1.8. In this case, the modification usually impacts only the component that is affected by the modification request, and it is possible to redeploy only the impacted component. This is a benefit that is particularly important for large systems. Of course, the achievement of this level

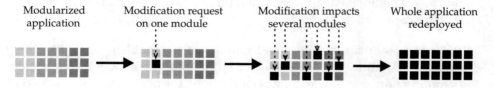

Figure 1.7 Maintenance in traditional systems.

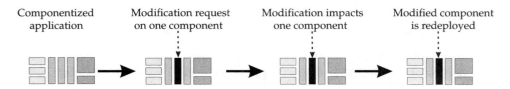

Figure 1.8   Maintenance in component-based systems.

of modularization requires an appropriate set of architectural and design principles and techniques across the development lifecycle and software lifecycle.

CBD covers all aspects of development. Component-based development can be approached such that all aspects of development are addressed using a small set of unifying concepts. An example at this point is that enterprise distributed components can be defined in such a way to include their own persistence aspects, and in such a way that database modeling and component modeling can be addressed together with a common set of principles, to the extent that there is no real separation between the two. We will discuss these powerful architectural concepts in Chapters 9 and 12. CBD also includes in a comprehensive approach all the modern technologies of distributed systems—for example, the support for multiple address spaces and systems on multiple platforms.

CBD covers whole software lifecycle. The theory of CBD addresses and informs the complete software lifecycle, not just the very important development lifecycle. It also covers maintenance, deployment, and customization: The whole software supply chain is affected and simplified by a component-centric approach. We even like to write user guides and online help with component-based thinking.

CBD reduces time-to-market. A mature component-based development will strongly reduce the time-to-market for a software development. This is particularly true when using component frameworks and component-based templates. Effectively, it will be possible to assemble new systems, easily, from existing components, reducing development time to a degree that today would seem incredible.

Today, a question is whether CBD really helps to establish a third-party market of components—a market of individual software components. As we aim to show, CBD according to the business component approach indeed addresses the technical and architectural issues. We also expect the business component approach to help software vendors in eventually providing complete catalogs not only of software products and software solutions, but also of individual enterprise components and component frameworks—as long as the evolution of such a market is not inhibited by other factors.

Evolution

We have argued that CBD is still a leading-edge approach and that it will evolve and mature over the next 10 years. This section discusses the kinds of things needed for evolution to occur—albeit at a fairly high level. First we examine the reality of software manufacturing today, and we briefly consider the variables affecting cost-effective software manufacturing. Following this, we highlight the risks in transitioning to CBD. Finally, the concepts, principles, and techniques presented in the rest of the book are placed in context by stating the longer-term objectives of CBD. These objectives describe where we want to get to—the vision—and are described in terms of the various phases of evolution from today to full CBD maturity.

Software Manufacturing Today

Developing software is very complex. Further, increases in complexity can be assumed to result in an equal increase in cost (at least as a first approximation). Indeed, Jones reports that developing software is so complex that more than 50 percent of large software projects are canceled, where *large* is defined as projects with more than 10,000 function points, and that the average large U.S. software project runs a year late, costs twice as much as planned, and performs below expectations [Jones 1994].

Developing large-scale distributed systems is even more complex. There are many reasons for this additional complexity—an explosive mixture of reasons that includes a combination of new technologies and the speed at which these are created and evolve, an exponential increase of the extra-functional requirements, the speed of business evolution and change, and new employment dynamics and patterns.

New technologies. Starting at the end of the 80s, the industry has seen a plethora of new technologies reaching the software development market: object-oriented technologies and approaches, graphical user interfaces, new operating systems, a new generation of middleware including object request brokers, and new generations of transaction processing monitors, to name a few. Each new technology required learning and reeducation. In recent years, this pace has further increased, with the introduction of the Internet, Java, e-commerce, and XML, to list only a few technologies that have profoundly affected not only the way software is developed but also end-user expectations. Technology evolves so fast that often during the evaluation cycle of a technology, new technology addressing the same space pops out.

Extra-functional requirements. Associated with these new technologies, influenced by them, and exacerbating complexity, are a set of new requirements outside the essential application function of the system. These include high levels of interoperability, user-interface friendliness, openness to various external accessors such as e-mail and workflow, and (again) Internet, e-commerce, and enhanced expectations in terms of such factors as quality, performance, scalability, and evolvability.

Functional requirements. At the same time, the new business reality leads to fast-evolving functional requirements. For example, in the order-processing area, it was enough for most companies to know that a given order had been shipped and would arrive in a few days. Today, the company often requires a delivery time of hours and full traceability through each step of the supply chain. This leads to a total rethinking of the way business is done and of the consequential information system support requirements.

Employment dynamics. All these factors are compounded by new employment and organizational dynamics. For example, consider the *2YL syndrome* factor (where 2YL stands for 2 Years' Loyalty). This refers to the fact that it is normal today for a software engineer to give a period of two years' loyalty to his or her employer before looking for greener pastures. Each individual technology needs three to six months to be absorbed, which means that an employee spending all of his or her time learning would, on average, be able to absorb four new technologies during the two years—as long as he or she did not work on anything else! Similarly, each serious software engineer should probably read at least five software engineering books a year to keep abreast of the evolution. Theoretically, it takes a month to read and absorb a book, two to three months to put it into practice and actually learn from it. Clearly a prospect such as this is not realistic. We are adding and adding capabilities and technical possibilities, without giving our architects and developers the time to fully absorb what they need to know. In addition, the people able to quickly absorb new technologies are often quickly promoted, ultimately removing them from the reality of development. In summary, changes in employment dynamics mean that the greater the technical complexity, the less able we are to handle it.

The evolution in the software industry from traditional systems to modern distributed systems can be seen as largely continuous, that is, new technologies and approaches have been introduced continuously and progressively. By *traditional system* we mean a system built using traditional development techniques, and by *modern distributed system* we mean a system that is built using distributed system development techniques, as defined earlier in this chapter.

From the point of view of a single organization the evolution is often perceived as a big gap, which we call the Tkach's Complexity Gap[7] as illustrated in Figure 1.9. The reason for this gap is that most organizations have development cycles typically lasting two to four years or even longer on a fixed set of technologies. By the time market forces require an organization to update its technologies and architectures, the industry has evolved so much that the organization faces a steep new learning curve and a real leap in complexity—and cost.

With this complexity gap added to all of the previous reasons for increasing complexity, organizations face a serious problem for the future. Ways of dealing with this growing complexity and cost are essential. Now the ability to develop quality software with all the required functional and extra-functional characteristics in a cost-effective way requires a combination of factors. It is not only a matter of technology or of methodology, but rather a complex cocktail of ingredients that must be mixed in a consistent way, so that it addresses all the ingredients as a unified whole. The most important factors influencing cost-effective software manufacturing are illustrated in Figure 1.10 and are as follows:

Integrated tools and development environments. These are required to manufacture software. In manufacturing terms, this corresponds to the machines and resources required to manufacture a product, and these are a critical aspect of mastering complex manufacturing tasks.

People and organization. Software manufacturing is, of course, a very people-intensive manufacturing practice, and the human factor is still the most important factor in this industry.

Software engineering practices. These include the methodology, development processes, and best practices required to have an organization use

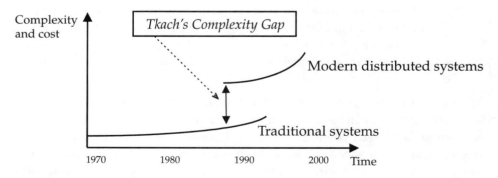

Figure 1.9 Tkach's Complexity Gap.

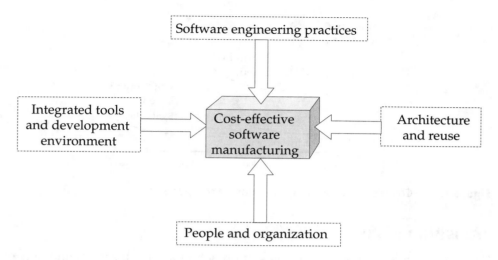

Figure 1.10   Influences on cost-effective software manufacturing.

the integrated tools and development environments to produce software efficiently.

Architecture and reuse. This refers to the set of architectural principles, patterns, and reusable artifacts and frameworks that support building software.

Although software manufacturing theory and practice have advanced a great deal in recent years, many organizations still struggle with the basic principles of software engineering. For them, software development is still a craft, and the software architect is still an artist. What is desperately needed is an organic approach to software manufacturing based on components, an approach that hugely reduces complexity for the functional developers and that has a high focus on cost reduction. This book aims to describe such an approach, especially in the areas of the technology, architecture, and development process aspects required for true component-based software engineering. These are important prerequisites for evolution to a mature industry. Of course, other aspects such as the creation of standards are also required, but these are secondary to the technological and architectural aspects.

The main objective in adopting CBD is to reduce complexity (and thus the costs) of development to the levels of the 80s, while still addressing all of today's needs. The objective is to achieve the curve shown on the right in Figure 1.11. At the same time, while moving through the transition to the new approach, risks must be recognized and managed.

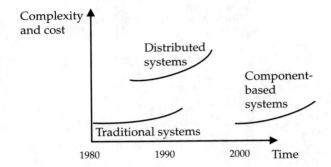

Figure 1.11   Complexity reduction using software components.

Transition Risks

Two major risks in adopting any new approach in an organization, and hence also risks in adopting a component-based approach, are to introduce a sharp cost increase over the transition time and to have the transition time last for years. By *transition time* we mean the time taken to move from a modern distributed system to a position where the benefits of a fully component-based system are largely realized (see Figure 1.12). The main costs of the transitions are due to the organizational learning curve and to the immaturity of current component-based technologies.

Because of this, an important objective of a transition to CBD is to control the costs of transition. Figuratively, the objective is to transform the situations shown in Figure 1.12 to those shown in Figure 1.13, where the peak of the transition curve is as smooth and low as possible and the transition time is as short as possible.

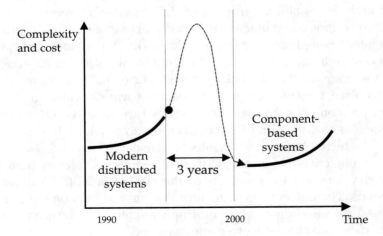

Figure 1.12   Transition risks.

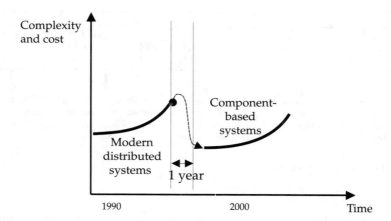

Figure 1.13   Reducing the transition costs.

The various considerations that can lead to a lower transition curve are addressed in Chapter 13. Briefly, they involve not only a proper methodological approach, but also an appropriate introduction of software engineering best practices, of the right set of architectural principles, of technologies and tools, of organizational learning, and finally of reuse practices.

CBD Maturity

What is required for CBD to move from a leading-edge to a mature approach? Currently, there are no significant technical aspects that prevent component-based development. All the individual technical capabilities exist. So what is missing, and why do we believe that CBD is still on the leading edge? Although all these necessary technologies exist, they do not constitute an integrated offering. Further, many of the individual technologies often do not directly support components. For example, most modeling tools and leading methodologies available on the market today are not truly component-centric. Furthermore, there is no architectural theory able to support very large-scale development—a hole this book aims to fill.

We like to think that this evolution and maturation are going to occur in phases as illustrated in Figure 1.14, obviously with some overlap (not shown). In the following discussion of the phases, we also address the user targeted by each phase.

Ability to build individual components efficiently. First of all, it must become technically simple to build enterprise components. The cost per individual component needs to decrease, and this will depend not only on the availability of the proper technology, but also—and mainly—on a set of architectural principles that supports this technology. Indeed, for it to

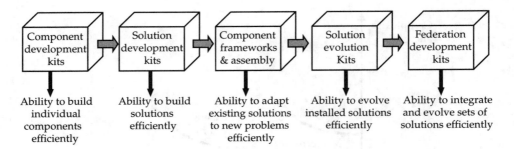

Figure 1.14   Maturity phases.

make sense to build individual components, the architecture and infra-structure—the socket—that these components need must be well known and accepted. The three leading technical models, that is, the CORBA component model, the various flavors of Microsoft component models, and the Enterprise Java Beans model, are all slowly evolving and maturing in this direction.

We are starting to see the appearance of *component development kits*, supporting all the aspects of designing, implementing, testing, and deploying individual enterprise components. Component development kits will mostly target the *component builder* and must also support the *component user*. These two users of the technologies have different needs in terms of support required:

- **The component builder.** From the component builder's point of view, what is important is being able to quickly, cost-effectively, and reliably build components. Ideally, a functional expert should be able to build a component without needing first to become a technical guru.

  For example, a very attractive aim is to provide the component builder with a modeling tool that supports creation of a specification from a business analysis perspective and generation of an executable prototype of the component, together with whatever is required to test the component. He or she should then be able to continually extend the component, adding functionality and generating the code for multiple platforms. During the development, he or she should be able to use a number of executable patterns and reuse many software artifacts previously developed.

  The component builder does not want to have to think about the internals—far less the building of—either the technical infrastructure or the development tools. He or she mostly wants to concentrate on building functional components as fast and efficiently as possible. Indeed, the less that has to be understood about the underlying technology, the better.

- **The component user.** From a component user's point of view, the ideal functionality would be the ability to easily add a component to the enterprise development. As we will see, this is fairly easy for user-interface components but is very complex for enterprise components. This could be achieved through a tool that allows a software component to be dragged into the system being developed. Such a tool would automatically take care of all import aspects, from checking semantics and consistency of specifications, to placing the right files in the right place around the system. It would rebuild if necessary all the parts affected by the import, take care of all persistence aspects, retest the system, validate that everything works as expected, and so forth.

Stated more generally, and considering the various levels at which we could consider pluggability (not only the traditional run-time pluggability, but also of requirements, or of design models, of testing specification, and so on), in an ideal world it should be possible to take a business component and plug it into the "system" with a single mouse click. Such an action would imply that its requirements models, its analysis models, its design models, its implementation, its run-time, and all other aspects have also been plugged in. At the same time, the functional designer should be able to concentrate on business functionality. He or she should not have to continuously worry about changing technology. An application or solution provider should not have to develop a technical infrastructure.

Whether this is a realistic objective is, of course, arguable. Developing the kind of mission-critical application addressed in this book is complicated and will stay complicated. But focusing on the set of tools, processes, and the whole mindset required to meet this objective is extremely useful. It drives a certain definition of what is good practice and what is not good practice.

Ability to build solutions in new domains efficiently. Over time, the principles required to assemble enterprise solutions using enterprise components will be directly supported by appropriate development kits. We call this a *solution development kit*. Such a kit will provide solutions to the challenges of managing a large set of enterprise components that are evolving iteratively and concurrently. It will provide for the proper management of large component-based projects, for their evolution, and for assembly of components to satisfy the functional and extra-functional needs of the business.

The main user of this kind of development kit will be the *component-*

based system developer. The developer of component-based application systems should be able to assemble the system in a build-to-order way. This could imply, for example, software development with turn-around times of days rather than years. If this refers to the full lifecycle, then it must also include validation aspects: Testing a large system can take as much time as developing it. The technical aspects of the maintenance cycle should take hours, or even minutes, rather than days or weeks.

Such productivity will require the ability to manage libraries of individual components and simple dependencies between these components as well as the ability to check in any component built using the component development kit.

Finally, the solution development kit will provide a full set of components that are common across one or more application domains. This is an essential part of making it cost-effective to start building an application for a new domain.

Ability to adapt existing solutions to new problems efficiently. Eventually, there will be component frameworks, component templates, component libraries, and even preassembled solutions available for each major domain. The focus of the development will shift from the ability to assemble systems from preexisting components to the ability to instantiate a component framework to address a specific problem. Adapting a solution to a new organization will mostly consist of instantiating existing solutions or parts of solutions and making minor modifications to them. Such prepackaged solutions should be very open and be accessible from any source, so that, for example, e-commerce is supported.

All this will require the ability to manage enterprise components that have complex relationships with each other. The management should occur from the point of view of the solution these frameworks and templates provide. The *component frameworks and assemblies* will come with out-of-the box solutions for at least part of specific business domains.

Ability to evolve installed solutions efficiently. All phases described so far still require the heavy involvement of software experts. Over time, the evolution of installed solutions must be addressable by the end-user organization itself, which may not have software technology expertise. An installed system must be able to support "100 percent maintenance," meaning continuous quick evolution performed directly by the user rather than by the producer of the system.

This will address the needs of the *solution buyer*, that is, the consumer of a component-based application system. He or she cares about the ease of deployment, configurability, evolvability, and, of course, the cost/benefit ratio.

Ability to integrate and evolve sets of solutions efficiently. The last maturity phase will consist of the ability to manage and concurrently evolve not only individual systems, but federations of systems. It will need to become relatively easy to evolve a whole set of cooperating solutions. We call this a *federation development kit*.

This will address the need of what today is the work of the *system integrator*. If we were able to see each application system as a component itself, the ideal for someone tasked with integrating or interoperating two or more systems is to be able to drag a whole system from a palette into a given environment and have everything just magically work.

Two important points of the previous list are that component-based development will mean different things to different players and that there will be a number of specializations. This, of course, is normal in a mature industry. But above all, assuming that our forecast bears some resemblance to what will occur, a mature CBD industry will mean a revolution in the way application software is developed, deployed, and used. Markets in components will become a reality; a make-to-order environment with miraculously short lifecycles will emerge; and development, deployment, and evolution costs will tumble.

Summary

A component is a self-contained piece of software that can be independently deployed and plugged into an environment that provides a compatible socket. It has well-defined and network-addressable run-time interfaces and can cooperate out-of-the-box with other components. Our particular interest in this book lies in the kinds of components that directly support reduction of the cost of developing large-scale distributed systems. These components are characterized by addressing the enterprise development needs, having run-time interfaces and network addressability, being of medium to very large granularity, and generally corresponding to a business concept.

Component-based development (CBD) is a software development approach where all aspects of the development, including architecture, all the phases of the development lifecycle, the supporting technical infrastructure, and even the project management are based on components.

CBD encompasses not only the new component technology but also a set of traditional approaches and techniques, including object-oriented development, database modeling, and years of experience in the development of large-scale distributed systems, and places all these at the service of the developer.

Today, CBD is primarily used as a way to assist in controlling the complexity and risks of large-scale system development, providing an architecture-centric and reuse-centric approach at the build and deployment phases of development. Over time, CBD will evolve to an approach in which all artifacts—including executable code, interface specifications, architectures, business models, and scaling from complete applications and systems down to individual components—can be built by assembling, adapting, and "wiring" together existing components into a variety of configurations.

The evolution of CBD from a leading-edge to a mature approach will occur in phases, starting off with the ability to build individual components efficiently. Then it will evolve through efficient building of component-based solutions in new domains, efficient adaptation of existing solutions to new problems, and efficient evolution of installed solutions by people with very limited technical knowledge. Finally, it will achieve the efficient integration and evolution of *sets* of solutions.

The real challenge in releasing the full potential of CBD is to define a coherent set of principles that will bring the whole of system development, including technology, infrastructure, distributed system architecture, methodology, and project management, into a single component-centric whole. The next chapter lays out an overview of an approach to meeting that challenge—the "business component approach."

Endnotes

1   For example, see [D'Souza 1998].

2   UML is the Unified Modeling Language, an OMG standard. For more information, see [OMG 1997b] or [Booch 1999].

3   For a definition of an object request broker (ORB), see, for example, [Orfali 1996].

4   CORBA stands for Common Object Request Broker Architecture, a widely used set of standards for distributed object systems defined by the Object Management Group. For more information on the OMG or the CORBA standard, see [OMG 1998e].

5   The first standard for a utility EDC was the OMG Currency Specification, submitted by SSA, Cyborg, and IBM, and co-authored by Peter Herzum [OMG 1998g].

6   XML stands for eXtended Markup Language—see [W3C 1998]. We will discuss this technology in Chapter 6.

7   Daniel Tkach, independent consultant specializing in component-based architectures, was the first person we heard clearly articulate this complexity gap.

The Business Component Approach

This chapter introduces a specific way of thinking about component-based development for the enterprise, which we call the *business component approach*. This is a whole new mindset: it is an approach to systems development that begins and ends with the *business component* concept. This chapter takes a high-level tour of both the business component approach and the business component concept, and it addresses the following major areas:

- The *levels of component granularity* within the business component approach. Each level of granularity corresponds to one specific category of component. Each category has specific characteristics. These granularity concepts are the core structural concepts of the business component approach.

- The *architectural viewpoints*. Our approach is strongly architecture-centric. In order to master the complexity of software development at industrial levels, it is important to adopt multiple architectural viewpoints.

- The *development process*. We introduce the key development process concepts, that is, how the structural concepts are addressed and applied in the development process. The really interesting part is that both the structural and the procedural concepts are based on the same single mindset. That is, the business component concept informs and shapes not only what is developed in the information system but also how the development process is managed. It is this mindset that we call the business component approach.

- What is meant by *business component approach*. Having briefly introduced component granularity, architectural viewpoints, and development process concepts, we can present the approach as a whole, its main characteristics, and its five "dimensions."

- What is meant by *business component factory*, that is, an efficient software development capability able to cost-effectively build and deliver business components.

- A simple *scenario* that describes how a distributed business system might be assembled in the (near) future using a set of independently produced parts (that is, as we shall see, business components).

- The *applicability* of the business component approach. There are different kinds of business systems, and we discuss whether the business component approach is equally applicable to all of them.

The rest of the book expands on the concepts introduced in this overview chapter. It also addresses additional associated areas such as architectural principles, design concepts, development lifecycle issues, implications, and so on, which arise from the business component approach and from the realities of distributed systems. Our aim is to provide sufficient detail to enable you to understand how this new approach to producing component-based distributed business systems can be used to set up an efficient software development capability—the *business component factory*—able to manufacture quality software at industrial levels quickly and cost-effectively.

Levels of Component Granularity

In this section we introduce the core structural concepts of the business component approach—that is, the levels of component granularity that define quite different categories of component. They are addressed in order, from finest-grained to most coarse-grained. They are as follows:

Distributed component. This is considered the lowest (most fine-grained) granularity of a component. It is a specific form of the usual concept of component in the industry—for example, it may be implemented as an Enterprise JavaBean, or as a CORBA component, or as a DCOM component. It is normally, but not necessarily, built using an object-oriented programming language (OOPL). The distributed component has a specific internal structure into which those OOPL classes fit or plug.

Business component. A component that implements a single autonomous business concept. It usually consists of one or more distributed components that together address the various aspects of distribution required by the business component. That is, the business component is a single artifact that may physically be deployed across two or perhaps more machines. The business component is the main concept around which the whole approach is centered.

Business component system. A group of business components that cooperate to deliver the cohesive set of functionality required by a specific business need. In other words, it is a system built out of business components.

When a business component system is encapsulated by being provided with clean interfaces designed so that the system as a whole can be treated as a black box, then it becomes a component in its own right. As such, it forms the largest grained component in the business component approach, and in this form it is called a *system-level component.* Designing a business component system as a system-level component is mostly useful when dealing with multiple systems or when dealing with the problem of business component systems that must interoperate as black boxes.

All three of the above are considered to be different kinds of software components, and each defines a quite different granularity level (as shown in Figure 2.1). A brief discussion of the pros and cons of the two main approaches to partitioning a given problem space into components, which can produce quite dif-

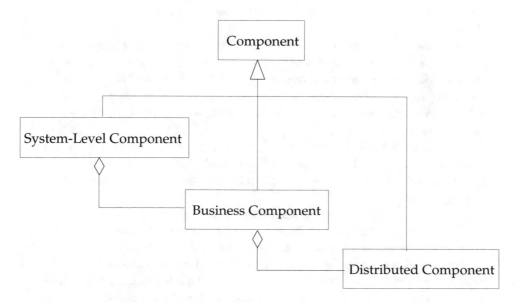

Figure 2.1   Component taxonomy.

ferent granularity outcomes, is given in the sidebar, "Component Granularity and Recursion."

There are two additional important levels of granularity that are not considered components in our approach. They are the language class (very fine-grained) and the federation of system-level components (very coarse-grained indeed).

Language class. We call a class in an object-oriented programming language a "language class." Language classes are used by a developer to build

COMPONENT GRANULARITY AND RECURSION

There are two general approaches to partitioning a given problem space into component form, both of which produce levels of granularity. First there is what might be called *continuous recursion*—the recursive application of object-oriented techniques (as, for example, advocated by [D'Souza 1998]). This is an analysis technique in which the problem space is partitioned by identifying very coarse-grained components; each very coarse-grained component is partitioned into components of a lower granularity and so on iteratively until the desired granularity is achieved. At each level of recursion, the same concept of component is applied.

Continuous recursion requires the designer to define how many levels to recurse, what role each level will play in the information system, what unique characteristics it must have, and how each level is to be packaged and deployed.

The second approach can be termed *discrete recursion*. While supporting strongly the concept that components are made up from smaller components, discrete recursion defines specific granularity levels. Each level identifies a unique category of component. Each category has specific characteristics that address the requirements for that level, including defined relationships with the other categories.

Discrete recursion is a powerful complexity-reduction concept for designers and developers: It predefines the number of levels, the role of each in the information system, its unique characteristics, and how components are packaged and deployed.

An important principle of the business component approach is its use of discrete recursion. Three major levels of recursion and hence categories of component are defined (Figure 2.1). These categories, which recursively represent business concepts, are explicitly targeted at those characteristics required for distributed enterprise systems. Such targeting significantly reduces design complexity, which is a major factor in successful component-based development for the enterprise.

something—in our case, a distributed component. While a language class is not considered a component, it is certainly a software artifact of fundamental importance.

Federation of system-level components. This is a set of system-level components working together to provide some business value. It meets the challenge of having heterogeneous information systems interoperate.

Distributed Component

The lowest granularity of software component is called a "distributed component." It is normally realized using a commercially-available component implementation technology such as COM, Enterprise Java Beans, or a Corba-Components product, and is described in detail in Chapter 3, "The Distributed Component." The term "distributed component" is used for a software artifact that has the following implementation characteristics:

- It has a well-defined build-time and run-time interface.
- It can be independently plugged into a run-time environment.
- It is *network addressable*, meaning that it can be addressed over the network at run-time. Distinguishing between network addressable software artifacts and those that are merely used in the implementation of the network addressable components is crucial for mastering the complexity of distributed systems.

A distributed component is assumed to be built using object-oriented technologies and following specific architectural, design, and implementation patterns. While normally composed of a number of language classes, as illustrated in Figure 2.2, a distributed component could also be built with other programming technologies. We shall return to these points in Chapter 3.

We will extend the concept of the distributed component and of its interface when addressing the business component in Chapter 4, "The Business Component." We will find that it makes sense to think of the distributed component as a concept that spans the development lifecycle and that has several aspects, such as different kinds of interfaces at each of design-time, build-time, and run-time.

In general, the nature of the distributed component is defined in this book from the point of view of the functional designer. The functional designer should not be concerned with technical complexities such as locating objects on the network, how data is communicated from a client to a server, transactional boundaries, concurrency, event management, and so on. Our definition of the distributed component abstracts these and other aspects and is largely technology independent. That is, we apply this definition whether we imple-

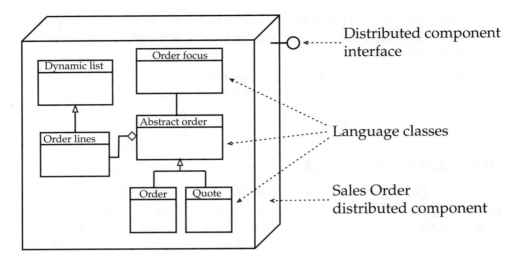

Figure 2.2 Distributed component and language classes.

ment the distributed component using DCOM or CORBA, or using some other middleware or component execution model.

Such abstraction must be supported, however, by an infrastructure that is mostly technical. Such an infrastructure is called a *business component virtual machine,* and a brief overview is provided a little later in this chapter, with a more thorough discussion in Chapter 8, "Technical Architecture." Such an infrastructure cannot yet be acquired as a commercial off-the-shelf product but can be implemented using a number of base "plumbing" technologies. In fact, the effectiveness of any new plumbing technology can usefully be assessed by its ability to support distributed components in their role of providing component-based development at the enterprise level.

Business Component

The *business component* is the single most important concept of our approach. Because this is an overview, we shall postpone a complete and unambiguous definition until Chapter 4. For the present, we can define a business component as follows:

> A business component is the software implementation of an autonomous business concept or business process. It consists of all the software artifacts necessary to represent, implement, and deploy a given business concept as an autonomous, reusable element of a larger distributed information system.

Let us analyze this definition, starting with its being a component that represents a single autonomous business concept, and then examining its in-built distributed system features ("an autonomous, reusable element of a larger distributed information system"). Following this, we focus on its applicability throughout the development lifecycle ("all the software artifacts necessary to represent, implement, and deploy a given business concept").

A component. A business component represents and implements a business concept or business process. It doesn't represent just any business concept, but those concepts that are relatively autonomous in the problem space. For example, the concept *customer* would normally be a good candidate, whereas *date* would probably not. It is implemented using software component technology—that is, as a composition of distributed components. It is itself a component, not only at deployment- and run-time, but also, as we shall discuss later in the book, during the development lifecycle. A business component is at the same time a software implementation of a single business concept. Being itself a medium-grained component, it is a unifying concept not only throughout the development lifecycle but also in its encapsulating distributed system features.

"Autonomous" does not mean isolated. As business concepts in the problem space relate to other concepts, for example, an *order* is by a certain *customer* for one or more *items*, so business components mainly provide useful functionalities through the *collaboration* with other business components.

In-built distributed system features. A distributed system is usually addressed by partitioning it into logical and physical tiers. The term *tier* is used here in the sense of *distribution tier*. You are probably familiar with the two-tier versus three-tier versus multitier debate.[1] We think of a distributed information system, and in particular an individual business component, as having four logical tiers (as illustrated in Figure 2.3). We name these tiers the *user tier*, the *workspace tier*, the *enterprise tier*, and the *resource tier*. They are analyzed extensively in Chapter 4.

Having four tiers (each implementable as a distributed component), the business component itself becomes a *unifying concept across the distribution tiers*. Consider, for example, a specific business concept, such as *Vendor*. Where is the vendor implemented in a distributed system? It may correspond to a few tables on the database (the resource tier), to some processing logic and business rules on a server somewhere (the enterprise tier), to some user-oriented editing on a PC (the workspace tier), and to a few panels and user-interface controls on a graphical user interface (the user tier). In this sense, any business concept is really implemented in a distributed system in a variety of places: the business concept *is* on the database, on the server , on the PC (in a client/server situation), and on the user interface. In a multiuser situation, as a concept, it is on multiple clients at the same time: The concept is distributed in the information sys-

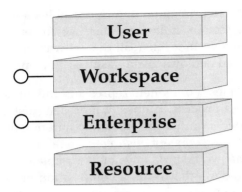

Figure 2.3   The four tiers of the business component.

tem, and it is the set of all places on which it is distributed that constitutes how the concept is represented in the information system. The business component concept enables us to think about and to develop all of these aspects as one unifying concept.

Throughout the development lifecycle. If we analyze how a given business concept is represented and implemented in a system, we discover that it appears as a wide variety of things, including the following:

- Analysis/design-time deliverables needed to express the given business concept and the various elements of the corresponding business component such as its interfaces, implementation, and dependencies. Deliverables could include an object model describing the business-related objects in the component, an entity relationship model of the persistent aspects of the component, a user-interface design, a definition of the dependencies of this business component on others, and so on.

- Build-time deliverables that implement the business component, such as the relevant part of the enterprise database schema, or language class definitions for the "server" and "client" specifically related to that concept.

- Deployment-time deliverables needed to install and run the business component over multiple platforms, for example, a set of software component executables (some implementing the "client" part and others the "server" part), configuration files, initial data, documentation, help files, and so on.

All of these deliverables represent some characteristic of a given business concept in an information system; expressed in another way, all of these deliverables *are* the business concept in the development lifecycle and in the implementation of the information system. Each development lifecycle phase is thought of as a particular viewpoint on the business component. In this sense, the business component *is* all the deliverables that are required to represent, implement, and deploy a given business concept in the information system.

The business component captures in a single software concept all these multiple aspects. It has a very specific form or "shape." In particular, it consists of a number of distribution tiers that map to an effective distributed processing model. This means that a single business component addresses both the client and the server. A second dimension is that the self-same concept is retained through the development lifecycle, as illustrated by the preceding list of deliverables. Thus we can see a business component as *being* the deliverables just described and also as a multidimensional software concept with different points of view at different distribution tiers and during the different phases of the development lifecycle. In this sense, a business component is a software implementation of a business concept and is itself a composition of software artifacts (including distributed components). Thus it unifies different concepts through the development lifecycle and the distribution tiers.

Another dimension is formed by each business component having a specific functional responsibility in a layered categorization of such responsibilities, from business process through the more static "entity" responsibilities down to utility functions. We briefly introduce these dimensions of the business component later in this chapter and expand on them in Chapter 4 , "The Business Component," and Chapter 5, "The Business Component System." As we progress through the book, we shall see how the business component starts as a single concept that maps directly to the business domain space, stays a coherent unit throughout the development lifecycle, and emerges at the end as a set of software components that can be independently evolved as business requirements change and develop.

Business Component System

A business component system corresponds to an information system or "application" in pre-CBD terminology—for example, an invoice management system or a payroll system. In business components terms, we define it as follows:

> A business component system is a set of cooperating business components assembled together to deliver a solution to a business problem.

According to our definition, a business component system is simply a set of cooperating business components able to provide a business solution, that is, to address a specific business problem in the domain space. It is here that we tie the whole business component approach in with real business domain needs. A business component system can be seen as composed of a set of normally simultaneously deployed business components. It implements one or more identifiable and autonomous business processes.

An example of a business component system that manages vendor invoices is shown in Figure 2.4, in which each box represents an individual business component.[2]

In order to better understand what a business component system is, let us describe how a given business transaction gets executed. The immediate objective is to give an initial understanding; a more formal explanation will be given in Chapter 5. Consider the simple design-level use case for invoice creation shown in Figure 2.5, which describes a process that merely records the details from a paper invoice received in the mail. The context of the use case is a rather traditional vendor invoicing system, where an invoice is created in the system when a paper invoice, for a product or service purchased, has been received.

Normally, the creation of the invoice would require the system to ask for the purchase order number, which would then be used to identify all the required information such as vendor, vendor's address, invoice amount, a product reference (to know what the invoice is for), and so on. For simplicity, the invoicing system described here requests all this information from the accounts payable clerk instead of from the system itself.

The main actions are represented in the sequence diagram in Figure 2.6, acting on the components identified in Figure 2.4. This sequence is provided as an initial sample of business component system behavior and does not necessarily illustrate good design. It also contains many assumptions and design principles that will be clarified, analyzed, and discussed in subsequent chapters. Finally, for simplicity, it assumes that the required information from the paper invoice has already been entered, so as to focus on the interactions between components rather than on those with the user.

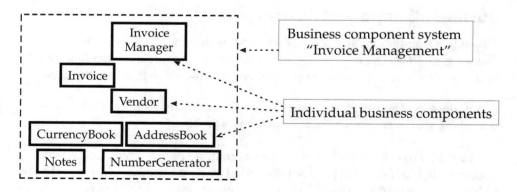

Figure 2.4 Example of a business component system.

Design Use Case: Invoice Creation.
Business Event: Invoice arrives in mail.
Description: Clerk manually enters the invoice data into the system on arrival of
paper invoice.
Narrative: The invoice creation starts by entering the vendor. The existence of the
vendor is validated. The address is entered and validated. The amount is entered in
the appropriate currency and exchange rate, and these are validated. A product
description is entered for reference. The system assigns a new invoice number, and
the invoice is created.

Figure 2.5   Design use case for invoice creation.

To create such a system from business components, whether preexisting or
not, various aspects clearly need to be understood—for example, how to identify, design, and implement business components, how to assemble a system
out of business components that have been partly developed internally and
partly developed externally, and what it means in practice to assemble the business component system.

But what is the difference between this system and any other system built
out of functions or objects? One important difference is that the business components illustrated in Figure 2.4 are not only the business components identified at design, implemented at construction, and tested during unit and
integration testing, but they are also the components seen at deployment. Each

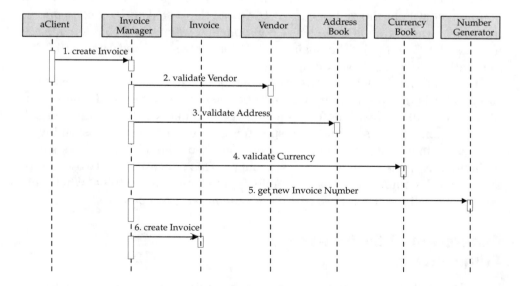

Figure 2.6   Sequence diagram for invoice creation.

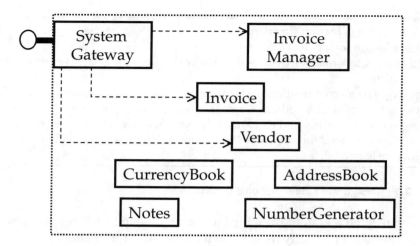

Figure 2.7   System-level component.

business component corresponds to a set of independently deployed run-time deliverables, can exist independently of other business components, and can be substituted by another component without, for example, re-linking the system. Thereby, in using components, the shape of the application changes forever. In the course of the book, we will explain what this means, its advantages, and its challenges.

Can a whole business component system be seen as a component? Certainly. It may be desirable to assign an interface, as illustrated in Figure 2.7 (where the interface is implemented by the *system gateway* component), to the business component system shown in Figure 2.4. We call this a *system-level component*, meaning a whole system treated as a component. System-level components are addressed in Chapter 5, "The Business Component System" and Chapter 6, "The Federation of System-Level Components."

The difference between a *business component system* and a *system-level component* is that the former is a white box assembly, whereas the latter is a pluggable black box with defined interfaces—in other words, a component. A business component system has a specific architecture—it is an assembly of business components. A system-level component, on the other hand, is seen by a client as a single large-grained component. This suggests that two or more system-level components may be able to interoperate usefully. When this occurs, we call the result a *federation of system-level components*.

Federation of System-Level Components

It used to be that the problem was "simply" to build a single application. Goodbye, happy days of the past. Today, the software industry is facing an order-of-magnitude increase in complexity by having to interconnect systems that in many cases have been built in total isolation by different companies. A large part of today's distributed system issues are thus due to the need to interconnect different systems, both legacy systems and new systems.

The world of software is evolving. Enterprises rely on information systems more and more, enterprises merge at a speed unheard of before, and a major obstacle to merging is often the time it takes to merge information systems. Partnerships are created, new business opportunities are found, virtual enterprises are created for short period of times, and so on. It is possible to think of a time when these virtual partnerships will be created in a matter of seconds and last for only minutes. Within a single enterprise, no one can address all aspects of the functionality needed, and there is a desperate need for quicker and simpler integration of systems developed by multiple partners. The bottom line is that an enterprise's approach to software development can no longer address only the problem of building an individual system; it must be fundamentally concerned with the problem of built-in openness and interoperability.

Does the business component approach help us to deal with this added complexity? Does it make the problem of collaborating business component systems any simpler? Technically, the answer is yes for any enterprise-level component technology. But unfortunately this is far from being only a technical issue; it also includes semantics, security, reliability, trust, and many other factors. These can be resolved, as is usually done today, in an ad-hoc way, but this does not resolve the challenge of building system-level components that are ready to collaborate with each other in a federation. Something more is required—a clear architectural model of how systems interact and a set of concepts, technologies, and principles that support it. Such a model, called the *seven-layer interoperability protocol model*, is presented in Chapter 6 and allows us to address what we call a *federation*:

> A federation of system-level components is a set of cooperating system-level components federated to address the information processing needs of multiple end users perhaps belonging to different organizations.

Figure 2.8 illustrates a simple federation of system-level components (the gateway components are not shown). The preceding definition may appear similar to the definition of a business component system, but it implies a few crucial differences: System-level components cooperate through federation rather than assembly, which implies a much looser connection between them; the level of granularity of the system-level components is much larger than the granularity of individual business components; and the system-level components may belong to or be built by different organizations. The challenge of federating system-level components corresponds to a large degree to the challenge of making systems interoperate. These subjects are addressed extensively in Chapter 6.

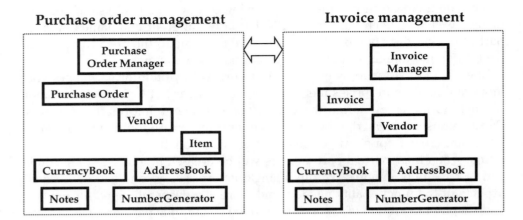

Figure 2.8   Example of a federation.

The componentization of systems introduces additional opportunities—and challenges. System-level components are meant to work together with other system-level components. When the federation of systems built by different vendors becomes the norm and not the exception, the challenge evolves from how to achieve interoperability to how to make interoperability and development of federations much more cost-effective. This implies a focus on minimizing the overall development costs and, among other things, simplifying overall system maintenance.

Now integrating system-level components may mean several things:

- Two independently developed systems that do not allow any internal modification and that must have a minimal set of contact points. In this case, whether the internals of the two systems are implemented in exactly the same way or in totally different languages and technology should not matter. For example, the two *CurrencyBook* business components shown in Figure 2.8 may have the same general purpose (of providing exchange rate calculations, calculating money amounts in different currencies, accessing exchange rate tables, and so on), but they may be implemented differently so that their interfaces are not identical. In other words, this federation would have 15 different business components.

- Two independently developed systems built using a common set of techniques, infrastructure, business components, application architecture, and also addressing common reduction in development costs, while still aiming to have a minimal set of contact points. For example, identically named business components shown on both sides of Figure 2.8 would be technically identical, so that where the two systems are deployed on the same architecture, there is only one copy of each business component (that is, the federation would have only 10 different business components).

These two meanings for integration are two different models that achieve similar ends. They also support different business models. The business component approach allows high levels of intersystem reuse and interoperability in the second case, but it is also a powerful conceptual framework in the first case.

Architectural Viewpoints

An important characteristic of the business component approach is that it is strongly architecture-centric. Most approaches to large-scale development today are architecture-centric: It is now generally accepted that an approach to large-scale distributed system development must be first of all architecture-centric, and that methodology and process should support rather than drive this point of view [Jacobson 1998].

"Architecture" is a term with many definitions and connotations. The following definition suits our needs:

> Architecture is the set of significant decisions about the organization of a software system, the selection of the structural elements and their interfaces by which the system is composed, together with their behavior as specified in the collaborations among these elements into progressively larger subsystems, and the architectural style that guides this organization—these elements and their interfaces, their collaborations and their composition. Software architecture is not only concerned with structure and behavior, but also with usage, functionality, performance, resilience, reuse, comprehensibility, economic and technology constraints and trade-offs, and aesthetic concerns. *[Booch 1999]*

Generally speaking, the term *architecture* can be seen as covering all aspects of a software architecture. All its aspects are deeply intertwined, and it is really a subjective decision to split it up in parts and subjects. Having said that, the usefulness of introducing architectural viewpoints is essential as a way of discussing, documenting, and mastering the architecture of large-scale systems.

The biggest obstacles to a true component-based market today are architectural in nature. The architectural viewpoints need to cover much more than technology in order not only to enable, but also to support[3] industrial-level CBD.

There are several different proposals on how to describe an architecture through viewpoints,[4] but we have found none satisfactory for the purposes of a component-based approach. Over many years, we have developed, tested in the field, and proposed to many practitioners the following four main viewpoints: technical architecture viewpoint, application architecture viewpoint, project management architecture viewpoint, and functional architecture viewpoint. In our approach, other viewpoints exist (for example the deployment architecture viewpoint or the system process architecture viewpoint), but these four are the most important to properly discuss the business component approach and the business component factory. We define these viewpoints as follows:

> The *technical architecture* is the architectural viewpoint concerned with the component execution environment, the set of tools, the user interface framework, and any other technical services and technical facilities required to develop and run a component-based system.

This viewpoint also includes what we call the *eXtended Integrated Development Environment* (XIDE), which is the term we use for the set of tools, development environments, compilers, and so forth required to develop a component-based system. The implementation of the technical architecture viewpoint is the *business component virtual machine*, and is addressed in Chapter 8.

> The *application architecture* is the architectural viewpoint concerned with the set of architectural decisions, patterns, guidelines, and standards required to build a component-based system that conforms to extra-functional requirements. It addresses the set of things needed, in addition to the business component virtual machine, to build a scalable system.

This includes the set of available generic application-level services and is centered on business components. For example, errors and error handling, business data types, generic structural patterns for distributed systems and for database architecture, and other application architecture aspects are all designed to take into account the nature of business components and the need to preserve autonomy of development and system-level development integrity. We address this viewpoint in Chapter 9, "Application Architecture."

> The *project management architecture* is the architectural viewpoint concerned with those elements needed, in addition to the technical and application architectures, to cost-effectively build a scalable large system with a large team. It includes the concepts, principles, guidelines, and tools (such as configuration management and performance measurement) needed to scale up development to industrial level.

Many people find this strange as an architectural viewpoint, until they really think about it. And indeed, this viewpoint is more concerned with the architecture of the development environment and of all the aspects required to build the system, rather than with the information system itself. This viewpoint is addressed in Chapter 10, "Project Management Architecture."

The *functional architecture* is the architectural viewpoint concerned with the functional aspects of the system, that is with the specification and implementation of a system that satisfies the functional requirements.

We address this viewpoint in Chapters 11, "Component-Based Business Modeling," and 12, "Component-Based Design."

Although we give a strong component-based flavor to these architectural viewpoints, they are of universal validity, and they are particularly useful in discussing any type of distributed system development.

Development Process

This section expands on some important aspects of the business component as a unifying concept throughout the whole software-product lifecycle, taking a 20,000-foot overview of the development process. An important objective of the business component approach is to provide, as far as possible, an isomorphic mapping between a given business concept and the deployed software component that represents the business concept in the information system. A unifying concept that applies throughout the development lifecycle is therefore essential. The business component approach defines this unifying concept, conceived at requirements analysis time, designed, built, and deployed into the run-time, to be the business component.

Conceptually, the development process can be thought of as an additional (orthogonal) viewpoint, the *temporal viewpoint*. Indeed, all four architectural viewpoints assume a different relevance depending on the specific development process phase in which they are used.

Main Characteristics

The main characteristics of the development process within the business component approach are that it is a *component-centric approach*, it is an *architecture-centric approach*, it has a *focus on autonomy*, it provides an *approach to collaborations*, it exhibits a profoundly *iterative nature*, it assumes *continuous integration*, and it is driven by *risk management*.

Component-centric approach. The main difference between the business component approach and any other development approach is that the business component approach is strongly *component-centric*. That is, the whole development process, as well as all architectural considerations and indeed any other aspect of the approach, are centered around the various levels of component granularity.

Architecture-centric approach. The business component approach and the development process in particular are strongly architecture-centric.

That is, the architecture viewpoints are used throughout the development lifecycle to drive the evolution of the system. In particular, a large part of the approach addresses the needs of the functional developer by clearly separating the responsibilities of the functional architecture from other architectural viewpoints. The development process presented in this book is mostly focused on these needs, assuming that the other architectural viewpoints have already been addressed.

Focus on autonomy. In a business component approach, the development process is centered on the autonomy of system-level components, of business components, and of distributed components. In following chapters we introduce additional concepts that focus on autonomy. The general mindset, which is further expanded on in Chapter 7, "Development Process," is that to obtain high levels of autonomy, appropriate steps must be taken to focus on autonomy at the appropriate levels at *each* lifecycle phase. Autonomy is not obtained as an afterthought, but rather it must be explicitly targeted at every development lifecycle phase.

Approach to collaborations. There are continuing tensions and dynamics in focusing on autonomous development of components. This occurs because the various levels of component granularity deliver useful function only through collaboration with other components. On one hand, there is the autonomous analysis, design, implementation, and testing of individual business components. On the other, it is necessary to preserve the integrity of the system as a whole, and of the various possible collaborations between these various units of autonomy. For example, a single business component is rarely useful to an end user.

A critical aspect of the approach is how to allow a focus on autonomy while enabling high levels of collaboration. Of particular importance is how to address the development and project management process while preserving the information system integrity (at all levels) and supporting the independent development of the various autonomous artifacts.

Iterative nature. The development process, through the ability to autonomously implement and evolve individual components, is highly iterative and incremental.

Continuous integration. The business component approach enables continuous integration throughout the lifecycle. A functional developer should be able to continuously develop parts of the system and get immediate feedback on the functionality and behavior of the system. Such continuous, iterative, and rapid development should not sacrifice quality. On the contrary, it should be easy at all times to check for quality without increasing costs, allowing the achievement of high levels of quality for a minimal price.

Risk management. The whole development process is geared toward best-practice risk-management. This is particularly important today, when very few organizations can be considered mature from a CBD standpoint.

Phases

How do we achieve these characteristics (which are further expanded on in Chapter 7)? Let us see at a high level what it takes from a development process point of view.

Through interviews, soul searching, or whatever magic it takes, we get an idea of the functionality we want to have in the system and gather detailed requirements. Without going into detail about what can and should be captured, note that it is important to organize these requirements around the business components of the system. Suppose the expected business components are the ones represented in Figure 2.4. Let us call this model a *business component system model* (BCSM), meaning a component-based model of the business system.

From the beginning, the software lifecycle is supported either by an in-house business component system model or by one acquired from the market (or a combination of both). If the project is started from scratch, then *before* requirements gathering, the candidate components of the system may be able to be identified, and a candidate BCSM drawn up. But how can the components be known before requirements gathering? The answer is that the candidate business components may follow known patterns and so can be identified with minimal information by following guidelines presented later in the book, particularly in Chapters 5 and 11. An analogy is found in the design of a new computer: The exact characteristics of each computer component may not be known, but, at an industry level, the kinds of components that make up a computer are certainly known; for example, everybody expects a computer to have a monitor, a network or external port, a hard disk, RAM memory, and, of course, a microprocessor.

Requirement gathering and use cases are thus organized around components. A business process analysis normally fits easily into a well-conceived business component system model. For example, system-level use cases and system-level processes are naturally owned by high-level components called business process managers. Generic use cases, in the Jacobson sense of use cases that capture commonality between other use cases, correspond to components that we call support process components; that is, components that implement reusable processes (see Chapter 11 for further detail on functional categories of business components).

Similarly, analysis, design, and implementation are organized by business component for all development aspects (modeling, conceptual, organizational, file structure, repository, and so on). For example, once the *Vendor* business concept is identified as a business component, it can be independently analyzed, designed, implemented, tested, and deployed. Furthermore, the project plan for system development can be organized in terms of business components, and even the directory structures and configuration management can be organized in terms of business components.

To a large extent, testing is carried out autonomously for each business component and, inside each business component, each tier of a given business component can and should be tested independently from other business components that use it. With some distributed component technology, a business component can also be tested independently of other business components on which it depends.

The results of applying these aspects of the development process include the following:

- A highly *reuse-focused development lifecycle* throughout all stages of development. When the business component approach is fully applied, a new project should be able to reuse (or buy from a third party) various levels of software artifacts at defined points in the lifecycle. This includes business component system models and business components, including their design models, possibly the source code, the (fully tested) executables, and even perhaps guides for deployment and use.

- *High levels of concurrency* in all phases of development, due both to the partitioning of the project into business components and the separation of concerns allowed by a strong architecture-centric approach. The functional specification, analysis, design, implementation, and testing of business components can be done to a large extent independently from each other. For example, the most used (and reused) business components in the system can be fully stabilized, thereby providing for better quality control from the bottom up. In addition, through separation of concerns, functional developers can focus entirely on their core competence, developing functional components, while technical developers focus on evolving the technical architecture.

- Concurrent, bottom-up, autonomous development also enables *subcontracted, multisite, partnered development* and allows fewer dependencies on detailed technical knowledge (as compared with a traditional object-oriented approach), directly supporting additional cost-reduction strategies.

Business Component Approach

We have introduced the levels of component granularity, the architectural viewpoints, and the development process. So what do we mean by the business component approach?

The business component approach defines a conceptual framework for large-scale distributed business system development and integration. It is a mindset, a way of approaching distributed business systems, a set of technologies, processes, guidelines, heuristics, rules of thumb, and techniques. It's more than just a methodology; it's a whole mindset about how application systems should be conceived, architected, analyzed, designed, structured, constructed, tested, managed, deployed, and evolved.

The approach takes its name from its core concept, the business component concept. But most of the principles and concepts described are *equally valid* even if you do not adopt the precise business component construct as described. We consider the business component approach as being a complete component-based approach for any enterprise development. It is a useful frame of mind in any kind of development, even if the business component is not directly represented in tools, development process, and execution environment, but rather is simply considered a logical concept.

The main objectives of the business component approach are the following:

- Limiting complexity and development costs by enabling autonomous development of large-grained software units—that is, distributed components, business components, and system-level components

- Enabling and supporting high levels of reuse at all phases of the development cycle (not only at build-time) and through all the architectural viewpoints and distribution tiers

- Speeding up the development cycle, first by allowing development by assembling preexisting components and second through a combination of enabling rapid system development, continuous integration, and high-quality development

- Delivering highly evolvable systems

- Enabling substitutability of components produced by different vendors, and ultimately enabling a market in components

A few years ago, people using structured design or entity-relationship approaches often argued that there was nothing new in object orientation (OO), that it was just a bunch of common sense applied to existing traditional technologies, and that people had applied these same principles for ages. Such arguments failed to capture the essence of OO: the whole new mindset it introduced and the new insights it brought. In the same way, some might argue that business components are just a rearrangement of existing technologies. The business component approach, however, is not simply a refinement of the object-oriented approach, but introduces a revolutionary mindset—with new challenges and new solutions—that builds nicely on today's capabilities (including OO) and provides an evolutionary path toward the industrialization of software.

No single aspect of the business component approach per se is new: To a large extent, the business component approach is simply a reorganization of existing concepts and techniques. The overall philosophy, though, is very different, and the whole mindset necessary to succeed is different. On one hand, it is a very comprehensive approach, covering all aspects of software development. On the other hand, it can be successfully applied to address just one specific aspect of development—for example, the development of enterprise-level components. The theory is comprehensive, but various points of view and dimensions, solutions, and technologies can be applied individually. In other words, it is not an all-or-nothing approach.

We have found that thinking of a system in terms of business components has proven to be an incredibly powerful conceptual tool. It greatly simplifies discussions, presentations, modeling, management, control of complexity, documentation, testing, and other aspects of development. At the very least, even if you don't plan to use the full set of concepts, the business component approach provides a highly useful conceptual framework for thinking about client/server and distributed business systems.

Of some importance is that the concept of the business component system supports a way to "chunk" the domain space. That is, faced with large monolithic integrated systems such as today's ERP systems, the business component system concept provides a natural approach to partitioning the domain space in a way that is directly relevant to the market as well as to development. Again, the business component concept provides a totally new shape for applications, and the whole concept of an "application" changes. No more do we have a monolithic application that must somehow be split up in order to distribute it. On the contrary, the system becomes a set of independently developed and deployable units, with a built-in distributed system architecture. This allows considerably more flexibility—for example, simple replacement of parts over time—in all aspects of the development lifecycle of a system, from conception to sun-setting.

Finally, it is a powerful model with which to reengineer the business process of functional development itself and then support efficient ways of addressing the organizational aspects of large-scale system development.

A Unifying Concept

The approach is based on the business component concept, a unifying concept that can be used to support software development starting at system definition and requirements gathering, and analysis and continuing through design, construction, deployment, and customization to subsequent system evolution with minimal transformations across the development lifecycle.

Appropriate processes, architectures, and tools can be built, centered around the business component concept, to directly address the needs of the business component approach. But even if the tools or the infrastructure do not directly support the business component approach, it is a very powerful way to think about applications, especially when trying to adopt component-based development (CBD) in large-scale distributed systems.

The business component approach, which has been developed and successfully applied over several years, includes a sophisticated software component technology for deployment and interoperability that can exploit current software component initiatives. At the time of writing, most component initiatives are aimed essentially at build-time components for developers, and they fall broadly into two categories: first, GUI- or PC/NC-oriented components and, second, components aimed at enterprise object model implementation. This latter category is still quite immature as a technology, and includes Enterprise JavaBeans, CORBA components, and the various Microsoft-based component models. These component technologies address a very important aspect of the lifecycle of a component-based system—the build/deployment time aspect.

If we are to address the multidimensional systems development problem for mission-critical, large-scale, multiuser, distributed business systems, we need a component concept that addresses the entire development lifecycle and the realities of distributed systems, as illustrated in Figure 2.9. Failure to address the whole lifecycle would prevent us from achieving the desired reductions in the total cost of development. The business component concept, as illustrated in Figure 2.9, covers both the distribution tiers and the whole development lifecycle. Combined with the other levels of component granularity, and the whole business component approach as described in this book, together with support by an appropriate business component factory, we can finally hope to greatly reduce the cost of development.

Development Costs

If we analyze the costs involved in developing a system using any technology or approach, it is evident that the implementation phase is a small part of the overall development costs. An approach and a technology that addresses only the implementation costs will do little to fundamentally reduce the total cost. Cost reduction is not only a matter of reuse, even if reuse at various levels may help. Reducing the costs of development requires a combination of a number of factors, including well-formed architectures, development processes, organization, and so on. These aspects, and how they relate to each other within the business component approach, are described in this book.

A large part of the costs of software development today lies not in the functional part of the development, but in the development and run-time infrastructures required on one hand, and on the costs of deploying, evolving, and

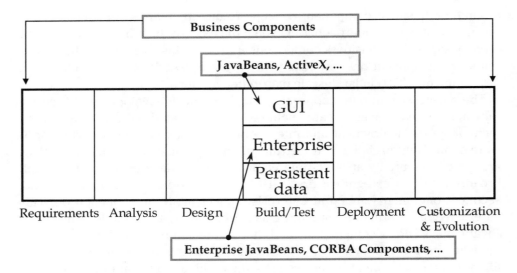

Figure 2.9 Business components cover the whole development lifecycle.

maintaining the system on the other. An approach that does not address the whole lifecycle of a system fundamentally will not reap all the possible benefits and costs reductions. This is one reason we prefer to use the wider *business component approach* term rather than the now-popular CBD (component-based development) term, which seems often to have a strong development-only connotation.

Minimal Dependencies

The definition of a business component stresses its autonomy. However, a business component cannot be isolated. It must collaborate with other business components in order to deliver the functionality required by the business. Collaboration together with autonomy means that a strong concept of minimal dependencies is essential. This is true not only at run-time, but also throughout the development lifecycle and the after-release lifecycles. A large business system cannot easily evolve if its software components have a large number of cross-cutting dependencies at any development phase, including run-time.

The business component approach has at its core the concept of cooperating components that are autonomous and large-grained, and that have minimal dependencies—from requirements analysis right through to system deployment, run-time, and evolution. This approach builds nicely on today's capabilities (including object-oriented and build-time component technologies), providing an evolutionary path toward the industrialization of software.

Five Dimensions

We can now clarify the *five dimensions* of the business component approach and the relationships between them. The five dimensions are the *levels of component granularity*, the *architectural viewpoints*, the *distribution tiers*, the *functional categories (or layers)*, and the *development lifecycle viewpoint*.

Levels of component granularity. At the start of this chapter we introduced the five main levels of granularity in terms of software artifacts as follows: the *language class*, the *distributed component*, the *business component*, the *business component system* (and its componentized equivalent, the *system-level component*), and the *federation of system-level components*. These levels of granularity are illustrated in Figure 2.10. Three of these are what we consider to be real software components, that is, the distributed component, the business component, and the system-level component. Part 1 of the book is structured around these levels of granularity.

Architectural viewpoints. The four architectural viewpoints already introduced are the technical architecture, the application architecture, the project management architecture, and the functional architecture. These viewpoints will be further detailed in Part 2 of this book, with the exclusion of the functional architecture viewpoint, which is addressed in Part 3.

Distribution tiers. The four main tiers of a business component and of a whole information system are the *user, workspace, enterprise,* and *resource* tiers. In Chapter 4 we discuss the meaning of the tiers at the business component level, and in Chapter 5 we discuss their meaning at the business component system level. There may be additional tiers, one of which is the *gateway tier* presented in Chapter 5. These tiers are *logical tiers*, as opposed to the *physical tiers* that will actually be used at deployment time. For example, there is the possibility of physically further splitting the resource logical tier in two separate deployment physical tiers,

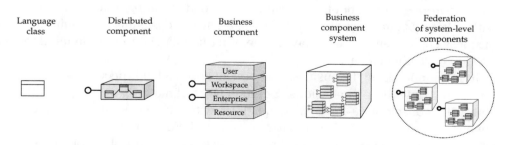

Figure 2.10   Levels of component granularity.

that is, the actual database and the run-time access to this database; or of combining the user and workspace tier in one single physical tier.

Functional categories (and layers). We introduce in Chapter 5 the three main functional categories of business components, which are the *process*, *entity*, and *utility* categories, and the additional *auxilliary* category. These categories are used to classify the business components into functional layers. We will see in Chapter 11 that we also define functional sub-layers of these layers. The term *layer* is used in this context in the sense of an *open layer*, that is, a layer that does not hide lower layers from upper layers (see the discussion on open and closed layering in Chapter 9). The functional category is a dimension orthogonal to the distribution tiers. Whatever its functional layer, a business component can have implementation aspects belonging to any of these tiers, as we will see in Chapter 4 and Chapter 5.

Development lifecycle viewpoint. The development lifecycle viewpoint can usefully be considered to be the temporal dimension. During development, the view of the four other dimensions changes according to the particular lifecycle phase from which they are considered. At each phase, a number of models may be useful to describe other dimensions. For example, at the analysis phase five models are useful to describe the *business component system* level of granularity, and these five models mainly describe the functional architecture viewpoint of the layers and tiers of the system. We will describe the development lifecycle dimension in Chapter 7.

Other dimensions could be considered. As for any information system, a business component system will mean different things and appear differently to various kinds of users and actors. In other words, and as always, different points of view show different characteristics. For example, a *business expert* mainly cares about the functionality of the system, the speed of configurability and of evolution, and the costs of the software. A *human-factors expert* sees only the business objects and components presented on a user interface and cares mainly about the way these are presented and the metaphors used. A *system integrator* cares about the facilities provided for integrating this system with other systems. A *functional developer*, while designing and building a business component system, may, on the other hand, need to keep in mind the previous five dimensions.

To fully understand the business component approach it is necessary to learn how to navigate these dimensions. A certain point of maturity occurs when the ability to consciously, easily, and quickly switch between the dimensions depending on the needs of the moment is acquired. For example, depending on circumstances, the system can best be seen as a set of distributed components or as a set of business components.

We suggest keeping these five dimensions in mind while reading the book. They are applied at many points—for example, when discussing the development lifecycle. The ability to easily analyze and separate the system being built in these dimensions is an important factor for a successful project using business components.

Business Component Factory

Suppose that we know how to build a business component, how to assemble a system out of business components, how to deal with interoperability, and how to integrate business component systems: Would we be ready to churn out components at a speed and cost unmatchable by our competition? Well, we have definitely gone a long way, but we are not done yet. Although components are buildable, there are still many aspects before efficient mass production and mass consumption of software are achievable. The main prerequisite is our ability to set up a business component factory.

> A business component factory is an efficient software development capability able to cost-effectively and rapidly mass produce high-quality software for the enterprise in a repeatable way.

The main subject of this book is how to mass produce software cost-effectively. We believe that component-based thinking and business components are necessary prerequisites.

The software industry is probably the only major industry that in most cases produces the factory, the manufacturing processes, and the manufactured products at the same time. And indeed what we do most of the time is continuously build and rebuild the manufacturing capability, the tools, and the manufacturing environment as well as the processes. This is a major reason for the soaring development costs, the over-long time to market, and the risks and complexity of development.

For software to become a commodity, or even simply to achieve high levels of repeatable development efficiency, we need a software factory that is separate from the products built using it. Such a factory would consist of a given standard development process, a technical architecture, application architecture, and project management architecture. These are the four main constituents of a mature business component factory, and each has a chapter devoted to it in Part 2. Such a factory allows functional developers to focus on what they know best—that is, to build business functionality. Figure 2.11 illustrates this, with two components, *Foo* and *Bar*, being developed in a software component factory. The factory is indicated by the four main areas that the developers use but do not have to build themselves—development process, technical architecture, application architecture, and project management architecture.

Indeed, from the point of view of a software producer whose strategic intent is to deliver a solution to a business problem through the use of software tools and infrastructure, a big part of what has to be built is perceived as a necessary evil. This is due to the immaturity of the industry, and is illustrated in Figure 2.12, where the strategic objective is to build an information system. In order to do this, the software producer usually has to produce a set of reusable components because today it is not possible to buy commercially produced enterprise-level components for most industries. And in order to build these components efficiently, it is necessary to set up a factory.

Using commercial off-the-shelf (COTS) business components introduces a set of interesting issues. These issues exist for integrating systems at any level, and they are the kind of issues that have made it difficult to integrate systems for years, independent of the integrating technology. These issues are discussed in more detail in Chapter 6. However, introducing a business component developed by a third party has consequences in the system where factors such as reliability, performance, scalability, security, and safety are concerned. This means that in certain domains with very high requirements in terms of these factors, a COTS business component may never be economically justifiable.

So far we have discussed concepts primarily from the point of view of the functional designer. We achieved this by abstracting a whole set of extremely important technical, infrastructural, and architectural considerations. In other

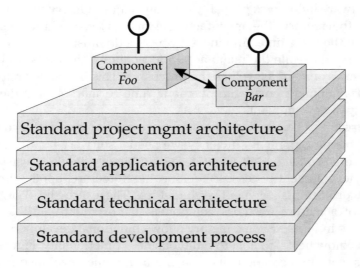

Figure 2.11   Focusing on functional development.

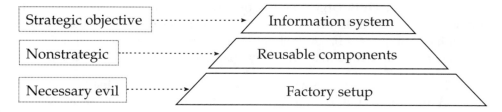

Figure 2.12   Producing a component-based solution today.

words, implementing a business component approach implies a set of technical requirements on the infrastructure. These requirements correspond to the need for the functional developer to concentrate on what he or she knows best, which is how to build the component functionality. For example, transactional behavior is assumed to be implicit or hidden from the functional developer. This means that we must have an infrastructure that delivers such transparency. We also assume a certain kind of persistence solution. This has to be properly supported by an infrastructure defined by the technical architecture. This part of the factory can be thought of as a "virtual machine"—a business component virtual machine (BCVM).

Business Component Virtual Machine

We use the term *virtual machine* in an extended sense. First we mean a runtime virtual engine capable of hiding specific operating system detail, as in the case of the Java virtual machine. But second, we imply all the tools and infrastructure required to specify, implement, test, and deploy software components such that the functional developer can focus solely on the functional challenge, while producing components that can run on many hardware architectures, middleware, database systems, and be easily federated or made to collaborate with other components.

In other words, the business component virtual machine (BCVM) is an infrastructure whose objective is to enable business components to be built independently of underlying plumbing and software technology considerations. For example, it should be possible to execute, with no change in functional source code, on a Unix or Windows NT or AS/400 system, using Oracle or Informix or SQL Server or whatever RDBMS is chosen, and using any run-time infrastructure desired, whether CORBA or DCOM/COM+ or EJB. Chapter 8 addresses the BCVM in some detail.

The BCVM includes a run-time infrastructure; a set of services, facilities, and frameworks; a set of development tools; and a user-interface framework. The operating system, ORB, DBMS, and so on, are also included. This is where the infrastructure market is headed, and it is what is needed for a cost-effective adoption of component-based technologies. Indeed, we expect that over time the concept of the virtual machine will expand in two main directions:

1. The level of abstraction will move up to cover not only what is today considered infrastructure, but also more and more ground in what is today considered to be the functional space. For example, we expect that the scope of the BCVM will eventually increase to include some of the reusable business components that we will encounter in the course of the book and that are mentioned in Figure 2.12.

2. The development lifecycle coverage of the BCVM will expand to cover not only build-time and run-time, but also, gradually, all phases of the lifecycle.

Scenario

Our scenario starts with the need to build an invoicing system very quickly—and cheaply. The invoicing system is required to manage invoices received from various vendors. During the (brief) analysis phase, a number of things have been identified, including the need for something that manages vendors; in turn, as part of managing vendors, we need something that manages vendors' addresses—an address book, say. It is decided to build much of the invoicing system in-house, but we suspect that we may be able to buy in the address book capability.

The features required of the system have been documented, and Table 2.1 defines the handling of addresses.

We browse the Internet to look for something that meets our needs. We happen to find something called "The Ace Address Book Component," which has the desired features, and we download it to our file system. Then we install it, bring up the application system that uses this component, and . . . done! Problem solved! Or is it?

Let us stop and think about this question: If we want to use a third-party com-

Table 2.1   Feature List for Address-Related Functionality

FEATURE NAME	FEATURE DESCRIPTION
Get address of person or organization	Ability to obtain a particular address of a person or organization, given the name of the person or organization
Create address of person or organization	Ability to create an address of a person or organization

ponent, for example, an address book that can manage addresses at an enterprise level, what would we actually be using? What kind of software artifacts would be required?

Before answering these questions, it may be useful to state a few assumptions we've made about the scenario:

- We assume that it makes sense to have a software artifact that manages addresses independently from the functionality related to the vendor concept. This assumption is revisited in Chapter 11, where the modeling of a business component system is discussed.

- The requirements ask for an address book able to manage addresses at an *enterprise* level: What does the *enterprise* qualifier imply? It implies data concurrently accessible both by different users (through a user interface) and by those parts of the business system that need address information. This probably also implies some form of shared processing. A logical consequence of these aspects is the need for a server program that provides for multiple concurrent access.

- We are trying to build a client/server system that allows three to four accounts payable clerks (this is a realistic average number for a typical accounts payable organization) to interrogate the system and enter invoices at the same time. This implies a system architecture along the lines illustrated in Figure 2.13.

- A GUI (graphical user interface) for the users is assumed, with all the features that constitute user friendliness. For entering or accessing the address of a given person or organization, a property page such as that shown in Figure 2.14 is assumed.

- Finally, we assume that the Ace Address Book Component is compatible with our system, meaning that it runs on the hardware, operating system, middleware, and database management systems that we have installed.

Our objective is to build the invoicing system in the quickest and cheapest way. This implies that the enterprise-wide Address Book component should be able to be used with minimal effort, ideally out of the box. Given the previous assumptions, the component itself could contain the following:

- As a minimum, the server run-time executable(s) for the address book.

- Documentation explaining how this component interoperates with other parts of the system (and since we are discussing distributed systems we assume interoperation through the network from a remote site). For example, how the invoicing system gets a particular customer address (to print a given invoice) from the address book server executable. This means that we need a precise description of the run-time interfaces to the address book, perhaps a specification description, and a header file.

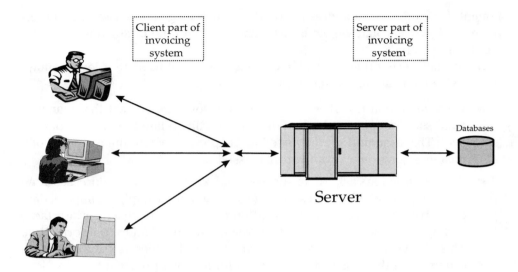

Figure 2.13 System architecture for the scenario.

- A default user interface implementation—for example, a Java bean that is preset to talk to the "server" part of the address book and that implements the property page described in Figure 2.14. This property page would probably not be used as a stand-alone window, but rather would be integrated into a property sheet, such as could be provided by a *Vendor* business component. In other words, an easy-to-integrate-into-my-system deliverable. If the business component did not include this, it would have to be implemented in-house, so increasing development costs.

- A specific set of tables so that the address book can persist its own data, and possibly some initialization data (for example, a list of all states in the United States). These tables (and any initial data delivered with the component) will need to be installed on the server together with the other tables in the information system, assuming that these are delivered for the specific database management system used for the rest of the information system.

- Perhaps various documents and additional files. They could include, for example, a help file, a user guide, an install guide, a document describing the main internal characteristics of the component (such as internal design, performance, and scalability aspects), and how it can be tested.

The business component may contain more than this, and we will meet several such additions in the course of this book. The preceding list indicates that our component is not simply a single executable. Rather it's a cohesive collec-

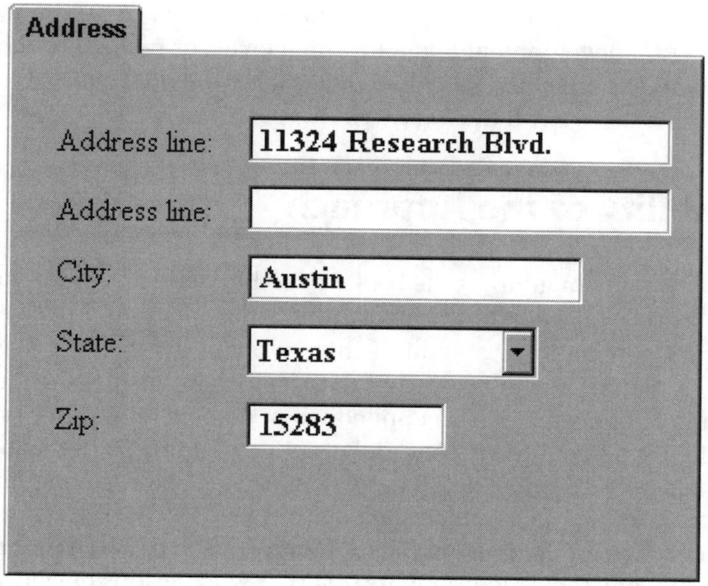

Figure 2.14   Address book property page.

tion of things that address the run-time end-to-end and that provide for build-time integration of the component with other parts of an application. The main point is that the deliverables required to (re)use, deploy, and run a third-party component in a client/server system are many. They cover many aspects across different architectural viewpoints and distribution tiers, including run-time, documentation, configuration files, and various deliverables intended to be executed on different machines.

The scenario illustrates that we are dealing with the business component across all phases of the development lifecycle. Our downloaded *AddressBook* business component was originally developed by gathering requirements for an *AddressBook* business component, designing an *AddressBook* business component, and building and testing an *AddressBook* business component. Now we are integrating and reusing that *AddressBook* business component.

Once the address book business component has been acquired, and supposing that we have built in-house the other business components needed to provide the required functionality, we could perhaps assemble the business component system depicted in the Figure 2.4.

Finally, suppose we had a whole theory, heuristics, guidelines, methodology and processes, architectures, and tools that would allow us to describe how a software concept such as our address book can elegantly be used to reduce the costs of development and better control the complexity of today's large-scale development. It might, for example, enable high levels of autonomous, iterative, incremental development and allow high levels of reuse throughout a software development lifecycle. If we had that, then we would surely be extremely happy. This is what we call the *business component approach*.

Applicability of the Approach

In this book we do not address the best way to build a word processor, a game, telephone switch software, or the algorithms for an elevator. All of these can be very complex applications, and all of them would benefit from a component-based approach. We are interested here primarily in business systems. While similar kinds of concepts can be applied when dealing with other types of systems, we do not present the theory and practice of doing so in this book.

Also, we do not explore in detail how to build the business component virtual machine, or the component execution environment, or the eXtended Integrated Development Environment using components. This is a subtle point: While we do address in detail their requirements together with various design aspects, we do not discuss how these requirements can be implemented using components. For example, an object-oriented modeling tool may support component modeling, but this says nothing about whether the modeling tool itself is built using component-based principles.

The business component approach is well suited to address many development situations and contexts of business applications, as we will briefly discuss in this section. This is so in spite of the various categories of business applications having fundamentally different characteristics and needs in terms of processes, architectures, and required infrastructure. In particular, we will briefly discuss online transaction processing (OLTP), batch, Web-based, and PC-based applications.

A large mission-critical application normally has parts that belong to the different categories. It is not unusual, for example, that some parts of a system must be treated as OLTP and some parts as batch. Rather than have two totally different approaches for the different categories, it should be possible to find commonality of approach across them, and the business component approach can provide this commonality.

The applicability of CBD and of the business component approach may also depend on the size of the application. For example, a small system with few evolution requirements, reduced expectations in terms of reuse, only 30 to 40 database tables (and an equal number of business language classes) can be developed in many ways. Where a proper component factory is not readily available, developing using a component-based approach may not be the least expensive way.

OLTP-Based Applications

This is the kind of system for which the business component approach has been primarily developed. We consider in the category of online transaction processing (OLTP) applications most core business applications, including large parts of the financial, logistical, transportation, and manufacturing functions. These applications are typically characterized by the following list:

- They are often large-scale, mission-critical, distributed business system applications, involving hundreds of classes and tables.

- They often have heavy concurrency requirements: hundreds or thousands of concurrent users in distributed locations and strong performance requirements, often requiring better than a two-second response time for 90 percent of user interactions.

- They have strong data consistency and integrity requirements, typically requiring transaction processing monitors, heavy-duty access to relational databases, and strong reliability, availability, and security requirements.

- They are often based on high levels of interaction with the user and a lot of small client/server transactions.

The business component approach works wonderfully for these kinds of applications. It is arguably the best way to develop OLTP applications today because it explicitly takes care of many existing development complexities found in such applications.

Batch Applications

The batch category covers very processing- and data-intensive applications. Typical examples are traditional Manufacturing Resource Planning systems or payroll systems. From a simplified point of view, these systems conform with the following pattern:

1. Load data into memory (sometimes all the data, sometimes one record at a time).

2. Perform a large number of operations and processes on the data.

3. Save results on disk.

4. If loading one record (or a few records) at a time, go back to step 1 until end of file(s).

These are normally systems with little user interaction and few requirements for distribution. They may be transaction based, but the transactions[5] are long transactions, each one lasting for perhaps 15 minutes or more, and they are mostly used to provide reliability, for example, to prevent having to redo several hours of processing after having reached a stable point.

Furthermore, these systems often have a requirement to be executed at predetermined times or when triggered by external events. They are also often required to log their mode of operation and provide notification of exceptional occurrences of events encountered while processing.

Many of the business component approach concepts and techniques that are used for OLTP applications, as well as actual deliverables, can be reused for batch systems. For example, the interfaces of existing business components can be used cost-effectively to provide for the loading of data required by a batch process. In addition, because a component always provides interfaces, then external systems (for example, system schedulers) can use those interfaces to drive a componentized batch system.

Web-Based and E-Commerce Applications

Modern information systems usually have to support Web-based access and enable various e-commerce aspects. This support is usually characterized by several of the following features:

- Supporting secure access to enterprise data through a Web browser, within an intranet, within an extranet, and from the Internet. Compared to the usual user–interface access, this implies higher requirements in terms of security, reliability, and availability, and also the ability to dynamically download to the remote machine not only data for local use, but also the programs that work on that data. This support is similar to that required for a mobile PC user, where the enterprise server(s) must assume, from the security point of view, that the PC is in an untrusted environment.

- Supporting secure cooperation between information systems of different organizations. This implies, among other things, high requirements in terms of accessibility, security, reliability, and availability.

The business component approach directly supports Web-based and e-commerce development. A business component system is, for example, naturally *open*, meaning that it is very natural to access it over the network. Of course, the extra-functional requirements must be appropriately addressed, but all of the concepts, architectural principles, the development process, and the design patterns, including the interoperability model presented in Chapter 6, can be directly applied to the development of Web-based and e-commerce-ready information systems. We will address considerations specific to these systems in various chapters, for example, Chapters 9 and 12.

PC-Based Applications

Of course, this will not apply to you, but we are constantly amazed by how many people believe that a distributed system is nothing but a PC application that is distributed. Some have been known to say that you can take a few objects, put some CORBA IDL interface around them, and suddenly obtain a scalable, performing, highly effective distributed system. This is a myth.

A PC system is a system substantially dedicated to a single user. Even if the user may want to simultaneously perform multiple tasks, there are no real concurrency requirements, or the few concurrency requirements there are may be addressed very simply. For example, a simple file-based lock on a file, with a message "This file is in use. Do you want to open it as a copy?" is more than enough in most situations. Similarly, PC-based applications have a very limited concept of transaction. "Transactions" here are very coarse-grained, such as a whole file, and are open for a long period of time, potentially hours. Certainly, you want to know that your transaction, in other words saving a file, has fully completed. However, once you have opened that document you are in full control.

Even so, the business component approach brings a useful mindset to the development of PC-based business applications. It still makes sense to think about the whole system in four tiers and to break the applications in workspace and enterprise business logic, especially if it is known that this application may one day become an enterprise-level application. The distribution tiers, the partitioning of the business space in components, the layering, and the other dimensions can all materially reduce the complexity of application development, even in a PC-only development.

Summary

This chapter has provided an overview of the business component approach, which is a powerful new mindset for the modeling, analysis, design, construction, validation, deployment, customization, and maintenance of large-scale distributed systems. Today this is the best way to build industrial-strength business systems, and it is an important conceptual framework for future industrialization of the software industry. The approach embraces the advantages of the object-oriented and distributed-object approaches. It is strongly reuse-based. One of the underlying philosophical principles is that any software artifact in a system should be defined in one and only one place, and it should be reused as many times as necessary. It provides a conceptual framework that supports strong levels of reuse across the development lifecycle and across various architectural layers.

The business component approach has five main dimensions:

Dimension 1: Levels of component granularity. These are summarized in Table 2.2, with the levels of granularity going from fine- to coarse-grained.

Dimension 2: Architectural viewpoints. These are summarized in Table 2.3.

Dimension 3: Development process. The development process in the business component approach is component-centric, architecture-centric, with a strong emphasis on component autonomy at the various granularity levels, factored by a precise collaboration model. The process is of a profoundly iterative nature, supporting continuous integration, and is driven by risk management best practices. It allows for high levels of concurrency and reuse.

Dimension 4: Distribution tiers. From a functional development perspective, business components and business component systems are seen in terms of four logical distribution tiers: the user tier, the workspace tier, the enterprise tier, and the resource tier.

Dimension 5: Functional layers. We will present in Chapter 5 the main functional layers and categories of business components: process business components, entity business components, and utility business components.

Table 2.2 Levels of Component Granularity

LEVEL	DEFINITION
Language class	A class in an object-oriented programming language used to build distributed components. It is not considered a component.
Distributed component	The lowest level of component granularity. It is a software artifact that can be called at run-time with a clear interface and a clear separation between interface and implementation. It is autonomously deployable.
Business component	Represents the software implementation of an autonomous business concept or business process. It consists of all the software artifacts necessary to express, implement, and deploy a given business concept as an autonomous, reusable element of a larger information system. It is a unifying concept across the development lifecycle and the distribution tiers.
Business component system (system-level component)	A set of cooperating business components assembled together to deliver a solution to a business problem.
Federation of system-level components	A set of cooperating system-level components federated to resolve the information technology needs of multiple end users often belonging to different organizations.

Table 2.3 The Architectural Viewpoints

VIEWPOINT	DEFINITION
Technical architecture	The architectural viewpoint concerned with the component execution environment, the set of development tools, the user-interface framework, and any other technical services and facilities required to develop and run a component-based system.
Application architecture	The architectural viewpoint concerned with the set of architectural decisions, patterns, guidelines, and standards required to build a component-based system that conforms to the extra-functional requirements.
Project management architecture	The architectural viewpoint concerned with the set of architectural and organizational decisions, and associated tools and guidelines, required to scale a development to more than 10 developers working together.
Functional architecture	The architectural viewpoint concerned with the functional aspects of the system, including the actual specification and implementation of a system that satisfies the functional requirements.

These five dimensions constitute the conceptual framework required to set up a business component factory able to efficiently produce business components with high quality and short development cycles.

Endnotes

1   For more information, see, for example, [Orfali 1998].

2   In Figure 1.1 these boxes were labeled "enterprise distributed components," since the business component concept had not yet been introduced. Chapter 5 discusses how this can be an acceptable simplification.

3   In this book, we adopt the [Stroustrup 1993, page 14] distinction between *enabling* and *supporting*: "A language is said to *support* a style of programming if it provides facilities that makes it convenient (reasonably easy, safe, and efficient) to use that style. A language does not support a technique if it takes exceptional effort or skill to write such programs; it merely *enables* the technique to be used."

4   See, for example, [Booch 1999] and [ODP 1998].

5   For batch systems, transactions are often called checkpoint/restart.

The Distributed Component

Chapter 1, "Component-Based Development," introduced our definition of *component*, and Chapter 2, "The Business Component Approach," described the several levels or granularities of components within the business component approach. This chapter deals with one of those levels—the level that most writers address today—that is, the technical unit of independent deployment that we call the distributed component.

The distributed component (DC) is, in granularity terms, the smallest component that provides network-addressable interfaces, and it is normally implemented using a commercially available component implementation technology such as CORBA 3.0, EJB, or COM/DCOM.[1] The name *distributed component* was chosen because of the specific way in which component implementation technologies are used—that is, with the application of design patterns and architectural principles that enhance portability and reduce complexity for the functional developer in the context of larger-scale distributed systems.

The DC is visible as a design artifact very early in the development lifecycle. It retains its identity and autonomy throughout development, ending up as the basic unit of software component construction and deployment. As such, it is a key implementation concept. It provides an answer to the question of what precisely the functional programmer actually builds. In this chapter we deal mainly with the build-time and run-time aspects of the DC; however, the discussion is extended in Chapter 4, "The Business Component," to cover the whole development lifecycle.

This chapter is structured as follows:

- First, the key distinguishing *concepts* of the distributed component are discussed.

- Second, the *internals* are examined; that is, we look at the DC as a white box[2] and examine its internal structure. This structure provides a clear separation layer between what the functional developer sees and those aspects specific to whatever component implementation technology has been chosen.

- Finally, the white box is turned into a black box, and several *externals* concepts concerning the DC's interface(s) are introduced.

As elsewhere in the book, our discussion adopts the functional developer's point of view, staying above the fine detail of implementation and technical infrastructure. Of course, the technical details of the different underlying infrastructures—the component execution environment and component technologies—do influence what can be done or not done, but they are in general consistent with and supportive of the concepts, principles, and patterns discussed here.

Concepts

The DC is defined as follows:

> A distributed component (DC) is a design pattern for an autonomous software artifact that can be deployed as a pluggable binary component into a run-time component execution environment. This design pattern is aimed at supporting high-productivity development for large-scale distributed systems. It is normally implemented using a commercially available component implementation technology.

When a DC is implemented, the resulting software component is called a *distributed component implementation*. However, the term *DC* is normally used for both the design pattern and the implementation, unless the context requires a distinction to be made.

The component execution environment is defined as follows:

> A component execution environment (CEE) is the run-time "socket" into which a distributed component plugs and within which it executes. The CEE consists of a defined set of services, facilities, and middleware, and it is the run-time part of the business component virtual machine.

The business component virtual machine (BCVM) is an implementation of the technical architecture. The technical architecture defines how, at all phases of development, technical complexities are hidden from the functional developer. The CEE, the technical architecture, and the BCVM are addressed in Chapter 8, "Technical Architecture."

The most important aspect of the definition of a DC (distributed component) is that the DC is a logical concept, a design pattern. This supports the adoption of a particular approach to the DC—that is, a way of thinking about components independently of a specific implementation technology. Indeed, a DC could be implemented (with a few constraints) using not only any of the current component implementation technologies, but even using noncomponent technologies such as RPC, traditional CORBA, or traditional transaction processing monitors. Of some importance is that this approach is a way to avoid the various contentions between providers of component implementation technologies and to bring the focus back where it belongs: on the functional developer's needs for the design and development of a component-based business system. As such, we dare to hope that the vendors of component implementation technologies may use this chapter (and others) as a requirement statement: This is what is needed to build high-performance and scalable systems in a cost-efficient way using component technology.

This section first presents an overview of the run-time DC in terms of the functional developer's point of view. Second, the main characteristics of the DC concept are presented, and finally the various categories of DC are briefly discussed.

Overview

In our approach, the DC is defined in such a way that the functional designer/developer needs to be concerned only with specifying interfaces, writing business logic, defining the mapping to any persistent storage, and invoking the services of other DCs. All other implementation aspects should not be his or her concern, but rather the concern of the technical architecture. Hence although a DC is built as a component as defined by a component implementation technology, it is shaped according to important design patterns and architectural principles that reduce complexity for the functional developer. The complexities largely hidden from the functional developer include both technical "plumbing" and distributed business system complexities. Figure 3.1, a run-time view of two DCs, *A* and *B*, illustrates the essential elements of a DC from the functional developer's viewpoint. In the figure, DC *A* is invoking DC *B* by sending it a message. Physically, the message is handled by the component execution environment (CEE); however, the figure shows the logically direct invocation. The essential elements are as follows:

Functional code. This is the code internal to the DC that the functional developer must write for the DC to provide the business function. Other parts of the DC can be generated or handled by generic code.

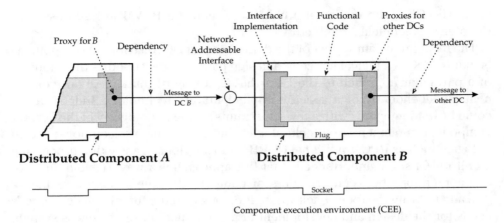

Figure 3.1 Distributed component essentials.

Proxy. DC *A* contains a proxy for *B*, which the functional code in *A* calls in order to talk to DC *B*'s interface. The proxy can typically be generated, and its code is specific to the component implementation technology.

Network-addressable interface. Each DC has one or more network-addressable interfaces. In Figure 3.1, DC *B*'s interface is shown. The interface(s) are implemented by an interface implementation.

Interface implementation. The interface implementation is what bridges the gap between the interface and the functional code. Like the proxy, it is specific to the component implementation technology used (unless a separate *dispatcher* is implemented—see "Internals" later in this chapter), and given appropriate build-time tools, it can be generated from the functional developer's interface specification.

Dependencies. When a DC *A* invokes *B*, then *A* is said to be dependent on *B*. Figure 3.1 also shows that *B* is dependent on another DC to which it sends a message. There are a number of different kinds of inter-DC dependencies. A major goal of the DC design pattern is to minimize these dependencies, not only at run-time but also at the various stages of development.

Plug. The plug allows the DC to be deployed autonomously into the provided socket of a run-time CEE, and it is clearly specific to the component implementation technology used. For example, the plug may call the CEE to inform the CEE when the DC has been loaded into memory. It should never have to be seen by functional developers, being automatically generated or provided by the component implementation technology's build tools.

Socket. The socket, which is part of the CEE, provides a number of services to the DC. For example, it supports the physical loading of the DC into memory and its recognition by the CEE. Physically, the socket often takes the form of low-level entry points that the DC must invoke.

Characteristics

As was mentioned previously, while the DC is usually built using the normal build tools provided by the chosen component implementation technology, it has a number of refining characteristics that extend and also constrain the conventional description of a software component. These are as follows:

- *Traceability* from business concept to run-time
- Support for *distributed systems*
- A clear "*black-box/white-box*" boundary between externals and internals, as seen by the functional developer
- *Separation of concerns* between functional code and the underlying "plumbing" of CORBA, COM, or other messaging middleware
- A clear *component model* for the functional developer

Throughout these five characteristics runs a constant concern for two important and distinct aspects of large-scale, mission-critical distributed business system development: first, performance and scalability across the development lifecycle—that is, the ability to quickly, reliably, and cost-effectively build large-scale systems using a large team of developers; and second, run-time performance and scalability.

Traceability

Although the DC can be used for a number of different purposes, the main purpose within the business component approach is to provide the component implementation within a given business component tier. The DC is an autonomous unit of design and construction, and as such provides direct traceability from business concept through analysis, design, construction, and deployment, with essentially no transformation.

By *no transformation* we mean that the concept of DC may appear at analysis, and it may be carried through to deployment as an autonomous unit. The concept is refined throughout the development lifecycle, but logically (and if desired physically) the DC at analysis is also the DC at design-, construction-, deployment-, and run-time. This traceability from analysis through to run-time is illustrated in Figure 3.2, where the business concept "Vendor" (identified at requirements capture) is implemented at the enterprise tier by an enterprise DC

(EDC) called *eVendor* (see Appendix A, "Naming Conventions," for the naming conventions used throughout the book). The figure also indicates that a DC consists of a number of language classes (the circles), one of which is often the major functional class within the DC. Such a class is called the "focus" class, and is further described in the later section, "Internals."

Compare this to what happens with other development approaches. In *traditional development*, transformations are the norm. For example, an analysis-time object model is transformed into a functional segment or package model at design-time, then retransformed at build-time into project deliverables often of arbitrary size, and finally transformed again for deployment into executable binaries. Each transformation results in artifacts that are quite different in their content from artifacts in the previous phase, although a good methodology will provide a mapping between them.

No matter how good the mapping, it is always the case that information is lost on transformation. This is one reason why so few analysis-time deliverables are actually updated when a required change is detected at design- or build-time. The *object-oriented approach* improves on traditional development because a concept identified at analysis as a class appears as a class also at design and at construction; however, it is lost at the last stages of build-time (if not earlier) when the classes are compiled into some set of modules, which have little or no relationship to the original business concepts, for deployment into the run-time.

The DC, on the other hand, enables a business concept to be mapped isomorphically from a tier defined at analysis-time through all phases of develop-

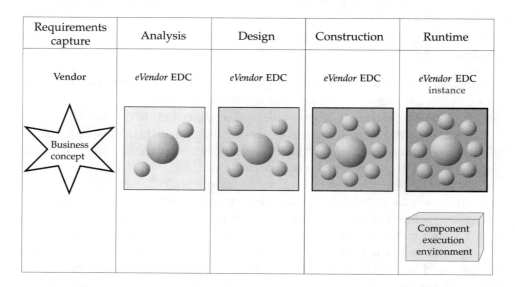

Figure 3.2 Traceability through development lifecycle.

ment right into the run-time. This is illustrated in Figure 3.3, where the business concept *"Vendor"* is represented at the top left of the figure by a business component. At analysis-/design-time, it is refined into a number of tiers (four are shown, although not all business components have all tiers). The diagram then follows the enterprise tier only and shows (top right) a further refinement, with two interfaces being identified. One interface provides services to any one specific vendor, the other to (perhaps large) collections of vendors.[3] The figure shows that the option has been taken to implement each interface by a separate DC. That is, in this example, the enterprise tier of the *Vendor* business component contains two DCs. Note that the number of interfaces per DC and the number of DCs per tier are design decisions, and the figure illustrates one of a set of possible design decisions. At the bottom right of Figure 3.3, the construction of the two DCs is shown, both eventually (bottom left) being linked into a single binary module that is independently pluggable into a CEE. Even though it is a single module, the CEE would recognize two components. Again, the number of DCs within a given executable binary is partly a design decision and partly a matter of the support provided by the underlying CEE.

Figure 3.3 illustrates how a single business concept—"Vendor"—ends up as a single server-side module that implements all the vendor business logic in the enterprise tier. In other words, the DC is traceable with almost no transformation (but with refinement) from requirements to run-time. At analysis-time, for example, the business component's distribution dimension enables early decisions to be taken regarding how many of the four tiers are to be implemented

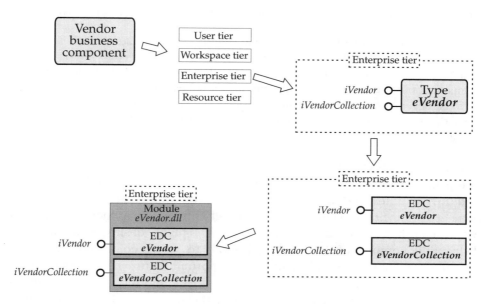

Figure 3.3 Distributed component development lifecycle.

and hence what DCs will be used to compose the business component. At construction-time, the business component will consist of a small number of DCs (plus other ancillary artifacts), all unambiguously identifiable as part of the business component. It is this kind of nontransformational traceability between business concept and the unit of code deployment that has been one of the longer-term objectives talked about in the industry for some 10 years or more. Figure 3.3 illustrates how, in the business component approach, all phases of the development lifecycle are involved in delivering against this objective.

Distributed System Support

The DC directly supports architecting, designing, implementing, testing, and deploying distributed systems. It does this through various important characteristics, which include location independence (that is, technical independence; an architect still has to take location into account for scalability and performance), middleware independence, network addressability, reduction of dependencies through provision of specific granularity guidelines, and the consequential clear boundaries between different build-time and run-time artifacts.

For example, the DC directly supports a crucial design guideline for distributed processing—that is, the necessity to distinguish between those things that are "network addressable" and those things that are not. At run-time, the DC has a well-defined middleware-supported reference—such as a CORBA Interoperable Object Reference (IOR)—that is visible to other software over a network. A DC also has a well-defined *external* identity (for example, "eVendor"), usable at run-time as well as at design- and construction-time and defined as follows:

> The external identity of a DC is a unique identity that associates it with its corresponding concept in the business domain. For example, the concept "vendor" in the business domain could be represented in the enterprise tier by an EDC whose identity is the string "eVendor." At run-time, a DC can be addressed by the functional developer using its external identity. The external identity is mapped to a valid component implementation technology reference by the component execution environment.

Thus the DC is explicitly intended to implement a network-addressable unit in business component systems—it has an external identity and provides one or more run-time interfaces to a run-time type. Of course, the physical presence of a network is not a requirement. Several distributed components can interact with each other in the same address space. It is highly desirable that moving a distributed component from being remote to being colocated should not require a recompile or relink. The really important feature is that, as far as the functional developer is concerned, colocated DCs and those in other address spaces or machines are invoked in exactly the same way. That is, in general, they are all treated as being located remotely. On the other hand, programming constructs such as language classes used to build the DC only invoke other constructs inside the DC. This means that language classes visible to the programmer at construction-time become nonnetwork-addressable objects at run-time. In this way, the distributed component provides in a very simple way for the necessary separation between those things that are network addressable and those that are not.

Black Box/White Box

A DC shares current component thinking in that it has a very clear *boundary* (its interfaces and dependencies) at run-time. Externally, the DC is seen as a black box. The most important objective for the DC designer is to properly define its interfaces and dependencies. The user of the DC should have to deal with only the interface and should never be required to have any knowledge of its internals—either at run-time or build-time. A DC is a white box only to the programmer who actually builds it. Many technologies, including distributed object technologies, make a point of separating interface from implementation.

We strongly support this distinction, to the extent that we see nothing unusual in two interacting DCs using different languages and underlying middleware technologies. For example, a DC implementation running on CORBA and built with C++ should be able to invoke a DC built in Java as an EJB. This is made possible by the CEE, which normally consists of not only a component implementation technology but also some additional "glue" code—a separation layer, discussed later in this chapter—to support the DC concepts described here. Any organization dealing in a serious way with distributed component technology will gain significant benefits from implementing this additional code. We hope one day that this will be provided directly as part of the commercial offerings of the component implementation technology providers.

A good example of the extent to which a DC is a black box at build-time is the treatment of proxies. This is illustrated by Figure 3.4, where two EDCs—*eVendor* and *eAddressBook*—are shown at build-time. Suppose the programmer of *eVendor*—let's call him Joe—needs to write code that will access the *eAddressBook* EDC in order to get the vendor's address (the design background to placing an address in a separate DC is discussed in Chapter 11, "Component-Based Business Modeling"). Through some appropriate tool, Joe sees *eAddressBook* as a black box and is able to access only those things that *eAddressBook* has specified as being "exportable." One of these things would, of course, be the proxy provided by *eAddressBook* so that other DCs can invoke its services. This proxy is produced as an integral part of producing *eAddressBook* and, as shown by Figure 3.4, may be exported to a build-time repository, from which Joe can import it into his *eVendor* functional code. The proxy is then said to have been exported to *eVendor*, which in turn is said to have "imported" *eAddressBook*'s proxy.

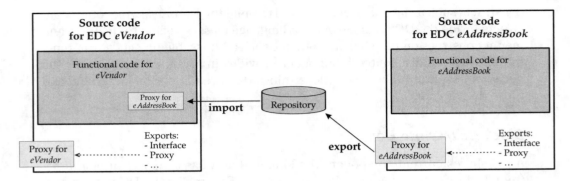

Figure 3.4 Proxy export at build-time.

Note that *eAddressBook* may well produce several proxies for the different interfaces it may have. Also, a given proxy may be produced in several programming languages where it is possible that DCs will be built using those languages.

Hence at build-time the only artifacts visible outside a DC are those that have been explicitly exported. If exported, the developer of another DC can import the artifact. At run-time, a called DC is never physically bound into the calling DC. Indeed, there are no compiled software language bindings between the two DCs. And in the case of a proxy, although it enables the programmer to treat the target DC syntactically like any other language class, he or she must be aware that the real target is not within his or her own build unit, and hence it cannot be thought of as being another local in-process construct.

When a DC is compiled and linked, the exported parts are generally not included, so that at run-time the DC consists of the functional code, plus other generated or generic artifacts such as the interface implementation, as shown in Figure 3.5.

A run-time application of the black-box principle is the treatment of language classes. The language classes used to build that DC are visible only within the DC. Indeed, there is a hard rule that language classes can never directly invoke another language class in another DC. Put another way, this means that there is no way to access a language class from outside the DC other than through one of the DC's interfaces. This strongly supports the concept of information hiding that helps significantly in mastering the complexity of very large projects.

Separation of Concerns

The distributed component has a programming model that provides many technical and system transparencies. For example, concurrency, threading, and memory management issues, as well as event and transaction management, are

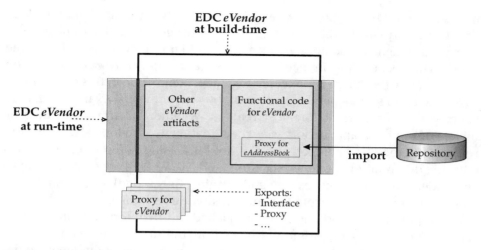

Figure 3.5   Build-time versus run-time.

hidden from the functional developer. These transparencies are provided by the component execution environment, a logical part of which is a separation layer within the DC; this is described in "Internals" later in this chapter.

Such transparencies are essential in providing the required separation of concerns between functional development and infrastructure provisioning. There are two main reasons for this approach. First, a functional designer should be able to concentrate on functional design and should not have to be concerned with underlying technical plumbing issues. Second, it enables source code portability across multiple different component execution environments.

For example, when invoking a method on a DC, the functional programmer should have to consider only two things: having a way to easily identify which component he or she wishes to invoke and what method to call. Ideally, taking the *eVendor* example, and assuming some method *get_vendor_information*, then the programmer should expect to be able to do something as simple as the following example, written in a type-based architectural style (where individual instances of a vendor are handled internally through instances of language classes, so that the DC at run-time represents all instances of the *Vendor* type—see Chapter 9, "Application Architecture," for the difference between a type-based and an instance-based style):

```
ieVendor a_vendor;
a_vendor.get_vendor_information(...);
```

The first line is an example of using a proxy—the type *ieVendor*—which represents an interface to *eVendor*. The first line then declares and initializes an interface *a_vendor* of type *eVendor*, where the DC's external identity ("eVendor") is an attribute of the proxy, so that the programmer does not have to know it (although an operation to access it would normally be provided by the proxy). The second line invokes the *get_vendor_information* operation on *a_vendor*. Note that there is no technology-dependent code in this example.

The technology independence shown by the previous example can be expected to be important for most readers. Whether software providers or builders of a custom application, we expect that many developers will face the problem of integrating components that are built using different technologies and using different component execution models. We thus advocate a component model that is, to a great extent, and certainly fully so at the functional code source level, independent from the implementation technology.

The programmer's model is further touched on in "Internals" later in this chapter. For the present, we now discuss how the functional developer perceives the component at run-time—which determines the component model that the functional developer must understand at build-time.

Component Model

There are two more important aspects of the DC component model that have not yet been fully addressed: First, the DC implements a type; second, the DC imposes a strong distinction between itself and its internal software construction artifacts, usually language classes.

The DC implements a type. A question that, at the time of writing, none of the component implementation technologies answers unambiguously is whether component technology is simply about a packaging technology around object-oriented (or other) code or whether the component implements a type in its own right. Consider the previous example of building the *eVendor* DC. A technically important conceptual question concerns the run-time nature of *eVendor*. Does a DC merely reflect an evolution of the RPC mechanisms that evolved in the 1970s and early 1980s? Is it just a kind of transaction program? Or does it in some way embrace the distributed object models that evolved in the late 80s and early 90s? It would seem that there are two possible answers:

1. *eVendor* is a lump of code whose in-memory image provides interfaces to language objects within it. By *language object* is meant a run-time instance of a language class—implemented using an object-oriented programming language, or OOPL for short. Such language objects may have multiple instances. The component *eVendor* itself, however, is merely the piece of code that contains the implementations of those object instances.

2. *eVendor* is a type that provides interfaces at analysis- and design-time and is refined into an implementation of that type at design-/build-time. How

eVendor is implemented internally is irrelevant. It might be implemented using a procedural language, with no objects in sight.

We adhere to the second of these two answers. A DC at run-time is the implementation of one or more run-time instances of a type (see the sidebar, "Build-Time versus Run-Time," for further discussion). We call such an instance a "component instance"; each component instance has an external identity such as "eVendor" (in a type-based architectural style—see Chapter 9).

The DC imposes a strong distinction. It is a crucial principle of modern distributed systems that there be a clear distinction between component instances and language objects. This distinction applies not merely at run-time, but right throughout the development process. The purpose of this principle is to provide strong support for a proper partitioning of the problem space while at the same time significantly reducing intercomponent message volumes and dependencies in order to support performance, maintainability, and scalability. A prime example of this distinction principle is that the DC is never passed by value; rather a reference to the DC is always passed (in a parameter on some operation). A language object is always passed by value, and it is never passed by reference. Where the complete state of a DC must be copied (for example, in order to be serialized), then that state is passed as data extracted by the DC from whatever internal structures and mechanisms it uses to maintain its state.

In the past, the industry has not made such a clear distinction between components and language objects. A starting assumption seemed to be that distributed object computing was all about applying RPC principles to OOPLs. The underlying concept was that you build an application and then tear it apart in order to distribute it. In turn, this meant providing language-centric bindings across a network between different pieces of the application. Only now is it being realized that this is essentially a blind alley: The truth is that distributed component computing has little to do with programming languages. In particular, design concepts used within an OOPL application often just do not scale at all into the distributed environment. For example, it is very common in an OOPL application to iterate over a collection of objects. Doing this sort of thing across a network, however, will usually guarantee that the system will perform appallingly badly. Again, language objects are very much the slaves of the application that binds them all together. Often a given language object's lifecycle and state are entirely at the mercy of its clients. Distributed processing, on the other hand, requires components that are masters of their own destiny. A DC is an adult in the computing world—responsible for its own actions, and for its own lifecycle.

One thing is clear: Before embarking on a business component project, it is necessary to understand the distinction between component instances and language objects. Unfortunately, at the time of writing, there is no well-accepted industry meta-model for these things. For example, looking at the COM/DCOM

BUILD-TIME VERSUS RUN-TIME

In discussing run-time instances, we need to distinguish between code produced by a developer, on the one hand, and the run-time phenomena produced by that code. Code built and shipped as a binary file is not the same as the run-time effects produced by that code when it is loaded into memory and run. For example, suppose a programmer uses an OOPL to build a simple application that contains a *customer* class. The source code for the customer class (and the rest of the application) is then compiled, linked, and run. At run-time, were I to peek into the computer's memory, not only would I see the machine code that implements *customer* (that is, the in-memory image of the implementation) but I would also see multiple instances of *customer*—say, 10. Of course, this does not mean that the programmer actually built and compiled 10 copies of the *customer* class, one for each run-time instance. What the programmer built was one customer class. At run-time, the multiple instances are actually handled by mechanisms provided by the OOPL development kit and included in the machine code during the compile/link process.

The important point here is that the programmer, when writing the code, must have an understanding of what happens at run-time. In a real sense, the programmer is producing a plan for what is required to happen at run-time. Indeed, as Szyperski points out, the process of software construction is nothing more than the creation of a plan as to how a computer will operate at run-time. "Software is different from products in all other engineering disciplines. Rather than delivering a final product, delivery of software means delivering the blueprints for products. Computers can be seen as fully automatic factories that accept such blueprints and instantiate them. . . . It is as important to distinguish between software and its instances as it is to distinguish between blueprints and products, between plans and a building." [Szyperski 1998, p. 8].

Although defined as a pattern, the term *DC* is also generally used to refer not only to a design/construction artifact but also to the corresponding run-time construct. We have done this in the same spirit as the term "object" is often used to mean a thing being built using an OOPL (a class) and also a run-time thing (an instance). It is sometimes essential, though, to distinguish between the DC at run-time and at build-time. For example, when speaking about the network address of a DC, it would be more precise to say that the component instance that is instantiated from a DC at run-time has an external identity whereby it can be invoked across a network. For this reason, where distinction is necessary, we call the run-time instantiation of a DC a "DC instance" or "component instance."

literature, it would seem that these questions are left for the developer to answer. The emerging CORBA Component Model does not (at the time of writing) seem to answer these questions either. But an answer is required; the DC concept, described in this chapter, provides one such answer.

Categories

Distributed components can be classified into four main categories according to their responsibilities in implementing one of the four business component tiers. This section briefly describes the characteristics of each category; additional detail is provided in Chapter 4, "The Business Component," Chapter 5, "The Business Component System," and Chapter 12, "Component-Based Design." Note that while the business component approach does not strictly require that all tiers be implemented using DC technology, we always assume that at the very least the enterprise tier is so implemented.

> **User DC (UDC).** This is a DC specifically built to display the user interface for a business component. A UDC may need to persist its data (such as window position and size and what business components are being viewed). This is so that, when a user closes down a client machine, things can be returned to the same state on the screen when the machine is restarted. The UDC is always located on the same machine as the physical GUI screen because it must be able to react to user events at GUI speed. In other words, the bandwidth between the UDC and the underlying GUI infrastructure is very high. The UDC gets its data from a workspace DC.

> **Workspace DC (WDC).** This is a DC built to support the needs of a single user, where application logic relevant to only a single user is required and where that logic cannot sensibly be provided by the user tier. A WDC does not need to support concurrent access by multiple users. The WDC may well need to persist its data. It does not need to have the persisted data accessed concurrently by multiple users, even if it may need to handle concurrent access by several user units of work initiated concurrently by a single user. The WDC is often physically located on a client machine such as a PC, but this is not mandatory. We will discuss this aspect further in Chapter 9. Bandwidth between UDC and WDC is typically much lower than between the UDC and the GUI. A WDC often gets its data from the enterprise tier—that is, from one or more enterprise DCs.

> **Enterprise DC (EDC).** The enterprise tier is arguably the most important tier because it implements the enterprise level. An EDC typically needs to be accessed concurrently by multiple users, and it requires persistence and transactional services. In Chapter 8, we discuss how the CEE provides these services more or less transparently to the functional developer. The EDC is similar in its internals to the WDC; both types are essentially business logic, with no knowledge of the edges of the information system.

> **Resource DC (RDC).** This is a DC uniquely dedicated to the management of shared resources. It does not contain any business logic. The most typical example of an RDC is a component that provides for database access. The

RDC gets and puts data when requested by an EDC. A given RDC is addressed by only one EDC.

In addition to these four kinds of DC, there are others that are important from a functional designer's point of view. Two of these are the following:

Gateway DC (GDC). This is a DC uniquely dedicated to be a gateway to some other service or component. For example, an external system or a legacy system could access business components using GDCs. We will further illustrate this in Chapter 4. The gateway DC can be seen as belonging to an additional tier, in a different dimension from the normal four business component tiers.

Testing DC (TDC). This is a DC that knows how to automatically test (and retest, and retest) a distributed component or a business component or a particular part of a business component. This may be purpose-built, or it may be scripted. Testing DCs are also useful for determining the quality of service of a business component, for regression testing, and for guaranteeing a given level of confidence in the deliverable.

In addition to these two, there are a number of components within the CEE that can and should also be built as DCs. These include generic implementations that are scripted to achieve various ends. For example, a generic workflow DC is sometimes very useful.

Internals

This section describes the internal characteristics of a DC. A major factor driving the internal design is to make things as simple as possible for the functional programmer, so that he or she is fully supported in being able to concentrate on business logic only. Such business logic is assumed, for the purposes of this section, to be implemented using an object-oriented programming language (OOPL). This is not, however, a hard requirement—a DC could be built using any programming language; in such a case, although the details presented in this section would change, the general structural principles would remain the same. A second important factor driving the internals design is the objective of source portability across CEEs (component execution environments). In this section, first we present the desired functional developer's model—a model that meets the objective of simplicity. Second, we discuss how functional code is strictly separated from code that interfaces with the plumbing of the underlying technology-specific middleware. Finally, the various internal parts of the DC—that is, the different categories of language classes used to construct a DC—are addressed, and a DC design style that guides distributed component developers in the design of DCs is described. The architectural and design rationale behind this structure will be expanded in Chapter 12.

The principles and concepts discussed in this section are independent of the underlying middleware technology. These principles and concepts are supported more or less directly by such technologies, but we have not yet found a middleware technology that disallows them.

Functional Developer's Programming Model

If we are truly to provide a dramatic improvement in software manufacturing productivity, then the functional programmer must be relieved as much as possible from having to be concerned with technical plumbing complexities. Put another way, support should be provided such that the functional programmer can concentrate solely on business logic. To achieve this, it is necessary to define the desirable level of abstraction for the functional programmer—that is, what it is desirable that the programmer should write. This is even more important where there is a focus on code portability across component implementation technologies; these technologies often seem to export complexity to the functional developer. A useful way to define the desired level of abstraction is to define a functional programming model. A functional developer's programming model defines the nature of the code that the functional programmer is required to write—its structure and its transparencies, together with the set of concepts that tell the programmer about the context for which code is being written. While the complete details of the DC functional programming model is beyond the scope of this book, in this section we briefly illustrate some of its main characteristics.

The starting point is to ask, "What is the least the functional programmer should have to do in order to implement the required business logic?" The DC functional developer's programming model is explicitly and intentionally a high-level programming model that both hides the intrinsic complexities of distributed component computing and also enables code portability, at least at the source level. We look at two facets of the programmer's mode: first specification, then the code.

Specification

Consider again the *Vendor* business component. Suppose a design specification has been produced, expressed either in some graphical notation such as UML or in some text-form specification language. If written in a specification language, the specification for the *Vendor* business component, focusing particularly on its enterprise tier, might look something like Figure 3.6. This sample specification language uses an OMG IDL-like syntax, but it differs from IDL,

```
module Vendor_Module
{
   BusinessComponent Vendor
   {
      enterprise eVendor, eVendorCollection;
      ...
   };

   interface ieVendor
   {
      set_address( ... )  raises BadAddress;
      ...
   };

   DistributedComponent eVendor
   {
      provides   ieVendor;
      publishes  AddressChanged;
   };

   DistributedComponent eVendor
   {
      uses           ieAddressBook;
      implementation ...;
   };
   ...
};
```

Figure 3.6   Business component specification fragment.

first, in that it assumes that the sequence of identifier definition is not important and, second, in that it allows cumulative definitions—a given identifier can be defined several times with the same keyword.

Consider the specification of the *eVendor* DC, indicated by the keyword DistributedComponent in Figure 3.6. The specifier has elected to differentiate between those aspects visible to a developer of another component using this specification, who would see only the externals (provided interfaces and events published), from those that are the concern of the internals developer (interfaces used and the name of the implementation). To do this, the specifier has specified *eVendor* twice. The parser for this specification language would combine both into a single specification, which would be loaded into a repository. Of course, it is preferable that some tool should be provided rather than forcing developers to write in a specification language.

Specification of the internal implementation of the DC would also be provided, but it is not shown in Figure 3.6. There are two aspects to such a specification. First, we wish to specify things like language classes, mapping of the provided interface to language class operations, and so forth. Second, the implementation may be more than one artifact. For example, the implementation may be a generic binary plus a configuration. Or it may be several binaries (for example, several Java .class files). In this case, the DC is, in fact, a defined collection of artifacts.

Code

Let's move on to the code seen by the functional programmer within a DC. We assume that the type-based architectural style (see Chapter 9) has been used for *eVendor*. Also, *eVendor* does not appear to store its address, but uses (as shown by the keyword "uses" in Figure 3.6) the services of the *eAddressBook* utility component, whose network-addressable external identity could be the string "eAddressBook". Consider the *set_address* operation in interface *ieVendor* shown in Figure 3.6. Let's assume that this operation does the following:

- Reads the Vendor's persistent data to get the address key (we assume a design where the key does not change when the address changes).

- Invokes *eAddressBook*'s *update* method to make the change in the address (the Address Book validates the address before performing the update and raises a *BadAddress* exception if the validation fails).

- Publishes an "AddressChanged" event. A good design question is why *eVendor* should do this rather than *eAddressBook*. We confess that we chose *eVendor* merely to make this example shorter.

The desired level of abstraction to handle this is illustrated by the pseudo-code shown in Figure 3.7, where *utility* is a well-known language object within the DC (described later in "Language Class Categories") that provides utility services to business logic. Lines 5 and 6 in the try block define first the Address Book's interface and next the data structure for vendor information. Line 7 loads the data for the vendor identified by *vendor_id*. The next line invokes the *update* operation on the Address Book DC to record the changed address. Finally, in line 9 the *utility* language object is requested to publish an "Address-Changed" event. Exceptions (indicated in line 11) and the required conformance with the error management framework could be handled by generated or generic code.

This code shows no awareness of the underlying component implementation technology, and hence it is source portable. In addition, it is extremely concise code. Some out-of-the-box component implementation technologies would require some 20 or more lines of code for this simple *set_address* method. Given that the business requirement was to do two things (set the address and publish an event), five lines of code (including definitions) are close to the ideal. But is that all? The objective is that this *should* be all. The functional pro-

```
set_address(VendorId vendor_id, Address new_address)   //   1
{                                                      //   2
  try                                                  //   3
  {                                                    //   4
     ieAddressBook        address_book;                //   5
     eVendor_information vendor_information;           //   6

     vendor_information = self.get_data(vendor_id);    //   7
     address_book.update(
                  vendor_information.address_key,
                  new_address);                        //   8
     utility.publish(ïAddressChangedÓ);               //   9
  {                                                    //  10
  catch { ... }                                        //  11
  ...
{                                                      //  12
```

Figure 3.7   Pseudo-code for the *set_address* method of *eVendor*.

grammer should not have to consider anything else. Technical complexities such as concurrency, database locking, thread management, transaction management, event handling, name service access, and other technical details should all be handled on the programmer's behalf. In addition, the programmer is not concerned with any of the specific detailed coding mechanisms that the component implementation technology often requires.

Although not delivered by commercially available software today, the level of programming abstraction illustrated is certainly technically achievable, and it is an important objective of the DC's separation layer, the building of which, for an organization going seriously into CBD, is certainly worthy of consideration.

Separation Layer

There are a number of middleware-specific coding constraints required of a component. For example, in many CORBA ORBs, programmers are required to include a parameter in each interface operation that carries ORB information. Again, ORBs in general have their own specific memory management rules concerning operation parameters. As a final example, COM strongly urges the programmer to return a specific technology data type (an HRESULT) rather than a business-related result. Hence the specific technical nature of the component implementation technology influences the precise shape of an operation signature, and this must appear somewhere in the coding of the DC. However, given appropriate tools that generate this code from a specification, all such code can be hidden from the functional programmer through a separation layer, based partly on the *façade* pattern, which "provides a unified interface to a set of interfaces in a subsystem" [Gamma 1995].

Thus a DC consists of two major parts: the source-portable code with which the functional programmer is concerned, and generated and/or generic code that is specific to the component implementation technology used and hence is nonportable. The latter provides the separation layer that plugs the gap between the developer's programming model, illustrated in the previous section, and the component implementation technology.

The separation layer is illustrated by Figure 3.8, which takes the *eVendor* distributed component as an example and shows the following:

1. A method or operation on *eVendor* is invoked by a calling DC (not shown in the figure).

2. The CEE (component execution environment) invokes *eVendor* 's interface implementation, which has a technology-specific operation signature—that is, a signature conforming with the technology requirements of the CEE. The interface implementation is part of the separation layer.

3. The interface implementation (which should normally be generated code) handles this invocation, deals with the technology-specific aspects, and passes it on to the business-specific method.

4. The business-specific method is written by the functional developer and has no knowledge of underlying technical idiosyncrasies.

   Where another DC must be invoked, then the process is reversed: The functional logic invokes a proxy for the target DC.

5. The proxy, which should be generated code and is part of the separation layer, drives the plumbing-specific requesting mechanisms to send the message to another DC.

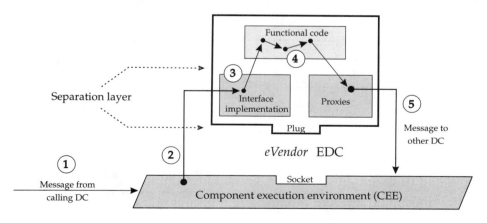

Figure 3.8   The separation layer.

Let's pause for a moment and consider the relationship between the separation layer and the CEE. Figure 3.8 suggests that they are quite different things. This is true from the point of view of, say, a systems programmer looking at the physical module structure of the code. From this viewpoint, the CEE in Figure 3.8 would consist of the component implementation technology produced commercially, plus some additional code produced by a third party or by an infrastructure team. The DC, on the other hand, including the separation layer, would be physically produced by the functional development group. From a different point of view—that of the functional developer at build-time—the separation layer is a part of the CEE. It is that part that normally would be automatically generated by tools or handled by generic code: It is not built by the functional developer, even if it may be used by him or her as, for example, in the case of proxies. This is illustrated in Figure 3.9, which distinguishes more precisely between the CEE and the DC. Figure 3.9 also suggests additional separation layer code, and (on each side of the socket) additional capabilities that may have to be provided to supplement the component implementation technology in order to provide the required level of separation (see Chapter 8).

In addition to source code portability and complexity reduction, a further advantage of the separation layer approach is that it allows us to make performance trade-offs. For example, there is a need for inexpensive inter-DC invocations within the same address space. To satisfy this need, generated or generic code can be included in the proxy part of the separation layer to assess whether the target distributed component is colocated and to take the appropriate action. This is particularly useful when the component execution environment is MOM-based (message-oriented middleware) for cross-address space (and cross-machine) communications but uses, say, COM for intra-address space invocations.

Providing a separation layer between the desired functional programmer's model and underlying technical complexities is of prime importance. For exam-

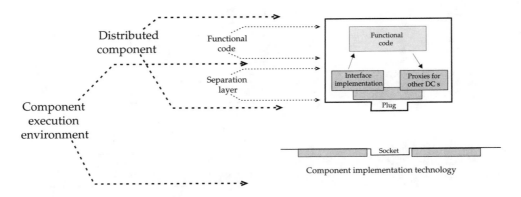

Figure 3.9   The functional programmer's view.

ple, consider line 5 of the *set_address* method shown in Figure 3.7. This provides an interface reference for the *eAddressBook* DC. Now the underlying component implementation technology may well first require that a name service be accessed, which returns some pointer. Then it has to be established whether the required component instance is active. If not, then it must be activated, and an interface reference must be retrieved. As far as the component implementation technology is concerned, all this has to be done by the programmer. Only then can the programmer invoke the Address Book's *update* method. But that's not all. The programmer must also conform to the component implementation technology's conventions about error handling, parameter storage rules (for example, when memory can be freed for a given parameter), and styles of parameter passing. The effect of all this is to require the programmer to know a great deal about the specifics of how the underlying ORB works.

In contrast, for our DC programmer, we state that invoking a method requires only that the programmer specify the interface type (*ieAddressBook*), the operation (*update*), and its parameters. Everything else is handled by the separation layer working with other parts of the CEE. When sending a message to another DC, the programmer is actually invoking a proxy within the separation layer that should normally be generated by the build tools. The proxy invokes generated or generic run-time code that handles the appropriate interaction with the component execution technology. In particular, the proxy can be tuned to specific technologies so that, for example, where they do not provide efficient activation, then the proxy (probably plus some separate CEE-provided run-time service module) can enhance activation efficiency, thereby significantly reducing network traffic.

In summary, the separation layer is a crucial player in providing the functional programmer with the required level of simplicity. There are other complexities, though—within the functional code—that must be handled. The DC concept also addresses these, as discussed in the next section, where the internal structural elements of the DC are considered—that is, the different categories of language class used in DC construction.

Language Class Categories

The two kinds of DCs most commonly seen by functional programmers are the WDC and the EDC. Of these two, the EDC is the most relevant for the enterprise. It is the DC category on which run-time performance and scalability depends. From a structural view, the EDC is the most complete: Other kinds of DCs can be illustrated by difference. For these reasons, this section centers mainly on the EDC. Although EDCs share many structural characteristics with WDCs, an important distinguishing characteristic of the EDC is that it manipulates the system's persistent storage through a resource tier.

EDCs, like any other DCs, are collections of language classes (LCs). A DC can be thought of as a micro-application, and so any pattern or type of class that is appropriate for an application tends to be appropriate for a DC. We can identify a few kinds of LC that usually appear again and again in a well-designed DC. Each of these kinds of LC has a well-defined role and has well-articulated relationships with other LCs. This not only provides the developer with a pattern, it also eases maintenance and supports evolution. The main LCs typically found in an EDC are shown in Figure 3.10, and this structure is the "default" EDC structure.

Figure 3.10 shows the resource-tier proxy as being of a slightly different kind than the other proxies. This is because resource-tier proxies have specific characteristics that other proxies do not have.

LCs fall into two categories following the distinction made in the previous section, "Separation Layer":

■ Business language classes. In Figure 3.10, the "cloud" shows the functional code where business logic is implemented. LCs that implement business logic are generally built by the functional developer.

Note that Figure 3.10 is a build-time picture. At specification-time, the developer of a DC sees its interfaces and, given appropriate tools, would map DC interface operations to business language class methods, so allowing the interface implementation LC to be entirely generated. Were

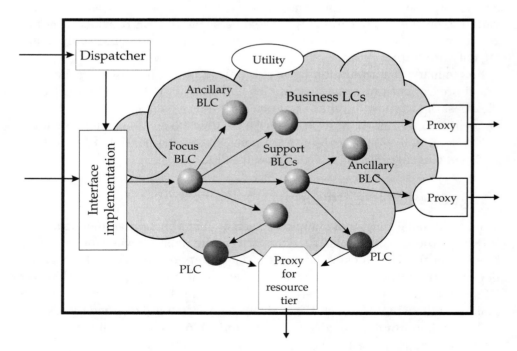

Figure 3.10 EDC structure.

Figure 3.10 to be redrawn as a specification-time diagram, then the interface implementation would appear much more strongly in the business logic area.

- Separation layer language classes—classes that are generated or generic and that make up the separation layer. Some of these classes may be seen and used by the functional programmer (the ones obtruding into the cloud in Figure 3.10), but they are never built by him or her.

Business Language Classes

Business language classes (BLCs) provide business data and/or behavior data—as opposed to technical or structural data—within the EDC, and they are further categorized in Table 3.1. Note that one particular category, the technical LC, while not business logic, is treated as a BLC because they are seen and used by the functional programmer and have nothing to do with the separation layer.

Focus BLC

The focus BLC is the business class that is central to a particular EDC. It is invoked only by the interface implementation (see "Separation Layer Language Classes" later in this chapter). Its responsibilities are directly those of the busi-

Table 3.1 Business Language Classes in a Distributed Component

CLASS CATEGORY	NUMBER PER EDC	DESCRIPTION
Focus BLC	One by default, but zero or more by exception	The focus BLC contains the business logic that implements the thing that the EDC actually *is*. For example, an Order EDC would have an Order focus BLC.
Support BLC	As many as required (may be none)	The support BLC contains business logic necessary for the EDC to do its job but that is not the responsibility of the focus LC. For example, an Order EDC could have an Order Header and an Order Line support LCs.
Ancillary BLC	As many as required	Ancillary BLCs fall into three categories: business data types, algorithm classes, and rule classes.
Technical LC	As many as required	Technical LCs are typically standard library classes such as lists, containers, and hash-tables. They are used in the implementation of business logic or to organize other classes. They do not do themselves implement business logic.

ness concept represented by the EDC (and by the business component). For example, the *eVendor* DC would have a focus BLC that encapsulates the essence of *eVendor*.

The focus BLC implements the core business logic and process flow. It helps to reduce the dependencies and interactions of all the other types of LCs. It is responsible for getting the business work done, and it structures the sequence of interactions with a set of support BLCs. This control or "mediating" role means support BLCs can be coded simply and without complex dependencies with other LCs embedded within them. This, in turn, makes the support BLCs more (potentially) reusable, as they will provide standard behavior and data, any complex collaborations being located in the focus BLC.

Often a given EDC will implement a single concept having a clear class that is the main focus of the implementation, such as an "Order" or an "Invoice." In such cases, the EDC will contain a single focus BLC. Sometimes (rarely in our experience) the EDC will end up as a small collection of things, placed in the same EDC for some reason. For example, a "Currency Book" EDC may contain three main concepts: exchanges between currencies (so needing the concept of exchange rate), maintenance of various currencies (for example, adding a new currency such as the Euro to the system), and performing calculations on money. In this case there could be three focus BLCs in a currency book EDC (and probably at least three interfaces as well). Note that the concept of "Currency Book" could well be a "discovered" business concept—that is, a concept that the business users had not thought of but would certainly have welcomed were it to exist.

Sometimes, the focus BLC at design time appears trivial, and it is possible that it will have nothing to do except forward method invocations from the interface implementation through to support BLCs. Although the focus BLC could be omitted in these cases, by default a focus BLC is assumed in order to provide for easier evolution and consistency. This results in the following simple guideline: By default, there will be one focus BLC (for example, "Order" in an Order EDC), but more than one focus BLC can be defined. However, situations where more than one seems to be required should be reviewed before a final decision is made.

Identification of focus BLCs is addressed in Chapter 11, where we discuss business modeling. Finally, although not shown in Figure 3.10, a focus BLC may use PLCs (persistence language classes—described in "Separation Layer Language Classes" later in this chapter) and talk through a proxy to another DC.

Support BLCs

A support BLC carries key business responsibility, such as handling a major subpart of an EDC (for example, Order Header and Order Line in Order EDC) or for validating business data. Often support BLCs in an EDC will be the minor or "dependent business objects" that are in close association with the focus

BLC. Note that it is possible for an EDC to contain a focus BLC but no support BLCs.

The following guidelines and heuristics can be used to identify support BLCs:[4]

- They are secondary to most discussions in that they are used only in conjunction with a focus BLC.

- They are often related to key PLCs (Persistence LCs—see "Separation Layer Language Classes" later in this chapter) in supporting the business process.

- They should represent basic behavior (for example, validation) associated with data held in a PLC.

Here is a suggested process that may assist with the design of support BLCs:

- Review the focus BLC business logic and identify what data is required to support its work. Where such data requires business logic separate from the responsibilities of the focus BLC, then this is a good candidate.

- Review the types of the EDC method parameters as they will indicate what PLCs may be needed. Any business behavior associated with those PLCs may then be allocated to support BLCs.

- If the behavior is simple maintenance—the so-called CRUD (create, read, update, delete) operations—and does not require significant behavior in the update or create methods, then a PLC may be sufficient and a support BLC may not be required.

- Try to avoid creating dependencies between the support BLCs unless this is a standard and consistent collaboration between a small number of support BLCs. "Dependencies" include method invocations so, in other words, try to avoid one support BLC invoking methods on another. Any such dependencies should be, as a default, delegated (pushed upwards) into the focus BLC. This means that all the coordination of behavior should happen through the focus BLC.

Ancillary BLCs

An ancillary BLC is a class used to implement business logic that is neither a focus nor a support BLC. Such classes are often generated or pulled from a class library; although used by the functional programmer in producing business logic, they are seldom if ever built by him or her. Three of the more important examples are data, algorithm, and rule BLCs.

Data BLC. A simple data structure class with little business functionality other than get/set. Sometimes it may be streamable, for example, to an XML string. A business data type (see "Externals" later in this chapter) is a good example of a data BLC. A business data type is normally generated rather than written by the functional programmer.

Algorithm BLC. A class (or set of classes) that allows a complex logical function or calculation to be factored out of a focus or support BLC if the behavior needs to be frequently accessed or included into other classes. It is the core functional logic that would carry out detailed or complex calculations, and it provides a simple "Do-It" interface.

Rule BLC. The reification of a specific business rule. Ideally, such rules should be "pluggable" from outside the EDC, so allowing clients to "configure" their EDCs with appropriate rules as business conditions evolve and change. Many rule BLCs may share a knowledge base. One example of a rule BLC is a pre- or post-condition on a method.

Technical LCs

While implementing a DC, as in any other application, there will often be the need to use classes that do not themselves implement business logic but that are needed to implement business logic or organize other classes. Examples are standard library classes—lists, containers, and advanced data structures such as hash tables. Such classes are termed technical LCs.

Separation-Layer Language Classes

The EDC's separation layer consists of a small number of different kinds of classes. These classes are ideally never built by the functional programmer, and they are often generated (assuming the appropriate specification tool support) or are based on generic code. Separation layer LCs are itemized in Table 3.2.

Interface Implementation

The interface implementation LC is responsible for implementing the EDCs provided interfaces. As a design principle, this language class should not contain any business logic.

The interface implementation receives messages from a client (calling) DC through its own proxy invoking one of the operations on one of its interfaces. It normally implements the operation by calling the focus class. From a functional designer's point of view, the interface implementation links the DC's interface to the business implementation. In a very real sense then the functional designer is concerned only with specifying the mapping between the DC's interface and the focus BLC. All other aspects can be taken care of by the separation layer and the CEE.

Exceptionally the interface implementation may invoke methods directly on a support BLC, when the support BLC provides a useful business function offered by the EDC interface. This has to be considered carefully, though, to make sure it is not bypassing key logic (including validity checks on data or sta-

Table 3.2 Language Classes in the Separation Layer

CLASS CATEGORY	NUMBER PER EDC	DESCRIPTION
Interface implementation	One	Implements the provided interfaces of the EDC; invokes the focus BLC.
Proxy	As many as required (may be none)	An LC that is a proxy for other DCs that this EDC talks to. That is, the other DCs implement the required interfaces of this EDC.
Persistence LC (PLC) and handle	As many as required (may be none)	The persistence LC (PLC) is a data-only class used to contain data that is to be read/written from/to a persistent store.
Utility	One	Provides a well-known object within the DC that BLCs can use for various services including cross-DC system capabilities (for example, issuing events or handling error structures).
Dispatcher	Zero or one	Handles a scripting interface where this is required.

tus) in the focus BLC. The interface implementation also normally manages the life cycle of focus BLC instances.

The interface implementation LC may also on occasion undertake the role of the dispatcher (see "Dispatcher" later in this chapter).

Proxy

Proxies are LCs that represent interfaces of target DCs (that is, DCs whose methods this EDC wishes to invoke). Proxies are classes owned by the target DC but exported at build-time to those DCs that wish to collaborate with the target DC. Each proxy provides a strongly typed interface to one or more interfaces of the target DC.

As a simple initial design rule, a proxy corresponds one-to-one with the DC interfaces. Depending on the underlying technology, however, various other alternatives can be adopted. For example, a proxy may be created for that subset of methods defined in an interface that are actually used by a given component, or an "intelligent" proxy may be created—that is, a proxy that performs some transformation or even applies some business rule before calling the interface. At the extreme, a proxy may even expose an interface that is different from the interface actually exposed by the target DC.

Persistence Language Class

A persistence language class (*PLC*) is an LC whose main purpose is to contain data that needs to be persisted to or read from a database. A PLC instance contains data retrieved from the database and/or data that is to be stored back onto the database through a persistence proxy or other mechanisms (see Chapter 12 for a discussion of persistence design). The internal nature of these classes is very similar to the business data types discussed later in this chapter. A PLC, together with the resource-tier proxy (shown in Figure 3.10), are mainly separation layer artifacts, and they are often generated. Together they hide access to the resource tier from the functional developer, and they assist in mapping between business logic and database access, so providing database independence.

Utility Language Class

The utility LC is instantiated at run-time as a well-known, singleton object within the DC. Its primary responsibility is to provide intra-DC nonbusiness services for business language classes. For example, it may provide an error object that accumulates errors detected within the DC. When an operation is completed and control returns to the interface implementation, then the interface implementation would check with the utility LC to see if there were any errors. If so, then the interface implementation would return the error using the appropriate middleware-specific error-handling mechanisms and formats. Another use of the utility LC is to allow BLCs to signal events in a simple way. This hides from the functional programmer the various mechanisms for driving an event management system provided by the underlying CEE. Other uses of the utility LC may be to manage introspection, quality of service, and static state (for example, the number of times this DC has being invoked or the number of transactions in which it has participated). Finally, the utility LC may contain the network address (that is, the run-time external identity) of this DC, should any business language class need to see it. In summary, the utility LC provides various common intra-DC services and in addition supports the DC's interaction with extra-functional services and facilities outside the DC—for example, passing events to the CEE—which the functional developer should not need to know about.

Dispatcher

The dispatcher provides the code that is actually invoked by the component implementation technology when the DC's interface is invoked; it is therefore necessarily specific to the particular component implementation technology used. In turn, the dispatcher invokes the interface implementation. On several occasions, depending on the detailed design of the DC internals, the dispatcher responsibility reduces to merely rerouting calls to the interface implementation. In this case, its role may be undertaken by the interface implementation, and there would be no dispatcher per se in the DC.

The dispatcher is also responsible for providing, where required, a scriptable interface to the distributed component. In this case it could, for example, parse a single incoming "execute" or "dispatch" message (which could be constructed as an XML string), extract the operation and any parameters, and then invoke the appropriate operation on the interface implementation. Exceptionally, and where performance allows, a DC may provide only a scriptable interface. In this case, the dispatcher may be merged with the interface implementation, and the DC's interface is that which is provided by the parsing mechanism of the dispatcher—which may, in even more exceptional circumstances, itself be scripted.

Externals

Many aspects of the DC's externals have been addressed previously in the section "Concepts." In this section, we address two particularly important aspects that are seen by users of a DC:

- The interface(s) of a DC
- The concept of pass-by-value objects as interface operation parameters, which we call business data types

These two aspects contribute to the minimal but necessary dependencies between DCs, but we postpone full discussion of such dependencies to Chapter 4, "The Business Component," and Chapter 10, "Project Management Architecture."

Interfaces

The OMG's definition of an interface is this: "An *interface* is a description of a set of possible operations that a client may request of an object. An object *satisfies* an interface if it can be specified as the target object of each potential request described by the interface" [OMG 1998e, Chapter 1; OMG's italics]. In this section, we adopt a slight modification of this definition in that "object" is replaced by "DC."

Generally speaking, a DC may have one or more interfaces. Each interface contains one or more logically related operations. The number of interfaces and operations, and their natures, is highly dependent on the architectural style (see Chapter 9) and design principles (see Chapter 12) adopted. Designing the interface is the most critical design decision in a component-based system because it implies a long-lasting contract for all clients of that interface. This is particularly so for EDCs (enterprise-layer DCs) because their interfaces can be accessed from anywhere over the network. As such, the detail of the interface operations has consequences on the performance, scalability, reusability, and evolvability of the DC.

For this reason, it is useful to design interfaces early in the development process. DC interfaces can be designed before the internals of the DC are designed and before the DC is built. In addition, certain interfaces, including generic interfaces (that is, interfaces that all DCs in a given scope must support), can be designed even without specific business components being identified. Finally, and following our general focus on the functional developer, interface specification should be able to be done without having to be concerned with underlying technical implications. As discussed earlier in this chapter in "Functional Developer Programming Model," the functional designer should be able to concentrate on only the business aspects of the interface specification. For example, methods on EDC interfaces are generally considered implicitly transactional by default. Again, technology aspects such as introspection, activation, deactivation, and so forth, which may require technology-level interfaces on the DC, should be handled by the separation layer and should therefore be hidden from the functional developer.

Business Data Types

The signature of an interface operation includes the operation name and a list of parameters. Each parameter is of a specified type. Where interfaces are based on the object-oriented paradigm, such parameters are primitive data types such as string or integer, or they are object-oriented classes. We call such a parameter a *business data type*.

> A business data type is a software artifact with a standard business interpretation that can be passed by value—that is, used as a parameter of an interface operation to a business component or used as an information element in a transmissions between components or systems. Typical examples are Address, Volume, and Date, but they can include more complex types such as Bill of Material.

The name "business data type" is chosen, first, to focus on its business aspects and to indicate its importance from a business perspective and, second, to denote its pass-by-value and data-oriented status. In a nonobject-oriented interface implementation, these would be simple data structures. In the following, we will assume an object-oriented paradigm for interfaces.

The definition of business data types is a critical activity in the specification of a DC and its interface(s). A business data type provides the business information needed by an interface operation. A business data type is normally designed with the following characteristics and design principles (we will expand on these in Chapter 12):

- It represents a small-granularity concept in the business domain. As a design principle, its internal structure tends to be flat, or if it contains nested business data or primitive types, it tends not to have them nested too deeply, often at just one level.

- It is always passed by value, never by reference, and it adheres to all of the semantics of the OMG's pass-by-value type (identified in IDL by the keyword *valuetype*). This means that a calling DC will always receive a copy of the state of the object, not a reference to it. This is analogous to a fax. Just as when a fax has been received, there are (at least) two physical copies of the same thing (one at the sender, one at the received end), so when a business data type is sent from one DC to another, there are two physical copies. And just as one of the fax copies can happily be written on without invalidating the original, so can one of the business data types be altered with no implication at all for the validity of the other copy.

- It is a capsule of data. Methods tend to be low granularity, often having only accessor methods ("set" and "get" on attributes) and a few additional standard methods such as "isValid". That is, a business data type is a class with a potentially complex but often simple data structure with simple behavior.

- It should be generated from a specification; it should seldom if ever be written by the functional developer.

- Although it has a business meaning that is well understood, this implies very little about its usage. That is, how it is used is determined almost entirely by its relationship to some other class within a DC.

- It should be totally self-contained. That is, it should not invoke methods on any other objects other than those that may be nested within it.

- It is owned at design and development time by one specific business component (see Chapter 10).

The second characteristic in the list—pass-by-value—is important, and it is the flip side of the DC situation. A DC at run-time is a component instance that is referenced or addressed through the network but is never passed by value. Once a client has a reference to a DC, it can request of the DC that it return business data types (by value) through the DC's interfaces. In this way, we achieve a separation that is of crucial importance for distributed systems—that is, we strictly divide instances into those that are passed by reference (DCs) and that implement larger-grained business concepts and those that are passed by value and that are the state of smaller-grained objects used in the implementation of DCs.

We return to some of the design principles for business data types and interfaces in Chapter 12. Meanwhile, Table 3.3 describes the key differences between DCs and business data types.

Business data types have been referred to in various ways by other authors and practitioners, whose terms include the following:

Table 3.3   Distributed Component versus Business Data Types

	DISTRIBUTED COMPONENT	BUSINESS DATA TYPE
Network address	Has an external immutable network identity, which maps to its network address. For example, may have a name such as "eVendor" that the CEE maps to a CORBA IOR (interoperable object reference).	Can contain a well-specified data instance (and thus identify a specific data instance), but has no network address. Cannot have (for example) a CORBA IOR. A reference to a business data type is valid only within a DC.
Operation parameter	Is always a reference to the DC. The DC itself is never passed by value.	Is always passed by value over the network. A reference to a business data type can never be passed outside a DC.
Associations	Can have associations with other DCs and can receive business data types from other DCs.	Can have associations only with other business data types within the confines of a single DC.
Nature of interface	Always assumes low (modem speed) bandwidth. For example, it is very unusual to find a reference to a DC being passed as an iterator.	Assumes high (in-memory speed) bandwidth. For example, it is quite normal to find a reference to a business data type being passed as an iterator between objects within a DC.

Dependent objects. This is the name given by some OMG members to a group of classes that includes our business data type; see [OMG 1999b, p. 8]. A dependent object has no external identity nor true independent behavior. From a different point of view, however, business data types are totally independent of anything, and they appear to be the most independent objects in the system: They are the only objects that can be freely passed from component to component and from system to system. In this sense, a better term might be *independent object*. Finally, the term *dependent object* seems implementation-oriented, rather than functional developer-oriented. For these reasons, we prefer a different term.

Network classes. This term refers to the fact that these are the objects whose state actually travels on the network between network-addressable objects. Indeed, while a business data type is not network addressable, it is network visible in the sense that it travels on the network and hence is "visible" with a suitable trace tool. We avoid this term because of the confusion it may generate (among network class, network visible, and network addressable) and also because it is still not, for our taste, sufficiently functional developer-oriented.

Summary

The distributed component (DC) is a key software technology concept within the business component approach. While a DC is normally built using one of today's commercially available component implementation technologies, an important difference is that the DC concept—the pattern that it defines—provides technology independence as far as the functional code is concerned. The reason for this is that we strongly believe that functional designers thinking about a component-based application should not have to worry about the "plumbing." That is, it should not really matter which technology is used for the implementation, especially because the expectation is that large systems will be built on multiple technologies.

Supporting this contention, the DC concept, through its separation layer and its defined internal structure, can do the following:

- Clearly separate (at all phases of development) business logic on the one hand, and the technical complexities inherent in today's middleware and development environments on the other.

- Provide an answer first to the programmer's question as to what should be built, and second to the designer's question as to the nature of the necessary network-addressable unit in a component-based distributed business system.

- Define object-oriented programming languages and language classes as being internal to a component and little to do with the external world of network-addressable component instances.

- Provide for source portability of functional code across underlying component implementation technologies. That is, the "plumbing" is hidden from the functional programmer, to the point where what the functional programmer writes can be ported across different ORBs and middleware messaging facilities.

Four different kinds of distributed component are identified, depending on their main characteristics and responsibilities within a business component: user DC, workspace DC, enterprise DC, and resource DC. DC technology can also be used in other defined roles, such as gateway DC and testing DC.

The internal world of the DC is informed by patterns that simplify its design and implementation. When building a DC using object-oriented languages, the following language classes are normally found: focus, support, ancillary, and technical. Additional classes in the separation layer of a DC are interface implementation, dispatcher, proxies, persistence LCs, and the utility LC.

The externals of a DC include interfaces and business data types, which are a particularly important aspect of an interface. Business data types are usually small-granularity, self-contained classes that are always passed by value.

In the next chapter we will extend some of these concepts beyond the definitions given here, but in a way that will better support us in our journey to master the complexity and costs of distributed business system development. For example, we will show how DCs collaborate and how they are used to implement a business component; in so doing we will add characteristics such as how the definition of a DC's interface can be extended to the whole development lifecycle.

Endnotes

1   In this chapter and elsewhere, we use the term "component implementation technologies" to refer to the group of commercially available component middleware technologies and their associated connectivity capabilities. These include CorbaComponents, EJB (Enterprise Java-Beans), Microsoft's COM and DCOM (with COM+ on the horizon), and Message Oriented Middleware (MOM). The OMG's technical work on CORBAComponents was completed in August 1999, and the specification is now available on the OMG's Web site [OMG 1999]. Several companies have already committed to implement it for at least Java and C++.

2   The terms *white box* and *black box* are used in their usual sense; that is, they refer to the visibility of an implementation's internals. White box implies that internal implementation details are visible. Black box implies that no internal details are visible; only the interface and specification can be discerned.

3   The set of all instances of a type (whether active or inactive) is sometimes called the type's *extent*. A collection is some subset of a type's extent.

4   We are grateful to Don Kavanagh for many of these BLC identification heuristics.

The Business Component

The business component is the fundamental concept of the business component approach. This concept has been applied to large-scale distributed system development since 1994, and has been used in various functional domains, including enterprise resource planning, manufacturing, supply chain management, and telecommunication. We believe this is the concept of component that is required to support a drastic reduction of the cost and complexity of software development. Of course, the concept alone cannot do this—it is not a silver bullet, but its use inside a comprehensive approach such as the business component approach has proved successful in the attainment of many of the objectives set forth in Chapter 1, "Component-Based Development."

An understanding of the business component's characteristics is crucial in appreciating how the concept can address the complexity problems inherent in large-scale distributed systems. Chapter 2, "The Business Component Approach," defined a business component as the software implementation of an autonomous business concept or business process; as consisting of all software artifacts necessary to represent, implement, and deploy that business concept as an autonomous, reusable element of a larger distributed information system; and as being a unifying concept throughout the development lifecycle and the distribution tiers. The concepts embodied in this definition are expanded and amplified in this chapter, which is structured as follows:

- The main characteristics of the business component *concept* are examined, by further analyzing the definition, discussing some important additional concepts, and presenting considerations about implementation aspects.

- The *internals* of a business component are described from the functional designer's point of view. This view exposes the anatomy of a business component and in doing so shows how DCs are used to compose the business component and how they collaborate to provide function to the end user.

- Business component *externals* are examined. This provides an understanding of how the business component can be considered as a black box not only at run-time but also across the whole development lifecycle.

- The life of a business component across the *development lifecycle* is briefly described. In doing so, some of the definitions and concepts related to the distributed component are extended to cover the whole development lifecycle in a way similar to the business component.

- We illustrate by a *scenario* some of the concepts presented so far in the chapter.

- The business component concept is compared with other *related software engineering concepts* such as the business object concept, the concept of module, and the UML concept of package.

Before proceeding, the reader should note that this chapter focuses on the business component as an individual component, rather than on how it is used to build systems or how it interacts with other business components. Chapter 5, "The Business Component System," addresses building complete systems out of business components and how a business component collaborates with other business components.

Concepts

This section addresses the main concepts and characteristics of the business component, and it builds on the brief discussion in Chapter 2. It starts by examining the constituent parts of the definition given in Chapter 2, and repeated previously in this chapter, then proceeds by discussing an important set of concepts that derive from and support this definition. Finally the main implementation considerations for the business component are presented.

Definition Concepts

We focus here on four parts of the definition: why do we consider a business component to be a component; why do we call it a *business* component; what does it mean that it consists of *all the software artifacts* representing a given business concept; and what is meant by *autonomous business concept*.

A Component

A business component is a component. Indeed, it satisfies all the characteristics that we presented in Chapter 1 when we discussed the definition of the component concept. In particular, a business component is a self-contained software construct that has a defined use and a run-time interface, can be autonomously deployed, and is built with foreknowledge of a specific component socket. Of course, because the business component is a composition of software artifacts, each of these terms has a specific meaning:

Self-contained software construct. A business component is composed of a set of software artifacts. It can include a broad set of deliverables, such as one or more distributed components (DCs), database definitions and schemas, documentation, specifications, and a number of other deliverables. All of the deliverables required to represent, implement, test, and deploy the business component throughout the development lifecycle are considered as not only belonging to the business component, but also as *being* the business component at the various phases of development. For example, the models required at analysis to represent the business component *are* the business component itself at analysis time: They are what is seen from the analysis viewpoint of the business component. Similarly, a test script that can be used to test the business component is what is seen from a testing viewpoint. These artifacts, rather than being thought of as an external representation, are considered an integral part of the software construct called business component. Hence the concept of a self-contained software construct acquires a meaning that extends throughout the development lifecycle and that gives the business component a lifetime coherence.

Run-time interface. The run-time interface of the business component will be defined later in this chapter as being the sum of the run-time interfaces of its constituent DCs. In this sense, the business component has not only a run-time interface but also an interface that can be appropriately distributed across machines and address spaces to satisfy the needs of the distributed system under development.

Autonomously deployable. Given an appropriate delivery mechanism, it is possible to deploy a whole business component, which is a complex collection of deliverables, as a single autonomous unit. The ability not only to rapidly develop but also to rapidly deploy complex software is becoming a critical requirement of modern software manufacturing. Meeting this requirement in turn demands a deployable unit that goes well beyond the simple installation of a single executable. This is what the business component provides: the ability to deploy a complex component as a single autonomous unit.

Specific socket. An important aspect of the whole business component approach is to master and reduce dependencies not only between components but also between components and the business component virtual machine (BCVM). A later section, "Externals," discusses the *business component socket* and the *business component plug* that cover both runtime and development-time aspects and that support our dependency management objective.

A Component for the Business

Not only is a business component a component, but it is also a direct representation and implementation in the solution space of a business concept existing in the problem space—a concept in the *business*. A business component fully implements—across the development lifecycle, the architectural viewpoints, and the distribution tiers—all aspects of a business concept (entity or process) of medium to coarse granularity. Hence the business component captures *both* the "pure" business concept *and* the realities of distributed systems in *one* concept.

Note that not all business concepts will be represented by a business component—only those that satisfy a given set of criteria (discussed in Chapter 11, "Component-Based Business Modeling"). The most important criterion is that the business concept be "real and independent" in the problem space. For example, a single pricing rule would almost certainly never become a business component; but a vendor, and all the information and rules required to manage the vendor, could well do so.

All the Software Artifacts

A business component represents and implements a business concept by encapsulating *all* its software artifacts. It encompasses and gathers together all such artifacts across the distribution tiers and development lifecycle phases. For example, even though a business concept such as "Customer" is deployed as several deliverables (because it is intended for a distributed system and may be implemented by more than one DC, each to be executed on different machines), it is still treated as a single deliverable (the business component). Thus the business component can be seen as a potent unifying and clustering construct that also has business meaning, and it is this extended clustering characteristic that enables a business component to represent a business concept in its entirety. This is a powerful concept that requires a specific set of development process principles, architecture principles, and design principles, which will be addressed in the course of this book.

Autonomous Business Concept

The definition of a business component emphasizes the "autonomous" representation of an "autonomous" business concept (whether business process or business entity). This captures an important objective of the business component approach—that is, to reproduce autonomous business concepts as autonomous software artifacts in the information system, without introducing additional dependencies and relationships between components for technical or any other reasons. Avoiding such dependencies is not entirely possible because, for example, the need to interact with a component execution environment (CEE) will require some software dependency between the business component and the CEE, although this may be a dependency that has no correspondence in the real world.[1]

Why do we use the quotes around "autonomous" business concept? Well, even in the problem space, business concepts are not completely autonomous. For example, a sales order cannot be initiated if a customer does not place an order. In the real world, a sales order captures information about the customer: Does this mean that the sales order is an autonomous concept? Yes, it is a real and independent concept, but it is not *isolated* because it is in a specific relationship with the customer. The ordering process has certain business constraints, such as the customer's having good credit. Such business constraints can be very complex, and they can lead to complex business relationships among concepts that are at first glance perceived as independent. For example, a change to a customer's address will generate havoc in the real world if a sales order placed by that customer still has the old address.

Given the relationships, dependencies, and collaborations between the real entities and real processes in the real world, these same relationships, dependencies, and collaborations are an essential aspect of any information system. For each form of collaboration at the business level, one or more corresponding dependencies will usually exist at the software level. For example, a customer issuing an order for a certain item will imply some form of software-level communication between the customer, the order, and the item. The focus of the whole business component approach, though, is to preserve and enhance the natural autonomy of the business concept.

This focus on autonomy is reflected in many ways. For example, because many relationships identified at analysis time turn out to be between language classes within a DC, the nature of the DC itself reduces the web of relationships and hence promotes autonomy. The architecture viewpoints enhance autonomy by properly separating concerns. The development process (described in Chapter 7, "The Development Process") is largely centered on autonomy. The business component itself, and its strong concept of black box/white box across the whole development lifecycle, is a powerful way to support autonomy. And in Chapter 10, "Project Management Architecture," we address the management of unavoidable dependencies, and we show why this is crucial for the success of a large-scale project.

Derived Concepts

The preceding characteristics lead to a number of derived concepts and characteristics, which also in turn support the definition of a business component. Although derived, these are not necessarily less important, and they address the business component ownership concept, the business component as unit of modularization, as unit of deployment, as unit of reuse, and as unit of management.

Ownership

Each functional software artifact of an information system is owned by one business component (or by one of its constituents). By *functional* we mean software artifacts that belong to the functional architecture viewpoint: This explicitly excludes software artifacts belonging, for example, to the technical infrastructure required to support the business components. Autonomy and minimal surface area between components are preserved by a strong management of the dependencies between business components. If a functional software artifact is needed by other business components, it is explicitly exported by the producer business component and imported by the consumer business component. This characteristic also makes the business component an important name-scoping mechanism.

Unit of Modularization

At one end of the development lifecycle, the business component supports a modularization and partitioning of the problem space into units that correspond to business concepts. These units are directly represented in what is deployable at the other end of the lifecycle. Hence the business component is not only a logical modularization concept, but it can also be directly found in the deployed information system and follows not only the development lifecycle but the whole software manufacturing cycle, including the software supply chain.

Unit of Deployment

The business component is an important unit of deployment from a business perspective. There are two aspects to this: First, each business component can be delivered in a form corresponding to what was identified at the requirements phase; second, the whole system is now composed of individually deployable components. A major complaint often heard from those responsible for installing and maintaining enterprise business systems is that every new release or even every new patch often requires the whole system to be reinstalled. A properly architected and implemented component-based system, and in particular a business component system, supports the deployment of only the changed parts (as shown in Figure 1.8 in Chapter 1).

Unit of Reuse

The business component is the fundamental unit of reuse across the whole development lifecycle, from requirements to deployment. It enables a level of reuse that goes well beyond construction-time reuse, which includes reuse of specifications, source code, patterns, and other build-time software artifacts. The business component concept provides a conceptual framework for achieving off-the-shelf reuse: For example, given a set of requirements and assuming that a specific business component that satisfies them is identified, then the business component concept supports acquisition of an appropriate business component and its installation in the information system with no development and with little testing.

Unit of Management

The business component is the unit of project management. The whole development process, the development environment, and the organization of teams, as well as task assignment, project planning, and project tracking can be organized around the business components that make up the system. Once the functional developer is assigned the requirements for a particular business component, he or she should be able to design, build, test, and deploy it autonomously. The developer's whole world is made up of a business component and the distributed components it contains, and this is reflected in all aspects of the project management architecture. The detail of how this is done is discussed in Chapter 10.

Implementation Considerations

To conclude this conceptual overview, we would like to express a few considerations about implementation aspects of the business component.

A business component, with its various architectural principles and concepts, can be implemented in any language or component implementation technology supported by the BCVM. In addition, different languages can be chosen to implement the DCs that make up a business component. Distributed components (and hence the corresponding business components) have been implemented, at various times and places, in Java, C++, C, Cobol, RPG, Python, Ada, Smalltalk, and even in such lesser-known languages as Rexx and Object Rexx.

Today, commercially available modeling tools and component implementation technologies do not directly support the business component concept. Applying the concept requires an appropriate set-up of the development environment. Depending on the level of support desired, this may require in-house tools and code-generation capability to be evolved, in addition to a meta-model that has the business component concept as a first-class citizen. An obvious question is whether the business component concept is useful when it is not directly supported by tools and component implementation technologies. The answer is strongly positive. The business component is a very powerful logical concept that can help reduce the complexity of large-scale development, independently from the level of support of the underlying development environment. It can be adopted in various degrees, where each degree can bring significant development benefit. For example, applying it during business modeling supports a proper partitioning of the problem space, as will be discussed in Chapter 12.

We have so far presented the business component as the representation and implementation of a business concept in an information system. It may in some cases be useful to apply the appropriate concepts, principles, architectures, and perhaps whole parts of the business component approach to the development of elements that are not related to business concepts. In other words, the business component can also be seen as an implementation technology. It does not necessarily always have to be used to represent an autonomous business concept, although this is by far the major strength of the concept. For example, suppose a project identifies a highly reusable element of the information system and thinks that it would be useful to implement it using parts of the business component approach. The fact that the reusable element does not represent a business concept is not, by itself, a good reason against putting the thought into operation.

Internals

This section describes the anatomy of a business component—that is, its internal architecture, structure, and constituent parts. The viewpoint of the functional designer/developer's perspective is adopted. From this viewpoint, no technical and infrastructural aspects are seen. Indeed, this view of a business component is ideally the only view with which the functional developer should be concerned.

Distribution Tiers

From the functional designer point of view a single business component consists of between one and four consecutive tiers, shown in Figure 4.1: the user tier (u-tier), the workspace tier (w-tier), the enterprise tier (e-tier), and the resource tier (r-tier). Each tier corresponds to a different *logical* area of responsibility. Each has a specific behavior and specific design patterns, and each addresses a separate area of concern. These tiers will also be discussed from a design perspective in Chapter 12.

User Tier

The user tier presents the business component on a screen and is responsible for all communication with the user. It is the u-tier's responsibility to implement and execute the panels and user interface controls of a particular business component. Not all business components are directly presented to the user; in other words, not all business components have a u-tier. The way a business component is presented to the user, and in particular which business component owns the user interface aspects of which business component, depends on the particular application architecture and functional architecture adopted for the project. For example, a project may decide that a user interface construct for data entry related to an "order" business component may be provided by another business component that implements the order entry business process. Physically, the user tier is positioned as close as possible to the underlying screen system software.

The user interface delivered with a business component can be considered as a default, "no-think" user interface. The business component distribution architecture makes it easy to develop a new u-tier that accesses the provided w-tier and through that the provided e- and r-tiers.

A user interface provided by one business component can be used by another business component. In this case, it does not need to be a full-blown user interface, nor does it need to be a self-standing user interface: It can be as simple as a user interface control. For example, the functional designer could decide that

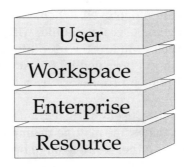

Figure 4.1   The four tiers of a business component.

a business component representing a customer would deliver for reuse by another business component simply a property page containing an entry field where a customer ID can be entered and a few fields to display a small amount of returned customer information, such as name, address, and credit limit. For entity components such as Customer or Vendor, a "search list" user interface control, such as a property sheet supporting the input of search criteria and returning a list of instances of that entity satisfying these criteria, is often provided as well.

The user interface could also be a configuration property sheet that would enable the purchaser (of the business component) to define and/or configure some of the functionality of the business component, as well as aspects of the database schema. Such configurability could apply to all tiers, so that, and if present, the user tier could be adapted to meet the needs of different groups of end users. Where this kind of configurability is provided, then a default configuration would typically also be provided, so that the purchaser is not forced to configure before making at least some use of the business component.

User interface technology is among the most quickly evolving technologies in the software industry. To say that a business component delivers its own user interface means usually that a specific technology, and often a specific and probably proprietary user interface framework, is assumed to be the target user interface infrastructure for that business component. Alternatively, the business component could deliver as many user interface implementations as there are targeted technologies and user interface frameworks: For example, technology-wise and depending on the targeted markets, it may have to deliver one user interface in Java, one in Dynamic HTML, and one in C++. Framework-wise, it may actually have to target a specific user interface framework built in Java, or a specific user interface framework built in Dynamic HTML, and so on. This may be considered unrealistic by many. Indeed, very little support is provided by the major commercially available user interface infrastructures for deploying autonomous components but at the same time allowing their user interface constructs to be mixed and matched. For example, suppose first an Invoice business component is deployed. When, later on, an Address Book is also deployed, then the Invoice user tier should, with only minimal reconfiguration, be able to include on its window the user interface construct (for example, a page of a property sheet) provided by the Address Book user tier. This cannot be done today without a proprietary user tier framework also being deployed.

The provision of a proprietary user interface framework would, of course, be a localized solution. Nevertheless, it may be deemed sufficiently productive, especially where it applies to either a single large business component system or, better, a jointly architected federation of business component systems. The ability for each business component to be delivered with its own user interface that would simply plug into the general (if proprietary) user interface framework would greatly enhance the reusability of the various business components built to that proprietary standard.

There is a tendency in the software industry to consider user interface development as totally separate from the server-side development. Professionals often specialize on client-side or server-side technologies, and development teams are often organized along what we consider "horizontal lines," which roughly reflect the distribution tiers of a three-tiered approach—the user interface, business logic, and database. We will discuss in Chapter 10 the rationale and advantages of a "vertical organization," along business components lines. Cost-effective software manufacturing must address both user interface aspects and other aspects of the business component in an integrated fashion, while still taking into account the many differences in user interface technologies and approaches. Using the business component concept as a way to properly assign responsibilities for the design, development, and testing of the user interface has proven to be very powerful. In other words, the business component concept is great for supporting rational and user friendly organization and partitioning of user interface development.

Workspace Tier

The workspace tier supports the user tier, implements local business logic (all business logic required uniquely to support the user and that does not need access to enterprise-level resources), and is responsible for interacting with the enterprise tier to access any enterprise-level resource needed to support the current user's work. This separation—keeping the business logic specific to a single user separate from the business logic specific to the enterprise—allows for different kinds of optimization, and it supports the highest levels of performance and scalability.

Access to enterprise resources should be the sole responsibility of the w-tier. The u-tier knows nothing about these resources. If the u-tier needs to present data deriving from the enterprise database, or if data entered by the user must be used to update the enterprise database, then the u-tier should always make a request to the w-tier. It is the w-tier that knows about enterprise resources. And it is here that the "logical" nature of the w-tier is best seen. Sometimes, for very simple user models (such as a green-screen-type menu/panel model) the w-tier has very little to do other than access a server. In this case, the w-tier and u-tier are often implemented as a single DC (or perhaps as some other construct). W-tier responsibility is still there, but it's bound in with the u-tier code. Good design will separate the u-tier and w-tier at the source-code level. And it is in this minimal w-tier case that the four-tier model can be viewed as collapsing into the traditional three-tier model.

The w-tier works as a single-user buffer—the "workspace" for that user. In other words, it is a workspace for any business processing that is unique to a single user, and which does not affect the enterprise as a whole. The w-tier may contain business state; for example it can be used under certain circumstances (see Chapter 9, "Application Architecture") to manage the state of business transactions being prepared. In addition, it may have user-unique persistent aspects. In a fat-client architecture, the w-tier normally resides on the client machine, but it could also be on the departmental or central server.

The w-tier can be implemented with several DCs, or it can be implemented as a single DC representing the whole of the business component's w-tier. It can also be implemented using a different component implementation technology than that used to implement the enterprise tier, or perhaps even by a noncomponent technology (for example, the w-tier could be implemented as a single Java application, while the e-tier is implemented using CORBA Components and C++). In a Web-based architecture, the w-tier could be implemented by the Internet application server.

Finally, the w-tier of one business component can communicate with the w-tier of another business component.

Enterprise Tier

The enterprise tier processes the core aspects of a given business component: It implements enterprise-level business rules, validation, and interaction between enterprise components, and it also manages the business aspects of data integrity. From the point of view of large-scale, mission-critical systems, this is the most critical tier because it contains most of a business component's business logic and because it is responsible for meeting a number of general enterprise-level requirements, including performance, scalability, reliability, and security of the information system. The e-tier generally needs to be accessed concurrently by multiple users, and it requires persistence, security, and transactional services. In Chapter 8, "Technical Architecture," we discuss how the CEE supports the EDC in providing these services to the functional developer in such a way that the functional developer can focus on designing and implementing business function.

Very often we find ourselves discussing the enterprise tier, in particular the EDC part of the tier, as if it were the only tier of the business component. For example, at analysis- and also at design-time, the term "business component" is often used when what is really meant is the enterprise tier of the business component. Even if imprecise, this is acceptable at a high level, and normally the context clarifies what is meant.

Resource Tier

The resource tier manages the physical access to shared resources. Data in shared databases is the most common form of resource, and this tier is responsible for bridging and mapping the functional developer's model inside the e-tier with the actual reality of the database implementation. Furthermore, this tier is also responsible for shielding the functional developer from the peculiarities of the various database management systems. For example, the coding of embedded SQL to access relational data would be in the resource tier.

Accessing the database is not necessarily the only responsibility of the r-tier. For example, the r-tier could also be used to access the Internet in a way that is transparent to the rest of the business component: A component managing currencies could request a real-time exchange rate from a remote Internet site through its own r-tier. This means that the business component can be built in such a way that, apart from the r-tier, it has no knowledge of how the exchange rate data is obtained—whether from a remote site or from its own database. In the remainder of this chapter, we consider only the case of the r-tier being used for persistence management.

The resource tier exists to hide and separate, as much as possible, persistence aspects from business processing aspects. It should be possible to change the database management system, and to a certain extent parts of the schema, without having to change the whole system or the individual business component. This is particularly important in product development, where the presence of more than one relational database management system is often required. Separating database management from the rest of the system also makes sense in custom development, in order to avoid tying into a particular software vendor, to enhance the possibilities of reuse across the system, and to enhance maintainability.

The mapping between the functional developer's model inside the e-tier and the database model is a major concern of the architects and designers of the system (and is discussed in detail in Chapter 12). Persistence aspects are the most critical and important aspects of a business system and will remain so for the foreseeable future. While it is possible to use some form of automatic mapping between an object-oriented model and the data for smaller systems that do not have stringent requirements in terms of performance and concurrent access to the data, in large-scale systems the database must be very carefully designed. Furthermore, for performance and scalability reasons, the current state of the art does not support the use of object-oriented databases for traditional large-scale systems with high rates of data entry and access. Unless stated otherwise, we assume the use of relational database technology whenever the r-tier is discussed.

In designing a business component to be autonomous, the single business component should own an *island of data*, that is, a set of tables that only the component itself can directly access, through its resource tier. It is indeed possible to draw the relational model of the persistence aspects of a single business component, and to build a whole business component system out of business components that are autonomous also insofar as the persistence aspects are concerned. In order to do this successfully, we have to apply appropriate architectural and design considerations (see Chapter 12), for example, the use of what we call *implicit foreign keys*, which are links that are logically considered to be foreign keys but are not explicitly declared as such.

With regard to the level of visibility of r-tier interfaces, the principle that this tier is accessible only by its own enterprise tier and is not directly visible outside of the business component is usually applied. This view of a single business component's persistent data as an island of data, accessible only through the interfaces of the enterprise layer, must take into account the reality of other information systems technologies. For example, report writers today require direct access to relational databases, and completely wrapping up the database tier and restricting access to the e-tier interfaces only would prevent this necessary access. We will address some of these practicalities when discussing the persistence challenge in Chapter 12..

From an implementation perspective, the resource tier can be implemented using distributed component technology, but this is a project-specific decision based on weighing all data access requirements. It certainly makes sense to model data access in terms of a separate logical tier, even if the final packaging might not implement this as a separate physical tier.

Distribution Tier Characteristics

Having presented the four main tiers, let us discuss some additional characteristics of their relationships and their role within a business component.

Figure 4.2 illustrates the different ways in which DCs interact within a business component. It is a sound architectural principle, corresponding to the principle of noncircularity that will be discussed in more general terms in Chapter 9, to have messaging (that is, the invocation of operations) always flow in one direction, namely from UDC toward the database, as shown by the solid lines in the figure. Hence a given DC in the figure knows nothing and assumes nothing about which DCs are on its left, nor does it invoke operations on a DC to its left. When a DC needs somehow to be informed about some event occurring to a DC to its right, then it subscribes to an appropriate event published by that DC, as shown by the dotted arrows in the figure. For example, a WDC might subscribe to some event in an EDC, so that it will be notified when the EDC publishes the event.

A given business component does not need to have all four tiers (although this is a common configuration), but if it has more than one, those tiers are normally in sequence. Figure 4.3 illustrates various examples of acceptable structures for a business component. Aside from the four-tier configuration, it is the first two in Figure 4.3 that are the most common. Other configurations may be found appropriate in some situations. Cases of nonconsecutive tiers (for example, only user and resource tiers) occur very rarely if ever (we have never yet

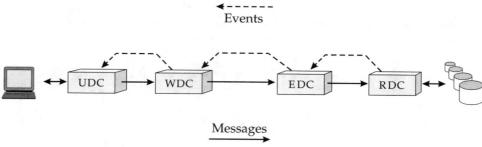

Figure 4.2   Inter-tier interactions.

encountered one). Also, as the functionality of a business component with less than four tiers matures over its development life span, there is sometimes a tendency for it to be extended to have all four tiers.

In Chapter 3, "The Distributed Component," we introduced various categories of DCs. Figure 4.4 illustrates a simplified meta-model explaining the relationships between these categories and the tiers presented earlier in this chapter. This meta-model reflects the following: A business component may have one tier of each kind, and each tier can be implemented by one or more distributed components. Cardinalities are not shown in order to simplify the figure because it is not always absolutely necessary that distributed component technology be used to implement a tier. This has not been shown in the figure. The only tier that is always recommended to be implemented using distributed component technology is the e-tier. In this sense, the u-tier, w-tier, and r-tier can have zero distributed components, in which case, if they exist, they would simply be implemented by some other implementation technologies not shown in this simplified meta-model. Because the e-tier is always assumed to be implemented using distributed component technology, it always has at least one DC.

If using DCs to implement two different tiers, the actual implementation technology may be different between the tiers. For example, the e-tier could be implemented using C++ and CORBA Components, and the w-tier could be implemented using Java and Enterprise Beans. Furthermore, the implementation technology between the distributed components of the same tier could be different: The internals of an EDC managing specific instances of a given business concept could be implemented using Java, while the EDC that manages

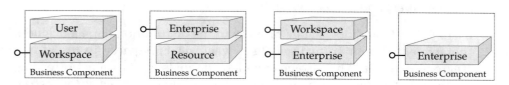

Figure 4.3   Examples of business components.

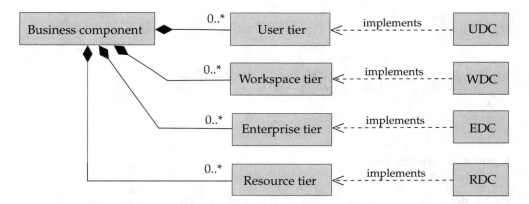

Figure 4.4   Tiers' and DC categories' meta-model.

collections of the same business concept (and hence belonging to the same e-tier of one business component) could be implemented in C++.

The anatomy of the business component presented so far is strictly from a functional developer's point of view. As discussed in Chapter 2, we assume a strongly layered architecture, in which each viewpoint addresses a set of considerations and each viewpoint can for the most part abstract from those addressed by other viewpoints. A more complete picture of the anatomy of a business component, which shows not only the functional viewpoint but also the technical architecture viewpoint (represented here by the CEE), under the assumption that each tier is implemented using distributed component technology, is shown in Figure 4.5. The interfaces will be explained later in this chapter.

The distribution tiers presented in the previous section are *logical tiers*. At run-time, these tiers can be deployed in a variety of ways. That is, the *physical tiers* can be different from these logical tiers. For example, as illustrated in Figure 4.6, the user tier and workspace tier could be deployed as a single physical tier (for example a PC), and the resource tier may be deployed as two separate physical tiers—the RDC on a server and a remote DBMS on a mainframe (of course, with careful design for scalability).

The discussion of the four distribution tiers has not so far included a number of business component deliverables. A more complete picture would add at least two aspects (as well as other deliverables, discussed later in the chapter), which can be considered as tiers in an extended meaning of the term "tier": the testing tier (t-tier) and the gateway tier (g-tier).

Testing tier. In addition to one or more of the distribution tiers, a business component should normally include whatever is required to test it and regression test it. Where some commercial tool is used to support testing, we have still found it useful to refer to this additional artifact as the *testing tier* (t-tier). Even though the t-tier does not appear at run-time, it can be on

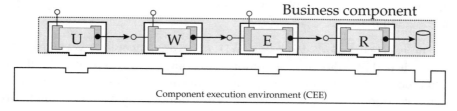

Figure 4.5 Business component anatomy from two viewpoints.

a separate machine at testing time and can be considered a testing-time tier in its own right. Indeed, with each business component and sometime even with each distributed component, a distributed component is often delivered whose only responsibility is to test the business component or one or more of its distributed components. We call this a testing DC (TDC).

Gateway tier. The term "gateway tier" is sometimes used to indicate a set of deliverables whose only purpose is to provide a gateway from external systems to a given business component. This logical tier can be located, at run-time, on a separate machine from the rest of the business component system. The g-tier, as we will see in Chapter 5, may need to follow different visibility and security rules than the internal tiers. This tier could, for example, deal with the firewall in an e-commerce application. The gateway tier, as with all other functional artifacts in the system, is assigned to and owned by a specific business component. In Chapter 5, we will also see that the presence of the g-tier for individual business components will depend on the particular solution adopted for interoperability of the business component system with its external world.

Distribution Domains

The four distribution tiers can be organized into two logical domains or areas of responsibility: the user workspace domain (UWD) and the enterprise resource

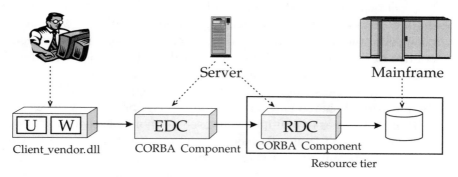

Figure 4.6 Examples of physical tiers.

domain (ERD). Each is specifically defined as being an area as seen by the functional developer.

- The *user workspace domain* (UWD) consists of user and workspace tiers, and it is that collection of computer resources whose responsibility is to support a single human being's view of system facilities through some user interaction/interface technology. This domain supports a single user through a presentation device such as a graphical user interface (GUI) or green screen. It represents the user's object model of the system.

  A GUI can support a number of such user models, from simple green screen-style menu/panel to full-fledged (and arguably easier-to-use) object-based user interfaces. In general, the more user-oriented the user's model, the greater the amount of business function dedicated to the user. And indeed, there can be considerable business function in the UWD. For example, consider a telephone salesperson user involved in a long and complex customer conversation. This may involve several potential changes to the enterprise's database. It may well be that no actual commits to the enterprise database have yet been made. Now, if the customer asks to stop the conversation and restart it tomorrow, then the system must store the incomplete user unit of work so that it can be picked up later. Clearly, to store the work temporarily and restart it later is likely to require significant functionality, as is the whole notion of tracking which particular business transactions have been accumulated for later issuance. This function is there to support a single user in the telephone sales activity. It is therefore the responsibility of the user workspace domain.

- The enterprise and resource tiers together form what we call the *enterprise resource domain* (ERD), which is that set of computing facilities within which state changes to important (probably concurrently shared) resources can reliably be made. The boundaries of the enterprise resource domain are defined by the boundaries of the underlying transaction management infrastructure software in its ability to manage ACID[2] transactions. Normally the "important resources" are those data managed by one or more database management systems (DBMSs) so that state changes to the data can always be committed or rolled back under the control of that or those DBMSs in an ACID way. In practice, today this often means a single DBMS on a single machine, although sometimes the DBMS may have distributed commit/rollback support. The ERD manages the integrity of shared enterprise resources and provides services based on those resources to multiple concurrent authorized requesters.

  Because the ERD always has associated with it a specific scope of integrity management, there can be more than one ERD in a given distributed information system. For example, where departmental servers are deployed in addition to an enterprise server (perhaps a mainframe), then there will probably be two ERDs. One handles "enterprise" resources whose scope is a single department; the other handles true enterprise-wide resources. In this case, it is assumed that each departmental server is a clone of each of the others. Sometimes this is not the case. For example, there may be two departmental servers for a single department, each with, let us assume, a different and isolated integrity management system. In that case (and by the assumption we just made), an ACID transaction running on one would not be able to handle a unit of work that ran over both servers. There would thus be two ERDs. Another example occurs where there is a divisional server in addition to departmental and enterprise servers.

Sometimes a UWD must access two or more ERDs for update, and so, by definition, there will be two or more ACID transactions running to complete that single UWD unit of work. In this case, it is good design to have the UWD coordinate the work across the ERDs. Clearly, if something goes wrong halfway through, and one of the ERDs has committed but not the other, then there cannot be a transactional rollback. The UWD must then arrange for compensating transactions to be issued against those transactions that committed. This coordinating responsibility is handled by the workspace tier in the UWD, never by the user tier.

Both UWD and ERD define domains of responsibility. To assign a given software artifact or a given implementation concern to one of the two domains, we apply two simple questions: "Does this support a single user, or is this an enterprise level concern?" and "Does this need to be within the transactional management?" Essentially, the UWD supports the user's model, the ERD supports the enterprise model, and the two models are different. While they may be closely associated, there will often be concepts in the user's model that have no correspondence in the enterprise model. One example comes from the "traveling user" scenario, where a user might work in one office on one day and in another the next day. It may be required that the user should be able to choose which of possibly several user units of work to work on. The business logic constructs (perhaps a collection of available user units of work) are highly unlikely to be reflected in the enterprise model (although there are those who would say that this would show an error in the enterprise model). These user units of work would have been stored on a server somewhere overnight—a good example of UWD persistence.

To further illustrate the different responsibility of the UWD and ERD, and their relationship to physical machines such as client machines and server machines, let us consider the following example. The advent of the Internet and the enhanced mobility of professionals in all business sectors today set requirements for high availability of aspects that used to be, by default, located on a single machine. For example, a configuration file identifying user interface preferences (such as a particular layout of icons on the user interface at system start-up) that used to be exclusively for one user can now be easily shared over a network using a distributed file system. A frequently asked question is this: Would this not be part of the ERD? The answer is negative: The fact that it is stored for convenience on a server, and even the fact that it is eventually shared between multiple users belonging to a given user group, does not mean that it is an ERD software artifact. This configuration file is there to address the needs of a specific user (even if this "user" is really a group of users sharing the same user profile), does not need transactional support nor true concurrent access, and hence is a UWD software artifact. Further design guidelines related to the two domains are presented in Chapter 12.

Externals

This section discusses the external view of a business component. Because we assert that the business component addresses the realities of the whole development lifecycle, it is necessary to analyze these externals at the various phases of the lifecycle, not merely at build-time and/or run-time.

Because one of the main objectives of the business component approach is to create *autonomous* software components, there is a strong focus on reducing as much as possible the surface area between any business component and its surrounding world. Now the surface area of a DC (distributed component), as illustrated in Figure 4.7, consists of interfaces, dependencies on other distributed components, and dependencies—in the form of the plug—on the business component virtual machine.

Similarly, the surface area of a business component consists of corresponding concepts of interfaces, dependencies, and plug. These are the subjects of this section.

Interfaces

Because a business component consists of a set of software artifacts (for example, distributed components), what do we mean by the *interface* of a business

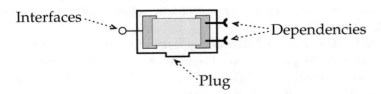

Figure 4.7   Connections to the external world.

component? To answer this, we start with the traditional concept of interface—that is, the run-time interface as specified by some interface definition language such as OMG's IDL[3]—and then progressively extend the meaning across the development lifecycle.

Before discussing the run-time interface, however, we need to define the different *levels of visibility* of DC interfaces, as illustrated in Figure 4.8. The three levels are as follows:

1. *Business component-internal.* Interfaces that are visible only within a given business component. A common example is where an EDC interface is visible only to a WDC within the same business component. This typically comes about when that WDC is the only artifact that is allowed to perform full maintenance on entities managed by the EDC. A specific functional example occurs where a WDC managing a stock item in a manufacturing enterprise is the only part of the system allowed to create a new item.

2. *System-internal.* Interfaces that are visible to other business components within the same business component system, but not to business components outside the boundaries of that system. For example, and building on the previous stock item example, an *eOrder* distributed component within an order management business component system may invoke a stock item interface as part of placing an order or to perform such read-only operations as verifying that a specific item exists. It is very unlikely that *eOrder* EDC, however, would be allowed to create a new stock item. In this case, the *create-item* operation on the stock item interface would not be made visible to *eOrder*.

3. *System-external.* Interfaces that are visible outside of the boundaries of the business component system. Such interfaces are either specific externally visible interfaces provided by the system's gateway business component, or they are a subset of the system-internal interfaces. For example, when a specific set of constraints deriving from the need for firewall security are imposed, then a small and predefined set of interfaces may be made available to other business component systems.

The level of visibility for a given interface may be predefined during development or in some case assigned by configuration at deployment. Most component implementation technologies do not provide direct support for these different levels of visibility, but it is relatively easy to enforce them through tools or project conventions.

With these visibility levels described, the run-time interface of a business component can now be examined.

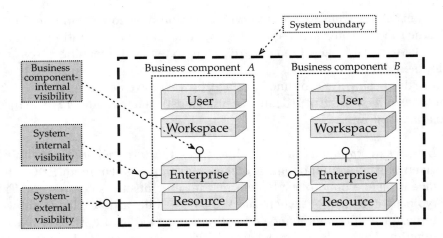

Figure 4.8   Visibility levels in a business component.

Run-Time Interface

At run-time, the business component appears as a composition of DCs that implement the business component's various tiers. Given this composition, the run-time interface for a business component can be defined as follows:

The run-time interface of a business component is the union of all system-internal and system-external DC run-time interfaces.

This means that the run-time interface of a business component corresponds to the union of the run-time interfaces of the WDCs and EDCs (and, in rarer cases, of the UDCs) that make up the business component, as illustrated in Figure 4.9. Just as the business component consists of a composition of DCs, so the business component's run-time interface consists of a combination of (externally visible) DC interfaces. The business component does not have a single run-time interface in a well-localized place: Rather, in that it addresses the needs of distributed development, its interface is a distributed concept—an extension of the traditional meaning of interface.

It may well be that at some point in the evolution of the software component

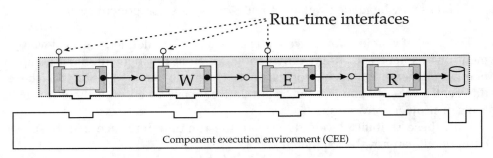

Figure 4.9   Run-time interface of a business component.

industry, the business component could develop an additional interface that would represent the business component as a whole rather than its constituent components. This would probably take the form of an introspection interface, able, for example, to return at run-time the business component version. Absence of such an interface, however, does not affect the usefulness of the business component concept.

Build-Time Interface

Usually, a run-time interface implies a build-time dependency between the consumer and the provider of the interface. For example, in order for business component A to invoke a given run-time interface of business component B, the business component A must be provided a proxy by B at build-time, and this proxy would be compiled and linked with A. This was discussed briefly in Chapter 3 in terms of an import-export activity: DC B declares the designated proxy as "exported," and DC A "imports" this proxy from B. Other artifacts, such as a business data type (see Chapter 3), may also be exported by B and imported by A. Chapter 10 introduces further elements of build-time interfaces.

The action of exporting a software artifact from a business component corresponds to the creation of a bridge, or of an access point, into an otherwise closed entity (the business component). Even if this access point does not correspond to an operation, as in the admittedly unrealistic but not impossible case of a business component exporting only a single business data type, this bridge can be thought of as being part of an interface. The action of importing an artifact at build-time from another business component can be thought of as invoking, at build-time, an import operation on that business component. In this sense, the business component can be said to have a build-time as well as a run-time interface.

The concept of build-time interface extends the interface concept beyond the traditional meaning of a set of run-time computational invocations whose signatures may be specified at design-time through an interface definition language. This extension significantly assists in meeting the objective of reducing the surface area of a business component at all phases of the development lifecycle.

The business component is thought of as a black box throughout the development lifecycle and as being persistent in its own private repository during development. The exported part of this private repository (that is, in our terminology, the development-time interface of the business component) is accessed during development by other business components that need to import some software artifact owned and exported by the business component. At build-time (and, as we will shortly see, at any other moment of the development lifecycle) we use this repository concept to enforce a crisp black-box/white-box distinction. Anything that another component needs from a target component must first be exported by the target. Conversely, nothing is available for import that the target has not chosen to export.

Thus, at run-time, the business component is visible to other components through its run-time functional interface(s); during development, it appears as providing development-time interfaces, as illustrated in Figure 4.10.

Depending on the kind of repository technology used, the idea of a business component having its own repository, corresponding to its development lifecycle persistence, may be a logical concept, or it may be a physical reality whereby each business component really has its own physical development repository. Either way, a very valid and useful viewpoint is the one that sees the repository (or, more precisely, the software artifacts stored in the repository) as *being* the business component.

Design-Time Interface

Let us take a step further, using the following example to illustrate the argument. When a business component provides run-time interfaces, it may be that all clients of these interfaces access them using a particular set of classes. These classes are not proxies, but rather a way of using a proxy that is common to all DCs invoking this interface. For example, to invoke an operation of a business component representing a currency book, a set of language classes dealing with a specific kind of currency formatting—that depends on the state of the calling component—may be needed. These classes are typically support or ancillary LCs (see Chapter 3).

Once this set of classes has been identified, it would make sense that they are designed, implemented, owned by, and maintained in one single place in the system. Because they are always used in conjunction with the CurrencyBook business component, it makes sense for this business component to own the set of classes. This set of classes is reused during the internal design of a business component that invokes CurrencyBook interfaces. Following the export/import model, it hence makes sense for the CurrencyBook business

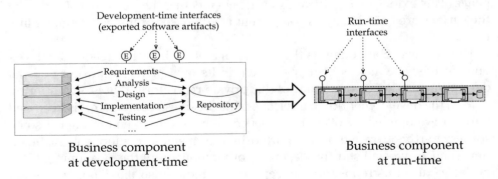

Figure 4.10   Business component repository.

component to export the set of classes and for a consumer business component to import them at design time. This is one example of a *design-time interface*, sometimes referred to simply as a design interface. A design-time interface can hence refer to or provide the specification for a set of classes that belongs to or is owned by a given business component, but it is only used in the context of another component. In the example in Figure 4.11, such a set of classes is always used to access a given proxy of a target DC.

By now it should be clear that the term *interface* is being used with a meaning that is a significant extension of the UML definition, whose context is interfaces that are invoked at run-time. In the last example, we applied the term *interface* to indicate design-time import of sets of classes, to be used to access a target business component in a predefined way. At development-time, these classes are owned by the target business component, but at run-time they do not appear as parameters on the target business component's run-time interface. Rather they are at run-time bound into and part of the calling business component. We will shortly give an extended definition of interface that covers this case. Let us first discuss the issue a little further.

Development Lifecycle Interface

We have so far seen run-time, build-time, and design-time interfaces. These interfaces provide access to software artifacts that a business component makes available, through some form of export mechanism, for use by other components. At run-time, an interface can also, of course, provide functional behavior, which may or may not return a software artifact. In general, it is possible to envision a whole set of software artifacts for which it may make sense,

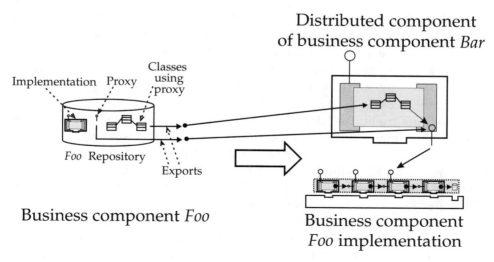

Figure 4.11   Example of design-time interfaces.

on one hand, to have clearly identified ownership, but on the other, and at the same time, to be able to make them available for use by other components at various times in their development lifecycle in a controlled way.

For example, when buying a commercial off-the-shelf (COTS) component, the buyer may want to check the acquired component's object model against the more general object model of his or her own system. In an ideal world, the buyer should be able to simply import the acquired component's model into his or her own object model and so verify name clashes, conceptual clashes, and any other point the buyer may be worried about. But the selling organization may want to make only part of its model visible, that is, the part that needs to integrate with the buyer's model. The selling organization may hence have an internal model, which it considered its own intellectual property and does not dream of showing to a buyer, and an exported object model that could be (depending on the maturity of the specification mechanisms) a subset of, or a view on, the internal model and that is sufficient for the verification needs of a buyer. This is conceptually the same as having a set of internal classes and methods and giving external access to only a few of them through a run-time interface.

Having given various examples of how the interface of a component can be considered as being invoked at development-time as well at run-time, we can now provide the following definition:

> An *extended interface* of a component describes a collection of access points to the component. An access point to the component is any software artifact (or combination of software artifacts) that, at any moment in the development lifecycle of the component, from any architectural viewpoint, or at any distribution tier, is exported at development time by the component.

This definition implies conceptually that a single operation—named, say, "import"—is always associated with each software artifact exported. In other words, when such a software artifact is imported, this operation can be thought of as having been invoked. However, a given access point has the same name as its corresponding software artifact (in the same general way as the names of C++ attributes imply the names of getter and setter operations).

In the UML "traditional" definition, an interface describes only actions or services. An extended interface, on the other hand, can be (informally speaking) a collection of things, where things (still, informally speaking) may include operations as in the UML definition. When it is necessary to distinguish between the traditional definition of interface and this extended definition, then the term *UML interface* or *extended interface*, respectively, is used.

This definition of extended interface has proven very convenient in the development of business component-based systems, even if controversial for some practitioners who are used to the more traditional definition. The important point is not so much the definition of interface; it is that to achieve autonomous analysis, design, implementation, testing, and deployment of a business component requires a focus on autonomy at all times during development. It is extremely useful to support this focus with clear black-box/white-box thinking across the whole development lifecycle, not only at run-time. This can be achieved through a strict definition of ownership of all software artifacts, a concept of a repository private to the individual business component, and by using export/import mechanisms at all development phases to allow for controlled access to selected artifacts from this repository, supporting a strict and relatively easy management of dependencies across the whole development lifecycle.

In other words, the business component is seen as a real component, with interfaces, throughout its development lifecycle—hence the requirement for the extended interface concept. This is particularly so given that the business component concept is multidimensional, and different viewpoints can be taken at the various phases of the development lifecycle and at the various distribution tiers. Because of this, a related concept of interface, which covers all development lifecycle phases and distribution tiers, is needed. Thinking of the business component as a black box, at any moment in the development lifecycle the developer can put software artifacts of various kinds—including specifications, models, source code, configuration files, and whatever else may be required to represent, design, implement, test, and deploy the business component—into this black box (that is, the business component). These artifacts are visible only to the owner of the business component. Should someone else wish to see an artifact of that business component at any given point in its development lifecycle, then she or he needs a specific permit to do so. Such a permit is an access point, and as few permits as possible should be given out.

Today the concept of an extended interface is seldom if ever directly supported by tools: For example, it is relatively difficult to model a business component in strict isolation with current COTS tools and then make available a selected subset of software artifacts (model elements) in an appropriately controlled way. But the frame of mind presented is very important in supporting the activity of continuously monitoring the dependencies and actually achieving the maximum possible autonomy for business components.

Using our extended definition of interface, we can now redefine what is meant by the interface of a business component:

The extended interface of a business component *is the union of all system-internal and system-external extended interfaces of its constituent distributed components and of the business component itself.*

Colloquially, we often just say that the interface of the business component is the union of all externally visible interfaces of the business component. It is the union of all the software artifacts that are seen when looking, at any phase of the development lifecycle, at the business component. In terms of our export/import model, it is the set of all software artifacts available for import from that business component. Because, as we have seen, the business component itself is built out of several other software artifacts, and in particular out of distributed components, its interface is strongly related to the interface of these software artifacts.

Dependencies

We have just seen how a business component provides interfaces to other business components at different moments in the development lifecycle. Each time a business component imports a software artifact from a target business component, it creates a dependency on this target business component.

A component *Foo* can be said to have a *software dependency* (often, when the context permits it, simply "dependency") on component *Bar* when *Foo* requires a software artifact from *Bar*. This can happen in any moment of the development lifecycle and for any distribution tier. The dependencies that are of greatest importance in the day-to-day management of a component-based project are the *functional dependencies*. But there are other kinds of dependencies, such as *technical dependencies* on, for example, the particular CEE used. Technical dependencies are part of the definition of the business component's *plug*.

Hence, a given business component provides interfaces *to* other components and has a set of dependencies *on* other components. In Figure 4.7, the elements affecting the external surface area of a distributed component were illustrated. We can now extend this to the business component. The external world of a business component is composed of interfaces, dependencies, and its plug. These are the three aspects that need to be properly designed and managed in order to enhance the autonomy of each component.

Dependencies on other business components can be analyzed at three levels of granularity: dependencies on other business components, dependencies on DCs of other business components, and the most detailed one, detailed dependencies at the individual software artifact level.

A serious software manufacturing capability must have the ability to track all dependencies of the components it builds. In order to properly track all the software artifacts that a given component depends on, we need appropriate concepts and tools. One such tool is what we call a dependency list, which is defined as follows:

> The *dependency list* of a given business component is a description of the set of all business components, their DCs, and their software artifacts on which the given business component depends.

A dependency list enables the navigation of the various software artifacts on which a given business component depends. Management of dependencies will be addressed in detail in Chapter 10.

There are dependencies between components that do not translate into direct software dependencies but that are still very important. For example, there are dependencies introduced by the application architecture (such as the defaults and overrides presented in Chapter 9), logical dependencies and database dependencies (both direct and functional), and dependencies generated by various artifacts (including documentation and help files). These dependencies can seriously constrain the development of a business component. Consider the case of a testing dependency. For example, let us suppose that, in order to properly test an invoicing component, we need a set of orders that are valid from a business perspective. The creation by hand of a valid order may be a very complex activity: Indeed, it could involve properly entering hundreds of fields for each individual order test case. Often, to test an invoice component, the tester may be required to create tens or hundreds of test cases. Hence, to manually create the necessary test cases may be very expensive, very complex, and somewhat error prone. Of course, appropriate tools to simplify the test case specification or even generation may be envisioned, but, in many cases, it may be much simpler and much more cost-effective simply to use the order business component to generate these test cases. After all, it is the job of the order component to create valid orders. This creates a dependency that does not translate into a software dependency: Before testing the invoice component, the project plan will require the development of the order entry component.

Socket

A component needs a well-defined concept of socket to plug into. What is the socket for a business component? The term *business component socket* is used to indicate the set of (extended) interfaces that the BCVM (business component virtual machine) makes available to the business component, and correspondingly the term *business component plug* indicates the combination of software artifacts that the business component provides to satisfy the interfaces provided by the socket.

The run-time portion of the business component socket is illustrated in Figure 4.12.

Given the distributed nature of the business component and of its interfaces and dependencies, the run-time socket for a business component is potentially distributed over multiple tiers and machines. In the figure, each tier requires an appropriate socket: The u-tier requires a user interface framework; the w-tier may require, for example, a Microsoft-specific component execution model; the e-tier will plug into a component execution environment for the enterprise, such as the CORBA Component model or the EJB model; the r-tier will plug into an appropriate persistence framework.

We have seen that we can apply interface and dependency concepts not only

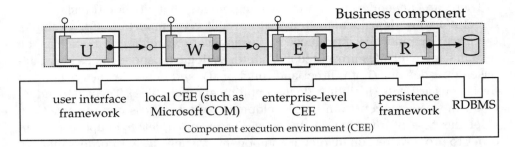

Figure 4.12   Socket of business component.

at run-time but also across the development lifecycle. Similarly, we can think of the socket as spanning the whole development lifecycle: To physically plug a business component into a business component virtual machine, there would be a socket at various predefined points of the lifecycle, each of which would provide interfaces whose semantics are to do with ensuring that the appropriate software artifacts, perhaps in one of several predefined forms, are provided by the business component being plugged in. The act of plugging in may also be more than a simple import into a repository. It may require action on the part of the BCVM. For example, it might be that during the plugging in of a newly-purchased design-time business component, its database schema must be combined with the larger system database schema.

Development Lifecycle

We have so far analyzed the internals of the business component and the externals. While analyzing the externals, we extended the concept of *interface* to cover the whole development lifecycle. In this section, we take a closer look at how the business component appears at various phases of the development lifecycle. This is done by presenting examples of the deliverables that are part of a business component at the various development phases. The presentation is very simplified and high level, and it will be addressed in greater detail when we present the development process in Chapter 7.

One of the strengths of the business component concept is that it can support development with minimal transformations, but with refinements, from requirements to deployment and beyond, including customization and maintenance. Figure 4.13 illustrates the construction aspects, from requirements to implementation, and also shows deployment. The phrase "without transformations" means that the business component identified at the requirements phase stays a business component during the whole development lifecycle. At each

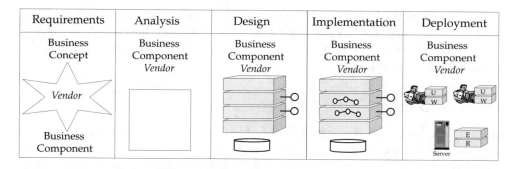

Figure 4.13   Development lifecycle.

phase, some additional aspects are defined and refined, but the self-same business component can still be clearly identified at deployment.

For each business component, a given development phase will typically produce three main kinds of deliverables: deliverables describing the context of the business components (which usually includes deliverables clarifying as much as possible the various uses of the component itself), deliverables describing how a user of a business component will see, or think of, or interact with it as a black-box, and deliverables describing specifics of the business component internals at that phase. In brief, context, externals, and internals. The distinction between these three aspects may not be very crisp during the requirements gathering phase, but it is an important frame of mind to adopt at all development lifecycle phases. The distinction becomes clearer with the maturity of the development and in later iterations.

Other practitioners more clearly separate external specification and internal specification in more or less sequential phases. At the high level of abstraction adopted for this discussion, the sequence is irrelevant, as long as at the end of each phase all deliverables are covered.

In the previous section, we also discussed how, at each development lifecycle phase, it is possible to think of the business component from a strong black-box/white-box point of view and crisply define what is inside and what is outside. Deliverables are assumed to be "normalized" across business components: Information is not duplicated, software artifacts are owned by one and only one component, and each business component is described with as little knowledge as possible about its potential users.

As in the rest of this chapter, the focus in this section is on an individual business component. Other deliverables are important when analyzing a system composed from several business components; however, they are not fundamentally important in discussing an individual business component. For example, the most important deliverable for a whole system is the model representing all the business components in the system. This model, apart from its relative importance in describing the context, on one hand, and the dependencies, on the other, is not particularly important when discussing an individual business component.

Deliverables

All of the deliverables described here relate to a single business component. It is important—for example, in project management—to have a way to address them as a whole. By associating them with the individual business component owning them, it is much easier to rapidly iterate the development of a business component and rapidly produce new versions of the business component. This, coupled with the whole architectural approach, allows the rapid development, in relative autonomy, of important parts of the system. At each phase, the business component is refined (not transformed).

Requirements

We introduced in Chapter 2 the hypothesis that the business components of the system under construction are known at requirements time, or at least very early on in the development lifecycle. This can be counter-intuitive, and this aspect is discussed in Chapter 7. Assuming for the moment that it is so, then it is possible to organize the requirements gathering around the business components.

The *context* will normally require, as a main deliverable, a diagram illustrating the dependent business components, and giving examples of how the given business component may be used by other components. At requirements, an initial high-level identification with no detail about specific dependencies is usually sufficient, although developers who do not understand the problem space may need to understand something about such dependencies, especially relationships.

The requirement description of a business component will usually include a list of features including both functional and nonfunctional requirements. Each feature may have, usually in a separate document, a detailed feature description or a set of monographs about particular sets of requirements that the business component must address. For a business component representing a process, an initial user interface prototype may also assist in capturing detailed requirements.

Analysis

The *context* defined at the requirements phase—mainly shown by the model of the components using and being used by the component under analysis—is refined if necessary. In addition, the business component may be described in the context of an initial enterprise object model focusing on the classes that are owned by the business component. For example, for an order business component, it may be a class diagram [Booch 1999], focusing only on the classes directly related to the order concept: This can be seen as a view of the global enterprise model, from the point of view of the component—that is, at the enterprise tier. Some of the language classes identified in this class diagram (typically, the focus class) may directly correspond to and help identify a business component, but there is not a one-to-one correspondence between the business component and the classes. For mid-level or highly complex business components, the context deliverables typically also include a set of high-level process models and/or use cases.

The *external* specification of the business component will include a user interface prototype (especially for process-oriented business components) and an initial specification of the run-time interfaces. At analysis, it is important to start differentiating between what can be seen internally and what can be seen externally. This is not only in terms of what will eventually become run-time interfaces, but also for a whole set of other software artifacts.

The deliverables may also include an initial object model of the *internals* of the business component (to be more precise, of the EDC, or WDC if there is no EDC/RDC), which is different from the object model adopted to describe the context: The internal model focuses on the internals of the DCs, starting to follow the patterns identified in Chapter 3, while the context enterprise object model focuses on the role of the concept represented by the business component in a wider context. Also, this phase produces an entity/relationship diagram of the island of data owned by the business component and the business rules implemented by the business component.

Design

At design, the business component consists of a detailed definition of all the known artifacts to be exported and imported, plus a detailed specification of the business component itself, as illustrated in Figure 4.14. At a high level, the most important parts of this specification are the user interface prototype and specification, the high-level design of the tiers (including the identification of the number and type of distributed components required to implement each tier), the detailed specification of the workspace and enterprise tier run-time interfaces, dependencies on other business components, and the persistence model.

At the end of this phase the deliverables will include the detailed internal object models of the various distributed components that constitute the business component—especially for the enterprise tier and the workspace tier, the complete relational model of the persistent data owned by the business com-

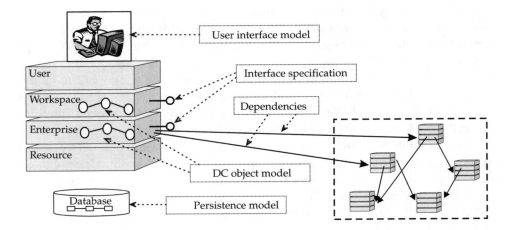

Figure 4.14   Specification.

ponent, and the design of the mapping between the internal e-tier object model and the relational model.[4]

An important design phase deliverable is the business component's dependency list, that is, the list of all the other components that this business component depends on, together with the exact identification of the software artifacts it imports from other business components.

It is not unusual, in a properly set-up component-based development environment, to be able at the end of the design to execute the interfaces. By this we mean that the information should be available to generate all the distributed components of the system as empty shells (either compilable, linkable, and executable or configured generic implementation), with no business logic whatsoever but with some minimal ability to execute dummy interfaces. This is very important for Rapid Component Development (RCD), discussed in Chapter 7.

Implementation

During implementation the actual coding of the business component's internals is performed. Of the set of implementation-time deliverables, the most important include the proxies for distributed component interfaces and the language classes that implement the distributed components themselves.

Additional deliverables may include various software artifacts that other components may reuse for their internal implementation but that are conceptually owned by this component; for example (and harking back to the example we gave earlier in this chapter when discussing design-time interfaces), the class header files and bodies that may be reused by components calling this component, or a set of user interface controls that other business components may reuse to make better use of this business component, and, of course, deliverables such as constants, error messages, and other things "owned" by the business component but reused by other components.

Testing

The business component architecture supports the testing of each aspect of the business component in relative isolation. Each phase of the development lifecycle will include various artifacts necessary to validate the component itself. For example, the design phase will include the design of the testing DCs. The implementation phase will include the implementation of the testing DCs. The testing deliverables will usually include test scripts, test data, test cases, and test plans. Each business component should deliver, together with the construction deliverables, whatever is required to fully test the business component and its own individual DCs.

Deployment

At deployment, the business component will appear as a set of executables representing the user and the workspace tiers on various client machines (for example, a set of laptops and desktop computers), a set of executables on one or more server computers, and possibly a set of database tables with some initialization data already loaded. An example of initialization data is the set of standard currencies (specific by an ISO standard) delivered with a Currency-Book component: There this no reason this data could not be part of the deliverables deployed at the customer site. An example of deployment is illustrated in Figure 4.15, which shows a business component at deployment as being deployed on three client machines, one server, and a mainframe. Typically, there will also be a set of other deliverables not shown explicitly in the figure, which could include configuration files, user guides, help text, installation guides, and any other deliverables that are required to use, execute, and administer the business component.

The development lifecycle exemplified in this section shows how there is a one-to-one relationship across the whole development lifecycle between an appropriate business concept and the business component that represents the concept. The functional developer starts to think in terms of this business concept at requirements and continues through deployment.

There may be project-specific, pragmatic reasons for which, even if possible, this may not be desirable. For example, the project may end up finding it easier to test two or three or more components packaged together in a project-specific way rather than the individual business components. Or, possibly for

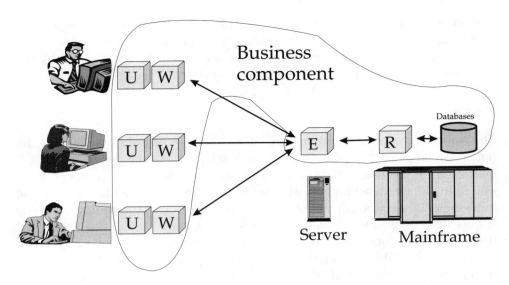

Figure 4.15 Deployment.

performance reasons, a single DLL implementing both the u-tier and w-tier of a business component during implementation and testing may be split into several smaller DLLs. These project-specific choices do not diminish the importance and power of the ability of keeping this one-to-one mapping.

AddressBook Scenario

At this point, several aspects of the example given in Chapter 2 are expanded, focusing on the same AddressBook business component introduced there but aiming to explain more clearly some of the things that the builder of this business component must provide. In doing so, one specific solution is given for a specified set of functional requirements. This solution is not claimed to be the best, but it is a useful, if basic, vehicle for the purposes of this section. There are many other possible solutions, and no solution is wrong unless it delivers less business success and/or lower net business benefit.

Two main aspects will be analyzed, under the assumption that we are building a client/server system where the client machine is a PC and the server machine is a Unix server. First, we integrate a user interface provided by a single business component into a bigger system. Second, we analyze EDC-to-EDC invocation—that is, how the e-tier of this component may be called by another component and what happens internally in the business component when it is called by other components.

User Interface

In a normal business application, there are a number of places in which an address needs to be shown, for example, when dealing with a customer, a supplier, a bank, a warehouse, or any entity representing a person, a location, or an organizational unit. Let us assume for simplicity that wherever in the system an address is displayed on the user interface, it can be displayed in exactly the same way. It would clearly be useful to develop this user interface once and for all throughout the system and reuse it everywhere an address needs to be displayed. Because we assume that we have an independent *AddressBook* business component managing all the addresses in the system,[5] the life of a functional designer/developer planning to use the address book component would be simpler if this reusable piece of user interface was delivered as part of *AddressBook*.

But an address alone makes no sense; it is always the address of something, for example, of a particular location or person. Consequently, from a development and even usability perspective, it could be argued that it makes no sense to deliver an autonomous user interface with the *AddressBook* business component. Rather it makes sense to deliver an individual control or a property page to be integrated into the user interface of other business components, which are assumed to be built in-house. Let us assume that this is possible, that the *AddressBook* business component provides a property page, and that it is integrated into the *Vendor* business component user interface, as illustrated in Figure 4.16.

This property page can be more or less easily integrated, to the point of true plug and play, depending on the implementation technology, the design, the user interface framework, and other considerations. Let us assume that in our case there is preferably none, but in any case minimal coding, compilation, and linking to integrate the *AddressBook* user interface into the property sheet developed for managing the vendor. To reduce the effort, we need the address property page to be delivered not only with a user interface layout, but also with all the code and designs corresponding to the set of events, messages, and processing needed to satisfy the various user actions. The point is that, even if commercially available development environments are making it a lot easier to develop user interfaces, it is still required, in order to associate the user interface with the business logic, to properly design, write code or scripts, test, and document the user interface. These things all take time and add to the cost of the development. It is to be hoped that the component we buy comes with all of this already done. Of course, some standards are needed here: The *Address-Book* business component must deliver a property page that is compatible with the user interface framework we are using for the rest of the system. We discuss user interface frameworks in Chapter 8.

An example of one of the many possible designs whereby a particular user interface layout can display and update data provided by the e-tier is presented

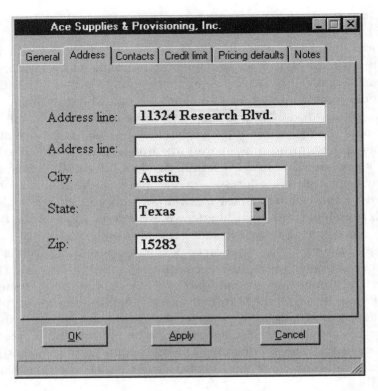

Figure 4.16   A property sheet managing a vendor with a property page managing an address.

in the sequence diagram in Figure 4.17. Let us also assume that the user requests the display of address data for a given vendor—in *Vendor*'s property sheet—in order to change it on behalf of the vendor. First, the user clicks on the address tab of *Vendor*'s property sheet (interaction 1 in the figure). This results in the focus moving to the address property page and (2) the address property page indicates to the *AddressBook* u-tier that the display needs to be refreshed. Let us assume that the *AddressBook* has not fetched the vendor's address data when the vendor property sheet was first displayed. In this case, the *Address-Book* u-tier (3) requests the current address information for the vendor from its w-tier. Let us further assume that the w-tier has not cached this data.

Earlier in this chapter, we discussed the logical nature of the w-tier. The code that calls the e-tier for data is *by definition* part of the w-tier, even if it's only a single line of code. In a thin-client situation, this may be all it is, and it would be physically bound into the same physical deployable unit as the u-tier. However, in a fat-client situation there may well be some amount of processing on the client machine in order to optimize and minimize the communication with the enterprise resource domain. In addition, invoking the EDC's interface (4) from

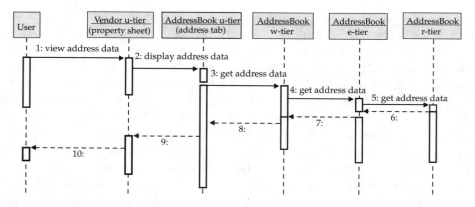

Figure A.17 Sequence diagram for user interface example.

the user workspace domain may require a translation of data input by the user into the format expected by the EDC, not to mention client-side data validation. These functions are by definition the responsibility of the w-tier. Such functions can help minimize traffic between the UWD and the ERD—for example, by avoiding having to invoke the ERD with data that is clearly invalid. This is not the case in this simple example, but it is typically the case in real life.

The e-tier needs to be able to somehow load and possibly validate the data from the database, and in a large-scale system this would advisedly be done through the crisp separation layer that is implemented by the resource tier (5). In this simple example, not much validation is required in the e-tier; the example implies mainly a simple read from the database. In normal cases of w-tier-to-e-tier communication, usually some kind of (potentially very complex) processing is required before the e-tier returns information to the w-tier.

This example demonstrates how a user interface can be usefully delivered together with a business component. In this case, a user interface for the address book business component is not a self-standing user interface, but it may be an address ActiveX control that implements a property page and that knows how to be integrated into a property sheet. The buyer of the *Address-Book* business component would clearly benefit if it were possible to buy, together with the rest of the *AddressBook* business component, this simple client-side control, such as a JavaBean or an ActiveX control, that was simple to integrate with the other parts of the system shown in the previous example and that would automatically take care of all the aspects interacting with the address book e-tier and r-tier.

EDC-to-EDC Invocation

In a real system, a given address will often need to be verified, or read, or even modified, as a result of processing in some other part of the ERD. Suppose, for example, that we are in the process of issuing an invoice and that before printing the invoice or the envelope for the invoice, the system needs the address for the vendor John Smith. Printers attached to a server are a shared enterprise resource, and hence they are one of the resources that the ERD addresses. Assuming that the *eInvoice*[6] EDC has received a request to print invoice #123 for vendor John Smith and has invoked the *eVendor* component to get John Smith's address, the subsequent possible sequence of calls is illustrated in the sequence diagram in Figure 4.18. This is an *inter-DC sequence diagram*, meaning a sequence diagram focusing on the flow of messages between DCs. In the figure, purely for diagramming purposes, we have abbreviated address to "addr".

Suppose for this simple example that the *eAddressBook*'s interface includes the operations described in Table 4.1, corresponding to simple CRUD (create, read, update, delete) maintenance operations. Many aspects of the interface specification, such as the exact errors raised or the result parameters, have been omitted for ease of presentation.

Let us briefly examine the internal operation of a minimalist address book EDC, which has only one business language class, that is, the focus class (see Chapter 3 for a definition). Figure 4.19 shows first (on the left) the proxy *ieAddressBook* (for the *eAddressBook* distributed component) that would have been imported into *eVendor*. The rest of the diagram shows intra-DC interactions within *eAddressBook*: the interface implementation class (*iieAddressBook*), the focus class (*feAddressBook*), and the proxy for the resource tier (*irAddressBook*).

In this simple example, the interface implementation class does little but pass the message to the focus class. Often an interaction such as that shown in Figure 4.19 will perform some processing as it progresses. The figure reflects this in that the business data type returned by the *rAddressBook* distributed component is shown as being different from that returned by the focus class and then by the interface implementation class to the *ieAddressBook* proxy. This may occur for a number of reasons. For example, the class of the *p_addr* instance (where "p" is used to indicate persistence) may contain an additional

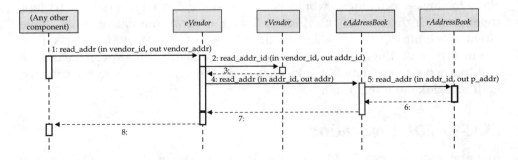

Figure 4.18   EDC-to-EDC invocation.

Table 4.1   Interface of eAddressBook

OPERATION NAME [7]	PARAMETERS	DESCRIPTION
create_address	in Address new_address, out AddressID new_address_ID	Creates a new address on the database and returns the new address ID.
read_address	in AddressID address_ID, out Address a_address	Returns the address identified by address_ID.
update_address	in AddressID address_ID, in Address new_address	Substitutes new address for the existing address identified by address_ID.
delete_address	in AddressID address_ID	Deletes the address identified by address_ID.
exist_address	in AddressID address_ID, out Bool result	Checks if the address identified by address_ID exists.

field that indicates the date of expiration of this address. The *feAddressBook* class may, before returning the requested address to the caller, check the expiration date against some internal business rule and decide whether to return the address. When it returns the address, it may return it as a business data type that does not contain the expiration date field.

Related Software Engineering Concepts

This section analyzes the differences between the business component and the related concepts of business object, module, and UML package.

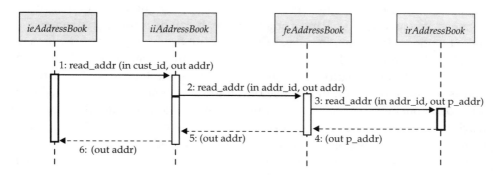

Figure 4.19   Intra-DC sequence diagram.

Business Object

The term "business object" has been widely used and abused. At least since 1991 people have been speaking about business objects. One of the authors published a book about the subject in 1994 [Sims 1994], in which the "business object" was very similar to the DC concept, with the added admonition that the DC should represent a business concept. What was missing (among a number of other things) was the unifying business component concept. What are the differences between business components and business objects? At the time of writing, a crisp and agreed-on definition of the term *business object* does not exist. Practitioners are using the term in two main and quite distinct meanings: first, the "object of the business" meaning; second, to indicate an implementation artifact—a particular software artifact that is used in a certain implementation approach and technology. These two meanings are often confused in discussions and presentations.

Object of the Business

We distinguish between "artifacts of the problem space" and "artifacts of the software solution space." By "artifacts of the problem space" we mean real entities, concepts, or business processes in the real world. Example of artifacts in the problem space are a paper document capturing the data for an order, a price, a real person who is a customer, or the order-entry process (possibly documented in a paper procedures manual) used to satisfy the needs of a customer. By "artifacts of the software solution space" we mean software artifacts created to support business activities as part of a software solution. The term "software solution" is used to differentiate a solution to a business problem that is of interest to IS developers from a solution that may not require the implementation as a software information system. Examples of artifacts in the software solution space are the implementation (in a software information system) of an order, a price, a customer, or the order-entry process.

When using the term "business object" in the meaning of an object of the business, it is an artifact of the problem space. It can be represented in a model of the business (for example, a class diagram), but a class *represents* a business object, rather than *is* a business object. And it can be implemented in a software solution, but the software solution *implements* a business object, rather than *is* a business object. In this use of the term, it would be perfectly acceptable for a business object to be implemented by a language class or by a distributed component in the terminology presented in this book. When identifying a business object, however, there is no predetermination about levels of granularity or implementation aspects. A money amount and an order-entry process are both business objects.

In this book, we use the term "business concept" instead of "business object" in its object-of-the-business meaning. The term "business concept" is applied to both entities (such as customer, price, and cost) and processes (such as the order-entry process). In addition, we apply as an integral part of the business component approach a specific concept of levels of granularity.

An Implementation Artifact

In this use of the term, a business object is a specific software artifact and also implies a specific implementation philosophy (that is, one specific chosen philosophy from among possibly many). In this case, the business object is a software artifact, an artifact of the software solutions space, with more or less well-defined characteristics. These characteristics are very similar to the concept of distributed object, with a few differences due to the fact that the business object is more specifically targeted at the needs of business system developers. In this meaning, the term "business object" has a very similar meaning to the "enterprise distributed component" concept.

Most of the software industry is today leaning away from using the term in this meaning. The more precise and well-defined term "component," especially when used together with a qualifier as in this book, is today preferred to both "business object" and "distributed object." The term "business object" is not used in this book.

Module

The term "module" is also used in at least two meanings. In the first meaning, it is used to indicate a partition of a problem space into a set of logical parts that loosely correspond to some form of software organizational mechanism. A "module" in this meaning may or may not have well-identified interfaces; it can be a logical partition, where by *logical* we mean that it may not correspond to any physical software artifact or organizational mechanism; it does not need to correspond to any well-defined architectural partition; and it can also be a purely marketing term. In the second meaning, "module" is used to indicate some lump of code or an executable that packages some set of perhaps unrelated software artifacts.

We view the business component as an extension and improvement of both these module concepts. On one hand, the business component is a specific way to partition a problem space, with well-defined architectural characteristics, that does correspond to well-defined software organizational mechanisms. On the other, the same business component corresponds to a well-defined and closely related set of source code files and executables. In fact, all the software artifacts that make up a business component are well defined and follow specific guidelines and principles. The term "module" is not used in this book other than (trivially) in a few specification language examples, where the OMG IDL syntax is followed.

UML Package

A package in UML is defined [Booch 1999] as "*a general-purpose mechanism for organizing elements into groups. Structural things, behavioral things, and even other grouping things may be placed into packages.*"

There are similarities and differences between the business component concept and the UML package concept, including the following:

- Packages are clustering mechanisms, like business components.

- Software artifacts "contained" within one package may appear in other packages in the form of "imports." This is similar to what happens in a business component, which has a strong import/export philosophy.

- Packages have an interface and implementation like business components. But unlike business component, "package" is a very generic concept, which can support various kinds of interface modeling and implementation but is totally nonprescriptive. The business component concept goes much deeper than the UML package in prescribing the kinds of interfaces and implementation structures and approaches, with the objective of tackling the challenge of highly productive, large-scale distributed system development.

- A package can be used to represent at least part of a given business component. But packages are not a key part of a development approach; rather, they are simply one of many tools. On the other hand, the business component approach is fundamentally based on business components, with a whole set of consequences, while packages are just one aspect of the object-oriented approach.

- Packages are not used for functional decomposition. They are logical concepts. As the term indicates, they were created as *packaging* mechanisms, not as a concept around which to organize the whole development. They could perhaps be used for functional decomposition, but there is no direct support for this, no body of principles that explains how to do it—and we don't know anyone who has tried it yet.

- Packages can be nested. In this sense, they support the *continuous recursion* concept presented in Chapter 2. On the other hand, business components are not nested: A business component cannot contain another business component. It can use another business component, and business components can be organized in various meaningful groups, as will be discussed in Chapter 5, but they are not nested. Of course, business components contain distributed components, and in this sense, a component can contain other components, according to the principles of *discrete recursion* presented in Chapter 2.

- Packages do not have identity or semantic scope. Business components do have identity and semantic scope. In this sense business components are perhaps more like UML collaborations.

Summary

A business component is the software implementation of an autonomous business concept (entity or process). It consists of all the software artifacts necessary to represent, implement, and deploy a given business concept as an autonomous, reusable element of a larger distributed information system.

Important characteristics of the business component concept are its strong concepts of software artifact ownership, of black box/white box across the development lifecycle, of architectural viewpoints, of distribution tiers; and of its use as a unit of modularization, of deployment, of reuse, and of management.

At first approximation a business component can be seen as being composed of four tiers: the user, workspace, enterprise, and resource tiers. These tiers are in defined relationships with each other: The messaging flow is always from u-tier to r-tier. Not all tiers need be present in a business component, and they are logical tiers rather than physical. The tiers can be organized into two distribution domains, the user workspace domain (concerned with the user's model) and the enterprise resource domain (concerned with the enterprise-level aspects, the boundaries of which are defined by the underlying transaction management). Two additional tiers are also defined, the testing tier and the gateway tier.

We apply an extended definition of interface, where an interface of a component is seen as a collection of access points into the component. Correspondingly, the interface of a business component is the union of all system-internal and system-external interfaces of all software artifacts of the business component. The business component is a black box across the development lifecycle, owning its own development repository, and any software artifact required by other components must first be explicitly exported by the business component itself.

An important aspect of a business component's externals is its set of dependencies on other business components. Such dependencies include not only functional dependencies, but also dependencies on the underlying BCVM socket.

A business component starts its life as a single construct at requirements, and it is still the same unit at deployment, customization, and maintenance. In this sense, the business component concept addresses the whole development lifecycle. The distributed component concept also lives throughout the development lifecycle.

We use the terms "business component" and "distributed component" instead of the more ambiguous term "business object." The business component concept extends the traditional concept of module, and it has similarities but also many differences with the UML concept of package.

The architecture of a business component solves some of the more pressing problems of distributed business systems and provides a number of design guidelines. To further the understanding of the business component, we must now consider its relationships with other business components and how it can be used to build whole information systems. We address these aspects in Chapter 5.

Endnotes

1   In the real world, there are some logical correspondences to the dependencies between a component and its CEE. For example, to be able to receive a sales order in the precomputer real world, you had to have in place a "CEE"—made up from things like pads of paper, envelopes, in/out trays, post boys, trolleys, store rooms, mail rooms, stationery stores, procedure manuals, franking machines, printing machines, elevators, pneumatic tubes, and so forth.

2   The term ACID stands for Atomicity, Consistency, Isolation, and Durability. The acronym was first used in [Harder 1983], to indicate changes to database status that are atomic in nature; for example, the changes are either fully committed and successful or are rolled back with no trace in the database. The term is explained in nearly every text on transactions or databases, see, for example, [Date 1995].

3   For more information about IDL and the process of defining interfaces in CORBA, see, for example, [Siegel 1996].

4   This description of the deliverables conforms to a given view of how to approach the persistence problem. Alternative views are discussed in Chapter 12.

5   The rationale, benefits, and disadvantages for having a separate component managing the addresses will be discussed in Chapter 11.

6   Throughout the book, when specifying interfaces we adopt the OMG style guide [OMG 1998b]. See also Appendix A, "Naming Conventions."

7   Readers coming from a technical infrastructure background may argue that some of the names of operation signatures in the table should be reserved for factory operations. A functional developer's point of view is adopted; these are perfectly normal operation names from that point of view. We will come back to these considerations in Chapter 9.

The Business Component System

The previous two chapters defined and discussed the distributed component and the business component. Now we can start to compose a system. Such a system is called a *business component system*, and it was defined in Chapter 2, "The Business Component Approach," as a set of business components collaborating together to deliver a solution to a business problem. This chapter expands on the brief description given then and is organized as follows:

- The main *concepts*, terminology, and characteristics required to discuss a business component system are presented.

- Attention is then turned to the *internals* of the business component system, from the point of view of the functional architecture.

- The *externals* of a business component system are discussed, including an introduction to the largest level of component granularity—the *system-level component*.

- Finally, the business component system is placed in the larger context of a complete information system, with some discussion on the pros and cons of the business component approach in this larger context.

Chapter 4, "The Business Component," dealt with the business component in isolation; this chapter analyzes collaborations between business components in the context of composing a system. In the process, there will sometimes be a need to switch between two levels of granularity—the individual business component and the business component system. Where necessary, the two are distinguished by the terms *business component-level* for the individual business component and *system-level* for the business component system.

Several aspects of the business component concept are mainly relevant in the context of collaboration within a system—for example, the functional categories. The system-level conceptual framework and terminology addressed in this chapter allow the discussion of these aspects to be completed.

This chapter presents many examples that illustrate the concepts discussed. The architectural and business modeling principles behind the examples given are not addressed, however, until Chapter 9, "Application Architecture," and Chapter 11, "Component-Based Business Modeling," respectively. Hence this chapter makes a number of significant assumptions about the structure of the system, its architecture, and what a "well-formed" system looks like. This means that, for some readers, some of the examples may appear to be arguable or may give rise to questions about structure and modeling that are not immediately answered. We ask those readers to bear with us while we build the conceptual framework.

Concepts

This section begins with an *example* of a business component system and discusses the functionality of each business component in the system. Using this example for illustration, additional concepts that are used in the rest of the chapter (and the book) are then presented: the *business component assembly*, the *product assembly*, and the *business type system*. Following this, and again using the example, the *component model* and *component diagram* of the system are introduced. Finally, and based on the concepts introduced, the overall distinguishing *characteristics* of a business component system are described.

Example

Figure 5.1 shows an example of a business component system—the same example shown in Figure 2.4 in Chapter 2.

A brief and simplified description of each business component in the figure follows, starting with *NumberGenerator* and working up. In reality, these business components would probably be of considerable complexity, and we ask the indulgence of the reader familiar with the business area used in the example to bear with us regarding the simplifications made.

>*NumberGenerator.* Generates, according to well-defined business rules, any sequence number needed in the system. In the business component

Invoice management

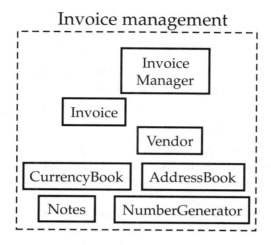

Figure 5.1   Example of business component system.

system shown in Figure 5.1, it is assumed that every time a new invoice is generated, a proper identification number (an invoice number) must be assigned, following unstated business rules. This is a generic need in business systems: In many cases, for example, on the creation of any new document such as a sales order, purchase order, or invoice, the system must somehow be able to generate an appropriate identification according to given rules (which may be configurable). This function can be collected in a "number generator" business component, which provides interfaces that return values for the various valid entity types and their associated management and maintenance. For example, invoice numbers are often required in sequence, and *NumberGenerator* could provide interfaces for the creation, retrieval, update, and deletion of sequences, following given sequence rules.

Notes. Enables one or more free-text notes to be attached to any entity in the system. A note is accessible at a user interface that shows the entity record to which the note is attached. Depending on the end use of the information, different types of notes are available. Two examples of notes in the invoice system are vendor notes (notes applying to a vendor) and invoice notes (notes specific to an invoice).

AddressBook. Contains location and other related information—for example, in addition to traditional address information, *AddressBook* also contains phone, fax, e-mail, and contact name information. It also ensures that only valid addresses are entered and that all entries are complete according to the address type associated with the address. For instance, an address requiring a contact must contain contact information.

CurrencyBook. Deals with all aspects of currency, exchange rates, and functions directly related to currency such as money arithmetic. The currency component provides interfaces to support the following:

- *Basic maintenance operations.* The creation, retrieval, update, and deletion of currencies, exchange rates, and rate types.

- *Conversion between currencies.* Converting amounts of money between currencies.

- *Money arithmetic.* Performing operations involving money in one or more different currencies. Simple integer or decimal arithmetic is not supported because it is not specific to currencies and money amounts.

Vendor. Holds information related to parties to whom the company pays money. This could consist of outside companies from which the enterprise buys items, but it could also include employees seeking reimbursement. *Vendor* provides a user interface for basic functions, manages any relationships created between different vendors, and manages access and retrieval functions for vendor information.

Invoice. Supports the creation and management of invoice-related financial transactions, including the maintenance of any relationships between the individual invoice transactions (such as invoices and related credit memos).

InvoiceManager. Encapsulates the invoice management process. While *Invoice* is responsible for storing and retrieving financial transaction information, it is *InvoiceManager* that coordinates the relationship between invoice records and the other components in the system. *InvoiceManager* either performs calculations required to transform data or requests those transformations from other components. *InvoiceManager* also maintains knowledge of relationships between related transactions stored by different components in the invoice lifecycle (for example, depending on the project design choices, it could own the relationships between invoice records and the payment records related to those invoices).

These descriptions raise many questions. For example, why were these particular business components identified and chosen at analysis- or design-time? What do address-related functions encapsulated in a business component mean? What is the database key of the addresses in the address book? If *CurrencyBook* is one business component, is it composed of three distributed components at the enterprise tier, since it encapsulates three major functionalities? What is hidden behind the term "book" in the name *AddressBook* or *CurrencyBook*? These and other questions will be addressed in Chapter 11.

Business Component Assembly

Chapter 4 introduced the concept of a dependency list for a business component, where it was defined as the list identifying the set of business components on which the given business component depends. Table 5.1 illustrates a simple example of a dependency list for the business component *Vendor*.

It is often useful to treat this set of business components—that is, a given business component and all the business components it depends on—as a unit. We call this unit the *business component assembly*.

> A *business component assembly* (BC assembly) is the transitive closure[1] of a given business component and the business components on which that business component depends.

From this definition, it is apparent that a BC assembly has one and only one top-level business component. Given its relative structural simplicity, its closured dependencies, and its normal size of between, say, 3 and 10 business components, it is a useful logical unit within the business component approach, and it is particularly appropriate as a project management unit, as discussed in Chapter 10, "Project Management Architecture." In addition, the BC assembly can be usefully mirrored at the DC level and is called a *DC assembly*. And just as the BC assembly has a dependency list, as illustrated in Table 5.1, so can a DC: A *distributed component dependency list* (DC dependency list) is the list of the DCs on which a given DC transitively depends.

Figure 5.2 illustrates the business component assembly corresponding to the dependency list in Table 5.1. In this simple example, where *Vendor* depends on *AddressBook* and *NumberGenerator*, the *Vendor* business component assembly is composed by {*Vendor, AddressBook, NumberGenerator*}.

The BC assembly is useful as the unit of development, testing, deployment, and release. In addition, it can be seen as a unit of evolution or maintenance—a whole business component assembly can be replaced by a new version with (given appropriate tools) a single operation. The unit of evolution/maintenance can, however, be of a smaller granularity. For example, we might deploy the *Vendor* business component assembly and later we might want to add functionality to, or even fix an existing feature in, the *eAddressBook* EDC. In this

Table 5.1 Dependency List for *Vendor* Business Component

BUSINESS COMPONENT	DEPENDENT BUSINESS COMPONENTS
Vendor	AddressBook, NumberGenerator
AddressBook	NumberGenerator
NumberGenerator	None

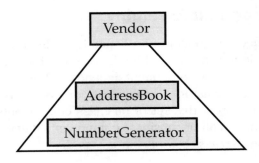

Figure 5.2   The *Vendor* business component assembly.

case, we could send out an update containing only a new version of *eAddress-Book* to be plugged into a running system.

As illustrated in Figure 5.2, it is useful to represent a business component assembly graphically in terms of a triangle. The business component at the top of the triangle names the assembly. We often jokingly refer to this as *management by triangle*, to illustrate the importance that this concept has in the management of the development of a business component system.

So far, we have seen a business component system in terms of a set of collaborating business components. Because each business component defines a BC assembly, the business component system can also be seen as a set of overlapping BC assemblies that are deployed and installed together in order to resolve a specific business problem.

A business component assembly may correspond to a business component system if and only if the system has one and only one top-level business component. A single business component that is not dependent on other business components is an acceptable degenerate case of a BC assembly. An example is the *NumberGenerator* business component shown in Table 5.1.

BC assemblies can intersect. Consider the very simple example of a business component system composed of business components A, B, and C, where both A and B depend on C. Suppose that, for some good reason, it is decided that two BC assemblies, {A, C} and {B, C}, are to be the two units of management. As shown in Figure 5.3, these two BC assemblies would intersect. If A is deployed separately from B, are two Cs deployed? No; intersecting assemblies do not usually lead to multiple deployments of the same business components.

A BC assembly could be thought of as including or nesting other BC assemblies. In the example illustrated in Table 5.2, the *Vendor* = {*Vendor, Address-Book, NumberGenerator*} assembly includes two other BC assemblies, the *AddressBook* = {*AddressBook, NumberGenerator*} and the *NumberGenerator* = {*NumberGenerator*} assemblies. Given the maturity of assembly technology today, however, it is not currently useful to see this in terms of nesting. In gen-

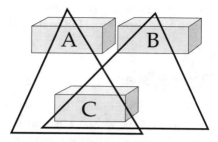

Figure 5.3 Intersecting BC assemblies.

eral, it is better to think of a BC assembly as containing only business components, not other BC assemblies. In this sense, a BC assembly is, to a large extent, only a (very important) logical and managerial concept. For example, in Chapter 10, the BC assembly concept will be found to be highly useful during configuration management and day-to-day task management.

Product Assembly

A *product assembly* is a set of business components that makes commercial sense to a software vendor or an in-house IS department as a distinct catalogue item or reusable asset for its intended customers. It is defined as follows:

> A *product assembly* is a set of one or more business components that can be delivered or sold to a consumer as a distinct, useful, and well-identified unit.

A product assembly often corresponds to a BC assembly. In some cases, however, the only thing that the constituent business components have in common may be that users want to acquire them as a single product. A product assembly, unlike a BC assembly, may have more than one top-level business component.

A business component system is also a product assembly, but not all product assemblies are business component systems. For example, a product assembly may be a set of generic business components that can be reused in the imple-

Table 5.2 Business Component Assemblies

ASSEMBLY NAME	ASSEMBLY
InvoiceManager	InvoiceManager, Invoice, Vendor, AddressBook, NumberGenerator
Vendor	Vendor, AddressBook, NumberGenerator
AddressBook	AddressBook, NumberGenerator

mentation of many different business processes, but it does not per se provide a solution to a defined business problem. Hence it would not be a business component system.

Business Data Type System

Chapter 3, "The Distributed Component," introduced the concept of a business data type. The *business data type system* is the set of business data types implemented by a given business component system. It is typically extensive and is, for developers of large systems, a fundamental concern. Three levels of business data type system can be discerned, corresponding to the three levels of interface visibility presented in Chapter 4:

1. An *internal business data type system*, sometimes referred to simply as the *data type system*, is the set of all business data types used in a given business component system, regardless of whether they are used only within a distributed component or whether they are an interface parameter. That is, the internal business data type system is the set of business data types seen by a developer who has full authority to look at the internals of all software artifacts within the given business component system. Normally, the internal business data type system is a large superset of the business data type system.

2. A *business data type system*, without further qualification, is the union of all business data types used in the interfaces of the distributed components within a given business component system.

3. An *exported business data type system* is the set of all business data types that are explicitly made visible outside of a given business component system. Normally, the exported business data type system is a small subset of the business data type system.

Component Model and Component Diagram

Figure 5.1 is a simple graphical representation of the business components required for our simplified Invoice Management system. This is a useful way to represent a business component system graphically, and it is called the *business component diagram* or BC diagram. The full component model of the system is called the *business component system model* (BCSM). This model belongs to the functional architecture viewpoint. A full BCSM consists of a number of models and documents, detailed in Chapter 7, "Development Process," and it is the most important model in a component-based development. The business component diagram part of it is the model that, in the various component-based projects we have worked on, always ends up being pinned to every project member's cubicle wall. It is the model that is most often used during any of the project's modeling or design discussions and brainstorming.

The BCSM is only one of the models used to describe a business component system: Other models include a business process model, an enterprise object model, a user interface model, and an enterprise persistence model. These other models are addressed in Chapters 7 and 11.

The BC diagram is a representation of two of the five dimensions of the business component approach (as a reminder, these are granularity, architectural viewpoints, distribution tiers, functional categories, and development lifecycle). It doesn't show but implies aspects of the other three—the levels of granularity, the internal tiered architecture of the individual business components, and the time dimension of component evolution during the development lifecycle. It does directly address the functional architecture and is one of its main representations. In addition it explicitly captures two very important aspects of the functional categories dimension, as illustrated in Figure 5.4:

- An orientation of the dependencies between these business components, in which any business component higher up in the model may depend on any business components lower down. Indeed, the placement of the business components on the component diagram is not arbitrary: It corresponds to a directed acyclic graph (DAG), in that a business component at a given level in the diagram can depend on business components at any of the levels below but cannot directly depend on a business component above. The DAG is indicated by arrows in the figure and is more fully addressed in the context of the *principle of non-circularity* in Chapter 9,

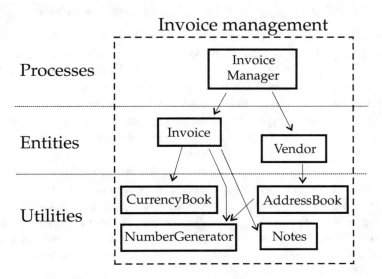

Figure 5.4   Characteristics implied by the BC diagram.

where the reason for this being a fundamental principle of architecting distributed systems is discussed.

■ An organization of the business components in the diagram by categories, where each category corresponds to a layer. Figure 5.4 illustrates the characterization of business components as belonging to the utility, entity, and process categories, which are the subject of the next section. These layers and direction of dependencies are what is referred to when we say that the system can be built bottom-up.

This two-dimensional model in reality can be thought of as representing a cut of the multidimensional space at the enterprise tier level, meaning that the boxes could represent the enterprise distributed components of the system. A section of the same system at another point in the space (such as the work-space tier) could produce a different BC diagram. This is equivalent to saying that unless otherwise specified, the BC diagram corresponds to the model of the EDCs of the system, and it is indeed often useful to think about it this way.

The BCSM is a living model. By *living model*, we mean a model that is constantly kept up to date to reflect any change done to the system that may affect the model. The BCSM may evolve and be refined at each phase of the development lifecycle, as well as at each iteration, and is up to date at each moment during the project. For example, Figure 5.5 represents the stylized evolution of a BC diagram. Initially, at the requirements phase of the first iteration, the diagram has two business components. During analysis, a new business component is identified and added to the diagram. Successive phases of the same iteration will work with this new component diagram. Components may be

---

LAYER

The term "layer" without qualification is used in this book to imply a functional layer, and it equates to an open layer. As we will see in Chapter 9, the term "open layer" is used, as opposed to the term "closed layer," to indicate the direction of dependency and not a hidden layer. For example, given three layers *A*, *B*, and *C*, with *A* at the top, then *B* does not hide *C* from *A*; rather business components in (belonging to) *B* may depend on business components in *C* but not on those in *A*. Business components in *A* may depend directly on those in *C*, as well as on those in *B*.

A layer should not be confused with a tier. The unqualified term "tier" indicates a distribution aspect—for example, the enterprise tier. The term "tier" is used when discussing distribution aspects within the application architecture viewpoint to indicate a logical tier as discussed in Chapter 4. Layers and tiers (or, more precisely, functional layers and distribution tiers) are two orthogonal dimensions; for example, a business component belonging to a given layer may have a number of tiers, typically four.

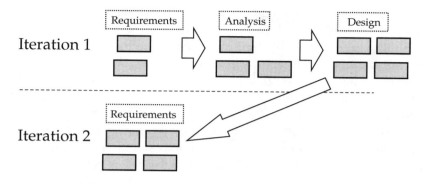

Figure 5.5 BC diagram evolution.

added, changed, or removed from the diagram for many reasons, including changes in requirements, prototyping, business component not relevant in an earlier phase, errors in modeling discovering additional business components, and so forth. If requirements must be updated, or when a new iteration is started, it is the most up-to-date BCSM that is used. At each phase of the lifecycle and at each iteration, the BCSM may change: From this point onward, the enhanced BCSM becomes the only BCSM for the system and the reference model for all future phases and iterations.

Characteristics

Having established a number of concepts, the main characteristics of a business component system can now be discussed. These are as follows:

- *Definitional implications*—that is, implications deriving from the definition of a business component system
- The way that the *shape of applications* changes
- The *Base* and *System* business components

Definitional Implications

A business component system was defined as a set of business components collaborating together to deliver a solution to a business problem. There are three important implications of this definition: First, any collaboration of business components that delivers a solution can be considered a business component system. The term *solution* is interpreted in the sense of implementing one or more business processes. In this sense, a business component system is a product assembly, but not all product assemblies are business component systems. There is hence a precise objective of the collaboration of business components: to resolve a business problem. A commercially available business component system would be useful as-is because it would implement a recognized business process, often more than one, with enough functionality to be used as an independently useful end-to-end process, which by itself is of value to an organization.

Second, based on architectural principles that will be addressed in Chapter 9, the collaborating business components are in a defined relationship with each other: They are a hierarchical set of collaborating business components, where the hierarchy is defined by the request of services. Any layer applies, with respect to any layer below it, the Hollywood principle: "Don't call me; if I need you I'll call you." Higher-level business components, in an application of the essence of the mediator pattern [Gamma 1995], act as coordinators for lower-level components, thereby reducing dependencies. Each layer has some level of business rules and processing, and each can be seen as a provider of services for higher levels and a requester of services from lower levels. This concept will be revisited in more detail in the next section.

Third, this definition is from the functional architecture viewpoint. But there are other viewpoints under which the system can be seen. We saw that each business component is composed of a set of tiers. From the application architecture viewpoint, this is also true at the system level: The whole system can be thought of as composed of four distribution tiers. These four tiers mirror the business component tiers presented in Chapter 4, but they are seen here at the system level, which better enables the analysis of system-level patterns and characteristics of the tiers. Indeed, any system, not only systems assembled from components, can be thought of in terms of four tiers and should, we believe, be architected that way.

The Shape of Applications

A business component system corresponds loosely to the concept of an application. Assembling a business component system can be seen as bringing together one or more top-level business components and their transitive closure, which consists of one or more business component assemblies. What is the main difference between this kind of system and a traditional system or traditional application built, for example, using an object-oriented approach—that is, based on classes? A component-based system is made up of components visible at run-time. The implementation of a component can be changed without having to change the rest of the system. This is not generally true with OO-based systems because the rigorous focus on autonomy is not present. Indeed, the whole shape of the application changes when using business components. One major change is that, from the same set of business components, different business component systems (applications) can be assembled without necessarily having to redesign at the detail level, or break code apart, or even recompile or relink the system. For example, using many of the business components described in the preceding invoice management example, a purchase order management system such as that shown in Figure 5.6 could be assembled. The shaded components in the figure are the same as those shown in Figure 5.1.

A frequently asked question is this: If invoice management is a business component system, and if the purchase order management is another business component system, what is the result of an organization's bundling them together in order to ship both as a single unit? The answer is that it is still a business component system. This is so because the result (see Figure 5.7) is what the project creates and eventually deploys as a solution to the problem that the project is trying to resolve—the target of the development project. Accordingly, a business component system implements one or more business processes, depending on the needs of the project.

Chapter 4 briefly introduced the concept of islands of data, in which each business component owns its own set of tables (at least logically) and is the only business component in the system that can access those tables directly. Other business components access them indirectly, through the owning business component's interfaces. A business component system can hence be seen as shown in Figure 5.8, where each business component owns its own logical database. This concept will be discussed extensively in Chapter 12, "Component-Based Design."

Base and System Business Components

Chapter 4 discussed the fact that a business component can be seen as a clustering mechanism and that all functional software artifacts in the systems are owned at development-time by a given business component. This concept of ownership is very important during development of the system (more so than at run-time), and it leads directly to the creation of two important and atypical

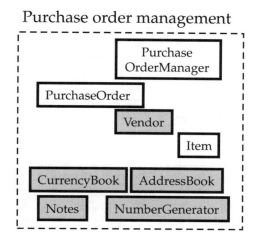

Purchase order management

Figure 5.6   A purchase order management system.

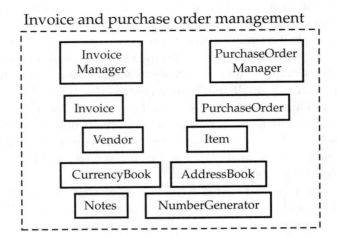

Figure 5.7 An extended purchase order management system.

business components that we introduce as an answer to the following two questions. First, if each functional software artifact in the system is owned by a business component, which business component owns the software artifacts on which all other business components depend, such as base classes or system-wide error definitions? Second, is there a business component that represents the system itself and/or that owns the software artifacts that are needed to represent the system at some global level?

These two questions are very real, and their answers become system requirements. The answer to the first is what is called the *Base* business component. The answer to the second is affirmative and results in what is called the *System* business component.

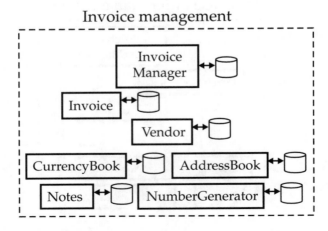

Figure 5.8 Business component system with islands of data.

Base business component.

- The business component *Base* contains all the software artifacts that do not belong to any particular business component but that are globally needed. Such artifacts include common libraries, common error definitions, constants, commonly used business data types, and so forth. *Base* has no knowledge of any of the other business components and is not dependent on them.

- *Base* is a degenerate case of the business component concept, in that it could, depending on the system and the technology used, have no run-time representation at all. For example, it may contain only a set of software artifacts to be used by other business components at development-time. Also, *Base* does not correspond to a business concept, at least not in the usual sense of the term. In a large system, it may be useful for the whole system to have a separate base business component for each business sector (see sidebar) or even business domain within the system. For example, in an enterprise resource planning system, it may be necessary to have a base component for the financial aspects, one for the manufacturing aspects, and one for the supply chain management aspects.

System business component.

- The business component *System* contains all the software artifacts of the system that must have a cross-system level of visibility in order to work properly but that do not belong to any of the other business components.

BUSINESS SECTOR

In many businesses, there are functional areas of concern that are normally and routinely identified as a whole, for example, manufacturing, logistical distribution and supply chain management, business financials, transportation, telecommunication, and so on. These are referred to as "business sectors." These business sectors may have dependencies among them, and it is difficult to define crisp boundaries between them. Each business sector may contain several business domains. The term "business domain" identifies a logical grouping of function or business processes. For example, supply chain management may contain the Order Entry, Billing, and Inventory Management business domains. In this chapter, the term "domain," without further clarification, is intended as a business domain in the meaning discussed here. Each domain may correspond to a business component assembly, but the correspondence can be loose and a given business component can belong to more than one domain.

A business domain should not be confused with a distribution domain (the enterprise resource domain and user workspace domain) presented in Chapter 4.

A typical example is an application desktop, that is, an artifact that supports user interface navigation throughout the whole system being implemented, and that effectively provides the user with visibility over the whole system.

- This component may also own all the software artifacts required to properly develop the system: For example, a system-wide configuration file could be placed in *System*. Typically, *System* also owns the system-level dependency list.

- In a large system (and as in the case of the *Base* business component), it is useful, in addition to a *System* component for the whole system, to have a separate *System*-like business component for each business sector or even business domain within the system.

While we have consistently found the need to define a *Base* business component, the need for one or more *System* business components is more dependent on the particular design of the application. The fundamental difference between the two components is that while all business components in a given system will normally depend on the business component *Base*, which is hence positioned at the very low end of the "food chain," *System* has global visibility of all the other business components in the system, establishing it high on the food chain. These two components can be thought of as useful "catch-all" components that experience demonstrates have an important role in a business component system. These two business components and their placement in the BC diagram are illustrated in Figure 5.9.

The business components *Base* and *System* are a good example of business components that do not correspond directly to a business concept in the problem space, at least in the traditional sense of the term. They are also a good example of something mentioned in Chapter 4, that is, that the business component technology can be usefully applied to things other than the implementation of real-world business concepts.

Internals

The best way to describe a large-scale distributed information system, is to use the Lasagna Model.

RADOUANE OUDRIHRI, 1992

This section provides a perspective on the business component system from a functional point of view. It does this by describing the three most important functional categories of business components, plus a fourth category, as we

Invoice management

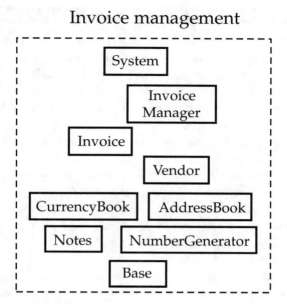

Figure 5.9   Component diagram with *Base* and *System*.

shall see. Assigning function to business components based on their category is not addressed here, nor is how to assign a business component to a category. This is left to Chapter 11, which addresses modeling a business component system, and which also discusses the criteria used in identifying business components. The focus in this chapter is primarily on describing each category and its distinguishing characteristics.

Earlier this chapter, we discussed how the BC diagram represented a set of business components belonging to specific categories and also how each business component belongs to a layer that corresponds to a specific category. The use of these layers reflects an important architectural principle of the business component approach, the *principle of noncircularity*, and strongly supports the mastery of the ever-increasing complexity of modern information systems. We use the Lasagna Model analogy to illustrate this principle of building and thinking of the system in layers, which also supports bottom-up and concurrent development of the business components in a system.

Business Component Categorization

There are three broad functional categories of business components, which were indicated in Figure 5.4 and are shown again for reference in Figure 5.10: process business components, utility business components, and entity business components.[2]

THE LASAGNA MODEL

Lasagna is an Italian pasta dish, built bottom-up by alternating layers of pasta and layers of cheese and tomato sauce (or other sauces). Each layer is built independently from the others but relies on the layers below to sustain its weight. Once broiled in the oven, the separate layers are linked together by the sauce and the cheese, and if you want to peel off a layer, other layers are, to various degrees, peeled off as well.

This is similar to what happens to a layered enterprise model. For example, an invoice business component can be laid on top of an address book business component. Because of the dependency of invoice on address book, lifting off the invoice will bring with it, as it were, the address book.

An important aspect of the lasagna model is that when modeling a given layer, the lower layers are assumed to exist, and their elements are not included in the layer being modeled. This simplifies what may otherwise be very complex modeling activities.

The *lasagna model* is a useful analogy, but only to a certain extent. For example, while with real lasagna it is impossible to substitute an intermediate layer by another layer without destroying the whole dish, it should be perfectly possible to replace an intermediate layer in a well-architected business component system without disturbing the other higher or lower layers.

The lasagna model might be said to complete the pasta analogies, adding to *spaghetti* code for highly intertwined code and to *ravioli* design for object-oriented systems. For those not familiar with Italian cuisine, *ravioli* is a particular kind of pasta that wraps around and embodies, hiding from view the meat or other fillings contained in the ravioli.

Utility business component. Represents one of the supporting concepts that are broadly required across many different business component systems but that are not the main entities on which processes depend. In the example of an invoice management system shown earlier in this chapter,

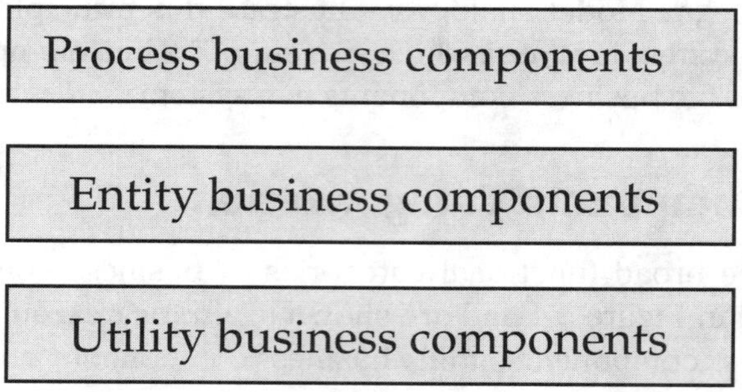

Process business components

Entity business components

Utility business components

Figure 5.10 Business component functional categories.

the *NumberGenerator*, *CurrencyBook*, and *AddressBook* business components appeared. These are all examples of utility business components.

Entity business component. Represents one of the main business concepts on which business processes operate and provides the services that support such processes and their business use (manage, maintain, group, link, select, present, convert, and so on). Examples of entity business components are *Invoice, Order, Product* (as in a manufacturing Product Data Management system), *Vendor*, and *Customer*.

Process business component. Represents a business process or business activity. In many cases, these components directly perform, or support human or nonhuman users in performing, a specific business/domain task. Examples are business components that implement the invoice management process, order management (that is, supporting the order-entry process), inventory management, or smaller support processes such as credit checking.

The previous three categories focus on the business components most relevant to the functional architecture viewpoint. A fourth category, *auxiliary business component*, is not shown in the figure, but it will be discussed later in this section.

In Chapter 4, we argued that the enterprise tier of a business component and the enterprise DC as the main element of this tier share many characteristics of the business component they belong to, to the extent that, at a certain level of abstraction, the business component and the EDC can be used as synonyms. An example is that, as illustrated in Figure 5.11, we can apply to EDCs the same functional layering we apply to business components.

The three categories correspond to the three main functional layers of business components, and these layers imply a direction of dependency as described earlier in this chapter: A process component may depend on entity and/or utility components, but neither of these will depend on a process component; an entity component may depend on utility business components but not on process business components; a utility business component does not depend on either entity or process business components. Because the layers are open, the dependency of a process on a utility business component does not need to be through an entity business component but can be direct.

Distribution tiers and functional layers are nearly orthogonal concepts: Why "nearly"? Business components in the same layer tend to have similar characteristics, while business components in different layers tend to have different characteristics, as illustrated in Figure 5.12. For utility business components, the persistence aspects are generally very important; on the other hand, they tend to have few complicated business rules and are mainly (but not only) data-oriented components. Of course, some utility business components may be dedicated to a specific cohesive set of business rules and may have no persis-

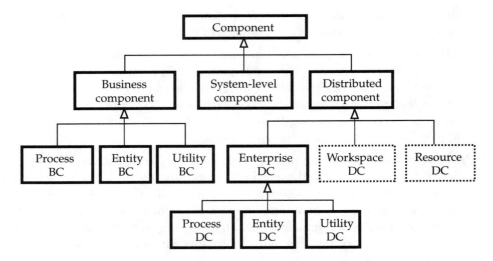

Figure 5.11 Functional classification applied to business components and EDCs.

tence. For example, were the money calculator function to be split out of *Currency Book* as a separate business component, then it would mainly be concerned with calculation and would probably have no persistence.

For entity business components, both the persistence aspects and the business rules can be very complicated. And finally, process business components usually rely on the entity business components for whatever persistence might otherwise be ascribed to them, and so they normally have low but not nonexistent persistence requirements. On the other hand, they have very important processing and business rules aspects. Their user tiers reflect to a large extent that processing and business rule importance.

These considerations reflect directly on the probability that a given distribution tier exists for a given category. For example, a process business component may have only a user or a workspace tier, or a relatively simple enterprise tier, while a utility component may have only a resource and a relatively simple enterprise tier.

The various aspects of each of the functional categories are now analyzed in more detail, with the aim of providing a better understanding of component-based system characteristics and helping the business modeler in identifying, given an initial problem, a set of candidate business components.

Utility

Utility business components (UBCs) are those that are most generally reused throughout various different business systems. They are normally collections of highly reusable services. Utility business components tend to be rather easy

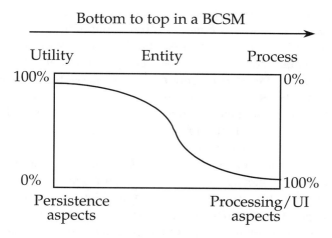

Figure 5.12 Relative importance of persistence and processing/user interface aspects.

to model and understand because they represent concepts that are quite autonomous or that can be modeled so as to be autonomous. They can usually be built with no dependencies, by concept or more often by design, on entity or process components.

Across domains, utility components tend to have very similar detailed characteristics in terms of required functionality. For example, the need to associate a note to any entity in a system is much the same in any business sector. Requirements for utility components tend to evolve relatively slowly (for example, a currency was a currency 20 years ago and still is a currency today, with the same detailed characteristics unchanged), and they are normally not part of the competitive edge of software solutions. Partly because of this, utility business components are also relatively noncontroversial, and they can be designed, implemented, and deployed relatively independently of business process considerations. Thus they lend themselves to in-depth standardization of interfaces and possibly even of internals such as the precise algorithms and database layouts used. Such components could support a third-party component market, eventually becoming part of a business component framework product.

The utility layer could include things that are not necessarily implemented using a business component approach (for example, not having four tiers), such as a component performing calculator operations and implemented as a JavaBeans or an ActiveX control, which is not a distributed component. Given the various characteristics of UBCs, we shall see in Chapter 7 that they can have a simplified or even specific development process. For example, because they are relatively autonomous, it is easy to test them in isolation.

When comparing an object-oriented analysis of the information system with a business component analysis of the same system, and depending on the designer, UBCs often do not appear as classes in the enterprise object model. For example, while an address concept often appears in an enterprise object model, it is very unlikely that an address book concept will. Again, a number generator is not usually found in an enterprise object model.

In a complex layered enterprise model, it is often useful to build the utility business components as an independent layer of the system and then forget about them. Other modeling can simply assume their existence, thus reducing the complexity of the overall enterprise model.

A utility business component in some cases manages entities that are logically "weak." For example, an *AddressBook* business component manages addresses, which are logically weak entities. According to the relational database theory, a weak entity is an entity that is not uniquely identified by its database primary key alone. A *logical weak entity* is an extension of this concept covering entities that, even if not implemented in a relational database as physically weak entities, have the characteristic of not being an independent concept in the real world. For example, an address is always an address of something, and a note is always attached to something.

Entity

Entity business components (EBCs) represent the main business concepts on which business processes operate. These correspond to the business concepts normally identified by object-oriented analysis of a given problem space and also by an entity-relationship analysis of the system. Examples include "Invoice" and "Item", but also concepts like "Price" and "Cost". The names "Price" and "Cost" may at first glance seem surprising; this is discussed in the sidebar, "The Naming of Names."

At a high level of abstraction, EBCs have similar and cross-domain characteristics in terms of required functionality: For example, an item is an item in all industries, and it needs to be engineered, priced, and sold. But behavioral details usually vary significantly from one business domain to another, and even from one corporation to another in the same business domain. For example, an item for what is called discrete manufacturing is substantially different from an item in what is called process manufacturing.

In any specific business domain, the related requirements for the fundamental structure of these entities tend to evolve slowly (an item was an item 20 years ago and still is an item). But the specific behaviors tend to evolve relatively quickly and some EBC behavior may well form part of the real competitive edge of a given software solution.

EBCs can *not* always be fully designed, implemented, and deployed independently of business process considerations. For example, both interface and implementation requirements of the concept "manufacturing item," embodied in the business component *Item*, may change quite radically depending on

THE NAMING OF NAMES

Names such as "Price" and "Cost" may at first glance seem to refer to perhaps simple abstract concepts that would not be candidates for realization as a business component. Such a name, though, does not refer to the abstract concept. In enterprise resource planning systems, for example, the calculation of an item's price often requires vast amounts of information and the application of complex rules. A business component that encapsulates such information and rules is likely to be named "price" or "cost" in preference to a name such as "price manager" or "cost manager." This is because we reserve the word "manager" for the naming of certain process components, and so do not apply it to entity components such as the ones being discussed. Again, some may argue that the calculation of price *is* a process. And yes, the actual calculation can be seen as a business process—or more precisely (as discussed in Chapter 11) a *support business process*—that might be called "pricing." In addition to processing, however, a great deal of support data must also be encapsulated. Indeed, there may be a need (see Chapter 11) for both a process component (which we would call, for example, *Pricing*), and for an entity component handling this support data, which we would name, for example, *Price*.

In the absence of industry standards, the naming of these entity components is, of course, subjective, and different approaches to naming have various advantages and disadvantages. For example, the name *PriceBook* could be used to indicate that this component is used as a real-world book of prices: that is, the information needed to calculate a price is looked up, and this information is then processed in a *Pricing* process business component. Similar reasoning applies to many of the business component examples presented, for example, *Cost* and *Tax*.

whether it is a discrete manufacturing or a process manufacturing item. The development of comprehensive standards for such concepts will involve controversy and compromises, as exemplified by the fact that it is often hard to standardize them within a single large-scale system design. Nevertheless, end users evince a strong interest in standardizing models and interfaces for these objects, in the business interest of improving out-of-the-box interoperability of diverse software assemblies.

It is unlikely that such components will become autonomous products of a third-party component market. Rather they are more likely to be contained in software systems and component frameworks aimed at supporting a particular collection of business activities. What can be standardized are the common characteristics exhibited by these components, together with the business information that is transmitted between collaborating systems. This would allow a system developer to provide access to those common characteristics.

Process

Process business components (PBCs) represent business processes and business activities. These components directly perform, or support human or non-human users in performing, a specific business task.

Business processes tend to have significant differences in functionality from one business sector/domain to another, and often from one corporation to another within the same business sector. Indeed, business process details are often considered to be part of the competitive edge of the business itself. This means that it can be difficult to adhere to standard business process components across business domains/sectors.

PBCs tend to evolve very rapidly, and it is often their ability to evolve at the speed required by the business that is the most important aspect of the information system. Exactly what process is performed, what approaches/algorithms are used to perform the process, what data is captured, how it is captured, how it is used, what data is produced, and how it is presented to the end user are all vital marketability issues in business software solutions.

It is typical for a single software product to support many options in these areas, in order to meet the needs of diverse customers. It is difficult to standardize process components and their interfaces within a domain, and it is arguably not even desirable at the industry level. On the other hand, it may suffice to provide standards for communication among business process implementations, and much of that communication is in terms of the business entity components previously discussed. In addition, it is useful to standardize general-purpose "process supervision" interfaces—activation, suspension, termination, and so on.

A PBC normally manages one or more use cases, as we shall see in Chapter 11. Process business components realize business concepts that are normally not found in an enterprise object model, for example, invoice management or processing payments. Traditional approaches usually place these in a business process model. The identification of a PBC, and of its responsibilities, is normally done using process modeling and/or use case modeling.

A process can, in some cases, be seen as a very complicated maintenance activity on entities. For example, an Order Management component is basically the maintenance of an Order entity; this maintenance happens to be extremely complicated and in this sense happens to be a whole process. In general, the separation of entity from process component is largely accepted; the precise point of demarcation, however, is often seen as being somewhat arguable.

Auxiliary

The preceding classification of business components, because it focuses on the functional point of view and on the business components most relevant for the enterprise, is one that has been found highly useful in practice. There is one more useful category of business component, the *auxiliary* category.

Auxiliary business components are those that are normally not identified by object-oriented analysis, but that are to be found in every well-constructed system. They usually support development or the run-time system, in various ways, and must be delivered as part of an industrial-strength system. An example is the business component we call *DatabaseIntegrityManager* that manages a very important aspect of any system: the integrity of the database. Not infrequently in the lifetime of a system, the database requires a clean-up, or the overall integrity and consistency of business data must be checked for some reason. To address these kinds of requirements, a database integrity business component could be provided. It would contain all the business rules, typically quite complex, used to determine whether the state of the system-level database is one of full integrity. Consistency may be lost in many ways: for example, the import of the data into a table, a data administrator using SQL to directly change a table, or even an error in application processing. The database integrity business component is not intended to be invoked during normal transaction processing by other business components.

Another example of auxiliary business components are those that monitor a system and support its operations—perhaps by reporting on performance (the *PerformanceMonitor* business component) or on frequency of errors.

The previous examples are all business components that do not represent business concepts and thus do not satisfy the definition of a business component. This is usually true for all auxiliary components. The term "business component" is still applied, as it is for other components such as the base and system business components that use business component technology even if not directly realizing a business concept.

Externals

Up to now, the discussion has centered on the business component system from the point of view of its internal composition, that is, for example, the kinds of business components used in its composition and its internal layers and tiers. This section analyzes the externals of the business component system, and it introduces the concept of system-level components. Collaborations of system-level components are considered in Chapter 6, "The Federation of System-Level Components."

Interface

The run-time interface of a business component system is defined as follows:

> The run-time interface of a business component system is either the union of all system-external interfaces of its constituent business components or the interfaces of its gateway.

There are two main ways in which a business component system can be provided with an interface: a black-box approach or a white-box approach.

Black box. An interface to the business component system is provided through a specific access artifact, of which there are two flavors: a *gateway* (see Figure 5.13) or an *interoperability adapter* (see Figure 5.14). Perhaps arbitrarily, the term *gateway* is used to identify an interface implemented at development-time, while an *interoperability adapter* is the implementation of an interface "after the fact," for example, after having deployed the system. An interoperability adapter may be specified and implemented by an organization different from the one that developed the original system. In the remainder of this section, the gateway is assumed, leaving it to the reader to extend the discussion to the case of an interoperability adapter. A gateway will totally hide internals of the system, and so a client of the gateway will be unable to determine whether the system is composed from business components or built as a monolithic system. This is similar to the encapsulation afforded by a DC, where internals are completely hidden from a user of its interface.

White box. An effective interface to the business component system is provided by allowing direct access to its constituent business components. This is done by exporting a selected set of business component interfaces so as to give them system-external visibility. Such interfaces will normally require a set of additional constraints to be imposed on them for security and other reasons. This may, in turn, demand that specific system-external business component interfaces be specified and implemented. In Figure 5.15 such constrained interfaces are indicated by the letter "C."

The specification and design of the interface for a business component system is often more critical than the specification and design of business compo-

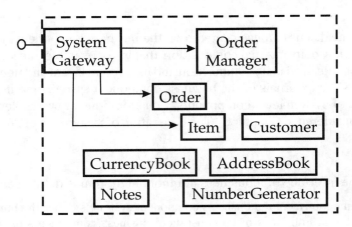

Figure 5.13   System interface provided by a gateway.

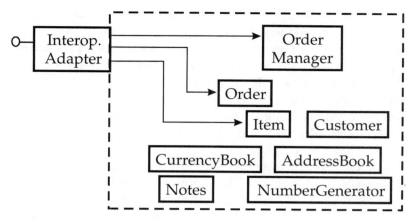

Figure 5.14   System interface provided by an interoperability adapter.

nent interfaces for the following reason. Very often, business component interfaces are designed to be used by trusted clients, that is, clients that are within the system and are conforming with a shared functional architecture. The system's interface, on the other hand, may be used by clients provided by other and even unknown organizations. In many cases, accessing software belonging to these organizations may not enjoy the same level of system trust as internal clients. Hence the interfaces will often be specified so as to allow their implementations to perform additional functional validation. The level of trust referred to here is not only a security matter, but also a functional architecture matter. For example, a client provided by the organization that invokes, say, a *create_order* interface may be assumed to have run a given set of business rules

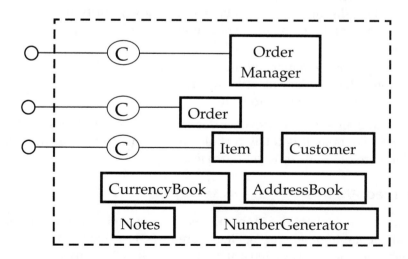

Figure 5.15   Exporting constrained business component interfaces.

before invocation. A client accessing software in other organizations may not have the capability to run those rules prior to invoking the system.

In addition, there are pragmatic reasons why some of the principles governing the specification of system-external interfaces are different from those applied to business component interfaces. For example, when the system's interfaces are driven by a set of conflicting requirements, such as those that arise when the needs and opinions of several different organizations must be taken into account, then the resulting interface design may often reflect compromises rather than best practice.

The implementation of a gateway as in Figure 5.13 may require a gateway business component. Should the gateway be particularly complex, the implementation might even consist of a set of business components. In the case illustrated by Figure 5.15, the interface constraint(s) for a given business component may be implemented by a gateway DC that is owned by the business component concerned. In this case, the union of all individual gateway DCs can be referred to as the "system gateway."

In both cases, the gateway may be much more than simply a pass-through interface implementation: A whole set of functionality may be provided by a gateway to the system, which would not normally reside in any of the system's functional business components. These functionalities could, for example, include the following:

- The ability to accept various data formats and transform them into the appropriate system-internal format. Examples include accepting business data directly and automatically from faxes, e-mails, EDI, or Internet-based communication.

- Management of the prioritization of incoming or outgoing requests, including the appropriate scheduling of low-priority and high-priority messages, and moving high-volume messages, when appropriate, to off-peak times.

- Access management, including activity history and log management, validation of the sender's identity, security management including the ability to work as a functional firewall.

The technologies and approaches for system-level interfaces are evolving rapidly. For example, it is today technically possible to provide systems with predefined proxies and with agent-proxies.

Predefined Proxies

Today, what usually happens is that target components provide proxies to the potential clients. In other words, clients are forced to adapt to the demands of the target component: They must use the proxies defined by the target. Over time, it is quite likely that client systems (or client business components) will be delivered with predefined proxies, and that it will be the target components that will have to adapt—to the predefined proxies. This will allow the delivery of totally self-contained components. Coupled with an appropriate run-time capability that can find the target dynamically, this will greatly enhance the possibility of true plug and play.

The introduction of predefined proxies, with their requirement that target components adapt to them, implies that the specification of dependencies (the target components) must be much clearer and more detailed than otherwise. Aside from provision of standard introspection interfaces, it will probably also be necessary to specify in greater detail such things as the allowable responses to operations invoked on a target component, and the realization of specifications in the predefined proxy such that dynamic checking can take place. In other words, especially careful design of predefined proxies would become crucial to their success.

Agent-Proxies

An agent-proxy,[3] while encompassing the same dynamic adaptation approach as the predefined proxy, turns things round so that it is effectively the client that adapts dynamically. Today, this approach has been implemented using Java, and other approaches are possible, including mobile agent technology.

An agent-proxy, illustrated in Figure 5.16, is a dynamic intelligent proxy that is downloaded into the client system at run-time from the target system. It is owned by, and may contain business logic belonging to, the target system, yet it executes in the client system's run-time environment and interacts dynamically as a peer with the requesting component. It represents the target component locally.

Given that an intelligent agent-proxy can be downloaded, there is an added possibility. That is, it can also perform application function that properly belongs to the target component, but that is "lent" dynamically to the client. This work would be done in the logical context of the target component, but physically it would be executed on the client system. Such an approach may well provide an answer to the problem of trustworthiness that was alluded to in the discussion of gateways earlier in this section.

In a future "post-scarcity era" [Orfali 1999], this approach could extend to the run-time the concept of extended interfaces described in Chapter 4. For example, in the scenario presented in Figure 4.11, the classes owned by the target component at development-time and executed as part of the client component at run-time could be implemented by an agent-proxy, owned by the target component and "shipped" to the client component at run-time, further reducing the development dependencies. Of course, using this approach there would almost certainly require greater network and computing bandwidth—hence the advantage of being in a post-scarcity era!

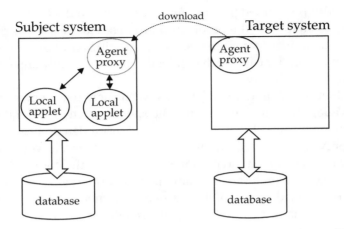

Figure 5.16   Agent-proxies.

System-Level Component

The previous two chapters have mainly addressed the lower levels of component granularity within the business component approach. This section addresses the level to which many business people, analysts, and software vendors implicitly refer when they speak of components: that is, a complete system as a very large-grained component. It is hence important to make a clear distinction between the following levels of component granularity:

1. *Business component and distributed components.* These coarser-grained components are intended to enable the speedy building of large-scale systems. A system built this way is not necessarily designed with interoperability with other such systems in mind.

2. *System-level component.* This very coarse-grained component is the third level of component granularity in the business component approach. It is a business component system that is specifically designed to interoperate with other systems, and it is constructed as a component in its own right.

Many practitioners equate a system-level component with a business component system having a well-defined external interface. This is formally incorrect. To be a component, a system must not only have a well-defined interface, but must also be easily deployable as an atomic unit, have its interface as the only way to access the services it provides (so enforcing the required strict black-box design), and must be provided with a plug that corresponds to a well-defined socket. In the rest of the book, all considerations regarding a system's interfaces will be discussed in the context of system-level components, although some may also apply to business component systems having a system-external interface.

Over some considerable time, and with significant technological and architectural improvements, it may be that the granularity of what is considered a system-level component will decrease. This may lead to a lesser distinction between system-level component and business component. Today a system is a very coarse-grained concept; in the future, it may be useful to consider a BC assembly or even an individual business component (typically, a process business component) as a system in its own right. This and other kinds of evolution will be driven by cost and complexity considerations. Today, a large business system such as an enterprise resource planning system can be expected to contain 350 to 400 business components but only some 30 system-level components. The latter is a very manageable number of components, taking in account that currently very little technical support is commercially available for system-level components. Should the future bring widespread technologies and architectures that support federations of systems, this will tend to drive system granularity downward, and it would result in a significantly higher number of system-level components, some of which may end up consisting of a single business component.

Chapter 6 provides further detail of interoperability between systems and examines the protocols required to enable interoperability as well as consideration of development lifecycle interfaces for system-level components.

The Information System

The focus up to now has been on how to build a mission-critical system using components in a cost-effective and rapid way. Other challenges that today's information systems must also meet include such widespread aspects as e-commerce, workflow, report writers, data warehousing, distributed systems management, and so forth. All of these add to the cost of building an information system, and they must be included in a comprehensive approach to software development. This section focuses on two of these challenges: e-commerce and report writers. These will highlight some interesting characteristics of the business component approach that can be generalized to the other elements of a whole information system. Indeed, through the following two examples, we also hope to illustrate how a whole third-party support market for large-scale information system could mature.

E-Commerce

Electronic commerce[4] is a catch-all term that covers a large set of very different requirements, technologies, and challenges. Broadly speaking, it covers all aspects of performing some form of commercial activity across information systems, using some form of computerized information exchange. There are two main forms of e-commerce today: business-to-consumers and business-to-business.

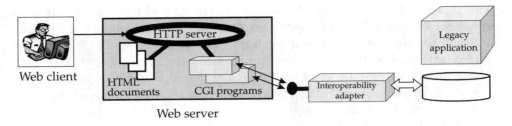

Figure 5.17   Traditional enabling of e-commerce.

Business-to-consumers includes all kinds of sales over the Internet, from a producer through some form of online shopping mall, more or less directly to the end consumer. This should by now be familiar to most readers, ranging as it does from selling books or airlines tickets over the Internet to online stock trading. The essence of this activity is interactive exchange of data between a Web browser and one or more servers. *Business-to-business* covers any form of electronic exchange of information between companies that supports a commercial activity. This kind of intercompany activity has been established for some time now, for example, through various forms of Electronic Data Interchange (EDI), and it is rapidly becoming cheaper and more available to small and medium enterprises.

Until recently, information systems have been dealing with the requirements of business-to-consumers e-commerce in an ad-hoc way: Legacy applications are in some way opened up to provide access from external systems through some form of interoperability adapter, as illustrated in Figure 5.17.[5] Interoperability adapters are further discussed in Chapter 6. Given the closed nature of many legacy applications, these interoperability adapters often access a database directly, and they can be quite complex applications in their own right.

With the advent of distributed system technologies, information systems are more naturally open. A business component system, and even more a system-level component, can today be considered to a large extent *e-commerce ready* given the fact that it directly provides network-addressable interfaces (see Figure 5.18) and is directly accessible from the external world, without the need for building complex interoperability adapters.

With the evolution and maturation of e-commerce technologies, commercial technical infrastructure offerings that support development of e-commerce capabilities in internal information systems will be soon available. Indeed, as shown in Figure 5.19, where the server is shown as being either HTTP- or CORBA-based or both, the technology prerequisites are already available today.

Technology alone is not enough to significantly reduce development costs and complexity. Development of the e-commerce parts of an information system must become an integral part of the development of the whole system, at all architectural viewpoints. Our expectation, which at the time of writing is already

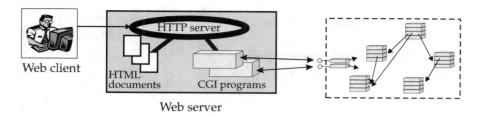

Figure 5.18   E-commerce with business components.

realized by visionary e-commerce organizations, is that fewer and fewer organizations will content themselves with merely adding some e-commerce capability to existing systems, but will move toward making the e-commerce system *the* core system, or at least have it directly developed as an integral part of the core system. The business component approach can greatly assist with this movement, and it also supports the functional developer in being able to focus on functional aspects only, without having to become a technology guru. In other words, adopting the business component approach can relegate the technical architecture—the glue—to its proper place, as illustrated in Figure 5.20.

A system such as system *B* in Figure 5.20 will export a proxy in order to allow other systems to gain access to it. This proxy should appear to the developer as any other proxy so far discussed. That is, it will hide underlying plumbing detail—in this case, characteristics that are specific to the e-commerce situation. Such a proxy is sometimes called an "e-proxy."

We have discussed here two levels of integrating the development of e-commerce in an information system: The first level of support concerns the ability of e-commerce technology to take advantage, or simply to properly use, component-based systems. The second level of support is where e-commerce technology becomes an integral part of a component-based architecture, to the extent that elements specific to e-commerce sink below the level of focus of the functional developer, becoming part of the BCVM. These two levels are a characteristic of many, if not all, technologies that have to encompass components: First, they somehow take advantage of the flexibility and advantages of com-

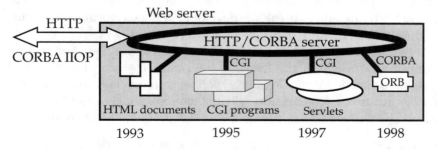

Figure 5.19   Evolution of e-commerce technologies.

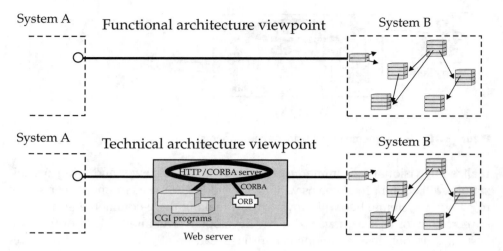

Figure 5.20 E-commerce and architectural viewpoints.

ponents; second, they evolve to the point that they are an integral part of the component-based approach.

Report Writers

Report writers enable a user to define online and dynamically a report on a database or part of a database. Commercially available report writers normally make certain assumptions about the way the database is designed. For example, they usually assume a relational database. In addition they often constrain the adoption of certain application-specific expedients in database design, such as giving a string field a meaning known only to the application itself. Examples of this latter expedient are having processing depend on certain hard-coded values in the database and provision of a dynamic or generic foreign key that points to different tables depending on the value of some application-dependent variable.

With current report writer technology, direct access to the database, rather than through the interfaces of a distributed component, is required. In this sense, current report writers tend to break the developer-defined layering that requires, as a design principle, that the only way to access a component's data is through its interfaces. This is an important point because, even at the cost of not applying component design principles, the reality of information systems is this: In order to achieve extra-functional requirements such as commercially available report writers, it is necessary to take into account noncomponent-based traditional approaches. The three main ways to deal with this problem today are these:

1. Deliver a set of default predefined reports, as appropriate, to each business component. This should be common practice, with the reports fol-

lowing standard patterns. The obvious defect of this solution is that it does not allow a user to design his or her own report.

2. Develop an in-house report writer, capable perhaps of limited user-defined reports, that knows about components and can either drive their interfaces or access the database in the knowledge of the islands-of-data approach taken by business components. Very few organizations can today afford this solution.

3. Allow the report writer to view the database as if it were a whole, rather than a set of islands of data, even if from a component-based development perspective each business component is still delivered with its own island of data, as illustrated in Figure 5.21. This usually implies that the various business components are delivered and deployed such that they share one single system-level database.

The solution we normally prefer combines items 1 and 3 of the previous list. This is helped through report writers usually needing only read access to data, so that integrity is not affected. Hence this solution is mainly a matter of the cost-effectiveness of the implementation.

Report writers are a good example of how the business component approach must take into account the constraints of commercially available technologies. Until component-based development has further evolved, to the point of interface standards that would support report writers to use only those interfaces instead of accessing a database directly, appropriate care has to be applied in the design and deployment of business component systems so as to enable use of commercial off-the-shelf report writers.

Summary

A business component system is a set of business components collaborating together to deliver a solution to a business problem. Business components can

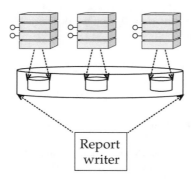

Figure 5.21   Different point of view on the database.

be seen as organized in business component assemblies. Product assemblies are collections of business components related by something that makes them useful to an end user or other consumer. The business data type system is the set of business data types appearing on interfaces implemented by a given business component system.

The most important description of a business component system is given by a business component system model, which at a high level is a two-dimensional description of a business component system. The business component system model is a living model; that is, it is always up to date at any moment in the development lifecycle.

A business component system, from a functional architecture viewpoint, can be seen as being composed of business components belonging to three main categories: process, entity, and utility business components. An additional important category is that of auxiliary business components. Two degenerate cases of business components are the *Base* component and the *System* component.

When provided with an interface, and designed and built so that it is deployable as a single unit, a business component system can be validly considered as being a component in its own right. Such a system is called a system-level component.

A complete information system must take into account a number of additional technologies, which include, among others, e-commerce and report writers. We believe that these additional technologies will typically evolve, with regards to component-based development, on two levels: First, they learn how to cope with existing components; second, they become, over time, an integral part of a business component approach.

In the next chapter, collaboration between system-level components is explored. Such a collaboration is called a *federation* of system-level components.

Endnotes

1   Transitive closure means that the full set of dependencies is included. Thus if business component *A* depends on *B*, *B* on *C*, and *C* on *D*, then the BC assembly will consist of *A* plus *A*'s transitive dependents: *B*, *C*, and *D*.

2   Chapter 11 presents a breakdown of each of these categories into a more detailed classification.

3   Thanks to Steve McConnell, president of OSM SARL, for the initial outline of this concept.

4   For more information on the technologies required to address e-commerce, see [Orfali 1999].

5   This and several other figures show CGI as a main technology, even though it is unlikely to last long as a technology of choice. We show it because it is widely used today, and it does indicate a general area of infrastructure functionality.

The Federation of System-Level Components

The three previous chapters navigated the concepts related to various levels of component granularity, that is the distributed component, the business component, and the system-level component. This chapter addresses how two or more system-level components can collaborate in a federation. Such a federation is defined as follows:

> A *federation of system-level components* is a set of collaborating system-level components federated to address the information processing needs of multiple end users perhaps belonging to different organizations.

The term *federation* conveys the idea of a set of autonomous or quasi-autonomous systems, independently developed and deployed, collaborating to provide a wider set of functionality for their users. In this chapter, however, we use the term to mean a federation specifically of system-level components. The federation challenge includes the general interoperability challenge on one hand and the e-commerce challenge on the other, and this chapter describes how a federation can address both. It is organized into the following sections:

- A brief introduction to the *business* aspects of the interoperability *problem*.

- The main *interoperability concepts*, providing a conceptual framework for interoperability, which is a prerequisite for addressing federation concepts. This framework consists of a seven-layer protocol model that helps illustrate and explain the interoperability problem. It applies to many development approaches, and it is not specific to the business component approach.

- The main *federation concepts*, including the characteristics of a federation whose constituents are system-level components working seamlessly together. Application of the seven-layer protocol model to a federation is also discussed.

- Finally, some of the main considerations in creating an *architected federation* are addressed.

The Business Problem

Even if the importance of interoperability among information systems has been a high-priority requirement for at least two decades, until recently the main problem of software development was to build a single self-contained system. Today, the ability for information systems to interoperate is a critical part of business reality, and it is seen as an important enabler for business innovation. Lack of interoperability is often seen as a bottleneck in the economic evolution of a business, both from the point of view of the enterprises concerned and of the software vendors providing the information systems.

For a modern enterprise, this is not only true looking inward, but also looking outward in terms of the partnerships an enterprise needs to survive and thrive in the market. Looking inward, if the enterprise needs to deploy a large scale distributed business system internally, there are only three fundamental choices:

1. Buy the whole system from a software vendor that provides all the functionality required

2. Custom-build the system

3. Buy a set of systems from multiple vendors, often with the objective of choosing the best-of-breed, and integrate them or interoperate them—or, more likely, ask a system integrator to integrate them

Given the improbability of any single software vendor being able to deliver on all requirements, and given the costs of building an application system in-house, the third alternative is currently receiving a tremendous push toward becoming the only effective reality.

From a software vendor's perspective, complete software solutions that address all of their customers' needs just cannot be afforded: There is a need to partner with other vendors and integrate their several systems to implement a given solution. This leads to a hard requirement for easy integration of systems developed by several partners. And even for a single product that has a well-defined focus and scope, and that does not at first sight need to connect to other systems, new technologies and opportunities, such as connecting to online banking and enabling Internet-based electronic commerce aspects, drive the vendor toward the need to interoperate.

The various process reengineering activities and creative ways of speeding up business processes all rely increasingly on technological support and particularly on the ability to receive information and share information processing rapidly, cost-effectively, and reliably. In addition, enterprises are not microcosms any more. They must look outward, whether toward an imminent merger where a large part of merger cost and risk derives from incompatible information systems or to be ready to partner in virtual enterprises.[1] And in either case, if the information systems of the respective organizations are to participate seamlessly in business transactions, it is imperative for all parties to have information systems that can either interoperate or be speedily integrated with each other, or both.

In summary, a comprehensive approach to software development cannot address only the problem of building individual self-contained and stand-alone systems any more, but rather must address fundamentally the problem of providing built-in openness and support for interoperability with as-yet unknown systems. That is, interoperability must become an explicit and high-focus aspect of architectures, development environments, and development tools, as well as of the entire development lifecycle of an information system.

Interoperability Concepts

This section introduces interoperability concepts that are of general applicability and that are prerequisites to the discussion of system-level component federations in the following section. In presenting these concepts, we use examples that involve two systems that could have been independently developed. Of course, if they were independently developed, then they would probably know nothing about each other, and it would be necessary to introduce some factor that would provide for their collaboration. However, the examples do not make this explicit; rather they simply assume the presence of such a factor where needed.

The section is organized as follows. First a powerful *interoperability reference model* is presented. This reference model is then placed in the context of the four *architectural viewpoints* used throughout the business component approach. Finally, the main *modes of interactions* between systems are introduced. This whole section is about interoperability in general, and it is not in any way specific to the business component approach, nor is it about system-level components.

Interoperability Reference Model

Interoperability presents very complex challenges, and meeting them requires some form of structure in order to reduce complexity. To address this challenge, the business component approach introduces a model called the *seven-layer interoperability protocol model* (often referred to as just the *seven-layer protocol model*). This model defines seven protocol layers (see Figure 6.1) through which two or more systems cooperate, and it provides a reference model for interoperability. Layers in the model are a combination of open and closed, and their position in the notional hierarchy is somewhat representational rather than necessarily implying specific dependencies.

The seven-layer protocol model can be used both for analyzing and for enabling interoperability and collaboration between systems. Each layer establishes one or more protocols that the two systems must respect in order to communicate and cooperate. An interoperability protocol can be defined as follows:

> An *interoperability protocol* is a defined set of rules, formats, and semantics that governs interaction between information systems.

At each interoperability layer, a given protocol represents the set of things that the two systems must agree on in order to enable various levels of collaboration—for example, transactional behavior. Such a protocol governs the cohesive set of interactions that can cross the boundaries of an information system. The protocols of interest here are not only those directly affecting the shape of particular messages between two systems, but also the various protocols that support such message exchanges in some way.

The seven-layer protocol model described here can be thought of as being loosely related to the ISO-OSI seven-layer reference model (see, for example,

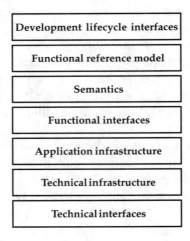

Figure 6.1   The seven-layer protocol model.

[Mullender 1991]), illustrated in Figure 6.2, which describes a set of protocols for inter-system connectivity, focusing mostly on low-level network software, communications adapter hardware, and on-the-wire aspects, all of which are today considered transparent to the functional designer.

The seven-layer interoperability reference model presented in this section focuses exclusively on the application aspects—that is, they fall into the OSI *Application* layer. It is interesting to note that, for example, Mullender [1991] dismisses the ISO-OSI Application layer as "all that remains to be done is for two sites to start sending messages." In the following, the term *seven-layer protocol model* will always refer to the application-level interoperability model defined in this section, and not to the OSI model.

An important point of the interoperability reference model is that it illustrates how the interoperability problem is not only a technical problem, but rather involves all the architectural viewpoints, including the development lifecycle viewpoint (which, as briefly discussed in Chapter 2, "The Business Component Approach," can be seen as a temporal architectural viewpoint). CORBA-based or TCP/IP-based connectivity may be necessary to support full-fledged interoperability between two or more systems, but they are far from sufficient. The seven-layer protocol model allows us to discuss interoperability concepts and standards independent of any particular vendor's interoperability solution.

Systems can interoperate in a range of ways, from the very basic, where each system communicates following very loose protocols and often involving protocol translations at each end of an exchange, up to full integration, where each system communicates natively—that is, using identical protocols at all levels, where the protocols are native to all the systems involved so that no protocol translation is required.

To enable interoperability between two or more systems, each protocol layer must be addressed, if only in a limited and ad-hoc way. Different levels of

Figure 6.2   The ISO-OSI reference model.

desired interoperability require different levels of protocol agreement at each layer of the model, making system interoperability very complex and expensive. Seamless interoperability, to the point of full integration between systems that may have been built by separate vendors, requires detailed agreement at all seven protocol layers. Having two or more systems interact according to a well-defined set of protocols at all layers of the reference model inevitably means that the systems must have been developed under the same architecture. The relationship between the architectural viewpoints of the business component approach and the seven protocol layers is addressed later in this chapter.

In the following text, each protocol layer is individually discussed. To simplify the argument, only two systems are considered, where the information system to be connected to another is called the *subject* system and the other system is called the *target* system. In many figures in this chapter, these two systems are identified by "S" and "T," respectively.

Technical Interfaces

The *technical interfaces* layer is the bottom layer of the model, and addresses the technical shape of the software mechanism used to access a target system. Agreeing on a protocol at this layer means agreeing to use a given technology for information exchange between two systems. Examples include using CORBA, RPC, or DCE for program-to-program exchanges, or using the SQL language to access shared data directly. A technical interface protocol may actually be a combination of two or more technologies, for example, using XML on top of a CORBA interface.[2]

This is the layer most software developers are familiar with, and is where technology has made the most progress over the last few years. The most important new technology in this space today is XML, which is addressed later in the chapter when we discuss the federation.

Three examples of technical interfaces are database-based, file-based bridge, and API-based. These three approaches can be used in isolation or in combination, depending on the desired level of integration.

Database-Based

Probably today the most common way to allow for systems to work together, given the prevalence of closed legacy systems, is to extract data from the database of a target system and to load the same data, with a set of possibly complex transformations to adapt it to the expected needs of the receiving system, onto the database of the subject system.

For people used to objects and classes, it is sometimes difficult to remember that many existing systems were not built with an object-oriented paradigm and that the rest of the world may not think in terms of an object that can be addressed and on which an action can be invoked. Similarly, when thinking of interoperability between systems, it can be difficult to remember that most systems simply do not have methods or APIs that can be called to access them internally. Most legacy systems are just not callable from the external world; they are not *open*. Using a PC analogy, this corresponds to a PC having no external port—neither parallel, nor serial, nor USB, nor Ethernet network access, nor any other way to connect to another computer.

The only way to interact with systems such as these, without heavily modifying them, is by somehow accessing the data they work on, for example by writing directly to their databases, as in Figure 6.3, or by explicitly developing *interoperability adapters*, as in Figure 6.4. Using the PC analogy, the first example corresponds to building a hard-wired access from an external PC into the hard disk of a target PC, the second to crafting a network port that accesses a hard-wired adapter accessing the hard disk of a target PC. Both solutions are feasible and are being routinely adopted, but they are awkward and far from economically sensible.

A standard protocol such as SQL or ODBC can be used as the technology to extract the data, but the complete solution to an interoperability problem obviously requires having knowledge of how the data is stored in the database, which corresponds to having knowledge of the database model. Defining that a system will use database-based technical interoperability does not imply a particular functional protocol or particular database schema. It simply implies that a technology such as SQL will be used to access this data, following a protocol defined by the SQL grammatical rules.

Writing directly to a database is high risk and very error prone because each piece of data on the database may have a whole set of relationships with other data, and the integrity of the database is absolutely critical for the proper functioning of the enterprise. The persistent data *is* the enterprise, under many points of view. This is why an interoperability adapter is required—to guarantee that this data is written in such a way as to preserve, at every instant, the business integrity of the database itself. On the other hand, to properly develop interoperability adapters able to write to the database while preserving the business-level integrity of the data requires an internal knowledge of the target

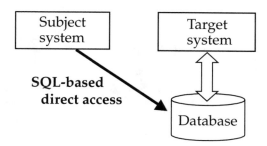

Figure 6.3   Database direct access.

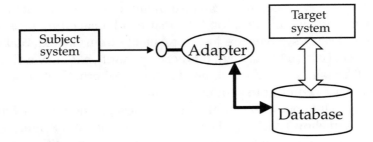

Figure 6.4   Database-based interoperability adapters.

system and can often result in design and implementation costs comparable to those of developing the target system itself. Very often, the interoperability adapter ends up duplicating business rules and functionality already available in the target system, with all the resulting costs when the information system is subsequently evolved.

Database-based interoperability is a very limited type of interoperability; it is a very ad-hoc solution requiring high levels of knowledge of the internals of the interacting systems. Furthermore, the two systems become highly tied together, and a change in one system can easily wreak havoc in the other system.

Nevertheless, we expect that in the medium term (two to three years) many systems will adopt database-based interoperability as the solution for interoperating and integrating with other systems, and they will eventually use *interoperability tables* (see Figure 6.5). An interoperability table (or file) is one that is explicitly designed and created for access by other systems. It has a published format and normally, when not read-only, has stringent conditions of use applied to it, both for the subject system and the target system.

File-Based Bridge

A bridged technical interface provides a point-to-point formalized and sometimes standardized set of technical interfaces to which both ends of an interaction must conform. In traditional implementations the bridged technical

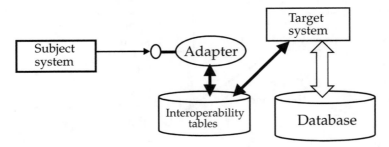

Figure 6.5   Interoperability tables.

interface has often been file-based, meaning there is a set of file formats that can be seen as standardized file-based interfaces. That is, the target system must write to the file following a certain format, and the subject system must read from it following the same format.

Traditional file-based interoperability solutions are often ad-hoc point-to-point solutions, providing for a simple integration process where the participants have to agree only on a file structure. This also implies that, if the subject system must communicate with several other systems, each connection is a point-to-point solution, and so the cost of designing, implementing, testing, and maintaining all the connections is extremely high. Furthermore, using traditional technologies, the interfacing mechanisms based on the standardization of the bridge have proved to be costly to implement, as shown by the limited success of EDI-like solutions, and often have poor performance characteristics. Technology evolution is rapidly making the file-based bridge (Figure 6.6) approach obsolete with the advent of more powerful and flexible technologies.

API-Based

In traditional API-based interfaces (see Figure 6.7) the target system exposes a set of interfaces or APIs that can be simply called by any user wanting to invoke a service of the target system, often through an adapter or a gateway. Instead of converting certain table data to new table data, the user is given a set of interfaces.

Today, many of the API-based interfaces between information systems are data maintenance oriented; that is, they provide for a safe way to perform database access reusing parts of the available programs. They do not perform a great deal of processing, but mostly allow easy data entry, with some guarantee of integrity from one program to another. Typical examples of the technical protocols applied are CORBA, DCOM/COM+, MQ, and RMI.

Technical Infrastructure

The ability to technically call an interface does not exhaust the set of technical considerations required to enable and support interaction between two systems. For example, for a subject system to call a target system, the target system must be up and running, or alternatively the target environment must know

Figure 6.6   File-based bridge.

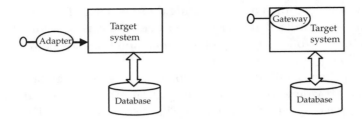

Figure 6.7　API-based adapter and gateway.

how to start the target system on receipt of a given call. How this activation works is one of the considerations with which the technical infrastructure is concerned. The term *technical infrastructure* covers all the considerations that technically support the communication between two systems, including aspects such as error handling, security, naming, transactions, and others, depending on the nature of the interoperability requirement. It also includes the technical aspects of workflow management, or of the various scripting capabilities that may technically enable and simplify the implementation of interoperability by coordination. Each of these topics can correspond to a specific interoperability protocol, and each of these protocols may or may not explicitly appear in the technical or functional interface.

The distinction between what is a technical interface and what is part of the technical infrastructure may be considered arbitrary, especially for systems not based on distributed system technologies. For example, when adopting an SQL technical interface protocol, connecting and disconnecting to the database could be seen as a technical infrastructure protocol because it tends to support indirectly rather than directly the point of view of the functional programmer. The distinction becomes more important in distributed component technologies because in order for the interfaces to be invoked, there must be a technical infrastructure in place to support the invocation, and this infrastructure may need to become very sophisticated, up to a full-blown component execution environment.

The many ways in which these services can be designed and implemented affect the characteristics of intersystem interaction, including the performance and scalability of the federated system. It is necessary to have a common technical infrastructure or framework in order to enable detailed levels of interoperability. Each protocol that is not shared between systems will need some form of translation of equivalence, and if this translation is not available, some forms of collaboration may be impossible. As an example, unless a target system and the technical infrastructure make available some transaction model, the subject system will not be able to access the target system in a transactional way. This deficiency may severely affect the collaboration capabilities of the two systems.

The various protocols of the technical infrastructure can normally be approached with two different architectural models, each at the opposite end of the interoperability spectrum:

Model knowledge. The subject system has knowledge of the technical infrastructure protocol of the target system, and the protocol is designed so that a subject system can, if it desires, adapt to the target's protocol through some form of translation. For example, the subject system may have knowledge that security is implemented through a specific parameter and data type to be added to each functional interface following certain protocols. Or it may know of a specific interface that it can invoke before each functional interface to start a transaction. The subject system may also decide to adopt this model internally, but this is irrelevant for its interaction with the target system (aside, of course, from eventually removing the need for the interoperability adapter).

Context-based (a.k.a. shared services–based). The subject and the target systems physically share a given set of protocols, and in an ideal case even the *context* for each protocol. For example, they are both part of a technical transactional framework in which both systems can access the exact context of the transaction at any time, or the context can be easily passed from one system to the other. Participation in a transaction in this case is not only through simple externalization of the transaction start and commit, but is very collaborative, leading to the possibility of both systems being part of a single transaction.

Application Infrastructure

At present, there is a gap between what the various vendors of technical solutions to interoperability provide and what real-world projects need. For example, each individual technical protocol of the technical infrastructure will require the definition or the knowledge of at least some project-specific convention. The term "application infrastructure" refers to the set of architectural decisions, conventions, interfacing decisions, and design patterns that are needed for a real-world project to support functional interoperability. Each individual protocol of the technical infrastructure potentially translates to a specific application infrastructure protocol. Given the almost total lack of standards in this particular area, each project ends up developing ad-hoc solutions, hence defining project-specific protocols that will often require a translation or adapter mechanism to support interoperability. For example:

■ Because there is a technical infrastructure, addressing security does not guarantee that two systems will be able to interoperate securely. The subject and the target systems must still agree on apparently trivial aspects such as the specific convention for the identification of the individual and groups participating in the exchange, or the specific business rules allowing access to certain groups and denying it for others.

- A given system will raise various errors or exceptions. When these are encountered, the receiving system must know what to do. Normally these errors can be technical (for example, the message did not technically succeed, due to a network failure) or functional (for example, a given order was not issued because the item is out of stock and in back-order[3]). The simple fact of sharing a technical means for communicating errors does not imply that a given error has the same meaning in the two systems and can be appropriately dealt with when encountered. Over time, industry-specific standards will evolve so that two systems will, for example, share a given standard application format for errors, and not only a technical format. In this case, a specific error code will mean exactly the same thing in both collaborating systems; for example, error "1002" could mean that a given customer order number did not exist. This can be considered an example of an application infrastructure protocol.

Functional Interfaces

Suppose a project identified a particular kind of technology to use for the definition of its interfaces, for example, CORBA IDL interfaces. This implies a certain technical infrastructure and a certain technical way to call this interface, but it does not presuppose anything about the kind of specific functional interfaces that will be provided. For example, whether an operation is a *get_order* or an *add_inventory* operation is not defined as part of the technical considerations. CORBA may specify, as part of the technical protocol, that, for example, an operation must have a name and (optionally) a set of parameters. The *functional interface* protocol, however, will specify functional names for the operation names and parameters.

This applies to non-API-based systems as well, even if the distinction may appear arbitrary. For example, in database-based interoperability with direct access to the data, the technical protocol is defined by the use of the grammatical conventions specific to SQL—for example, that the statement starts with a "SELECT" keyword—while the functional interface protocol corresponds to the detail of the individual SQL statement used—for example, the specific table and column names that need to be accessed.

The form of technical and functional interfaces are, for traditional technologies and also for most distributed system technology, directly related: The functional interface specification uses the conventions of the technical protocol to specify the desired functional operations. The technical protocol deals with the fact of using CORBA or RPC, but it says nothing about the specific instance of interface. The functional protocol specifies what exactly is desired from that specific interface. Decisions about the two levels of protocol are usually made by two different roles in the organization (typically, technical architect and functional architect), and at different moments of the development lifecycle. With current technologies, it is possible to fully define the functional interface without committing to a particular technical interface.

The definition of a functional interface can be done in terms of the *type of processing* the target system provides—such as specific maintenance or processing operations, or in terms of the *type of data* that the target system can exchange—such as the ability to exchange a specific kind of sales order. Different standardization bodies tend to focus on one or the other: For example, the OMG specifications focus on processing interfaces, while EDIFACT and X12 focus on data exchange standards. In an API-based interface, these two aspects are reflected in the signature of various interface operations, that is, in the definition of particular operation names and data (parameters)—and relationships between operations—provided for a target system to request services.

In traditional interoperability, the subject system mainly requires what we call *entity data*—data about a given business concept—from the target system. More recently, the interaction between systems is about higher-level collaborations; for example, fulfilling a given business transaction that no single system can perform alone. In the first case, the subject system would mostly need to create, read, update, delete, or check for existence data from the basic entities of the target system, which typically require only a dialog with maintenance-oriented programs. The second case is mostly a collaboration at the business process level, in which interoperability may even have to be driven by a user interface dialog.

Semantics

The fact that a system can receive information does not mean that it knows what to do with it or what it means. Having agreed on the functional interface protocol, it is also necessary to agree on the exact semantics of each interaction. The following example should clarify the issue: Suppose that the subject system provides an API such as:

```
create_order(in order, out result)
```

This could have several meanings, including the following:

1. The target system simply creates an order record on a database, where the record will store basic information about the order. There is no association between this operation and the eventual dispatch of goods

ordered to the customer. The remaining parts of the target system are not informed of the arrival of the order record; the order is not scheduled nor are goods allocated. Therefore the caller will get no feedback on whether the order was accepted by the business and is in process. The caller may get feedback on whether the order data provided on the operation was valid. To get feedback about, for example, the dispatch date of the order, the caller would have to invoke some additional interface, or the target system may have to use some form of event notification mechanism, whether through a formal event management system or by polling some database containing order result data.

2. The target system creates the order in the business sense. The order is actually scheduled and goods are allocated as a direct consequence of the creation and as part of the implementation of the creation. The caller can receive, as a direct result of its operation, information about the business outcome of the operation.

Questions about the exact semantics of interfaces, such as whether *create_order* actually allocates stock and schedules the order, are less than obvious from inspection of the interface only, but they are of extreme importance from a business perspective. The interface may be the same in both cases, but the state in which the system is left after the transaction is very different, and the meaning of positive feedback to the caller is very different in each case. In the first case, it may mean only that the message was received successfully by the target system; in the second case it may also mean the customer will have a certain degree of confidence in receiving the ordered goods in a timely fashion. So the same interface, even having agreed on all lower protocol layers, may have totally different semantics.

There are various solutions to this. Once an appropriate level of specification of the semantics involved in one system is available, it is possible to implement semantically aware gateways or implement some form of semantic bridging. In the near future, the system should be able to be interrogated about the level of interfaces provided, and a time can be envisioned in which the system can also be interrogated about the semantics implemented. This is already technically possible, but it would require a level of standardization well beyond any level addressed today. At present, solutions to this problem, even using industry-level standards such as Edifact or X12, involve costly point-to-point agreements between the system implementers.

Functional Reference Model

So far, the discussion has been mostly centered around the interfacing aspects of interoperability and mainly adopting the point of view that the problem of interoperability can be reduced to adapters and bridges between adapters. Even when discussing the semantics problem, we argued that it was possible to some large extent to address it purely by adapters, once the target semantics are known. In reality, the interoperability challenge affects the whole system, and it is especially dependent on the level of integration required by the federated system.

For example, suppose that the subject system can successfully read customer information from the target system: There is not much the subject system would be able to do with this information if the length of the customer ID field on the subject system is always 10 characters but is 36 characters on the target system. Independent of translation or adapters, if the target system meaningfully uses all 36 characters, the subject system will just not be able to use this information properly. No bridge or translation mechanism, even if the project fully masters the semantics of the exchange, will resolve this.

This is a simple example of interfaces potentially having a very direct relationship with the internal models of the systems involved in interoperating, to the extent that the two influence each other. There is just so much that can be done using adapters and gateways. If the cooperating systems do not share a detailed functional reference model, their ability to interoperate is reduced to a minimum common denominator of functionality. This means that, in order to envision a world in which information systems are easily integrated and assembled from parts built by independent software manufacturers, there is a need for sharing not only technical interfaces and technical infrastructure, application infrastructure, and even functional interfaces and semantics, but also the same functional reference model, including the same detailed model of all the points that need to interact or are impacted when two or more systems interoperate.

Thus the existence of a functional reference model is a prerequisite for full interoperability. Often it is wholly implicit, as in the context of SQL access to a database: The only way a SQL statement that accesses a target system's database can be written is where the developer knows the details of the actual schema of the database. This knowledge corresponds to an implicit knowledge of the target system's functional reference model.

Development Lifecycle Interfaces

There are cases where a subject system needs to decide early in the development lifecycle with which of one or more target systems it will interoperate. In such cases, addressing the interoperability challenge requires the capabilities of systems involved to be verified for interoperability as early as possible in the development lifecycle. Furthermore, the need to synchronize the development of systems required to interoperate is becoming common. Both these aspects are pushing the interoperability challenge into the early phases of the development lifecycle.

For example, the builder of a subject system may require the ability, using the modeling tools used for its internal development, to analyze in detail the business models of one or more of the planned target information systems—models that may well have been produced using different modeling tools. In other words, for two or more interacting systems to have high levels of interoperability, it is necessary that both run-time and development-time interfaces follow well-defined protocols. The concept of business component interface was extended in Chapter 4, "The Business Component" to the development lifecycle, and the concept of system-level interface can be similarly extended. This is what is meant by *development lifecycle interfaces* in Figure 6.1. For example, for interoperability to be enabled during design and development of the system and not only at run-time, it must be possible to exchange the specification of a system itself between systems that need to be integrated or to interoperate.

The development lifecycle interface protocols may also cover the needs of deployment, such as the exact definition of the correct logical or even physical location of relevant files that will allow two systems to interoperate as expected.

Relationship to Architectural Viewpoints

There is a direct relationship, illustrated in Figure 6.8, between the four architectural viewpoints, used throughout the book to analyze other information system aspects, and the seven layers of the interoperability reference model. For this present discussion only, the project management viewpoint is subsumed into a development lifecycle viewpoint, including the role that it has at both development and deployment.

The four viewpoints, in the interoperability context, can be described as follows:

Technical architecture viewpoint. Addresses and illustrates the various technical aspects of interoperability, which includes the possible types of technical interoperability and the infrastructural considerations that enable interoperability. As illustrated in Figure 6.8, the technical architecture viewpoint includes two protocol layers: technical interfaces and technical infrastructure. Depending on the protocols chosen at each layer, these two layers may be highly independent or tightly coupled.

Application architecture viewpoint. The application architecture viewpoint corresponds to the *application infrastructure*. It addresses the gap between what technology provides in the technical architecture viewpoint and all other nonfunctional aspects that are needed for interoperability

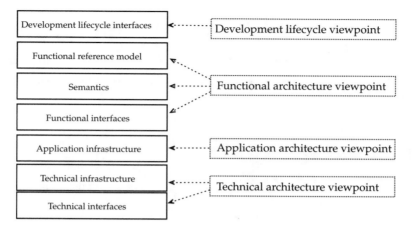

Figure 6.8   Reference model and architectural viewpoints.

between systems possibly developed by separate organizations. These considerations are not functional or are arguably not part of what should be the main concern of the functional developer, and they are included under the application architecture viewpoint.

Functional architecture viewpoint. The functional architecture viewpoint addresses all aspects required by two systems to cooperate successfully in providing a given level of functionality. The three protocol layers of relevance for the functional architecture viewpoint are functional interfaces, semantics, and functional reference model. These layers address very different but related aspects, and an interoperability solution cannot be implemented without some aspects of all three protocols layers being addressed. Figure 6.9 illustrates the different areas of concern: The functional interface is concerned only with the actual interface, the semantic layer goes further into the two communicating systems to achieve semantic consistency in the communication, and the functional reference model encompasses the whole body of all the systems involved.

Development lifecycle viewpoint. To enable rapid and cost-effective cooperation between two or more systems, it can be important to analyze the interfaces and interoperability aspects early on in the development lifecycle. Indeed, cost-effective interoperability is achieved by pushing the interoperability challenge to the early phases of the development lifecycle, rather than addressing it as an after-the-fact challenge. This is achieved by properly analyzing all the development lifecycle deliverables that will affect run-time interoperability as early as possible. This and other forces, for example, the need to properly coordinate teams using different development lifecycle tools, will require what can be called *development lifecycle interoperability*, that is, interoperability not so much at run-time, but

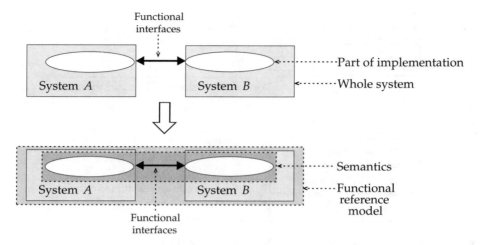

Figure 6.9   Functional protocol layers.

between the various tools and repositories used or produced at development time.

Interaction Modes

Each of the seven protocol layers may correspond to one or more protocols. For example, the technical infrastructure may have a protocol for security, a protocol for transactions, and so on. Each of these protocols and each layer may be specified and implemented using a certain *mode of interaction*. There are four main modes of interaction, presented in Figure 6.10: the *integrated* interaction, the *bus-based* interaction, the *bridged* interaction, and the *coordinated* interaction.

In the following, the interaction modes are described and exemplified in terms of adapters, but they could in most cases be equally well described in terms of gateways. The distinction between adapters and gateways was introduced in Chapter 5, "The Business Component System."

In an *integrated interaction*, two systems share a protocol. For example, two independently developed systems, not originally intended to interoperate, may be extended by the addition of ad-hoc interoperability adapters. These adapters, illustrated in Figure 6.11, would usually be point-to-point adapters, and they would be specifically built to address the needs of the particular interoperability problem. A typical example of an *integrated* interaction is the use of a common database for interoperability purposes.

A *bridged interaction* is a point-to-point interaction in which the two systems agree on a common format, possibly different from the formats of the subject and target systems. The bridge does not usually implement any intelligence, and it can be seen as an external protocol definition to which both

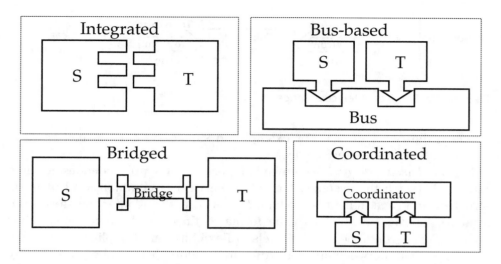

Figure 6.10 Interaction modes.

the subject and the target must conform. Using a PC analogy, it can be considered as the cable that connects the parallel ports of two PCs. There are typically at least five parts involved, as illustrated in Figure 6.12, where it is assumed that neither the subject nor target systems, both independently built, were ever intended to collaborate. Both may need to be extended with an adapter, either already provided by them or custom built. The difference between these adapters and those in an integrated interaction is that in the bridged case the adapters perform any required transformation to the standard format defined by the bridge protocol (or set of protocols). The bridge may be seen as an external protocol to which both the subject and target systems must independently conform.

The advantage of this approach is that if there are industry-standard or at least widely known bridges, then any two systems that implement adapters for that bridge should be able to interoperate at the protocol level defined by the bridge. This can significantly reduce the number of different kinds of bridges required.

In a *coordinated interaction*, the subject and target systems exchange data through a coordinator, as illustrated in Figure 6.13. In many cases, the coordinator may be a separate application that coordinates the interoperation

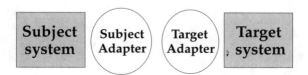

Figure 6.11 Integrated interaction mode.

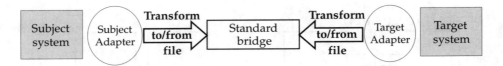

Figure 6.12   Bridged interaction mode.

between the two systems. For example, in simple systems, it may be code implementing a user interface desktop.

In a *bus-based interaction*, shown in Figure 6.14, the protocol does not flow directly between the systems, but rather between a common level of infrastructure and each individual system. In this case, the adapter transforms the system's internal protocol into the format defined by the component's bus socket. This permits the highest levels of flexibility, but it implies an architectural agreement between different software vendors that may be prevented by economic or strategic considerations. Interoperability with bus-based interactions is usually built into the system from the beginning. As a comparison, a bridged solution is often implemented after the fact. Highly cooperative systems will eventually require bus-based interaction. A bus-based solution can be used to implement any of the other interaction modes. Furthermore, several systems can share the bus concurrently, thereby providing a multipoint solution, whereas a bridged solution is point-to-point by definition.

Within a single interoperability situation, different protocol layers can have different interaction modes. Furthermore, even within one particular protocol layer, certain protocols can be addressed using one interaction mode, while other protocols can be addressed using another. For example, it is not uncommon to find a system that is both bus-based and bridged or, as illustrated in Figure 6.15, coordinated and bridged at the same time. There is often a prevalent interaction mode across the various protocol layers, and people often generalize and talk of the systems as interacting in that prevalent mode.

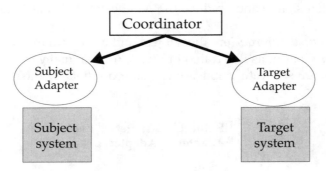

Figure 6.13   Coordinated interaction mode.

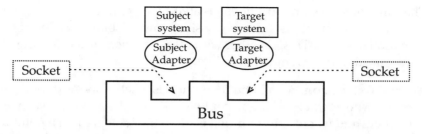

Figure 6.14 Bus-based interaction mode.

Federation Concepts

Armed with the interoperability concepts presented in the previous section, this section can now address the main concepts related to a federation of system-level components. This is done first by analyzing the *characteristics* of a federation, second by discussing *tagged data* and *XML* (which has become an important de-facto standard for component-based interoperability), and finally by *profiling* the seven-layer protocol model. This section does not consider modeling or design principles for federations, which are addressed in Chapter 11, "Component-Based Business Modeling," and Chapter 12, "Component-Based Design," respectively.

Characteristics

A federation of system-level components is a set of cooperating system-level components (SLCs). These SLCs cooperate through federation rather than assembly, which implies a much looser connection among them. The level of granularity of the SLCs is much larger than the granularity of individual business components. And the SLCs may belong to or be built by different organizations.

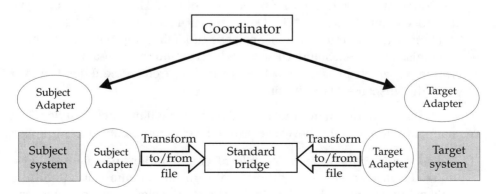

Figure 6.15 Two systems coordinated and bridged.

The huge business opportunities created by e-commerce are causing many organizations to move as fast as possible toward building "Internet-ready" information systems. This, together with other reasons, is accelerating the evolution from ad-hoc to architected federations:

Ad-hoc federation. An ad-hoc federation is a set of loosely connected systems, whose interoperation could well have been unforeseen by their builders and whose interworking is often implemented on a point-to-point basis. Usually, an ad-hoc federation has no model describing the federation as a whole; rather the various parts of the federation evolve independently and without any federation-level knowledge of individual system evolution. The success of a federation depends on the individual systems having been architected and designed in such a way as to be not only open, but also resilient in the context of unforeseen modes of cooperation. Two systems that were independently developed by different vendors are very unlikely to conform to the same architecture, or to a well-thought seven-layer protocol model.

Until recently, federations have been mostly ad hoc, even though addressing the interoperability challenge in an ad-hoc way has shown itself to be extremely expensive, complex in both development and in maintenance, and a threat to reliability and security. Systems involved in an ad-hoc federation often implement ad-hoc translation of protocols at several protocol layers. Each interface to a different system becomes a unique case, with some level of reuse if done properly, but often with significant differences between each case. Partly because of this, interface testing is very costly, and high-performance requirements are unlikely to be satisfied.

Architected federation. Leading-edge organizations are today starting to approach federations in a architected way. Developing the federation is addressed as an explicit (complex) task, and as an integral part of the development of a solution to a business problem. This requires appropriate processes (Chapter 7, "The Development Process"), tools (Chapter 8, "Technical Architecture"), and business modeling approaches (Chapter 11). It also requires a standard architectural set-up (at least across the federation) to which all systems will conform. The architected federation will be further discussed later in this chapter.

The SLCs of a federation interact according to a small number of styles. The three main interaction styles between system-level components are as follows:

1. *Master-slave collaboration.* A style of collaboration in which one system—the master—is clearly the initiator of all communication and the only active partner, while the other system—the slave—is a passive partner, a service provider. The master initiates all communications and all

requests to the slave. Let us use a simplified example that should be familiar to the reader; suppose you are banking online. Through a modem, the subject system (you, the master) establishes a master-slave connection with the target system (the bank, the slave) and performs a certain set of operations (a withdrawal or deposit), at the end of which the subject system (you) closes the connection. A typical e-commerce architecture is master-slave, where the cardinality is n:1; that is, many systems (the masters) connect to a single system-level component (the slave). In ad-hoc federations, it is also normal to have cascading master-slave configurations (see Figure 6.16), in which each master-slave is unaware of the existence of the other configurations.

This last is a good example of a federation of business component systems, rather than of system-level components: Indeed, a federation of system-level components implies an easily manageable and controllable set of systems. Ad-hoc federations are rarely considered to be good examples of federation of system-level components.

In Figure 6.16, the exchange between master-slave SLCs is shown as a unidirectional exchange. In reality, in most cases there is a requirement for both systems to be able to initiate a communication. In order to satisfy the requirement of unidirectionality, this is usually done allowing one of the systems to raise events rather than to directly call the subject system, as illustrated in Figure 6.17. This technique is assumed for other figures in this chapter.

2. *Coordinated collaboration.* A style of collaboration, illustrated in Figure 6.18, in which all exchange of information between two or more system-level components is done through a coordinating entity, usually (assuming the coordinating entity is implemented using some form of component technology) a system-level component itself but at times simply a business component or a distributed component. The coordinating entity is called Component Manager in the figure. Coordination can also be implemented using a scripting language, using workflow interoperability, or by custom development. In the figure, the coordinator communi-

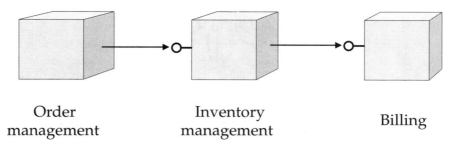

Order
management

Inventory
management

Billing

Figure 6.16   Cascading master-slave configurations.

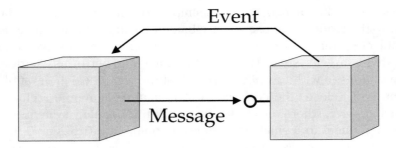

Figure 6.17 Messages and events.

cates using messaging with each coordinated system-level component, whereas each system-level component, in order to guarantee unidirectionality of messaging, communicates with the coordinator using events.

3. *Peer-to-peer collaboration.* A style of collaboration in which the participating systems can freely and directly invoke each other and initiate an exchange of information, as illustrated in Figure 6.19. This style enables maximum collaboration flexibility, but it is also the most complex (and expensive) to develop, test, deploy, manage at run-time, and maintain. The biggest architectural disadvantage is that peer-to-peer collaboration can break the important noncircularity architectural principle (see Chapter 9, "Application Architecture") if the collaboration is not carefully architected. Peer-to-peer collaboration is very similar to human collaboration, and it is intellectually very appealing. By analyzing an ideal interaction between two systems, we can deduce that the communication will often need to be bidirectional. Any of the two systems may need to receive information or ask for information from the other.

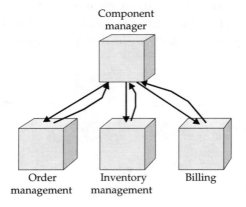

Figure 6.18 Coordinated collaboration.

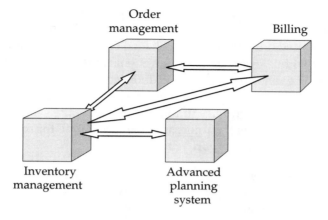

Figure 6.19   Peer-to-peer collaborating systems.

In a federation of average complexity all three aspects may be present. Figure 6.20 shows an example where the following conditions exist:

- The user may want to perceive the federation as a whole system through a single user interface, which is sometimes called a *federation desktop*. This is an example of coordinated communication.

- At the same time, behind the scenes, the different systems may need to communicate directly to each other. This may be done using a peer-to-peer interaction style.

- One or more systems may also need to contact a remote system for some point-to-point communication. In the figure, the order management system calls, for example, through a simple modem line, to a bank in order to update the organization's own accounts. This is an example of a master-slave interaction style.

These three styles are an orthogonal dimension to the interaction modes pre-

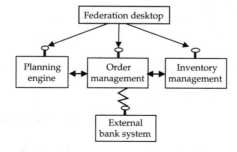

Figure 6.20   Mixing styles.

sented earlier. Indeed, a master-slave or a peer-to-peer style can be implemented using any of the interaction modes. The coordinated collaboration style can be implemented only through a bus-based or coordinated interaction mode.

Examining two business component systems and the various ways they can collaborate with each other, four main federation patterns can be identified: black boxes, some level of white boxes, integrated through a set of common components, or fully integrated. All four cases will make sense in different circumstances. Let us analyze the four cases in more detail, for example, given the two systems represented in Figure 6.21.

Black-box interoperability. (See Figure 6.22.) In this case, each system sees only a set of interfaces, following given protocols at the different layers. It does not really matter whether the two systems are internally implemented using business components or using traditional technology, or whether they have the same components in their implementations. The business component approach makes it much easier to provide a gateway or adapter to the system, making the design and implementation of black-box interoperability relatively painless.

White-box interoperability. (See Figure 6.23.) Assuming that both systems are implemented using business components, it is possible, if desired, to directly address an internal business component. This interoperability solution makes assumptions about the presence, behavior, and identity of the various business components in the systems involved. For example, in Figure 6.23 the purchase order management system knows it can communicate directly with a specific component of the other systems, that is, with the invoice component of the invoice management system. If the two systems have common components, then in white-box interoperability they are replicated both at build-time and at run-time in the two systems.

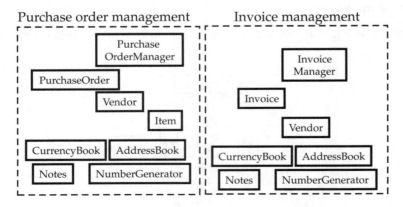

Figure 6.21 Two business component systems needing to interact.

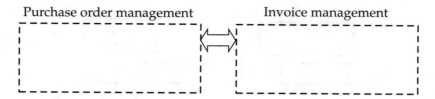

Figure 6.22   Black-box connection.

Using common components. (See Figure 6.24.) In this case, the systems of the federation share the components that are common. These common components could themselves be seen as part of a system that could eventually be built and supplied by a different software supplier than those responsible for the purchase order management and invoice management systems. The common components system can be thought of as a *functional bus*. The reuse of these common components raises the bar of reuse across the development lifecycle, with some relevant impact on the overall cost and complexity. It corresponds to sharing not only the relevant aspects of the technical architecture and application architecture, but also important parts of the functional architecture.

Full integration. (See Figure 6.25.) In this case, no business component is duplicated in the two systems, and the two systems cease to be considered, at least at run-time, as separate systems. This level of interoperability/integration requires a good instantiation of the first six layers in the protocol model. With full integration, the border between system-level component interoperability and business component interoperability becomes thinner. To be precise, the term "full integration" implies that the two systems have been built using the same set of architectural and development lifecycle protocols across the seven protocol layers, which, of course, cannot be directly implied from the figure.

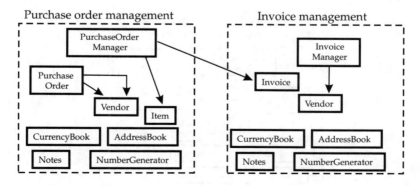

Figure 6.23   White-box connection.

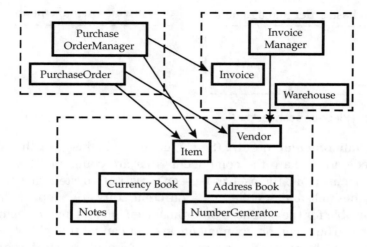

Figure 6.24 Using common components.

Tagged Data and XML

An important interoperability issue is that of exchanging business data in a flexible and resilient manner, while avoiding the technical drawbacks of brittle interfaces. A powerful approach to this problem, called *tagged data*, exists today and makes effective use of the XML standard[4] that is being rapidly adopted by the software industry. This approach, originally known as "semantic data," is not specifically a CBD technology, but perhaps proves its full power within a CBD architecture, where resilience in the face of change and evolution is so important. This section first describes the problem in more detail, second reviews the tagged data solution that supports a level of interface flexibility unreachable with other approaches, and third discusses how tagged data is used in other areas, its pros and cons, and the extent to which the functional programmer is affected by its use.

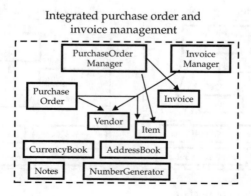

Figure 6.25 Full integration.

Problem

A great deal of the business data exchanged today is in the form of data structures. Other forms (complex documents, audio-visual streams, and so forth) are also exchanged, but at the heart of business data are the relatively small collections of formatted numerical and alphanumerical data that carry information such as prices, quantities, short descriptions, costs, and dates. In handling such data, two important resilience requirements are being increasingly met, especially in e-commerce and virtual enterprise situations. These requirements illustrate well the capabilities of tagged data, and they are as follows:

- The ability to *evolve* interfaces without forcing all users of those interfaces to evolve at an identical speed.

- The ability for data structures to be *passed through* various recipients, where each recipient has knowledge of a part of the data structure, but no single recipient necessarily has prior knowledge of the entire structure. This requirement is met, for example, in negotiation exchanges, where all agreed items must be carried with the "contract" but where each participant may need to agree only on the part of it relevant to that participant.

Both of these capabilities are badly impeded by the brittle interface problem. This arises because most interface technology today assumes that an operation name is compiled to a specific entry point in the target code and that the position and type of each parameter in the operation signature must be matched by any caller (although minor additions at the end of a signature are acceptable by some technologies). For smaller distributed systems, or those that do not change rapidly, this is manageable. In the case of rapid business evolution or where (as with virtual enterprise systems) new systems must be connected as quickly as possible, any small mismatch can not only cause immediate failure of communication but can also be difficult to find.

For example, suppose the following operation was available through an SLC gateway interface:

```
update_vendor_information(in string          vendor_id,
                          in VendorInformation vendor_information);
```

Further assume that the business data type *VendorInformation* has the structure shown in Figure 6.26.

Now suppose the *update_vendor_information* operation is invoked from another SLC. As long as the caller provides a data structure that exactly matches the structure expected, all will perhaps be well—provided the caller does not switch values; that is, for example, the caller does not place the street data in the city slot. Were the caller's version of the address part of the structure to be sequenced state, city, street, zip, then the invocation would succeed—and be wrong! Current interface technology checks only for type safety—that is, in

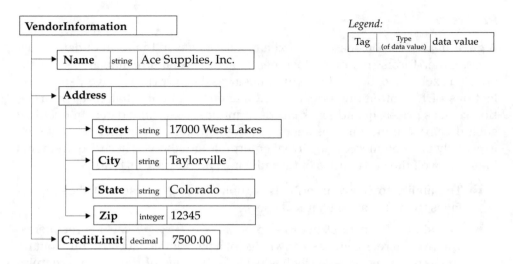

Legend:

Tag	Type (of data value)	data value

Figure 6.26 Sample *vendor_information* structure.

this example, that the first three members of the structure are strings and the last an integer. The names given to each item of data in the structure (that is, "street," "city," and so on) are not taken into account—indeed, they are not even sent; only the raw data is physically transmitted between the caller and the target. For example, if the address of the vendor were 17000 West Lakes, Taylorville, Colorado 12345, then what would physically be sent across the wire would be something like this:

```
(16)17000 West Lakes(11)Taylorville(8)Colorado000012345
```

The figures in parentheses are the lengths of the following strings. In other words, while the binding (between the caller and the target) may be type-safe, it is not semantically safe.

Another example of brittleness concerns type matching. Suppose, for example, that the caller defines *zip* as a string. In this case, the invocation would fail, even though it was correct in the business sense, because the primitive data type (string) used to carry the zip code was not the same as the integer type expected.[5]

Another area of fragility is versioning. Suppose the *Address* part of the structure is changed to include a country. Now suppose a caller with an old address structure invokes a target that has been updated with the new address structure, or vice versa. In either of these cases, the interaction would fail using traditional interface technology, which assumes that all targets (perhaps an SLC supplied to the market and bought by many customers) and callers (other SLCs bought perhaps from different suppliers or developed in-house) will be updated at the same time. But how is that change sent to users and consumers of the interface, when its developers do not even know who or where they are? Yet this is the nature of fast-evolving virtual enterprises.

The previous examples illustrated the essence of the brittle interface problem. Many people think that this problem cannot occur because all developers using an interface will merely ensure that they get the correct header file or IDL file that defines the interface in low-level detail. In a fast-changing business world, where systems are required to begin interoperation with as little set-up delay as possible, and where interfaces can evolve, this may not be a viable solution. Versioning of interfaces is often proposed as the solution to brittle and nonresilient interfaces. Although this can be useful to a certain extent, systems based on traditional interface technology may become overloaded by the resulting version management load, especially in the face of rapid change and evolution.

Solution

Tagged data provides resilience capabilities that address the brittle interface problem by separating out the various concerns. The essence of the solution is to send meta-data (data about data) with the data itself. Instead of meta-data, however, the word "tag" has become popular in the industry, and the data that is being sent is called "tagged data." The de-facto standard for representing tagged data is the eXtended Markup Language (XML). Now a recognized and increasingly widely used standard, XML provides a huge array of capabilities that allow all sorts of documents, including Web pages containing dynamic links, to be described in a standardized way. It is being widely adopted, not only for Web use, but also for many interchanges requiring data transfer, such as case tool interchange. Many standards bodies today are starting to use XML to express their standards. Like many other uses of XML, tagged data[6] uses a small subset of XML capabilities to provide for the transmission of business data as a very simple and sometimes very small "document." In XML notation, the *vendor_information* data shown in Figure 6.26 might look like this as it traveled between the caller and the target (with data values in bold for readability):

```
<VendorInformation>
    <Name>Acme Supplies, Inc.</Name>
    <Address>
      <Street>17000 West Lakes</Street>;
      <City>Taylorville</City>
      <State>Colorado</State>
      <Zip type="integer">12345</Zip>
    </Address>
    <CreditLimit type="decimal">7500.00</CreditLimit>
  </VendorInformation>
```

This whole XML fragment is technically a single string. Hence the technical interface might look like this:

```
update_vendor_information(in string vendor_id,
                          in string xml_vendor_information);
```

In handling this data, the target component would parse the string *xml_vendor_information* and would pull out the various pieces of data by name. Let's consider how tagged data addresses the two capabilities referred to at the start of this section.

Evolution. Suppose that, for some reason, the interface provider changes the sequence of address data items to state, city, street. A caller with the old interface would provide the old sequence of street, city, and state. The target would perform an operation on the received XML string to retrieve the data value corresponding to just "street" in "address," and so forth. Hence the correct data items would always be retrieved regardless of their sequence. Notice that the nesting levels must be adhered to, however. But well-designed XML structures easily reflect business reality, and nesting inside structures is not normally a problem (although there may be other reasons to minimize nesting).

Suppose also that the interface provider is evolved such that the type of the zip code is changed to string, perhaps to handle international zip codes. A calling component using an integer to represent the zip code could make a successful call because the target would merely convert the integer value provided to a string.[7] Not all type mismatches can be handled this way; but many can, and all that cannot be handled can be detected, and an appropriate error returned.

Finally, suppose the structure were to be further evolved, so that the target system interface is updated to include a "country" field. If the calling system has the old version of the interface definition, then there would be no *country* tag or associated value sent. In this case, the target component would detect the absence of the *country* tag, and if a value could be defaulted, it would carry on. Otherwise an error would be raised, which (if the error system is well designed) would include a reason. At least the system manager of the calling system would be informed precisely why, and where, there had been a failure.

The resilience provided by tagged data for the interface evolution problem does not mean that all requirements for interface versioning disappear. It does mean that the number of versions tends to be much lower and hence considerably more manageable.

Pass-through. As a simple example, suppose that the previous example is reversed. Instead of the target component being evolved to provide a *country* tag, suppose the calling system includes a *country* tag, but the target component is not expecting it. In this case, the target will simply not look for it, and the extraneous tag will be ignored. Now let's consider this capability further. Suppose a federation is created where the provider of the *update_vendor_information* interfaces—say *SCL-A*—is one of several SLCs and is quite uninterested in a *country* tag. Suppose *SLC-A* does pass information it receives on to *SLC-B*, which *is* interested in the *country* tag. In this case, due to the use of tagged data, *SLC-A* can be quite insensitive to the presence of a *country* tag in the address structure and in its interface, but it can still pass the correct information to *SLC-B*. This approach can be extended to enable much more than one simple tag to be passed through, and is precisely what is required in some of the new negotiation and contracting interchanges being proposed for e-commerce. Of course, the SLCs in such a federation must be designed for pass-through.

Some may see the resilience provided by tagged data to be too free and easy. Resilience, however, can always be constrained where necessary (whereas the opposite is not generally true). For example, a target could search for tags it does not recognize and optionally return an error; arguably this is part of a higher-level protocol to do with the resilience of the contracts between the systems.

From these examples, several conclusions about the nature of tagged data can be gleaned. First, tagged data is "strongly tagged" rather than "strongly typed." That is, the meaning of data is derived from its tag rather than from its position and sequence in an untagged structure. This clearly means that both ends in a communication link must agree on the tags and on the general structure of the data. Tags are checked at run-time rather than at compile-time. What is checked is not (for example) that the fifth data element is an integer; instead, it is the presence of the tag *zip* inside the tag *address*. Second, the traditional responsibilities of caller and target are reversed. Instead of the caller being forced always to conform precisely with the detailed interface of the target, it is the target that can adapt to the data provided by the caller. Strongly tagged data implies type checking at the level of the tag (or label) given to the semantics of the data. This ensures that what is needed is there, regardless of data sequence within a given level of a structure,[8] and it provides support, for example, for the predefined proxies described in the last chapter. Third, the target can adapt to missing tags as long as a default is provided by the target itself.

Advantages and Disadvantages

To the authors' knowledge, tagged data was first used to address interoperability in the early 90s. Even before that, in large-scale enterprise systems, similar approaches are known to have been adopted specifically to solve interoperability between systems where the systems were fast-evolving in a quasi-independent way. This is clearly a main advantage of tagged data.

Tagged data has also been found advantageous in areas other than interoperability, and it can be productively used at a much finer level of granularity than inter-SLC communication. Many of the advantages derive from the ability to write generic code that is configurable and that adjusts itself to specific situations at run-time. Areas where tagged data has proved its worth range from highly configurable user interfaces through provision of standard generic interfaces for WDCs, to configurable resource-tier code for prototyping and initial testing of EDCs. Other advantages that justify the rapid and widespread adoption of this technology include the readability of run-time data (when security does not dictate encryption!) and the switch from compile-time to run-time checking, with the additional flexibility this provides for interfaces.

Furthermore, tagged data is highly appropriate as a basis for scripting a component. A DC could provide, as illustrated in Figure 6.27, both traditionally typed and tagged data interfaces. The latter could contain the operation name in a tagged data structure together with the data. For scripting, a generic "execute" interface would be invoked. Within the DC this would be handled by the dispatcher, which would then call the traditionally typed interface. Such an approach provides considerable flexibility, allowing for the advantages of scripting and at the same time providing strongly typed interfaces. A DC then becomes, as it were, bilingual, able to handle both kinds of requests for the same service, providing not only the flexibility and resilience of tagged data but also the (slightly) higher performance of traditionally typed interfaces.

Finally, on the subject of advantages, tagged data is especially useful for message queuing systems where the precise technical format of application data carried on a message is not predefined. It really comes into its own when the underlying communications mechanisms are heterogeneous. For example, consider a system that employs both message queuing and one or more strongly typed mechanisms such as DCOM or CORBA. Tagged data provides a common and higher-level approach to data exchange, and it means minimal conversion when boundaries are crossed.

One apparent problem in using tagged data is that the functional programmer has to learn to parse and build tagged data structure programmatically. The complex programming task of parsing XML can be done, however, by automatically generated code in the separation layer of the distributed component, as shown in Figure 6.27. In this way, the functional developer needs to see only traditional typed interfaces. This introduces a clear distinction between the actual interface of a tagged data-capable DC and the interface seen by the functional developer. In other words, there are two "levels" of interface (indicated by Level 1 and Level 2 in the figure), so reinforcing the separation between techni-

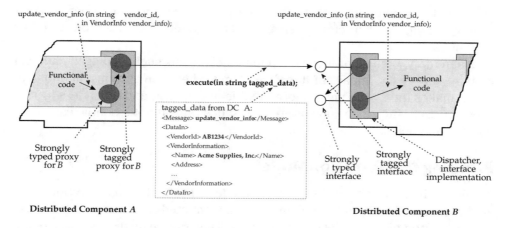

Figure 6.27   Level 1 and Level 2 interfaces.

cal interfaces and those seen by the functional developer, making the function code in a distributed component even more independent of the component execution environment.

Finally, tagged data lends itself not only to repository-based development, but also to repository-based run-times, where meta-data is accessed online. Indeed, e-commerce, and its requirement for resiliency, is driving the increasing use of XML for intercompany information exchange. Security aspects of sending data "in clear"—together with the meta-data that allows at least some interpretation of the data—are being addressed through encryption.

One of the main perceived disadvantages of tagged data is performance. First, if implemented above the level of a component execution environment such as an ORB, then data is marshaled and demarshaled twice—once by the ORB and once by the code used to access the XML-formatted data. Second, the XML data format is wordy, and it uses greater network bandwidth than pure data values. Performance tests using operational data, however, have shown that, in many cases, the resulting performance loss is negligible compared to the end-to-end message times, which often include database access. Furthermore, various techniques exist to reduce this overhead. In addition, we believe that the trade-off between performance and flexibility in this case is generally heavily weighted in favor of flexibility.

A second disadvantage is that tags must be agreed on between all interoperating systems. This almost certainly means the use of repository technology, which may reverse the disadvantage, in that it forces a focus on agreement not only of tags, but also of their semantics. Finally, tagged data is not a panacea. For example, it does not address the problem of a 36-character order number being sent to a component that requires a 10-character order number and that cannot handle 36 characters even if the two systems do agree on all other semantics.

In summary, the use of loose-coupling mechanisms such as tagged data can certainly lower the impact of interface changes between systems, and in general it makes interfaces much more flexible and robust, and much less brittle. Properly used, such mechanisms are a most desirable if not essential capability for interoperability.

Profiling the Protocol Model

In this section, the seven-layer protocol model is profiled for a federation. That is, the interoperability reference model is instantiated for the specific context of a federation of system-level components. This is done by discussing specific solutions, approaches, and, if applicable, standards. The discussion will not go into detail on the various architectural viewpoints, which is the subject of Part 2 and Part 3 of this book.

Technical Interfaces

Independently of the specific technology adopted, by definition system-level components provide well-defined API-based interfaces. The interaction and collaboration between system-level components is always and only carried out in terms of these interfaces, without relying on alternative, less flexible approaches such as file-based or database-based approaches.

Two aspects are rapidly becoming de-facto standards in the software industry:

1. All component-based technologies adopt a bus-based interaction mode. For example, CORBA adopts for each exchange between a subject system and a target system the model illustrated in Figure 6.28 (see, for example, [Siegel 1996]). As we saw in the previous section, a bus-based interchange is the most flexible interaction mode.

2. For system-to-system communication, or in our case for system-level-component-to-system-level-component communication, the data is formatted as tagged data. Furthermore, a specific formatting language, XML, is used as the formatting technology for information exchanged as tagged data, independently of the carrier mechanism. For example, CORBA can be used for the communication, using input and output XML strings. XML can be used on all communication technologies, from DCE to EJBs.

Technical Infrastructure

Various technical infrastructures exist at the time of writing, but they do not (as discussed in Chapter 8) directly support a true component-based model, or they

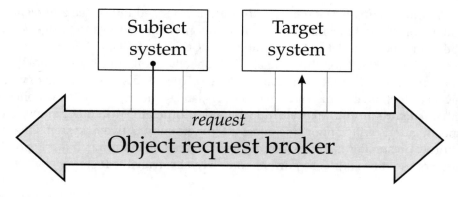

Figure 6.28 A CORBA request.

tend to address it at the distributed component level of granularity rather than at the SLC granularity discussed here. Recent infrastructures such as the CORBA component model or the Sun EJB component model improve this situation, but federation technical architects are still required to adapt the generic offerings of these component models to the specific needs of their federation.

There are efforts to address this gap: For example, Cummins [OMG 1999b] outlines a view of how a technical interoperability infrastructure may look in the future. This level of specification is very much required, but it addresses only the bottom two of the seven interoperability protocol layers. The gist of the model proposed by Cummins, from a system point of view, can be interpreted as shown in Figure 6.29.

The recent advances in distributed system technologies hugely simplify the technical aspects of creating open systems. First of all they naturally support technical openness for a system: The industry has now clearly defined network-

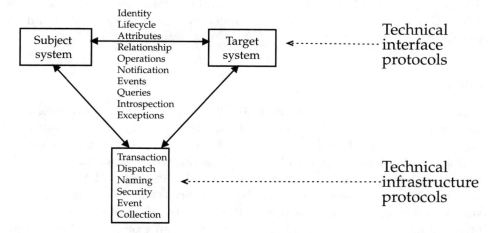

Figure 6.29 One approach to technical protocols.

addressable software elements, with formally defined interfaces and clear protocols for the technical interfaces, and even predefined ways to bridge some of the component models—for example, the CORBA to COM OMG specification (see [OMG 1998e], for the official OMG specification, and [Rosen 1998] for a good discussion on this particular challenge). There is also a definition of various levels of technical infrastructure protocols, and some aspects of the application infrastructure, in third-party products and in official OMG submissions. These specifications will support technical interoperability between systems that rely entirely on standards. Infrastructure aspects are still maturing, but it is possible and not too difficult to use current commercially available technologies.

Application Infrastructure

No standard application infrastructure exists today. This is true both at the individual system level and at the global federation level. Commercial off-the-shelf products exist that provide the most important aspects of the application infrastructure, for example, Forté (see www.forte.com), which, of course, requires the adoption of its own proprietary infrastructure. Most organizations today, however, choose to architect and implement the application infrastructure as an ad-hoc, in-house solution.

Functional Interfaces

Industry-level standards for this protocol layer exist, but most of them are not currently component-based. This is the space addressed by most functional interoperability organizations, including EDIFACT, X12, the domain part of the OMG, and many others. The first example of a truly component-based standard in this area was the OMG Currency specification [OMG 1998g]. The incredible business push given by the needs of e-commerce has accelerated the standardization effort.

Semantics

This is the protocol layer that, under the e-commerce push, is evolving more rapidly. Nevertheless, at the time of writing, there are very few standards, and they are for selected business domains. Hence, most organizations end up addressing this protocol in an ad-hoc way. Leading-edge organizations adopt a repository-based semantics definition, which in the case of XML would include at least a tag dictionary that could be used, across development teams, to secure agreement on the semantics of the system's tags. Indeed, the semantic protocol layer acquires a specific importance when exchanging information using tagged data (with XML formatting) in that the participating systems must agree on the semantics of the tags for the information exchange to succeed.

Functional Reference Model

Various standard organizations have tried to address this protocol layer at the business modeling level. For example, the Supply Chain Council (for more information, see www.supply-chain.org) has produced a supply chain reference model (SCOR), which is very useful if somewhat high level. Based on our current knowledge, however, no business sector currently has a *component-based* reference model, which must hence be defined in-house by organizations wishing to properly address this protocol layer. Chapter 11 addresses this subject further.

Development Lifecycle

Consider an organization that wishes to federate two system-level components, where at least one was obtained from a third party. For mission-critical systems, a certain level of confidence in the third-party system is needed before installing it for production use. This requires various check-points that normally include not only the ability to run detailed test scenarios, but also to perform a detailed set of usually complex and time-consuming reviews. The checkpoints may include such activities as comparing the database models. Whatever tools the third-party system provides for this purpose, it is unlikely that they will be the same as those used by the obtaining organization. Sharing models is one of the problems that, under different perspectives, both the UML [OMG 1997b] and XMI [OMG 1998f] standards have tried to address. These are two very important standards in our domain, and they will hugely benefit business software producers, even if at first sight (at least from the interoperability perspective) XMI is mainly of interest to modeling tool vendors.

Table 6.1 summarizes an example of a recommended profile, at the time of writing, for the seven-layer protocol model applied to a federation of system-level components.

As can be seen from this table, at the time of writing many protocol aspects require an in-house implementation. Of course, the more that federation builders rely on in-house protocols, the less hope there is for a thriving market of federatable SLCs. At the time of writing, there are no component-based standards for the application architecture, and few for the functional architecture, although many existing functional standards are being rapidly evolved toward being expressed in XML. On the other hand, as mentioned in the previous section, there are two important OMG standards, UML and XMI, for the development lifecycle viewpoint.

Table 6.1 Profiling the Protocol Model

PROTOCOL LAYER	INTEROPER-ABILITY MODEL	MODE OF INTER-ACTION	STANDARDS
Technical interfaces	API-based	Bus-based	CORBA, COM+, EJB, MQ-Series, XML.
Technical infrastructure	Context-based	Bus-based	EJB Component Model, CORBAComponent Model.
Application-level infrastructure	Shared model	Bus-based	No standard exists yet. Products exist, such as Forté. Typically developed in-house.
Functional interfaces	API-based	Bridged or Integrated	Space covered by OMG domain standards, Edifact, X12, OAG, and others.
Semantics	Context-based	Bus-based (in particular, repository based)	Standards are starting to appear for specific business domains. Evolving very rapidly. Typically developed in-house.
Functional reference model	Shared model	Bus-based (in particular, repository based)	Space covered by SCOR. Typically developed in-house.
Development lifecycle interfaces	Shared model	Bus-based (in particular, repository based)	Initial aspect addressed by the UML and XMI standards. All other aspects currently in-house.

Architected Federation

An *architected federation* is a federation of system-level components, where the federation is carefully architected and developed as a whole. This section addresses the main characteristics of the architected federation and high-level aspects of the architecting process. Development process considerations are addressed in Chapter 7 and those of business modeling in Chapter 11.

Characteristics

The theory and practice of modeling and architecting a federation as a whole are still in their infancy. Although some experience, tools, and techniques are available to address interoperability between two or more systems, there is little to support the concept of a set of systems as parts of a whole, in which the whole is properly architected, managed, and evolved. Indeed, to treat the federation as a whole is perhaps the most complex task of software engineering today. Just the sheer amount of functionality in any federation is beyond the ability of any single human to handle.

Component-based development and the whole business component approach are the best way available today to deal with this complexity; indeed, the kind of complexity-reduction approaches provided by the business component approach are an absolute prerequisite to addressing the architected federation. The concepts, principles, patterns, and techniques that have been presented so far, in the context of the business component approach, to manage business components and individual business component systems should extend to managing federations.

Theoretically, to architect a business component system and to architect a federation do not appear to be very different, aside from the problem of scale. There are, however, a few important differences. By applying the principles of the business component approach, it is possible to architect a business component system that is highly integrated *and* highly modular at the same time. Even if the individual business components were to be built by independent organizations, the detailed architectural characteristics they must have are usually dictated by a single architecture team within a single organization. Given the "coarse but not very coarse" granularity of the business components, it is relatively easy for the business components not only to follow this architectural model, but also to participate in an assembly that will provide a functionally cohesive business component system. The cooperating business components can participate in very strict and well-defined collaborations, in which each business component can make strong assumptions about what other business components provide or not.

On the other hand, to architect a federation using system-level components requires a very different conceptual approach. System-level components tend to be very loosely coupled and highly autonomous, and they will often be developed by different, unrelated organizations. Hence, the choice of the protocols at each layer, as well as the definition of the interfaces and the development of the interoperability adapters, will be dictated not only by good architectural and design principles and/or the typical extra-functional requirements such as flexibility of the interfaces, looseness of the communication, costs, performance, and scalability, but also by business decisions and political skills of the organizations involved.

The typical extra-functional requirements such as performance and scalability, play differently at the federation and at the system level. For example, although performance and scalability are theoretically very important for the federation, in practice today many users are willing to trade off other, more mission-critical characteristics to the detriment of performance and scalability. In many real-world instances of system-to-system communication, aspects such as security are overwhelmingly more important. The low expectations set on response times by the Internet contribute to low performance objectives. We expect this to change, with users becoming educated as to the lack of a real technical reason for low performance in system-to-system communication, and with software vendors maturing their implementations of federations of systems.

There are three levels of federations: the intra-enterprise, extra-enterprise, and inter-enterprise federation.

Intra-enterprise federation. A set of systems federated to address the internal needs of one enterprise. Many organizations today face the challenge of bringing under control a large number of traditionally isolated systems. These systems usually run on a proprietary network internal to the enterprise (an *intranet*) and are composed of *enterprise-local* SLCs, meaning SCLs that, even if built by external organizations, are executed locally to the enterprise. Of course, "locally" is to be interpreted in a logical sense because the enterprise can be a highly distributed one.

Extra-enterprise federation. A federation established to address the need of a virtual enterprise. Such systems usually run on what can be seen as a network internal to the virtual enterprise (an *extranet*) and are composed of *enterprise-local* and *enterprise-remote* SLCs. The partners of the virtual enterprise can share (and usually have a high interest in sharing) architectures, factory setup, development process, and actual deliverables like business components and even system-level components.

Inter-enterprise federation. Addresses the needs of an e-commerce federation, in which a given enterprise, in no particular partnership with any other, needs to participate in some kind of business exchange. The participants in the business exchange should not have to have any development-time knowledge of each other. The only thing that they should need to share are the run-time interoperability protocols (all protocols layers with the exception of the development lifecycle interface).

Each federation level requires a different approach. For example, each level usually corresponds to a different level of trust between the participating organizations and hence requires different levels of security. In particular, the extra-enterprise federation challenges can be enormously complicated by the different corporate cultures and the different business goals of the participant organizations.

The type of processing that a given SLC in a federation will perform drives the kind of interoperability solution appropriate for that SLC as a participant in the federation. For example:

Planning engines. A planning engine will often need to load a large amount of data at the start of a request for service, perform a planning process typically in batch, and give the results back to the target system at the end.

This type of processing requires functional interfaces optimized to read and write very large amounts of data easily.

Business transaction-based systems. Compared with planning engines, order-entry systems or billing systems, for example, need to interact at a much smaller granularity of data. Such systems normally require a more collaborative kind of processing, requiring feedback from the target system on the results of the business transaction.

Electronic banking systems. An interaction with an online banking system is usually of a very limited kind. It may require a specific set of interfaces to deal with scheduled transactions (for example, repeated at a given moment or scheduled for specific moment). It often has very simple interfaces, with high security requirements.

Architecting the Federation

At a high level, there are three important aspects to architecting a federation: clearly defining the seven-layer protocol model, properly preparing the individual SLCs for federation, and properly addressing the federation as a whole.

The Seven-Layer Protocol Model

The definition of the seven-layer protocol model corresponds to a large extent to the definition of the federation architecture (at all architectural viewpoints), but with a strong focus on the collaboration between the SLCs. Ideally, as a complexity-reduction strategy, it should be possible to agree (at the federation level) on unique protocols for each protocol type (for example, agree that CORBA and XML are to be used for each SLC-to-SLC exchange), or at least to a reduced set of equivalent protocols. In practice, corporate politics, the rapid evolution of protocols and technologies, and the length of the typical federation project all frequently dictate an outcome of more than one protocol instance for each prototype.

As discussed previously, the availability of industry standards applicable to federations is still evolving. Figure 6.30 illustrates this evolution. The gray area in each layer estimates where standards and direct industry support for that layer are available today, and it attempts a prediction on their evolution in the years to come. As can be seen, at the time of writing the only layer that has significant coverage is the technical interface layer.

In the absence of industry-level standards covering all the federation needs, an organization that decides to properly architect the federation will need to define an enterprise-specific set of protocols, at least at the intra- and extra-enterprise levels. Luckily, the definition of each layer in the seven-layer proto-

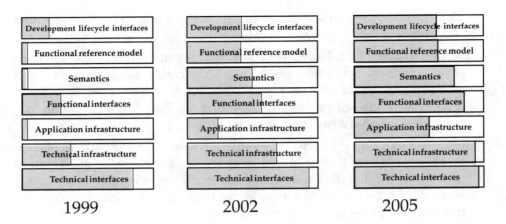

| 1999 | 2002 | 2005 |

Figure 6.30 Evolution of architected federation.

col model can be addressed with a certain independence, although there are linkages especially within the same architectural viewpoint.

The main challenge of architecting a federation lies in moving from integration of preexisting systems to the development of systems that are intended from the start to participate in a well-defined federation architecture. To a large extent, defining the first three levels of the seven-layer protocol model corresponds to defining a federation factory set-up. While this book mainly discusses factory set-up for business component systems rather than for federations—so reflecting the current focus by most component-based developments at the time of writing—over the medium term the federation factory set-up will become an important consideration.

On the other hand, for a federation, the functional and application protocols are more important than the technical protocols. To a large extent, it is possible to architect a federation in such a way that the functional and application protocols are fully defined, while the exact definition of the technical protocols are left for later implementation. Given an appropriate functional architecture and application architecture, it is much easier to bridge two systems at the technical level.

Preparing an Individual SLC for Federation

While architecting and developing a business component system, or a system-level component, steps can be taken to make its federation easier. Often today, and especially given the relative immaturity of system development using components, organizations are focused only on piecing together the system, rather than also considering that the system itself will be part of a bigger whole. The following is a list of the more obvious things that will help prepare a system to become federated:

- Include federation considerations from the beginning of the development lifecycle. A system-level component is thought of and designed for federation from the beginning. For example, when defining the error-handling framework, include virtual enterprise considerations in the definition of error identifiers, rather than making assumptions such as "since there will never be more than 99 business components, it will be enough to prefix all errors with two characters indicating the component they originate from."

- As much as possible, use any appropriate federation-level protocols internally in the system as well. For example, adopting internally the same transactional model established for the federation will make it simpler to have federation-wide transactions. Conversely, if a federation-level transactional model is not defined, adopting a very flexible transactional model that makes as few assumptions as possible on the caller will make it easier to extend this transactional model to the federation. The objective is to avoid protocol translation as much as possible.

- Design interfaces to be as modeless as possible (see Chapter 11). A *modeless interface* is an interface in which the operations can be called in any order or sequence without affecting the result. Do not assume a trusted source or operation invocations that follow precise rules. The SLC must be designed with a paranoid approach to reliability, resilience, and security.

- Assume there will be interest in system-internal events. That is, clearly define all system-level events in which any external system may wish to register interest.

- Apply the same almost paranoid focus on componentization, autonomy, and reduction of external surface area as is applied to business components in a business component system.

Federation as a Whole

The last high-level aspect of an architected federation is the need, mainly for intra- and extra-enterprise federations, to develop, manage, and evolve the federation as a whole. In this case, the focus shifts from the points of contacts between systems toward the global aspects of the federation, for example, from the interface functionality to the global functionality delivered by the federation.

The challenge becomes the coordinated development of a set of system-level components as a cost-effective and reliable software manufacturing. Indeed, it is possible to reduce the cost of the development of a set of systems by sharing such things as the factory set-up between the different system developments.

Once this focus is adopted, most of the things that are important when addressing the business component system as a whole become important also at the federation level. Here are a few examples:

- The single most important model of the federation is the functional reference model, which corresponds to or at least includes (as is discussed in Chapter 11) a federation-level component model. This is the model that defines the static composition of the federation.

- There will be a need for managing deliverables that refer to the federation as a whole rather than any individual SLC of the federation. For example, the proper deployment management of the systems involved in a federation will require a federation-level dependency list that captures the exact constitution of the federation at each relevant point in time.

- All the concepts defined for the business component system can be extended: For example, the federation will have SLC assemblies (as the system had BC assemblies), a federation-level business data type system, a definition of all errors at the federation level, and so forth for most of the subjects discussed in Chapter 5.

- In particular, the "plug" concept introduced in Chapter 4 will need to be extended. SLCs belonging to an intra- and extra-enterprise federation are best thought of as being provided with a plug that fits the federation socket. On the other hand, the exchanges between SLCs in an inter-enterprise federation are best thought of as occurring through a *port* rather than a *plug*.

The architected federation will eventually need to be supported by appropriate tools, which we call a *federation development kit*. This development kit must be able to deal easily with complex software artifacts such as sets of SLCs. This is yet one more reason why the level of abstraction delivered by the business component concept is so important; we will need to extend it to be able to deal, in a very near future, with federations.

Summary

The subject of interoperability is becoming one of the most prominent issues in the software industry, and it is bound to acquire increasing importance, given the role that e-commerce is playing and will play in our economy.

The seven-layer interoperability protocol model provides a conceptual framework to address the technical, architectural, functional, and development lifecycle architectural viewpoints of two or more systems participating in some form of federation. From the bottom up, the seven layers are: technical interfaces, the technical infrastructure required to support the technical interfaces, the application-level infrastructure needed on top of the technical infrastructure, functional interfaces, semantic aspects, the functional reference model, and finally development lifecycle interfaces. Each layer can have more than one protocol. Protocols at each of the first six of the seven layers, even if implemented in an ad-hoc way, are required for two or more systems to cooperate. The seven-layer protocol model is applicable beyond the business component approach. It acquires a particular prominence in the case of a federation of SLCs, since this will both support and further drive the requirements for high levels of interoperability between independently built systems.

Systems can cooperate according to four interaction modes: integrated, bridged, coordinated, and bus-based. Using a bus-based approach, the other three modes can be simulated. Furthermore, systems interact in three main styles: master-slave, coordinated, and peer-to-peer. Master-slave and peer-to-peer can be implemented using an integrated, bridged, or bus-based approach. The coordinated style can be implemented using only bus-based or coordinated modes.

A federation can be ad hoc, which usually means a set of system-level components that are cooperating under the pressure of external events, but without a specific a-priori federation plan. Or it can be architected, meaning that the federation is addressed as a whole, and its architecture and evolution are properly planned as a whole. Furthermore, it is useful to classify a federation as intra-enterprise, where the systems are federated to address the needs of one single enterprise; as extra-enterprise, where the federation is established to address the needs of a virtual enterprise; or as inter-enterprise, in which autonomous systems need to participate in some form of business exchange.

To establish a federated architecture requires instantiating the seven-layer protocol model for the federation, properly preparing each individual system-level component for federation, and addressing the various deliverables at the federation-level.

This chapter concludes Part 1, in which the conceptual framework for the business component approach has, we hope, been established. That is, the main concepts, dimensions, and levels of granularity that support the development of large-scale distributed and component-based systems have been defined. In Part 2, the focus moves to setting up the component factory and to the principles, techniques, and approaches that support efficient and cost-effective manufacture of such systems.

Endnotes

1   A definition of the virtual enterprise concept can be found at the National Industrial Information Infrastructure Protocol (NIIIP) Web site (www.niiip.org).

2   For more information on any of these technologies and others, check out the excellent [Orfali 1999].

3   To be precise, this is a normal business event and not an error. A project can decide to report this event using the same technology adopted to report technical errors, and for this reason it is here imprecisely referred to as an *error*.

4   See [W3C 1998] and, for example, [Harold 1998].

5   This is not, of course, an argument against type safety, which is essential in many computing situations. It is, however, an argument about excessive low-level checking when first it is not required, and second it can not check the important business-level things. In other words, different levels of binding should be used in different situations.

6   At the time of writing, the specific subset of XML that is tagged data has not been standardized by the various standards bodies, although both W3C and OMG are working toward it, albeit by different routes. See [OMG 1998d] and www.w3.org.

7   For one approach to handling the recording of type in XML-formatted tagged data, see [OMG 1998d].

8   Some implementations of tagged data have provided for finding a given tag regardless of depth of nesting as well as of position at a given level of nesting. This approach is generally not as safe, but it can be useful in some circumstances—for example, where the target merely needs to know if the data includes at least one *phone* tag.

Component Factory
Set-up

Part One described the conceptual framework for the business component approach and defined what it is that we want to build. Knowing this, we can now start to set up the component factory—an efficient production capability able to produce software components in a cost-effective way. Part Two describes the factory setup challenges that confront most organizations wishing to manufacture components. Because real component factories are currently in their infancy, factory setup is likely to be an integral part of most component-based developments today, and the factory will evolve together with the first few functional development projects.

The topics addressed in Part Two are not about producing domain-specific functionality, but rather address only factory setup—the production capability. Of course, different organizations will have more or less refined factory setups, but the principles presented are of general validity. The main architectural viewpoint that Part Two does not address is the functional architecture, which is concerned with actually producing and assembling components, and it describes production rather than factory setup aspects. Part Three is dedicated to the functional architecture viewpoint.

Setup of the factory involves four major viewpoints, as illustrated in Figure P2.1. Each chapter in Part Two addresses a separate viewpoint, as follows:

Chapter 7: Development Process. In order to build the factory, we need an idea of the development process, that is, *how* components will be manufactured and assembled. The business component approach defines a methodology framework, based on which various manufacturing processes can be defined. Each manufacturing process is specific to a need; for example, each level of component granularity should be addressed in a specific way. The development process may be seen as external to the factory itself because given a factory it is possible to associate multiple processes with it. On the other hand, it is still an important aspect of the

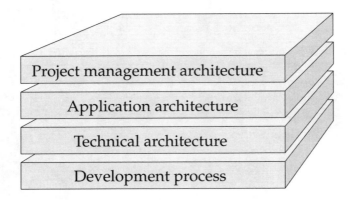

Figure P2.1 Setup viewpoints.

setup, and the layout of the factory may be optimized according to the targeted process. Chapter 7 provides an overview of the key elements of a process within the business component approach.

Chapter 8: Technical Architecture. Having defined the characteristics of the development process that the component factory should enable, the first step of factory setup is to define the technical architecture that will support and provide tools for the things that we want to produce, and to build an implementation of that architecture. This implementation is called a business component virtual machine, and it includes both the run-time environment and the development-time environment required to build components at industrial levels and with the desired technical characteristics. This aspect of the factory setup involves the definition of the tools, machinery, and basic materials required for the manufacturing process.

Chapter 9: Application Architecture. To build a large-scale system requires a certain view of how the parts of the system should look and of how they should interrelate. Together with a set of design principles presented in Chapter 12, "Component-Based Design," this chapter defines the architectural principles and the main collaboration patterns that can be used to build a system that scales and that satisfies extra-functional requirements. In manufacturing terms, this viewpoint defines the structure of the final product.

Chapter 10: Project Management Architecture. This viewpoint addresses what is needed to optimize the production process so that a large team of people can work concurrently and efficiently using the factory. While the application architecture is about building a run-time scalable system, the project management architecture is about building a development-time scalable manufacturing capability. In this sense, it is about the architecture of the factory rather than the architecture of the product.

There is some level of subjectivity in assigning principles and concepts to one architectural viewpoint rather than another; the separation is not always precise; and many topics appear in several viewpoints. The architectural viewpoints presented reflect a number of years of experience in component-based development for the enterprise, together with knowledge transfer of this experience, and they have proved extremely useful. But when all is said and done, as discussed in Chapter 2, "The Business Component Approach," everything is part of the architecture, and as long as a project addresses all of the various topics, their exact assignment to viewpoints is of secondary importance.

Development Process

There are two ways a project can fail: by not following a development process, and by following a development process.

FRANCOIS DEVERDIERE

Chapter 2, "The Business Component Approach," introduced an overview of the development process for a business component system, and Chapter 4, "The Business Component," presented various aspects of the development process for an individual business component. This chapter expands on the methodology and development process for component-based development in general and business component-based development in particular.

The objective is to describe, at a reasonably high level of detail, those aspects of the development process necessary to form a good understanding of the business component approach from the development viewpoint. This is done mainly through a pragmatic description of the development aspects that are specific to the business component approach, with examples of particular deliverables being given. Additional important considerations for the development process, including software configuration management and version control aspects, as well as the more general project management architecture for component-based development, are addressed in Chapter 10, "Project Management Architecture."

Although not essential, useful prerequisites for this chapter include a background in software engineering and a general understanding of software development methodologies and lifecycles, in particular object-oriented development methodologies.[1]

The chapter is organized into four main sections:

Concepts. This introductory section briefly introduces three levels of development process granularity for software manufacturing and presents 10 golden characteristics of a CBD process.

Construction. This section focuses on construction aspects, from requirements through implementation, and exemplifies them for a transitional organization.

Validation and Verification. This section focuses on validation and verification aspects that address the challenge of producing a complete and correct set of deliverables, again exemplifying them for a transitional organization.

Iterations. Having described the main concepts and deliverables, we can discuss some of the characteristics of iterations, both at the individual business component level and at the system level.

Concepts

The ultimate objective of the business component approach is to reduce costs and master complexity across the whole software supply chain, from manufacturing to deployment and evolution. This requires an appropriate conceptual framework, which was established in Part One of this book. In turn, this conceptual framework informs the methodology framework and the individual development processes, or, as we often prefer to call them, the *software manufacturing processes*. A proper establishment of manufacturing processes is important as a first step in a component factory set-up. This chapter focuses on those aspects of the business component approach that deal with the methodology framework and manufacturing processes,[2] and this section describes two main conceptual foundations: the main *manufacturing processes* and the most important development characteristics of the business component approach (which we call the *10 golden characteristics*).

Relying on a common methodology framework, the business component approach encompasses a set of manufacturing processes, which address the different categories of deliverable within the software lifecycle. Each manufacturing process provides pragmatic and direct support for the concerns of the various kinds of developer and assembler, and it can have multiple routes and be adapted in various ways. The manufacturing processes can also be seen as methodology components, which can be assembled by each project into a concrete, project-specific methodology tailored to project-specific needs. This chapter will mainly address one specific process, called Rapid System Development, that can be seen as a combination of the basic manufacturing processes.

Manufacturing Processes

The three basic manufacturing processes in the business component approach correspond to the three levels of component granularity. These processes are:

Rapid component development (RCD). The development process for thinking about, building, and testing an *individual* business component. In an organization that focuses on selling individual business components or distributed components for reuse and assembly by other organizations, RCD is the only manufacturing process that really matters. Although the term "rapid component development" could be applied to other levels of component granularity, we use it to mean specifically the business component granularity level.

System architecture and assembly (SAA). The development process for architecting, assembling, and testing a system using business components. The name captures the two main aspects of the manufacturing process for a business component system: the architecting part and the assembly part. This manufacturing process includes, when appropriate for the project, architecting a business component system as a system-level component that is planned to interoperate with other systems. Given the strong focus on assembly using preexisting business components, this process will also include guidelines on how to properly identify, analyze, compare, and eventually buy those preexisting components.

Federation architecture and assembly (FAA). The development process for architecting, assembling, and testing a *federation* using system-level components. This manufacturing process is expected to become important in the medium term (two to three years); in the short term, most component-based developments will be targeted at building systems rather than federations of system-level components. This is not to diminish the current importance of federating distributed systems that are not system-level components.

A mature component-based organization will differentiate clearly between these three levels of development process granularity, while at the same time properly addressing the important interrelationships and dependencies among them. Most of the organizations using CBD, however, at the time of writing are, with respect to CBD, transitional organizations. A *transitional organization* in this context is an organization that is just starting to adopt CBD or at most is still on one of the various learning curves. A transitional organization today, given the current maturity of the component-based industry and the lack of commercially available business components, needs to consider the development of a system at the same time as it defines and builds its components.

The typical transitional development process, called *rapid system develop-*

ment (RSD), is the development process that will be exemplified in this chapter. This process is a good example of how the basic processes introduced previously can be combined for specific needs. Indeed, RSD is a specific process using elements of both RCD and SAA, where there are few or no preprovided components, and development of a system will address all granularity levels. This approach is hence particularly appropriate for transition situations. In describing RSD, we make two unrealistic assumptions: that both legacy considerations and the nonfunctional architectural viewpoints can be ignored. These assumptions enable us to focus entirely on component development from a functional viewpoint and also to lay out the concepts within which the remaining chapters of Part 2 can describe the requirements placed on the other architectural viewpoints.

The exact detail of the RCD part of the RSD process will depend on the category of business component being developed: For example, a process model will make sense for a process business component, but in most cases it will not make sense for a utility business component.

It is useful, albeit a gross simplification, to represent the RSD process as a v-cycle (or V-shaped development process, named after the "V" shape in which it is usually represented) illustrated in Figure 7.1 (see also [Coleman 1993]). The v-cycle has proved a convenient way to introduce many concepts and deliverables, but it is a simplified and linearized representation of a complex development process reality. At a first approximation, the construction aspects correspond to the left side of the v-cycle, and they cover the requirements, analysis, design, and implementation phases. Testing aspects, which, together with review aspects, are part of validation and verification, correspond to the right-hand side of the v-cycle. The terms used in Figure 7.1, where "BC" is short for business component, are explained in the course of the chapter.

The keyword "rapid" is used repeatedly, and it indicates the ability to develop

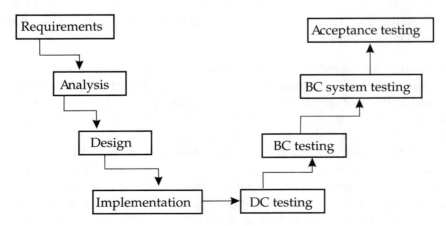

Figure 7.1 Transitional development process as a v-cycle.

a component, system, or federation by performing short and quick iterations that provide incremental functionality. The two biggest risks of rapid development or at least iterative approaches are, first, compromising the quality of software releases and, second, continuously reworking the same deliverables. There is a fine trade-off between the necessity of exploring requirements and managing risks, on one hand, and the necessity of ensuring high-quality, correct, and complete final deliverables, produced in a cost-effective way, on the other.

Enabling high levels of rapid development requires an approach that conceptually and architecturally directly supports autonomous, iterative, and high-quality deliverables, as well as strong tools and development environment support. For example, as will be seen later in this chapter and in Chapter 8, "Technical Architecture," the development environment must provide not only high levels of code generation (relieving the functional developer from the low-level details of the technologies used), but also a set of additional capabilities to relieve the developers from repetitive tasks, to the extent of including over time lower-level components, such as utility and entity components.

The development environment hence plays an important role in any development process. Although the main aspects of a development process are obviously independent of the development environment, in a mature and optimized software production capability, the available tools play an important role in influencing the *detailed* aspects of a development process. For example, as discussed later, we have found it very convenient to set up the whole process in such a way that each business component can be developed both by generating as much of its internals as possible and by enabling validation and verification of its behavior and of the behavior of its constituent DCs as independently as possible from other parts of the system.

Other manufacturing processes are important, but they are not discussed here. For example, the development of the component execution environment requires a manufacturing process that, even if it would strongly benefit from the adoption of the same methodology framework and have many common characteristics at the high level, would have significant detailed level differences.

10 Golden Characteristics

This section recapitulates and expands on the main development process characteristics presented in Chapter 2. The component-based development process is characterized by the following *10 golden characteristics*.

1. *Component-centric approach.* The main difference, at the time of writing, between the business component approach and other development approaches and methodologies is that the business component approach

is strongly component-centric. By this we mean that the whole development process, as well as all the architectural considerations and any other aspects of the approach, is centered around the various levels of component granularity. For example, requirements and analysis deliverables are organized as much as possible around business components. Design, implementation, and testing are performed by a team organized around a business component. Within this strong focus, a very important role is played by both distributed components (the main constituent elements of a business component) and the BC assembly (other business components on which a given business components depends).

2. *Architecture-centric approach.* The business component approach and the development processes in particular are strongly architecture-centric. By this we mean the architecture viewpoints are used throughout the development lifecycle to drive the evolution of the system. In particular, a large part of the approach addresses the needs of the functional developer by clearly separating the responsibilities of the functional architecture from other architectural viewpoints. The development process discussed here is mostly focused on these needs, and so illustrates requirements on the other architectural viewpoints.

3. *Focus on autonomy.* In a business component approach, the development process is centered on the autonomy of the system-level components, of the business components, and of the distributed components. The general mindset is that to obtain high levels of autonomy, appropriate steps must be taken to focus on autonomy at the appropriate levels at each development lifecycle phase. Autonomy is not obtained as an afterthought, but rather it must be explicitly targeted not only at every development lifecycle phase, but also in the set-up of development processes and the factory itself, including the various architectural aspects.

4. *Approach to collaborations.* A critical aspect of the approach is how to allow a focus on autonomy while enabling high levels of collaboration. There is continuing tension in focusing on autonomous development of components. This occurs because the various levels of component granularity deliver useful function only through collaboration with other components. For example, a single business component is rarely useful to an end user. Focusing on reducing dependencies to achieve autonomy goes side by side with properly acknowledging and explicitly managing, throughout the development lifecycle, the various collaborations and associated software dependencies. On one hand, there is the autonomous analysis, design, implementation, and testing of individual business components. On the other, it is necessary to preserve the integrity of the system as a whole and of the various possible collaborations between these various units of autonomy. Of particular importance is how to address the

development and project management process while preserving the information system integrity (at all levels) and supporting the independent development of the various autonomous artifacts.

5. *Iterative nature.* The development process supports, through the ability to autonomously implement and evolve individual components, a highly iterative and incremental process. For this to be cost-effective, the development environment philosophy must support fast iterations through the lifecycle. Fast iteration applies both to development of a single component and to rebuilding the system after a modification. The implication is that it should be possible, for example, to rapidly develop, check, modify, calculate dependencies, and if required regenerate and rebuild the system. This can be enabled only by integration and streamlining of processes and tools (further addressed in Chapter 10) at all the lifecycle phases so that they support RSD and enterprise-level (as opposed to user-interface) prototyping.

6. *High levels of development concurrency.* Previous characteristics support the ability for separate teams to design, develop, and test parts of the system in isolation from and concurrently with other teams, while still preserving system-wide integrity. This is an essential element of rapid development and directly supports the objective of cost-effective software manufacturing.

7. *Continuous integration.* The iterative nature of component-based development must also be supported by a continuous integration approach throughout the lifecycle. A functional developer should be able to continuously develop parts of the system and get immediate system-level feedback on the functionality and behavior of the system, while concentrating on building the system's function rather than on technical details. Such continuous, iterative, and rapid development should not sacrifice quality. On the contrary, it should be easy at all times to check for quality without increasing costs, allowing the achievement of high levels of quality for a minimal price.

8. *Supporting risk management-driven development.* The whole development process is geared toward best-practice risk management. Developing an information system is complex. Developing a distributed information system adds to this complexity.[3] Today, CBD projects have an even higher risk due to the current immaturity of the field (although this may change rapidly). We are not the first and will not be the last to advocate development driven by risk-management considerations, especially risk-management techniques that enable high levels of joint development; immediate feedback on the project status to allow continuous validation and verification of the various design and implementation decisions; and

small, rapid iterations in which all the trivial details of development are taken care of by appropriate tools and processes.

9. *Strong focus on reuse.* Reuse applies at all phases of the lifecycle, starting with requirements. Reuse is to a large extent a natural occurrence in the business component approach because all levels of component granularity are built with minimal external dependencies and hence have a much greater probability of being applied to many situations with minimal effort. In particular, reuse is directly supported by the strong focus on the business component as the stable unit of problem-space partitioning and by the strongly architecture-centric nature of the approach.

10. *Component development as product development.* Building business components is very similar to the better software product development. A good product development differentiates itself by a strong focus on quality, documentation, and support, in the context of the product being used by a variety of users in different situations. Business components are products that will be reused in as many places as possible, and hence they justify a stronger-than-normal focus on quality and on other product-oriented characteristics. In the precomponent world, processes for developing a product were very different from those for developing a one-shot application. This difference tends to disappear in the business component approach.

These characteristics directly influence many practical aspects of the development process. For example, in order to achieve fast iterations without sacrificing quality, mature and optimized organizations give prominence to the deliverables that are "living documents." A *living document* is one whose importance keeps it always up to date. In other words, the development process places such importance on its role within the development environment that it is naturally kept up to date. For example, a relational data model from which a schema is generated is always an accurate and up-to-date description of the database. On the other hand, an entity relationship diagram drawn to clarify requirements but that does not feed into any generation ability will soon be obsolete. Optimized processes are built around living documents.

Construction

Because of its particular relevance for the component industry over the next two to three years, the focus of both this section ("Construction") and the next ("Verification and Validation") is on the rapid system development process (RSD). In this process, the business component system and its individual business components are, as far as possible, built concurrently.

The term "construction" denotes the left side of the v-cycle, from requirements to implementation. Before discussing each phase in some detail, three factors should be clarified: how the development process provides *concurrent focus* on both system and business component levels, the availability of a *component model* early in the development lifecycle, and how each phase produces what is required to *verify and validate* the phase itself.

Concurrent focus. Initial requirements and analysis usually address system-level aspects. Toward the end of the analysis phase, the focus of the project will shift from system-level modeling to the individual business components; at the start of the design phase, development is subdivided into business components, where each business component is assigned to an individual team (see Figure 7.2). At this point, it is as if a new development lifecycle starts from requirements again for the individual business component: Each business component can be individually analyzed for functional completeness, and new business component-specific requirements may be added. Given that both development lifecycles exist at the same time, most types of deliverables need to exist both at the individual business component level and at the system level. For example, each business component may have its own island of data (see Chapter 12, "Component-Based Design"), but it may also be important to be able to verify the integrity and consistency of the overall database model, and hence to have a system-level view of the database that includes all the individual islands of data as if they were a single database. A good tool would enable a developer to switch between the two points of view, for all the appropriate deliverables, at the click of a button.

Component model. Already at the requirement-gathering and analysis phases, the main deliverables start to be organized and assigned to the business components. This makes a strong (and controversial!) assump-

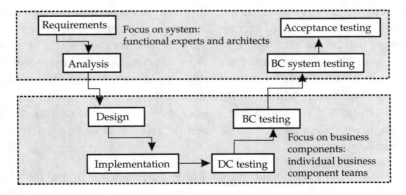

Figure 7.2   Main focus of the different phases.

tion: It assumes that a component model is available very early in the development lifecycle, perhaps even before starting the project. Thinking of other mature industries, this is an obvious statement: The parts that make up a computer or a car are well known before a project for defining a new computer or a new car is started. For example, when designing a new PC it is assumed that the PC will have a given set of components, such as a monitor, a hard disk, some kind of floppy disk, a certain number of external ports, a keyboard, and so on. The individual components may change over time, or they may not even be present in certain particular designs—for example, the keyboard may be replaced by a voice-only input device or a touch screen—but the underlying component model for a standard PC is pretty well established in the computer industry.

In the software industry, however, component models are not yet established. In a few years, we expect that there will be publicly or commercially available component models for many business domains. While we wait for Godot [Beckett 1996], it is possible to draw an initial component model very early on following the principles and patterns presented in Chapter 11, "Component-Based Business Modeling." This candidate component model can be used to start organizing the project around the candidate business components. For example, features and their corresponding market requirements, as well as use cases, can be assigned early on to individual business components. This is particularly important for large projects in which just navigating through the enormous volume of requirements can rapidly become a challenge, and a rational and logical organization—following an easy-to-understand partitioning of the problem space—may be of great help. Assigning requirements deliverables to business components helps decompose both requirements and function into well-partitioned areas, thereby keeping complexity under control through the implicit divide-and-conquer strategy provided by business component concepts.

Verification and validation. Each phase of construction produces, as an explicit deliverable, a precise and detailed specification for how that phase will be tested (see Figure 7.3). Although presented in a component context, this approach to test specification is a characteristic of any mature development process. There are, however, detail-level differences in its application within the business component approach; for example, consistent with the business component definition, and to support complexity management, test specifications are organized by business component.

We now analyze each development phase by providing examples of the general kinds of deliverables, which in reality can be very project-specific, in the requirements, analysis, design, and implementation phases.

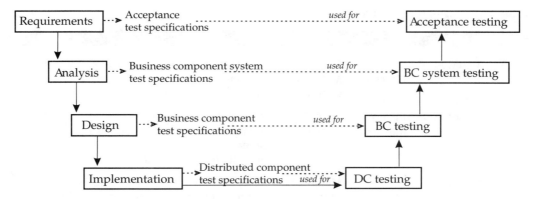

Figure 7.3 Construction phases and test specifications.

Requirements

During the requirements phase, the functional and extra-functional require-ments of the system are gathered[4] using traditional techniques such as reverse engineering, existing documentation, various types of interviews with cus-tomers, sales force, internal experts and industry analysts, benchmarking of the competition, and so on. For present purposes, a "customer" is loosely defined as the source of the requirements definition; in a software product development organization this may be the internal product management group rather than an external customer. The set of deliverables produced may include the following:

- A feature list, which lists the system-level features, typically with a few lines describing each feature, and often in spreadsheet form, as exempli-fied in Table 7.1. "Ver" in the table is an abbreviation for the system release version at which the feature will be released, "P" stands for prior-ity, "Ref" is a reference number uniquely identifying the feature, "BC" indi-cates the name of the owning business component, and "Status" indicates the particular development status of a feature. For example, feature *IMO-001* is currently in testing, while *IMO-015* is still being designed. The fea-ture list is further discussed shortly.

- A market requirement description, normally half to one page of text or more, for each feature described in Table 7.1. This can grow to become a self-standing document—a monograph on a particular functional or extra-functional topic, which may cover a whole set of features on multi-ple business components. An example of a market requirement descrip-tion for one particular feature is presented in Figure 7.4.

- An initial business process model of the system, which includes the rough scope of the system, a description of the system's main processes, and a set of models such as a process hierarchy, process threads, description of

Table 7.1   Fragment of Feature List for Invoice Management

VER	P	REF	BC	FEATURE	DESCRIPTION	STATUS
1.0	1	IM0-001	Invoice Manager	Three-way Match Invoice	Three-way matches between purchasing, receiving, and invoice information.	Testing
1.0	1	IM0-006	Invoice Manager	Special Charge Process	Pay noninventory charges associated with specific purchase order lines. Charges can be by lot or relate to quantity received.	Testing
1.0	1	IM0-011	Invoice Manager	Multiple Currency	Accept vendor invoices rendered in a currency other than the operating currency, including the use of date-sensitive exchange rate and foreign exchange reservation.	Design
1.0	1	IM0-015	Invoice Manager	Log Invoice	Allow entry of invoices that will be held from payment pending further user intervention. Journal entry creation is optional.	Design
1.1	1	IM0-057	Invoice Manager	Memo Invoice	Add information to invoices that already exist in the system. These transactions may affect the invoice amount and may create journal entries.	Review
1.1	1	IM0-045	Invoice Manager	Void Invoice	Reverse the effect of an earlier invoice. After the invoice is voided, it will no longer be considered as payable.	Review
1.1	1	IM0-062	Invoice Manager	Reactivate Invoice	Reinstate an invoice that has been voided and make it eligible for payment.	Review
1.2	4	IM0-065	Invoice Manager	Override Calculated Discount Amounts	Allow the user to change the discount amount available during invoice entry.	Review

the system's internal and external actors, and so on. This deliverable starts off with things identified during requirements, but it is refined and completed during analysis. See, for example, [Allen 1998] for an introduction to business process modeling.

■ An initial set of use cases for the system. A few considerations about use cases in the context of the business component approach are provided shortly in the section "Use Cases." For more information on use cases, see

---

Feature: Special Charge Process   **Reference Number:** IM0-006

Pay noninventory charges associated with specific Purchase Order lines. Charges may be by lot or relate to quantity received.

This feature applies to invoices related to purchase orders only. When goods are purchased, there are often incidental charges related to specific items. These charges may be blanket amounts or may have a quantity relationship with the item quantity received. In either case, attaching indications of these charges to a purchase order line item constitutes approval on the part of the purchase order originator for payment of these charges. At the time the charges are included, the purchase order originator will also provide information regarding pricing, quantities, and general ledger accounting.

During the invoice entry process, the user will have the ability to view, select, and process these charges. Ideally, processing the charges will not be dependent on processing the items the charges relate to. User will have the capability to process all the charges that apply to the invoices in progress. User will then have the ability to view all changes processed before concluding the invoice.

Figure 7.4   Example of market requirement description.

[Jacobson 1995] or [Schneider 1998]. Depending on the complexity of the problem space and on the maturity of the development organization, this may replace the business process model.

- An initial user-interface prototype. This is often the best way to quickly focus the requirement gathering activity while obtaining immediate and concrete feedback from the end user.

- An initial set of business rules that the system must satisfy, organized by business components.

- An initial business component system model, and particularly the component diagram as exemplified in Chapter 5, "The Business Component System," Figure 5.1. See Chapter 11 for a discussion on how to identify business components and choose the right granularity for them.

- The test specification for acceptance testing.

Consistent with rapid development objectives, a project can, of course, decide to start the next analysis phase before the requirements phase—and in particular the test specification—is fully complete. There are advantages (such as a more complete and correct requirement specification) and disadvantages (such as a delayed analysis start and the possibility of discovering and better clarifying requirements through iterative development) in waiting until the test specification is completed before moving forward. In this sense, some practitioners go as far as to think about each development process phase as something that is started at some point in time, but is actually closed only at the end of the project!

The exact requirement deliverables produced by each project will depend on a variety of things, including the complexity of the requirements, the level of the customer's involvement in requirements definition, and both the customer's maturity (from a software development's point of view) and availability. Some customers are perfectly happy to stay at the feature list level, whereas others want to participate in the detailed design of the system. Thus the precise definition of the deliverables of the requirements phase can be very context-specific. For example, it may or may not be necessary to have requirements deliverables totally separated from any development consideration. In this chapter, the term "requirements" is used to indicate what the customer has signed off on, that is, the version of the requirements produced or used internally by the development organization.

The following two subsections highlight a few component-specific characteristics of feature lists and use cases.

Feature List

A feature list is a high-level summary of the functionality of a system or of an individual component. Feature lists can be used in a multitude of ways, for example, as a simple project-level, or even executive-level, description of the system-wide functionality. In a sense, a feature list-based development process can be adopted; that is, a feature list can be used to support sizing, estimation, planning, management, tracking, reporting, and testing of the project throughout the development lifecycle. In several contexts the feature list has been used as the main traceability management tool across the lifecycle. Some practitioners equate a feature list to a list of use cases, which may be accurate for some projects. A feature, however, can in general correspond to more than one use case; conversely one use case may correspond to multiple features.

All features are assigned to, or "owned by," a business component. As we have seen, this implies that a candidate BCSM exists very early in the development process. Each business component will have its own feature list. A feature often has implications on more than one business component, and it is assigned following this simple rule: The feature is owned by the business component that owns the main business rules of the feature. This usually means that the feature is owned by the business component that is higher in the hierarchy of functional categories. Because a high percentage of customer-defined requirements are normally requirements on processes, features directly corresponding to customer requirements tend to be assigned to process business components.

When thinking about the implications of a feature, or when designing the business components to support a feature, it is not unusual to determine various new functionalities and features required by the business components involved, which can be recorded as new features against the individual business components. For example, the creation of a given order by an *OrderManager* business component implies the ability of a *NumberGenerator* to generate a sequence number for entities of type "order."

When does feature detailing stop? The practical level of detail at which it makes sense to stop thinking in terms of features and start thinking only in terms of interfaces, operations, design, business rules, and so on is highly project-specific. The trade-off is normally given by the fact that the feature list must be a practical management tool, rather than a sizable management overhead on the project. A very rough guideline might be to start questioning the level of detail when there are more than 500 system-level features for a specific business domain.

As for other deliverables, it is important to be able to switch easily between the system-level view and the business component-level view of the feature list. The system-level feature list is given by a selective union of all the feature lists at the business component level. The selective union guarantees that a feature that appears in multiple business components is included only once. This implies that the number of features important at the system level is considerably less than the number of features given by a proper union of the feature lists of all the individual business components. As a practical example, an average of 30 features on a single utility business component can be expected, an average of 60 on a single entity business component, and an average of 70 on a single process business component. In a large system, this could lead to 400 to 500 system-level features, although the proper union of all business component feature lists might produce a few thousand.

Use Cases

Use cases relate directly to features. As for each feature in a feature list, a use case is always owned by or assigned to a business component, and more specifically a process business component. A process component owning a use case usually needs other components to carry out the use case. System-wide use cases, at the highest level, may be owned by the *System* business component (presented in Chapter 5), but these are relatively rare. In most cases, it is not difficult to identify the owner of a process or of a use case.

There is often a need to extract common parts of use cases, which can be reused in multiple use cases. A typical example of such a *generic use case* is the credit checking use case, which can be used within a higher-level use case, for example, entering an order or shipping a product to a customer. Such a use case can be a complicated process that is not directly useful as an independent business process—of course, if you are a credit-checking agency, this is your main process. Typically, generic use cases are owned by a support process component (one of the subcategories of process business components described in Chapter 11), and often the identification of a new business component belonging to this subcategory is directly supported by the identification of a generic use case.

The analysis and refinement of a use case will often discover new requirements on the various business components involved, leading, for example, to additional features in the feature list. This is a good example of the phenomenon that production of any given deliverable, in any phase, may often lead to improvements in or completion of other deliverables in the same or other phases.

A process business component can typically own more than one use case, as it can manage more than one business process. The implications on granularity will be discussed in Chapter 11, where we will also see that this is project dependent. For example, the *OrderManager* business component may manage not only the order-entry use case and process, including the allocation of the goods, but also the deletion of an order and even, if the project so requires, the higher-level lifecycle of the order from creation to shipment, billing, and closing.

As described, for example, in [Jacobson 1995], use cases can be refined during analysis to support the definition of candidate interfaces, which, of course, in our case are business component interfaces. A component can also be an actor in a use case.

Analysis

During the analysis phase, a set of models of the information system is created, describing the system under different points of view, as illustrated in Figure 7.5. These models include the following:

- The analysis business component system model (BCSM), including the BC diagram and a business component responsibility description. This model, as we saw in Chapter 5, is a living model; that is, the analysis model at one iteration is an enhancement of the requirement model, but it becomes the requirement model at the next iteration.

- The refined business process model (BPM), detailing and completing the initial process model defined at requirements to capture the behavioral aspects of the system.

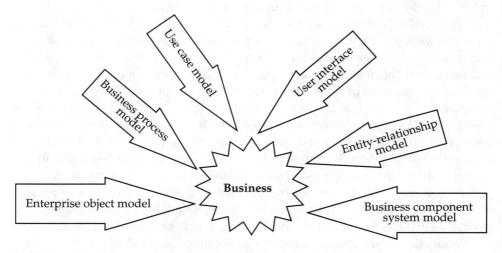

Figure 7.5   Modeling the business (software analyst point of view).

- The detailed use case model (UCM). As mentioned previously, in many projects—depending on the complexity of the problem space and on the maturity of the development organization—this may totally replace the BPM. The use case and business process models are collectively referred to as "process models."

- The enterprise object model (EOM) of the system, that is, an object-oriented model of the business. This is usually a complex set of models and documents, but as a rough first approximation, the term is used here to indicate the class diagram of the system.

- The user interface model (UIM). Even if mostly a prototype, it is useful to think of this as an executable model. It is jointly developed with the end users.

- The entity-relationship model (ERM). This model describes the conceptual view of the database. Many object-oriented practitioners do not see this model as an analysis deliverable; however, it can be successfully included in the analysis phase, directly reflecting the importance of the persistence aspects in the development of business systems.

These are different views on the same reality, that is, of the problem space corresponding to the business system being modeled. All these models contribute information required for the detailed test specifications for the business component system. At analysis even more than at requirement definition, it is useful to organize the deliverables around the components in the BCSM. For example, each deliverable related to the user interface is assigned to a specific component.

Enterprise Object Model versus Component Model

The enterprise object model (EOM) and the business component system model (BCSM) are two of the models used to describe a system. These two models are strongly related to each other, but they are at a different granularity and have different objectives and a different importance in the development lifecycle. They are *not* simply a refinement of each other, but rather two different and related points of view on an information system.

The EOM, usually together with the process model, is often considered to be the most important model for "understanding the business," and indeed a business model of the problem space, from the point of view of the software analyst, can be fully effected using a combination of a process model and an EOM. The BCSM, on the other hand, is the fundamental model of the information system—used for requirements analysis, project management, design, acquisition, reuse, and new development. At a simplified level, the EOM captures all the business concepts of the system, their main characteristics and structure, and their relationships; the BCSM is currently used mainly to show the components of the system.

Both the BCSM and the EOM derive from the same set of requirements, and in practice a project will generally consider one of the two first. We prefer to build the initial BCSM first, then use it to define the detail of the EOM. This has two main advantages: First, the EOM still describes the business but is cast into a "component shape." That is, the main diagram will show the focus classes and their support classes grouped together. Where a support class is used by more than one focus class, then it is associated with a specific focus class, thereby starting to reflect ownership by a specific business component (identified by the focus class). Second, it is common for some distribution aspects to become visible during requirements definition (business modeling) or in the early phases of analysis. The EOM has great difficulty in capturing such information, and it is often lost. The BCSM, on the other hand, can capture this very easily by annotating a business component with the tiers it will probably have. The information is not lost. This, in turn, can assist greatly with the development of the user workspace domain.

Organizations that have adopted object-oriented approaches will, on the other hand, have a tendency to address the EOM first. This approach presents a few risks because it tends to postpone component thinking and implicitly pushes toward thinking of components as packages of classes.

To think of components as packages constructed from a preexisting object model is a particularly widespread misconception. For example, Booch states, "A component typically represents the physical packaging of otherwise logical elements" [1998, p. 343]. Let us be clear: There is no way that the desired characteristics of autonomy can be achieved if a component is seen as just a matter of packaging preexisting software artifacts. Autonomy must be designed into the components, and the autonomy considerations must be an overriding concern of the entire development process in order to achieve the desired levels of independence, granularity, and reuse. Nevertheless, it is useful to think of each business component in the BCSM as *containing* a set of classes—as a form of package that starts life at analysis time, or possibly even before that.

Suppose that, for some reason, you start with, or are given, an enterprise object model (EOM) of the system. An EOM equates roughly to a software-less object-oriented model—a representation and description of the objects of the business often done for the purposes of better understanding the business rather than describing a software implementation of the business itself. The question is, how can we use an EOM to identify business components? Which patterns dictate which set of reusable analysis artifacts in the EOM are part of a given business component? The main concept used is the *focus* language class (introduced in Chapter 3, "The Distributed Component"), which is a grouping concept for classes in an EOM. Given the link between focus objects and business components, identifying focus objects corresponds quite closely to identifying business components. Consider Figure 7.6, which shows a simplified EOM on the left, with the three dark classes being focus objects. It can be seen that there are many dependencies between the classes. Using a grouping approach defined by the focus object concept, the right-hand side of the figure shows how three candidate business components are drawn around three groups of classes. Some of the classes are in more than one group. This implies that they will become support or other non-focus classes. Separating out the right-hand part of Figure 7.6 results in the three separate groups shown in Figure 7.7.

It can be seen that the high coupling of the EOM in Figure 7.6 has reduced markedly. This occurs because many of the dependencies, including all of the inheritance dependencies, have turned out to be contained within a business component, and so they are not visible outside. The lower part of Figure 7.7 shows a cleaned-up version of the upper part. Or, rather, it shows a BCSM.

The EOM is often flat. The position of the classes on a class diagram does not imply a layering, but rather it is a direct representation of the business reality in which all the relationships between business concepts are captured and described. The use of inheritance does provide a kind of hierarchy, but it does not correspond to the functional layering of the business component approach, it tends to be of low granularity, and it is class-specific (rather than system-wide as in the case of the BCSM). On the other hand, the BCSM is explicitly and purposely layered.

Usually the EOM is mainly data driven and not behavioral driven, meaning that it is mostly a static and structural description of the business, relying on process and use case models to describe the behavioral aspects. Under this assumption, the EOM is not the best model to identify the process business components. Also, there are often no focus objects in the EOM for utility business components. There are focus objects in the EOM for entity business components, and there are focus processes in the BPM for process business components. Utility business components correspond to centers of reusability, and they are usually only support concepts as far as the object-oriented model of the system is concerned. Hence, as discussed in Chapter 11, other approaches may be needed to identify utility and process components.

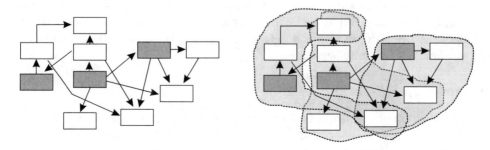

Figure 7.6 From EOM to BCSM (part 1).

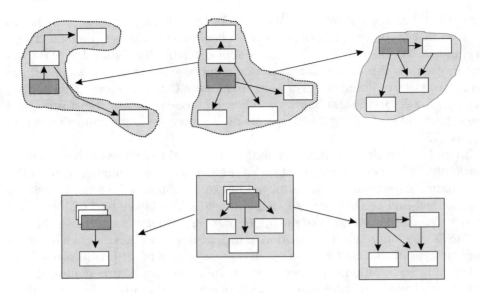

Figure 7.7 From EOM to BCSM (part 2).

Design

At the design phase, the focus shifts decidedly toward the business component. At this point, the business component system model allows design and development to be assigned to small teams (typically two to three persons), each one responsible for a specific business component.

The initial design of a business component includes the identification, at each distribution tier, of its constituent distributed components. Each business component is further specified and designed, as shown in Figure 4.14 and reproduced for convenience in Figure 7.8, in terms of its interfaces, the internal object model of its EDCs and WDCs, its persistence model, its user interface, and, very importantly, its dependencies.

The specification of a business component can be seen as a combination of an *external specification*, a context (in particular a *dependency specification*), and an *internal specification*. While a convenient way to illustrate the design phase, this breakdown is not as clear in practice because in many cases the three cannot be cleanly separated.

External Specification

The external specification of a business component is the set of software artifacts required by the user of that business component (as illustrated in Figure 7.9). The strong focus on autonomy makes it important for the surface area of the external specification to be as small as possible. The following heuristic can

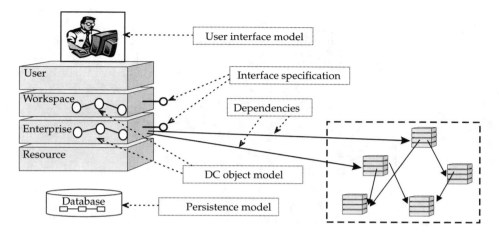

Figure 7.8 Specification of a business component.

be used to determine whether a deliverable is part of the external specification: A deliverable of a business component *Foo* belongs to the external specification if a change in this deliverable directly impacts any of the business components using *Foo*.

The external specification is the most important aspect of a business component's definition. The main feature of this specification is the exact definition of the business component's EDC and WDC interfaces, which, of course, implies the determination of exactly which DCs are required by the business component. The user interface specification also belongs to the external specification, as well as the description of any functional aspects and potential uses of the business component.

Each operation of a component's interface needs to be specified in terms of its signature, which includes the operation name, parameters, and the business data types of these parameters. Interface definitions may also include pre- and post-conditions, invariants, errors that may be raised together with their informational messages, the meaning and use of each parameter, events published, and any functional or external constraints on the implementation of operations.

The technical and application architectures often define a set of default interfaces that each distributed component must or should deliver (see Chapter 12). Hence during design, it is mainly the additional business interfaces that are defined.

The external specification also includes the test specification for each interface and each operation, with the testing preconditions (including the initial state of the database) and postconditions, expected results, and expected state in which the database should be left. This may turn out to be somewhat time-consuming for entity and process components.

The exact set of external specification deliverables is project-specific, and it

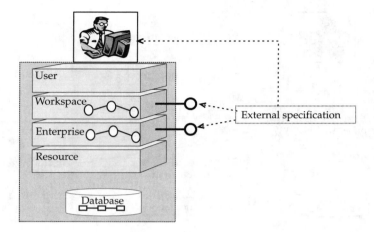

Figure 7.9   External specification point of view.

will depend, for example, on the level of formality required by the specific activity, as exemplified in Table 7.2.

Dependency Specification

Specification of dependencies is a critical step in the specification of a business component, and it consists of the identification of those interfaces required of other business components—that is, the identification of dependencies on other business components. This also, and importantly, provides a definition of the participants in the business component's BC assembly (see Figure 7.10). The dependency specification is not considered part of the external specification because a change in the list of dependencies of a component *Foo* may not directly affect a component using the component *Foo*. Neither is it included in the internal design specification, which is focused more on the definition of DC internals.

The dependency specification includes a defined dependency list, together with identification of the exact interfaces and operations required. Also, each dependency may be illustrated by an inter-component sequence diagram specifying the flow of the processing.

Internal Specification

When the focus shifts to the internal design of a business component, most of the externally-visible decisions have already been taken. The internal design may include any kind of model the designer believes useful to describe the business component and its distributed components, but it usually includes at least

Table 7.2 Activity versus Specification

ACTIVITY	ACTIVITY OBJECTIVE	EXTERNAL SPECIFICATION
Prototyping	Risk management, for example, a technical or functional proof of concept. Not necessarily targeting completeness and correctness.	Definition of interface signatures, with some high-level textual explanation and maybe examples of how the interface can be used.
Industry-level development	Large-scale development, eventually with detached teams, but all working within the same architectures and targeting completeness and correctness.	Full definition of interfaces, plus detailed test cases as acceptance tests.
COTS components	Definition of the external specification of a component that will be used by another team to assemble an integrated system.	The industry-level development specification plus detailed specification of interface semantics and possible inclusion of certain detailed internal specifications.

the internal object model of the distributed components and the persistence model, as illustrated in Figure 7.11.

DC Object Model

The DC object model is intended to describe the internal design of the DC. Depending on the level of detail desired, it can consist of a set of deliverables. The various techniques used in normal object-oriented modeling may all be

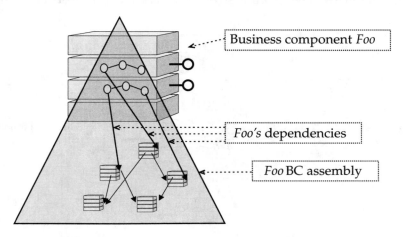

Business component *Foo*

Foo's dependencies

Foo BC assembly

Figure 7.10 Dependencies and BC assembly.

used here. Note the huge complexity reduction due to the strong black-box/white-box component concepts: This is a well-scoped modeling and design issue—the implementation design of well-defined interfaces. It is also like the design of a rather small and simple application. An additional reduction in complexity derives from the existence of clear design patterns for DC internals, as described in Chapter 3.

It is often possible to reuse many parts of the EDC's object model in that of a WDC. This is especially so where the WDCs and EDCs are implemented using the same technology. In this latter case, various aspects of the implementation can also be reused.

We saw in Chapter 3 how EDCs are usually the most important part of each business component. Focusing thus on the enterprise tier, the minimal deliverable is the EDC business language class diagram (the kinds of classes that could be included were presented in Chapter 3). Some of the other deliverables that could be expected to be found in an EDC object model could include the following:

- A description of the overall design approach, objectives, and alternatives for this specific DC.

- One or more intra-DC sequence diagram(s), typically used to describe the interaction between business LCs and to illustrate particular processing scenarios within the DC. It is usually very useful to clearly separate intra-DC from the previously mentioned inter-DC sequence diagrams.

- A detailed description of the business and technical language classes involved in the class diagram, including a detailed description of their methods, signatures, and relevance, a detailed description of each method parameter, preconditions and postconditions, information on any implementation expectations, and so on. Pragmatically, the level of precision and

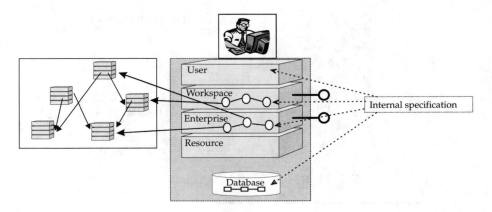

Figure 7.11 Internal design specification point of view.

formality of LC method specifications is less important than that for DC interface operations, given the limited visibility of the class-level interfaces.

- Pseudo-code, scenarios, or any other deliverable useful to specify what is needed to implement the most relevant processing aspects and business rules.

Component Persistence Model

The persistence model for the component usually includes a persistence object model and/or a relational data model that describes the data storage accessed by the EDC through its resource tier. Each project will choose its preferred approach, and the various options and their advantages and disadvantages are described in Chapter 12. We have a strong bias (the reasons for which are explained in Chapter 12) for defining the relational data model and then generating the persistence object model from it, and this is the case assumed in the next section, "Implementation." The design of the relational data model can be done following well-known database modeling techniques (for example, see [Date 1995]).

Implementation

During the implementation phase, the functional developer provides, according to the DC object model, the implementation of the interfaces specified at design. The focus is on the internals of a business component and of its distributed components. Usually, a business component is part of a BC assembly and has dependent components. If so, implementing a distributed component that is not at the very bottom of the BCSM requires deliverables from dependent components, typically at least their proxy for proper compilation and their runtime for testing and execution.

For example, consider implementing an *Invoice* component that is at the top of an *Invoice* BC assembly {*Invoice, CurrencyBook, NumberGenerator, Notes*}. Compiling and linking the *Invoice* component, to say nothing of formal testing, requires deliverables, at least at some level of completion, from the dependent components, for example, *CurrencyBook* and *NumberGenerator*. Interestingly, this statement implies that the implementation of the invoice component corresponds in reality to the integration of a part of the system, that is, the *Invoice* BC assembly. This has important consequences on how CBD projects need to be managed, which is the subject of Chapter 10.

In line with business component approach assumptions, the implementation phase should consist of a series of quick iterations, in which many of the technical and architectural details are taken care by the development environment. The implementation phase consists mainly of implementing the business language classes that realize the business function of the various distributed components and of initial testing of those classes and of the DC that contains them.

Examples of sets of activities within this phase that have been used in real-world large-scale projects can be identified. The following is one such set, and also illustrates what a typical component-based development environment set-up should provide for the functional developer.

1. The first step could be to establish the execution environment for the DC to be built, for example, the *Foo* EDC. This can be achieved by implementing a testing DC for *Foo* (as discussed in the next section "Validation and Verification") together with the *Foo* DC itself realized as a component faker. A component faker is an extremely light implementation of a component—either automatically generated or a configuration of a generic DC that simulates the behavior of *Foo* without actually executing any business logic or reading any data from the database. The faker DC, when invoked, could return data read from a simple developer-provided data file, which contains simulated data compatible with the return parameters for each *Foo* operation. This step is really a preparatory step that ensures that *Foo* will be easily testable. This approach also allows any user of *Foo* to perform a "faked integration," meaning an integration that relies on a "faked" copy of *Foo*, but where the user is able to use the actual *Foo* interfaces.

2. The objective of step 2 is to reach, as fast as possible, a state where the whole system is up and running from end to end—at least in an initial nonrobust prototype form. To do this, and relying on the relational data model and the component persistence model, the developer could generate *Foo*'s resource tier code, its proxy, and the persistence language classes needed for maintenance-oriented interface operations. In a properly set-up component-based development environment, this could go as far as automatically generating a default *Foo* implementation, using the interface specification, on one hand, and the persistence specification, on the other. This default implementation would be a prototype, not usable for any serious integration because obviously it does not have any real business logic or robust code. It would be sufficient to replace the faked component of the previous step with one that could do simple data entry on a real test database. Where the development environment does not provide for such automatic generation of a simple (and executable) default implementation, this step would consist of the implementation and testing of the *Foo*'s main maintenance interfaces, with little if any attention paid to the robustness of the internals. When this is completed, a start can be made on the continuous integration approach.

3. Relying on their interface specification, this step provides a simple implementation of the calls made by *Foo* to its dependent components. The developer could rely on faked versions of these dependent components should their usable implementations not yet be available.

4. At this point, by rapid iterative development and continuous integration, the implementation of *Foo* is moved forward through iterative removal of the faking aspects, by actually integrating all the dependent components, and by completion of all internal code according to the design specification and satisfying other constraints such as coding guidelines. At each step, it is possible to compile, link, and execute the *Foo* DC and its BC assembly.

5. While the various DCs composing a BC are being addressed in the way described previously, the implementation of the main user interface events and subsequently the end-to-end test from screen to the database can take place. This provides for all the main aspects of the business component to be in place.

6. Any interface not addressed previously can be added to the business component by iteratively implementing it according to the project priorities, for example, driven by the user interface or by the requirements of other components.

7. This step involves progressively bringing the whole component to the desired level of quality and robustness and performing all the required tests. As for any technology, the code required to implement all the internal error handling and exceptional conditions may easily be more than five times the amount of code required for the "normal" paths.

At this point it should be clear that the implementation of the distributed components and business components, the distributed component testing, and the business component testing should not really be treated separately in a component-based development. The description of the development lifecycle as a v-cycle is thus a simplification, valid at a certain level of abstraction but not correctly representing all the complexity of a real-life development.

Finally, the previous implementation steps require the support of an appropriate development environment. Given the clear architectural layering of the business component approach, this development environment, based on experience to date, is an achievable objective. Such an environment also allows the project manager, if so desired, to see design, implementation, and testing as a continuous flow, in which design specification can be executed very early on, through the generation of fakers and of default implementations, so providing immediate feedback to the designer, providing a strong check for completeness and correctness, and supporting continuous and iterative implementation.

Validation and Verification

This section discusses the validation and verification[5] of a rapid system development process, including the review process and test execution. As noted previously, in a mature organization test specification occurs during the construction phases, and is part of the preparation for validation and verification rather than part of the validation and verification itself.

The cost of fixing an issue or error in the lifecycle becomes higher the further down the lifecycle it is identified. Figure 7.12 illustrates the approximate relative costs of fixing an issue at the various points in the development lifecycle; similar graphs can be found in many publications, for example [Humphrey 1995]. Indeed, successful projects very often install a rigorous review process of the various deliverables of the project in order to intercept as many issues as possible as early as possible in the lifecycle. In a system with strict requirements for high quality, literally all deliverables should be properly reviewed; however, such a level of reviewing can be harmful in dynamic projects, and there is a fine trade-off between the need to keep the process as dynamic and flexible as possible and the need to intercept issues early and so retain control of the process. The exact level of reviews must be carefully matched against the needs of the exploratory nature of software development, especially for transitional organizations.

Reviews

The traditional distinction between different kinds of review[6]—including functional reviews, design reviews, technical reviews, architectural reviews, and process-oriented reviews—is still very applicable to components. In general, each development lifecycle phase should terminate with a review, as illustrated in Figure 7.13. Furthermore, the advantage of a business component view of the world for the review process is that the domain to be reviewed is nicely partitioned into well-scoped parts (the business components), and the interaction between the parts is easily traceable and controllable given the clean interfaces between them and the strong focus on dependency management. The business component has proved to be a good level of granularity for design reviews in

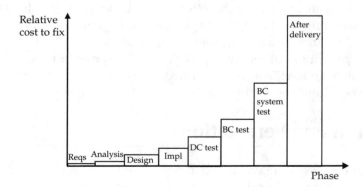

Figure 7.12 Fix cost versus development lifecycle phase.

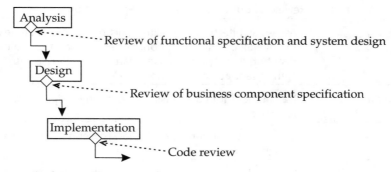

Figure 7.13   Examples of reviews.

that it provides enough but not excessive material for a single cost-effective review. The distributed component granularity level is more appropriate for code reviews.

In this section, three examples of reviews that have been found to be particularly useful are briefly described. These are the review of a business component specification from a functional point of view (Table 7.3) and from an architectural point of view (Table 7.4), and a code review of part of a business component implementation—the EDC—from a functional point of view (Table 7.5). "Functional" here refers to the objective of assessing the correctness and

Table 7.3   Functional Review of a Business Component Specification

Objective	Assess the functional correctness and completeness of the given business component specification relative to a given scope, feature list, market requirement description, and other functional documentation.
Suggested time	Ten to 20 minutes for each feature or for each business rule per reviewer, depending on the business component's functional category.
Input	Business component specification (covering all the aspects of design).
Constraints	Project scope document, feature list, market requirement description, and other existing documentation
Tools and prerequisites	Functional domain experience, high-level understanding of business component approach, ability to read a business component specification.
Exit criteria	Review of each feature and business rule assigned to the subject business component.
Output	List of issues (including questions) on the subject business component.

Table 7.4   Architectural Review of Business Component Specification

Objective	Assess architectural and extra-functional appropriateness of the overall business component design and of its individual distributed components, with particular regard to the component persistence model.
Suggested time	Half an hour for each business component operation per reviewer.
Input	Business component specification (covering all the aspects of design).
Constraints	Technical architecture, application architecture, and project management architecture guidelines; design guidelines.
Tools and prerequisites	Knowledge of distributed systems architectures and design, detailed understanding of the business component approach.
Exit criteria	Review of each EDC method assigned to the subject business component.
Output	List of issues (including questions) on the subject business component.

completeness of the function, whereas an architectural review addresses such aspects as conformance with mandated architecture principles, good design principles, and extra-functional requirements.

"Suggested time" in the table refers to the time taken by an individual reviewer to understand and prepare comments on an item. Process business components normally take a longer time than the average because they not only have more features but also more complex features. Utility business components normally take a shorter-than-average time.

The review example in Table 7.5 was chosen to illustrate a further advantage of the business component approach, namely the ability for a functional domain expert to carry out code reviews. An obvious prerequisite for any code review is for the reviewer to be able to read code. Given the strong focus on architectural viewpoints, the source code implementing the internals of a distributed component tends to be very readable and directly related to functional aspects. This can result in it becoming feasible to have functional experts review the source code from a functional perspective—especially because it is much easier to learn to read code than to write it. We have been successful in rapidly training functional, nontechnical people (for example, a domain expert working on the system definition from a functional viewpoint) in the art of reading DC code. This appears counter-intuitive, but it has proven extremely powerful and cost-effective in a number of situations.

Over time, an organization should evolve a reference checklist for reviews, as very briefly illustrated in Table 7.6 for the architectural review.

Table 7.5   Functional Review of EDC Implementation

Objective	Assess functional correctness and completeness of the distributed component code relative to a given scope, feature list, market requirement description, business component specification, and other functional documentation. The review includes the persistence aspects.
Suggested time	Half an hour for each DC operation per reviewer.
Input	Source code.
Constraints	Project scope document, feature list, market requirement description, business component and distributed component specification, and other existing documentation.
Tools and prerequisites	High-level understanding of the business component approach, ability to read a business component specification, ability to read DC functional code.
Exit criteria	Review of the source code implementing each feature and business rule assigned to the subject distributed component.
Output	List of issues and questions on the subject distributed component.

Testing

In a business component approach, many of the traditional principles of testing[7] acquire a new flavor. For example, the traditional distinction between unit testing and integration testing is not appropriate: Testing an entity business component or process business component corresponds to a certain level of integration testing when viewed from the BC assembly perspective, but it can

Table 7.6   Example of Architectural Review Checklist

SUBJECT	WHAT TO CHECK
Technical Architecture Point of View	
Error handling	Does the error handling cleanly separate business errors from communication and database errors?
Persistence	Is the persistence layer properly isolated?
…	…
Application Architecture Point of View	
Global principles	Is the noncircularity principle respected?
Interface implementation	Is there any business logic in the interface implementation?
…	…

be considered unit testing when viewed from the point of view of clients of the business component. Because this happens at all layers of the component diagram, it becomes misleading to adopt the terms "unit" versus "integration" testing. Hence, given the component-centric approach, testing is organized and presented in terms of the levels of component granularity, as in the v-cycle illustrated in Figure 7.1. Furthermore, given the strong focus on autonomy across the whole development lifecycle, it will not come as a surprise that one of the big advantages of a component approach is the ability to individually test components before releasing them to the remaining parts of the system. This is further supported by the use of a set of component-specific techniques, which includes component fakers.

In any development approach, the cost of testing can be extremely high, both in terms of test specification and of test execution, to the extent that it can overshadow the costs of construction. It therefore becomes very important to optimize the testing process—not by doing less testing but by doing it more efficiently—and to balance this with the costs of not testing. The testing framework set-up is as important as the development set-up, and it should allow for an effortless repetition of any facet of a given test, directly supporting the motto "test early, test often." Testing costs can be thought of as 50 percent specification and 50 percent execution, assuming that the costs of execution are paid only once. This emphasizes the importance of easy and automatic regression testing.

Every DC executable should be delivered with a way to test it automatically. This can be achieved in several ways, including the provision of a generic testing DC, the provision of a specific test DC, or third-party test tools. These three solutions all have advantages and disadvantages. We have a bias for the specific testing DC approach, where, in a mature and optimized development, much of the implementation of the testing DC can be done through generation and reuse. This approach can deliver the highest levels of quality because a detailed test of a DC may require replicating whole business scenarios.

Automating testing is fairly simple for utility business components, but it can become extremely complicated and require a detailed database set-up for entity and process business components. Indeed, an ability to regression test business components and distributed components usually requires having the database represent a specified business state at the beginning of each test. Automatic regression testing hence requires not only the ability to easily and rapidly reset the database to a predefined status, but also the ability to automatically compare both the results of test operations and the end-of-test database state with a predefined "correct" outcome. The potentially complex activities of resetting the database to a predefined state and comparing database states are made easier if the "islands of data" concept is adopted for component-based development, since the database is then particularly well scoped.

To enable iterative development, it is important to be able to automatically regression test the system as a whole. This requires that techniques adopted for regression testing individual components can be easily and rapidly integrated at the system level. Ideally, a system-level regression test should be initiated with a single mouse click or command, which should reset the database for each individual component, run the proper sequence of individual tests, automatically check the individual tests results, and clearly report any incorrect result.

We now move to a brief discussion of testing of the distributed component and the business component. In addition, some component-specific aspects of a quality plan are described. There are, of course, other kinds of testing including the testing of language classes, performance and scalability testing (including volume and stress testing), concurrency testing, acceptance testing (often performed as part of the hand-off to the customer or to another team), installation testing, usability testing, and random (or subjective) testing. These are not separately addressed because they are not specific to a component-based development.

The main terminology used in the following discussion is shown in Figure 7.14 (which focuses on the right side of the v-cycle and where "UI" means user interface).

Distributed Component

In the business component approach, there is a need to extend the traditional concept of test coverage. In a DC, test coverage can be seen at two very different levels:

Intra-DC. For example, we define a *language class method coverage test* to perform the testing of all the language class methods inside a DC, making sure that each is invoked at least once.

Inter-DC. For example, we define a *distributed component operation coverage test* to perform the testing of all the operations of a given DC's interface, making sure each is invoked at least once.

In many projects with average quality requirements, to focus formal tests and coverage testing on the inter-DC aspects brings satisfactory results at a good cost/benefit ratio. Consequently, as a default approach in case of limited

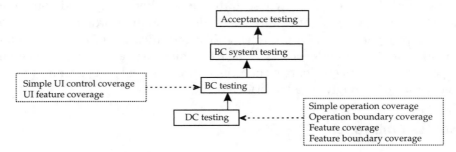

Figure 7.14   Testing process terminology.

resources, we tend to invest the money in an appropriate review process and in formal testing down to the inter-DC level, and we minimize intra-DC testing. In the following, the term "DC testing" refers to testing a DC exclusively through its run-time interface. A thorough DC test, including all its interfaces and operations, is very cost-effective in helping ensure high quality levels. There are several levels of coverage in DC testing, including the following:

Simple operation coverage. Each operation in each interface is executed at least once.

Operation boundary coverage. Each operation is called at least for all boundary conditions.

Feature coverage. Each documented feature in the feature list of the DC is tested at least once. This translates into a set of formal test cases for the interfaces.

Feature boundary coverage. Each documented feature of the DC is tested at least once for every boundary condition.

Each testing level usually includes the previous levels. For example, a thorough feature boundary testing will in most case also address all the other levels of coverage. The various levels of testing are usually performed by different parts of a development organization. For example, the DC developers could execute the simple coverage and boundary testing, while functional experts might carry out feature testing.

From a testing point of view, each DC can be thought of as a client/server microsystem in which the proxy is the client and the DC implementation is the server. It is useful to apply the separation-of-concerns principle to testing; that is, as far as possible the server is initially tested independently from the proxy. The extent to which this can be done depends largely on the technology: For example, a probe supporting informal tests of the server can be developed without using the proxy. This is made significantly easier when tagged data is used for communication between DCs. Because the proxy is expected to be entirely generated, testing the server in isolation in a single address space or on a single machine can eliminate the many issues that arise when distributed communications have not yet been fully implemented. It is still important, however, to perform a proxy-level test before release. The specification of this test should be identical to the server-level test, aside from the possible explicit inclusion in the specification of tagged data structures. A proxy-level test is normally specified in terms of strongly-typed interfaces only.

Business Component

Having tested the individual distributed components, few important things remain to be tested at the business component level: For example, the distributed component testing would not normally have covered user interface testing. The following levels of coverage are useful at the business component level:

Simple user interface controls coverage. The implementation of every control (widget) and every field on the user interface is executed. This consists of entering data in each field of each panel that is part of the BC assembly user interface. Normally both mouse-oriented and mouse-less operations are covered. Simple user-interface controls coverage tests the basic functionality of the user interface rather than business functionality. It does not necessarily access data, is normally performed by an analyst, and is often a very rapid test. For example, testing a large system with perhaps 200 panels at this level of coverage can take as little as two days, depending on the user model implemented. The exit criterion is for each field is to be exercised at least once.

User-interface feature coverage. Each feature of the business component is executed at least once, from the point of view of the user interface. An analyst performs this (without necessarily using a written test case), and the activity could take on the order of five minutes per feature. In a mature and optimized organization, testing will be supported by a user-interface record and playback tool that automates UI-level regression testing. Such tools become more important where a user-interface infrastructure allows business component user tiers to be mixed and matched, so that several different business component u-tier constructs can all appear in the same window, for example, as multiple property pages on a single property sheet.

Quality Plan

Before concluding this section, it is worth commenting on the quality plan. In order to build a quality plan, quality requirements must be carefully weighed against their costs and against how mature the development capability set-up is and the extent to which requirements are understood. For example, there is little point in thorough functional testing in early iterations when requirements are discovered during the iterations themselves. Table 7.7 gives an example of the decision-making process relating to the kinds of tests that should be included in a test plan. Decisions are also influenced by the category of business component (where "U" stands for utility business component, "E" stands for entity business component, and "P" stands for process business component).

Iterations

This section addresses the iterative nature of the development lifecycle in the business component approach. An explicit objective of the development

Table 7.7 Reviews and Tests versus Quality Targets

	PROTO-TYPING	INDUSTRY-LEVEL DEVELOPMENT	COTS COMPONENTS
(Other reviews…)			UEP
BC spec functional review	EP	UEP	UEP
BC architectural review	E	EP	UEP
DC code functional review		EP	UEP
(More reviews…)			UEP
Random informal test	UEP	UEP	UEP
Simple operation test	UEP	UEP	UEP
Operation boundary test		UEP	UEP
Feature test	UEP	UEP	UEP
Feature boundary test		UEP	UEP
Simple operation test	UEP	UEP	UEP
Simple UI control test		P	UEP
UI feature test		UEP	UEP
…			UEP

process is to support quick iterations and concurrent development. This objective is directly supported by the focus on autonomous development of business components. Development iterations can be seen in terms of individual DCs, or of business components and BC assemblies, or at the level of a system-level component (SLC). As an example, consider two levels of iterative development—iterative business component development within a single SLC release and iterative SLC development—as follows:

1. Iterative and concurrent development of business components *within* an individual system release. Within any particular system release, individual business components and each distributed component are developed iteratively and concurrently. This means that, if the system release is just one iteration in the life of the system, this particular iteration contains a set of BC-level iterations. This is illustrated in Figure 7.15, where "A" indicates analysis, "D" design, "I" implementation, and "T" test; and where Process, Entity, and Utility correspond, respectively, to the process layer, entity layer, and utility layer.

   The figure shows two BC-level iterations within a single system-level iteration. It also implies that any business component in the utility layer may be analyzed, designed, and even coded and tested before any work starts on entity-layer business components. Utility business components have many characteristics that make them particularly suited for autonomous development. Their requirements are generally easily understood without a broad business domain knowledge, and, hence, a start can be made on gathering their requirements while those of the system as a whole are still being finalized. Given their minimal dependency on other parts of the system, the whole utility layer can often be developed, tested, and released independently of the remaining business functionality. This enables bottom-up development even in a large-scale system, once the technical architecture, the application architecture, and the project management architecture have been defined. In this sense, an organization could start the component-level and system-level development lifecycles concurrently.

The same principle applies to some extent between the entity and the process layer. Furthermore, once a first internal release (a release to another part of the development organization) of the utility layer has occurred, in order to enable proper implementation and testing of the entity and process layers, the project may start development of the second release of the utility layer without the first BC-level iteration of the entity and process layers necessarily having to complete.

2. Iterative and concurrent development of system-level releases. An efficient production capability will support not only internally iterative building of a single system-level release (as illustrated in Figure 7.15), but also the iterative build of different system-level releases, as shown in Figure 7.16, with different iterations starting concurrently or at least overlapping for some extended period of time. The figure illustrates that, to some extent, work on a subsequent external project release can start before the previous release has completed.

The iterations incrementally build on business components at a lower functional layer. This has various advantages: For example, components lower down in the hierarchy will tend to be very stable and of high quality

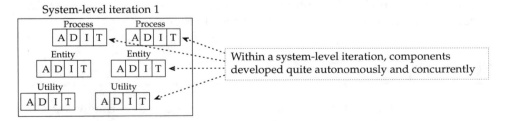

Figure 7.15 Iterative business component development within a system-release.

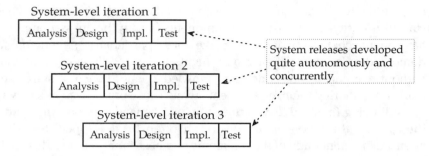

Figure 7.16 Iterative system releases.

after a few iterations, leaving the development to focus on the quality of smaller pieces of the system.

Iterative development is a powerful concept, but it can easily become a management nightmare, especially in a large-scale development. The iterative nature of the development process, at the various levels of granularity, requires an appropriate project management architecture and development environment setup to scale up to a larger-than-10 team, as will be discussed in Chapter 10.

The previously described levels of concurrent and iterative development have always been desirable, but they are now directly supported by the business component approach. All the parts (the business components and distributed components) of the system have such levels of relative independence that it becomes technically and architecturally feasible to launch concurrent system-level and BC-level iterations, pushing the rapid development of the system to extreme limits. The limitation to concurrency and numbers of iterations becomes the ability of the organization to properly staff and manage the project.

It is useful to think of the various iterations following what we call the "T-model." The project is organized as a set of iterations progressively larger in scope, where there is a relatively wide functional coverage at the top end of the development lifecycle, but each iteration of the system addresses a relatively narrow slice of the project down through the lifecycle (see Figure 7.17). The choice of slices is governed by risk assessment considerations. At each iteration, both the cross and the stem of the "T" cover a progressively wider functional area and a deeper part of the development lifecycle.

Summary

The business component approach includes a methodology framework and a set of default manufacturing processes that can be composed to address the various needs of developing organizations. The basic manufacturing processes are rapid component development, system architecting and assembly, and fed-

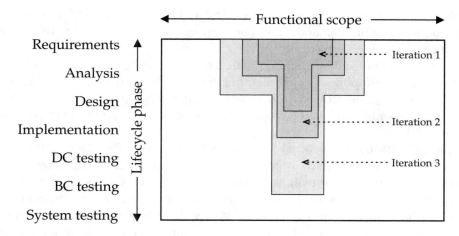

Figure 7.17   Example of T-iterations.

eration architecting and assembling. An important manufacturing process, obtained by combination of the rapid component development and of the system architecting and assembly processes, is rapid system development, which both covers the needs of a transitional organization and addresses concurrent building of a system and its constituent business components.

We can also view the development process in terms not only of different development processes for the different levels of component granularity, but also of different kinds of development processes for the different functional layers. For example, the nature of a utility business component allows for a differently optimized development process than that of a process business component.

The 10 golden characteristics of the component development process are: being a component-centric approach; being at the same time an architecture-centric approach; focus on component autonomy as an overriding concern; the particular approach to collaborations and consequent dependency management; the iterative nature of the development; high levels of development concurrency; the continuous integration approach required by the previous two characteristics; direct support for risk-driven development; the strong focus on reuse; and that the component development should generally be approached with the same mindset as good product development.

For a rapid system development, the construction phases (which include requirements, analysis, design, and implementation) are organized around business components, as regards approach, deliverables, and teams. For example, each feature is assigned to a particular owning business component. Requirements and analysis focus on specifying the functional aspects of the system and the collaborations between components. The external specification, dependency specification, and the internal design of business components and distributed components are the focus of design. Implementation of a distributed component can be seen and should be managed, at any layer of the BCSM, as a continuous integration activity.

The validation and verification aspects, including reviews and testing, are organized by component as are all other activities in the development lifecycle. Testing a component often equates to testing the component assembly. Real-world successful processes have an iterative nature that can be described using a T-model.

Armed with the conceptual framework presented in Part One of the book, and with the development process concepts introduced in this chapter, we can now discuss the three remaining parts of setting up a business component factory. Chapter 8 discusses the technical architecture and the business component virtual machine and Chapter 9 the application architecture required to produce industrial-strength business components and business component systems. Finally in Chapter 10 we conclude the factory set-up by discussing what is required to scale the production to very large teams.

Endnotes

1   For further reading, see [Sommerville 1989] for software engineering, [Henderson-Sellers 1994] for software lifecycles, and [Booch 1999] for object-oriented methodologies.

2   The methodology framework and manufacturing processes use, when appropriate for a component-based development, UML 1.3.

3   As per our discussion of Tkach's complexity gap in Chapter 1, "Component-Based Development."

4   For more on requirements engineering, not specific to the business component approach, see [Sommerville 1997].

5   For more information on validation and verification, see [Boehm 1981] or [Sommerville 1989].

6   See [Hollocker 1990] for a useful presentation on software reviews.

7   For further readings on testing, see [Myers 1979] or [Kaner 1996].

CHAPTER 8

Technical Architecture

Previous chapters have assumed that the functional developer is concerned only with those things that *directly* implement the business solution. Examples of such things are designing month-end account balancing; calculating sales tax for a given customer who orders a specific product sold under a specified promotion; defining the vendor-related data items needed to create an invoice; and designing the presentation of, and end-user interaction with, a view of a vendor. That is, we have assumed that the functional developer enjoys a view of the development world that exposes only the design and implementation of direct business logic. Technical considerations that are necessary to build business systems, such as the design and implementation of transactions, thread management, GUI complexities, multithreading, persistence, and so on, should be hidden.

Such a view of the development world is not just a nice-to-have view; it is an important part of our vision of reducing time-to-market and development costs by an order of magnitude. Practitioners who are familiar with the fine detail of building functional code directly on today's ORBs know how there is a myriad of technical complexities in developing distributed computer systems. The functional developer does not need to be exposed to them, but rather should be provided, at each development stage, with a separation layer; that is, an environment that hides technical complexity and supports portability. We call the set of concepts behind such an environment the *technical architecture* of the business component factory, and we define it as the architectural viewpoint concerned with the component execution environment, the development tools, and any other technical capabilities required to develop and run a component-based system.

For a business component factory, the technical architecture is the set of architectural principles, models, and design patterns that defines an environment in which technical complexities, at all phases of development, are hidden from the functional developer. Having defined the conceptual framework in Part 1, and various aspects of the development process that guide manufacturing in Chapter 7, "The Development Process," addressing the technical architecture viewpoint is the first step in building the component factory.

The objective of this chapter then is to illustrate the various aspects concerned in the technical set-up of the component factory. The chapter is organized in the following sections:

- An introduction to the main *concepts* relevant for the technical architecture. This focuses on what the technical architecture viewpoint covers, on the portability issue, and on some of the technical alternatives in implementing the separation layer discussed in this chapter and in Chapter 3, "The Distributed Component."

- The *technical core*—the underlying run-time technical capabilities that derive from the requirements of the functional developer's programming model. It hides technical computational complexities, such as component activation, threading, and memory management, from the functional developer.

- The run-time *services and facilities*. Numerous design problems are met when building a distributed business system. Many of these are computationally complex, and they include such things as persistence, transactions, and event management. Often the same solution pattern can be used for many different implementations. In order to avoid exposing their inherent complexities to every functional developer, they must be supported by the technical architecture as a defined set of services and facilities, which hide business system complexities from the functional developer.

- The *extended integrated development environment*—the set of tools, development environments, compilers, repositories, associated services, and so forth required to develop a component-based system while maintaining the functional developer's desired level of abstraction.

Throughout this chapter, the scenario illustrated in Figure 5.1—an invoice management business component system—is used as a framework for developing the various arguments. Also, this chapter uses the following distinction: A *functional DC* is one that is implemented by a functional developer and that directly addresses business-oriented concerns. A *technical DC* is one that makes use of the DC implementation technology to implement some technical consideration that helps hide technical complexities and so makes the life of the functional developer that much easier.

Concepts

The implementation of the technical architecture should provide the functional developer with a separation layer—that is, an environment that hides technical complexity and supports portability at each development stage. And it should provide this separation layer according to the functional developer programming model discussed in Chapter 3. The set of concepts behind such an environment is the technical architecture. An implementation of such a complexity-hiding environment is called a *business component virtual machine*, and it is presented in the next section. The following sections address two important conceptual aspects of the business component virtual machine: namely, *portability* and *implementing the separation layer*.

Business Component Virtual Machine

The business component virtual machine[1] is defined as follows:

> A business component virtual machine (BCVM) is an implementation of the business component technical architecture.

A virtual machine is an environment that hides the nature of the underlying environment from a user and that is aimed at making the use of that underlying environment an order of magnitude more simple. Today, perhaps the best-known example of a virtual machine is the Java VM, defined as "an imaginary machine that is implemented by emulating it in software on a real machine" [SunSite 1999]. This is a complete target run-time environment for people writing Java compilers, and it hugely simplifies the portability problem (among other things). Another virtual machine is the DOS Command Prompt in Windows 98, which simplifies the running of a DOS program on the Windows 98 operating system.

The term "virtual machine" is used in a similar manner, but we extend the term to cover all the aspects that are needed to allow a functional developer to manufacture components focusing on the concerns of its pertinence. A hallmark of a virtual machine is that, for a given area of concern, it provides a complete environment that hides or hugely simplifies the underlying environment. As we shall see, the BCVM provides the functional developer with this characteristic. Indeed, the BCVM supports a business component developer over the development lifecycle and across distribution tiers.

Figure 8.1 illustrates the concepts that together make up the BCVM. The technical core addresses what is required by an individual distributed component at run-time, while services and facilities address what is required for distributed components and business components to properly collaborate. It is in the area of services and facilities that technical DCs are typically found. The technical core, together with services and facilities, provide an integrated execution system for DCs and for business components. They make extensive use of a chosen set of underlying enabling middleware, including component implementation technologies and, not shown in the figure, DBMSs, transaction managers, and so forth. Because they make up the run-time part of the BCVM, there is often a need to refer to them as a single entity—what the functional developer programmer assumes will be there at run-time. For this reason, the two together are named component execution environment (CEE).

The extended integrated development environment represents the development-time support. The dream of an integrated development environment supporting rapid development has existed for probably 30 years. Although implemented for environments such as transaction processing in the past, it has been technically feasible for distributed components only perhaps in the last 10 years, and only recently it has become not only technically feasible, but also economically viable.

Finally, the figure also shows where the concept of a "technical infrastructure"—a term used elsewhere in the book to refer broadly to some underlying middleware, whether component-oriented or not—fits in: The technical infrastructure within the business component approach is the CEE.

Consistent with the rapid system development process outlined in Chapter 7, the focus of this chapter will be on the BCVM as something that supports the design, build, deployment, and running of business components. Software technology companies produce commodity products such as transaction monitors, ORBs, DBMSs, message queuing, load balancing, modeling tools, design and

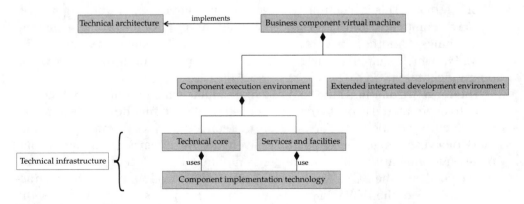

Figure 8.1   Major parts of the technical architecture.

build tools, methodologies, and so on. Ideally, the BCVM would integrate these commodity products, and it would provide a complete development environment through all stages of development, including the development kits described in Chapter 1, "Component-Based Development." We particularly like the term "business component virtual machine" for the manufacturing connotation it carries: The BCVM can be thought of as the tools and "machines" needed to carry out our component manufacturing process in the world of software manufacturing.

Creating the BCVM is a software technology development task, undertaken by technical architects, software technologists, and methodologists, and it makes as much use of the commodity products as possible. The customers for the BCVM are, of course, functional developers who use the BCVM to design, build, and run business components. Their customers, in turn, are business domain users who use business components in their live system to deliver business benefit to their organization.

At the time of writing, while most parts of the BCVM can be acquired commercially and are individually fairly mature, it is not possible to acquire the whole BCVM as an integrated offering. Hence organizations wishing to set up a true component factory will need to provide an integration of commercially available CEE parts to suit their needs, together with some additional in-house "glue" code. Indeed, there is no general agreement, and before this book (to the knowledge of the authors) no published description, of what should be included in this BCVM. This chapter aims to illustrate, justify, and exemplify the BCVM. In the space available, however, we are not able to go into detail on all aspects of a BCVM, so only a few relevant examples of each aspect are discussed. Over time, the BCVM will evolve upward, so that at some point, our definition will become "The BCVM is an implementation of a factory set-up."

As mentioned in Chapter 3, the CEE is the run-time infrastructure that provides sockets into which DCs plug. But a DC also includes a separation layer, which includes the plug itself. Hence the functional developer's viewpoint of the CEE often includes the DC separation layer. Although an implementer of the technical architecture must, of course, keep the two separate, in this chapter we generally take the functional developer's viewpoint, and we use the term "separation layer" to mean a combination of the DC separation layer, any glue code required in the technical core, and whatever technical DCs may be necessary in implementing the services and facilities. This is illustrated in Figure 8.2.

The main run-time construct supported by the BCVM is the DC, described in Chapter 3. As may be recalled, the DC defines the developer's desired level of abstraction—the level that enables the developer to ignore underlying technical complexities. In doing so, it establishes several fundamental concepts—concepts that not only directly support distributed systems, but also synthesize the disparate concepts of software components and distributed objects.

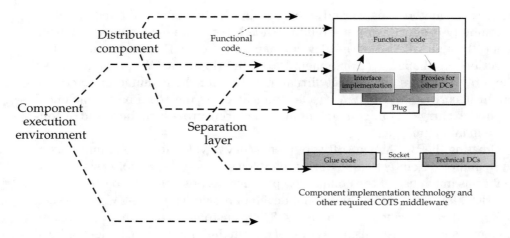

Figure 8.2   Functional developer's view of the separation layer.

One of these concepts, and an implication of complexity hiding, is greater potential for portability.

Portability

The technical architecture not only hides complexity, it also enables portability. For example, a BCVM based on the technical architecture would provide the functional developer with everything needed to take a third-party business component and deploy it in his or her system, whether at analysis-/design-time, construction-time, or run-time.

The portability challenge addresses the ability to easily deploy on one or more environments, a component having been specified, developed, and tested on a different environment. "Environment" includes various technical areas: platforms, source code, databases, database access, network/middleware, and user interface, to name a few. There are different kinds of portability: source level, which requires the component to be compiled and relinked in order to be ported; binary or run-time, which permits a port without recompilation and relinking; and development lifecycle portability, which refers to the ability to port a component across development environments rather than runtime environments. The business component approach, with its emphasis on extended interfaces at development time, places high importance on portability at all phases of the lifecycle. This is enhanced through the technical portability potential provided by the DC design pattern.

In this section, however, we address the first base of portability—that is, the ability technically to port functional source code to a different component execution environment. This is currently the most important aim of portability, and its two main aspects are portability *across CEEs*, which support the same programming languages, and where the same languages are not supported, concepts that support *language neutrality*.

Across CEEs

The major benefit of source portability is to have single source for the code written by the functional programmer. For example, an organization may wish to use different component implementation technologies in its distributed system, and it may also desire source code portability across them. Portability across CEEs can be addressed using different types of solutions. Today, individual portability solution providers address parts of the portability challenge; for example, the major RDBMS vendors provide solutions in such a way that it is possible to develop on one environment and access their database on multiple environments, and the major ORB providers suggest that it is possible to develop on one environment and run on others. But no individual provider addresses all aspects of portability required for a proper component development as described in this chapter. Hence, depending on the level of CEE functionality targeted, component factories will need to integrate portability solutions, usually relying on the usage of separation layers, of code generation, and of repositories. This challenge is addressed here from two angles: DC-level and BC-level.

DC-level. Referring back to Chapter 3, we see that the functional code is only part of the DC. The separation layer (see Figure 3.8 in Chapter 3) is intended to be CEE-specific and to be automatically generated. Because the function code has nothing in it that is CEE-specific, then it can be ported across different CEEs. This is illustrated in Figure 8.3, where the *eVendor* EDC is shown being ported between two CEEs *A* and *B*. The separation layer on the left binds with CEE *A*; that is, it is specific to CEE *A*. This is shown in the figure by the same striping pattern on both the CEE and the DC separation layer. To port to CEE *B*, the separation layer is regenerated from the specification, and then the functional code is recompiled with the newly-generated separation layer to reconstitute the *eVendor* EDC so that it will run on CEE *B*.

BC-level. The previous example focused on what is required for an individual DC to be ported across CEEs. However, a BCVM also needs to address the challenge of porting a whole BC across CEEs, as illustrated in Figure 8.4. Here we see that not only do DCs have to be ported, but several other portability concerns must also be addressed. For example, DBMSs must be compatible not only at the level of DB access code within the resource tier, but also in terms of DBMS facilities such as triggers that are assumed to be available. Again, the user tier aspects of the CEE must also provide com-

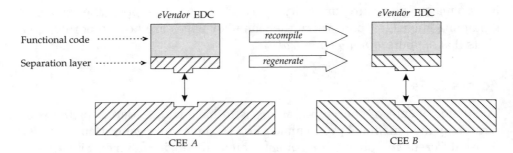

Figure 8.3 Porting a DC to another CEE.

patible sockets. It is unlikely that complete portability for business components will be reached in the short term, since such a goal is likely to be reached only with the emergence of appropriate standards. DC portability, however, provides at least a start and makes it feasible to begin considering a portability strategy for complete business components.

Now one of the objectives for the CEE is to be "language neutral." Figure 8.3 assumes that both CEEs support the same languages. What happens if they don't?

Language Neutrality

DCs should in principle be able to be written in any language, whether object-oriented or procedural, compiled or interpreted. Support for a range of languages is what is meant by a CEE being "language-neutral."

Because the function code must be able to be invoked by, and to call, the separation layer at the language level, portability is possible only as long as the target CEE supports the language used to write the functional code. "Support" means being able to generate a separation layer in the same language, and supporting the language bindings between the resultant DC and the CEE (because

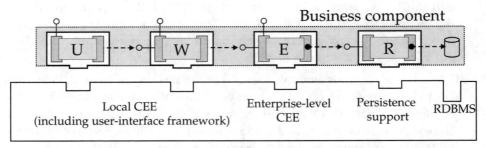

Figure 8.4 Porting a business component to another CEE.

the technical bindings between a DC and the CEE may vary across different CEEs). Suppose the EDC in Figure 8.3 is written in a language not supported by CEE *B*? In that case, the DC will not be portable. Lack of language support inhibits portability, unless it is possible to overcome this constraint by providing a "language adapter" to map a supported language into a nonsupported language. This is illustrated in Figure 8.5, where *eVendor*, written in language *L*, is able to be ported to CEE *B*, which does not support language *L*.

The port is enabled through a language adapter—a "stub" written in a supported language, language *M* in the figure. To do this, it is necessary to split the separation layer into two parts—each part in a different language.[2] One part is in the DC's native language (shown by vertical stripes in the figure); the other is the language adapter. Both parts are generated, or the language adapter may be a generic implementation. Microsoft has recently espoused this latter approach for building COM components with scripting languages. The language support adapter is a system-provided generic DLL called *scrobj.dll* [Esposito 1998]. The functional programmer sees only the functional part of the DC written in language M.

Of course, the ideal situation would be to have one or (a few) more binary binding standards supported by all CEE vendors. This is unlikely to happen in the near future, so the most that can be done is to make the DCs as source-portable as possible. It is interesting, though, to speculate that a combination of tagged data-oriented interfaces and language adapters may provide a possible future path to binary portability.[3]

Implementing the Separation Layer

There are two main alternatives in implementing the separation layer: to choose a single development environment and run-time environment or to allow multiple development environments and run-time environments. Even in

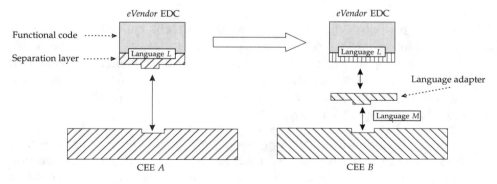

Figure 8.5 Portability and language neutrality.

the first case (for example, in the case of choosing a Microsoft development environment), at the time of writing, a considerable amount of work is required to properly attain the objectives of simplicity and separation of concerns while still supporting the desired functional developer programming model and achieving some level of cost-effective software manufacturing and scalability. In the following, we will assume that multiple run-time and development environments are targeted, which is likely to be normal for most component factories set-ups.

Implementation can be done in a range of ways, some more development-scalable than others. At one extreme, the separation layer is directly implemented by hand every time it is needed. For example, a set of guidelines and design patterns are provided, and each time a proxy is needed it is hand-crafted according to these guidelines. This approach, although highly error-prone and time-consuming, does minimize the initial costs of the factory set-up. For anything other than very small projects, this approach will result in continuing high costs over time.

At the other extreme, all aspects of the separation layers are generated from the specification produced by the functional developer. This approach (which is the approach that has been implicitly assumed so far in the book) requires at the time of writing a substantial initial investment, but it greatly reduces development costs and complexity over time. It usually involves creating or extending the modeling tools, as explained in the last section in this chapter, creating a meta-model of development and run-time concepts in a repository, a specification language (either a user interface-based or a text-based language), and the creation of appropriate code generators. All of this needs to be done while keeping priorities straight: Today, many projects end up spending a large part of their budget not so much in building the system, but in gold-plating the factory.

Technical Core

This section describes the main features of the technical core of a CEE as regards hiding technical computational complexities, and also the work required to develop the separation layer. A detailed and complete discussion of all aspects of a CEE is beyond the scope of this book. Only a few relevant examples are chosen, to illustrate various aspects of this implementation. In particular, the following aspects are covered:

Component invocation. All component implementation technologies provide some form of invocation. This is an example in which the separation layer must simply abstract from the various peculiarities and provide a model that is portable across component implementation technologies.

Component lifecycle. This is similar, in that the separation layer can quite simply abstract from the various peculiarities of the component implementation technologies, but it is slightly more complex than in the previous case.

Concurrency. The ways the various component implementation technologies address concurrency affect the details of each CEE.

Asynchronous messaging. This is an example of how the separation layer can provide a very useful mechanism, although it can be complex to implement when the various component implementation technologies do not directly support it.

Dynamic inheritance. This is an example of how the separation layer can actually provide extremely powerful functionality, not provided by most of the component implementation technologies.

Component Invocation

The CEE must support a high level of simplicity in component invocation. For example, suppose a functional programmer wants to invoke the *update_vendor_information(...)* operation of the *ieVendor* interface of the *eVendor* component. Suppose further that the specific vendor is identified by its vendor number "AB123." At the level of abstraction occupied by the functional programmer (whom we expect to be a domain specialist), this should be all the information needed to get that particular vendor's name. The functional programmer might therefore find it natural to write something like this:

```
ieVendor a_vendor;
a_vendor.update_vendor_information("AB123",
                                    VendorInformation vendor_info);
```

NOTE This style of operation invocation carries the identification of the vendor instance as a parameter. Should this seem not intuitive at first glance, please look ahead to Chapter 9, "Application Architecture," where we discuss two important styles of component design: type-based and instance-based. This example assumes a type-based style, where the component encapsulates a type (the *eVendor* type), whose extent is all vendors. Although this particular component, an entity component, might in some circumstance be thought better implemented following the instance-based style, in this chapter we have chosen to adopt the type-based style for all examples.

In the first line, the programmer defines *a_vendor* as an instance of the proxy class *ieVendor*. The component name itself ("eVendor") is part of the generated code in the *ieVendor* proxy class. Thus the name does not appear in the functional code (the functional programmer, however, could read it in the documentation of the *ieVendor* proxy). The second line invokes the *update_ vendor_information* operation on the vendor component, providing two parameters: first, the identity of the specific vendor—in this case, the Vendor Number "AB123"—and, second, the business data type containing the new data.

Now, some readers may consider the preceding code to be perfectly normal. Others may think that the apparent absence of the usual minutiae of managing parameter memory, connecting to an ORB, obtaining interface pointers explicitly, and using a name service all indicate that large chunks of code have been omitted. In fact, the preceding example is the most that should be required by a functional programmer, other details being hidden by generated code and by the CEE (see "Functional Developer's Programming Model" in Chapter 3).

One aspect of the preceding code sample is that the naming issue is largely hidden. Naming relates to how a functional programmer sees the run-time identity of another component. The principle is that a distributed component should be able to have a name that is human readable and relevant to the business domain. Thus a *Vendor* component should be network-addressable by a name such as "eVendor" (the enterprise-tier component). If instance-based, then the name should be able to accommodate an instance name such as the vendor number. In either case, where the component implementation technology does not directly support externally-meaningful names such as "eVendor," then the separation layer should provide code to access a name service, find the associated object pointer or component handle, possibly cache it for later use, and so forth.

Component Lifecycle

From the point of view of the functional developer, a distributed component instance is considered to be an adult in the component world, and it is hence responsible for its own actions and for its own fate. That is, a DC is largely responsible for its own lifecycle. By component lifecycle we mean mainly activation and deactivation. These operations are usually handled by code in the separation layer, and the functional developer is rarely if ever concerned with them.

Activation

The functional developer's programming model described in Chapter 3 requires that the functional programmer should be able to invoke an operation on a component without first establishing whether the target component actually "exists." When does a component not exist? Suppose that the underlying component implementation technology perceives the component instance as an object instance. Such instances are technically in-memory things. A component instance is technically "nonexistent" when no trace of it is in memory—although its persistent data may be sitting on disk somewhere. If the target component instance is not in memory, then before an operation can be invoked on it, it must be "activated"; that is, its code must be located and loaded, memory allocated and initialized, and any state re-established.

From the point of view of the functional programmer invoking an operation on a component, all this should, however, be transparent. If the component instance is not active at the time one of its operations is invoked, then the CEE (possibly in conjunction with the separation layer in the DC) should activate it on behalf of the functional programmer. Where the underlying component implementation technology does not provide this function, then additional function in the technical core and/or separation layer must do so. This is a good example of why the technical core may need to be more than a component implementation technology. In addition, to avoid unnecessary network traffic, the activation process is best handled—as far as is allowed by the component implementation technology—on the target system.

Deactivation

When the component instance is no longer required, it must be "deactivated"—that is, removed from memory and any persistent state saved, memory reclaimed, and code unloaded. Deactivation is crucial for scalability, especially for the instance-based style. Without it, memory can become full of unused component instances; the system would slow down and would eventually stop—or crash! The ability for the CEE to deactivate components that are active but not being used is known as garbage collection (not to be confused with language-specific garbage collection mechanisms).

There are a number of interesting situations where the target distributed component must be made aware of the fact of activation or deactivation. This means that the component must provide an "Activate" and a "Deactivate" operation. These operations are an example of what the BCVM should normally generate as part of the DC's separation layer.

In summary, component life cycle operations should generally be transparent to the functional developer, who should not be concerned with technology-level matters such as activation and deactivation. Similarly, although garbage collection is often of crucial importance in enabling scalable systems, it is certainly not something with which the functional developer should ever be concerned. In other words, an important role for the CEE, together with the separation layer, is to hide the complexities inherent in component lifecycle management from the functional developer.

Concurrency

The concurrency problem occurs when a single piece of code must handle two threads of control at the same time and in the same address space. That is, the operating system may schedule two threads, both of which need to execute the same piece of code, concurrently. This is no problem if the two threads are in separate address spaces (processes), since the operating system takes care of duplicating all technical aspects of the code. The situation becomes more complicated when the two threads are run within a single address space, as is normally the case, at least for server-based components.

Managing concurrency is a highly technical subject, and if it is handled by other than highly skilled software engineers, is hugely error-prone. Clearly this is an area that should be handled on the functional developer's behalf by the CEE. Suppose, for example, that at time *t1* the *update_vendor_information* operation of the *eVendor* component is invoked by some client component. Suppose also that it takes *m* microseconds to execute the *update_vendor_information* operation. Now suppose that at time *t2*, which is less than *m* microseconds after *t1*, another client invokes the *eVendor* component. What happens? One thing is very clear. The CEE must provide standard solutions to this problem.

Solutions that depend on ensuring that only one thread runs at a time (a "single-threaded solution") do not scale up. Hence multithreading through different DC instances in the same address space (and hence quite possibly through the same DC code) must be allowed for. However, a solution where several threads can run concurrently but only one thread at a time is allowed to run through a given component instance can easily lead to deadlock, and so is not a viable solution. Another solution, used extensively in transaction monitors for at least 25 years, is to have the technical infrastructure block a second thread on a single component instance until the functional programmer does some well-known function (for example, invokes an operation on another component instance), at which point the component instance can be reentered by the second thread. This approach is often called "serial reusability" because it results in various parts of the code being reused (by different threads) serially. Although the serial reusability approach has been used with some success in the past, there is a problem with it: Where a component instance is stateful, then it is possible for the second thread to change the state of the component instance such that when the first thread returns from invoking another component instance, the state for the first thread has changed. This does not conform with the principle of least astonishment (see Chapter 9) for the functional programmer.

Because concurrency is intimately bound up with transactions, further discussion of possible solutions is postponed to the "Transactions" section later in this chapter.

Asynchronous Messaging

There comes a time in the life of every designer of distributed systems when he or she yearns for asynchronous messaging. Synchronous messages have blocking and serialization semantics that are often just what is required. But sometimes, there is a need to break an interaction and to request that something be done in another interaction sequence. One very common place that this needs to be done is in interactions between a UWD and an ERD, for example, to provide rapid feedback and return of control to the user tier in order to avoid blocking the code that implements that tier. Without such capability, many implementations of the user tier could find that the user interface "freezes" until the request to the ERD completes. When asynchronous messaging is not made available, then developers often resort to using event channels—not for events, but merely as a useful mechanism that has the side effect of breaking the interaction sequence.

Thus, although synchronous messages will suffice for many situations, real systems also generally need asynchronous messaging.[4] The recent OMG adoption of asynchronous messaging supports this contention [OMG 1998a]. Hence the CEE should provide an asynchronous messaging mechanism that is simple for the functional programmer to use and understand. "Simple" means two things:

- The functional developer of a component should never have to know whether that component is invoked synchronously or asynchronously by a client component. Experience in providing both synchronous and asynchronous messaging has proved to us that this level of transparency is essential if code is not to become ridiculously complicated.

  Conversely, the programmer of a client component instance should always be aware of whether that component issues a message synchronously or asynchronously. Otherwise, the programmer gets hopelessly mixed up about what is and is not returned at the next sequential instruction.

- The programming model must be simple. For example, suppose some component needs to read information from *eVendor*—say by invoking *eVendor*'s *read_vendor_information(...)* operation. A synchronous invocation might look like this:

```
ieVendor a_vendor;
VendorInformation vendor_info_out;
a_vendor.read_vendor_information("AB123", vendor_info_out);
```

where the parameter *vendor_info_out* is an "out" parameter—that is, one that is for information provided by ("pulled out from") the target component. The code for invoking the same operation asynchronously might look like this:

```
ieVendor a_vendor;
VendorInformation vendor_info_out;
a_vendor.read_vendor_information_async(
        "AB123",
        vendor_info,
        "vendor_read_response");
```

Here, the suffix *_async* is attached to the operation to be invoked. The proxy will actually invoke *read_vendor_information* asynchronously and return control immediately to the functional developer's code. The CEE handles the asynchronous technicalities based on the facilities provided by the underlying component implementation technology. The third parameter in the sample code illustrates one way the separation layer could provide for responding to asynchronous requests: it represents the operation to be invoked when the response to the asynchronous message is returned from *eVendor*. This could work as follows (other approaches are also possible). When the *read_vendor_information* message is received by *eVendor*, the required business data type is returned on the normal return of control, as if invoked synchronously. The CEE (together with the separation layer) would cause a separate message, containing the returned business data type, to be sent back to the invoking component. On receipt, the separation layer in the invoking component would map the string "vendor_read_response" (specified by the third parameter in the sample code) to its *vendor_read_response* operation.

Implementing the above scheme when the component implementation technology does not support asynchronous invocation can become quite complex. Implementing on a MOM (message-oriented middleware), on the other hand, is simpler. In addition, a MOM would normally support further considerations such as time-based scheduling of messages to be addressed.

Dynamic Inheritance

The ability to extend a delivered distributed component so that new facilities can be added, or existing facilities can be modified in some way, is a desirable feature of a CEE. By "delivered" we mean that the DC has been compiled and linked, and it may also have been deployed. Extension after compile/link means that built-in OO language capabilities cannot be used as a general solution (unless perhaps all DCs are written in Java). Hence a solution must be language-independent; without this capability, a DC could be extended only by modifying its source code and then recompiling and relinking. This would mean retesting the DC, and it would also mean redeploying it—to possibly thousands of systems—with all the associated system management implications. Therefore some mechanism other than built-in language capabilities must be used, and this in turn implies that the extensibility requirement is best satisfied at the binary level. Then the DC being extended does not have to be touched.

Binary extension means that a user can purchase a third-party extension and apply it without being forced to go back to the IS department (or his or her favorite DC supplier) and ask them to reengineer and redeploy the extended DC. It also means that extension could be done in a programming language other than that used for the DC being extended. We call such a highly useful facility "dynamic inheritance,"[5] and it has two major advantages:

- It allows users to apply third-party extensions without touching the DC to be extended.

- It enables common code to be shipped as a "base" DC; that is, a single DC containing extra-functional code common to all or most functional-level DCs. Such a DC would be "extended" by functional DCs. This allows the functional DCs to have much smaller footprints than they otherwise would. It also means that base DC capabilities can be modified without having to touch the functional DCs. This is clearly hugely useful in reducing maintenance and redeployment effort.

The extension concept can be considered as a combination of the OO inheritance and the component delegation (as found in COM) concepts, but it can be applied to complete shipped binaries. It does not involve language facilities because by definition what is required is outside the scope of a single language. For example, if it were desired to extend a Cobol DC with one written in Python, then this should be able to be done. To the functional programmer, the extension concept can be presented as delegation within a component instance. As far as the underlying CEE implementation is concerned, either delegation or implementation chaining can be used. Figure 8.6 illustrates the functional programmer's view.

In Figure 8.6, the original *eVendor* distributed component has been extended by a new *eSpecialVendor* component. The CEE would ensure that these two components make up a single group as far as any client component is concerned. The group's network address would still be "eVendor." When (1) a client such as *eInvoiceManager* invokes an operation on the *eVendor* component instance, the message is technically routed (2) to the *eSpecialVendor* EDC. Its separation layer then either routes the message to the functional code within *eSpecialVendor* or delegates (3) to the *eVendor* component (4). In turn, the message may be routed to *eBase*.

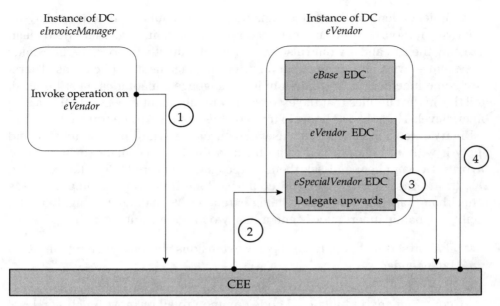

Figure 8.6 Extension through dynamic inheritance.

This facility is especially useful when component frameworks are considered. The base DC can be built to handle several technical complexities such as interfacing to event management services, handling simple persistence (for example, in the UWD), managing some aspects of the component lifecycle, and so forth. The base DC would be placed above the functional DCs in the delegation chain, as shown in Figure 8.6, so that framework-related operations could be delegated.

Dynamic inheritance can be implemented using existing facilities in some component implementation technologies. In all cases, to preserve the pluggability of the individual components, added meta-model constructs, and glue code may be necessary. For example, with COM, a particular use of delegation can be employed.

Services and Facilities

The technical core described in the previous section hides many computational complexities from the functional developer. However, a number of additional capabilities are required, which typically derive from the fact that the target for development is a distributed business system. Many of these capabilities are common across the majority of business systems, and some are highly complex. And again, many of these are provided by individual vendors at the time of writing, but not as an integrated offering covering both the technical core and these services and facilities. Hence, following our goal of hiding as many complexities as possible from the functional developer, an organization should carefully consider how these should be addressed in order to achieve the desired levels of cost-effective and scalable development. The technical core section permitted us to illustrate several examples of the kind of things, specific to an individual DC, that a BCVM should provide. This section exemplifies more complex aspects, usually involving multiple DCs and whole business components, and also more obviously cutting across multiple architectural viewpoints. It briefly describes the problems and indicates requirements on solutions for what we consider to be the most fundamental services and facilities:

- Transactions
- Error handling
- Events
- Persistence
- Megadata
- User interface framework

Transactions

The word "transaction" has several meanings in our industry. This section addresses "ACID" transactions,[6] while "business" transactions, which might consist of multiple ACID transactions, and which can span multiple UWD-to-ERD invocations, are addressed in Chapter 9. In this section, the unqualified term "transaction" will refer to an ACID transaction.

The most important thing the CEE should do for the functional programmer in the area of transactions is to make them transparent. This is preferably achieved through a simple transaction model that provides a useful amount of function for many situations, but that can be bypassed by an experienced developer when required. Such a model, which has proven powerful enough to enable building large-scale component-based systems, could serve as a default, and its main assumptions are as follows:

- A distributed component should run in the context of an implicit transaction. An *implicit transaction* is one that is initiated by the CEE on behalf of the functional developer as a consequence of a given (well-known) action implemented by a functional developer. Hence a transaction is started by the CEE when an operation invocation enters the ERD (remember that the ERD is defined as the logical space within which a transaction can run). The execution of the message (by one or more component instances) will run in that transaction. Such a transaction is implicit, since its initiation is done outside the scope of the DC, and neither the DC separation layer nor (especially) the functional developer has anything to do with it. When all processing is completed, the transaction is terminated by the CEE, which sends commit or roll-back messages to the participating DCs, and then performs the actual commit or roll-back. The DC separation layer should provide default behavior for commit/roll-back messages. Thus the functional developer gets involved only when it is absolutely necessary from a functional point of view. The result is returned to the caller (typically, a DC in a UWD). The only thing that the functional developer of the calling DC need do to cause a transaction to be run is to invoke an operation on the ERD.

This model assumes "stateless" DCs. That is, a DC run-time instance does not maintain state between transactions. This is further discussed in Chapter 12, "Component-Based Design."

■ Within a transaction, EDC-to-EDC invocations share, as a default, the same transactional context.

■ The ERD within which the transaction executes maps physically to a single server address space (partly for performance reasons and partly as a result of limitations in the underlying resource managers used).

■ When during a given transaction a DC issues an asynchronous message, then the message is issued as a new transaction sometime after completion of the given transaction. Also, because it is useful for events to be published asynchronously (see the "Events" section later in this chapter), then the notification resulting from an event being published is also a separate transaction.

The system requirements for transaction processing have been well understood for over 20 years in the industry (some would say 30). Until recently, component implementation technologies and transaction monitors were not integrated, and the choice for many organizations was either to sacrifice the use of component technology and use a traditional (noncomponent-based) transaction monitor, or to build a home-grown transaction infrastructure (based usually on native DBMS transactional capabilities) to support distributed components. The distributed component world is now beginning to see the emergence of appropriate transaction monitors. The approach is generally to provide a technical core that does much of what previously was left to the functional programmer—that is, thread management, activation policies, database connection, and other "server plumbing." Recent component implementation technologies such as EJB (and CORBA Components at the time of writing) call this a "container." With such increasing integration, today it is becoming possible to base the CEE transaction support on commercially available products.

Threads, Serialization, and Concurrency

One of the most important aspects for scalability is to avoid serializing component requests and transactions. Serialization occurs when the transaction management software causes requests (operation invocations) to be queued up. Sometimes this is to ensure that only one transaction is physically running at any one time in an address space; sometimes it means that any component instance is in only one transaction at a time, regardless of how many requests are waiting for it, and regardless of the capability of the operating system to handle greater concurrency. The problem with serializing transactions is that serializing access to data should be left to the DBMS. Most modern DBMSs can handle multiple concurrent accesses to the same data by providing their own internal ACIDity and by providing appropriate APIs so that concurrency can be optimized. If the transaction manager does not work with the DBMS, then this can result in needless queuing, with its consequential impact on scalability.

In essence, the question is, why serialize outside the middleware, one of whose functions is to serialize requests? All this does is to slow the system up. The essential principle for any CEE implementer is to allow the underlying DBMS to handle serialization of requests against data. How do we deal with this? This is essentially a concurrency problem, in the context of transactions. In general, there are three main approaches to handling the problem while providing the functional programmer with as simple a programming model as possible:

Block all potentially-concurrent transactions. Impose a single-threading policy so that only one transaction is allowed to run in a given address space at any one time. Once a transaction is started, other transactions are blocked until the running transaction is completed. This approach is neither scalable nor high-performance.

Block the component. Allow a given component instance to participate in only one transaction at a time. This means that other transactions that need to use the component are blocked or bounced. Note that a given component may be reentered within a single transaction, and therefore the concurrency issues are still present.

Clone the component. If a component is already in a transaction, then have the infrastructure clone that component so that the new transaction can use the clone. This actually means that a given component or component instance is copied for the purposes of a transaction. Ideally this should be transparent not only to the functional developer but also to the system-wide component naming and name resolution mechanisms. We have had some success in using two variants of the cloning scheme; the "Component Cloning" sidebar gives some additional detail. Cloning essentially provides to components the equivalent of transaction programs run under transaction monitors. It also is a superset of the component pooling notion prevalent in some of today's transaction monitors. For example, Microsoft's MTS provides (or at least plans to provide) a restricted form of component pooling. At the time of writing, and as far as the authors know, none of the various component implementation technologies provide a fully concurrent facility for components in such a way as to provide a simple programming model for the functional developer. Support today can require involvement by the functional programmer at a significant software engineering level. The challenge is to move this to the separation layer and/or CEE, away from the functional developer, and still provide full concurrency. Thus to provide a simple programming model and at the same time provide scalability for high-performance systems, organizations currently may have to build themselves the additional (quite complex) CEE glue code that would be needed.

COMPONENT CLONING

Consider a given component instance. It doesn't matter whether its design is type-based or instance-based. The functional developer, when building the component, should not be concerned with technical concurrency matters. However, at run-time, the component should not block or serialize concurrent requests for its services. Blocking and serialization are handled by the underlying transaction and/or database manager, and it's certainly not sensible to do it twice. This means that multiple requests must be allowed to enter the code concurrently. Implications on functional code, however, should be hidden.

A transaction processing monitor (TPM) hides concurrency issues by running a given transaction program in a different thread for each incoming request. Any in-memory data storage required by the transaction program is tied to the transaction (that is, the thread), not to the program code. All that has to be done by the functional programmer to provide for this is to follow some simple and well-understood design rules. For example, in general do not use static variables. When these rules are followed, the transaction program code, which typically is thought of as having behavior only, is stateless. Stateless code is very simple to run concurrently.

A component instance, on the other hand, may have state. If multiple requests are allowed to enter the code concurrently, then the state could change under the programmer's feet, as it were, and without the programmer's knowing about it. The concept of serial reusability (described in "Concurrency" earlier in this chapter) considerably alleviates this problem but does not remove it. Again, even if the component design is stateless, there may be small pockets of state hanging around. For example, a C++ object may have been created on the heap, and its reference held as part of the component's state. In any case, it is clearly better to provide a general solution rather than several solutions each appropriate for only one design approach.

A solution based on the well-tried TPM approach suggests itself, and that is to tie the instance's state to the transaction. To the author's knowledge, there have been two quite different approaches to this in the past. One approach clones the state only, rather than the whole component; the other clones the whole component. The fine detail of the mechanics of these two approaches is beyond the scope of this book. To illustrate how this can work, we sketch the essence of the first approach, assuming a transactional environment, with full commit/rollback capabilities, as follows.

First, the memory for each component's state is managed by the CEE, and focus and support business language classes are built accordingly. Ideally, the parts of these language classes that cooperate with the CEE are generated as part of the separation layer, so that this aspect is transparent to the functional developer. The effect is that the state can be associated with a transaction rather than directly with the component. Suppose that the component receives a message on some transaction *tx1*. The separation layer checks to see if a golden copy of the state has been created. If not, then this implies that the component's state has not yet been set up, so the component does this during its activation—for example, by getting data from its resource DC. From the functional developer's point of view, this state is held in business language classes. In fact, the separation layer makes a golden copy and associates another copy (at least logically) with the current transaction, after which the component begins to process the message within *tx1*. Now let's assume that a second message—on a second transaction *tx2*—enters the component before the first has completed. The separation layer checks to see if a golden copy of the data has been created. It has, and so a transaction copy is made and associated with *tx2*, which now starts its processing within the component, changing its data and writing it to persistent storage via its resource DC. Let's now assume that *tx2* completes before *tx1*. When *tx2*'s "Commit" message is received from the CEE, the separation layer checks to see whether the golden copy has been changed by another transaction. In this case it has not, and so the golden copy is marked as changed by *tx2* and an OK is returned to the Commit. Now *tx1* completes. When *tx1*'s "Commit" message is received from the CEE, the separation layer checks to see whether the golden copy has been changed by another transaction. In this case it has been changed, the golden copy is left unchanged, and an Error is returned to *tx1*'s Commit. The CEE then rolls back *tx1*.

The preceding is a high-level view of a general approach, and it does not answer all the detailed questions that the knowledgeable reader may have. However, we hope that enough has been said to indicate that the cloning approach may be a fruitful avenue for future exploration. In particular, the whole approach is handled by the separation layer and CEE working in conjunction with the underlying transaction management product, and the functional developer has very little, if anything, to do.

Error Handling

Consider the implementation of *eVendor*'s *read_vendor_information(…)* operation. What should the functional programmer do if an error of some sort is found? This is a very simple question, but it is loaded with implications. The overall system requirements for error handling almost certainly include the following:

- Pass all errors back to the requester so that, if necessary, an analysis can be made.

- Provide application-defined error codes and descriptions (the descriptions will be references to string tables so that national language support can be provided).

- Log all errors found; provide for logging in both the UWD and ERD.

The functional programmer should not have to deal with all these requirements as well as handling the functional code. Error handling is a CEE facility. But it is a facility that cuts across various layers and usually is addressed in separate, often inconsistent ways by the various providers of component implementation technologies. For example, the conventions followed by a DBMS may very well be different from the assumptions of ORB providers. And although it is indeed possible to build an error-handling framework, this should not be the work of the functional developer, but rather it should be the work of the technical architect and application architect (as will be seen in Chapter 9). All the functional programmer should be required to do is to identify when the error occurs, pass the required error information to the CEE facility, and then return to the caller with an indication that an error occurred. This process can be wrapped into the phrase "to signal an error." The code that the functional developer might write to implement the *read_vendor_information* operation could look something like this:

```
read_vendor_information(string          vendor_id,
                VendorInformation vendor_info)
{
  try
  {
    // Try to find vendor information.
    ...
  }
  catch
  {
    // Vendor with id vendor_id does not exist:
    utility.add_error("EVNDR-003", vendor_id)
  }
}
```

If the vendor identified by *vendor_id* does not exists, then an error is signaled by throwing an exception, which is caught in the *catch* block. Here, the functional programmer invokes an *add_error* operation on a "well-known" object in the DC—the utility language class within the DC's separation layer (see Chapter 3)—passing an error number ("EVNDR-003") and the value of *vendor_id*. The fact that an error occurred is returned to the caller.

For this approach to work, the technical error-handling framework should specify a standard internal DC design. A BCVM-defined business data type, able to contain a list of errors, and managed (transparently to the functional developer) by the utility language class, could accumulate the errors. When control returns from the DC, the "error" business data type would also be passed back to the calling component. Here it would be handled by the proxy. The code that invoked the *read_vendor_information(...)* within the calling DC, on seeing that an error has been returned, may also signal an error, and so on. Experience suggests that such a business data type can be usefully constructed using tagged data to hold the various nested errors. Another approach uses a list of error objects that are defined by the technical architecture and that also provide the ability to add context-specific information such as *vendor_id* in the preceding example. Either approach can help avoid a type explosion, where each different error has its own type. Such an explosion can occur easily when different errors have different numbers of attributes. Some may have more than two as additional information is provided. For example, a file name that is not found, or a table name, and so on.

Events

From the functional developer's point of view, a simple event model is needed. To simplify the presentation, events that may be generated automatically by the CEE or by generated code are ignored: The focus is on what, if anything, the functional programmer sees. Again, a top-down view is taken: First we ask what is the simplest thing the programmer can do, and then we see if it can be supported. Such support is the job of the CEE, which in turn will drive any underlying event mechanisms provided by the component implementation technology. In addition, event persistence is handled transparently by the CEE (functional events must be persistent; that is, they must not be lost).

To illustrate what a CEE may have to provide on top of component implementation technologies, a simple model—the publish/subscribe model—is chosen. This model requires no polling by the functional programmer, and experience has shown it to be a readily-understood model. Both subscription to an event occurring to a specific named DC and subscription to an event channel are supported.

Suppose the functional programmer of the *eVendor* DC wishes to publish a "changed" event when some aspect of *eVendor* changes. The functional programmer already knows about the utility language class (see Chapter 3), so there is no need to introduce other objects such as specific event channel proxies. Instead, the programmer asks the utility class to handle everything. For example, the functional developer might provide the code along the following lines to publish the event required:

```
update_vendor_information(string          vendor_id,
                    VendorInformation vendor_info);
{
  // try update of vendor vendor_id
  // if successful, then:
  Utility.publish("Changed");
  ...
}
```

Of course, a typed event object rather than a string could be passed to the utility language class. In addition, the preceding code assumes that the event will be notified to subscribers to *eVendor*. A functional programmer subscribes to an event either by subscribing to a specific component by name or to an event channel. Consider a distributed component *A* that is interested in "Changed" events that occur to *eVendor*. Here is what the functional programmer of DC *A* might write, using DC *A*'s utility language class to do the plumbing work:

```
Utility.subscribe("eVendor", "Changed");
```

There are several ways in which the functional programmer of a subscribing component could see an event notification. One simple approach is to define a standard operation (for example, "notify") that the CEE will invoke whenever an event to which this component has subscribed is published. The functional programmer then provides this operation, along the general lines of the following pseudo-code fragment:

```
notify(Event e)
{
  if ( e.name == "Changed" )
  {
    /* handle this event */
  }
  if ( /*some other event*/ )
  ...
}
```

The preceding code could be generated, leaving the functional programmer to fill in the blanks, as it were.

There are many possible variations on the preceding event-handling code. The essential thing is to abstract as much as possible into the CEE, making event handling a nonevent for the functional programmer.

Event notifications are generally issued asynchronously. That is, the utility class invokes synchronously a CEE-provided mechanism (for example, an *eEventManager* technical DC provided by the CEE.). If the DC is transactional, then a published event must be rolled back should the transaction fail. The CEE should provide for this, perhaps by holding the event until the end of the transaction, and then publishing it asynchronously. An *eEventManager* DC can provide a wrapper for the underlying event management middleware, instead of binding this wrapper into every DC. This reduces the footprint of all functional DCs.

Persistence

The persistence challenge is probably the single most important aspect of the category of systems addressed by this book. In such systems, everything revolves around the database.

Persistence is a very generic term. In a business application, there are, in reality, very different categories of data that may need to be persisted, for different reasons and possibly requiring different technologies and architectural solutions. These categories include business data persistence, which is what most people think about when they discuss persistence; data warehousing, which adds an historical perspective on business data; recovery support, meaning data that is made persistent to guarantee that the system will come back up properly after going down for any reason; configurations and preferences, for example, each user may want to record a specific layout of the screens or some particular business configuration that he or she usually uses to run the system; and meta-data, meaning data about the application, components, business rules, and data itself.

This section will discuss one very important class of persistence solution, called *framework persistence*, that relies on components being able to externalize their state. This solution can be used, for example, to address recovery support or configuration and preferences. It is also particularly appropriate for, and will be exemplified as applied to, UWD components. An alternative approach, called "component-managed persistence" which is more suitable for the e-tier, is discussed in Chapter 12.

Framework persistence is one of several component frameworks that can be provided by CEE services and facilities. It aims at providing almost fully automatic persistence, with as little involvement by the functional programmer as possible. The only thing that the functional programmer needs to do is to provide implementations for two operations: internalize and externalize. In some circumstances, the use of tagged data to hold component instance state can result in these operations being able to be automatically handled by the separation layer, thus making persistence wholly transparent to the functional programmer.

The following provides one example of how framework persistence could be implemented. The main concept is that when a component instance is activated, it is handed its state on an "internalize" message. When the component instance is deactivated, it is first sent an "externalize" message, the component returning its state in some streamed form such as tagged data. Thus the component merely has to provide an implementation for "internalize" and "externalize" messages, and the rest is done automatically by the framework.

Figure 8.7 is an interaction diagram that illustrates the framework. It assumes that the CEE provides for dynamic inheritance (see the earlier section in this chapter, "Dynamic Inheritance"). Thus in this example the component instance at run-time is composed from a functional DC (*wVendor* in the figure) and the "base" DC (*wBase* in the figure) that handles the component instance lifecycle.

The top part of Figure 8.7 shows the complete interaction sequence for "activate," including the returns of control. The distributed component *wVendor* is shown as dynamically inheriting from *wBase* by the small arrow between the *wVendor* and *wBase* boxes at the top of the figure. In the body of the figure, there are three styles of arrow: solid (a message to the component instance), dashed (a message delegated to another DC within the dynamic inheritance delegation chain), and dotted (return of control). Return-of-control messages are labeled with a notation to show from what message control is returning. Thus "r > 4a" means the return of control from message number 4a, which is the "internalize" message delegated to *wBase*. This framework depends on data being passed as tagged data, which enables the delegate component to be generic and polymorphic. The sequence of operations for "activate" is shown in Table 8.1, where the left-most column shows message numbers from Figure 8.7.

Figure 8.7 shows the interaction sequence for "deactivate" at the bottom, this time without the returns of control (dotted-lined arrows) being shown. The general idea is as for "activate," but in reverse, with *wPersistence* being invoked with a "save_data" message.

The effect of this framework is that the functional DC (*wVendor*) processes only the "internalize" message. This message has a single parameter of a string containing, in tagged data form, the data to be internalized.

The pros of framework persistence are the following:

- Much less for the programmer to do—merely provide the implementations for the internalize and externalize operations. And where these can

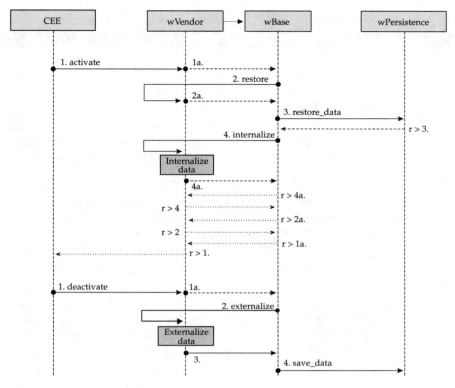

Figure 8.7 Framework persistence.

be generated from some form of specified mapping appropriate to UWD persistence, then the programmer has nothing to do.

- A simple generic persistence mechanism that is particularly useful in the UWD. For example, where the user tier has been implemented using DC technology, this approach to persistence for window positions and so forth has been used very successfully.

The cons are as follows:

- Because the framework requires several interactions within the delegation chain for each access to persistent data, it can be slower than component-managed persistence (that is, persistence managed by the DC itself). This performance degradation is generally acceptable in the UWD, but can become important in the ERD.

Note that the two approaches can be intermixed within a single DC. They can also be intermixed within a component delegation chain: one DC can use component-managed persistence while another can use framework persistence. This can, for example, be useful where the base DC uses framework persistence

Table 8.1 Sequence of Operations for "Activate"

#	OPERATION PERFORMED
1.	The CEE sends "activate" to *wVendor*, which ignores it other than to…
1a.	…delegate it directly to *wBase* (that is, *wVendor* does not process this message at all).
2.	*wBase* sends a "restore" message to "itself" (that is, to the bottom of the delegate chain—in this example, *wVendor*). This allows any DC in the chain to handle its own data restore if it wishes and to ignore the framework.
2a.	The "restore" message is delegated to *wBase*.
3.	*wBase* sends "restore_data" to the *wPersistence* component. The *wPersistence* component (a kind of local RDC in the UWD) retrieves the appropriate data from some form of persistent storage.
r > 3.	Return of control (to *wBase*) occurs from inter-DC invocation 3. The return carries with it data retrieved from the database by the *wPersistence* component.
4.	*wBase* then sends an "internalize" message to "itself." The data retrieved by *wBase* from *wPersistence* is passed on this message as a string parameter containing tagged data. On receipt of this message, *wVendor* extracts the data it needs, and…
4a.	…delegates the message in case the delegate DC (*wBase* in this case) wishes to process it.
r > 4a. to r > 1.	The process now unwinds, and control is returned to the CEE.

for configuration and other non-functional data, while a functional DC in the delegation chain uses component-managed persistence for business data.

Megadata

By *megadata*[7] is meant the management of potentially large collections of data. In any business system, it happens often that it is necessary to send a large list of data from one tier to another or from one software component to another. This set of data can be bigger than the physical limit of a single message, or it may be of indeterminate size. Another example is where the user tier is required to present a list of possibly thousands of items. In either case, specific patterns are required to properly manage the data. In general, the megadata problem exists when there is a dynamic amount of data to be handled with the risk of reaching some technology-specific limit. Examples of such technical limits are the maximum size of data in a single component-to-component message, memory size on a client machine, and memory size on the server machine. These three categories can be thought of as three main design points for solutions to megadata. Other constraints include network bandwidth and minimum required screen response times.

The megadata challenge is a good example of a challenge that all business systems face, but that is not directly or completely addressed by any of the component implementation technologies providers. Indeed, it requires a megadata framework that crosses the distribution tiers and the architectural viewpoints.

This section discusses megadata as it applies to retrieving large amounts of data from an ERD into a UWD. This is a very common situation in distributed systems, and it is an end-to-end problem, with implications from the user interface right through to the organization of data in a shared database. The megadata challenge also occurs when retrieving large amounts of data into a domain other than the UWD, for example, by a gateway business component that manages requests from an EDI link or at times in EDC-to-EDC communication.

There are three main problem areas in a typical ERD to UWD scenario:

1. Scalability

2. Staging

3. Instance overload in the UWD

The functional programmer should ideally be concerned with none of these problems. Experience to date suggests strongly that it is possible to handle all the complexities associated with solving the preceding problems in a framework, such that the functional programmer can safely ignore most if not all of the complexities. Each of these problem areas is briefly described, and possible solutions are proposed.

Scalability

When accessing a large amount of data on the database for transfer to some requester, it cannot be assumed that all data can be retrieved using a single SQL command. If it were, then search loads on the database would be too high, and the returned data, in a single stream, would block up the network. The result would be a significant hit on response times across the system and for the requesting user in particular. In addition, retrieving all data risks flooding the UWD because, in the general case, the hardware accommodating the UWD is much smaller than that available to the ERD.

The conclusion is that large amounts of data should be sent on several messages from the ERD to the UWD: The data must be "chunked." This then raises the question of whether the chunks should be sent from the ERD one after the other (streamed megadata) or sent in response to specific requests only (paced megadata). These two options are illustrated in Figure 8.8.

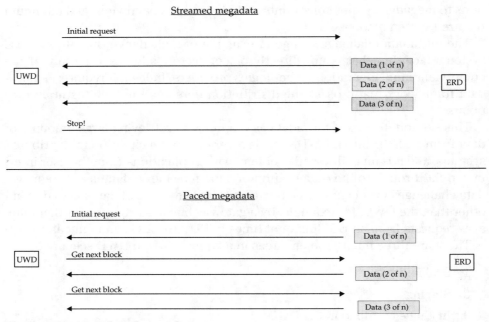

Figure 8.8 Megadata flow options.

Streamed megadata. Shown at the top of the diagram, the UWD requests a large amount of data. The ERD accesses the database and sends the data back one chunk after another. It is up to the UWD to determine what to do with the chunks as they arrive. The UWD can interrupt the process by sending a "stop" message.

Paced megadata. Shown at the bottom of the figure, this relies on the UWD specifically requesting each chunk. This introduces another design point: Who defines what "next" means? If it's a component instance in the ERD, then that component instance must remember where the last chunk ended and where the next chunk should start. This means that state for each requester is held in the ERD, and the ERD's operation is bound to the UWD's state. In general, this is an *extremely* bad idea. So what we do is have the requester define what "next" means. This implies that the ERD component instance provides an interface something like this:

```
interface VendorMegadata
{
   read_multiple_vendors( in  string     start_key,
                          in  long       max_number,
                          out VendorArray vendor_data );
...
};
```

Of course, some necessary aspects are omitted from this interface, but it's sufficient to explain the essentials. So, the UWD component instance invokes the *read_multiple_vendors* operation on the first invocation, perhaps providing a null *start_key* to indicate "start at the beginning." An array of up to *max_number* vendor records is returned in *vendor_data*. The last array element contains the last key provided. When more data is needed, the UWD component instance invokes the same interface but provides the last-retrieved key as *start_key*, and so on. Thus the ERD component instance retains no state between the two invocations. Note that this approach requires the ERD component instance (and the DBMS) to be able to search from a provided start-key, even though that *start_key* value may not exist. This is to allow for row deletion by another user in the database between invocations. Note also that as data is retrieved within the ERD from the database, only one cursor needs to be kept open by the ERD component and then only for the duration of a single request from the UWD.

Between the two approaches, we generally prefer the paced approach because it gives more control to the UWD, is generally less complex at the UWD end, and is no more complex at the ERD end. Note that the maximum number of rows to return is defined by the requester. This provides more control over the amount of data returned, that control being exercised where it counts most—at the requester end.

Some designs for handling megadata rely on counting the number of hits in the database before returning anything. This is so that if the number of hits is very large, then an index can be returned, perhaps with the first chunk of hits as well. An algorithm for this approach is provided in *Business Objects* [Sims 1994, p. 184]. Counting is efficient only if there is an index on the column to be counted. Where requesters are allowed to specify any column or set of columns on which to search, then this will probably result in unacceptable overhead— or a much larger number of indices than normal!

Staging

Consider the scenario where a user wants to see a list of vendors on the GUI, where only a subset of the data from each row in the database is displayed. Now consider Figure 8.9, which shows the various places, on an end-to-end solution, where data can be staged—or "duplicated"—or "cached."

A shows data visible in a list on the screen. The data in this list is physically in a GUI control such as a list box or a grid (and, not shown, it's also physically copied in the screen buffer deep down in the GUI system software). *A* is a visualization of the list *B* that is in user tier memory. The user scrolls up and down this list (*B*) with effectively immediate response time. List *B* is copied from a

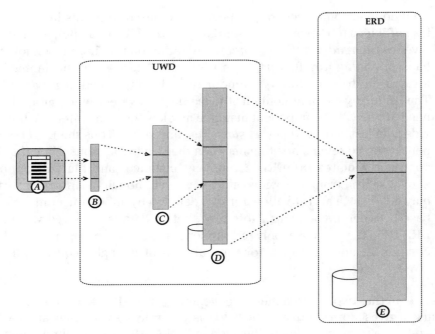

Figure 8.9 Data staging.

workspace tier component instance, which holds a larger list C in memory. This component instance might also cache an even bigger list locally on disk (D). Finally, the workspace component instance requests data from the ERD (E). The ERD does not cache data as a result of workspace requests. (Of course, the database shown as E may indeed be a copy or extract of an operational database. This consideration is outside the scope of megadata.)

The arrangement shown in Figure 8.9, although useful in a number of situations, is not the only one possible. For example, the workspace disk cache (D) may be omitted. A useful general-purpose framework can be built using this arrangement. It is also possible to make this framework generic, so that the UWD parts of different business components can all share the same generic megadata-handling DCs. Such generic DCs could be configured by business component to conform to a small number of different patterns of cached data. In general, it is a combination of user interface design and physical system design that determines the specific design to be used within the UWD. For example, the user could be led to believe that he or she can scroll across the whole of the list D. If this is so, then, in order to avoid sticky (possibly very sticky) scroll bars, the data has to be fed very quickly from the workspace tier. This almost certainly means keeping the workspace tier on the same machine as the user tier.

Many people worry about data duplication between the database and the GUI. This is most often a needless worry because duplication will occur. Accept it and make sure it's appropriate. Data "duplication" is essential in distributed computing, and the general megadata solution is a good example—especially considering that in most cases the data is read-only. Remember that when data is copied, the copy is not the same data. Even if identical bit for bit, it's still different data, and does not necessarily have to be kept in sync with the source data. Changing one does not mean you automatically have to change the other.

Instance Overload in the UWD

Megadata solutions are often used to present the user with a list of data items (for example, customers or vendors). Such lists contain only a few of the data attributes of the item shown. For example, the list might show Vendor ID, Name, City, and Zip. At this point, a problem appears. On the one hand, it would be much better not to download *all* the data for, say, the 500 vendors displayed in the list. On the other hand, the user may well want to think of each list item as "the vendor." That is, when the user double-clicks on a vendor, the full details of that vendor (or a large subset) should be displayed. Many occurrences of the megadata problem have these characteristics, which can be summarized as follows:

- The user requests a list containing many more items than can be displayed on the screen.

- The user model requires that the user should perceive each item as an "object" (that is, it can be double-clicked, picked up, dropped on, dragged over, and so on).

- For performance and resource utilization reasons, all items cannot be instantiated when the list is retrieved.

The first two items in this list seem to imply that all details of each item should be retrieved just in case the user wants to see all the details of a particular item, or if a drag/drop operation would require some data not in the visible list on the GUI. This would seem to imply that the details for each item should be activated as component instances or as language class instances. In either case, for large lists, the network load is likely to be excessive, and the numbers of instance activations may cause performance problems—hence the third item in the previous list, which presents a problem if the first two items in the list are to be satisfied. It is an intrinsic part of a megadata framework to handle this problem, and other related challenges, on behalf of the functional programmer.

User Interface Framework

The user tier is probably the most underestimated area of distributed systems. To some designers, the user interface is merely a visualization of data on a server, and its implementation is hence no more difficult than using a GUI layout tool. To others it is the universe, and all else is merely a trivial matter of someone else providing the data to display. Both these views are extremes, and both can easily lead to disasters in the UWD. What is initially often seen as merely data visualization usually turns into a complex system of multiple windows, complex widgets, detailed editing and mapping code, drag/drop, interprocess communication mechanisms (to avoid the whole of an enterprise's user tier to run in one address space on a PC), and complicated efforts to avoid blocking (the "sticky mouse" syndrome). In addition, there is the challenge of actually interacting with one or more ERDs, handling workflow constructs, tool selection, and language selection, as well as providing for the required user friendliness.

The main point here is that the user tier needs some serious thought. The first thought is that this whole thing is far too unproductive for the functional developer. What is needed is a framework and infrastructure that enables functional developers to develop user tier and workspace-tier components just as easily as ERD ones. A well-designed CEE should provide several things for the user tier, including the following:

- Clear separation of layout from GUI-related code, such that layout can be changed without changing any functional DC code—and preferably without having to redeploy it.

- Support for a defined user's model by generic technical DCs, so that in, say, 80 percent of cases, the functional developer need not write user tier DCs—because they are merely configured.

- Ability to handle event notifications from the workspace tier, for example, when a workflow workspace DC requires a view of some other WDC to be displayed.

- Thread management so that the user interface is not blocked; that is, the user should not find the GUI frozen when least expected.

There are a number of viable designs for the user tier infrastructure. Figure 8.10 illustrates one such design, which addresses a requirement for platform portability across Wintel and Unix. The implementation language is assumed to be Java.

The separate parts of the infrastructure are as follows:

GUI system infrastructure. System-level infrastructure as provided by Microsoft, Sun, and so on, together with GUI microcode and hardware. The GUI system infrastructure provides APIs and frameworks for the experienced GUI technology programmer. It will often be platform-specific.

CEE GUI infrastructure. A thin CEE-provided layer that may be significantly implemented using COTS (commercial off-the-shelf) tools and/or software. The purpose of the CEE GUI infrastructure is to do the following:

- Separate the platform-specific GUI system infrastructure from the platform-independent CEE-provided user model DC.

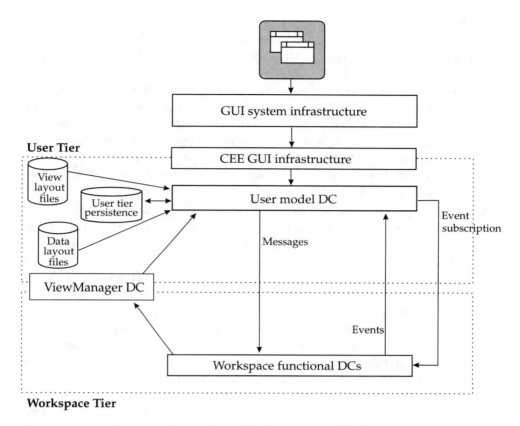

Figure 8.10 User tier infrastructure.

- Support GUI constructs in a way that maps to the component concept, so that the user tier of a business component may be physically installed without impact on any other business component's user tier.

The implementation of this layer is platform-specific, but it provides a platform-independent user model to its users. It provides a pull model, so that GUI widgets "pull" data from data elements in the user model DC (an example of the principle of noncircularity). This layer also registers interest in data state events published by the user model DC.

User model DC. This is a CEE-provided technical DC that is generically-coded and that implements the user model. Different user models require different support frameworks. For example, an object-based user model is quite different in the capabilities it must support from a menu-panel user model [Sims 1995, 1996]. This DC also handles screen layouts, generated by a COTS layout tool, and user tier persistence. Persistence is needed, for example, to remember what views the user had visible when he or she powered off, so that the views can be reconstituted when the user powers on. Data displayed on the GUI is provided to the CEE GUI infrastructure from data elements held in this layer. When a data element changes, an event is published.

The user model DC requests data from a workspace DC. (We assume that the user model is such that workspace DCs are required; if not, then the workspace responsibilities could be implemented within the user model DC.) In addition, it subscribes to change events in workspace DCs, so that changes there can be reflected on the GUI. Note that the user model DC can be designed as a single configurable generic DC usable by all business components.

View manager DC. This is a CEE-provided technical DC that enables views to be surfaced as a result of activity in the workspace tier. To do this, it first provides a "show" operation that takes a workspace tier component instance name. Second, it determines which user tier of which business component should be used to show a view of the provided workspace component instance. Third, it causes this view to be surfaced. At this point, the view can populate itself from the workspace DC. Logically, the view manager DC straddles the user/workspace tiers because it "knows" about DCs in both tiers. Where the user and workspace tiers are physically separated (in different processes or even on different machines) then this DC would normally be physically positioned with the user tier. Also, the GUI layout for a visualization can be passed programmatically to the view manager DC, thus providing a way to minimize the number of files on a PC and allowing central management of views.

Further internals detail of the user tier infrastructure provided by the CEE are beyond the scope of this book. Suffice to say that the kind of infrastructure described has been built and has proved highly productive. It allows for interesting expansions, such as automatically determining a view layout from the shape of the data in the user model DC.

Extended Integrated Development Environment

An efficient production capability must be supported by an appropriate development environment. The development environment is defined as including the whole set of tools required to construct, verify, and validate a business component and a business component system: We call this the *Extended Integrated Development Environment* (XIDE), referring to the fact that this should include not only commercially-available IDEs but also, in an integrated environment, what is required for assembly and development across the development lifecycle. This section focuses on what is required to quickly build an industry-level version of a component-based system. Chapter 10, "Project Management Architecture," will address the requirements on the development environment that derive from the needs of a large development team.

An example of a XIDE for component-based development is represented in Figure 8.11 and is based on the development process presented in Chapter 7.

Each phase of development has its own focus and toolkit. The development environment in this example relies on a repository and on software configuration management (SCM) tools. Here we discuss repository-based development, leaving the SCM perspective to Chapter 10. In the example shown in Figure 8.11, the project has decided to have the requirements phase managed through documents and spreadsheets. Given the current state of requirement management tools, this can be a reasonable choice. A consequence of this is that the requirements deliverables are not directly integrated into the overall development environment. Hence conventions and guidelines are used to track requirements through the development lifecycle.

Analysis and design should be supported by appropriate tools. In the example, we indicate an object-oriented analysis and design tool, a data modeling tool, a graphical user interface prototyping tool, and what we call a component specification tool (CST), further discussed later in this chapter and again in Chapter 10. The usual cycle, code-build-test-debug, is today supported by a multitude of excellent IDEs. And multiple testing tools are available on the market.

All these tools are individually available on the market as independent (not integrated) offerings. New standards, such as UML and XMI (also mentioned in Chapter 6, "The Federation of System-Level Components"), are creating the

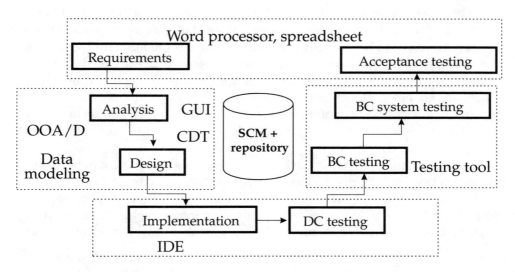

Figure 8.11   Example of an XIDE.

conceptual support that will make it much easier to achieve a commercial integrated offering, but at the time of writing this can be obtained only with some project-specific XIDE integration effort.

Let us consider, starting from a simple example, what it means for the XIDE to be integrated. This will be further covered in Chapter 10. Suppose that while modeling the database, the *CurrencyBook* business component defines, in a table *t_currency*,[8] a column (field) "currency_mnemonic" of database type string and length 3 alphanumeric characters. Examples of possible values are "USD" to indicate US dollars, "LIT" to indicate Italian lire, and so forth [ISO 1995]. Suppose that this is the primary key, which is also used to identify currencies in other tables owned by other components. These other tables should have the same definition of this field. In a large system in which this kind of thing may happen literally hundreds or thousands of times, it is important that the location of the master definition of a given field is well known. Where required, how to easily modify it in the system should also be well known.

Furthermore, there will be a need to have a corresponding attribute in many language classes defined in the object-oriented model. It is a project-specific decision whether this is just a string or a full-blown *currencyMnemonic* object (or something else): The important point is that this definition should be consistent not only across a given business component, but also across all business components. Last but not least, because this field will probably appear as a parameter (or part thereof) in a distributed component interface, a similar concept will need to exist in the implementation of other business components; thus, there is a requirement for consistency of this definition across the system.

The point of this example is that, in an efficient production capability, many aspects of the construction are related to each other and should be linked, more or less directly, to each other while, on the other hand, directly supporting the need for autonomous development. What starts out as a separate area of concern turns out to be a development environment integration problem where the whole set of tools should be integrated or should at least feed into each other in some useful way. This includes the tools for component modeling, database modeling, object-oriented modeling, testing; and also the IDE, the repository, the software configuration management tool, and so forth. This is especially true given our focus on rapid development. In Chapter 10, we will add a versioning dimension.

Chapter 7 identified the main characteristics of the development of a business component system, which can be summarized as follows: to build the system iteratively through assembly of concurrently developed high-quality business components and distributed components. This description captures the following important aspects of a development environment supporting this development:

- It should support the rapid, autonomous development of *individual business components*. In this sense, for each business component the functional developer should be able to specify and immediately generate an executable deliverable. For example, as discussed in Chapter 7, the specification of a DC's interfaces should permit the generation of a component faker and (together with the testing specification) of a tester DC. The database model and persistence mapping specification should allow the addition of a default (very simple, maintenance-oriented) executable implementation of the DC; and the specification of the DC's internal object-oriented model should permit, at each iteration, the progressive build of the functional DC while being able to execute the DC. All of this, of course, should happen in such a way that the DC, and the containing BC, is portable as described earlier in this chapter (for example, across different component implementation technologies).

- It should support the management of the whole development at the *system level*, supporting the view of the individual business components deliverables at the system level (for example, the ability to view the database model of the whole system at an integrated level).

- The previous two points, coupled with the need of rapid functional development, lead to the requirement to be able to shift quickly between the business component and the business component system point of view.

- Furthermore, in a mature environment, all repetitive aspects should be automated and simplified. For example, it should be possible to rebuild the whole system with a single command. The rebuild should include regeneration and retesting. This leads to the requirement for tools to be scriptable, in such a way that some of their behavior can be automated to some level.

- Given the high costs of testing, it is natural to target tools that diminish these costs. In a rapid system development, the development environment should enable easy modification of the software artifacts that impact a given test (for example, the impacted test specifications and the related testing scripts). It is possible to a large extent both to generate automatic testers and to link specific test cases to a specification in the tools.

At the time of writing, there is no environment available on the market that supports the kind of component-based development described here, but both authors have been involved in designing and building such an environment for the in-house consumption of large software vendors. Such an XIDE should ideally have all parts of the development environment feed into each other. We have discussed continuous integration and the concept of living documents: The development environment must support both these aspects. This requires repository-based development, as will be illustrated in the subsection "Repository-Based Development." It should also have a strong concept of distributed component (and if possible of business component); that is, it should have a concept of distributed component as a first-class citizen in its meta-model. This concept should abstract from the particular implementation technology at the specification level.

Component Specification Tool

Given the importance of the definition of component interfaces, it would be natural to have tool support for this specification, and this tool is called here a Component Specification Tool (CST). Many commercially available object-oriented modeling tools claim to have this functionality, but at the time of writing, few if any of them seem to be wholly appropriate for serious component-based development. Reasons for this range from weakness in the definition of the component concept to the lack of integration with other CBD tools.

A good CST would have three main aspects: support for the definition of component interfaces, support for the management of dependencies, and support for generation of at least that part of the separation layer that provides the portability across different CEEs. The second of these is addressed in Chapter 10, and it is not considered further here. In addition, the tool should be able to feed and receive information to and from the other tools in the XIDE.

Interface definition. This should exclude the various technical peculiarities of the underlying middleware such as COM or CORBA Components, allowing the functional developer to define technology-free interfaces. This approach is feasible today, but given the lack of a technology-independent component specification standard, obviously leads to a proprietary solution.

The interface definition could be supported by an appropriate textual language, along the syntactical lines of OMG's IDL or Microsoft's MIDL, rather than by a proper user tool. We refer to such a specification language as a component specification language (CSL). A tool could superimpose on the specification language project-specific conventions, defaults, and so forth, making the specification much less error-prone and consistent.

Separation layer generation. We have already discussed the criticality of using, as much as possible, code generation to simplify some of the complex aspects of the implementation of distributed systems. Ideally, a functional developer should not have to worry about any component implementation technology aspects but should be allowed to focus purely on the specification of business functionality. For example, the CST should have all the information required to allow for code specific to the component implementation technology to be generated.

Repository-Based Development

Software professionals use the term "repository-based development" in different ways, and with different meanings. For example, the term may refer to the need to have a central place usable by all tools in the development environment to share related information, but it may also indicate a repository to store semantic definitions of tags for tagged data to be used for interoperability aspects. In this section, we use the first meaning.

Repository-based development can be both very healthy and very risky for a project. While the notion of bringing under control the many different results of the various development environment tools is very appealing, it is also very easy to get to the extreme that all parts of the development are so highly tied to each other that it becomes very difficult to modify anything without impacting larger parts of the system. A repository-based development that adopts a strong component-based approach can resolve this issue. This requires, as discussed briefly in Chapter 4, "The Business Component," the ability to view each business component as owning its own repository, either logically or physically, and the application of a strong export/import model at all phases of the development lifecycle.

Typically, tension exists between having a central repository and having one repository per business component. For example, consider the following issues with data types:

- If a central repository is used for data types, it is very simple to use existing types anywhere in the system because they are just "available" for use by everybody. On the other hand, this central repository may need to be updated frequently (creating an unstable development environment); this may create a "broader surface" for interfacing business components because typically this "central" data type definition produces one big header file that needs to be included by everybody needing the data types, potentially requiring a recompile/rebuild of the system every time it is modified.

- If every business component has its own repository (logically if not physically), and if the elements of the repository are imported/exported to other repositories when needed, some of the problems and constraints of a single central repository are resolved. On the other hand, in the previous example, it is less simple to just use data types because some conscious action to import them from the proper business component must be taken.

Furthermore, the use of a repository for each component requires that it is not only possible but also easy to combine the various repositories into one bigger repository at different development phases. This is typically required in order to retain all the benefits of a centralized repository to manage development integrity and consistency—for example, to manage consistency across the whole development or to see a system-wide view of various models. That this system-level repository is not used to generate global files to be reused by everyone, but rather is used to verify system consistency, means that a broader surface area between components is not created.

Summary

The technical architecture is the architectural viewpoint concerned with the component execution environment, the development tools, and any other technical capabilities required to develop and run a component-based system, and it addresses the first step in a component factory set-up. The aim of the technical architecture is to provide a separation layer that hides technical complexity from the functional developer and supports portability. In other words, the aim is to provide the functional developer with an environment within which he or she can focus entirely on business function and can have little or no concern with any software engineering aspects. We call the set of concepts behind such an environment the *technical architecture* of the business component factory. The business component virtual machine is the implementation of the technical architecture.

The business component virtual machine includes the component execution environment and the extended integrated development environment. The component execution environment consists of the technical core and a set of services and facilities. To a large extent, the technical core addresses what is required by an individual distributed component at run-time, while the services and facilities address what is required for distributed components and business components to properly collaborate.

The business component virtual machine should hide from the functional developer all the technical complexities of component development, including as many portability issues as possible—portability across platforms, databases, network and middleware (including the various component implementation technologies), and user interfaces. The virtual machine corresponds to the implementation of a separation layer, which may require the creation of a meta-model of the development and run-time concepts required for component-based development, as well as the creation of code-generation capability to quickly address separation layer coding needs.

The technical core includes the main technical capabilities related to the execution of a given distributed component. These include component invocation, management of the component lifecycle, hiding from the functional developer the various concurrency issues, and providing useful features such as asynchronous messaging and dynamic inheritance.

Services and facilities address all the remaining technical aspects required to build a large-scale business system, such as transactions, error handling, event management, persistence, megadata, and the user interface framework. While many of these are included at the time of writing in commercially available component implementation technologies, others such as the megadata framework require an appropriate set-up by the component factory builders.

The extended integrated development environment supports a rapid system development across the development lifecycle. Ideally, it should consist of a set of tools, covering all parts of the development, and feeding and receiving development information to and from each other through some form of development repository. In a component-based development, it should be possible to see this repository as logically or physically owned by each individual business component, while still having the ability to quickly gather a system-level view of the appropriate deliverables to validate system-level architectural and design consistency.

Endnotes

1   We are indebted to Don Kavanagh for the term "business component virtual machine."

2   This is not possible for all languages; the language must have some specific underlying technical capabilities to do with how a compiled and linked module written in that language can be bound to a module written in another language.

3   SSA's Business Object Facility submission to the OMG [OMG-1997a] aimed at providing for such binary portability across same operating systems. Clearly binary portability across operating systems is not possible today, and it is likely to remain so for some time to come.

4   One school of thought believes that distributed component systems should be built entirely using asynchronous messaging. Prins has built a large-scale distributed system using asynchronous messaging only. "All objects must run and cooperate concurrently. There is no implied master-slave relationship; all objects will cooperate on a peer-to-peer basis." [Prins 1996, p. 27].

5   See also [Szyperski 1998, p.193], [Abadi 1996, p.46], and [OMG1997b].

6   The term ACID stands for Atomicity, Consistency, Isolation, and Durability and is further explained in Appendix B, "Glossary." The acronym was first used in [Harder 1983], and is addressed in many texts on transactions and databases; for example, see [Date 1995].

7   The phrase "megadata problem" was coined by Oliver Sims some 10 years ago in an IBM internal paper.

8   We adopt an arbitrary convention of indicating a table name by t_<name>, see appendix A, "Naming Conventions."

CHAPTER

9

Application Architecture

We are well underway in our factory setup. We have now established a conceptual framework for the products (the components) we want to build, and we have discussed the process for building these products, which is an essential part of defining the factory. We have also discussed the kinds of machines and tools (the technical architecture) we need to perform our software manufacturing. This chapter will help us define the structural guidelines for the components—that is, the application architecture.

The *application architecture* is the architectural viewpoint concerned with the set of architectural decisions, patterns, guidelines, and standards required to build a component-based system that conforms with extra-functional requirements. It addresses the set of things needed, in addition to the business component virtual machine, to build large-scale systems. This includes a set of generic application-level services that are centered on business components. Examples are errors and error handling, business data types, and generic structural patterns for distributed systems. These and other application architecture items are all designed to take into account the nature of business components, the need to preserve autonomy of development, and system-level development integrity.

The intent of this chapter is to describe the main application architecture principles required by component-based development, and illustrate the nature of an application architecture through a few examples of what it addresses, without any pretense of an exhaustive treatment of this extensive and interesting subject. It is assumed that we can take technical infrastructure and technical architecture considerations as given. While not realistic, it enables a focus to be placed on the most relevant issues from the application designer point of view.

The application architecture can be viewed as the set of principles, architectural styles, patterns, application-specific guidelines for using the technical architecture properly, and the more generic set of guidelines and standards required to support the building of a large-scale application that globally satisfies the extra-functional requirements and, in particular, some of the application architecture aspects necessary for the scalability and high-performance requirements of the following development context:

1. Large-scale (hundreds or thousands of language classes and database tables), mission-critical distributed business systems

2. Heavy use and strong performance requirements (for example, less than two seconds' response time for 90 percent of user interactions, thousands of concurrent users in distributed locations)

3. Strong data consistency and integrity requirements (typically requires transaction processing monitors or equivalent system, plus a heavy-duty access to relational databases)

In this chapter, the following aspects of the application architecture are discussed:

- *Application architecture principles*. Two important architectural principles, the principle of noncircularity and the principle of architectural normalization, and a number of other principles are presented.

- *Application architecture styles*. There are two main styles for an application architecture based on components, type-based and instance-based, as well as a set of other architectural style considerations.

- A set of *collaboration patterns* for large-scale distributed systems built out of components. As examples, we present the challenges of business transactions, default management, overrides management, and how to deal with validations and where to allocate them.

- Filling the gap between the *technical architecture* and *the functional architecture*. A set of application-side (as opposed to pure technical infrastructure viewpoint) aspects for the various services and facilities is presented in Chapter 8, "Technical Architecture." As examples, we discuss error handling and the issues related to setting up an enterprise-wide system, as well as a set of guidelines and project standards.

There is not an exact line between where the technical architecture viewpoint finishes and the application architecture begins: The two viewpoints have a strong influence on each other, and the difference between the two evolves in time, with more and more conceptual aspects becoming more known and thus technically addressable. An ideal BCVM should eventually evolve to cover more and more application architecture aspects (see Figure 9.1), in the same way that operating systems are including more and more aspects that would never have been considered part of the operating system until just a few years ago.

Again, over time and across organizations, there is not an exact line between architectural principles and design principles (presented in Chapter 12, "Component-Based Design"). We take the following pragmatic if subjective approach to defining the difference: The application architecture influences both the whole shape (or at least large parts) of the system and how business components and distributed components collaborate. Design principles tend to be specific to an individual business component, and they influence its shape and that of distributed components. This is far from being an exact distinction, and it can sometimes be seen as quite arbitrary and subjective. What is certain is that both application architecture and design play a crucial role in satisfying extra-functional requirements such as scalability and performance. In this sense, both this chapter and Chapter 12 can be seen as two aspects of the same thing.

Finally, there is not an exact line over time and across organizations between application architecture and functional architecture. Generally speaking, the application architecture describes the mental model required to successfully design and build a distributed system, and shapes the functional architecture. The application architecture may define both high-level and detailed principles that govern system and component structure; the functional architecture is concerned with the functional patterns and principles required to define and build the exact functional deliverables according to this structure. For example, in the business component approach, the application architecture prescribes the four distribution tiers, while the functional architecture prescribes

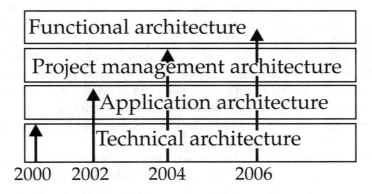

Figure 9.1   BCVM evolution.

the functional layering of utility, entity, and process components. As a more detailed example, consider an application architecture error definition that defines an error code format as "errors must consist of a pair {<component mnemonic>, <error code>}." This is instantiated in the functional architecture viewpoint as a specific string value for each business component (such as "ORM, 42" for the error "42" of the *OrderManager* business component).

In a custom-application development, the amount of time and energy available to properly define the application architecture aspects are often limited. A set of trade-offs, which should ideally balance risks and pragmatic business considerations, often leads to compromises on this important aspect. This can arguably be a good approach in a few cases, under the perspective that a good solution is not so much the most well-designed solution, but the solution that achieves the business objectives. On the other hand, this approach usually significantly adds to the risks of the project. Often, the project sets up the technical infrastructure, spends some time on the tools, and then takes off into the many problems of functional development. The application architecture evolves with maturity, and its absence is often the main cause for significant and costly system-wide modifications, as well as of project failures.

Like many other aspects of the business component approach, the application architecture is geared toward supporting the autonomy of the business components and of their development. Within the application architecture subject, there are various aspects that have to be carefully considered in order to prevent unexpected links and dependencies between components popping up unexpectedly.

Architectural Principles

This section presents a set of architectural principles. Two important architectural principles, of universal validity and not specific to the business component approach, are the principle of noncircularity and the principle of architectural normalization. These are required to argue some of the concepts in the remaining parts of the chapter.

Many readers will be familiar with these principles because they have been applied by software architects and application designers probably for decades, and they may look or sound like just plain common sense. Still, we are constantly reminded that common sense is not necessarily common. If nothing else, presenting them here should help illustrate various important aspects of the business component approach.

Two clarifications about application architecture and design principles: First, *principles are not dogmas*, but rather they are stated in order to know when to break them. Second, *principles are not always universal*, but rather are sometimes context-dependent. A different development context can lead to a different set of principles. The most important thing is enlightened pragmatism: As one of the authors likes to say, "*If it works in practice but not in theory, then the theory is wrong.*" For example, over time, the definition of what constitutes a *good component* should be driven by usability, and other extra-functional considerations, which can sometimes rightfully lead to decisions that appear contrary to the principles outlined here.

Noncircularity

A circularity, or more precisely a *circular dependency* between two software artifacts, exists when these two software artifacts are able to invoke each other or in some way depend on each other. A circular dependency may exist at any lifecycle phase. We consider circularities the mother of many evils in software development. The following principle is probably one of the simplest, most important, and most neglected principles of large-scale architectures in any technology, not only for distributed systems. It applies at all architectural viewpoints, distribution tiers, functional layers, and lifecycle phases and it is this: *Circularities should be avoided in any available way, including by architecture, design, development process, and others.*

This principle takes many equivalent forms. For example, it is sometimes expressed as the Hollywood principle: "Don't call me, I'll call you if I need you." Again, it has been expressed as the need for proper and clean architectural layers, with "each layer below providing clean interfaces to the layers above." This is also a principle that, when broken at run-time while accessing a database, may lead to deadlock. It is also important to understand that a circularity can causes problems at development phases other than run-time.

A typical example of circularity problems is as follows: Two different components are developed by two different teams, but they depend on each other. A modification to one component usually requires a modification to the other component, as well as the testing of both components. This leads to a potentially nonconverging development process.

At the business component system level, this principle can be usefully expressed as the Directed Acyclic Graph (DAG) principle: It should be possible to trace a DAG between business components in the BCSM. This implies that the relationship between two components is unidirectional (no circularities are allowed between components) and that the component space is not flat. It also implies that components are not created equal—they do not participate as peers in a democracy; rather there are managers or coordinators and managed or coordinated—there are masters and slaves. This currently leads, in the information world only, to a simpler world. By applying this principle, dependencies between business components and between the distributed components that implement them are much reduced and are made predictable.

The principle of noncircularity can appear to be broken when analyzing a given component as a whole, but not really be broken. Figure 9.2 exemplifies what appears to be a circularity when analyzing dependencies at the business component level but that turns out not to be a circularity when dependencies between distributed components are analyzed.

This example points out how the ability to detect whether circularity exists will ultimately depend on the sophistication of the tools. Sophisticated tools could allow large sets of cross-dependencies between two business components that appear as circularities at some level of abstraction but that are not actually circularities at a detail level. As a general rule, though, the system will be a lot simpler to manage if the principle is enforced at the business component level.

This principle impacts how we think about components, and it drives many architectural and design decisions. It has been implicitly applied throughout this book at various levels of granularity. For example, all previous examples that showed business components at the various functional layers have also illustrated their constituting a DAG, as exemplified in Figure 9.3. In addition, it has also been implicitly assumed that the tiers and distributed components inside a business component belong to a DAG. The tiers always follow the rules exemplified in Figure 9.4, where it is applied top-down: The user tier of a given business component can call its own workspace tier, or the workspace tier of another component, but it cannot be directly called by any other workspace tier. The workspace tier can call its own enterprise tier, or the enterprise tier of another component, but it cannot be directly called by any enterprise tier. The enterprise tier can call another component's enterprise tier, or its own resource tier, but it cannot be called by any resource tier.

The noncircularity principle may be applied as a logical principle: There are various ways in which the principle can be technically relaxed, that is, allowing some level of physical circularity while still enforcing the logical noncircularity. We do not consider the principle broken if event or notification mechanisms or other technical ways to enforce logical unidirectionality (typically relying on the CEE) are used.

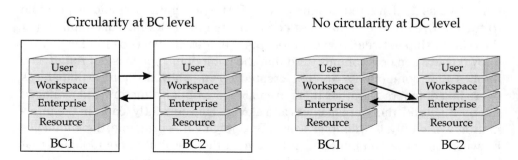

Figure 9.2   Apparent circularity.

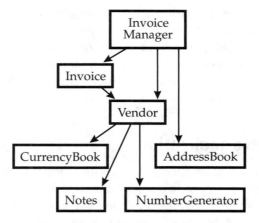

Figure 9.3   Legal dependencies between business components.

A lower functional layer may know about some concept belonging to an upper layer in the functional category hierarchy if that concept is "pushed down" to a lower level. For example, the project may decide to have the business component *Base* manage currency codes (the list of currency codes an organization assumes are valid, such as "USD" for US dollars, "LIT" for Italian Lire, and so forth). These codes may need to be used by the business component *AddressBook*, which is below the business component *CurrencyBook*, which naturally owns the currency code concept. "Pushing down" the currency code aspect of the currency concept to the *Base* component does not break the business component definition, but it does allow the noncircularity principle to be respected.

The previous example is a pragmatic approach of general validity to facilitate the respect of the principle: Often, what would break the principle is the own-

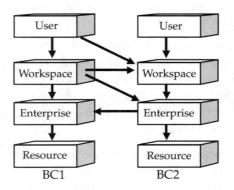

Figure 9.4   Legal dependencies between distributed components.

ership of attributes and business codes. By pushing down these attributes to lower-level components, the circularity is removed. Using similar approaches, it is always possible, either by architecture or by design, to have a business component system respect the principle of noncircularity. The noncircularity principle can be relaxed in mature architectures and systems, as will be discussed later in the section "Peer-to-Peer Components."

Architectural Normalization

The principle of normalization and the various normal forms of the relational model are well known; it even has a mathematical formalization. But this principle is in the reality of general applicability, particularly for both object-oriented modeling and business component modeling. The principle states that each software artifact should be owned by one and only one "location," and the objective should be to architect the system without any repetitions. The term *location* in component-based development indicates a specific level of component granularity.

Examples of the applicability of the principle are as follows:

- The business component system model should be normalized, both at the functional level and at the software artifact level. Functional-level normalization implies that each function is performed by one and only one business component; software artifact-level normalization implies that each software artifact is owned by one and only one business component. The same principles that apply to "good" database design apply to component modeling, too. There should be no repetition, and dependent aspects that are only indirectly dependent should be factored out.

- The internal object-oriented model of each component should also be normalized. The normalization principle can support good object-oriented modeling, at least as a guideline to challenge the design. Of course, in many practical cases the normalization principle can be broken without great loss.

- The system should be normalized across the architectural viewpoints. Each concept and software artifact should belong to only one viewpoint; that is, a given concept or artifact should be assigned to its most natural viewpoint. For example, a decision should be made as to whether the utility language class in a DC belongs primarily to the technical architecture or to the application architecture.

A system is either constrained by architecture or non-normalized. Mastering the consequences of the normalization principle will enable the architect to break the principle when required. Indeed, there are various levels at which the principle can be rightfully broken because this principle can under certain circumstances play against the autonomy principle. For example, typically at the federation level, a certain amount of redundancy is not only unavoidable, especially in ad-hoc federations, but may also help in maintaining the loose connection of the system-level components.

Other Principles

This section discusses a set of other architectural principles, which have been used so far in the book or will be used later. These are layering, consistency, temporal cohesion, and least astonishment.

Layering

Layering is a powerful approach to complexity reduction. It comes in two flavors, closed layering and open layering. In a *closed layer*, each layer in the layered solution can directly speak only to the adjacent layers. In an *open layer*, each layer can speak with layers that are not adjacent, but usually this is done following a well-defined set of rules (for example, the noncircularity principle). Closed layering is usually used to build solutions by several parties, and it often leads to duplication of codes or artifacts. Consider for example layers *L1*, *L2*, and *L3 (L3 at the top)*, where *L3* uses *L2*, and *L2* uses *L1*. When closed layering is adopted, an interface provided by layer *L1* must be duplicated in layer *L2* if *L3* needs to use it. The advantage is that each layer needs only to know about the layer directly below it in order to work. When open layering is applied, *L3* can use *L1* directly, as well as using *L2*. Open layering is more flexible, but it needs additional principles and management to be effective.

Consistency

This simple principle is a powerful complexity-reduction tool. Any system is much simpler to deal with if its parts (in our case, components) behave and look according to common rules. Chapter 12 will apply this principle to define what a well-formed and a well-behaved component is. The autonomy of the business components and distributed components is enhanced by their consistency at the system level.

Temporal Cohesion

This is a particular application of the well-known "high-cohesion/low-coupling" principle. Rather than applying the cohesion principle in design terms (software artifacts that are related at design should be together), the principle is applied temporally: Software artifacts that are used at the same time should be together. Temporal cohesion and design cohesion lead to different advantages and disadvantages through the lifecycle. The application of the temporal cohesion principle usually leads to better development-time and run-time performance, but it has some impact on the maintainability of the system.

Least Astonishment

The principle of least astonishment relates to the outcome, including side effects, of some set of actions that a person is taught, or led, or instructed to perform. The principle states that the less someone is astonished by an outcome, then the better the set of actions has been designed. In general, this means that side effects are minimized. For example, consider a programmer who first does something that sets the state of the component he or she is writing, then invokes an operation on some other component, and after that checks the state. At run-time, the expected outcome would be that the state has not changed, whereas the converse would be at least a little more astonishing. In this case, whatever had caused the state to change would have broken the principle of least astonishment.

Architectural Styles

This section describes the main application architecture styles and patterns used for component-based systems. The two main styles for DCs are these:

1. *Type-based style.* Also known as "service-based," in this style the components are *manager-like* (or *coordinator-like*) components, in the sense that each component implements a type and manages a set of instances of this type, where these instances cannot be directly addressed over the network.

2. *Instance-based style.* The components represent actual instances of the concept they implement, for example, the specific sales order for customer John Smith having a sales order number APS18584. The specific instance is directly addressable over the network.

These two kinds of architectural style can to some extent be combined, yielding a powerful combination for large-scale component development.

Later in the section, a third style, the *event-based* architectural style, is presented. This style is orthogonal to the type- or instance-based styles, and it is in contrast to the normal synchronous invocation style.

All three styles can be combined by a mature business component factory, but each architectural choice has a greater or lesser consequence on the kind of technical support needed from the BCVM, on the choice of the best design patterns, on the modeling approach, and on the characteristics of the delivered application. Hence using more than one approach at the same time implies a more complex set of requirements on the technical infrastructure, and more generally on the whole software development including the maturity of the organization itself. These styles are presented here mainly under the point of view of their application architecture impact, with some example of their technical architecture consequences.

None of these styles directly impact the functional modeling choices in terms of granularity of the components and how they are identified (although we will see some indirect consequences), but they do differ, as will be discussed shortly, in terms of assignment of the detailed ownership of software artifacts. The component diagram tends to be the same in the various cases, but the detail assignment of responsibilities may be different.

Type-Based and Instance-Based Styles

In this section, the two styles are first described. Following this, the subsection "Applicability" discusses the use of the styles, and the subsection "Comparison" compares and contrasts the two styles on the assumption that each style is synonymous with the following mindsets. An *instance-based mindset* is one that thinks in terms of small-grained instances of classes with many interactions and dependencies between them. Such a mindset is not infrequently found among designers coming directly from an object-oriented programming background. A *type-based mindset* is one that thinks in terms of program units that handle all instances of some type, with few dependencies between the program units. This mindset is often found among designers experienced in using traditional transaction processing systems.

The term *mindset* is used to indicate a typical way, frequently observed in practice, of using a given architectural style, where this typical way does not necessarily correspond to the best way. Indeed, each style can be used in other ways, possibly more optimal for certain contexts that the mindset presented. In particular, the subsection "Comparison" analyzes the effect on design and complexity that can result from a wholly instance-based mindset. This is done to explain the advantages and disadvantages of the two mindsets when applied to larger-scale distributed component systems.

Type-Based

In previous chapters, the type-based application architecture style has been assumed: Business components have always represented a business type rather then a business instance. For example, the Invoice component was really *managing* a set of invoices rather then *being* a specific invoice. We have used the simplifying, if potentially misleading, naming convention that an "Invoice" business component is what manages any set of invoice instances or that an "Item" component is what manages the set of item instances.

Each component in the system is seen as a service provider representing a type that acts as an instance-manager.[1] An *instance-manager* provides a set of interfaces that contain information to internally identify and work on a particular instance of the type or on a collection of such instances. It does not provide direct network addressability to individual instances of a business concept. For example, a type-based *Invoice* component would manage the entire set of invoices in the system.

Type-based design leads to a certain interface style, typically with proxy interfaces following the pattern *component.operation_name (in id_of_instance, in or out someData)*. For example, the following pseudo-code illustrates how a component would invoke a type-based Invoice component (this example is a combination of the interface definition and the code that would be used to invoke the proxy):

```
ieInvoice invoice_manager;
invoice_manager.create(in invoice_id, in invoice_data);
invoice_manager.read(in invoice_id, out invoice_data);
invoice_manager.list(in search_criteria, out list_of_invoices);
```

The first parameter of each invocation gives the identity of the instance to be accessed or a set of criteria to identify some number of instances. The second parameter is data (either "in" or "out").

The type-based style is probably the most conservative and risk-free of the various styles today. It has the most mature technological support, and it is the smallest leap for many organizations to take, being the most intuitive approach for developers used to traditional client/server development. We know of several scalable component-based systems built using this approach.

Instance-Based

In an instance-based component architecture, component instances corresponding to conceptual instances (for example, order 123 for customer John Smith) can be directly addressed over the network.

This leads to a certain interface style, typically with interfaces of type *component_instance.operation_name (in or out someData)*, where the identification of the instance is part of the identifier of the component itself. For example, and where the first statement creates an instance of the proxy for an invoice instance identified by the string "I01512":

```
ieInvoice an_invoice("I01512");
an_invoice.create (in invoice_data);
an_invoice.read(out invoice_data);
```

The management of collections in an instance-based style requires a collection component, which is effectively a type-based component that manages collections and has interfaces such as:

```
ieInvoiceTypeManager invoice_manager;
invoice_manager.list (in search_criteria, out list_of_invoices);
```

Other reasons for creating a type-based component to manage functionality associated with an instance-based style include factory operations for instances. The type-based component associated with the instance-based component is sometimes called a "type manager."

It is worth clarifying three interpretations of the term *instance* when it refers to a component:

1. When there is a need to differentiate the component at build-time from the actual code image in memory at run-time, many practitioners use the term *instance* for the run-time. To differentiate from other meanings of the term, when necessary we qualify this as *the run-time instance of the component*.

2. A component can provide the implementation for an instance of a business concept, for example, "Invoice number 123 for customer John Smith." This is what we refer to as a *component instance*, and it is the meaning being discussed currently. Note that this is probably the meaning most commonly associated with the term *distributed object*, but given the many other connotations this term has, we prefer not to use it.

3. An exact copy of a given component can, depending on the technology, be instantiated more than once in memory for load balancing, performance, distribution, and so forth. This is true not only for a component representing a type, corresponding to a manager or coordinator of instances, but even for a component instance discussed in the preceding point. This case is referred to as *cloning* rather than instantiation, to distinguish it from other uses of the term. In this case, the term *component clone* is used to refer to the instance. More precisely, this can be expressed by saying that *a given run-time component instance can be cloned for extra-functional requirements*.

Applicability

When discussing the functional categories of business components in Chapter 5, "The Business Component System," we introduced the fact that it makes sense, for the different functional categories, to consider the use of instance business components. In particular, as illustrated in Figure 9.5, adopting an instance-based style mostly makes sense for entity business components, while utility and process business components, for different reasons, make sense as type-based components (also known as service-components). For a process business component (aside from instances of workflow, on one hand, and clones created for performance reasons, on the other), it is difficult to think about a logical meaning of an instance. For a utility business component, often the granularity of the objects that are managed by the component is so small that it does not make sense to consider them as network-addressable components, for example, an address or a currency object.

In this sense, the instance-based style is usually not used in a "purist" way—that is, building all components as instance-based. Rather it is a matter of allowing certain components of the system to be built as instance-based, and others as type-based. This approach can indeed be looked on as "purist" itself because it applies good software engineering principles and makes the best use of the available set of design concepts.

Furthermore, the preceding discussion makes the most sense when applied to the *enterprise* tier of the DCs. When the usage of the two architectural styles across the distribution tiers is considered, the tendency presented in Figure 9.6 is often reached. That is, aside from the functional category the business component belongs to, the user and workspace tiers are often thought of primarily in terms of instances (assuming the project decision is to use component technology in the implementation of these two tiers). For example, the user tier and the workspace tier of process components are often thought of as instances of some piece of user work. The resource tier, on the other hand, is often thought of as more naturally type-based. The enterprise tier follows the lines illustrated in Figure 9.5, and it is normally the tier that determines which style the business component is considered to be in.

In the industry today, there is some debate as to whether object instances should be network addressable; that is, should they have their own well-defined network identity? On the surface at least, all the main component implementation technologies seem to implicitly suggest an instance-based style. Any component execution model that supports an instance-based style, however, automatically supports type-based because the technical requirements for a type-based style are a subset of those for an instance-based style.

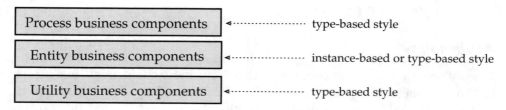

Figure 9.5   Architectural style by functional category.

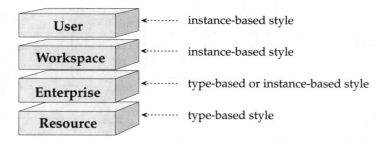

Figure 9.6   Architectural style by distribution tier.

Comparison

This section does two things. First, it explores the differences between designing with a type-based mindset and designing with a wholly instance-based mindset. One of the main hallmarks of the latter is that component instances are naturally thought of as having state across their lifecycle. Second, in exploring this difference, the intrinsic characteristics of each style are described.

Type-Based

A typical behavioral pattern of a type-based component architecture is shown in Figure 9.7. The distributed component *ManagerDC* acts as a manager component[2] in the pattern, while the components below act as managed distributed components, and hence they are simply indicated as *ManagedDC*. In the figure, only one language class is shown within a component (in reality, there are many language classes; this is just an idealization).

At time *t1*, some processing in a language class in the manager component results in the managed component being invoked: as a consequence, the information "s," corresponding to some kind of state, is transferred (for example, as a business data type) from the managed component to the manager component. During the remaining part of the transaction, there is no state in the managed component and the managed component has no recollection that it was activated, unless there have been changes to the database. At *t2*, the example illustrates how further processing of the state or information "s" can be done entirely within the manager component, and at *t3* the manager component may collaborate with other DCs, for example, to verify some additional business rule or ask for some additional data. Very often, as occurs at time *t4*, at the end of the transaction some state is transferred back from the manager component into the managed component, in order for the managed component to persist it.

An example of this for an invoice management system is illustrated in the sequence diagram in Figure 9.8. In this example, a WDC calls the *read* operation on *eInvoiceManager*, which calls *eInvoice* to gather and return the data to *eIn-*

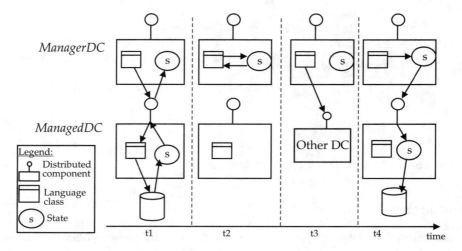

Figure 9.7 Typical type-based behavioral pattern.

voiceManager. When *eInvoice* has done this, it has neither state nor any recollection of having returned the *btInvoice* information, and under all points of view it is not any more an effective participant in the transaction—its role is finished. At this point, *eInvoiceManager* can perhaps perform additional operations on the data or call other business components for additional information (for example, *eCreditChecker* in the sequence diagram).

The previous scenario is further illustrated in Figure 9.9. The state passed from the managed DC *eInvoice* to the manager DC *eInvoiceManager* corresponds in this example to a business data type *btInvoice* (where "*bt*" stands for business data type).

The example in Figure 9.9 is also useful to illustrate an interface pattern. Type-based systems tend to have a repetition of maintenance interfaces from

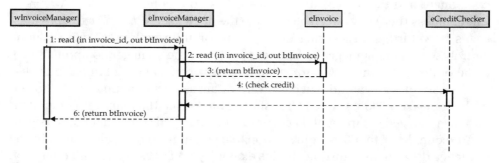

Figure 9.8 Sequence diagram for invoice manager.

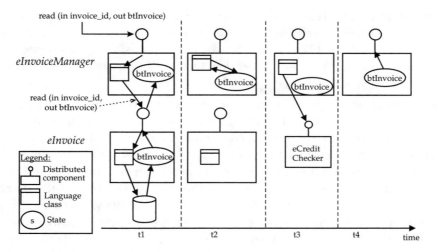

read (in invoice_id, out btInvoice)

eInvoiceManager

read (in invoice_id,
out btInvoice)

eInvoice

Legend:

Distributed
component

Language
class

s   State

t1   t2   t3   t4   time

Figure 9.9 Pattern corresponding to sequence diagram.

process components to entity components, meaning that the same interface can be found on both the manager and managed DC, for example, the operation *read (...)* in Figure 9.9. The two interfaces have usually very different responsibilities and hence different implementations; they also differ in terms of the level of visibility their implementation has with regard to other components. Interfaces on processes, corresponding to the execution of a given business transaction, are also found as CRUD interfaces on entities. In the preceding example, the *read* invoice operation appears both at the *InvoiceManager* component and at the *Invoice* component, with very different implications. The *InvoiceManager* will ensure that the *Invoice* is compliant with all the system-wide business rules; the *Invoice* component is mostly concerned with the proper creation of invoices on the database, which is a complicated operation in an industry-quality system.

A system architected using a type-based style lends itself particularly well to be built bottom-up where each component has a very deterministic and relatively simple behavior: It is invoked, it performs some processing as a consequence of the invocation, and it returns a result, with no internal state retention. The system is often assembled using stateless[3] components (although this is not a necessary consequence of using the type-based style). A given transaction is made up of a sequence of calls from one component to the other, where each call is performed as a service, and there is no expectation that any of the involved components maintains any internal state in memory once it has completed the particular service it was asked to perform.

Let us analyze a few characteristics of the type-based style. We will perform a similar analysis in next subsection for the instance-based style.

Component lifecycle. The activation and deactivation of components in memory can be a relatively rare occurrence. For some systems, it is even conceivable that all components are activated at start-up or connect of the system and that they are never deactivated during the lifetime of the system.

Identification. A type-based component is identified over the network by a static identifier. Once this identifier is obtained, for example, in a simple system through a well-known configuration file, a client of the component could use the identifier for many purposes including working on different instances managed by the type component. The component identifier has no relationship whatsoever with anything that is stored on the database regarding the instances managed by the type. This provides for a clean separation of concerns: On one side is identifying the service provider; on the other side is identifying the data on which that service needs to insist.

Name service and relationship service. The name space for the component is quasi static, and there is relatively little use of a *name service* or of a *relationship service.*

Roles. At least as supported traditionally by the component execution environments, roles may be avoided at the component level. For example, in a type-based component, it is easier to build a generic, all-encompassing Order component to cover different kinds of orders such as quotes, sales orders, or purchase orders, rather than build a component implementing some sort of "base order" concept and later extend it, through some kind of role or behavioral inheritance concept. Nevertheless, using roles in business modeling or even in the internal component design and implementation is very useful even in a type-based style.

Transaction management. Transaction management is relatively straightforward. To a large extent, especially if the type-based style is coupled, as usually happens, with stateless components (addressed in Chapter 12), it is concerned only with the database, and any transactional behavior can be handled by CEE-provided implicit transactions.

Collection management. Given the high levels of coupling and cohesion involved in the collection management functionality when compared to the instances that are parts of these collections, in a type-based style it is perfectly natural to manage both from within the same type-based component. Megadata considerations (introduced in Chapter 8) may, however, lead to assigning the collection management function to a separate *collection component.*

Testing. It is relatively easy to test each component: It is possible, and relatively easy often even at compile time, to deterministically identify the set of components potentially involved in a given transaction and to design a test coverage accordingly.

The type-based architectural style is particularly well suited for business components and distributed components having more than one focus object, for example, a *CurrencyBook* managing both currencies and exchange rates.

To summarize, this is a relatively simple but effective style, supported today by various technologies. It is actually quite easy to architect a system as consisting of components in a type-based style even with nondistributed object technologies such as traditional transaction processing monitor systems. Why bother with other architectural styles? Good question. We will try to answer it in the next section.

Instance-Based

A typical behavioral pattern of an instance-based architectural style can be described as in Figure 9.10; note the differences with Figure 9.7. At time *t1*, some processing in a language class in the manager component leads to the managed component being invoked: As a consequence, information corresponding to some kind of state is loaded into the memory of the managed component. During the remaining part of the transaction, if the manager component needs some information it can access the state of the instance-component: for example at *t2*, the manager component needing to do some more processing on the state will go to the managed DC. Very often, as occurs at time *t4*, at the end of the transaction the state is persisted by the managed component, without needing to transfer it back to the managed DC, as was required in the type-based scenario.

An instance-based architecture, when compared to a type-based style, places additional requirements on the technical infrastructure.

Component lifecycle. The lifecycle to be managed is now the lifecycle of the instances, not, as was for the type-based style, only of components corresponding to types. Instance components can be created for the duration of a transaction or even just for part of a transaction. The management of the component lifecycle hence becomes an important aspect of the technical architecture and of the component execution model required. As part of this lifecycle management, the problem of the automatic garbage collection of run-time distributed objects must be resolved; today this is still not handled well by all of the component implementation technologies.

Identification. The identifier of an instance component is usually composed of two parts, the type and the instance part—for example, "order/APL1234." There is often a great temptation to strongly link this instance identifier to some internal aspect; for example, use the instance part to actually identify the data on which the invocation needs to occur. A

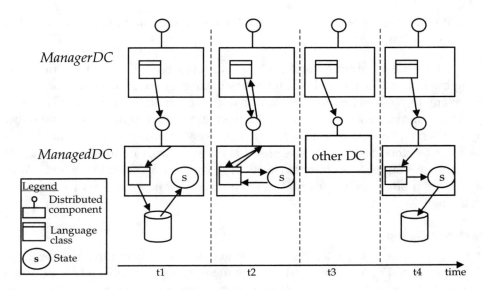

Figure 9.10   Typical instance-based behavioral pattern.

choice that works for simple systems is to use, as the instance identifier, the primary key of a row in a database (usually corresponding to the persistence data of a focus object), leading to a direct link between the name of the component instance and the structure of the database. While this can lead to some simplification, it breaks the architectural layering and separation of concerns. Two models of interaction result, with instances of data depending on the modeling role of the data:

- If the instance corresponds to a database primary key, it is identified as *id_of_instance.operation_name (out someData)*, where the identifier of the component instance is used to exactly identify the data on which the operation is supposed to execute.

- If the data that needs to be accessed is that of some subsidiary concept, not implemented as a component (for example, an order line), the component will provide an operation such as *id_of_instance.operation_ name (in id_of_auxiliary_instance, out someData)*.

The point here is that for many situations, especially for entity components, an instance-based approach often results in two interface patterns, while the type-based approach uses only one. Further, where the instance name is a primary key, then the instance-based approach ties component identity tightly to a resource-tier concern, breaking the technical layering and the separation of concerns, and potentially causing a ripple effect of database model changes in one component to changes to other components. Such tight binding can be, in general, acceptable for smaller systems, but not for large-scale development.

Name service and relationship service. Depending on the particular architectural substyle adopted, services like the *naming service* and the *relationship service* may become more important. The instance-based mindset can result in a whole modeling tendency toward lower granularity components and requirements for navigating dynamically from one instance of one component to another instance of another component, much in the same way done during a database join or complex query. Note that in a type-based architecture, the whole system can easily be built without making any use of a relationship service, given the static nature of the relationships between components in this style.

Roles. The point just discussed similarly applies here: The temptation to use roles, corresponding to the object-oriented modeling ability of assigning a specific type of responsibility to an entity, is great for many practitioners using an instance-based style. We will comment on these points in the next subsection, when comparing the instance-based and type-based styles.

Transaction management. For instance components, and under the instance-based mindset, the concept of transaction may be seen as needing to include the state of the instance components themselves—and not only the state of the data on the database as is the tendency with the type-based mindset. This implies extending to the component instance state all the traditional challenges associated with transactions; for example, locking, deadly embrace, commit, and rollback all have to take the state of the component instance into account. A good treatment of this subject can be found in [Sessions 1996].

Type component. In the type-based style there is a need for only one distributed component to implement a given concept in, say, the e-tier, with the possible exception of a separate type-based component required by megadata collection management aspects. In an instance-based approach there is a need to have both the instance-component *and* what might be called a "type manager" component. This component would manage factory functions, could also contain and manage any metadata information applying to instances, and more generally could manage any information that extends over a set of instances. Such aspects could often be automatically generated by the development tools based on a specification. In the instance-based style, megadata considerations may sometimes lead to a third component (a type-based component) dedicated to the megadata management.

Collection management. This is usually done by a type manager component. For performance reasons, the type collection component should not access the instance components for gathering the required data; rather it would directly use the resource-tier component of the business component. Given the high levels of coupling and cohesion involved in collection management when compared to instance management, in a type-based style it is natural to think of handling both within the same distributed component. On the other hand, considerations such as megadata (introduced in Chapter 8) may lead to the assignment of the collection management function to a separate collection component.

Testing. Theoretically, there is little difference in the ability to test a component in a type-based or in an instance-based style. Pragmatically, various complexities may creep in, depending on the level of technical infrastructure support and design principles used. For example, when coupling a type-based style with stateless components, the result of the test can be found either in the return parameters or in the new state of the system, which is represented by the appropriate database data. In an instance-based approach, when coupled with a stateful mindset as is often done, the result of the test must also include the new state in which the various component instances are in at the end of the test. This increases the complexity of testing, and it could lead to systems with some greater level of unpredictability.

Pros and Cons

Both styles are of crucial importance for enterprise-level component-based development. Given the importance of the topic, it is useful to analyze in more detail the differences between the two styles and to discuss how the instance-based style is being adopted. The difficulty in this analysis is that both styles can be applied in very different ways: The discussion here is based on our observations of what we consider (perhaps wrongly) at the time of writing to be the typical way of using these styles—that is, reflecting an instance-based or type-based mindset.

Philosophical aspect. To a large extent, the two styles differ in their day-to-day use by practitioners in one main philosophical aspect: The type-based is seen as an extension of the traditional system modularization; the instance-based is seen as an extension of the object-oriented approach.

To all of us who have been widely exposed to object-oriented principles, the instance-based may feel, on the surface, more natural: It becomes conceptually possible to build a system using true objects, and it is intellectually satisfying and elegant to extend to a complex distributed system the traditional principles of the object-oriented approach, not only encapsulation, polymorphism, and inheritance, but also various object-oriented patterns, using roles, relationships, and so forth. This is, after all, the *distributed objects* revolution!

In projects using the instance-based mindset, we observe a strong temptation to lower the granularity of the instance components and of their interfaces. For example, the use of "getter and setter" methods, or the implementation of each nontrivial object as a distributed object, is seen. Objects tend to have the same granularity as, or be just a little bit bigger than, objects in a nondistributed object-oriented application. There is often no clear and design-enforced separation, supported by metamodel concepts, between objects that are "network addressable" and objects that are not. In addition, it becomes natural to have components built using the rather purist principle of "one focus object per component." This can easily lead to an explosion in the number of component types, which can do much harm to both development-time and run-time scalability.

Instance components as distributed objects. The temptation toward lower-granularity components is often coupled with the temptation to approach the design of a business system as if it were enough to take a set of objects, put some IDL interface around them, and . . . voilà, a distributed system. This approach may work to some extent for a small distributed system having few constraining requirements for performance and scalability. For the kind of large-scale system we are targeting, where large implies both a large development effort (from 20 to several hundred developers working on the project/product) and high-level performance for large numbers of users, the complexity of cost-effectively reusing, managing, designing, and perhaps most of all, deploying and managing at runtime, a very large number of distributed object types may be beyond the ability of many software organizations. The type-based style, together with the type-based mindset, however, can scale to development organizations of 400 to 500 people and 200 to 300 business components, and there is no reason to believe that it would not scale beyond that.

Requirements on BCVM. The two styles translate into a different set of requirements in terms of tools, development environment, component execution model, and so forth. For example, most of the modern component execution models address the needs of distributed objects and the instance-based style. Because the requirements on the technical architecture of the type-based style are a subset of the requirements of the instance-based style, it is always possible to use these component execution models to adopt the type-based style.

An additional consideration is the ability to implement a component execution model that abstracts from the details of the various component implementation technologies. Because it is possible to use a type-base style in all existing component implementation technologies, and because a type-based style uses fewer of their specific characteristics, it is generally easier to build a common abstract model using a type-based style than using an instance-based style.

Persistence. Where the instance-based mindset results in lower component granularity, persistence aspects can become a key differentiator between the two styles, in that an instance-based mindset is less likely to think in terms of islands of data and tends to use framework persistence (see Chapter 8) for business data. It may also become more natural to think that persistence should show explicitly in component interfaces. On the other hand, given the granularity that tends to be chosen as optimal in the type-based mindset, having simple save-restore operations at the component level for data persistence is severely suboptimal. It may make sense at the distributed-object level, assuming that it is desirable to have one functional distributed object take responsibility for another's persistence—a questionable proposition.

So is everything a disadvantage? Well, not at all: An instance-based architectural style, if used with a mindset that says let's use the best of each style as appropriate, can be extremely powerful, especially in two important areas: encapsulation (and hence, in some sense, modeling) and performance.

Encapsulation. The instance-based style allows for more proper encapsulation of design and code. The logic tends to be truly localized. In Figure 9.7, the manager DC ends up knowing and needing to use many software artifacts that are owned by the managed DC. In Figure 9.10, on the other hand, at run-time these software artifacts are still mostly managed by the managed component.

Performance. It is possible, using an appropriate architecture and design, to reach higher levels of performance using an instance-based style. The trade-off is extremely subtle and requires some architectural and organizational maturity, but an instance-based style can lead to higher levels of achievable concurrency, lower network utilization, and fewer requirements for load balancing. Because concurrency is at the instance level rather than at the type level, there is less risk of two requests arriving at the same time for a given component instance.

In conclusion, both styles have advantages and disadvantages. Most of the disadvantages are directly related to what we have called the "mindset" of the style. This mindset is very common in the component industry, but it is not necessarily an intrinsic characteristic of the style. For example, the instance-based mindset often leads to medium or low-granularity, stateful component instances, but there is nothing that would prevent the same style from being used for very coarse-granularity, stateless component instances.

When properly applied, the instance-based style leads to a system partly build out of type components, partly built out of right-granularity, network-addressable component instances. While it can be more difficult to tune the system, potentially the system is more flexible and cleaner, and it may provide for greater concurrency. The trick is moderation: Instead of using the instance-based style as a solution in search of a problem, it is important to introduce component instances when they best resolve a particular problem or design challenge. In most cases, a combination of the two styles, without a purist mindset, will lead to the best component solution.

Event-Based

In real life, events happen. A customer calls on the phone, an order is returned unexpectedly, a shipment arrives. This can be quite naturally modeled and implemented using *events* in the information system. In a component-based system, events can be used for a multitude of aspects, and it is a powerful technology to enhance the autonomy of the components.

The main principle of an event-based style is that, because of the decoupling provided by the event concept, business components do not speak directly to each other; rather they raise and receive events. In a pure event-based architecture, events are used as the sole mechanism for communication between components. This allows a strong technical decoupling between components, but it leads to a less deterministic behavior or, more precisely, to a behavior that is equally deterministic but in which the order of calls is much more difficult to track (but see [Prins 1996]). In reality, business component systems can usefully take advantage of hybrid models, in which a given component uses events as a means of communicating only in particular circumstances.

It is useful to keep in mind two levels of component granularity—the federation of business component systems (or of system-level components) and the business component system. Events are an essential aspect of flexible communication between system-level components (with some minimal glue code handling the interest registration), and they can be successfully used within a business component system as well, but with some restriction.

Within a *business component system*, events are mainly used in the following ways:

1. As a refresh mechanism. For example, where a copy of some frequently accessed data is moved to a given location for performance reasons, the data copy can register interest in any modification of the master data, in such a way that if the master data is updated, the local copy can be refreshed following the appropriate business rules.

2. As a notification mechanism to a user tier. For example, an event can implement workflow-like kinds of interaction, in which the user is notified that a certain document is waiting for his or her approval.

3. To implement referential integrity between business components (see Chapter 12).

4. To implement what corresponds to an event in real life, especially as far as component-to-component communication is concerned. This is the meaning most interesting for this discussion.

The event-based style, which is orthogonal to the type-based and instance-based styles, is usually applied for a limited set of communication between entity and process components. Even if this technique appears theoretically very promising, and it has been used for parts of large-scale systems, to use it as the only means of communication between components in a system can lead to systems that are difficult to develop, test, and manage. For smaller-scale systems, this may still be in the realm of the ability of the organization, and it also has many advantages (for example, components built with a pure event-based style tend to be very autonomous and resilient).

A number of technical mechanisms can be used, including publishing, broadcasting, interest registration, and so forth. The most effective approach is probably the publish-subscribe approach. Here, a component can *publish* an event, and any component can *subscribe* to (or register interest in) a given event or event category. When a component has registered interest in some event, and that event occurs and is published, then the subscribing component is sent a *notify* message by the system.

In a federation of system-level components, events can be used as a valid alternative to having outgoing interfaces: A given system X publishes the list of events it can generate, and another system that is interested in working with system X simply needs to subscribe to these events. This leads to very autonomous system-level components or business components. Indeed, in an architected federation, a combination of events and direct invocation can be used to properly structure and architect the federation.

Event-based technology in component implementation technologies is now fairly mature, but it is not yet fully integrated with industry-strength middleware. Ideally, the lowest level of coupling between systems is obtained if they all have to go through an asynchronous message-based exchange (see [Prins 1996]). Often a hybrid model is adopted, corresponding to a combination of the three architectural styles presented so far. This is the perfect support for a mature business component system. The trade-offs for when to use events and when not to are usually based on development-time and run-time performance: Using events too extensively leads to complicated development, and both events and asynchronous calls—at least in the same address space—are slower than direct calls.

Architectural Patterns

This section describes two architectural patterns implicit in the preceding discussion. These two patterns are architecting the system using components as coordinators and architecting the system using peer-to-peer components.

Components as Coordinators

Within a given business component system, each business component can be seen as a coordinator for the components it depends on (that is, the components in its BC assembly). For example, in Figure 9.3, the Invoice Manager component can be seen as coordinating (directly or indirectly) all the components below it. In turn, the Invoice business component can be seen as coordinating all the components below it and as being coordinated by the Invoice Manager.

Each coordinator can be seen as a combination of the implementation of a mediator pattern and a façade pattern (Figure 9.11). The *mediator* pattern "define[s] an object that encapsulates how a set of objects interact. Mediator promotes loose coupling by keeping objects from referring to each other explicitly, and it lets you vary their interaction independently" [Gamma 1995, p. 273].

The *façade* pattern "provide[s] a unified interface to a set of interfaces in a subsystem. Façade defines a higher-level interface that makes the subsystem easier to use" [Gamma 1995, p. 185].

Each component using other components and being used by other components can be seen as a mediator for the used components and as providing a façade to the using components. Each coordinated component can be seen as providing data for its coordinator, and the system is built out of progressively

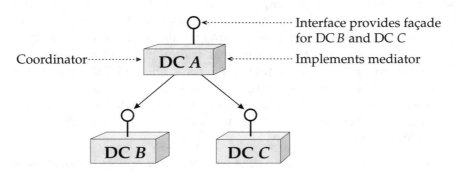

Figure 9.11   Coordinator as façade and mediator.

more complicated coordinators, each providing a more business-meaningful set of functionalities to the functionality above.

Simple systems can be built applying this principle to create just two layers [Jacobson 1995]: coordinator and coordinated. In this case, it becomes easy to configure the system: Without any impact on the coordinated components, it is possible to simply tweak or change the coordinators. A meaningful-size system, however, cannot be cost-effectively built out of only these two layers. Each business concept relies on other business concepts to be meaningful, and correspondingly each functional layer needs to do the same: A nonmonolithic information system is naturally composed of multiple layers, and forcing it into only two layers can be done, but doing so defeats many of the componentization purposes. The coordinator pattern also leads to a dynamic between coordination and autonomy, between ability to configure and ease of reuse:

- On the one hand, it is useful to extract the business rules and as much coordinator capability from lower-layer business components, basically pushing up in the DAG as many responsibilities as possible. This permits architecting a very configurable system: Because business rules and processing tend to be owned by business components quite high in the hierarchy, changing these business rules and processing logic while impacting as few components as possible turns out to be quite easy. This approach leads to a very clean separation of concerns between passive, maintenance-oriented components and more active, process-oriented components. Coupled with other techniques such as externalizing the business rules (see Figure 9.12), this can lead to very configurable systems. This advantage can also become a disadvantage: Building a process component can in this case be quite difficult because much of the business logic needs to be implemented in the process component, and the entity component tends to be very simple and, although reusable, not so useful.

- On the other hand, pushing the responsibilities down, basically making each layer responsible, as much as possible, for the coordination of the layers below it, makes for more auto-contained components. In this case, each component owns the business logic that directly concerns it and that it can handle. All components in the system tend to have some level of intelligence. It is easier to use and reuse these components because the user has less to do. But it is less easy to adapt them to specific business processes because the business rules are now spread out across different components.

As usual, the best solution is a pragmatic and appropriate application of the two aspects, making the right trade-off between maximizing component autonomy and pushing business rules toward higher layers in the component diagram.

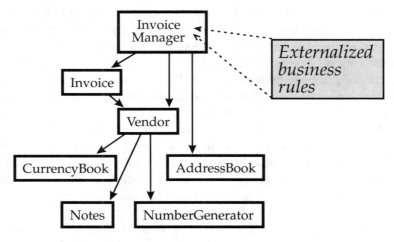

Figure 9.12   Externalizing business rules.

The type-based, instance-based, and event-based styles lend themselves in varying degrees to support a coordinator-based approach. It is particularly natural to implement coordinators using a type-based approach, which leads to BCSMs similar to the one illustrated in Figure 9.3.

Peer-to-Peer Components

We have so far always presented a business component system as composed of a DAG. Some may think that it would be generally desirable to have components interact as peers, but this is not the case and does not reflect what actually happens in the real world. Many concepts in the real world do not interact; they are passive participants in the interaction, and they are in a defined relationship with other concepts. For example, orders in the real world do not interact; they are acted upon. They are just pieces of paper. Addresses do not interact. On the other hand, organizations do interact as peers, as do trading partners and information systems. The point is that there are hierarchies of interactions, and having, for example, an order manager component as a coordinator of the order, item, and customer concepts actually reflects the real world, where a human actually might write on the order the various details to do with item, customer, and so forth. It is only in a limited set of situations that a peer-to-peer relationship would reflect what happens in the real world, and these situations tend to be higher up in our component hierarchy, at the process level.

If the "real world" peer-to-peer relationships are mapped into the information system world, this would hence lead to a mixture of coordinated relationships and peer-to-peer relationships, with a prevalence of coordinated relationships in the lower layers of the component diagram and more peer-to-peer relationships in the process layers of the component diagram. The peer relationships may occasionally need to be implemented by exchanges that are peer-to-peer at the technical level, which would require appropriate technical infrastructure support (mainly the ability to perform reentrant calls).

The peer relationship is acceptable when there is a limited and small number of components using this style. In these cases, development can still be kept under control, and it is possible to simulate the peer-to-peer calls in such a way that the various peer-to-peer components are still autonomously built. For example, it is an acceptable model for many SLC interactions in small federations.

We have also found that, once the whole system is built based on a strong DAG concept, a mature organization can relax the noncircularity constraint for a limited number of interactions within a business component system. Business component systems can be built without this, but in some cases the architect may decide that the added complexity is worth the price. This usually works best at the top-most process layer, in which the main processes are allowed to exchange peer-to-peer messages with other top-most processes, while still using a DAG concept for all other business components.

If for some reason an organization decides to widely adopt peer-to-peer configurations across components, many considerations presented so far need to be modified. First of all, the BCSM will tend to flatten, since the main reason for a hierarchy such as the one presented in Figure 9.3 is to reinforce unidirectionality of invocations. In order to keep the system manageable, other approaches may be needed to reduce complexity, such as implementing the whole utility layer as a set of reusable classes, and thus entity components may reuse the utility aspects in terms of a class library rather than as a set of run-time components. But this, of course, reintroduces other complexities and inflexibilities that a component-based approach avoids.

Collaboration Patterns

This section presents a set of component-based patterns, referred to as *collaboration patterns*. These patterns address various ways in which business components can collaborate. The section illustrates only a few examples, namely the management of business transactions, of defaults and overrides, and of validations, with the intent of showing the kind of challenges and thinking required to preserve the autonomy of individual components while allowing them to collaborate at the same time. Many other collaboration patterns exist;

probably the most notable is the treatment of deletions of data from the database in a component-based system, where the data to be deleted has some form of dependency on data owned by other components, and in general how to deal with referential integrity (addressed in Chapter 12).

Collaboration patterns usually span multiple business components and multiple distribution tiers, and if not approached carefully they can contribute to unfortunate levels of high cohesion between business components. A proper approach to these structural patterns is of fundamental importance for enabling autonomy of the various levels of component granularity.

Business Transactions

Chapter 8 discussed various aspects of transactions, where the term "transaction" was always intended as an ACID transaction (the unqualified term "transaction" will continue to have this meaning in this section). Often, however, there is a need to manage a set of interactions with the system that correspond to what an end user would consider a business-meaningful transaction—for example, entering an order or creating a bank account—and that encompasses several ACID transactions. Such a business-meaningful set of interactions is called a *business transaction*.

A business transaction often encompasses more than one transaction and may involve several business components over a long period of time. It is a specific form of collaboration between business components, and there is often a requirement to give the end user the ability to easily work on the business transaction until its full completion or cancellation, for example, through a consistent user interface across the whole business transaction. For their execution, business transactions need a collaboration of multiple business components as well as of the distribution tiers of individual business components.

There are a number of approaches to business transactions, depending on their nature. Two examples are as follows:

- In simple cases, it is possible to implement a whole business transaction as a single transaction, for example, where there are no requirements for intermediate storage of data for business reasons in the ERD. In this case, as illustrated in Figure 9.13, the w-tier can accumulate data from the u-tier and perform simple business logic and validation on it, until the u-tier (via a user interaction) declares that the business transaction is ready to be sent. At that point, the business transaction is sent as a single ACID transaction to the ERD. In this case, there is no real impact on the business component system architecture or on the performance and scalability of the system. Canceling the business transaction is easy—it simply requires discarding data held in the w-tier.

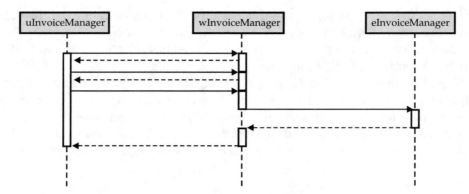

Figure 9.13 Simple business transaction.

■ Where there are functional or extra-functional requirements for intermediate storage of data (that is, during the business transaction itself), and
where this data needs to be shared among multiple users, it is not possible to use the previous approach. In this more complex case, there is a
need for sending the data to the ERD through multiple ACID transactions.
Because of this, and because of the requirements for intermediate visibility of the data to multiple users, the intermediate state of the business
transaction must be managed on the ERD, typically through some form of
temporary storage. It could be managed using stateful EDCs, but, as will
be discussed in Chapter 12, the use of stateful EDCs can have unwelcome
side effects.

An example of a complex business transaction is the order-entry scenario illustrated in Figure 9.14. Customer John Smith phones to order a set of items. He
orders the first item, and the system is built in such a way that as soon as he asks
for that item, it is reserved for him and preallocated. This requires an update to
the database in the ERD. John proceeds until he has completed his order, at
which point the business transaction is concluded and the order is finalized.

In this case, temporary storage of data in the ERD is required for the intermediate states. This temporary storage could be implemented as a separate
table (or set of tables) dedicated to record the intermediate states, or as a particular set of tuples on a "live" table (or set of tables). The latter case would
probably require the addition of one or more attributes to indicate the different
states of the order (for example, a flag that indicates that the order is "prealle-
cated" rather than "allocated"). This is quite a simple and cost-effective way to
manage the state of the entities affected by the business transaction: state-
management through adding an attribute to the table corresponding to the entity
component that is the focus of the business transaction—that is, the order.

If the business transaction is interrupted for any reason, and if the end user

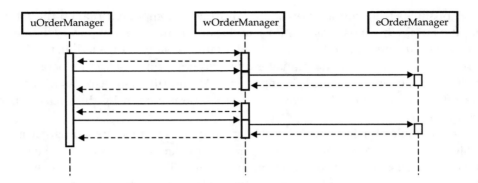

Figure 9.14 Complex business transaction.

decides to undo it, then the system needs to take appropriate actions to guarantee the business integrity of the system.[4] In simple cases, this action involves a number of compensating transactions to undo the effects of the previous transactions. That is, the data stored as a consequence of the business transaction on the database is removed; this can be seen as a business transaction rollback. Given the complexity of the data that can be involved in a business transaction, it may be impossible to reset the state of the database automatically to what it was before the business transaction started. In complex cases, the "undoing" of a given business transaction may even require a totally new processing scenario, such as in the case where the reason for canceling the business transaction needs to be asked of the end user and the reply recorded. This might come about where a quality system requires the reasons for cancellation to be recorded. In turn, this can require that once the order-entry business transaction is started, the data associated with it is kept in the database, and any attempt to interrupt the business transaction will lead to starting a new business transaction, "order cancel."

The choice between various implementation solutions for business transactions strongly depends on the complexity of the business transaction itself. Generally there is a trade-off between ease of design, implementation, testing, and maintenance on one hand, and run-time performance and scalability on the other. For example, in the case where a temporary table (or a set of temporary tables) is added to a business component, then at the commit of the business transaction, a potentially large amount of data needs to be copied from one table (the temporary table) to another (the "live" table). In complex business transactions, this may require multiple tables or even multiple business components. In some case, the temporary storage may even need to become part of other business transactions, which need to search for very similar data on multiple tables. On the other hand, managing business transactions by relying on the "live" tables may make the "live" tables unnecessarily complex and large.

A business transaction is owned by a process component (called the *focus process* of the business transaction), and it often stores its temporary data in a *focus entity* component. In a typical order-entry business transaction, the focus process would be the OrderManager business component, and the focus entity would be the Order business component.[5] All intermediate aspects of a business transaction should, whenever possible, be recorded by the focus entity component.

Very complex business transactions will require intermediate storage by multiple business components. Such business transactions require very careful business transaction architecture and modeling. The components involved in the business transaction become strongly related to each other, and they may all have some related temporary intermediate data that cannot usually be considered "stable" by other business transactions or processes.

From a distribution tier perspective, it is important to do the following:

- Whenever possible, implement the business transaction as a single ACID transaction. This is the most inexpensive and simple solution.

- When a single ACID transaction is not possible, try to minimize the amount of temporary storage, and if possible assign it to a focus entity business component, which makes it easier to keep temporary data under control and properly managed.

- If multiple business components must be involved in the temporary storage, model and architect the business transaction very carefully and thoroughly.

The business transaction collaboration pattern also has significant impact on how the user interface needs to be designed. The end user often expects to have some indication that he or she is currently performing a consistent set of actions, which are part of a whole. This is often referred to as a *logical unit of work*, or sometimes a *user unit of work*, and a complex business transaction may actually correspond to multiple logical units of work. There are various complexity-reduction strategies, though, and a prominent one is to ensure that only the critical parts of the business transaction are actually part of the user unit of work. For example, secondary updates, such as an update of the customer's address while the customer is inside the order-entry business transaction, could be committed separately from order entry and would not necessarily be rolled back if the order business transaction were to be canceled. This points to a UWD able to handle concurrent user units of work, together with an appropriate user model. For the roll-back of the business transaction, it may be much simpler, and in some cases may even add to usability, to require the user to manually perform an explicit "delete" action on data rather than try to have the system automatically manage business transaction roll-back.

A mature BCVM may well implement some form of direct support for business transactions, in terms of support at the user-interface level, support at the modeling level, and some form of record-playback to support the business transaction reversal or confirmation (roll-back or commit). This may turn out to be a very complex support, and it will not be enough to fully cover the most complex situations, but rather will address the 80 percent of cases that are simpler to deal with, leaving to the application designer the question of how to deal with the complex cases. In many cases, it is more cost-effective (meaning through application architecture and the work of the functional developer) to deal with all business transactions manually, rather than implement this BCVM support, unless it is delivered as part of a commercially-available technical infrastructure.

In summary, the important point is that a solution to the various issues of collaboration patterns, such as the business transaction, impacts multiple aspects of the development lifecycle, cuts across the distribution tiers and the functional layers, and involves multiple components. Properly managing these aspects assumes an appropriate granularity choice for business components and distributed components, and is required for component autonomy to be preserved.

Default Management

Default management is a common requirement in business systems. It should be addressed consistently throughout the system and, if not architected properly, easily leads to the introduction of unnecessary dependencies between business components.

The challenge arises from the fact that often a given entity in the system has defaults with regard to another entity. For example, a customer may have certain preferences in terms of which items are ordered, and these preferences need to be recorded somewhere in the system. If it were not for these defaults, the customer concept and the item concept could be considered, to a large extent, fully autonomous. It would only be at the moment of issuing an order for a given customer of a certain item that a link is created between the customer and the item concepts, and thus between business components, and this link may be owned by a "coordinator" component such as the order in this example.

Default management creates static links between components, which translate into software dependencies and make the assignment of the ownership of software artifacts more arguable. An example will clarify this discussion. Let us suppose that the business transaction for order entry goes through the following steps:

1. A customer is identified in the UWD.
2. The system sends the customer ID to the ERD.
3. The following default information is returned:

   - The warehouse the customer usually orders from
   - The type of items the customer has most recently ordered
   - The address to which the customer wants the wares shipped
   - The type of payment the customer prefers
   - For specific items, a specific configuration that is the preferred configuration for that item

For the default information to be retrieved, it clearly must be stored somewhere, but where? Some of this information is highly item-specific, and it requires detailed knowledge about the internal existing configurations of items; on the other hand, it is information specific to a given customer, and the item component may have been designed so that it has no knowledge of the concept of customer.

Deciding which component owns the business logic to manage the defaults, as well as the particular data belonging to specific instances of defaults, should be supported by a default management collaboration pattern. For example, the following rules can be applied:

- The management of a specific default is assigned to the component corresponding to the actor owning that particular default in the problem space. If this rule is followed in the preceding example, it is the Customer business component that owns the management of its own item-related defaults and is responsible for properly identifying these defaults.

- Applying the temporal cohesion principle, the data for a specific default is stored together with the data with which it is most temporally coupled. For example, the detailed configuration of an item may belong to the Item component, but the information linking this data to a specific customer, such as the identifier of that particular information, may be stored in a customer table within the Customer component since it is (temporally) used at the same time.

In any case, the specific solution for the default management often requires design and implementations that are spread across more than one business component, and it requires a collaboration pattern that must be consistently followed within the system. This is one more example of functional requirements needing solutions that can affect the whole system, and that must be adopted by all business components involved in the collaboration for a successful outcome to be achieved.

Overrides and Historical Data

Suppose a given entity has some defaults with regard to another entity, or that the system can propose a certain default answer to any enterable piece of information according to given business rules. In some percentage of cases, the end user will decide to override these defaults and enter a different value. When this happens, it is important to properly record the new value and be sure to use it throughout the system when appropriate.

For example, a customer ordering an item may have certain preferences, or the business rules may specify that certain fields are automatically entered, but, to add flexibility to the system, it should be possible to override these values and record the overridden values in the database. These are things that, as do defaults, affect component autonomy.

Depending on the complexity and maturity of the system, overrides may amount to very complex processing. For example, in a flexible order-entry system for an agile manufacturer, the system may need to be able to record a wholly order-specific item configuration. A particular configuration may be used for one and only one order, and the architect may decide that this information logically belongs to the specific order, which would require the ability by the Order component to deal with that very specific item data, well beyond the simple recording of the identifier of the item that is being ordered.

The required solution patterns are very similar, and they can actually be seen as a specific case of the patterns required to resolve *historical data management*. This term refers to the need to record a certain amount of information for historical purposes, such as for auditing or quality-control purposes or for explicit functional requirements, as required by the increasingly popular customer-profiling applications. This information typically belongs logically to multiple components, but by applying the temporal cohesion principle, it can be usefully implemented as belonging in one place.

Without going into detail, all of these collaboration patterns require an approach of the following kind: (1) properly define what can be done by non-functional viewpoints (for example, what can be done by the technical architecture and what by the application architecture that can simplify the life of the functional developer) and (2) strive to architect and design the patterns in such a way that the autonomy of the business components involved is preserved as much as possible, while still allowing for a proper collaboration. For example, by thoroughly applying the consistency principle, the complexity involved in these patterns can be reduced. A properly designed collaboration pattern should fit naturally in the existing component architecture: It is a good rule never to add a functional business component only for the needs of a collaboration pattern, but instead always try to find the right owner of the various parts of the pattern.

Validation

It is important in any information system to have a high degree of confidence in the data stored on the database. This can be obtained through a proper approach to the validation of this data. It can be important for the overall consistency that the way these validations are performed follows a consistent set of patterns across all the business components of a given system.

Validation should occur as close as possible to the generation of the validation request. It is possible to categorize the requirements in terms of validation as follows:

Simple formatting validation. This can usually be performed within the particular user interface control that supports data entry. For example, a text-entry control may support *masks*, which could specify that only positive integers are accepted or even that the particular order ID requires the first three letters to be alphabetic and the other nine to be numeric. Usually, individual controls on the user-interface framework should be able to check this kind of thing automatically.

Datatype validation. These validations require knowledge internal to a given data type. For example, a date with a month number 15 is an invalid date, and either the date user interface control or the data type "date" should be able to validate this.

System-parameter-dependent validation. An example of this is a date in one of the allowed formats, or in the only allowed format for that system, such as "mm-dd-yyyy." This kind of validation is still very simple, but it requires the execution of a business rule (perhaps at initial install time) that cannot be totally self-contained in a given data type because it requires access to system-wide information. In a fat-client implementation, the system-wide information can be made available both on the PC and the server, and hence this validation can be performed "locally" to the need with minimal other resources involved. This type of validation can also include *business code validation*, which can easily account for 20–25 percent of the processing time of an OLTP application. The term "business code validation" refers to ensuring that a value is a valid member of a predefined set of values such as country code, state code, currency code, unit of measure code, and many others. For example, while entering an address the system may want to check that the particular state entered is a valid state.

Functional validation. This normally requires access to another business component or to some database data. For example, checking when a particular customer exceeds his or her credit limits may require the order-entry component to access the credit-checking component. This is the only type of validation that a functional developer should really be concerned about. The application architecture should, as much as possible, provide standard answers to all the others.

In a typical distributed system, the types of validation just described require progressively more access to other resources and components in order to be validated. To preserve as much as possible the autonomy of the individual business components, it is very important, first, that the architecture supports the functional developer in focusing on the functional validation and, second, that an overall validation philosophy is defined for functional validation.

For example, it is important that all the system's components assume either that the received data is valid (so there is no need to validate it as soon as it is received) or that it is invalid, which typically would lead to validating it as soon as it is received. The first solution requires that the business components trust the other business components to have somehow properly validated the data before they send it; it leads to higher-performance systems and to smaller business components, but it also requires strict architectural guidance to prevent the system from becoming unreliable. The second solution leads to the risk of having the same validation performed multiple times, but it also leads to more independent and robust individual business components. The important principle here is not to mix and match the validation philosophy, but rather to clearly define it and consistently apply it.

From the BCVM to Functional Development

This section describes an additional and very important aspect of the application architecture: bridging the gap between what the BCVM provides and the needs of the functional developer. The BCVM is designed to hide complexity from the functional programmer, and to this aim it provides the technical core, plus a set of services and facilities as described in Chapter 8. The vast majority of the BCVM deliverables, however, require some additional defining to be made 100 percent usable by the functional developer. This may be simply some project-specific convention; for example, a very complete security framework may require some project-specific convention regarding how to name the groups at the various security levels. Or it may be some more fundamental aspect, as exemplified in this section for the error-handling and the data-type system, both good examples of the kind of considerations an application architect should apply. Many other examples could have been chosen, including persistence, tagged data labels, internationalization, application-specific caching, and so forth.

These subjects cover application development aspects that turn out to have an influence that cuts across multiple business components, impacts component interfaces and intercomponent dependencies, and ends up affecting the overall shape of the application. These are some of the many development subjects affecting multiple architectural viewpoints (see the sidebar, "Knowledge Management for Complex Projects").

Over time, the current trend of operating systems and middleware providing higher and higher abstraction levels will ultimately push the BCVM to a higher abstraction level, and many of the application architecture aspects covered in this chapter will become part of the BCVM. Ideally they would be defined industry-wide as standards, actually supporting or enabling the application architecture protocol layer for interoperability and relieving each single project from the costs and pains of having to design and build the support for these in-house.

Error Handling

Error handling is something that, even if the technical solution is delivered as part of the technical architecture, needs further system-wide work by the appli-

KNOWLEDGE MANAGEMENT FOR COMPLEX PROJECTS

Appropriate knowledge management of a large-scale project can be one of the factors leading to successful completion of the project. Indeed, the sheer amount of information produced within a project can be too much for any individual to master, and appropriate techniques to organize and capture knowledge must be adopted.

Adopting architectural viewpoints to organize the complex space of a software project is an extremely powerful way of mastering complexity and reducing it to manageable terms. At a first level, each deliverable is assigned to a viewpoint and is in direct relationship with other deliverables belonging to that viewpoint. This viewpoint often corresponds to a specific role, with associated expertise. For example, the technical architecture is the realm of the technical architect.

However, deliverables belonging to the same subject (for example the error handling subject) can also often be seen in other architectural viewpoints. Hence, it is extremely useful first to structure knowledge management by the architectural viewpoints, but second, at the same time, to organize individual subjects through *architectural monographs.* An architectural monograph is a cohesive presentation of a subject that captures in one place all aspects of that subject, independent of the architectural viewpoint to which that aspect belongs.

This dual organization of knowledge management can be easily supported by Web technology, in which the hyperlinked knowledge management is primarily organized by architectural viewpoint, and secondarily by monograph, where the secondary structure is superimposed on the primary structure using hyperlinks with a minimal duplication of information.

Such dual organization of knowledge can be visualized as a kind of architectural Rubik's cube, as illustrated in Figure 9.15.

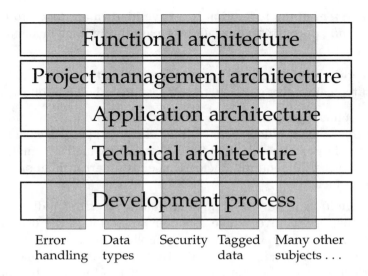

Figure 9.15 Architectural Rubik's cube.

cation architect for the solution to work properly. For example, the BCVM may specify how to handle errors at the component interfaces, or at the interface with some third-party persistence mechanism, but may not specify what is required for applying error handling across the architectural viewpoints, the distribution tiers, the development process, and the functional layers. CORBA for example, given its focus on interfaces, specifies how to deal with errors in IDL, but not how to deal with errors inside components or across a system. This is far from sufficient to resolve all the error-handling issues in a distributed system, and the application architect is usually left to develop internal patterns, implementations, and guidelines, which we refer to as the *error-handling framework*.

This framework must address the various levels of component granularity:

- The internals of each distributed component (intra-DC framework), taking into account that multiple errors may be raised internally in the course of processing a particular transaction.

- Error handling within a business component (intra-BC framework), which must take into consideration that only some of the errors identified within a DC may be of interest outside of the DC.

- Error handling within a business component system, and how the whole system acts consistently on determination of an error.

- The federation framework, in which the error handling is seen across a whole federation. Of course, if the federation is not an architected federation (see Chapter 6, "The Federation of System-Level Components"), each system in the federation will have its own approach to error handling, and appropriate translation or pass-through mechanisms must be defined.

Focusing on a single business component system, the error-handling framework must typically cover a variety of subjects, including the following:

- Development process aspects: at what phase and how should errors be identified and specified such that they can be properly used across development. For example, it should specify exactly which information (and in which format) is required to clearly specify an error in an operation of a DC interface.

- The definition and eventual implementation of error-handling implementation patterns. For example, Chapter 8 mentioned the use of a utility class, inside every DC, that would collect information about errors encountered during internal (to the DC) processing of an operation. This information would be sent back to the caller of the operation at the conclusion of the operation itself. In addition, an error-handling framework should specify how language classes should transmit error information or at least the fact of an error to each other, how the external parts of the system (such as other DCs or the database) should return error information, and how to deal with it, including how to deal with the various types of severity, how to distinguish between informational messages and errors, and so on. Last but not least, the framework should specify clearly the guidelines for passing errors back to the DC's users, in such a way that the surface area between DCs is reduced as much as possible.

- The overall error-handling framework across the distribution tiers of an individual business component, across the business components inside a single business component system, and across a federation of system-level components. For example, for the individual business component, the framework should specify how the errors are returned to an EDC's proxy, what the developer of a WDC should do to intercept the error, how the error should be displayed to the end user, including the initial information and also what to do if more information is required; that is, a flexible error-handling framework should be able to display a list of related errors, rather than only an individual error, and zoom in on request on the detail of specific errors. In addition, an advanced error-handling framework might even suggest solutions to an error in the list, or it could run the end user through a wizard-like scenario to fix the error.

- The design and format of the various kinds of functional errors, the definition of appropriate error hierarchies and error ownership, and the specification of associated naming convention and ownership. Appropriate naming conventions for the errors themselves is an apparently trivial aspect but a good example of how small things become important in a large-scale development. All business components should follow the same convention, so that, for example, interoperability is made easier. One possible way to identify errors is by a "(business component, code)" pair: (ORM, 42) could stand for business component OrderManager, error number 42. Other conventions can be used to identify intra-DC errors at the language-class level.

- How the framework deals with the interface to legacy systems or to third-party systems, and to ORBs and DBMSs. Database management systems, for example, usually report several thousand defined errors. Each of these errors could be raised by the persistence layer in given circumstances, and in most cases the only thing the error-handling framework can do is to propagate this error to the user, transformed into something meaningful to the user. In a few selected cases, the error-handling framework may decide to handle the error: For example, the "not found" DBMS error is typically intercepted and managed, rather than simply passed along.

- Where to log errors—usually required in multiple places in a distributed system. A client/server system, for example, typically needs to log errors both on the client and on the server, so as to guarantee that in the case of failure of the server, it is possible to define what happened by looking at the client log.

Error-related source code can amount to 50 percent or more of the total (hopefully generated) source code. Often the difference between a prototype and an industry-quality system lies only in robustness, which is often due to a proper error-handling strategy and implementation. It is hence important to design the error-handling solution so that it implements and evolves easily and quickly. Over time, an organization finds that many error-handling aspects can be generated or addressed with technical tricks such as the use of programming language macros that can significantly reduce the amount of code needed to check the most common errors.

Consider the sample business component system fragment shown in Figure 9.16. The error-handling framework may, for example, specify the following:

- Any error returned by the database is checked for severity. If it is above a certain severity, the transaction is aborted, and control is returned with the appropriate information to the *eOrderManager* DC, which will return to its w-tier a list of the errors encountered.

- If the database does not return any error, or if the EDC is able to deal with the error, then control stays within the EDC (for example, *eOrder* if it is *rOrder* reporting an error) until the EDC discovers that it cannot deal with the error. Errors within each DC are accumulated in their own DC-global error object (that might be managed by the utility language class) and are not usually passed from language class to language class.

- Each EDC may own its own error log or rely on a system-wide log DC. This log DC may be built as part of the deliverables of the application architecture, or it may be one of the services and facilities in the CEE.

- Each EDC may have an error interface, containing the operations that allow it to deal with the error-handling framework. For example, each EDC may provide an interface that returns additional information related to a specific error code, such as exactly which operation caused it or even the full text of the message associated with the error. Traditionally, this information was better managed on the UWD, but the needs of component-to-component interoperability require in some cases that this information be available also in the ERD. For example, a logging DC could provide the function that accesses a business component's resource files and pulls out text in an appropriate language. The previous example takes the view that many aspects of the error framework are managed by the respective business components: Alternatively, a project may decide to have a system-wide DC to provide this capability.

- The *wOrderManager* must also be able to provide logging and detailed error information, possibly without having to cross the distribution domain boundaries.

The definition of errors normally includes *functional errors*, such as credit limit reached, item not available, or some violation of business rules; *application errors*, such as input validation, method preconditions and postconditions, class invariants, and so forth; and *technical errors*, such as "keyboard not found: press any key to continue," or a server unavailable, or any error generated by the technical core, a service or a facility, or third-party systems such as ORBs or DBMS. In business component-centric approaches, each error could be assigned to a component. Functional errors are usually owned at develop-

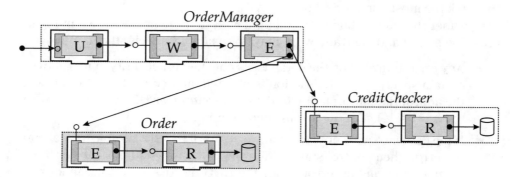

Figure 9.16   Error handling in a business component system.

ment time by a specific functional component, while application and technical errors are usually assigned to the business component *Base*.

The error-handling framework must also deal with a set of other constraints. For example, the messages must be stored in such a way to adapt to internationalization requirements. Or error objects should be able to accept parameters, in order to pass relevant information about the cause of the error that is discoverable only at the time of the error. All of this shows how an apparently simple subject like error handling can easily cut across the various dimensions of a development.

Data Type System

The concept of business data type was discussed both in Chapter 3, "The Distributed Component," and Chapter 5, from the point of view of distributed component and system-level component interfaces. From an application architecture perspective, though, the problem of data types goes well beyond the problem of the interfaces: The whole internal design and implementation of the distributed components must deal with data types. This is from the mapping between the internal object-oriented model of the component to the persistence aspects to the actual internal implementation to the relationship with the proxies to other components, and how all of this relates to the datatypes defined in third-party middleware and RDBMs. We globally refer to this problem as the problem of the definition of the "internal business data type system" (see Chapter 5), which is referred to simply as "data type system" in this section. This is strongly related to, but not equivalent to, the business data type system discussed in earlier chapters: The business data type system is focused on the definition of the business data types that can be shared between components; the data type system is concerned with all aspects of the data type framework of a system, whether it is internal to a DC or not.

A complete definition of a type system is a pervasive problem of the business component system architecture, influencing several architectural viewpoints and requiring, for a proper definition, a broad understanding of the interrelation of these viewpoints and a high dose of pragmatism. Note that data types, and the need to eventually convert data types from one architectural and application layer to the next, can lead to very costly and error-prone implementation, and they can also affect various extra-functional requirements such as performance. In systems with very high performance requirements, the data type system turns out to be a critical point, once the database access and network access aspects have been addressed. For example, in 1995 one component-based system was going through a very detailed development-time and run-time performance analysis. The project had developed a very powerful string class, but the performance analysis proved that less than 10 percent of the string class was being used across the system. Removing all the unnecessary functionality from the string class produced unexpected benefits across the whole system: compilation times were greatly reduced, footprints were reduced, and there was an all-round performance boost.

Data types come from a multitude of sources in a large-scale development, and we use the following two terms:

Base data types. The basic data types that are delivered to the application designer by the BCVM, assuming that the BCVM has already made any necessary abstraction from the various data types delivered by languages, component implementation technologies, and RDBMS. The base data types are known by the development environment, and they are defined by a technical architect and not by the functional designer or functional developer. Examples of base data types include character, integer, decimal, string, and also, depending on the BCVM, date, time, and other more business-oriented types. The base data types can also include, depending on the project, the basic complex types like arrays and lists.

Component data types. The data types that the component developer defines for internal purposes. These correspond in structure, granularity, and intent to the business data types; but they are used internally. Usually, a business data type corresponds to a component data type, but the reverse is not always true. Component data types can be very complex. For example, an item data type could be composed of more than 160 parameters, as can an order type or even a simple order line.

The data type framework must cover aspects similar to the error-handling framework. It must properly interface to third-party systems such as ORBs and DBMSs. It must take into account legacy systems. The development process aspects must be clearly defined; for example, when can a new base data type be added, and when can a new component data type be added? As for the error-handling framework, this is a subject that is deceptively simple, but that in reality cuts across the various dimensions of an information system.

Standards and Guidelines

With growing project sizes and the growing need to interoperate with other systems, the need for a precise definition of aspects that are trivial for smaller-scale system becomes obvious. This includes standards and guidelines covering such diverse subjects as the user-interface look-and-feel, naming conventions for all aspects of the development (from business components to data types, from errors to tagged data), precise conventions for the form and appearance of the interfaces, coding guidelines, and so forth. There is a thin line, though, between a file cabinet full of overly constraining processes and guidelines and the ability to effectively tackle a large project.

Many practitioners consider these deliverables part of methodology and quality assurance. A simple rule to define whether a certain deliverable is part of one of the architectural viewpoints or of other aspects (for example, the development process) is this: If the deliverable is normally defined by an architect, it belongs to the architecture. In this sense, many standards and guidelines are part of the application architecture.

The development of these deliverables adds to the costs of large-scale projects, either because they are normally not properly planned for or because of the amount of rework required when the need for project-wide consistency is eventually clearly identified.

Summary

To build a large-scale system with high run-time performance characteristics, the application architecture needs to be carefully considered.

The main architectural principles are these:

- Circularities should be avoided in any available way. The possible ways include architecture, design, development process, and others. It should be possible to trace a DAG not only between business components in the BCSM, but also within any individual business component.

- The principle of architectural normalization should be applied. For example, the business components system should be normalized as much as possible; software artifacts should be assigned to one and only one component.

Other principles include the layering principle, the consistency principle, the temporal cohesion principle, and the principle of least astonishment,.

There are two main architectural styles for a component-based system: type-based and instance-based. The type-based style is the most straightforward and risk-free, and it often has an associated mindset particularly oriented toward very large-scale systems. Instance-based architectures add powerful possibilities, but they require a certain level of maturity to avoid their pitfalls, and today they are still supported discontinuously by technology. There are several flavors of these two choices, including event-based architecture.

Collaboration patterns, focusing on how business components collaborate to provide various aspects of a business system, must be properly architected to prevent them from crippling business component autonomy. Collaboration patterns include aspects such as business transactions, default management, override management, and validations.

Most of the services and facilities provided by the BCVM need to be properly bridged and profiled in an often project-specific way. Two good examples, both of which must be properly addressed, are the error-handling framework and the data type system. Apparently trivial aspects such as standards and guidelines, including naming conventions, are important deliverables of an application architecture.

Endnotes

1 On a technical note, a type-based component is often implemented as a logical singleton instance of the type. Function associated with the type itself is often included in the same component.

2 Note the important distinction between a *component manager*, which manages a set of underlying components, and an *instance manager*, which manages a set of instances, typically instances of language classes.

3 Stateless components will be addressed in Chapter 12.

4 The difference between data integrity and business integrity: an ACID transaction guarantees that the database is always left with data that is in a consistent state (*data integrity*). It cannot guarantee, though, that the data is left in such a way that it reflects completion of the business transaction as a whole (*business integrity*).

5 Chapter 11, "Component-Based Business Modeling," will discuss how it is often possible to identify process-entity pairs that are strongly related, as in this case of the OrderManager and the Order components.

CHAPTER 10

Project Management Architecture

Previous chapters introduced the development process, the technical architecture, and the application architecture. These concepts help us to set up a factory of business components able to produce a large-scale system with high-performance characteristics and run-time scalability. The last step in the setup of the business component factory and an important aspect of large-scale development in general—particularly so for business component-based development—is the *project management architecture*.

The project management architecture (PMA) addresses the concepts, principles, guidelines, policies, and tools required to *cost-effectively* build a scalable and high-performance system *with a large team*. In other words, the PMA is the architectural viewpoint concerned with development cost-effectiveness and scalability. It includes all that is needed to scale up development to industrial levels by large teams often distributed across multiple locations: how the project is managed, the project organization, the structure of the development environment, software configuration management and versioning, and team composition and size. By large team is meant a team of up to a few hundred (or perhaps even a thousand) developers, although a more usual size would be between 10 and 50. The principles and approaches required for a team of 10 to work *cost-effectively* together on component-based development are to a large extent the same as those required by an organization of hundreds. Indeed, a team of 10 people concurrently developing business components and assembling them into a system encounters many of the same issues that a much larger team would face.

The chapter is organized in the following sections:

Concepts. Introduces the main concepts and principles needed to understand and discuss the project management architecture.

Software Configuration Management (SCM) and Version Control. The better-known part of the PMA. This section describes concepts, development process, and an integrated software configuration management strategy from the point of view of the business component approach.

Dependency Management. Introduces a dependency model, which includes a categorization of the dependencies between components, and a model of how to manage these dependencies. This is of crucial importance in achieving the target of reducing dependencies, on one hand, and properly managing the unavoidable dependencies deriving from the necessary collaboration between components, on the other.

Completing the Development Environment. Completes the description of the development environment to include various additional considerations about the roles of the physical structure of the development environment, and of additional PMA-related tools.

Project Manager's Model. Discusses the organizational principles of architecture-centric development, various project management views including the role of the architecture team, and the organization of teams around business components.

The concepts and principles presented in this chapter reflect one particular PMA that has proven useful on large-scale projects and has been refined over time. We believe that this PMA will save you time and make for much more agile development. It works especially well in supporting an organization that fully adopts the business component approach, that is, adopts the business component concept as a first-class citizen in the meta-model. The principles are of general applicability, and we believe they can be adapted without particular difficulty to any enterprise-level component-based development.

Many of the detail examples in this chapter are based on the state-of-the-art of tools at the time of writing. In particular, we assume a "today" environment where repository and SCM products have not yet reached the level of maturity forecast by many industry watchers. In this current environment, the file system itself will be an important part of an overall PMA "repository" strategy, and so in various places in this chapter, both the discussion and various examples are in terms of not only SCM and repository capabilities but also the native file systems provided by Unix or NT. Furthermore, all the examples presented in this chapter assume that the DAG principle is strictly enforced.

Concepts

The PMA is the final step toward supporting the objectives of the business component approach, such as autonomous component development and quick system assembly. Even though many aspects of the business component approach that support these objectives are in the other architectural viewpoints, the objectives would not be easily achieved without the principles and management infrastructure described in this chapter. To some extent, the PMA viewpoint defines the architecture of the development rather than that of the information system itself. However, the PMA directly and indirectly influences the other architectural viewpoints, and it is the glue that holds everything together and allows the full benefits of the business component approach to be achieved. Many of the promises of the business component approach cannot be fully achieved unless the PMA is set up consistently with and complementing the other viewpoints.

Is a PMA required? Yes, absolutely, especially if there are more than 10 developers working on the same project (but usually the need is felt with as few as 5). Nevertheless, many benefits of component-based development can be reaped without a full-scale instantiation of all the concepts described in this chapter. While some level of a PMA is always needed, some of the detailed aspects are required only for organizations wishing to optimize their development and reach the order-of-magnitude improvements in cost-effectiveness promised by the business component approach.

The need for a PMA can be a tough sell because its importance and consequences often become obvious only when many other parts of the factory have already been set up, and the development focus finally shifts to the rapid delivery of complete and correct function. Many organizations first focus on the technical architecture and infrastructure required to develop a large-scale component-based system. Only later in the project do the issues targeted by the PMA become critical for the success of the project, very often obliging the project team to rethink many of their decisions—mainly those about how the project is managed, but also those affecting other architectural viewpoints. This leads to delays and increased costs. The PMA viewpoint is also routinely neglected in technological evolution, to the extent that, over the years, we have learned to test the maturity of a given new technology or new development approach by simply asking the question: What kind of support does it give to large-scale development? New technologies focus primarily on the support needed to build a system and only secondarily do they address what it takes to scale their use to a large development team.

The problems addressed by the PMA and by the SCM part in particular are not new and have been described to some extent (see, for example, [Humphrey 1990] or [Whitgift 1991]). What is new is the degree to which the resolution of this problem becomes a critical aspect of lowering the risks of project failure and enhancing the cost-effectiveness of a CBD project. Indeed, the business component approach is a victim of its own success: Because it becomes relatively easy to develop, concurrently and iteratively, individual business components, an old problem of software development—the necessity to version-manage software artifacts, in particular components—becomes magnified. There may be multiple versions of each business component, depending on the versions of other business components, possibly developed and owned by teams that are physically remote. Therefore, it becomes critical to put in place appropriate solutions to prevent this old-new complexity from destabilizing the project. Many aspects that are considered trivial in a small development can become bottlenecks and cause failure as soon as the project scales up to a larger team. For example, in a C++ development, there is a need to keep the shared header files synchronized, but at the same time avoid having to recompile code each time another part of the system is changed. When a system contains millions of lines of code, this recompilation can be a major consumer of time.

Some core principles underlie the project management architecture. As always, these principles should not be taken dogmatically but should be applied with common sense. They are as follows:

- The business component is the most important project management unit. That is, the development environment is organized around the concept of business component, project plans are organized around business components, tools recognize the business component as a first-class citizen, and task assignments are business component-centric.

- A business component is not only the representation of a business concept or a run-time concept, but it is also a grouping of analysis, design, coding, and run-time software artifacts. It can be seen as a "bucket" for all the software artifacts related to that business concept.

- The three main levels of component granularity—distributed component, business component, and system-level component—must always be taken in account. Professionals involved in the development of a component-based system often need to quickly shift points of view across the levels of granularity, that is, to rapidly shift focus from the business (or distributed) component to the system and vice versa. For example, at analysis, the views of each component's island of data (see Chapter 12, "Component-Based Design") should be able to be consolidated into a system-level database schema. Again, the project manager should be able to quickly switch between day-to-day task assignments at the DC granularity to a picture of the system development status as a whole, appropriate for executive reporting.

- Each functional software artifact, and its specification, is "owned" by a single business component. This means that there is always one and only one place in which the golden copy of a software artifact can be found. A given version of a software artifact is never stored twice in a given version of a system. Most artifacts related to the technical architecture or the application architecture are owned either by the BCVM or by the *Base* business component, and they will not be addressed in detail in this chapter.

- The ownership concept is supported and strengthened by strict accessibility constraints throughout the development lifecycle. If business component *A* needs to use an artifact owned by business component *B*, that artifact must be made available by *B* through an explicit exporting action and must be explicitly imported by *A*.

- Autonomous component development requires the reduction of surface area across the lifecycle between business components and DCs, and at the same time explicit management of the unavoidable dependencies between them. The granularity of import/export actions mentioned in the previous bullet stems from the important trade-off between minimal surface area, on one hand, and management overhead, on the other hand.

- All deliverables are organized according to the business component architecture and stored in a business component-centric way. Even such things as overall project standards and architectural deliverables can be assigned to a business component: the *System* business component. To support rapid development, storage of a business component's deliverables may require that their logical location is physically easy to reach. For example, there is often a need to check, in rapid succession, the analysis, design, and implementation deliverables of a business component.

- Development should be set up in such a way that changes to a given component must be explicitly accepted by other components that depend on the given component. It is not acceptable that a component under development is made unstable by a change in a different component. This is important to enable truly autonomous component development: If not held to, the development of a component would risk being continuously interrupted and made unstable by the development of some other component (see section "SCM View of Development Process").

- In order to achieve rapid component development, it must be possible to develop each component with minimal waits for other parts of the system. This requires that almost any action should be able to be performed while developing or even prototyping a given component. For example, it must be possible, with minimal impact on the rest of the system, to add a business data type, a new table, a new interface, a new error code, or whatever is needed to complete that component.

- Rapid development requires the ability to rapidly update all DCs in the system affected by a change, including retesting the DCs, rebuilding and retesting the various assemblies involved, and rebuilding and retesting the whole system. This is especially important in the relatively rare case of a change having a pervasive impact, for example, where some new function impacts multiple components. It should also be possible to analyze the impact of a change *before* it is made. In a cost-effective software manufacturing capability, the ability to perform an extensive impact-analysis is important.

- Detached development must be directly supported. Detached development means development in which different parts of the system are developed by teams that are in physically different locations. For both economic and practical reasons, detached development is a reality of the software industry today, and it is one that the business component approach is particularly well positioned to address once the project management architecture is in place. Note that different functional categories of components are not all equally suited for assignment to (or being outsourced to) a detached team. For example, utility components are usually the easiest for a detached team to develop.

There is an ideal PMA, which would support independent, concurrent, and rapid development of components by any number of teams (possibly in different locations). And then there is reality: The current state of the art for software configuration management (SCM) systems, development tools, repositories, and integration of the three is some way from the ideal. A good PMA is always a combination of a clear model for large-scale development and a great deal of pragmatism.

Software Configuration Management and Version Control

SCM and version control are the most traditional parts of the project management architecture. The reason they are only a part, and not the whole, is that the traditional focus of SCM has always been change and configuration management, rather than the larger challenge of organizing and managing a project and its development environment so that a large team can work efficiently. This challenge includes aspects such as planning, tracking, estimating, and sizing the project. None of these are traditionally seen as part of SCM.

This section introduces some SCM-related terminology, discusses characteristics of the development process under the SCM point of view, and finally examines some of the factors involved in setting up an integrated SCM strategy that relies on commercial SCM systems, development repositories, and also file systems.

Terminology

This section clarifies terms and concepts used in this chapter. Because some of these terms are simple at first glance but can have many implications, a progressive approach to their definition is adopted in which, starting from an intuitive definition, details and precision are progressively added. The terms relate to dependency lists, to component versions, and to external system release.

Dependency List

The *dependency list* of a component *Foo* identifies the set of all the components on which *Foo* depends, as well as the detailed software artifacts implementing each dependency.

The dependency list is often used to identify dependent components, rather than the whole set of detailed software artifact dependencies between components. When the distinction needs to be made explicit, the dependency list used to identify only required components is called the *component-level dependency list*, while the dependency list showing all required software artifacts is called the *detailed dependency list*. The examples in this chapter focus mainly on DC assemblies and DC dependency lists, but the discussion can be easily extended to other levels of component granularity.

A *versioned dependency list* is a list that, rather than stating "component *Foo* depends on these components . . ." states, "version nnn of component *Foo* depends on these versions of these components." An example of a versioned dependency list for a distributed component is given in Table 10.1. For each component in the column "Distributed Component" in Table 10.1 and in the

Table 10.1   Versioned Dependency List for a Distributed Component[1]

DISTRIBUTED COMPONENT	VERSION	DEPENDENCY LIST
eVendor	v102	eAddressBook v101 eNotes v105 eCurrencyBook v99 eNumberGenerator v101

following examples, the corresponding entry in the "dependency list" column reports only the direct dependencies of each component.

When building a layered system or a strongly reuse-based system, there may be a hierarchy of dependencies: A given component *A* uses a software artifact from another component *B*. In turn, *B* may require some artifact from *C*, which creates an indirect dependency between *A* and *C*. A *closured dependency list* is a versioned dependency list for which all the indirect dependencies have been calculated, as shown in Table 10.2. Here we see that *eAddressBook* brings in the *eBase* distributed component to the closure of the list. Distributed components not having any other component in their dependency list, such as *eNotes* in the table, are considered *leaves* of the dependency list. Often for simplicity the term "dependency list" is used to mean versioned dependency list and/or closured dependency list, leaving the precise meaning to be determined by the context.

A *consistency set* is a closured dependency list whose components are known to work with each other and thus constitute a consistent set. Usually, either by management decision or by technical limitation, there is only one version of each distributed component in each consistency set, and in this sense Table 10.2 is an example of a consistency set. There are technology approaches, such as using tagged data in interfaces, that makes it technically possible to have more than one version of a component in each consistency set (and in the deployed information system), as illustrated in Table 10.3. For example, if *eAddressBook* v101 is upgraded to v102, and it is known that *eVendor* will not need the new functionality of *eAddressBook* v102 or alternatively that the use of tagged data in *eAddressBook*'s interface makes *eVendor* insensitive to this particular change, then it is not strictly necessary to create a new version of *eVen-*

Table 10.2   Closured Dependency List for a Distributed Component

DISTRIBUTED COMPONENT	VERSION	DEPENDENCY LIST
eVendor	v102	eAddressBook v101 eNotes v105 eCurrencyBook v99 eNumberGenerator v101
eAddressBook	v101	eNotes v105 eBase v98
eNotes	v105	
eCurrencyBook	v99	
eBase	v98	
eNumberGenerator	v101	

dor. This allows for some flexibility during development and deployment, but it makes management more complex. It is good project management practice, however, to retain consistency across the system by deploying only one version of each component.

This does not mean that one of the great advantages of components should not be exploited. For example, if *eAddressBook* v102 provides some significant new function for end users but requires no change to components using it, then it can be deployed by itself, without having to redeploy the other unchanged components, and, of course, in any given system there would still be only one version of *eAddressBook*. Individual deployment of upgraded components significantly reduces the granularity of maintenance and can make upgrading a much more attractive proposition. There are, of course, SCM implications of this, and these are touched on in the discussion of "branching" in the subsection, "SCM View of Development Process."

Various tools implementations could take different approaches to versioning. For example, a developer working on a given project may find it useful to equate "*eVendor* depends on *eAddressBook* v101" to "*eVendor* depends on *eAddressBook* v101 and higher." For simplicity, the dependency lists in this chapter reflect the most constrained use; that is, a component depends only on the versions that appear in the dependency list.

In many cases, such as when modeling the system, when discussing the system as a whole, or during an executive meeting, the component-level dependency list is at a perfect level of information content and is often used as

Table 10.3 Consistency Set Allowing Multiple Versions of Each Component

DISTRIBUTED COMPONENT	VERSION	DEPENDENCY LIST
eVendor	v102	eAddressBook v101 eNotes v105 eCurrencyBook v99 eNumberGenerator v101
eAddressBook	v101	eNotes v105 eBase v98 eBase v95
eNotes	v105	
eCurrencyBook	v99	
eBase	v95	
eBase	v98	
eNumberGenerator	v101	

a simple high-level description of the system at a particular moment in time. It corresponds to a large extent to the level of information presented in a component diagram (as shown in Figure 5.1 in Chapter 5, "The Business Component System"). On the other hand, as soon as the project needs to use the dependency list for day-to-day development purposes, it becomes necessary to use the detailed dependency list because there will be a need to know exactly which interfaces and software artifacts are part of a given dependency. The detailed dependency list also enables a full impact analysis to be carried out.

Dependencies may be different at different points in the development lifecycle. For example, they are different at deployment-time than at build-time, and an optimized development process will usually manage these differences. This will require different views of the dependency list, or different dependency lists, in the different phases of the development lifecycle.

Component Versions

Several terms are required for discussing versioning: distributed component version, business component version, business component system version, and work-in progress version.

Distributed Component

A distributed component version consists of a version of all the software artifacts necessary to design, implement, and deploy the distributed component, together with the information required to precisely identify its consistency set.

A given DC version also identifies a versioned distributed component assembly (the set of DCs on which the given DC depends). Indeed, the term "distributed component version" is sometimes used to indicate a specific distributed component assembly. For example, Table 10.2 shows not only the software artifacts required to build *eVendor* v102, but also all the other distributed components, and their versions, in the *eVendor* assembly. This assembly is referred to as "eVendor assembly v102."

A distributed component can be in several versions at the same time, and so it must be possible to support an *eVendor v002* at the same time as an *eVendor v003*. The limits to the number of versions allowed for each component should be purely technical, such as the size of hard disk space available, and not given by tools and infrastructure.

Based on experience to date, a new version of a given distributed component is normally created every two to three weeks, but the mechanics of creating a new version should be so efficient, in order to support the rapid development requirements, that it should be theoretically possible (at least technically) to create a new version in less than a minute. Creating a new version includes such things as moving all the appropriate files to the physical location of the new version and informing the development environment that a new version has been created, which means updating all scripts and all dependency lists to point to the correct versions.

Business Component

A business component version consists of a version of each of the business component's four tiers, the information required to precisely identify its consistency set closure, and any other deliverables owned by the business component. All the software lifecycle deliverables of the business component are also part of a given business component version.

Identifying a business component version also identifies the BC assembly. Thus the term "business component version" is often used to indicate a particular version of a business component assembly.

A given business component can be in several versions at the same time. For example, the development environment may be required to support a Vendor business component version n at the same time as a Vendor business component version $(n + 1)$. The limits to this should be purely technical, such as the size of hard disk space available, and not given by tools and infrastructure.

In a mature project, a new version of a given business component is normally created every two to three months. To support rapid development requirements, though, it should be technically possible to create a new version in a few minutes or less.

Business Component System

A business component system version consists of a defined version of each business component in the business component system. A new version of a given business component system is normally required for any internal release of the whole system.

Business component versioning can also be used to support identifying and managing the different releases of the system. The business component named "System" (described in Chapter 5) may represent the whole business component system; that is, each version of this business component may represent a version of the system because its dependency list can be used to unequivocally identify which business components (and which versions) belong to that particular version of the system.

Work-In-Progress

Each of the levels of component granularity can have a work-in-progress version, which is simply the version that is currently being worked on. Given the iterative nature of the development process, in a mature PMA there can be more than one work-in-progress version of the same component at the same time.

External System Release

An external system release is a business component system version that is deployed or released to the end user. It is a consistent set of versioned business components assembled to the required level of proven quality, and packaged together with a set of deliverables often not required for internal releases, such as user guides, install tools, and so forth. In many cases the release will include significant legacy deliverables and infrastructural deliverables. An external release, when compared to an internal business component system release, may require a different set of tools, processes, and infrastructure. It may also require the following:

- A different level of quality when compared to an internal release (a release internal to the development organization for project management purposes). Even though any release should have the maximum possible quality, internal releases may have priorities other than quality, such as proving a certain technology, and so may be of lower quality than an external release.

- Availability on a platform different from the development platform. For example, the development platform may be NT, while the release may be generated and (extensively) tested on Unix. Such cross-platform requirements are an important reason for delivering the source-level portability described in Chapter 8, "Technical Architecture."

- A different level of packaging compared to other phases of the development. For example, at external release time, the release manager may decide to release, instead of the 42 executables corresponding to EDCs on the server side used during design/development, a much smaller number of executables for systems management reasons. Or at external release time, the performance team decides that, instead of one single DLL for each WDC, they need to generate a set of DLLs for some reason and assemble the binaries with different code optimization from the ones used during development. Logically, this has no impact whatsoever on functionality and behavior. Packaging several distributed components into one executable may also be required to reduce the overall memory footprint. Every business component may contain repeated "code" (this is highly technology dependent), due, for example, to application architecture considerations such as error handling, base classes, and so on. Given that the footprint for object-oriented implementations, especially when heavily based on generation, tends to be quite big, it may be an important concern to optimize it.[2]

SCM View of Development Process

This section briefly summarizes the high-level concepts of the component development process from the point of view of software configuration management (SCM). The general development process philosophy is one of *continuous integration of autonomously developed components*.

Such development leads to the need for managing multiple versions of the same component and for supporting easy and rapid creation of new versions. Given the highly iterative nature of business component development, each software artifact in each component may evolve in different versions and at a quite rapid pace.

It is important to differentiate the problem of SCM by the levels of component granularity. Different techniques can be adopted to manage versioning within a distributed component, within a business component assembly, or for a system-level component. The fact that the system is composed from conceptually autonomous components allows a single distributed component to be managed as a microcosm, while collaborations of components need different management techniques and principles, and perhaps a different toolset.

Each business component or DC can be thought of as being on a timeline, on which from time to time a "drop" (a formal internal or external release) of the component is done. A drop is never modified other than in exceptional circumstances such as the correction of a blocking bug, and then under strict management control. "Users" of that component should use only a drop and never a work-in-progress version. This rule allows both the owner of the work-in-progress and the owners of other components to work without directly affecting each other. Figure 10.1 illustrates this and shows four releases of the business component *eVendor* and of its assembly. Each black dot in the figure represents a drop. The first release, Rel 1, contains only the address book assembly and is considered preparatory work for the release of the e-tier of the *Vendor* business component assembly. The second release, Rel 2, is the first release in which the whole e-tier is present, and it also contains a new version of all the components in Rel 1. The third release, Rel 3, differs from Rel 2 only in that it contains a new version of *eVendor*. The fourth release, Rel 4, contains a new version of each component in the *eVendor* assembly.

A modification of a drop corresponds to branching in traditional SCM systems, as illustrated in Figure 10.2. While releasing Rel 2 of the address book assembly, a fix is required to the *eNotes* component in Rel 1. The fix is released

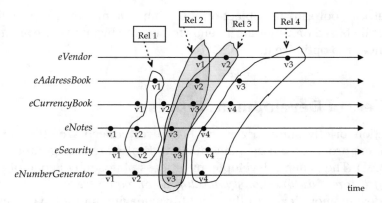

Figure 10.1 Timelines and drops.

as Rel 1.1, which is Rel 1 plus version 2.1 of *eNotes*. At the same time, Rel 2 goes ahead with version 3 of *eNotes*. Thus there are two branches of released assemblies at the same time: Rel 1.1 and Rel 2. The fix is merged back into normal releases with Rel 3.

From an SCM perspective, normal principles of large-scale development are applied. For example, we mentioned that as a general rule a change in a dependent component must be explicitly accepted by declaring in a new version of the dependency list that the new version of the dependent component will be used. This rule guarantees stability and autonomy of development. An exception to this rule is during the short "stabilization" periods, occurring right before release of a BC assembly or business component system, during which it may be decided—with full knowledge of the risks involved and of how to manage these risks—that it is acceptable to depend on a work-in-progress version of a business component or DC.

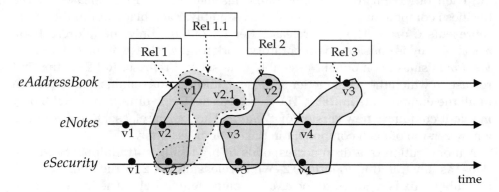

Figure 10.2 Branching.

Integrated SCM Strategy

Software configuration management is well known in traditional software development. It is also well known that to scale up a project to a large team requires proper SCM procedures to be in place. There are powerful SCM systems on the market today to support traditional SCM procedures, and some of these tools are well integrated with commercial IDEs. The question, however, is whether the current state of the art of SCM systems is enough to support the kind of development described in this book.

SCM systems do not currently have the same capabilities as repositories, and vice versa, because they do not address the same requirements. SCM systems are particularly powerful in managing source code and files, but at the time of writing are less appropriate as the integration point for tools built by different vendors such as database modeling and object-oriented modeling tools. These tools often rely on a repository-driven integration where the tools to be integrated, as well as possibly the tools built in-house, use, extend, or define a common meta-model in a development repository and rely on this repository for much of their versioning and SCM needs.Even if repositories provide some support for SCM procedures, at the time of writing they do not have the same sophistication as SCM systems or the same level (with regard to SCM support) of out-of-the-box integration with leading IDE systems.

The result is that today a CBD project is normally required to use, for different but related purposes, both SCM systems and repositories. An organization must not only properly integrate them (in a more or less ad-hoc way since integration is not yet readily available on the market) but also carefully choose the set of procedures required to make the development flow smoothly. In addition, even the most powerful SCM system is not a file system, and it may not be completely integrated and/or open to all the tools required to efficiently and cost-effectively run a large-scale project. Over and over again, due to various pragmatic considerations, projects have ended up using a combination of a repository, an SCM system, and a set of ad-hoc tools and procedures based directly on the file system to manage the software configurations and versions of the many software artifacts in the system.

The conclusion is that, not only at the time of writing but probably in the medium term, an organization wishing to reap all the benefits of component-based development may have to define an integrated SCM strategy relying on an ad-hoc integration of commercially available (or even in-house) SCM systems, development repositories, and other tools and approaches. As part of this integration, there will inevitably be some direct use of the file system.

Based on this conclusion, the following presents a number of examples of the kind of considerations that an integrated SCM strategy must address. In the long term, it can be assumed that repositories will become the sole center of the development universe. For simplicity, the following will focus on a strategy valid for the medium term, assuming that software artifacts are managed through a combination of a commercial SCM system, a repository, and manual procedures and policies based directly on the file system.

An integrated SCM strategy must answer several questions; the two main ones are these:

- Where is the golden copy of each software artifact stored? As an example, the project may decide that the golden copy of all deliverables managed by repository-based tools will be stored in the repository. Source code is either tool-generated or written by functional developers. The golden copy of all tool-generated source code will be managed and stored directly in the file system, and not managed through the SCM system. However, the golden copy of all source code written or manually modified by the functional developer will be stored in, and version-managed by, the SCM system. The golden copy of all deliverables that are not source code and not modified through the IDE, such as documents and specifications, will be stored either in the SCM system or directly in the file system. The latter is often preferred because the various versions of these deliverables are often managed using the capabilities of the tools—for example, a word processor—used to produce them.

- Which level of version granularity will be known to the various tools? Even assuming that each developer-modified source code file is versioned using the SCM system, it may be convenient to consider various levels of version granularity, corresponding to the levels of component granularity. For example, for SCM systems having the concept of "project," it is often useful to check in and check out at the same time all files that will be modified in the same modification session. A version granularity that has proven very convenient as a good compromise in size and management overhead is the DC version granularity. Often, for example, when correcting a bug, multiple source files belonging to the same DC are modified in rapid succession. It is very convenient to create in the SCM system (assuming it supports this) a project that corresponds to a DC and check out and check in all files of the DC at the same time.

The answer to the second question also addresses the business component in that its four tiers normally evolve at different speeds, and the dependency lists of the different tiers usually differ from each other. Thus from the point of view of tool integration it makes sense to version at the distributed component level as well. Indeed, we apply the following rule: The DC version is the lowest level of version granularity that is of concern from the tool integration perspective. Whether an individual DC development decides to use the SCM system to further manage versioning at the file level is transparent to the overall project.

Of course, this does not mean that finer-grained artifacts should not be versioned. In fact, the DC version granularity level nicely allows for management of individual software artifact versions within a distributed component. This could be done using a DC-level "bill of material" (in the manufacturing industry sense), that is, an internal dependency list that shows versions of each individual software artifact. For example, in a C++ development environment the bill of material can be implemented by the makefile. Last but not least, the DC version of granularity is such that a small team of two to three people could work on the same version of a DC at the same time. This is the number of people that can easily and pragmatically coordinate and still rapidly develop software, even where a project decides not to rely on SCM systems for file-level source control.

Based on the this approach, a specific integrated SCM strategy could involve directives such as the following:

- The SCM system can be used for check-in and check-out, assuming the main check-in/check-out granularity is the distributed component. Within the SCM system, distributed components are grouped within their respective business component. In particular, the SCM system can be used to version all the source code modified by the functional developer directly in the IDE.

- The repository can be used as the main way to version all the *specification* and *modeling* aspects. The versioning capabilities of the repositories are used to manage the versions of deliverables produced by the modeling tools.

- Each individual software artifact within a DC version (after having been checked out from the SCM system), as well as the dependencies between DCs, is managed mainly outside the SCM system and outside the repository, for example, through strict guidelines governing how a physical file system directory structure is to be used (as illustrated later in this chapter).

- The SCM system is organized around business components and distributed components. We will see later how this needs to parallel the structure of the directory tree in the file system. Each business component is owned by a team, and this is the team that is allowed to check in and check out component deliverables, create a new release, and work on the component.

To "check out a whole DC" could have the following implications:

- All and only the files that are "owned" by the given DC are checked out. Not all the files constituting a DC need be under SCM, so only some of a DC's files could be involved in the check-out.

- A given DC references the files on which it depends but that are not "owned" by the DC. These files are stored on the shared file system in the location of the owning DC, and not in a project-global "release" directory. For example, the C++ header file for the proxy of an EDC *eFoo* is stored in *eFoo*'s directories and referenced (not copied) by the makefile and "include" statements of a distributed component *eBar* that uses *eFoo*.

These considerations will be expanded in the section "Directory Tree Structure" later in this chapter.

Dependency Management

Dependency management is the set of concepts and tools that allow proper management of dependencies in a component-based development. Dependency management for a specific project goes through the following:

- The definition of a *dependency model*, which includes the identification of the possible categories of dependencies between components and how the project intends to manage dependencies.

- The development of appropriate tools to manage these dependencies. An example of this is the Component Dependency Manager introduced in the next section, *"Extending the Development Environment."*

Appropriate dependency management is critical for a large-team CBD project, for example, to ensure closure when something is shipped or to support impact analysis when a modification is needed. Given the levels of targeted concurrent and iterative development, each autonomously developed component can exist in several versions at any one time, and it can depend on components that may be at different version levels at any one time. Without proper management, the level of complexity becomes too great for effective development.

Dependency Model

A *dependency model* is an explicit description of the dependency categories between components and of how a project will deal with these dependencies. This implies an explicit description of which software artifacts have visibility outside a component at a given level of granularity. In the following discussion, only dependencies at the functional architecture viewpoint are considered, and not those between a component and BCVM deliverables.

Depending on various parameters such as size of project, stability of deliverables, organizational maturity, and so on, different approaches to managing dependencies will be appropriate. Some of these dependencies can be automatically calculated, in some case with minimal information, while others are better managed explicitly. The exact trade-off between the two choices is project- and technology-dependent. At first glance, allowing the system to automatically calculate dependencies looks attractive. However, a closer analysis shows this can present many issues for large systems, in that automatic dependency definition can be time-consuming and error-prone, as well as promoting the idea that interfaces can be designed without serious thought about dependencies, and hence indirectly contributing to an increase in surface area between components.

An explicit and selective *import/export model* for dependency management is probably one of the best approaches, and the remainder of this section assumes this approach, which defines the following basic process:

1. A component B "exports" a software artifact x by designating it as available for use by another component.

2. A component A "imports" software artifact x from component B by stating that it will be used by A.

3. Component A then uses software artifact x.

The two main objectives of the import/export model are to support the reduction of surface area between components and to support the management of unavoidable dependencies. These objectives are achieved by strictly enforcing (through the use of the import/export mechanism) the idea of ownership of software artifacts. This, in turn, directly supports an explicit and conscious effort to reduce dependencies. It also leads to better support of impact analysis and reduced change impact, and it ultimately enhances the ability to develop components independently.

The dependency model should recognize the different dependency categories, so that it can reflect the totality of dependencies that a given component has on other components. The following presents two main categories: direct dependencies between components and "derived" dependencies, that is, dependencies that derive from the development environment.

Let's first discuss direct dependencies. For the purposes of this discussion, assume that some EDC A depends on EDC B and thus, more generally, on the business component containing EDC B. EDC A may "use" EDC B in a number of ways, which include the following:

Operation invocation dependency. In order to invoke an operation on EDC B, EDC A must know and access (and thus "import") one or more software artifacts from EDC B, for example, its proxy, business data types, and error definitions. A dependency on a run-time interface is perhaps the most traditional example of dependency. It is referred to as an *operation invocation dependency* because the implementation of EDC A (in our example) depends on the availability of a set of software artifacts required to invoke EDC B. Such artifacts are imported by EDC A through EDC B's extended (development) interface.

Internal design dependency. A certain number of artifacts from EDC *B* may be reused to facilitate the internal design implementation of EDC *A*, quite aside from the invocation of operations on EDC *B*. These artifacts would typically not appear in the run-time interfaces of EDC *B*, and they may not even be part of the EDC *B* executable, but rather may be used only inside other DCs. An example of this was given in Chapter 4, "The Business Component," when discussing design interfaces (see Figure 4.11 in Chapter 4): that is, a set of classes that a subject component[3] can reuse within its own code, so making it easier to interact with a target business component. If this set of classes is generic enough to be reusable across the system, it would naturally be owned by the target component and be made available to the rest of the system through an export mechanism. The master version would continue to be owned by the target component, and it could be required that any modification be explicitly accepted by the components using it. This kind of dependency is an *internal design dependency*, given the need to take such things into account during component design, in this example design of EDC *A*.

Interface specification dependency. In order to define an interface for EDC *A*, a certain number of artifacts from EDC *B* may be reused, for example, business data types or tags. This corresponds to the concept of *interface specification dependency* and is so called because it is a dependency not at the EDC *A* implementation level, but only at the EDC *A* interface level, appearing when specifying EDC *A*'s interface. Note that the dependency list for interface specification dependencies is usually different from that of operation invocation dependencies.

Figure 10.3 shows how the dependencies of *Vendor*'s run-time interface can be different from those of *Vendor*'s internal implementation. Why is the previous distinction between direct dependencies important? Well, for example, in a detailed impact analysis, a modification to *NumberGenerator* could impact the implementation of *Vendor* but not its interface. Making an explicit distinction,

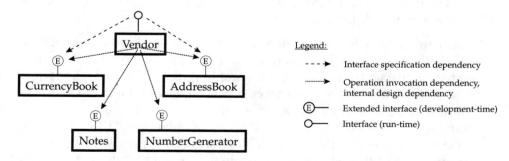

Figure 10.3   Direct dependencies between components.

and having the tools that are able to verify and manage this distinction, is critical in getting an exact picture of the surface area between components and in evaluating which indirect dependencies are created when another component decides to invoke *Vendor*'s interface.

The previous example also illustrates how the same conceptual dependency may appear several times during development—at various points in the lifecycle—as a different kind of software dependency. Let us further illustrate by addressing the other main category of dependencies, that is, derived dependencies resulting from the development environment. Supposing the project is using a textual specification language called, say, Component Specification Language (CSL), and that a repository is used to support at least code generation. Let us also assume that the usage of CSL, rather than a graphical user interface, is the main way of entering information into a development repository. The following derived dependencies can be identified in this scenario:

Specification-time dependency. In order to load the CSL definition of *eVendor*'s interface (say *ieVendor*) into the repository, there may be a need for other CSL files belonging to the same or other business component to be preloaded. For example, suppose that *btCurrency* is a business data type defined in some specification file and that it is owned by the *CurrencyBook* business component. Further suppose that *btCurrency* is used in the definition of a *read_vendor (…)* operation in one of *ieVendor*'s interfaces. This represents an interface specification dependency, but it also implies a dependency between the physical files containing the specifications. The former is a dependency on a software artifact—the *btCurrency* implementation—while the latter is a dependency on the file containing the specification of *btCurrency*. One area where this latter form of dependency manifests itself is in the way the repository handles the various specification files. If the repository is not able to accept input in any order, it will require, as some compilers do, that the specification file containing the *btCurrency* specification is loaded before the *ieVendor* interface specification file. This then creates a load order dependency, perhaps exhibited through some form of "file include" capability for specification files.

Compile dependencies (generated from repository). In order to use another component's business data type in an interface, the declaration of the business data type must be available, which in C++, for example, would require an explicit statement to include the header file declaring the business data type in the header file of the code implementing the interface. This creates a dependency, first, on the DC owning the declaration file to be included and, second, on the declaration file itself. In an ideal world, a repository would be able to directly manage this kind of dependency, in such a way that the functional developer has to worry only about the specification dependency. In practice, that is, in the medium term, a specification dependency will manifest itself as a dependency (at development) between the two files: the one containing the declaration and the one including the declaration. Assuming that both files can be generated from specifications in the repository, the code generation must also generate the appropriate includes, so reflecting explicitly the dependencies between files.

As an example, consider the interface *ieVendor*, which uses the *btCurrency* business data type. This business data type must be known by the proxy in any component invoking *ieVendor*. Hence (depending on the particular technology) dependency may well be created between files at compile time, where these files are generated from specifications contained in the repository.

The point is that not only must a dependency model have a clear picture of specification dependencies, but unless it has a clear, well-architected code-generation strategy explicitly focused on the reduction of dependencies, the project is at risk of creating unnecessary dependencies through code generation that can have a significant impact on the development. The concern of the project management architect should hence be not only the types of dependencies, but also the mechanisms used to minimize these dependencies in the generated code.

Compile dependencies (not generated from repository). There may be software artifacts that are added outside of the repository, for example, those created directly through use of an IDE. These are highly project-specific, but they may result in compile dependencies that the repository is not aware of. An example of this is a particular error code related to the *btCurrency* business data type that the project decides to add manually and not through the repository. This particular example may be seen as a bad project decision, but the fact is that there is often a pragmatic necessity to make decisions of this kind given either the immaturity of the repository meta-model or simply because of the flexibility this solution can give in particular contexts. This corresponds to intercomponent compile dependencies, which the repository has no way of knowing about, that need to be managed appropriately.

In a detailed dependency model we would expect to find dependencies related to each layer of the seven-layer protocol model introduced in Chapter 6. Indeed, these categories of dependency exist between any two applications or parts of applications needing to cooperate: They are not CBD-specific. On the other hand, in CBD we aim to obtain autonomous development, and each dependency is a threat to this objective. Each category of dependency may have some technical or architectural way to lessen the influence of the dependency itself. For example, through proper usage of tagged data, it is possible to introduce various degrees of freedom in component interfaces and so enhance autonomy. But this flexibility comes with a price, which is one more thing for the project management architecture to manage.

Exporting

As part of the dependency model, and assuming an explicit export/import mechanism to manage intercomponent dependencies, an *export model* must be developed, and the mechanism to manage it must be defined. *Export* means the ability to "mark" a particular software artifact of a given component as available for other components to use. This implies that only software artifacts marked as exportable can be used by other components. Other software artifacts cannot under any circumstance be used by another component.

To export a software artifact does not mean that it is physically moved. In fact, it is much better never to physically move or copy a software artifact outside of the component that "owns" it. A consequence of this principle in, for example, a C++ development environment, is that the makefile used to build a particular DC would refer to software artifacts owned by other DCs, typically located in their respective file directories.

There are a number of artifacts that a business component may want to share or export for public use at different moments in its development lifecycle, such as the following:

- Individual interfaces. A project may even decide to export individual operations within each interface, but when this is the case, the correctness of the interface granularity is open to question.

- Language classes exemplified as design dependencies in the previous "Dependency Model" subsection.

- Business data types, or tags when using tagged data, typically to be used in the context of an interface. It is sometimes useful to think in terms of direct and indirect export. An example of indirect export is a business data type exported only because a certain exported interface requires it. On the other hand, a subject component may need to use a business data type independently of any access to its owning business component; this is an example of direct export.

- Errors, that is, the list of errors that a given component may raise, together with associated error codes and messages.

- User interface elements, such as a user interface control or user interface panel to be reused by another business component.

- Constants, resources, and so on, that other components may need or want to reuse.

Importing one or more of the software artifacts exemplified in the preceding list is a typical example of the use of build-time or compile-time extended interfaces (see Chapter 4), and normally these kinds of software artifacts (particularly the ones related to proxies) are addressed as a priority by an export model. The following are examples of software artifacts that can also be considered to be exportable in a mature export model:

Data models. This is a totally different level of extended interface, typically exported from the database modeling tool. Before integrating a target component into the system, it may be required to verify the validity of the data model (or of any other model) within the context of the assembly into which the target component is to be imported.

Testing artifacts. The target component may have a set of automated test scripts that need to be integrated into the automated test scripts of the assembly into which the target component is to be imported.

Initialization data. If the target component exports definitions of data types to be used at the database level, a set of initialization data for these types may need to be exported as well. For example, the *CurrencyBook* may have the ability to export the list of currencies defined by the ISO standards.

Importing

A component may choose to import any of the software artifacts exported by another component. A software artifact can be imported from another business component or distributed component only if it has previously been explicitly exported (made visible) by that other component. A subject component usually needs to import different software artifacts at different times in the development lifecycle.

An importing component should not change an imported software artifact, but rather if a change is required it should ask the exporting component to change it and reexport it, usually from a new version of the exporting component. Any exception to this rule should be carefully managed.

The granularity at which a given component will export software artifacts on one side and import them on the other (the two are not necessarily the same granularity) is a trade-off between such things as management effort, development simplicity, and interface surface area. For example, from one perspective it could appear superficially attractive—and easy to do—to gather all the business data types into one logical or physical file (in the repository or file system, respectively). Any developer needing a business data type would just include this single file. On the other hand, every time a new business data type is added, or an existing one modified, all components in the system would probably be impacted, even if merely because they would need to be rebuilt and retested. This is clearly undesirable, and there must be a way to limit this impact. One approach is to build or acquire a tool able to analyze the interface specifications and create a file containing all and only the business data types that are actually used by a given component.

In order to reduce the surface area, it must be possible to import *selectively*. That is, it must be possible for an importer to specify a subset of the software artifacts exported by a given version of a component and to import only that subset. For example, if more than one interface is exported by a target component, a subject component must be allowed to import only one of them.

It must also be possible to check the indirect dependencies of what is being imported, that is, to calculate the closure and show the surface area caused by the extent of the indirect dependencies. For example, when importing an interface from a business component, this interface may, from a development perspective, be part of a specific consistency set. To be able to easily verify the consequence of an import action is an important factor in the management of dependencies and in the analysis of different strategies for dependencies reduction.

As an example of this impact, consider the two consistency sets shown in Tables 10.4 and 10.5.

Table 10.5 states that *eVendor* v103 requires *eAddressBook* v102 rather than v101. Suppose a subject component using *eVendor* v102 decides take advantage of a new function in *eVendor* v103. Suppose also that this new function has nothing to do with *eAddressBook*. Nevertheless, because *eVendor* v103 depends on *eAddressBook* v102, then to import an interface from *eVendor* v103, and

Table 10.4   Consistency Set

DISTRIBUTED COMPONENT	VERSION	DEPENDENCY LIST
eVendor	V102	eAddressBook v101 eNotes v105 eCurrencyBook v99 eNumberGenerator v101
eAddressBook	V101	eNotes v105 eBase v98
eNotes	V105	
eCurrencyBook	V99	
eBase	V98	
eNumberGenerator	V101	

Table 10.5   Consistency Set with Different Versions

DISTRIBUTED COMPONENT	VERSION	DEPENDENCY LIST
eVendor	V103	eAddressBook v102 eNotes v105 eCurrencyBook v99 eNumberGenerator v101
eAddressBook	V102	eNotes v105 eBase v98
eNotes	V105	
eCurrencyBook	V99	
eBase	V98	
eNumberGenerator	V103	

hence upgrade to using *eVendor* 103, it may also have to upgrade to *eAddress-Book* v102 and also to the appropriate versions of other dependent business components as indicated in *eVendor* v103's consistency set. The dependency model must define what happens in these circumstances.

Dependency Dynamic

A phenomenon that we have observed in the evolution of real CBD projects is what we call the "dependency dynamic," exemplified here as it applies to business data types.

Each functional software artifact is assigned to a business component. In the case of business data types, the *Base* business component typically owns a few system-wide business data types, such as Date and Time. Other business data types will be assigned to business components following various principles such as high cohesion. While developing a business component, for example, the *CurrencyBook*, a set of new business data types not provided by the *Base* component may be needed. Suppose it's decided that these are conceptually owned by the *CurrencyBook*. An advantage of this decision is that *Currency-Book* can go ahead and add these business data types without having to wait for any other component owner to add them. Even if the assignment of any particular type to any particular component may be challenged, *it is a desirable characteristic of a component-based development that each component can add a business data type to the system,* retaining ownership of this business data type for as long as needed (or until an architect decides otherwise) to test and stabilize the exact nature of this business data type. This approach supports a team developing a component to continue forward without waiting for other teams.

Once the business data type has existed for a while and its role is well established in the system, an analysis of dependencies might indicate that it would be better owned by another component. Mostly this other component is below (in the DAG) the component currently owning the business data type, and moving it downward may lead to a slight readjustment of dependencies, usually leading to a reduction in the overall dependency count.

What was just described is a quite typical occurrence in large-scale component-based development, and it is a good example of the dependency dynamic. This is a typical ownership dynamic in a CBD system: Over time, many atomic software artifacts such as business data types tend to migrate downward. These software artifacts may have been created as part of a given component simply for convenience of rapid development or because at the time that component appeared to be their appropriate owner. Through usage, or through architectural reviews, the project may decide that these software artifacts are better owned by other components, usually leading to a reduction in dependencies and in a more agile component diagram. In order to support the dynamic nature of CBD, as well as the requirement for autonomous development, it is important that this dynamic is facilitated by the extended integrated development environment.

The example of business data types can be extended to most atomic software artifacts that are exportable—for example, errors definitions, constants, and user interface controls.

Example

In this example of dependency management we assume that the component specifications are done with a text-based language called "Component Specification Language" (CSL) and that a repository is used to support at least code generation. The assumption of CSL enables us to illustrate in a simple form some of the aspects that surround dependency management and the import/export model. The principles illustrated are general, and the challenges exposed by this example apply also in other cases, for example, in the case of a GUI-based tool providing a direct user interface into a development repository.

An important principle of the project management architecture is that it must be possible to modify each deliverable and any software artifact of a business component or DC with minimal impact on other artifacts. For example, modifying a persistence language class in a given business component should have no influence whatsoever on the interface specification, or on compilation or runtime aspects of the given component or of the components using it. Hence it is important to separate out those things whose modification can impact other components because of their dependencies and those that do not. In the present example, this is done through the specification of each business component being created as a number of standard CSL files, including the following:

BusinessDataTypes.csl. This file contains the definition of all the business data types used in the business component's interfaces. The file defines each leaf attribute of each business data type as being of a base data type defined in the system-level bcvm.csl. This means that this file depends on the BCVM. If nested business data types are allowed, this file may also depend on business data types defined in the *BusinessDataTypes.csl* file of other business components.

Tags.csl. If using tagged data, this file would define the list of allowed tag names (and their descriptions) and the correspondence (or at least the default correspondence) between each tag and a business data type defined in *BusinessDataTypes.csl* or a base data type.

BusinessDataTypeList.csl. This file contains all of the "list" or collection business data types appearing on the DC's interface. Each list is defined as a sequence of a business data types defined in the component's *Business-DataTypes.csl* and with a tag name defined in the component's *Tags.csl*.

Interfaces.csl. This file defines the exportable interfaces of the component, including operation names and arguments. The interfaces defined in this file may use any of the data types or tags defined in the previous three files or similar definitions from the corresponding files of other business components.

In order for a code generator to correctly generate code for a given DC based on these specification files, all the required data must be in the repository. This means not only consistent, complete, and correct specifications in the above four files, but also all corresponding files containing artifacts imported by this DC from other business components. Other CSL files, containing specifications of artifacts internal to the business component, and which should never be exported, are also required. For example, required files include these:

Plc.csl. This file defines the persistence language classes that map to the r-tier, and through that to the database, possibly using the tags previously defined in this component's *Tags.csl*.

Edc.csl. This file defines the EDCs in the business component's e-tier. A corresponding file would exist for each of the other tiers and is not shown in this example.

Bc.csl. This file defines the business component itself and, among other things, would specify the DCs that make up the business component.

Consider the EDCs shown in Table 10.4. Suppose a skeleton executable version of *eVendor* is required and that there exists some set of build tools that can generate code and compile/link a skeleton EDC from a specification provided in the previous files. We'll call this set of tools (which would in reality include some form of repository) "the tool." Now, as shown in Table 10.4, *eVendor* v102 depends on *eAddressBook* v101 and *eCurrencyBook* v99 (among others). The following would typically be required:

- In order for the tool to successfully process *eVendor*'s CSL, that of *eAddressBook* and *eCurrencyBook* must also be processed—and probably has to be made available first (many tools are single-pass!). If so, then this implies that the exported CSL from DCs lower in the DAG must be loaded first.

- Because each of the various CSL definitions should reside in one and only one business component, the tool should avoid copying *eAddressBook* and *eCurrencyBook*'s CSL into the file-system location occupied by *eVendor*'s CSL. Rather the tool should know, for example from a dependency list, where to find each required CSL file and load it appropriately. Should the tool retain some memory of what artifacts in *eAddressBook* and *eCurrencyBook* have been referenced, then on a subsequent use of the tool, this can enable it to automatically pick up changes to the two required DCs. The question of how the tool knows where to find the CSL files is one of the subjects of the next section.

Completing the Development Environment

Chapter 8 introduced an extended integrated development environment suitable for a business component approach. This chapter has further elaborated on the development environment through the integrated SCM strategy discussion and the analysis of the relationship between SCM systems, repositories, and file systems. This section completes the discussion about the extended development environment, by first illustrating the challenges of physically structuring the development environment and properly defining the directory tree structure; second, by introducing the characteristics of a tool—named *Component Dependency Manager* (CDM) for the purposes of this book—able to manage the dependencies; and finally, by discussing the importance of scripts to automate many of the repetitive tasks of a component-based project.

At the time of writing, not only is the project management architecture often ad hoc, but various tools provide solutions to large-scale development that are often incompatible across the tools themselves, and this fact alone is often one of the biggest obstacles to development environment integration and to an effective project management architecture. Companies setting up an efficient software development capability today need to build this environment as a layer on top of commercially available tools. This layer safeguards projects from becoming unmanageable, or at least from being less cost-effective and less development-time-scalable. The trade-off is between initial setup costs and much higher ongoing "hidden" project development costs.

Directory Tree Structure

The "Integrated SCM Strategy" section argued that for various practical reasons it happens often that the file system and a proper structuring of the computer-based development environment play an important role in software development. Readers familiar with large-scale development will be aware of how this apparently simple problem, if not addressed, is responsible for many project issues and ongoing difficulties. This section presents the principles behind a proper design of the directory tree structure for a component-based development.

For simplicity, examples illustrating these principles assume a development in which business components are implemented using C++ and the NT/Unix development environments. The concepts presented, however, are of general applicability and can be applied to other contexts with minor modifications, for example, a Java-based development that takes into account the heavy dependence of Java on specific file locations. Most of the examples are given in terms of DCs for simplicity, but they can easily be extended to the business component granularity level. A further simplification is to focus on the software artifacts of the functional architecture viewpoint only; that is, other artifacts such as BCVM deliverables are not considered.

The following further assumptions are made:

- A component-based development will benefit from having a standardized environment structure for the development of each component. Given the importance of properly integrating various tools in an extended development environment, the tools usually must be made explicitly aware of the directory structure in order to automate tasks such as code generation directly into the appropriate location. We exemplify here some structuring principles on which these standards may be built.

- There is a *shared environment*, that is, a place in the file system that is accessible by the whole project and common to all developers. This contains internally released code, that is, code that a developer deems usable by other developers on the same project (rather than product-level code that can be delivered to end users). The shared environment is managed using conventions and guidelines through, for example, a shared area and a common shared drive, in conjunction with an SCM system.

- The structure of the shared environment and the structure of the SCM system should be directly related and, of course, be component-centric.

To a large extent, they should be organized following the same principles while taking into account their respective strengths. For example, in many SCM systems it is relatively easy to create a new version of a file by recording only the delta of difference between the new and the previous versions, while this is very difficult to do in the file system.

- The shared environment *lives*. The most efficient, simple, and safe way to set-up a component-based development is by having the functional developers work directly out of the shared environment, rather than copying the component and working on it on a local workstation. This can be managed simply in such a way that during development, this shared environment becomes a "remote personal environment" for the developer working on a specific version of a component. As soon as the developer wishes to release the version, and assuming, of course, that the component has gone through all appropriate quality checks, the developer can simply *drop* the component by stopping any work on it and create a new version on which to continue work. When a component is dropped, it is frozen and cannot normally be changed further. This can be effected through native file system access rights.

The last bullet may appear counter-intuitive, and it warrants some more discussion. Autonomous development of a given component usually depends on software artifacts being developed as part of other components owned by other teams. This is a natural consequence of the collaborative nature of components. In order to be able to compile, link, and also run a given DC, all the DCs belonging to the assembly of the given DC need to be readily available. To move them all to a workstation can be time-consuming and error-prone. Furthermore, given the expectations about how often the code-compile-link-run-test cycle will be performed, the need to reset the environment to correctly make use of a new version of a DC developed on a local workstation may become an error-prone inefficiency. The term "resetting the environment" includes making sure that all dependency lists are updated, all makefiles are updated, all scripts are updated, and so forth—and this applies in general to any part of the development environment that makes use of a specific directory or file location. It is much safer, error-free, and development-scalable for development to be managed out of a shared file system, in which continuous integration is completely ingrained in day-to-day development expectations. It also makes for easier backup/recovery procedures.

This approach reflects the philosophy that rapid system development is facilitated by limiting the steps required to produce any deliverable in the system and accepting that there will be a greater number of versions. This approach corresponds to a large extent to the creation of a new development sandbox at the beginning of each new component version and the transformation of the sandbox into production by a simple drop of the sandbox. We have also experimented at length with an alternative approach, in which something is developed in a physically separate sandbox and then physically moved into a production area. The conclusion is that the first approach is more efficient and easier to implement, and it better supports both larger teams and more complex development.

Based on these assumptions, the following example of a directory structure for a development environment describes where information is placed and explains the various structural levels starting at the top, with each level having a defined purpose.

Root level. Logically defines where the shared environment is located. The root level can be used to divide the project into the functional development projects, the BCVM aspects, and if applicable, software artifacts belonging to any preexisting non-component-based legacy system. For present purposes, these other aspects are ignored, and it is assumed that functional development projects all have the same root, exemplified as "$r:\backslash$", where r is a logical shared drive established system-wide by convention. This is an example of a simple trick (working with a common shared drive established by convention) that pragmatically resolves several problems in an NT-based development environment. For example, detached development may be achieved simply by mapping a different "root" on a separate physical machine to the same letter: By convention, all the detached participants use the same root to indicate where the project files are stored.

Business component level. The development environment should be organized around the concept of business components, as illustrated in Table 10.6. This has proven to be very practical, even merely from the point of view of enabling a simple and intuitive (even to nontechnical people) path to finding software artifacts.

Table 10.6 Business Component Level

ROOT	BUSINESS COMPONENT	COMMENT
r:\		
	\orderManager	the *OrderManager* business component
	\pricing	the *Pricing* business component
	\system	the *System* business component
	\base	the *Base* business component
	...	other business components

One of the apparently trivial aspects that can cause enormous grief to a large project concerns naming conventions, particularly naming conventions for files and directories. In this example the convention is that the names of business components and distributed components in the file system start with a lowercase character and follow the C++ convention of using uppercase to separate words, for example, orderManager.

Business component versions. Each business component is a separate and distinct deliverable and is versioned. However, introducing an explicit directory level for each version can be too constraining, because, for example, it becomes nonintuitive for a given version of a distributed component to belong to two different versions of a business component. A solution to this problem is to manage each business component version without explicitly creating a directory level for it, using a combination of project guidelines and an SCM tool. A set of version-specific business component dependency lists supports clear identification of the constitution of each business component version. These dependency lists could be physically located in the business component's directory; for example, *<root>\OrderManager\dependency list_v003.txt* is the dependency list for v003 of the Order Manager business component.

All the documentation that is version independent can be located directly in the business component's directory. This includes overall design artifacts that are not specific to any of the business component's tiers, such as the feature list. If it was decided to trace the purpose of each business component version, this can be addressed pragmatically with a text file or document that describes each version and allows for the reconstruction of the development history of that particular component. Such a file is a good candidate for the business component's directory, for example, *<root>\OrderManager\versions.txt*.

Distributed component level. Below the business component level is the distributed component level. This level defines the internal organization of the directory structure of the business component, and it is where the various kinds of DC that make up a business component will be located. Within a given business component, the development is organized by tiers, as shown in Table 10.7 for the Order Manager business component. This particular example shows a project-specific decision where all testing for all DCs is assumed to be managed from a single location in each business component, the *tOrderManager* directory.

Distributed component versions. Distributed components are independently versioned, and the shared file system directory structure could reflect this, as illustrated in Table 10.8.

Table 10.7 Distributed Component Level

BUSINESS COMPONENT	DISTRIBUTED COMPONENT	COMMENT
\orderManager		
	\documents	Contains all specifications and documents pertaining to this business component
	\eOrderManager	
	\wOrderManager	
	\tOrderManager	Contains all the test specs, the data used for the test, the testing sources, and testing executables
	\common	Contains artifacts that are common to all the tiers, for example, the CSL for the PLCs

The distributed component version provides a location for developers to place a shared, working directory. The assumption was made that development of a DC occurs out of the shared file system: From a practical standpoint, to change the status of a work-in-progress version of a DC into a released version (which corresponds to creating a drop of that DC) may be as simple as changing the file access rights for that version at the operating system level. The evolution of SCM systems, and their increasingly transparent integration with commercial IDEs, is moving toward enabling very advanced ways to manage distributed component versions.

Distributed component internals. This level holds all the software artifacts owned by a given version of a DC. Assuming a C++ based development, the entire level could correspond to an IDE project (or an old-fashioned makefile), with the contained levels being individual C++

Table 10.8 Distributed Component Version

DISTRIBUTED COMPONENT	VERSION	COMMENT
\eOrderManager	\v004	Version 004 of eOrderManager
	\v005	Version 005 of eOrderManager
	\...	
\wOrderManager	\v003	Version 003 of wOrderManager
	\v004	Version 004 of wOrderManager

Table 10.9 Distributed Component Internals

DISTRIBUTED COMPONENT VERSION	DIRECTORY STRUCTURE	COMMENT
\eOrderManager\v002	\	All manually edited C++ code to be at this level
	\Debug	All the object and executable files with debug information
	\Release	Same as above without debug information
	\gen	Contains the generated code, with the exclusion of exported artifacts
	<DC-specific files>	Any additional DC-specific file could be located here; for example, a DC run-time configuration file, the DC dependency list, and so on
	\businessTypes	Contains the generated business data types
	\proxy	Contains proxy source code, which can be exported to other DCs
	\plc	Contains persistence framework code
	\csl	All CSL files
	…	

subprojects. The example in Table 10.9 is based on some unstated assumptions about the component model and technology used.

Optimization of the development environment requires it to know where certain files are placed. For example, if an organization were to build a script able to search for the dependency list of each business component and distributed component in order to rebuild the system, the script must be able to find the dependency lists, and this may require some organization-wide convention such as placing these files in well-known locations and giving them well-known names, consistently across the organization. This requires being able to describe the location of these files to the development environment or establishing precise conventions known to the infrastructure and the tools about the placing of these well-known files. Examples of such files could include the following:

- The *DC dependency list*, placed at the DC version level, which is itself identified by precise conventions or configuration files.

- The *run-time configuration file* of the DC that defines other DCs with which this DC collaborates, which database the DC must connect to, and any other information required at run-time for this DC to execute properly. This file could be placed under the version of each DC.

- Eventually, a run-time configuration file for each business component, placed under the version of each business component.

Component Dependency Manager

The dependency model presented in this chapter would benefit from a tool able to directly support it. Such a tool would be required to manage, across the development lifecycle, the versions of the system being developed, the versions of the components, and the dependencies between components. This tool is referred to here as a Component Dependency Manager (CDM), and it is often part of (or at least related to) the Component Specification Tool briefly outlined in Chapter 8. This section discusses the characteristics of such a CDM.

First of all, a CDM must be able to create and manage a *business component dependency list* such as that presented in Table 10.10.

Two features are illustrated in this example. First, the business component dependency list indicates which other business components this particular component depends on (the items in the list starting with a capital letter indicate business components). Second, this particular dependency list also shows the version of the DCs that make up this business component. Alternatively, the two features could be separated into a dependency list and a kind of bill of material.

Each line in the "Dependency List" column corresponds to a component, and the CDM should be able to navigate to the dependency list of each component, based on its knowledge of the directory structure.

The CDM must also be able to support the creation and management of a DC dependency list such as that presented in Table 10.11, which is a repeat of Table 10.2 except that the version of the business component virtual machine (*bcvm*

Table 10.10 Business Component Dependency List

BUSINESS COMPONENT	VERSION	DEPENDENCY LIST
Vendor	v02b	AddressBook v02b
		Notes v02b
		CurrencyBook v02b
		NumberGenerator v02b
		eVendor v102
		wVendor v101

Table 10.11 Versioned Dependency List for the *eVendor* DC

DISTRIBUTED COMPONENT	VERSION	DEPENDENCY LIST
eVendor	V102	bcvm v042 eAddressBook v101 eNotes v105 eCurrencyBook v99 eNumberGenerator v101

v042) is explicitly included. The exact version of the BCVM is an important part of the consistency set of a given distributed component, and it unequivocally identifies such things as exactly which version of third-party middleware, third-party DBMS, or IDE was used for this particular DC version. In this example, the simplifying assumption is made that it is enough to specify the BCVM version for the root of the assembly.

Given the dependency list in Table 10.11, the CDM must be able to determine the indirect dependencies (or dependency closure), by analyzing the dependency lists of the dependent components, producing a closured dependency list as shown in Table 10.12.

Based on the previously described capabilities, the CDM will be able to navigate across the levels of component granularity. Starting from a system-wide dependency list, stored, for example, in the *System* business component, the CDM will be able to identify each and every component in the system and per-

Table 10.12 Closure of a DC Dependency List

DISTRIBUTED COMPONENT	VERSION	DEPENDENCY LIST
eVendor	v102	bcvm v042 eAddressBook v101 eNotes v105 eCurrencyBook v99 eNumberGenerator v101
eAddressBook	v101	eNotes v105 eBase v98
eNotes	v105	
eCurrencyBook	v99	
eBase	v98	
eNumberGenerator	v101	

form, or support other tools in performing, any appropriate action on these components. Eventually, it should be possible to give the system dependency list to the CDM and have it direct the appropriate parts of the BCVM to reload the repository, regenerate (in the right places) code and other software artifacts (makefiles, configuration files, and so on), recompile and relink the whole system, and even automatically rerun regression test—and all of this with *one* command. This may seem like dreamland, but a capability approaching this level has been created in the past by one of the authors.

The CDM could also provide the following capabilities:

- Determine dependency consistency. That is, the CDM should be able to verify that there are no circular invocations and no business component participating twice at two different version levels. Consistency is determined by a set of rules that can change from project to project, since rules such as whether it is acceptable to find two different versions of the same DC in the system are project-dependent. However, managing this, where not disallowed for some technical reason, would mean introducing new concepts, such as "equivalence sets." An equivalence set is a set of versions of a component that are considered equivalent for providing a given interface—a concept not addressed in this chapter.

- Starting from the dependency list, generate the appropriate artifacts (such as an IDE project file or makefile) used to build the entire business component system, and also build other "global" items such as the global database schema.

- "Open" a given dependency list for a given component, and provide a visualization of which software artifacts can be exported by each of the dependent components (in that specific version). It should also be able to check the consistency of the dependency list, the bill of material, or the IDE project file or makefile.

- Selectively define which of the available exportable artifacts has been in a specific component. The objective of selective export and import is to minimize the surface area between DCs.

- Support a detailed impact analysis.

There will often be a need to change a version of a dependent DC in the list of dependent components. This could have several implications for the CDM:

- For each DC, the list of available versions should be displayable, and summary information for each version should be available, including its development history and its exportable artifacts.

- The selection of a new desired version implies that the CDM checks if all the software artifacts previously imported are still available. Appropriate warnings should be given if apparent inconsistencies are found.

■ The user should have the opportunity to refresh, and then automatically rebuild, the whole DC assembly with the new version of the dependent DC.

Scripts

Another type of tooling required for a large-team project is a set of scripts to facilitate day-to-day work. Whether they are implemented in Visual Basic, Perl, a Unix shell, or some other technology, the development of scripts is often responsible not only for an appreciable amount of normally nonplanned setup and development cost, but also, and paradoxically, for important cost-savers. In this section, three examples of scripts that are normally required are illustrated: rebuilding an individual DC, building a BC assembly, and creating a new version of a DC. The section ends with a list of other useful scripts.

Rebuilding a Distributed Component

For the work-in-progress distributed component, it must be easy and optimized to rebuild the current version of the distributed component. "Building" here includes not only compiling and linking but also regenerating the code (and in our earlier example, even reprocessing the CSL). This requires a command-line interface to tools and is ideally fully performed with a single command.

Single-command rebuilds can be achieved by defining a bill of material or by extending the makefiles to include aspects such as regenerating all the required deliverables, recompiling the complete distributed component, and logging all errors. Whether the build should stop on encountering an error should be specifiable on the command line, with the default being to continue the build.

Rebuilding a Business Component Assembly

Similarly, for the work-in-progress business component assembly, it must be easy to rebuild the current version of the business component assembly. "Building" has the same meaning as for rebuilding a distributed component, with the obvious difference that a business component is more complex. For example, given a dependency list for some product assembly, a script should be able to do the following:

■ Check the consistency of the list, verifying, for example, whether there are unacceptable circularities or components appearing more than once. For all components appearing more than once, the script should be able to check that all the instances of the component have the same version.

■ Regenerate all the required deliverables, and recompile the whole assembly. This step will also, for each distributed component in the assembly, make use of the script described in the previous subsection "Rebuilding a Distributed Component."

■ Log all errors. It should be specifiable on the command line whether encountering an error should stop the build (not stopping being the default).

Creating a New DC Version

In an average-sized project of about 60 business components, some 150 to 200 DCs can be expected. Hence a new version of a DC is likely to be created each day. From a development perspective, given the number of times that a project may need to create a new version of a DC, it may be worthwhile to automate the technical creation process. A script could be created to perform a full copy of a version of a DC into the new version following any project creation rules. Such rules must take in account the integrated SCM strategy. A pragmatic example is that often SCM systems manage versioning through the file rights: For example, a file that has not been checked out may be in read-only mode in the file system, but it may be in read-write mode when checked out. A copy command may want to copy only the files that are not versioned using the SCM system or to copy all files while ensuring that SCM-managed files are copied as read-only, hence forcing the functional developer to check them out if any changes are to be made.

Other Scripts

Many other scripts can exist; a large number of development tasks can usually be automated to some degree. Some automation may, of course, be done by the third-party tools. A few examples of additional scripts are these:

■ A script to quickly create a new version of a run-time database. This new version could be built using a database schema that is the union of all the islands of data in a BC assembly. The creation would also properly set all the access rights and even load the new database from a set of initialization data. This would make creation of the run-time database painless, and even rapidly achievable without the intervention of an expert database administrator.

■ The previously described script is only one of many database-related scripts that can be created. For example, Chapter 7, "Development Process," described a testing environment that required the ability to easily set and reset the database to a given data content, and to compare data content with some predefined data content, in order to verify that the result of a test complies with the expected result. To do this by hand is so error-prone and time-consuming that without proper automated support it may not be cost-effective.

- A script that would automatically create a business component directory structure according to the project rules.

- A script that cleanly archives and/or deletes a development version of a DC. Given the rapid pace of creating new versions of distributed components, keeping the development environment clean is a task worthy of automation.

- Scripts that deal with the interface with the SCM system—for example, automating check-in/check-out of a business component or distributed component.

Project Manager's Model

The term "project manager's model" indicates the conceptual model and particular mindset that a manager approaching a component-based development should have to ensure proper coordination. This model consists to a large extent of all the elements presented so far; this section highlights a few of these aspects through a discussion of the development organization and of the project management views on a project. The section ends with the description of a new role: the software ecologist.

Development Organization

There is no such thing as the perfect organization. In a business component factory, the development organization must be very dynamic, and the concept of what is the *right organization* may change quite rapidly over time. Nevertheless, there are a few principles that are extremely powerful and have been applied successfully. Not only is the development environment organized around business components, but also the whole development can follow this business component-centric approach. At the risk of some repetition, let's discuss what this means to the project manager.

First, a bold statement: the business component approach allows for business process reengineering of the whole of software development. Business process reengineering (BPR) is a well-known buzzword [Hammer 1993] that emphasizes the principle that an organization's business processes should be directly aligned to the needs of its customers. Each business process should produce something of value for the customer, and the whole organization should be structured to enable these processes to be executed rapidly, with quality, and autonomously. There is, of course, much more to BPR, and also to its relationship with what we are describing here, but one relevant question is this: Is it possible to apply BPR to software development? Yes, it is. How? By breaking away from the traditional organization of software development and by organizing development around units of deployment that deliver value to the end user, that is, the business component—a software concept that implements function and meets requirements directly relevant to the end user.

A traditional software development organization follows what we call a *horizontal* dimension. Teams are organized along distribution tiers, in areas of technical experience. Such an organization typically has user interface experts developing the "client" side of the information system, server experts developing the "server" side, database experts developing the database model, and interoperability experts developing the interoperability adapters. Functional experience is separate from the developers, and no one in the organization really has a clear overall or detailed picture of customer needs or of how the various parts of development really relate to each other. This kind of organization usually is justified by the long learning curves required to absorb the various technologies, and it leads to many checks and controls, hand waving and responsibility shifting, as well as time lost simply waiting for the right resource to be available.

On the other hand, a business component development is organized around units of delivery that bring value to the end user, that is, the business component. Every business component is owned by a small team, typically not more than three developers, which is totally empowered and has all the capabilities for constructing and testing their business component from requirements to final delivery. The whole process is optimized in such a way that this happens with minimal interruption, minimal need for external control and checks, and minimal waiting for other teams. The whole project can be sized, estimated, planned, and tracked in terms of business components and distributed components.

In the business component approach, software development follows a *vertical* dimension corresponding to the functional features implemented by a whole business component, rather than the more traditional horizontal dimension. This is an important if controversial organizational principle. For example, rather than organizing development in terms of user-interface developers and server-side development, it can be successfully organized along functional lines. While the often radically different technologies used on the client and server sides often demand detailed experience of a specific technology, the architectural viewpoints work together to allow the functional developers to concentrate, with a simple and effective programming model, on delivering function.

Such an organization requires that all developers have some level of exposure to all aspects of business component development. To keep such an organization running efficiently, the functional developer must have available a pool of subject experts able to deal with specific problems outside the developer's technical or functional experience. In this sense, a BPR of software development enhances the need for an architecture team but also changes its role, which shifts from normative to supportive. While each member of the development team should target a broad but perhaps shallow experience in all aspects of the development, the architecture team provides a center of excellence in specific subjects, and a group of people able to keep the autonomous development of the various parts of the system coherent and pointing in the right direction. In this sense, the organization is strongly architecture-team centric. Further, the architecture team is tasked with producing deliverables—often including real working software—of direct and immediate relevance to functional developers.

Within this eclectic view, each professional may still have a preferred specialization and a preferred focus, for example, domain expert versus technical expert and client expert versus server expert. But the whole organization benefits from targeting the wider combined experience, which could ultimately allow the organization to become a true *learning organization* [Senge 1990]. This is immeasurably assisted through the BCVM hiding most if not all of the complex underlying technologies so that the functional developer can focus on the implementation of business function.

Adding the project management architecture to the set of architectural viewpoints calls for a chief architect who is very conscious of the organizational and human aspects of the proposed architecture levels. In a business component approach, an architect will not achieve the upper-most level of competence without having been exposed to the organizational and managerial aspects of architectural decisions. The difference between a traditional architect and an architect/manager is that the architect/manager considers the organizational viewpoint an integral part of the project.

There are many other advantages of this BPR of software development. Let us mention just one more: organization by levels of component granularity allows for a learning path that leads to productive work in record time. Relatively junior people can be assigned the relatively easy and relatively risk-free task of implementing well-defined DC interfaces. Within the boundaries of this interface implementation, they can explore and become exposed to different aspects of development while quickly contributing to the overall picture through the delivery of DCs. As their experience grows, they can be progressively exposed to the design and implementation of business components, business component assemblies, and whole business component systems.

Project Management Views

The advantages of project management being organized around business components is illustrated by the various points of view that can be adopted. For example, starting from the business component system model, the project is sized, estimated, planned, and tracked in terms of the following views:

Business component system view. The highest-level view, in which the system can be seen as a list of business components, abstracting the internal details of individual business components and their architectural structure. This is the level at which an "executive summary" of the project plan and progress is shown. A good time scale for this view is at the month level.

BC assembly view. Defines what is required to develop an individual business component, and also defines its proper development sequence. This view concentrates on the component's external dependency graph with less attention to the system view and the internal architecture of a given business component. That is, the BC assembly view enables evaluation of the availability and dependencies of required software artifacts produced by other teams. A good time scale for this view is at the week level.

Business component view. Defines how to develop the individual parts of a business component—primarily its distributed components. A good time scale for this view is at the day-to-day level, and this is the granularity appropriate for day-to-day task assignment.

Software Ecology

Everything we have said so far points to the importance of a new role in software development. This role is a particular evolution of what is believed today to be the role of the software architect. We call this role the "software ecologist."

An ecologist is a scientist of the environment. The particular objective of ecology is to understand the laws that enable the various parts of the environment to evolve autonomously while at the same time interacting with other parts, directly or indirectly. The environment is so complex that no ecologist can comprehend all the detail of the whole environment. But there are laws and principles that can allow houses to be built in isolation, houses to be build as part of a larger city plan, cities to evolve in harmony with the surroundings, and so forth. Does this sound familiar?

The traditional role of the software architect is no longer sufficient. While defining an individual house, the architect may lose sight of the city. In software terms, while defining the individual component, the architect may lose site of the system or of the federation. A new professional role is required: the software ecologist, able to have all levels of component granularity evolve harmoniously and in a sustainable way, without limiting the ability of each individual component to evolve autonomously.

Summary

The project management architecture (PMA) addresses the concepts, principles, guidelines, policies, and tools required to *cost-effectively* build a scalable and high-performance system *with a large team*, that is, a team with between 10 and, say, 200 developers. A good PMA is always a combination of a clear model for large-scale development and a great deal of pragmatism.

Software configuration management is the better-known and perhaps traditional part of a PMA. An integrated SCM strategy that exploits the strength of SCM systems, repositories, and file systems while at the same time directly supporting the objectives of a rapid, iterative development of components to be assembled into solutions is required. This integrated SCM strategy can be supported by the extended integrated development environment addressing the new requirements created by cost-effective software manufacturing.

Dependency management is another important part of a PMA. It includes a precise model of the dependencies between components and a model about how these dependencies should be managed. Explicit and selective import/export is one very effective approach to dependency management.

The extended integrated development environment must (at least at the time of writing) rely on a well-defined directory tree structure that organizes all deliverables of the system around the levels of component granularity, allowing all tools to easily identify the location and work with these deliverables. A component dependency management tool could, for example, use this standard directory tree structure and the dependency list of the various components, to navigate the system and provide a wealth of capability to speed up the development.

Finally, the project manager must have a model of how to manage a project compatible with the various principles described and, in particular, with the project management architecture. This will be a model where, for example, the development organization as well as project planning and tracking are structured around business components, allowing for a powerful business process reengineering of the whole software development organization.

This chapter concludes Part Two, which described the setup of the business component factory able to support dramatic reductions in development cost and complexity. Part Three assumes that the factory is now ready to be used and concentrates on the functional architecture—on the modeling and design of the components to be manufactured.

Endnotes

1   See Appendix A, "Naming Conventions," for naming conventions.

2   There is no theoretical reason for this example of packaging for footprint to be required, but from a practical perspective this has been an important consideration for many projects we have encountered so far, especially those that built C++ classes with no thought for footprint. Also, common code involved in such repackaging should be checked for thread safety.

3   Chapter 6, "The Federation of System-Level Components," introduced the terms *subject* and *target* to mean client and server but with no location implication; a "subject" component is the term used for a component that invokes an operation of another "target" component.

PART

Three

Manufacturing Component-Based Software

We are now ready to start manufacturing component-based software products. Part One presented the conceptual framework of the business component approach, and Part Two described the setup of an efficient software production capability—the business component factory. Part Three now addresses the main modeling and design considerations in using the factory to produce business components, business component systems, and federations of system-level components. In other words, Part Three largely focuses on the *functional architecture* viewpoint. It discusses the construction of a system assuming that the other architectural viewpoints have been fully addressed. After all, the business component factory is there to support the functional developer, who can then concentrate on developing function that satisfies the needs of the business. Part Three, with a concluding chapter that looks beyond manufacturing to the question of how to get started, is structured accordingly:

Chapter 11: Component-Based Business Modeling. The first stage in the production process is to model the system. This chapter discusses how business modeling is related to and influenced by the business component approach. It goes into further detail on the various functional categories of business components and how to identify them, and it examines other aspects of component modeling.

Chapter 12: Component-Based Design. Given that a model of the target system has been produced, the focus now moves to design. And although the business component concept encapsulates a distribution architecture, there is still work to be done to realize that architecture, to say nothing of other extra-functional requirements placed on the system. This chapter presents some of the main design principles supporting development of components that embody those desired extra-functional characteristics. In so doing, this chapter directly complements Chapter 9, "The Application Architecture."

Chapter 13: Transitioning. An organization's first venture into cost-effective software manufacturing using component-based development requires it to take on broad new concepts, techniques, and skills. Over the next several years, most organizations will be faced with the question of how to transition, in the most cost-effective way, to component-based development. This chapter discusses the key concepts in transitioning and how the new skills and know-how can be acquired.

CHAPTER 11

Component-Based
Business Modeling

What kind of thinking is required when a business problem is to be modeled using the business component approach? Is there a set of patterns, models, or other support that can make it easier to address the complex task of modeling a business? Is the thinking required in the business component approach any different from that for any other approach? If yes, why would the particular software development approach influence the modeling of the system? This chapter addresses these questions by focusing mainly on those modeling aspects specific to component-based development. It does not pretend to address the business modeling problem in general. Further, to simplify the presentation flow, the focus is on business modeling for custom development rather than for software product development. The difference between the two is that the business model for a software product does not represent one specific reality, but rather a whole class of realities. Hence it must be particularly generic and adaptable, which adds greater complexity to the business modeling activity. With this simplification in mind, the chapter is organized as follows:

Concepts. Explains what it means to do business modeling using a component-based approach, and various aspects of partitioning a business space.

Identification strategies. Presents heuristics on how to identify business components, as well as on how to evaluate an existing business component system model.

Modeling the processes. Business process modeling is perhaps the most important part of business modeling. In particular, workflow-based modeling, rule-based modeling, and modeling using process business components are discussed.

Modeling the entities. Addresses various considerations for modeling entity components such as those that capture the business concepts of trading partners and contracts.

Utility business components. Discusses modeling the highly reusable but relatively simple concepts captured by utility business components, and presents two simple examples dealing with addresses and zip code handling.

Concepts

Modeling a business is one of the most complex activities in building an information system. In recent years, many different approaches to business modeling have been proposed. One that has been receiving much attention is *process-driven modeling*, in which the business is analyzed in terms of the main business processes.[1] It is now generally accepted that business software should directly support and be aligned with the business processes of an organization, and this is the implicit assumption made not only in this chapter, but elsewhere in the book. Process-driven modeling using business components, which in their own right prescribe a specific way of partitioning and representing a business system, is a particularly powerful way to bridge business modeling relatively seamlessly into system design and implementation.

This section first presents a few considerations about the different roles of the business modeler and functional architect. Second, it discusses the main constructs used in modeling a business. It then briefly analyzes how to model a federation, then addresses the partitioning of a business component system. The section concludes by showing how each of the functional categories—process, entity, and utility—can be further partitioned into subcategories.

Business Modeler versus Functional Architect

There can be two very different objectives for the business modeling activity, and this can give rise to misunderstandings. The two can be characterized by the business modeler mindset and the functional architect mindset.

The *business modeler*'s objective is to produce a model of the problem space that can help in identifying business challenges and business opportunities. This may be required for reasons that have nothing to do with a software implementation of the modeled business. The business modeler's final deliverable is a business model—usually a paper (or tool-based) model—which can be considered as a product in its own right. The business modeler is seldom concerned with software implementation, and the kinds of trade-off that he or she makes are related to the level of detail necessary to remove ambiguities from the model and to achieve its business purposes. In order to remove ambiguities, the business model often contains a level of detail that a software designer might consider as belonging to a detailed design phase. If the business modeler has a reuse objective, it is to reuse business models, business frameworks, and business patterns.

The *functional architect*, on the other hand, when modeling the business, aims to support the production of a software application. The objective is to understand the business in order to properly structure the information system, not to find business opportunities. Business modeling in this case is simply a means to an end, not the final objective. The final deliverable is the functional architecture, and business modeling is only one of the things that the functional architect must take into account in order to specify the system. Since it is simply a means to an end, the functional architect's business model can achieve its purpose while being, from other viewpoints, incomplete, too abstract, or ambiguous. Precision is reached in the design phase. If the functional architect has a reuse objective, it is mainly to reuse design and implementation artifacts, or whole components in component-based development.

Both the business modeler and functional architect's points of view are correct and valuable in their own contexts. There are two sources of misunderstanding. First, the two mindsets often use the same modeling terminology, and they speak about the same deliverables, but with different semantics. Second, the deliverables of the two mindsets are often confused. For example, if the business model produced by the business modeler is taken as a high-level design, there will be a problem: The business modeler often does not have a sufficient understanding of large-scale distributed system development issues to be able to produce a high-level design defining functional structure, and it often does not even have this as an objective. On the other hand, the functional architect often does not have enough understanding of the business side to be able to properly define the business model.

For projects having the resources and the time, the ideal is where the model produced by a business modeler is taken as pure input to software development. That is, it is only one of the things taken into account when gathering system requirements, and it is not considered to be a high-level definition of the structure and design of the information system. In this case, the business model is seen as external to the software development (as it should be). There are, of course, benefits if the concepts described by a business model are the same as those described by the functional architecture. It would be in the interests of both parties to share a common set of concepts, semantics, and so forth, and to develop them together, in a joint business modeling activity. Whichever approach is adopted, it should be an explicit objective of business modeling activities to clearly separate the two areas of concern—that of the business modeler and that of the functional architect. However, even with this strong separation of concerns, the transition from the business model to the functional architecture specification will be much smoother if a mapping is taken into account from the start.

Over time, functional reference models or business component system models for given domains may well become publicly available. Reuse of such component models will be useful for both the business modeler and the functional architect. In addition, much of the support given by the business component approach to the functional architect can be equally useful to the business modeler, especially as a way to partition and help master modeling complexities. In this sense, the component-based approach better bridges the world of the business modeler with the world of the functional architect.[2]

One difficulty in keeping the two points of view separated stems from the fact that, before design specification, the business problem is rarely clear in all its numerous facets. Feedback from a given iteration during design or implementation is of fundamental importance in establishing the real requirements of the system, in better understanding the costs of implementing known requirements, and hence in basing new requirements on a realistic cost/benefit analysis.

This chapter assumes the point of view of the functional architect rather than that of the business modeler. Hence when the term *business model* is used, it is the functional architect's view of the business model rather than the business modeler's that is meant. From this viewpoint, it is very hard—perhaps even undesirable—to define a business model without taking the realities of componentization and distributed systems into account. Thus it is perfectly acceptable to introduce, very early in the business modeling activity, the business component system model.

Main Modeling Constructs

In order to map a domain space into a functional specification for a system, four main modeling constructs are used (see also the excellent paper by Riemer [1998]). These are business processes, business entities, business events, and business rules, and they are defined[3] as follows:

Business process. A business process is "a collection of activities that takes one or more kinds of input and creates an output that is of value to the customer" [Hammer 1993, p. 35]. An example is the order fulfillment business process in a manufacturing enterprise.

Business entity. An entity of the business that one or more business processes require for their successful operation. Examples are order, item, and customer entities, again for a manufacturing enterprise.

Business event. An event that triggers one or more business processes (including simple changes to an entity). For example, *customer orders a book* is a business event for a bookseller.

Business rule. A rule that governs the behavior of one or more business processes (including changes to entities). For example a business rule for a bookseller might be *if customer's credit card is valid, accept order for book.*

As a generalization, the key software constructs of the business component approach can directly capture these modeling constructs. Hence entity business components correspond to business entities, process business components correspond to business processes, operations or software events on entity or process business components correspond to business events, and the processing that governs the behavior of entity and process components corresponds to business rules. The opposite is not always true: For example, not all business entities will be implemented as individual business components, and not all business processes will be implemented as process business components.

The four modeling constructs represent aspects of business that evolve at different speeds in the real world, and hence in their corresponding software implementation. In addition, the speed at which business concepts change is not necessarily linked to the speed at which their realizations or content evolve. This is illustrated in Table 11.1, using the example of an invoice management process. Evolution speeds are indicated as *slow* if a change is not expected for more than two years, *medium* if change can occur in six months to two years, and *fast* if change can occur in less than six months.

Where the nature of the business itself is changing—for example, migrating from a product-based organization to a service-based one, then all aspects of the business may be required to change quickly. In this case, rapid evolution of the whole information system may be needed. While there is no magic in component-based development, it is certainly the case that a well-established business component factory will assist that evolution more than most other forms of software production.

Table 11.1 illustrates an important point: The identification of components corresponds to the identification of aspects of the information systems that are relatively stable. By organizing the system and the development around components, specifically business components, stability is enhanced and hence complexity is reduced.

Currently, the speed at which these business aspects evolve in software is

Table 11.1 Evolution Speed of Modeling Constructs

MODELING CONSTRUCT	CONCEPT	CONTENT
Business Process	*Slow*: An invoice management process existed 10 years ago and will probably exist in 10 years.	*Fast*: Usually the sequencing of processes or their detailed contents changes. This is related to business rules.
Business Entity	*Slow*: The invoice concept existed 10 years ago and will probably exist in 10 years.	*Medium*: An electronic invoice requires different content than nonelectronic invoices.
Business Rule	*Medium*: New business rules are created with relative frequency, and existing ones may cease to exist.	*Fast*: This is usually directly related to content changes in a business process, and for certain problem spaces, change may even be on a daily basis.
Business Event	*Slow*: The kinds of business events that may occur do not change significantly at a certain level of abstraction—for example, the arrival of a payment.	*Medium*: The exact meaning of each business event, and hence of the corresponding operation or software event, may change over time. For example, it is only recently that electronic payments have become widely accepted.

generally highly unsatisfactory. The software industry is often the bottleneck preventing rapid business evolution. On the other hand, it is sometime *desirable* that the evolution of the software implementation does not exactly map to the evolution of the corresponding concepts in the business spaces; in some cases it is this difference in speed that allows a breakthrough in the business. For example, many industries are now adopting an invoice-less approach, where invoices are not explicitly exchanged between trading partners, but rather there is only an exchange of a set of minimal data, such as the arrival of a shipment causing a payment according to certain business rules. Many business transactions are now invoice-less in the real world, but this fact does not automatically imply that the same thing happens in information systems. In most cases, information systems still create invoice records internally for their own accounting purposes, and it is largely due to this being able to be done with minimal external information that allows an external process to be invoice-less. The information system is about enabling, not necessarily slavishly mapping, the real world.

Modeling a Federation

When addressing an industry as a whole, such as transportation or manufacturing, that industry is often broken down into coarse functional areas. For example, Figure 11.1 illustrates a simplified example of a customer-facing organization in manufacturing/distribution. A given functional area may then be further broken down, as illustrated in Figure 11.2 for the ERP/supply chain. Such representations are called "functional reference models" or FRMs for short.

The FRM of a given industry is the set of models that represent the industry as a whole, including the main areas of functional concern and the main aspects of the functional interfaces (not shown in Figures 11.1 or 11.2) between these areas. Chapter 6, "The Federation of System-Level Components," discussed a particular case of FRM—a federation of system-level components. This section presents a simplified discussion of FRMs from a component-based point of view.

An industry's FRM often has little if anything to do with the results of analysis or design in the domain. Further, the functional modules of the FRM are seldom if ever traceable in any meaningful way to implementation structures. For this reason, and from the IT point of view, FRMs are often seen as merely initial positioning diagrams, to be discarded when serious work starts, as marketing diagrams, or perhaps as useful introductory pictures for people new to the industry.

If we consider an FRM not only as a high-level, marketing-like reference model, but also as the model of a federation of system-level components, then we can start to make the FRM a useful part not just of the development process, but of the whole representation and implementation process of a major area of concern.

Today there is no agreed format for representing an FRM, but generally the

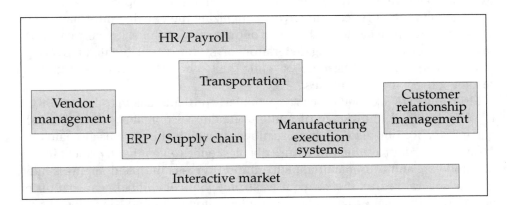

Figure 11.1 Example of functional areas in manufacturing/distribution.

Configurable Ledger	Accounts Receivable	Advanced Remittance Processing	Promotions, Deals, and Pricing	Configurable Order Management	Release Management	Planner's Assistant	Master Production Scheduling	Just-In-Time/Repetitive
Enterprise Structures & Consolidations	Credit & Deduction Management	Draft Management	Sales Performance Management	Billing & Sales Analysis	Outbound Logistics	Manufacturing Data Management	Material Requirements Planning	Capacity Planning
Currency Translation	Budgets & Analysis	Accounts Payable	Purchasing	Inventory Management	Forecasting	Configuration Management	Advanced Process Industries	Shop Floor Control
Multiple Currencies	Fixed Assets	Cost Accounting	Performance Measurement	Warehouse Management	Distribution Resources Planning	Formulation Assistant	Quality Mgt, Laboratory Management	Plant Maintenance

Enterprise financial applications	Supply chain management applications	Multimode manufacturing applications

Figure 11.2 Example of ERP/supply chain system.
Courtesy of System Software Associates, Inc.

representation should include a diagram showing the main parts of the federation at a high level of abstraction, as illustrated in Figure 11.1 and Figure 11.2.

When modeling a federation of systems, there are two extreme cases: first, the case in which all systems exist before the federation definition is started and, second, the case in which no system is assumed to preexist, for example, where a standards body creates a standard FRM for a given industry or when an organization defines the "to-be" reference model without being constrained by the existing systems. Of course, in most real cases of companies transitioning to component-based development, the FRM will be a mix of the two situations, in which the majority of systems have been defined and built using traditional technologies, while the others may be migrated or redeveloped using CBD.

Modeling in the first case involves recognizing the existing information systems and drawing a model of them and of their relationships. In many cases, the "as-is" model of the existing federation of systems will highlight overlaps, redundancies, and inconsistencies, while the "to-be" model will be targeted at resolving these inconsistencies.

Modeling in the second case is a particularly difficult task in today's reality. It involves detailed knowledge of multiple functional domains, not only of the current reality but also of the directions in which the various domains are evolving in order to avoid premature obsolescence (given that a project involving modeling and subsequent implementation across multiple domains is likely to take several years). It also requires strong political ability because if different partner companies have already implemented or intend to implement different parts of the federation, there must be a common vision behind it. It is thus typically an effort that can be successful only in a very cooperative situation, such as in a standardization body like the Object Management Group (OMG). Often a model of a federation will be a hybrid of the two cases.

A major advantage of the business component approach is that it supports at one and the same time the functional description of an industry and the initial decomposition into candidate software artifacts—the system-level components. That is, the FRM can be used also as an SLC federation model, describing a federation of systems having the following characteristics:

- The parts represented in the high-level structural model are system-level components. In this sense, the FRM not only describes the logical parts of the federation, but these logical parts actually correspond to components, which can have interfaces.

- The FRM describes a federation in terms of peer-to-peer system-level components. That is, the FRM rarely implies a functional layering. As the industry matures, however, business component thinking will assist with the layering (see "Layering" later in this chapter).

- Given the strong possibility that the different parts of the federation will be built by different companies, and given the reality that there are no cross-company architectural standards, pragmatic rules usually replace good architectural principles. For example, there is a real possibility that function will be duplicated across systems in the federation. Today this is an inevitable characteristic because it is this duplication of functionality that permits different companies to develop their systems autonomously. Over time, we believe that the various industry groupings will (slowly) move toward a well-architected, standardized, and normalized industry federation.

- The use-cases required to describe or test the federation are cross-system in nature. They are called federation use cases to distinguish them from system-level use cases (see Chapter 7, "Development Process").

- Given the current level of maturity of the component industry, an FRM will often represent a set of loosely coupled component-enabled legacy systems (rather than well-defined system-level components). Most effort will go into providing component-like interfaces to systems that may be closed monolith and into achieving correct functionality. In many cases relatively little effort can be spent addressing performance or other extra-functional requirements.

In order to enable the modeling of a system that is meant to work together with other systems at some level, possibly (in an ideal world) out of the box, the system must be built according to a given architecture, and if possible with the same component factory setup. This is illustrated in Figure 11.3: System 1 and System 2 can be functionally modeled to work together only if they already

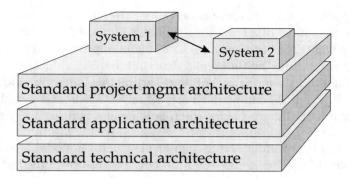

Figure 11.3 Two systems requiring a standard component factory setup.

share the component factory setup or if the component factory setup for each of them can be bridged. Furthermore, the system-level plug-and-play vision will require a common federation component model for each industry.

The idealized process for defining the components of a federation can be seen as follows:

1. *Model the federation.* This includes identifying the system-level components and the main functional interfaces required between these system-level components. In the short-to-medium term, each system-level component will need a mostly ad-hoc set of interoperability protocols to interoperate with the other systems. In the longer term, an industry-wide focus on component-based development should lead to a progressive normalization of the functional reference models.

2. *Model each system-level component.* This includes a strong focus on the interfaces of each system, and the identification of the internal business components of each system.

3. *Model each business component and/or distributed component.* This was touched on in Chapter 3, "The Distributed Component" and Chapter 4, "The Business Component," and is further discussed later in this chapter.

Partitioning the Business Space

One of the most critical aspects of the analysis of a new information system is how to turn the complex reality of the problem space into a model that is simple to discuss and that supports a focus on individual meaningful parts. Because any domain grows quickly beyond the understanding of a single individual, a way to master this complexity must be found. A useful strategy to adopt is the *divide and conquer* principle: good partitioning of the domain space is fundamental for every aspect of an information system, and it is particularly important in breaking down complexity into manageable pieces. There are two important dimensions of partitioning: *chunking* and *layering*.

Chunking

Chunking is the partitioning of the problem space, such as order fulfillment, into a relatively small number of parts that represent the main business processes of the information system. A simplified example of chunking for an order fulfillment business process (including accounts receivable) is given in Figure 11.4. Component-based modeling directly supports chunking through the granularity levels of the system-level component and the business component.

Layering

Layering is the partitioning of the problem space into a set of open layers (the definition of *open layer* was given in Chapter 5, "The Business Component System"), as illustrated in Figure 11.5. The processes identified through chunking rely on these layers to accomplish their functionality. In this figure, the *Order-Manager* component implements the Order Entry process of Figure 11.4.

The ability not only to model a functional area (or part thereof) in terms of layers of components, but also to be able to design, implement, and deploy the system in this way is a quite recent achievement in our industry. In traditional information system development, each functional area is typically a "stovepipe" monolithic application, with no well-structured internal partitioning (or at least not a partitioning that could translate into a corresponding packaging, deployment, and run-time partitioning), and often integrated through a single, large database. The evolution in thinking, from traditional stovepipes to component-based, is shown in a stylized way in Figure 11.6.

The two forms of partitioning—chunking and layering—can also be seen as two different levels of granularity of partitioning: at the higher level of granu-

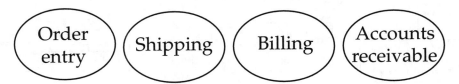

Figure 11.4 Chunking for order fulfillment.

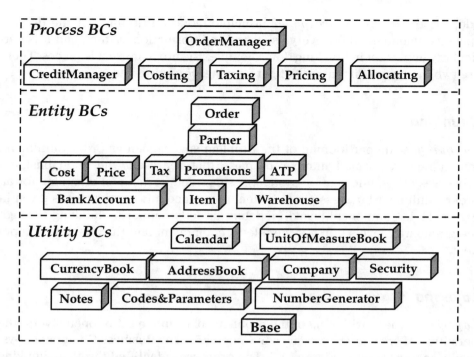

Figure 11.5 Layering of the order management process.

larity, the system is a set of interacting processes. When it is required to analyze the processes in more detail, the layering becomes important.

Is there a right way to partition a business space? The truth of the matter is that *any way you partition the business space is wrong from some point of view.* There will always be some business scenarios that are made difficult if not impossible to implement without rearranging the components, given a particular partitioning of the system. But some partitions are more elegant and change-resilient than others. The *best* partition is a matter of applying the best compromise between current and future development costs, performance and

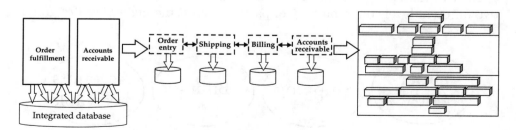

Figure 11.6 From monoliths to components.

scalability, flexibility of the solution, and other similar constraints. We argue that a component-based partitioning of a problem space is best because it gives a partitioning strategy that equals the power of other strategies but also maps directly into development strategies and hence architectures and technologies. Also, a good business component system model provides double resilience to changes in requirements through its process-driven structuring and its functional layering.

An information system implemented by applying an appropriate partitioning strategy presents many advantages for rapid development, especially after the first iteration. Figure 11.7, where the gray boxes represent the first release of a given information system, illustrates how, in order to build the first process business component, the various deliverables corresponding to the architectural viewpoints may have to be built as well. However, as illustrated by the white "new process" in Figure 11.7, once the first process business component is built, new processes can be built very rapidly because most of the software artifacts required to build them have already been not only defined but also implemented. Keeping this strong reuse-centric approach enables new processes—and also new systems—to be built very rapidly.

This is an additional justification for setting up a component factory, that is, setting up the bottom four layers in the figure. Once the setup is done, and after one iteration in the functional architecture, any extension of the system is very rapid and low cost. The whole setup provides for maximum reuse across the architectural viewpoints, the distribution tiers, and the functional layers.

Note that, for many organizations, it is the process components, and possibly some of the entity components, that are strategic. Most organizations would be

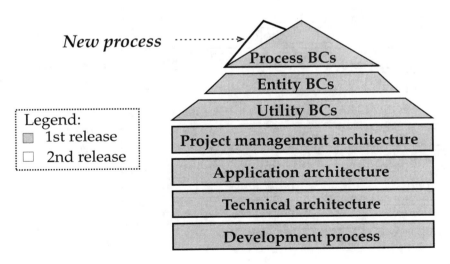

Figure 11.7   Evolving a component-based system.

perfectly content only to build those things that give some competitive advantage, such as business-specific processes. In this sense, many business components can be considered nonstrategic, and if it were possible to acquire them commercially, there would be no hesitation.

Functional Subcategories

Chapter 5 presented the three main functional layers or categories for business components: process, entity, and utility. It is possible to define subcategories of these main categories, as shown in Figure 11.8, which is Figure 11.5 with explicit subcategories added on the right of the figure. These subcategories are open layers in the business component system model, just as process, entity, and utility layers are. Separation of a system's business components into subcategories is not as universally valid as the main classification into utility, entity, and process components, but it has proven useful in a number of occasions. It is presented here in terms of further support of the business modeling activity, and the example in Figure 11.8 should not be seen as a strict codified set.

Starting from the bottom of Figure 11.8, the first two subcategories are part of the utility layer. As a reminder, components in this layer are those of general applicability that most business systems need to deal with.

Support utilities. Tend to address general support functions such as generating sequence numbers, associating notes with entities, managing system parameters, and so forth. These support business components are not usually identified in an enterprise object model.

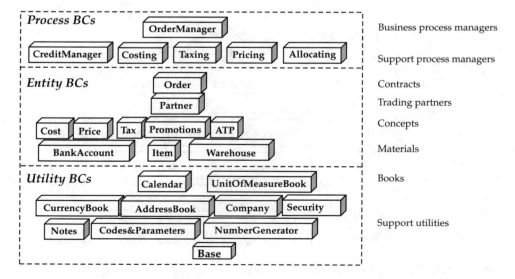

Figure 11.8 Functional subcategories.

Books. Things that in the past would be supported by paper books. For example, currency exchange used to be based on books that listed various currencies and their exchange rates, looking up an address required an address book, and units of measure and their conversion factors were found in a book.

The next four subcategories are part of the entity layer. As a reminder, these are components that correspond to the business entities on which business processes act.

Materials. The bread and butter of an information system. In a manufacturing system, this layer could include *Item* and *Machine*, whereas in a financial system it could contain resources such as *BankAccount*. These are the main tangible entities that business processes require.

Concepts. Concept business components represent logical or conceptual entities, such as price and cost, that do not correspond to something tangible in the physical world. As mentioned in Chapter 5, when representing something like *Price* as a business component, this does not mean such a simple price as in *the price of this book is $39.99*, but rather refers to the information and rules required to dynamically calculate the price of any manufacturing item.

Trading partners. The various organizational entities that participate in any business transaction, for example, *Vendor* or *Customer*.

Contracts. Also known as "Business Documents" (the term "contracts" comes from [Hay 1996]), these are the documents on which the system will do work, and they could include *Invoice*, *SalesOrder*, and *PurchaseOrder*.

The next two subcategories are part of the process layer. As a reminder, process business components implement the system's business processes.

Support process managers. These components implement processes that are often reused by other business process components. Support process managers often correspond to the "reusable" or "generic" use cases. An example of this category could be the *CreditChecker* component.

Business process managers. Components managing the "main" business processes of the system or domain. These are often the highest level in the functional layering, and they tend to be of direct relevance to the end user. This subcategory layer is the only one visible when discussing the chunking of the problem space. A business process manager is a component that corresponds to one business process, or more in the case of highly related business processes. For example, nonpurchase-order-related invoice entry and purchase-order-related invoice entry are 70 percent similar, have high cohesion and low coupling, and could be managed by a single business process manager.

Figures 11.9 and 11.10 show examples of subcategories from two different domains: supply chain management and finance or general accounting. While the order of subcategories in these examples is not the only possible one, it is one that has been found to be useful in practice.

Identification Strategies

This section describes approaches and heuristics useful in identifying the candidate business components of a system and in evaluating them. The discussion is presented in three parts:

- Considerations about the appropriate granularity for a business component

- Jump-starting the identification process—that is, a set of heuristics for business component discovery and identification

- Evaluating a business component system model—how to assess the "goodness" of a BCSM

The approaches and heuristics presented here do not guarantee that two people partitioning the same domain will arrive at the same conclusions, but they do generally result in a certain level of uniformity in the resulting business component system models produced. The focus of this section is business component identification. Once identified, the next step is to assign responsibilities (for function) to them, but this is not addressed in any detail. Many traditional

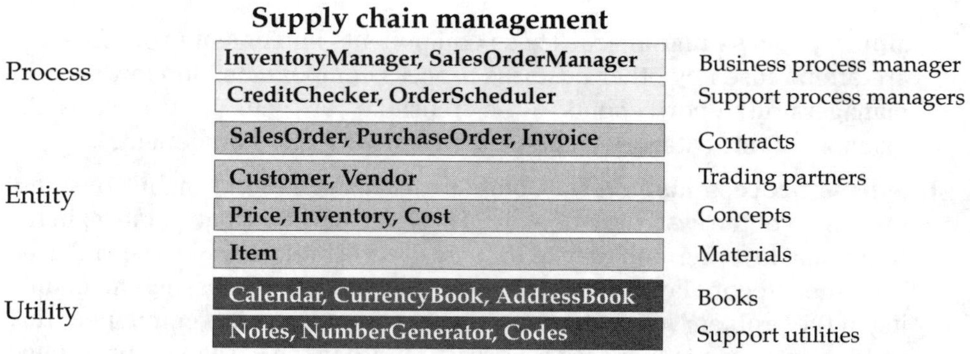

Supply chain management

Process	InventoryManager, SalesOrderManager — Business process manager
	CreditChecker, OrderScheduler — Support process managers
Entity	SalesOrder, PurchaseOrder, Invoice — Contracts
	Customer, Vendor — Trading partners
	Price, Inventory, Cost — Concepts
	Item — Materials
Utility	Calendar, CurrencyBook, AddressBook — Books
	Notes, NumberGenerator, Codes — Support utilities

Figure 11.9   Subcategories in supply chain management.

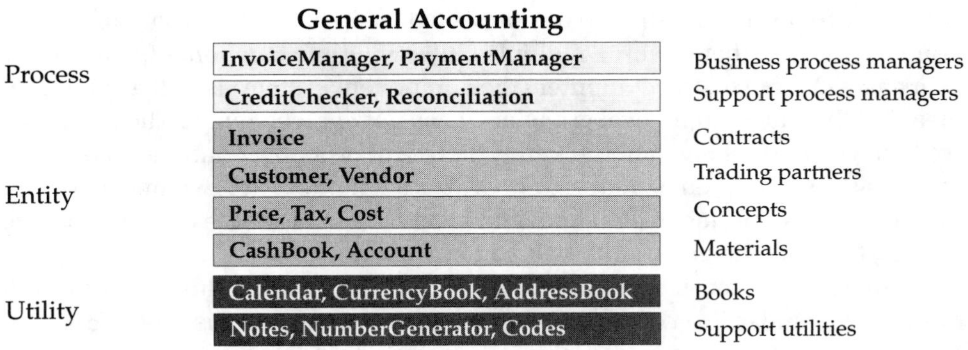

General Accounting

Process	InvoiceManager, PaymentManager	Business process managers
	CreditChecker, Reconciliation	Support process managers
Entity	Invoice	Contracts
	Customer, Vendor	Trading partners
	Price, Tax, Cost	Concepts
	CashBook, Account	Materials
Utility	Calendar, CurrencyBook, AddressBook	Books
	Notes, NumberGenerator, Codes	Support utilities

Figure 11.10   Subcategories in finance.

techniques for assigning responsibilities, for example, the object responsibility game [Wirfs-Brock 1990], can be extended to components.

Granularity

A business component can be defined as a software reification of a business concept of appropriate granularity. The key question, of course, is what does "appropriate" mean. Answering this question is probably the most important aspect of designing business component-based systems. It can also be controversial because there is no such thing as the "right" granularity in a context-free sense. In other words, the meaning of "appropriate" varies by context, and in any given context, there will be granularities that are wrong. For example, in the context of ERP systems, it would be wrong (or at least highly inappropriate) to make each address instance or each currency instance an autonomous network-addressable component.

Even in a given business context, the appropriate granularity may evolve with the maturity of the market, ways of doing business, technologies, and so forth. What is appropriate today may not be so 3 to 5 to 10 years from now. For example, if speed of finding a vendor becomes more important than long-term relationships with vendors, and if electronic negotiation mechanisms become viable, then instead of a *Vendor* business component, we may find *Negotiator* and *NegotiatingParty* business components, and the whole concept of vendor may become less relevant. Alternatively, the development of industry standards may result in some set of entity components and utility components becoming completely standardized within an industry. In that case, they may be bought off the shelf as a single business component (perhaps the "invoice set") with a reduced set of interfaces. Although not an exact analogy, such a possible future evolution corresponds to what has happened in the computer hardware industry, where today it is possible to buy on a single chip (a single autonomous component) function that required multiple chips (multiple components) just a few years ago. Of course, the computer (the component system) is still a computer, meaning that the system-level granularity has not evolved much. The former is, we believe, more likely than the latter; there will probably continue to be technical reasons why even were the standardization in the latter example to occur, providers will continue to ship individual components for ease of maintenance. That is, the upgrade granularity will still be important.

Furthermore, even if it is natural to expect that each industry sector will eventually standardize on an evolving set of components, this will take some time. Each sector would first evolve its own standards and may choose its own specific levels of granularity, which may differ from that of other sectors dealing with the same business concept. Only when each sector's standardization efforts mature, and it is possible and cost-effective to consider similar concepts that have been standardized in other sectors, is it likely that the software industry will see the birth of a cross-sector set of common components. Until this happens each vertical domain, and in the medium term each organization, will probably define its own components with a granularity to suit its particular purposes.

In any given context there is a *preferred granularity*, and the next section suggests a set of heuristics (some of which have already been discussed in other chapters) for identifying what this is.

Identification

What heuristics and guidelines are there to identity business components when starting out in applying component thinking to a development project? Probably the most useful starting point is the following:

> Good candidates for business components are those business concepts that are *real and independent* in the business domain.

"Real" means that the concept is both used and well understood by business domain people (as opposed to IS people). It is not abstract. A "real" concept is a type whose instances are actually used in the business, as opposed to an abstraction of that type. For example, in a manufacturing business, "customer," "address," and "invoice line item" would probably be real, while "legal entity," "location," and "collection member" would not. That is, a business person would assert that while a "customer" is a common everyday concrete thing, a "legal entity" is not (although there might be agreement that, hypothetically, it's a good supertype of "customer").

An "independent" concept is one that can be talked about by business domain people without first saying to what it belongs. That is, its scope is implied and understood, and it is probably that of the business or of a major division within the business. For example, in a manufacturing business, a "customer" probably does not have to be qualified, so it's independent. "Address," on the other hand, must be qualified to be meaningful, for example, "customer address" or "supplier address."

It is important to avoid confusing user interface constructs with the core enterprise concepts. A process for identifying objects on an object-oriented user interface for the purpose of building a user interface prototype was presented in [Sims 1994]. This process is not suitable for identifying business components. For example (and still thinking of a manufacturing business) it may well be that order-entry people might like the facility to pick up an order line and drag it to another order to avoid re-entering data. This would suggest that at the user interface (and perhaps also in the w-tier) an order line is real and independent. That may be so, but this does not translate automatically to the ERD. In fact, an order line would almost certainly not be an independent concept in the business domain, and hence it would not be considered as a good candidate for a business component. Aside from this, identifying an order line as a business component would probably be technically suboptimal in terms of performance and system load.

Other heuristics that support the "real and independent" guideline are as follows:

- The business components should satisfy *market demand* or be *easily marketable*. There should have been interest shown in them, or they should be believed to have some utility as components. The "market" may be internal to the software development organization; that is, if there are enough internal requests for a given concept to be delivered as a business component, then this is a good indication that perhaps it should be a business component.

- The components must be perceived as *highly usable and reusable*. This characteristic, as most of the others, must also withstand the test of time: Components must continue to "feel right" over time.

- A business component should be at a level of granularity that will support autonomous development by two to three people through the development lifecycle. *Autonomous development* is an extension of the "low coupling-high cohesion" principle, and in general it reflects the software engineering principles for good modularization.

- A business component must satisfy one or more of the *cohesion* principles, which include the following:
  - Temporal cohesion is where the business components must provide for stability at development time and subsequently at evolution time.

Stability refers to both the business models and the software artifacts. Things that evolve at the same speed are good candidates for belonging in the same business component, as illustrated in "Default Management" in Chapter 9, "Application Architecture." The two different points of view (development and evolution) are important for different players. The development point of view is important in the factory because it supports development cost reduction, but it is less important from the end users' point of view. The evolution point of view is important for end users.

- Functional cohesion occurs when business components package together a set of logically related functions. For example, order creation and order deletion are two different but very related processes in an order management system, and they should be considered for inclusion in the same business component. In general, this principle is what drives the concept of a "focus object," which was described in Chapter 3.

- Run-time cohesion occurs where it makes technical sense to run things in the same address space. For example, it does not make sense to decompose into different business components something that does compute-intensive processing. Such processing is typical of planning and scheduling engines, such as MRP (material requirements planning).

- Actor cohesion indicates the fact that the users of a given component should be similar. If very different kinds of actors or components, at very different levels in the DAG, need to invoke very different requests on a target component, this may be an indication that it should be separated into different components or subsumed into other components.

- Business components should correspond to *units of stability*. The identified components should be the most stable things in the system. Their content and exact functionality may change, but actually splitting a component in two, or packaging two components into one, can be an expensive operation in a component-based approach. Components are analyzed and looked on as "islands," and the focus is on what would make them become units of independence.

- Business components may also correspond to a "discovered concept." This rule applies particularly to utility components. Some useful business components are those that might not immediately leap to the modeler's eye as real and independent. When their characteristics are brought to the attention of users, however, they often find them useful and wish they were real. For example, the Notes business component is a component of general usability and is perhaps less likely than most to be discovered during traditional modeling. On the other hand, it may be argued that it directly corresponds to the Post-It™ concept.

Following these heuristics, certain components will often just pop out as obvious choices, while others will appear over time. With a growing component mindset, both developers and end users will, over time, find it increasingly easy to identify business components.

The problem of identifying business components, and also enterprise distributed components, differs depending on the functional category of business component under consideration. There is a direct relationship, which can be used to jump-start the component identification process, between the process, entity, and utility component categories and the models required to describe a business (see Chapter 7, Figure 7.5). Based on this relationship, the following guidelines are useful:

■ Chunking can be driven by a good process model and by thinking in terms of ownership of use-cases. The process models are the main models to identify, gather requirements, and decide about which components should be part of the process layer and with what content. Process business components are normally expected to appear as the main processes in the process models.

■ Directly related processes are good candidates to be owned by the same process component. As a rule of thumb, two processes can be considered directly related if they seem to have more than 70 percent in common or if they operate on the same entity or entities.

■ Use-cases and process models are usually naturally centered on focus processes. A *focus process* is a process that is the focus of a given set of activities. A focus process usually operates on a set of entities, one of which often clearly stands out as the main recipient of the process and is often called a *focus entity*. Focus process and focus entities often come in pairs, and as a general principle they are in a one-to-one relationship: If another process is identified that clearly has a given entity as a focus entity, that process is a good candidate to be managed by the previously identified focus process. For example, the order-entry process could be assigned to an *OrderManager* business component (the focus process) that operates on an *Order* business component (the focus entity). An order deletion process would usually also be assigned to the *OrderManager* business component.

■ The enterprise object model is the main model for identifying the business components that should be in the entity layer, for deciding their overall content, and for gathering their requirements. Entity business components are normally expected to correspond to the main entities in the enterprise object model.

- Utility business components are mainly identified based on experience, rather than on any of the preceding guidelines. Look for the utility business components defined in this book: It is highly likely that, if you accept the architecture principles illustrated here, they, or something close to them, will apply in your domain. New utility components that capture particular sets of reusable services can be added during a project. Utility components are identified mostly by commonality, experience, and reusability.

Evaluating a Business Component System Model

What rules enable a developer to assert that a given business component model is good? The skills required to define a BCSM are architectural in nature, and we have noticed that over time component modelers acquire an instinctive capability to identify components and assess if existing component diagrams are good. First, consider whether the initial component diagram is useful in studying the system and running use-cases against. The objective is to see whether the use-cases will work, as opposed to optimizing or designing them in detail.

Aside from the problems found by running use-cases against the component diagram, there are also a few useful quantitative guidelines, which act as *indicators* of something wrong in a component model:

- A distributed component has on average 10 business language classes, but a few may have up to 200. If there are fewer than 5 or more than, say, 150, there may be problems.

- The typical number of business components in any given business domain is a few 10s, say, 30 to 40. (As a reminder, a business domain, such as Order Management, was described in Chapter 5 as being part of a business sector, for example, supply chain management.) Normally, in most domains we would expect 10 to 20 utility business components, 15 to 20 entity business components, and 10 to 20 business processes.

- A big project that covers several domains could have about 200 to 300 business components and between 10 and 30 system-level components. Of the business components, 15 to 25 in the utility layer can be expected, 80 to 100 in the entity category, the rest as process business components. This is a sign that utility business components are highly reusable across domains (as are entity components, but to a lesser extent) and that over time most of the new components will be process components.

TIP At a minimum, one to two appropriately skilled people will suffice for the initial identification of the candidate business components for the whole BCSM for an average-sized development of, say, 60 to 80 business components. A very large-scale system, with 300 to 400 business components, may thus require two to three people in the identification phase. Once the components are defined, one person can easily part-time manage and maintain a whole business component system model for a large-scale system. Although the initial model can be built by a few people, it is usually better to include all the senior members of the team in the definition phase because it is a very good team-building exercise. This is especially so if the component diagram is being annotated—with tier, persistence, and other information—and validated against use-cases. Further, when this is the first business component development in which the team is involved, then it becomes essential for all senior people in the team to be exposed to business component identification. There is no better time to informally inculcate the business component approach in particular and component thinking in general.

Modeling the Processes

This section further discusses various ways in which the process layer can be developed, and it addresses *workflow management* and *rule-based modeling*, as well as *process business components*. The differences between these three approaches are compared, to show how component-based thinking provides a unifying conceptual framework that can blend all three approaches or styles into a powerful problem-solving combination. Finally, components as finite state machines are analyzed.

Workflow Management

The Workflow Management Coalition defines a workflow as "the computerized facilitation or automation of a business process, in whole or part" [WFMC 1995]. Workflow management (WFM) is defined by the OMG as being "concerned with the automation of procedures where information and tasks are passed between participants according to a defined set of rules to achieve, or contribute to, an overall business goal" [OMG 1999c]. It is implemented by a workflow management system, defined as "a system that completely defines, manages, and executes 'workflows' through the execution of software whose order of execution is driven by a computer representation of the workflow logic" [WFMC 1995].

At the core of workflow management systems is a workflow enactment service that manages the execution of instances of defined processes, scheduling them, assigning or reassigning them to the appropriate participant at the right time, invoking applications, tracking activities, and so forth. Workflow-driven information systems are process-driven systems, in which business processes and the order in which sequences of activities should be executed are highly configurable, and new processes with new actors relatively easy to create. An important factor in the success of WFM systems is their provision of scripting languages—usually fronted by a visual GUI tool—used to define the various workflows and business processes. Scripts are typically interpreted at run-time, are definable by appropriately trained end users or business analysts, and do not necessarily have to be provided by IS developers.

There are three main areas where workflow systems and component-based thinking can be mutually highly supportive. The first is where the workflow management system itself is treated as a business domain and is implemented as a set of business components. To the authors' knowledge, this has not yet been done, and it is not addressed here. The second area is in the use of the workflow scripting language, and the third is the ease with which business components can be used for workflow-related purposes. This section focuses on the last two of these three.

Some workflow scripting languages have the ability to encode business logic as well as define workflows. Where this is the case, there are two ways in which the workflow scripting capability can, in conjunction with business components, be extremely useful; they are as follows:

1. *Process implementation.* In this case, WFM scripting is used as a way to (relatively) quickly build or modify a process, without necessarily requiring the original developer of the underlying component system. This is illustrated in Figure 11.11. The WFM scripting language, which must be able to implement all aspects of business logic, is used for the implementation of entire business processes, for example, Invoice Manager in the figure. Potentially the whole process layer can be defined outside of component implementation technology, possibly as a flexible set of workflows managed and supported by the WFM system. This approach could work for simple systems, but for larger systems we have found it more cost-effective and easier to implement at least a part of the process layer using component implementation technology and to use workflow-based process implementation only for the upper-most process coordination layer.

2. *Workflow-based integration.* In this case, WFM is used as a way to (relatively) quickly integrate two systems through the implementation of a coordination layer which, because it is a workflow script known to the WFM system, can be managed by that system. This is illustrated in Figure 11.12. In this figure, we show two system-level components coordinated through a workflow-based layer. The example would be similar if it were

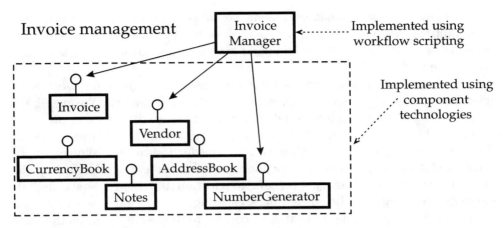

Figure 11.11 Workflow-based process implementation.

business components (rather than whole SLCs) belonging to the two different systems that were being coordinated.

Workflow-based integration can be a (relatively) simple way to address many interoperability demands, but Chapter 6 illustrated how a close integration between systems can be a complex challenge. For example, in a more integrated approach, it may be required to provide for the need for data integrity among different systems: If the workflow drives two SLCs that live on different

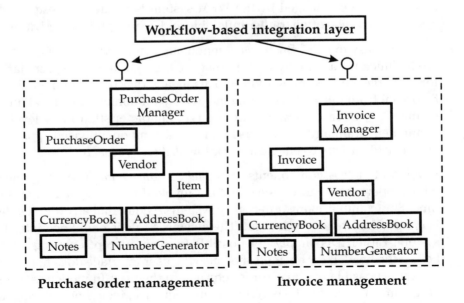

Figure 11.12 Workflow-based integration.

unconnected resource managers, having a complex business transaction spanning multiple systems either fully executed or totally rolled back may not be
possible or is, at least, difficult to manage without an extraordinary software
engineering effort.

Let's now turn to how business components can be used for workflow-
related purposes. First, does component-based thinking help when using WFM?
Yes. Unless the domain being modeled is small, there is still a need to properly
partition the domain to master complexity and assign workflows to well-
defined and well-scoped parts of the system. This leads us to the following functional architecture principle: Independently of the implementation approach,
as a way to master complexity, it is useful to partition the business space, including all the modeling of the business processes, using a component-based approach.

The preceding principle translates, of course, to the requirement on the various implementation technologies (including workflow) to support to some
extent a partitioning of the business space into components of appropriate
granularity: We actually use this as one important requirement to judge the usefulness of specific technologies to develop software related to business processes.

Second, does a component-based implementation help when a workflow-
driven approach is required? Yes. Information systems can be more or less
"workflow-ready" depending on a variety of factors. The following levels of
"readiness" could be provided:

- Level 0: Ad-hoc. The workflow management is somehow glued on top of
typically closed monolithic legacy systems. The granularity of the activities that can be managed by the WFM system is whatever these legacy
systems provide—often, rather inflexible and coarse-grained activities.

- Level 1: "Easy to call." Business components can provide interfaces that
are technically easy to invoke and that are the right interface granularity
for activities defined by workflow. This means that the components can
be driven from the WFM scripting language with minimal technical interfacing. Easy-to-call interfaces are a direct characteristic of any level of
component granularity, so at this first level, a component-based approach
can be said directly to enable a workflow-driven approach.

- Level 2: Modeless components. A *modeless component* is a component
whose operations can be meaningfully invoked in any sequence at any
time. For example, many order-entry systems require that an order header
is entered before any order line. This business rule is engrained into the
system: Either it is simply not possible to even attempt entering a line
before the header, for example, because the user interface does not allow
it, or it is possible but an error is returned to the user. In modeless order
entry, information can be entered in any sequence, including entering an
order line before any other order information. Modeless components may

appear simple to achieve, but in reality they lead to additional modeling complexity (see also "Components as Finite State Machines" later in this chapter). Evolution and change in workflows and in workflow management are greatly simplified by the presence of modeless components because it is particularly easy to rearrange processes in any sequence.

- Level 3: Fully workflow-based system. In this case, all components work seamlessly with the WFM system. Workflow is an integral part of all component considerations and development. This requires that all components be modeless, that most business processes are managed by the WFM system, and that the WFM system is an integral part of the BCVM, so that, among other things, component invocation is a native aspect of the workflow scripting language.

It can be expected that a level 3 capability may emerge in the medium to long term. When it does, then the WFM system will not be an external add-on to a BCVM (or vice versa), but rather they will be inherently integrated.

A fully workflow-enabled system will start to blur the current distinction between scripted workflow activities, on one hand, and entity-based business logic on the other. That is, it will push workflow-based aspects into the maintenance processes of the main entity business components in the system. One consequence of this is that the functional architecture will change to better enable workflow, both at the process and at the entity level (and even in some cases at the utility components level). Another will be the breaking down of business processes into steps that can be performed in any sequence, so enabling businesses to evolve processes much more rapidly.

Rule-Based Modeling

Often users need to be able to quickly adapt the business rules and business logic encapsulated in processes to new requirements that were not foreseen when the system was designed and built. Such a requirement may arise at installation or during subsequent normal system usage. In simple systems, this may be addressed by replacing the whole process layer with a layer that is appropriate for the new processes. In more complex systems this would be too expensive, and other approaches are required.

One approach is rule-based modeling. This is a lesser-known approach to building highly configurable processes, and it has its roots in the Artificial Intelligence field. It involves expressing much of the business processes logic in the information system in a rule-based language, relying on a rules engine (a.k.a. inference engine) to evaluate and execute those rules at run-time. Rule-based engines (such as Computer Associates' Aion [CAI 1999]) are usually composed of a proprietary development environment, which includes a rules language and a run-time inference engine that efficiently evaluates the rules.

There are two main ways to use rule-based modeling. In the first, directly supported by rule-based products, the business logic is expressed in terms of its rules, and the processing logic comprises those rules being executed by the rules engine while respecting defined logical constraints. In this case, the approach is strongly rule-centric rather than process-centric. The second case assumes the use of rules with components, and it is less directly supported by commercially available rule-based engines. The focus is on processes, where each component has the ability to externalize its rules such that they can be modified without affecting the rest of the system. New rules, or modifications to existing rules, should be able to be written and tested separately, then plugged into the information system without requiring any modification to the existing distributed components. This could provide for highly configurable business logic within DCs. Consider, for example, a Pricing component. The pricing rules are already encapsulated in this component. Simply by modifying the business rules of the Pricing component, and without touching other aspects of the system, a broad category of Pricing configurability requirements can be satisfied. The key technical requirement is that the inference engine can be invoked without having first to bind it into a specialized monolithic application.

How does this relate to component-based development? Well, as for WFM, unless the system is relatively simple, there is a need to master complexity and properly partition the problem space, and this can be usefully done by applying component-based thinking. Although rule-based systems allow for a certain level of componentization, their capabilities in this area are typically not comparable to the level of sophistication provided by current component implementation technologies. However, as long as the rule-based development and run-time environments allow for both calling and being called by other parts of the system, a rule-based process layer can be integrated with a component framework.

Rapid Evolution

From an end-user perspective, perhaps the most dramatic change over the past few years is the significant shortening of business lifecycles, with the concomitant need to adapt faster, to respond positively to new business requirements, and to manage the rapid evolution of business processes. Indeed, many industry experts today assert that change is the only constant in the current business reality. This has several important effects on software development priorities. Ideally, an information system should be designed in such a way that it can be instantly adapted to any new business process the end user may want to instigate, any change in existing business process, or any rearrangement of existing business processes to create new ones.

This section first discusses various levels of configurability (using the term in an extended sense to cover a range of customizations and modifications alternatives) in a business component system. Second, it considers how the two approaches previously discussed—workflow and rule-based—compare with the business component approach in their ability to provide for rapid modification and/or configurability, so that fast implementation and evolution of business systems can be achieved.

Configurability. There are many ways to configure a system so that it delivers what is required, ranging from tweaking installation parameters to custom-building code that will slot into and extend an existing system. For a business component system, a useful categorization of business process configurability is as follows:

- *Predefined configurability.* Some organizations require only a set of basic, general-purpose business processes for quasi "out-of-the-box" low-cost installation. This requirement can be addressed by a fully functioning business component system, where the business processes are configurable to some extent—in a controlled way—such that they preserve the integrity of the system. The organization must be prepared to adapt its processes to those provided by the configurable out-of-the-box solution. Modifying the supplied processes would be managed through a set of predefined parameters, whose values can be modified to configure the business processes in predefined ways.

- *Framework-constrained configurability.* The business component system provides a functional framework—a set of process, entity, and utility business components that are not intended themselves to provide a solution (although a default solution would normally be provided), but with minimal additions can provide a number of different solutions. This is suitable for businesses that need to constantly evolve and adapt to changes in the business reality of their customers, but that are content to do so within the constraints of the functional framework provided by the information system. Such a business would instantiate the framework, with as few modifications as possible or with smaller implementations of its own process components, so providing its own tailored solution.

- *Process reimplementation.* In this case, the needs are beyond what a functional framework can provide by simple configuration or minor modifications. Rather, a whole new set of processes must be designed and implemented. This configurability level can still take advantage of a component framework, typically reusing the utility and entity business components. This level of configurability, which should include the possibility of a complete change in the operating mode of the information system, is required by businesses that need the ability to adapt their processes to any level of change, including changes unforeseen when their information system was designed.

- *Component system reimplementation.* In this case, no existing component framework satisfies the needs, not even at the entity level. Indeed, some businesses require that not only single processes but also entire parts of the information system need to be configurable. This could be taken to the point where the only things that can be reused are the main utility business components plus development frameworks, leaving the business to build the new business-specific entity components and the process managers needed.

Comparison. Let us compare the three approaches to modeling and implementing processes—as workflows, rule-based systems, and process business components. The key to fast adaptability in most of the preceding situations is the speed with which process components can be developed, modified, and deployed. Does taking one of these alternative approaches make any difference?

Table 11.2 compares the various approaches to process implementation and configurability in terms of speed of development. The "Implementation Approach" column lists the three approaches. The column "Initial Development (immature)" indicates a company that is approaching a given business space without previous knowledge of the implementation technology for the various approaches. The column "Initial Development (mature)" indicates a company that is approaching a new business space, but that has prior experience of the particular technology. The column "Evolution" indicates a company that needs to evolve an existing system and is mature in the use of the particular technology in the business space being addressed. The "Combination" row refers to an implementation in which all the three implementation approaches are combined. This table is very context-specific because such factors as the specific technology used and the maturity of the using organization all strongly influence the outcomes, which are given here only as an indication of the relevant considerations.

The table illustrates how a first implementation using either workflow or a rule-based approach involves a relatively small learning curve. The organiza-

Table 11.2 Comparing Process Implementation Options

IMPLEMENTATION APPROACH	INITIAL DEV. (IMMATURE)	INITIAL DEV. (MATURE)	EVOLUTION
WFM	Medium-slow	Rapid	Slow in large systems
Rule-based	Medium-slow	Medium	Slow in large systems
Pure business component	Medium	Rapid	Rapid
Combination	Slow	Rapid	Rapid

tion needs to absorb a new technology and a new way of thinking about modeling, design, implementation, and testing. Once these hurdles are over, a new implementation is rapid for workflow and medium speed for rule-based. Unless combined with components, however, these implementation approaches do not scale very well. They provide strong support for simple systems or for small parts of large systems. To a large extent, adopting a rule-based approach can be seen as a "white box" approach to the modification of existing systems. On the other hand, WFM can be seen as a "black box" modification of the system, given a focus on coordinating existing components or component systems. Both approaches can have an important role in the development of large business systems.

The table also shows that adopting a pure business component approach is relatively fast. The adopting organization may have already gained experience through building utility and entity components, and the step to process components is a small one. Several things make the use of process components competitive with the other approaches:

- The ability to build process business components reusing many parts of the existing system without fundamentally affecting the design of the system.

- Most modifications or configurability requirements often affect only a single business component or business component assembly.

- Implementing a process business component uses the same technologies as other business component categories and is hence very cost-effective (assuming an appropriate extended integrated development environment as presented in Chapter 8, "Technical Architecture" and Chapter 10, "Project Management Architecture").

A combined approach may require a steeper learning curve because all the aforementioned technologies must be learned. But once the organization has climbed the learning curve, this is a very good way to rapidly implement a system and new business processes, providing systems and components that are very resilient to change. The approach scales very well, and through its strongly reuse-focused philosophy supports development of new systems without ever having to start from scratch. The implementation of a new process, in addition to reusing all the components it depends on, usually has at its disposal many reusable classes, reusable patterns, and even reusable BC-internal frameworks that make development of a new process very affordable.

Conclusion. The ideal situation is a mix of all technologies and approaches discussed in this section, seamlessly supported by and integrated in the BCVM and applicable to the different problems. The combined power of a component-based approach, of scripting, of a workflow engine, and of possibly externalizing business rules, leads to extremely configurable systems that are highly resilient to change and in which even sweeping changes can be rapidly implemented.

Components as Finite State Machines

A component may need to be explicitly designed and implemented as a finite state machine (FSM) for various reasons, including the following:

- Business transaction management. Chapter 9 discussed adding flags to the database to manage state for the various entities that were part of a business transaction. The management of these flags, or of business transactions in general, can be modeled as an FSM.

- Modeless components. The section "Workflow Management" discussed how modeless components are components in which the operations do not have to be invoked in a predefined sequence. Implementation of a modeless component is helped significantly by an FSM model that defines the valid set of states for the component and the transformations required to move from one state to another. This is not only applicable to workflow-based systems, but more generally modern information systems are often implicitly required to be as "modeless" as possible. By "implicitly" we mean that while there is not necessarily a market requirement, there is an extra-functional requirement that derives from general usability and flexibility requirements.

- Many today argue that modeling using business events leads to more autonomous and well-architected systems. When components are modeled and implemented as FSMs, business events are more easily mapped into the system.

A component implemented as an FSM is organized in terms of states and state transitions. The execution of an operation usually involves a transition from one state to another. Each state is meaningful in a business sense, and states can be reached in different ways and by multiple routes (sequences of operations). In the example of the order (see the section "Workflow Management"), it is perfectly meaningful to have an order line entered before any other order information. This may appear to be common-sense, and a first reaction may be, well, but shouldn't the information system be designed like this anyway? That may be so, but very often systems are designed assuming a certain relationship between interfaces and a certain sequence of calling them; this required sequence is usually reflected in a strict sequencing on the user interface as well as in other parts of the system implementation; and this can simplify the design (and often, for the nonexpert end user, it can also enhance the usability of the user interface).

Let us consider an example, applied to a manufacturing *Item*. Figure 11.13

shows the traditional (simplified) manufacturing cycle: The item is engineered, priced, built, and sold. The sequence of states is quite standard, and it is followed in order: An item cannot be sold before it is priced, nor priced before it is engineered. Traditionally, business rules about sequence are built into the information system (that is, they are often hard-coded in one way or another). Hence the pricing module would simply refuse to access any item that had not been engineered. As far as the system is concerned, an item not engineered simply does not exist. In a traditional manufacturing "item" lifecycle in an ERP system, an item having only engineering information (and that as such cannot be sold) would most probably be considered to be in an "incomplete business state." The order-entry user interface would not even display the item in an item search. In a traditional implementation, the sequence in Figure 11.13 would be reflected in the database model, the user interface, and the business logic. Even though this simple case can be thought of as a state transition diagram, it does not require an explicit FSM for its design and implementation.

In an FSM-based style, the item is always in a state that makes perfect sense from a business perspective. Figure 11.14 shows a modeless item lifecycle, where operations can be performed in nearly any sequence. The product can be priced or sold before it is engineered, or built before it is priced, or sold before it is built. The system does become more complex to model, implement, and test, but there is a great deal more flexibility.

The modeling principles required to make this a cost-effective implementation change the way of thinking about the components involved. Modeling constructs must be thought of in terms of states, leading to a redefinition such as the following:

Business event. An event that triggers a change in the state of the business. Even apparently "read-only" events may cause a state change; for example, a simple inquiry could well lead to a record being made of the fact that interest in something was expressed.

Business process. A collection of activities that implements a business event and in doing so changes the state of the business in such a way as to produce an output of value to the customer. A business process not only holds the state of the business event, but it also initiates actions that can change the state of business entities.

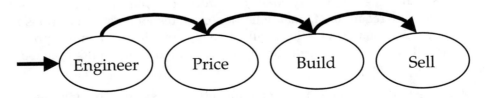

Figure 11.13   Traditional item lifecycle.

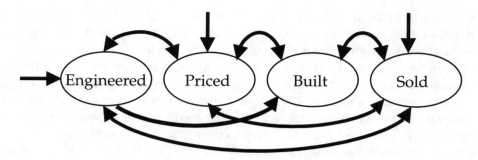

Figure 11.14   Item lifecycle as a finite state machine.

Business entity. An entity of the business that changes its state as a consequence of its being used by a business process.

Business rule. A rule that governs one or more changes of state.

Adopting an FSM-based style means that finite state machine modeling and implementation become a primary objective of development, and an explicit deliverable of analysis and design for each component. This has consequences on the database design, on the various distribution tiers, on the user interface, and even on interoperability. Examples of consequences can include the following:

- Flags and attributes to reflect state, and sometimes whole classes, are added to the DC internal implementation to support state management. In simpler systems, these correspond typically to attributes of a DC's focus class. In a more complex system, one or more classes within the DC will be required to explicitly manage the state.

- Correspondingly, flags and work-in-process tables are added to the database model, for example, to persist intermediate states in a business transaction.

- The user interface tends to be totally modeless. Potentially, any window can be displayed at any time, in any sequence. This provides power users with very flexible user interfaces, but it could be perceived as complicated by an occasional user (for example, an Internet user).

- FSM software, preferably code generators or technical language classes, is usually required. Manual definition of states and state transitions for other than simple situations can be highly complicated and error-prone. The BCVM should provide direct support for modeling, building, and executing FSMs.

If it is assumed that all business components in the system are built this way, then the objective of having a set of quasi-autonomous components working together that can process operation invocation in many different sequences without breaking can be achieved. Systems built this way are very resilient. The trend toward FSM-based systems is inevitable, and FSM-based implementations will be required as part of an overall component-based strategy.

Modeling the Entities

Chapter 5 described various characteristics of entity business components. This section first discusses "BC-level collaboration," that is, collaboration between the tiers of a business component. Following this, three examples of modeling options for entity business components are presented. These examples, taken from the supply chain management sector (but similar considerations apply elsewhere), are chosen to illustrate the kinds of modeling and implementation decisions faced by the functional architect and functional developer. The first is of two related concepts, vendor and customer, that belong to the functional category *trading partners* and illustrate the modeling decisions and trade-offs when two concepts are very close. The second example looks at the functional subcategory *contracts* and illustrates a specific example of the concept of a collaboration pattern—the header-detail pattern. The last example addresses when to separate related function into two or more business components, and it is illustrated using the two related concepts of *item and price*.

Collaboration within a Business Component

This subsection presents two concepts, strictly related to each other: BC-level collaboration and BC-level framework (where "BC," of course, stands for business component).

BC-Level Collaboration Pattern

A BC-level collaboration pattern is totally contained within a business component. Chapter 9 presented various examples of collaboration patterns involving several business components. Because an individual business component is assembled out of a set of distributed components and other software artifacts, at times it is useful to discuss collaboration patterns that are totally contained within a business component. These patterns are specified in terms of the set of software artifacts, across all tiers of the business component, required for the pattern itself.

The important point is that patterns are usually described either in terms of their underlying data models (see, for example, [Hay 1996]), their object-oriented model (see, for example, [Coad 1995]), or their specific implementation in one or more programming languages (see, for example, [Grand 1998]). In a distributed system, and more particularly in a component-based system, the tiers are often in close relationship with each other, and when they are, they must collaborate strictly to achieve not only maximum scalability and performance, but also ease of development. Figure 11.15 illustrates this in a stylized way, assuming a collaboration pattern that extends from the user interface to the database and showing the conceptual relationships between the internal implementations of each tier, which in reality, given the strict component encapsulation, would be translated into operation invocations.

A BC-level collaboration pattern needs thus to be described in terms of multiple deliverables addressing multiple distribution tiers. An example of a BC-level collaboration pattern is a header-detail pattern that could be used by orders, invoices, requisitions, and so forth. Such a collaboration pattern has a representation in the database model describing the tables for this pattern; this database model must somehow be reflected in the specification of the object-oriented model in the e-tier; in turn, this model must collaborate with the object-oriented model in the w-tier, which in turn has a representation on the user interface (and hence the u-tier). In addition, the collaboration pattern may describe such things as how exceptional conditions and errors are dealt with and various alternative implementations.

A BC-level collaboration pattern is a powerful approach for increasing productivity, and it is one more trick in the reuse bag of tricks that go with the busi-

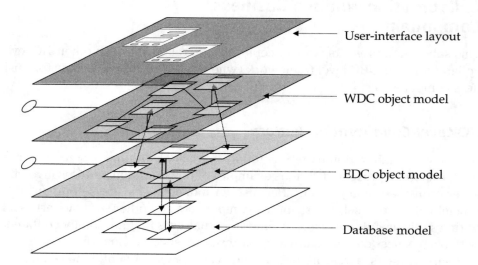

Figure 11.15   BC-level collaboration pattern.

ness component approach. A BC-level collaboration is often implemented through a BC-level framework.

BC-Level Framework

A BC-level framework is a combination of software artifacts that can be easily applied to resolve a particular design problem within a business component. It usually implements a BC-level collaboration pattern, and it directly supports rapid development by providing many or possibly all of the physical deliverables required to implement a pattern. For this reason it is sometime called an *instantiatable pattern*. It allows a combination of software artifacts, which apply across the distribution tiers, to be instantiated with minimal effort and possibly without coding effort.

A BC-level framework can be applied to multiple business components, with minimal or no change. It must also deal with practical aspects such as the namespace for tables: If all islands of data (see Chapter 12, "Component-Based Design") are to be installed in a single database, then for a BC-level framework that includes tables, the BCVM must ensure that when instantiating the framework in different business components, tables that would be duplicated are given different names.

Trading Partners

The term "trading partner" is used to indicate a participant in a supply chain management business transaction. The two main types of trading partners are vendors and customers. A vendor or a customer can be a person or an organization. Any business system needs to deal with the concepts of people and organization, and their various relationships and roles. The basic concepts to be modeled (person, organization, department, party, and others) are described in the literature (for example, see [Hay 1996]). Any of these basic concepts tends to translate to a small number of language classes and is of a granularity that, based on the criteria presented earlier in this book, would be too small to be considered as an individual business component.

On the other hand, both a vendor and a customer, when seen as a whole, including the basic concepts and their relationships, are very complex entities, and they translate into remarkable modeling complexities. In an advanced information system, a trading partner may need to be described in terms of its own real-life organizational internals, which can be worldwide and can include unique and complex structures. These structures may differ depending on the various business functions such as sales, distribution, billing, and so forth. Furthermore, the description and use of a specific trading partner may need to cover credit ratings, payment preferences, delivery conditions, ordering defaults, and many other features. A complete implementation of a trading partner is certainly at a complexity appropriate for a business component. For example, in one large supply chain management system of the many business components in the system, the *TradingPartner* component was the largest, with more than 200 business language classes.

A customer or vendor can have multiple subtypes; for example, a customer can be a ship-to-customer, a bill-to-customer, a pay-to-customer; or maybe an employee who is also a customer or a vendor who is a customer. These subtypes, depending on the project-specific philosophy, could be implemented as roles.

The basic requirements and design for both vendor and customer are usually very similar. Most differences are historical and terminological rather than conceptual. It is certainly possible to define their common designs as basic modeling patterns, and possibly even as a BC-level component pattern. However, the real question, given that their concepts are not only related but also very similar, is how to model them. There are at least two levels of component modeling decisions that are usually discussed in this case:

1. Let us assume that vendor and customer are different components: Should the subtypes be modeled and implemented as different components? Or as roles? Or in some other way? Should they be modeled as one or six different (hence having different network identities) components, and what are the trade-offs for each?

2. Should vendors and customers be the same component or different components? Because they share the same basic designs, structure, and concepts, wouldn't it make sense to merge them into one single "Trading-Partner" business component?

These kinds of decisions affect important parts of the functional architecture, as well as the kinds of interfaces provided by components, and even their implementations. The answer to the first question, which was about subtypes, is that it is highly inadvisable to model them as multiple components at a subtype level. They share too many characteristics and reusable parts for this to be effective. Many practitioners argue that this can be easily modeled and flexibly implemented using roles. While this may well be appropriate for an object model inside a distributed component, the idea of using roles at the distributed component level, given the level of granularity and mindset suggested here for the distributed component, is almost meaningless.

The answer to the second question should be based on an analysis of the overall implementation, maintenance, and evolution costs both at the component level and at the system level. Because the two concepts (vendor and customer) present many similarities, these costs will depend heavily on the degree of software artifact reuse. The following are examples of artifacts that could be reused, based on the initial hypothesis of two different components:

Object-oriented design pattern. In this alternative, the similarities of the two concepts are analyzed, and a common reusable design pattern, typically addressing the e-tier, is developed and provided to each component development team. Each team must then provide all the other aspects—pattern implementation, user interface, component interfaces, database model, and so forth—at the design level and at the implementation level. The two components will then need to be independently tested and deployed.

Language-class framework. In addition to the object-oriented design pattern, a corresponding set of business language classes, implementing parts of the pattern, is provided. Each team reuses this set, although each still has to design and implement all other aspects of its component. Both teams, however, may reduce costs through reusing provided artifacts for important parts of the e-tier implementation, as well as testing costs associated with these artifacts.

BC-level collaboration pattern. The specification of the pattern covers all the common aspects across all the distribution tiers. In this case, the two teams share much of the design costs not only in the e-tier, but of the whole business component. The resulting consistency between the two components also simplifies maintenance and evolution.

BC-level framework. The actual framework implementing the collaboration pattern is provided. Each team simply instantiates this framework to create their own component. In this case, much of the cost of development is shared. Of course, building for generality has its own costs. But if this approach is supported by the BCVM, the costs of building the collaboration pattern, providing the corresponding BC-level framework, and instantiating it to build two separate business components, for example, *Vendor* and *Customer*, can be much lower than designing and building the two components separately, without reuse.

What happens if a single component is built? How are the cost dynamics affected? Well, it depends, but before discussing it let us point out that the decision is not only a cost-related one because providing one rather than two components can also lead to different functionalities. For example, a single component for the two concepts—or for the single concept "trading partner"—can directly provide features that two separate components cannot, such as the ability to store common data just once and easily have a vendor act as a customer and vice versa without duplication of data. The decision may therefore depend on the features desired.

If a single component is built, the entire component is delivered as a run-time reusable artifact. Other teams can simply use this single component. Within the single component, the designers may decide to keep the two concepts of customer and vendor separated, or to further push the abstraction and provide interfaces directly (and possibly, only) at the trading partner level. This decision would lead, as a simple example, to interface alternatives such as the following:

- Each interface carries the partner type, with possible values "vendor" or "customer," as in:

```
get_partner(in id, in PartnerType, out information);
```

- Each concept has its own set of interfaces, as in:

```
get_vendor(in id, out information);
```

The decision can also be affected by the maturity of the development organization. The complexity of modeling a trading partner for genericity and of the resulting interfaces is nontrivial. In addition, the combination of the two concepts into a single "trading partner" concept is counter-intuitive for many functional experts who may be used to thinking of them as separate concepts. It also pushes the modeling and implementation of the sales cycle and the purchase cycle to be a mirror of each other, with consequences (not explored in this book) that may go well beyond the trading partner component itself.

An organization that is beginning to climb the component learning curve may find it easier to model the two concepts as separate entities and eventually merge them some time later. Of course, in many cases this pragmatic approach will mean that they will never be merged. Then again, the whole question may never come up. In many practical cases, the implementation of a system is focused either on the sales side or on the purchase side and hence really only requires one concept, either the vendor or the customer.

Experience suggests that it is more cost-effective, in the medium to long term, to address the problem by implementing a single component. The decision about the different interfaces will depend on the particular situation, but by default the concepts should be kept separate at the interface level. This assertion has been supported by actual measurements and complexity metrics (of course, heavily context-specific) based on a complexity model and change-impact model developed by one of the authors.

Contracts

The functional subcategory *contracts* is the highest sublayer of entity components in the business component system model. Examples of contracts, also called *business documents*, include customer order, purchase order, and invoice. Their precomputer real-world counterparts were pieces of paper, each with a legal meaning: Each establishes a contract between two or more trading partners. They usually have a corresponding process (for example, customer order entry or even customer order fulfillment). Contract component implementations can be very complex. If trading partner entity components can be the largest components in a supply chain management system, contract components are often the most complex, and also the ones with the most stringent extra-functional requirements. Normally they are the first ones to create scalability, performance, and concurrency problems. The reason is quite straightforward: Take, for example, an average order, with 10 order lines. Each order line contains a great deal of complex data. If the system is required to accept 100 orders a minute, then it must accept 1000 order lines a minute.

Contract entities are often the principal entities in a business process. As a result, they often appear in a process-entity pair: The particular contract is the principal entity in a process that is mainly built around that entity. For example, Order Management is built around the Order, Purchase Order Management is built around the Purchase Order, Invoice Management is built around the Invoice. Creating any of these contracts, which can involve multiple ACID transactions and can extend over a considerable period of time, possibly involving several users, corresponds to a business transaction. As seen in Chapter 9, a business transaction is often able to be captured as a system-level collaboration pattern. For example, it is quite usual for the process component to implement the u-tier, a corresponding w-tier, and a process-level e-tier acting as the enterprise-level business transaction coordinator, while the contract implements an e-tier acting as the contract data manager and an r-tier that is the main resource tier in the business transaction.

The design of a contract is an example of a BC-level collaboration pattern, called the "header-lines" pattern. Given that the user interface is owned by the corresponding process component, this collaboration pattern is mainly an ERD pattern. Each contract usually consists of a header and a collection of lines. In the case of a sales order, the header contains information at the order level, such as the customer, the total price of the order, the requested delivery date, and so forth. Each line contains the item ordered, the quantity, the price, the lead time, and other information.

The complexity of the header-lines pattern is very different (at the time of writing) when applied to business-to-consumer e-commerce as opposed to an internal order processing department using a fat client system (similar considerations apply to the case of business-to-business e-commerce). In the former case, orders tend to be very simple, with few order lines and minimal information (for example, an order for one or two books placed on a Web-based bookstore) that can be satisfied by a single request sent to the server. In this case, the complexity can be addressed through a BC-level collaboration pattern. In the latter case, it can have almost any level of complexity, and a solution will usually involve several business components. A system-level collaboration pattern specifying a business transaction for this latter case could do the following:

- Describe how this particular pattern instance implements the more generic business transaction collaboration pattern.

- Provide a complex user interface header-detail pattern, for example, a property sheet with several pages for the order header and a property sheet with several pages for each order line. This user interface is owned by the process component, such as *SalesOrderManager* (probably using u-tier artifacts belonging to the *SalesOrder* business component). In a complex situation, creating an order may require 5 to 10 ACID transactions for each order line and 10 to 15 for each order header.

These transactions require proper support by the w-tier and e-tier. Even a "simple" validation of an order can require the involvement of several business components.

Whether looking at the simple case or at the complex case, the design and implementation of the *SalesOrder* business component itself can be addressed through a BC-level collaboration pattern, often addressing e-tier and r-tier only and "nested" within the system-level collaboration pattern. The BC-level pattern could, for example, prescribe the following:

- The typical EDC interfaces provided by the pattern

- A typical design for the object model implementing this pattern, in our example the object model within the *eSalesOrder* EDC

- The typical database layout for the pattern

Now, all contracts have very similar high-level characteristics: Why would they not all be encapsulated in a single component? Is there any difference when compared to the Vendor and Customer example? This is a case in which experience shows that, even if the design pattern is very similar, and definitely worth designing once and applying for all contracts, at the detail level contracts are very different from each other. In addition, contract entities are in direct and strict collaboration with their respective processes. To put them all in a single component would create complexity monsters. Hence it is most inadvisable to attempt to provide a single component for several contract types.

Given the complexity of each component, would it be worth breaking them up further? Not really. For example, throughout the book, it has always been assumed that the order and the order lines belong to the same business component. This is a direct consequence of the application of the various rules illustrated in the section "Identification Strategies." For example, order lines are not independent, nor do we ever expect, in a COTS component market, that anyone would wish to buy an order line component.

Price and Item

The section "Trading Partners" showed an example of very similar concepts and some of the associated modeling trade-offs. This section illustrates how modeling decisions are affected when concepts are related but not similar. Again we use an example taken from the supply chain management sector, this time the concept of "item" and the related but quite different concept of "price" (price of an item). Should these be in the same business component, or should they be in different ones? The thinking involved in deciding this question is a good example of a modeling decision that, although context-dependent, arises not infrequently.

To make sense of this example, it is necessary to clarify that the software artifacts related to an item price can be quite complicated. In order to calculate the price of an item in a nontrivial information system, the system requires information that can, for example, cover the definition of a base price (a set of rules that are item- or customer-specific), the definition of discounts or increases on the base price, a set of cost rules, various types of price depending on seasonal aspects, specific promotions (such as "two for one"), and so forth.

In many systems, the features corresponding to *Item* can be used quite independently from pricing considerations, and they are certainly complex enough to warrant a place of their own. The various activities surrounding the definition of an item and of the price for that particular item are usually done by different actors in the system, and they are also done at different times. The two concepts are used by different components in the system: For example, while *Item* is one of the most accessed components in the system, *Price* is usually accessed only when issuing an order. By applying the rules in the section "Identification Strategies," it can be decided that the two concepts should belong to different components.

In addition, it may even be necessary to distinguish between a *Price* business component and a *Pricing* business component. *Price* could contain the data required to calculate a price for an item and also perhaps the business rules directly related to that data. A *Pricing* business component could contain the business rules and the processing logic required to calculate the various prices, which could depend on quantity, discounts, promotions, and a number of other considerations.

Hence, given the overall objective of reducing dependencies in the system, facilitating the development of quasi-autonomous components, and reducing the impact of future modifications, a good solution may be as follows:

- First, applying the actor and temporal cohesion principles, to separate *Price* from *Item*. This leads to a significant simplification of the dependencies in the system.

- Second, again applying the actor and temporal cohesion principles, as well as the process/entity separation principle, to separate *Price* from *Pricing*. This further simplifies dependencies within the system. Indeed, most components only need to read a price, rather than calculate it. The few components that need to calculate it are usually very high in the functional hierarchy. This separation enables a *Price* component, able to manage and provide *Price* information, to be relatively low in the DAG, while the *Pricing* process component is higher.

Utility Business Components

In Chapter 5 we introduced the concept of utility business components. This section presents two brief examples of this functional category: the *AddressBook*, to illustrate the concept of *weak components*, and the *ZipCodeBook*, to show a simple example of a very autonomous component.

Address Book

Each business system must deal with addresses. On the surface, an address seems quite straightforward to design and implement. However, addresses are becoming a relatively complicated part of each system. Today, every person usually has multiple telephone numbers, multiple location addresses, multiple e-mail addresses, temporary addresses, Web addresses (URLs), and so forth.

All of this could be managed through a BC-level framework, including a set of language classes, design specification, and tables. Each component needing to deal with addresses could relatively easily instantiate this framework in the component and add the corresponding tables or columns to the database. On the other hand, this would prevent a single point of address management within the system and would make maintenance more difficult. This is because every time some address-related function needs to be modified, there would be many places in which this modification would need to be applied, and hence also multiple components that would need to be retested and reshipped.

Can all addresses be managed by a single component—say an *AddressBook* component? Yes, this is possible, but a certain way of thinking about the autonomy of such a component is required. Addresses are a typical example of a weak entity, meaning an entity that is used only in association with another entity—for example, a customer's address or the address of a warehouse.

There are two main ways to think about an address book: normalized and denormalized.

When *normalized*, only the address is stored in the address book, and not the information about the address's owner. In this style, each address is a complete address, less the information about its owner. The primary key of the address is a nonbusiness-meaningful key, which could be automatically system generated. Any query on an address first of all needs to query the component using the address book. It is always at least a two-step process, as illustrated in Figure 11.16: The *InvoiceManager* cannot directly access the *AddressBook* to look up an address but must request it through the *strong entity* on which the address depends in that context. The associated strong component, such as *Vendor* in Figure 11.16, has a cross-reference table relating each individual vendor to its address. This design also easily allows for a single address to be owned by many actors.

In this case, the address book is what is called a *weak component*, meaning that it has no meaning or purpose if not used through another component that provides the missing information. A weak component is a component that manages a set of entities that are logically weak—even if the database representation has an independent primary key and hence does not conform to the definition of weak entity in relational database modeling theory. Note that a weak entity does *not* need to be implemented as a weak component.

When *denormalized*, each address in the address book contains information fully identifying the owner of the address. There is redundancy of information between the user component and the address book, which also implies additional complexity in maintaining data integrity over time, and more risk of breaking the DAG (see Chapter 9) between components if particular care is not applied.

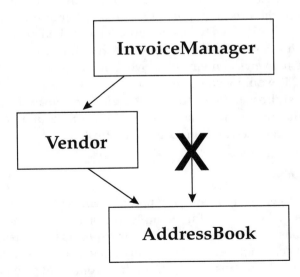

Figure 11.16 Two-step address look-up.

In both cases, the advantages of defining an address book as an autonomous component are that it provides a single fully functioning component that has a single point of maintenance rather than many, there is a centralized place that manages all the addresses in the system, and a single address can be applied to different actors. This is both powerful and cost-effective. The main disadvantages are the initial cost of development and some performance penalty.

How is it possible to model an address book in such a way that a single component can manage all kinds of addresses, provide proper management of relationships with the other entities, manage the integrity of the database, and still satisfy the various extra-functional requirements? It might appear, especially in the denormalized case, as if the address book component would need to know a great deal about components above it and so would appear to break the DAG, rather that be positioned toward the bottom of a business component system model as we have always shown it. Indeed, it would seem that there is a contradicting requirement: This component would need to be low in the DAG because it is used by so many other components, and yet it needs to be high because it appears to need to know about many concepts, for example, customers, vendors, and warehouses, among others.

This is a dependency pattern that happens relatively often. A component that would naturally be positioned low in the DAG appears to need to know about concepts, usually individual fields, belonging to components above. In the previous denormalized case, the *AddressBook* may need to store the information that an address is for a specific entity type, for example, to satisfy queries such as "What are the addresses of customers in Chicago?" The following principle helps minimize dependencies: It is useful to reassign ownership of some business data types to the *Base* component (or to another appropriate component usually low in the DAG). This business data type can then be used by any other component, in this case the *AddressBook*. Information stored in an instance of this data type will always come from above. For example, when *Customer* creates an address, it would also provide a piece of data encoded with the information that the address belongs to a customer. The *AddressBook* would know nothing about this data other than it is a token for a certain type. In this way, dependencies are reduced and the DAG is not broken.

Zip Code Book

ZipCodeBook is a very simple component that deals with zip codes. A single zip code is simply a piece of data; for example, the string or integer "60202" is the zip code for Evanston, Illinois, USA, and corresponds to a business data type. This component features responses to queries such as "to which city does this zip code correspond?" or (in the u-tier) "fill in automatically city and state once the zip code is entered."

This component has enough "autonomous" characteristics to be usefully separated out from *AddressBook* or any other component. An address will, of course, still have zip codes in it, meaning a zip code attribute for each address, but it does not need to contain all the logic to deliver the above function. Such a component is of sufficient general interest and has enough particular functional characteristics to become an autonomously built business component, potentially with its own prepopulated database or file. It can be designed, implemented, tested, and deployed fully autonomously, and once built it can easily be instantiated in multiple contexts and in multiple locations even within the same system. Given the particular nature of its data, which very rarely changes after installation, it can be deployed with its data at install time. Wouldn't it be nice if all components were of this kind?

Summary

Modeling a business is one of the most complex activities in building an information system. The business component approach helps master this complexity through its approach to partitioning and its focus on units of stability. An analysis of the main modeling constructs—business entities, business processes, business rules, and business events—shows that the ones that map directly to components and/or interfaces have high stability characteristics.

A functional reference model can be expressed, at various levels of detail, in terms of system-level components and business components. This helps bridge the functional description of an industry sector to a high-level breakdown into software artifacts. When modeling a federation, especially in the common case of different companies building the different systems, pragmatic rules often replace good architectural principles: For example, replication of functionality, to be avoided when architecting a single system, is often unavoidable in a federation and can help different companies to evolve their systems autonomously.

A given problem space can be partitioned in two ways: chunking and layering. Chunking is the partitioning of the problem space, such as order fulfillment, into a relatively small number of parts that represent the main business processes of the information system. These parts can, if desired, each correspond to a system-level component. Layering is the partitioning of the problem space into a set of open functional layers. The processes identified through chunking rely on these layers to accomplish their functionality.

When partitioning a system, the right partition is a matter of applying the best compromise between current and future development costs, performance and scalability, solution flexibility, and other similar constraints. Component-based partitioning gives a partitioning strategy that not only equals the power of other strategies but also maps directly to development strategies and hence architectures and technologies and provides extra resilience to change in requirements through its process-driven structuring and its functional layering.

A functional layer can be further partitioned into a number of functional subcategories. A categorization that has proven useful in several domains identifies two utility subcategories—support utilities and books; four entity subcategories—materials, concepts, trading partners, and contracts—and two process subcategories support process managers and business process managers.

There is a set of heuristics supporting the identification of business components of appropriate granularity, the main one being that the business concepts reified into business components must be real and independent in the business domain. Also, a business component should satisfy market demand (where the demand is possibly internal to the organization), should be highly usable and reusable, should support autonomous development, should satisfy one or more cohesion principles (temporal, functional, run-time, and actor), and should also correspond to a unit of stability.

As a way to master complexity, the component-based approach is useful in partitioning the business space, including modeling of the business processes, regardless of the implementation approach. Modeling and implementation perfection, as it were, will be attained when all the ancillary technologies, including workflow-related technologies and rule-based related technologies, are seamlessly integrated into a component-based approach and when the application developer will be able to use any of these technologies to model, design, and implement an information system that is component-based from requirements to delivery and evolution. The most scalable and resilient solutions today require components to be thought of and modeled as finite state machines.

A BC-level collaboration pattern is a collaboration pattern totally contained within a business component. It is often described by a set of collaborating deliverables, including data models, DC-internal object models, interfaces specifications, and user interfaces. This collaboration pattern can be implemented by a BC-level framework. Business components belonging to the functional subcategory of trading partners are a good example of components for which it can be better to use a single component than a BC-level framework instantiated in multiple components. Business components belonging to the functional subcategory of contracts are a good example of components for which the most cost-effective implementation is obtained through a BC-level collaboration pattern or even framework.

An *AddressBook* utility component is an example of a component implementing a weak entity, either as a weak component or as a denormalized business component. A weak component is one that is generally used in combination with other components. A *ZipCodeBook* is a good example of a component that can be a wholly autonomous component.

Endnotes

1   For more information about organizing the business around the business processes, see [Hammer 1993]. For an overview of how to represent the business processes of an organization, see [Allen 1998].

2   See also the work of Eric Aranow [1998].

3   In the section "Components as Finite State Machines" a definition of these concepts in terms of state and changes to state is introduced.

Component-Based Design

The internal design of a distributed component was discussed in Chapter 3, "The Distributed Component." This chapter addresses external component design in the context of inter-component collaborations, whether inter-tier within a business component or between business components themselves.

To a large extent, this chapter complements the concepts and principles set forth in Chapter 9, "Application Architecture," and is set in the same development context, that is, large systems with high performance and scalability requirements and providing concurrent access to databases. Design principles are to some extent context-dependent, and those appropriate for large-scale systems may be relaxed for smaller systems having less stringent scalability and performance. For example, the traditional two-tier approach (see [Orfali 1999]) may permit fast development of a small application but may also have difficulty scaling. A distributed system that is not strongly designed for run-time scalability is practically guaranteed not to scale.

The chapter is organized in the following sections:

Mindset for large component-based systems. Discusses the particular mindset required for scalability and performance, together with some of the principles for designing large component-based distributed systems.

Interfaces. Illustrates the characteristics and cross-system standards required to build components that are easily usable.

Business component. Presents design principles and considerations for the internals of a business component.

Persistence. Analyzes the persistence aspects required by enterprise-level components.

Mindset for Large Component-Based Systems

Cost-effective construction of a component-based distributed system that will scale and perform requires a combination of technology, architecture, development process, and more. No single principle will enable this objective to be achieved; rather it is a question of a whole approach to business system development and of a particular mindset. In this chapter, we will refer to this simply as "the mindset." While most of the chapter is dedicated to this mindset, it might be useful to start by illustrating some of its important characteristics, that is, those that directly address distributed system realities, granularity, component autonomy, and scalability priorities.

Distributed System Realities

The design of a scalable distributed system must take into account the constraints that arise from the fact that the system is distributed. Design decisions are affected by the fact that a system is distributed. For example, designing an interface knowing that it is to be used only within a single address space is not the same as designing it for access over the Internet, an intranet, or even between address spaces on the same machine. And the problem goes beyond interface design, given the number of variables that can influence the scalability and performance of the system, and given that the particular shape of an interface implies and is to a noticeable degree influenced by the overall design approach.

There are two particularly important aspects of the mindset, deriving from the realities of distribution. First, it is important to consider how information is communicated between components and how components are referenced. Second, it is important to minimize the number of invocations across a network.

Components exchange information by value. The components themselves are never "passed," but rather, when required, a way to reach them—a reference—is passed. Traditional programming languages present the concepts of pass-by-value and pass-by-reference, as do component implementation technologies. For example, many object-oriented patterns and practices strongly suggest that references to object instances should be provided as operation parameters. This enables a requester to gain access to an object provided by a target object and then operate on it directly. In the business component approach, we prefer to think in a subtly different way: Given the strict encapsulation desired by the mindset, and the autonomy desired for the components, any information exchanged among components is always passed by value, and the only things that should be addressable through a reference are the components themselves.

One way of expressing this would be that data is always passed by value and components are always passed by reference. Even if literally correct, however, the mindset suggests that components should not be thought of as being "passed" because this may have connotations of the whole component instance being somehow moved from one place to another. Rather components are thought of as never being moved. When invoking a component instance, a reference to it may be obtained, and in certain circumstances it may be necessary to pass this reference (which is, of course, a value) to other components.

This subtle but strict distinction encourages a mindset in which components are large, rather clumsy "things" that are in a specific logical location and don't really move, and information is light and agile—a piece of data that can easily be shipped around over the world. Of course, there are a few gray areas (for example, mobile agents), but the mindset described is useful as a guideline in designing scalable systems.

Minimizing network access. If a target component is located in a space remote from a subject component, a request to the target component would be across the network. Many object-oriented patterns assume that all objects are local. In a distributed system, they often are not, and this must be taken into account. Because remote access is much slower than access within the same address space, techniques to reduce the frequency and size of the network access must be built into the specification of the system.

In particular, accepted object-oriented patterns should be checked to ensure that they do not imply unnecessary network accesses. For example, one particular pattern concerns the use of iterators. Suppose, in an object-oriented application, an object *Foo* contains a collection of *Bar* objects. Following good encapsulation principles, only *Foo* should know how to iterate over this collection. A common pattern to allow other objects to iterate over *Bar* objects is for *Foo* to provide an interface allowing any other object to retrieve an iterator. Within the same program, this is a highly useful pattern because it avoids other objects having to include their own *Bar*-specific iterator in their implementations. Used across a network, however, this design can cause huge overhead and can seriously harm performance.

Assuming *Foo* to be a distributed component, the iterator example is best handled by *Foo* providing interface operations that allow iteration to be done inside *Foo*. For example, suppose a common requirement is to find the *Bar* objects with the highest values of some data value owned by *Bar*. An interface operation that *Foo* might provide could look like this:

```
get_best_bars(in number_of_bars, out bar_data_list);
```

A requester would then invoke *get_best_bars(...)* and would receive a small collection of business data types representing the desired set of *Bar* objects—all with one network interaction. These business data types would be internalized into some business language class within the requesting component.

This approach is not only dictated by performance. If network performance were equal to in-process performance, then it would still be good design because it reduces dependencies between components.

Component Granularity

The design must take in account the particular level of component granularity being designed. The detail design is different according to the levels of component granularity. For example, there is a difference between the best rules for SLC-to-SLC communication and those for EDC-to-EDC communication. At the SLC level, no assumption can be made about whether entities share the same architecture. One implication is that primary keys in interfaces must be business meaningful: It is highly unlikely that the different SLCs will agree on a federation-wide usage of, for example, a database-generated primary key. On the other hand, at the EDC level, system-generated primary keys can be used in interface because the system, built according to a well-known architecture, would know how to resolve them.

Another example: in SLC interfaces, nesting of business data types can be useful in reducing complexity. As will be seen in the section "Interfaces," within a single system complexity is sometimes better addressed with lower levels of business data type nesting.

A further difference between the interface of an SLC and that of an EDC is that the SLCs must follow the requirements of the market, and usually SLCs (or if not a true SLC, then a component-wrapped legacy system) are built by different vendors following different internal architectures. This leads to generic interfaces that assume loose connections between components and sometimes to the provision of different kinds of interfaces for the same functionality. On the other hand, an EDC is typically built for a specific architecture and can hence be much more optimized in terms of what is actually delivered.

A consequence is that, because no architectural assumption can be made about the callers in a communication between systems, an SLC interface is often provided by an adapter. On the other hand, and still respecting the logical separation between interface and implementation, the designer of a distributed component's interface has to take strict account of the application architecture and design underlying the system's implementation. Put another way, and as illustrated in Figure 12.1, an SLC interface may give fewer clues about the implementation architecture compared to the interface of, say, an EDC.

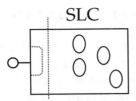
SLC

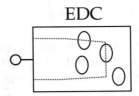
EDC

Strong separation between interface and implementation architecture.
Use of adapter.

Interface relies more on certain predefined architectural view.
It "intrudes" more.

Figure 12.1   Intrusion of SLC and EDC interface.

The design must use discrete recursion. This principle was discussed in the sidebar "Component Granularity and Recursion" in Chapter 2, "The Business Component Approach." It is sometimes argued that components can contain other components that can recursively contain other components and that all these components are of the same kind. This answers none of the questions concerning granularity: what is a good build unit, what is a good deployment unit; what is a good domain-chunking unit. To answer these questions, the business component approach states that granularity is discrete. A system-level component cannot contain other system-level components—although it can contain business components. A business component cannot contain other business components; rather it *cooperates* with other business components. A business component does contain distributed components. Finally, distributed components cannot contain other distributed components but can contain language classes (visible only at build-time). Each level of granularity has specific architectural and design characteristics that need to be taken in account, as illustrated in Part 1 of this book.

Autonomy

The emphasis of component-based design is autonomy. The emphasis of reuse-based design is reuse. This is a subtle but important difference. In a component-based system, even if creating reusable components is very important, the emphasis is on the independent development of "autonomous" components that perform complete functions through minimal interfaces needed to connect the components into a larger information system. This emphasis is due to the principle that autonomy must be explicitly targeted through the development lifecycle in order to be achieved. In a reuse-based system, the emphasis is on design of the shared elements that will be used to build a set of software modules providing the business functions. Not all reuse is about autonomy of the reused parts, and hence designing for reuse does not always imply design for autonomy.

In a component-based system, encapsulation is strictly enforced. Encapsulation must be designed into the component, and each component must be reviewed to make sure it shows as little as possible of its internals. The only way that internal objects, functions, or services may be accessed is through the component's interfaces. From an external point of view, nothing of the component's internals is visible, whatever the external viewer may care to imply from a study of the interfaces.

Scalability Priorities

The main elements influencing the extra-functional characteristics of a distributed system can be prioritized, as shown in Figure 12.2. This figures illustrates how the most important aspect of a scalable system is access to the database, then the client/server interaction, then network access and bandwidth, and then the scalability of e-tier components. These elements are mostly part of the enterprise resource domain.

In addition, there are some well-known general design principles, which include the following:

A transactional system will scale better if it is composed of many small ACID transactions rather than fewer large transactions. The definition of what constitutes a small transaction is very context-dependent, but as a general guideline it is small if it transfers less than 2K bytes over the network and lasts less than a second or so. This simple rule guarantees that the database is locked for only a very short period of time by any single transaction. Less time locked corresponds to more transactional power (see [Eeles 1998, pp. 186-189] for a review of why this is so).

In any system, there are often a few transactions that can potentially generate serious problems, and design resources should be focused on these as a priority. For example, in an order-entry system these are usually the transactions responsible for the individual order line entries, which are not only fairly complex but are also by far the most frequent.

Scalability requirements should be weighted against their development and maintenance costs. There is some level of correspondence between scalability and development effort. The most scalable systems are fat-client systems

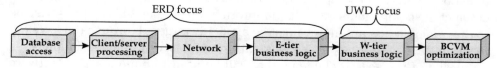

Figure 12.2 Design priorities for performance and scalability.

in which both the client part and the server part (normally containing the UWD and ERD, respectively) are strongly optimized to take advantage of their respective processing power and characteristics. These kinds of systems are also often the most expensive to develop and maintain.

Interfaces

An important long-term asset for a component manufacturing organization, and one of the biggest issues in developing component-based systems, is the definition of component interfaces. For simplicity, we will focus our attention primarily on enterprise distributed component (EDC) interfaces.

This section first illustrates two important characteristics of interfaces (interface independence and multiple interfaces), then analyzes the need for standards and what these standards could be required to cover, and finally discusses two important aspects of interface operations—business data types and tagged data.

Characteristics

The elements required in the specification of an interface depend on the metamodel of the interface itself. The metamodel assumed here is illustrated by the fragment shown in Figure 12.3. Two aspects of this metamodel are particularly important: interface independence and multiple interfaces.

Interface independence. In our examples so far, we have always shown an implicit one-to-one relationship between an interface and a distributed component. This is a useful simplification, but it can also be an unnecessary constraint. As illustrated in Figure 12.3, an interface can exist (for example, at specification time) independently of any attribution to a given component. In addition, a given interface may be implemented by more than one component.

The ability to specify an interface without having to define which component implements it can be useful in certain circumstances. For example, given the iterative nature of development, it may happen that a specific function that will be implemented by some component has been identified, but it has not yet been decided which specific component will provide it. Or a system may provide for an interface to be implemented by several components, leaving the decision as to exactly which component will provide it at run-time to some install-time system configuration.

Figure 12.3   Fragment of interface meta-model.

This ability is particularly useful at the SLC level of component granularity, but less so at the distributed component level. In the business component approach, interfaces are frequently considered to be directly associated with specific components. In general, the following guideline is useful: *Assume as a default that an interface is always owned by one component.* This simplifies the architectural model, particularly at the beginning of an organizational transition to a component-based approach.

Multiple interfaces. Most component models today allow for the specification of multiple interfaces for each distributed component, as indicated in Figure 12.3. Indeed, an industrial-level component can have a large number of operations, and these need to be organized to master the complexity. Different users of the component usually require only a few of these operations, normally grouped by subject. For example, most users of a currency book will access the interface only for exchange rate calculation, and few would use the interfaces for adding a new currency to the system. Multiple interfaces help to better partition the function of a particular distributed component and also to reduce the logical interfacing surface area.

The functional designer of a component will experience added effort in identifying the appropriate set of interfaces, specifying a name for each and defining the collection of operations owned by each. This is not particularly significant in a small project, but in larger projects many interface changes are due to simple adjustments in the ownership of operations by interfaces and in the proper choice of interface partitioning. Many changes in a component's interfaces impact other components and result in instability. Due to this, it may be advisable, at the beginning of an organizational transition to a component-based approach, to assume that each component has only one interface.

The added complexity that arises from multiple interfaces also appears at the functional developer's level. With one interface per component, the developer has only two concepts: components and operations. Code of the following kind would be seen in functional logic that invokes, for example, both the *exchange* and *add_currency* operations of a *CurrencyBook* component:

```
ieCurrencyBook the_currency_book;      // define component interface
the_currency_book.exchange(...);       // invoke an operation
the_currency_book.add_currency(...);   // invoke another.
```

In the case of multiple interfaces, the functional developer must be aware of all three concepts—component, interface, and operation. Although code will be similar, in the developer's mind there is a little more to be understood. The preceding example would need to be subtly altered as follows:

```
ieCurrencyExchange    currency_book;   // define an interface
ieCurrencyMaintenance currency_book2;  // define another
currency_book.exchange(...);           // invoke an operation
currency_book2.add_currency(...);      // invoke another
```

Standardizing Components

Traditionally, the main objective of good design has been to cost-effectively build a given system satisfying its functional and extra-functional requirements. Two additional objectives for component-based development are to make it simple to develop components themselves (the subject of much of this book) and to make life simpler for the developer who uses components. This last objective requires the provision of easy-to-understand and well-specified interfaces corresponding to a clean and scalable architectural model. Achieving this, in turn, requires consistency across interfaces—which requires standards.

Distributed components and business components, and to a lesser extent system-level components, require and are a part of a more general architecture. As illustrated in Figure 12.4, they not only provide a set of interfaces, but they also plug into a specific socket, where by socket we mean a specific set of protocols and conventions. It is hence important to define exactly, both for a successful plug and for a successful collaboration between components, how a component should be formed and how it should behave. In other words, it is important to define precisely what a *well-formed* and a *well-behaved* component is.

A well-formed component can be plugged into the system without crashing the system, while a well-behaved component, once plugged in, does something useful and behaves in a predictable manner when collaborating with other components in a system. In other words, a business component can be well formed without reference to other business components, and well-formedness can be assessed through inspection. A mature development environment should be able to automatically validate if a business component is well formed, and even automatically generate artifacts in conformance with the standards required for well-formedness. On the other hand, a component is well behaved in relationship to other components and to the BCVM it requires. Consequently, it is very difficult to state that it is well behaved without examining its collaboration with other business components, and nearly impossible to verify whether a business component is well behaved without actually testing the component and its collaboration with other components.

Well-Formed

The term "well-formed business component" indicates a business component that follows the constraints on its form or appearance that are defined by the socket (the BCVM) and the application architecture. A well-formed component can be plugged into the system without crashing. To enable this requires an exact definition of the various protocols with which the business component must conform at run-time. This definition would cover aspects such as standard categories of interfaces, including those expected on each component by the

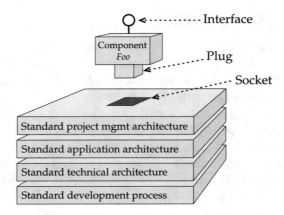

Figure 12.4 Socket, plug, and interface.

architecture and by the socket, standard naming conventions, and standard interface design patterns.

Categories of Interface

Generally speaking, each business component will require several of the categories of interface, which include the following:

Business entity lifecycle. These are interfaces supporting the management of business entities within a component. A business entity (see Chapter 11, "Component-Based Business Modeling,") is usually implemented by one or more business language classes. For example, a business entity managed by the *Order* business component could be an order line, an order header, or, of course, an entire order. Business entity lifecycle interfaces are also referred to as CRUD interfaces (where CRUD stands for "create, read, update, delete") and can include related interfaces such as a check for existence. Examples of business entity lifecycle interfaces for EDCs include the following:

create<name of entity>, such as *create_currency*, with the expected consequence that a new entity of the *currency* type is created in a persistent form (that is, on the database).

read<name of entity>, such as *read_currency*, with the expected consequence that an entity of the *currency* type is read from the database and returned to the caller.

update <name of entity>, such as *update_currency*, with the expected consequence that an existing entity of the *currency* type is updated on the database.

delete<name of entity>, such as *delete_currency*, with the expected consequence that the specified entity of the *currency* type is deleted from the database.

exist_<name of entity>, such as *exist_currency*, an operation that would verify if a given currency exists in the system.

A business component can manage more than one business entity, and a set of CRUD operations is usually required for each business entity managed by a component. For example, an *eOrder* EDC may have CRUD interfaces for the order header and the order line.

Collection management. These are the interfaces that manage sets of instances of the business entities managed by that particular component.

Functional interfaces. These are the interfaces that provide for specific processing in a component. An example of a functional interface on a currency book component could be the calculation of an exchange rate.

The preceding three categories are the typical output of the functional interface specification. The following are interfaces that may be required by the factory setup:

Component lifecycle. These include activation and deactivation of the component (see Chapter 8, "Technical Architecture"). Default implementation of these interfaces may be automatically provided by the BCVM. When creating a distributed component there may be a certain set of actions required by the component framework or by system function. These operations are at the distributed component level: They do not operate on the business language classes and concepts managed by the component, but rather work on the component itself. The component lifecycle deals with such things as how a distributed component is instantiated and how it is loaded into memory (activated) when needed. The business entity lifecycle, on the other hand, is concerned with aspects such as the persistence of the managed business entities (on a relational database).

Socket operations. These are interfaces that the BCVM may require by each component, mostly to deal with its services and facilities. These can include security, error handling, help (for UWD components), licensing, transactions, logging, audit trail, event registration, and so forth. Depending on the socket, and hence on the particular architectural model adopted, some of these may be part of other interfaces; for example, error handling may require only an additional error data type in each operation signature, as opposed to specific error handling interfaces.

Configurability. These interfaces are explicitly dedicated to support the configurability of the component, often through modification of configurability parameters. For example, the component may provide an interface that has the single objective of allowing a user to decide between sets of domain-specific business rules, such as adapting a tax component to a set of predefined tax rules for a specific country.

Introspection. These are interfaces that can be used to interrogate the component about its own behavior or state or to provide information about any meta-data held by the component. This may permit the user to dynamically discover which interfaces are available on the distributed component or to discover specific conditions in the component itself. For example, for performance tuning, it may be useful to be able to query the component itself about how many times a certain operation is invoked in a certain scenario.

Dispatch. Where a component supports scripting, it should provide a standard "dispatch" (or "execute") interface that, for example, could be of the form:

```
dispatch(in  string     operation,
         in  TaggedData in_parameters,
         out TaggedData out_parameters);
```

A client component invokes *dispatch*, providing the name of the real operation to be invoked in *operation* and the input parameters for that operation in tagged data format (*in_parameters*). Information returned by the real operation is placed in *out_parameters*, also in tagged data format. The implementation for the *dispatch* operation can be handled within the DC's separation layer, and it will typically construct a call to itself to invoke the real operation required. It is important that all components that provide a scripting interface should conform with the same standard dispatch-style interface.

The larger the number of interfaces required as a standard by the BCVM, the less sense it would make to have small granularity components because the overhead alone may prove not to be cost-effective—one more argument in favor of components of coarse granularity.

Naming Conventions

Many developers dislike naming conventions with varying degrees of intensity. Their absence, however, usually causes a great deal of grief and pain on large projects. Naming conventions include aspects such as interface style standards (such as the ones used in this book [OMG 1998b]), as well as conventions for business data types, standard abbreviations, and standard words for certain concepts (such as the choice between "CurrencyFactory," "CurrencyManager," or "CurrencyController"), the CRUD methods, and many others.

Interface Design Patterns

Consistent behavior across a set of components requires the definition of system-wide interface design patterns. Indeed, there are various typical situations that the designer may face and that could benefit from standardization. For example, where a set of component operations that provide the same functional feature have different parameters depending on precisely which kind of business entity is being operated on, then a single way of handling this should be defined. An example of design alternatives in this situation can be found in interfaces associated with exchange rate operations. An exchange rate may be of several kinds—a spot rate (say, at 09:00 EST), a contracted rate, a rate that depends on the amount to be exchanged, and so forth. Interfaces on a currency book component that use exchange rates may require different parameters depending on the kind of exchange rate. For example, if the exchange rate depends on the amount exchanged, then an amount needs to be provided, but if it is a contracted rate, then the contract number would be required. A functional designer addressing such interfaces should have guidance on which of various alternatives should be used. Such alternatives include the following:

- One operation for each kind of exchange rate, where the parameters depend on the kind of exchange rate. The different combinations of "kinds" will lead to a high number of operations but will allow each function to be performed with one invocation of a stateless server. For example, the following could be the operation for a contract-based exchange.

```
exchange(in  Money      money_from,
         in  CurrencyId currency_id,
         in  string     contract_id,
         out Money       money_to);
```

In this example, *money_from* is the amount and currency to be exchanged, *currency_id* is the target currency, *money_to* contains the resulting amount, and *contract_id* identifies a specific contract defining conditions for the exchange. Another kind of exchange that did not require a contract but perhaps requires a time for a spot rate would mean a different operation signature.

- A group of operations where a single given attribute is set by a specific operation. The requester would invoke the appropriate number of attribute-setting operations and then would invoke the operation involving the exchange rate. This approach keeps the number of operations linear with respect to the growth in the number of parameters affecting the exchange rate, but also gives a linear increase of the number of operations to be called for a single transaction and makes the target component stateful. For example, the previous interface could be delivered by two operations, such as:

```
set_contract (in  string contract_id);
exchange(in  Money      money_from,
         in  CurrencyId currency_id,
         out Money       money_to);
```

This kind of thinking is typical of some object-oriented approaches, but it is seldom if ever appropriate for an enterprise-level component-based approach, in which operations should be at the transaction level and each operation should carry out an action with a specific business meaning.

■ A tagged data string as the operation parameter. This reduces the number of currency exchange operations on the component to one because the functional parameters to be used are all within the tagged data string. A simple programming interface could be provided by which the functional designer could parse simple tagged data strings. This case would lead to an interface such as:

```
exchange(in TaggedData input, out TaggedData output);
```

■ A mix of a tagged data parameter and strongly typed parameters. This approach could use tagged data only for the variable parameters and would keep the number of operations to a minimum (possibly one in our example), while still providing some form of flexibility. For example:

```
exchange(in  Money      money_from,
         in  CurrencyId currency_id,
         out Money      money_to,
         in  TaggedData variable_parameters);
```

Whatever approach is chosen, a system-wide and/or project-specific strategy should be defined for how interfaces with variable data should be designed, and a well-formed component should conform to this strategy.

Well-Behaved

A *well-behaved component* is a well-formed component that behaves as expected by the architecture it is plugged into. Requirements for well-behavedness include that the interfaces expected on each component behave predictably, consistently, and with well-known semantics common across the whole information system. This can be achieved through the standardization of the design of the categories of interface presented in the previous section. Indeed, for each category of interface defined in a well-formed component, and often for each specific category of operation within each interface, it is possible to define, within a certain architecture, the generic behavior and the semantics of the interface. For example, a project-wide standard could define the semantics for a generic *delete* operation. This could include the definition of the errors the operation can generate and the exact definition of the state in which the database is left, for example, whether it is a hard delete or a soft delete. Any instance of this operation, such as *delete_item* for the *Item* component or *delete_vendor* for the *Vendor* component, would conform to this definition.

Business Data Types

Chapter 3 introduced the business data type concept, as well as an initial set of related characteristics and design rules. This section analyzes the business data type from the wider perspective of business component interfaces. This is important because business data types are the primary carriers of business information throughout a system. Figure 12.5 illustrates the route taken by business data types through the tiers of a business component from the database to the user interface.

For example, let's assume that an end user asks to see something such as details for a specific vendor. If the required data is not cached in one of the tiers, then the request is effectively passed through the tiers until it reaches the r-tier, where data in a row in a table is read into some format within the r-tier. From there it is returned to the EDC, in which the data will appear as a persistence language class, often with some kind of transformation. This persistence language class, or some transformation thereof, is usually used in some business rule before being transferred into a business data type. In some implementations, the persistence language class may *be* the business data type itself. This business data type is then returned to a w-tier, where it may go through some additional transformation and processing. It is then returned to the u-tier and finally displayed on the user interface.

Because real-world entities are quite complex, a business data type may well have more than 100 attributes. If each transformation made during the data's journey though the system were to be done through manual programming, then the development process would be extremely error-prone. This is because it is so simple to misspell a single attribute when dealing with hundreds of them or to assign wrongly during the transformation. Furthermore, errors at this level can be very difficult to identify. Hence much of this process should be automated through precise tool-enforced rules and code generation, but this cannot be done without design.

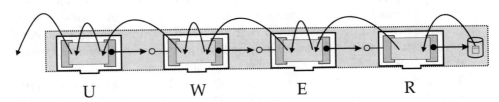

Figure 12.5   Data from database to user interface.

When designing business data types for an EDC's interface, we apply a set of design guidelines. These have evolved over some years of practice and making errors and, although subjective, should provide at least a useful illustration of the main kinds of design considerations. They are as follows:

Primary key inclusion. The business data type should include the primary key for the business concept it represents. This, of course, does not apply to business data types representing weak entities such as volume or date, but rather applies to those representing concepts such as order, item, customer, and so forth. For example, assuming that the contact name is the primary key, a simplified address business data type could be defined as follows:

```
BusinessDataType btAddress
{
    string contact_name;
    string address_text;
    string city;
    string zip_code;
    string country;
};
```

The primary key may be duplicated as a separate parameter in an operation signature. For example:

```
read_address( in string contact_name,
             out btAddress an_address);
```

This form of interface provides for consistency and readability, and also for an associated simplification in the coding of both the operation invocation and the operation implementation. It is arguably preferable to the following:

```
read_address (inout btAddress an_address);
```

where *an_address* contains the *contact_name* data when considered an *in* parameter.

Consistency with database. Business data types should conceptually match the structure of a well-designed database. This rule should lead to a clean, normalized, and easier-to-master business data types system because presumably the database will have been normalized and will have been designed to reflect the actual needs of the business. Consistency with the database will also promote least astonishment and global consistency, The rule implies that, at least as a default, a business data type should not include data from more than one table. This, however, should not be taken to the extent of directly tying business data type definitions to the database schema.

Nesting minimization. Nesting of business data types is discouraged. By nesting is meant the ability to define one business data type in terms of others—that is, to have a business data type contain another business data type. Use of lists of business data types, such as lists of order lines, is not considered nesting. An example of nesting would be the following:

```
BusinessDataType btVendor
{
   string     vendor_id;
   string     name;
   btAddress vendor_address;
   . . .
};
```

In this example, the business data type *btAddress* (defined previously) is part of the definition of the vendor business data type *btVendor*. This is a typical example of something that may seem a good idea when analyzed in isolation, but it has disadvantages when looked at in the wider system context. At first glance, nesting may seem a way of successively applying higher and higher abstraction levels. That is, a concept *btAddress* is defined, and it may seem natural to use it when defining other concepts such as *btVendor*. It is in reality, however, more complex to deal with nesting across the whole development due to the end-to-end (screen-to-database) nature of data, especially under the assumption that a relational database is used on the backend. Unless directly supported by code generation, the manual implementation of mapping into nested structures and subsequent reading from nested structures can defeat the benefits of nesting.

A preferable alternative to nesting is to have separate parameters, as shown in the following sample interface specification fragment:

```
update_vendor (in string            vendor_id,
               in btVendorInformation vendor_information,
               in btAddress          vendor_address);
```

where *vendor_address* is a separate parameter rather than being contained (nested) in *vendor_information*.

Nesting is, of course, necessary for base data types such as integer, string, or BCVM-defined data types such as Date or Time. Also, nesting may be allowed more readily where the BCVM knows how to manage business data types end-to-end, including, for example, generating the code required to map a nested business data type into the database and how to marshall/demarshall nested business data types to tagged data format where required. This effectively would require that frequently used data types should be added, by technical developers, to the BCVM and delivered as part of it. The nesting guideline is applied more strictly when dealing with multiple components: Business data types that contain data from more than one component should never be nested, and combining data from different business components into one business data type should be avoided. Indeed, just as each business component should correspond to a separate business concept, so in general a business data type should represent one single concept. Adherence to this guideline avoids controversy over business data type ownership and supports system consistency.

Self-containment. Business data types should be totally self-contained. They should not invoke any method of any other class, nor operations of other components.

System-wide consistency. System-wide conventions and semantics for given business concepts, and identification of specific instances of business concepts should be defined. For example, a system-wide convention could be adopted whereby currencies are identified by a string mnemonic (the value "USD" for US Dollar, "LIT" for Italian Lire, and so forth). This noticeably simplifies the definition of interfaces across an entire system. If not assumed system-wide, then all interfaces dealing with currencies must deal with several different approaches to currency identification, ending up duplicating interfaces to allow for multiple ways of data identification. This principle applies to all cases where there is more than one way to identify a business concept instance in the database and in the system. Another example is where a specific person can be identified through both a system-generated ID and his or her own social security number. Component interfaces are simplified if it is known across the system that only one of these means of identification is used.

Boundary values. Handling of boundary values must be defined for each base and business data type. Examples of boundary values are Null (the value has been set and it is no value), Unknown (don't know—a value has never been assigned), Indefinite (no upper or lower bound), and Range (maximum and minimum values).

Tagged Data

The flexibility and interface resilience provided by tagged data (introduced in Chapter 6, "The Federation of System-Level Components") are so far unbeaten by any other technology. Use of this technology in interfaces presents challenges that require careful treatment. When using tagged data, a large part of the interaction between two components relies on their sharing the same tag. Hence the mindset needs to switch from thinking in terms of types to thinking in terms of tags or, as expressed in Chapter 6, from thinking in terms of *strongly typed* interfaces to thinking in terms of *strongly tagged* interfaces.

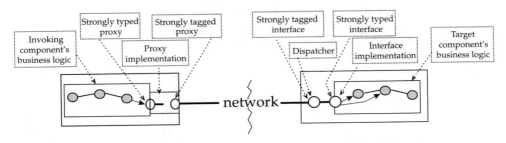

Figure 12.6   Strongly tagged and strongly typed interfaces.

Chapter 6 presented the case for having two levels of interface. The "level-1" style allows for direct manipulation of tagged data, and it may not be appropriate for functional developers, partly because parsing tagged data can be a complex programming task. The "level-2" style provides a mapping from tagged data to the typed interfaces in the DC's separation layer, so providing the familiarity of typed interfaces for functional developers. In many cases, there are clear advantages in providing both a strongly typed and a strongly tagged interface. A typical structure to enable this is illustrated in Figure 12.6. The functional developer of the subject component on the left interacts with a proxy that presents a strongly typed interface, hiding tagged data. The target component on the right provides both a strongly typed and a strongly tagged interface. The dispatcher and the interface implementation hide the details from the target component's functional developer, who has to worry only about the implementation of strongly typed interfaces.

When appropriate tools are used to generate the separation layer, then the effective functional developer's view is as shown in Figure 12.7, where it can be seen that the functional developer is concerned only with strongly typed interfaces.

The fact that the functional developer does not have to deal with marshalling and demarshalling tagged data from and to types does not mean that he or she can ignore tags. Suppose, for example, that a functional developer specifies a strongly typed interface such as:

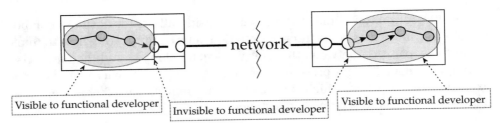

Figure 12.7   The functional developer's point of view.

```
create_order_header (in btOrderHeader order_header);
```

where the parameter is:

```
BusinessDataType btOrderHeader
{
  int    order_number;
  int    customer_number;
  int    pricing_customer;
  string order_company;
  string order_currency;
  real   exchange_rate;
  ~      // many other attributes
};
```

The attributes of this business data type have to be mapped into tags for the level-1 interface, and these tags should be human-readable. It makes a great deal of sense to adopt the convention that tags are generated from the attribute names or vice versa. Without such a convention, each designer must somehow specify his or her own mapping. In either case, he or she may not be allowed to arbitrarily pick the attribute names but rather, given the need for a correspondence between attribute names and tags, would be required to use established system-wide conventions for each business concept. Attribute name consistency is a good design guideline independently of the use of tagged data, but it becomes a strict constraint when using tagged data and requires a data dictionary specifying either the tags, from which, following precise rules, the appropriate attribute names can be defined or both the tags and the attribute names.

The discipline of having to use a data dictionary of tags does not come easy in some organizations. Functional developers who are used to choosing their own names for interface parameters must now work with the tag repository to ensure that the appropriate tag is used. If the appropriate tag is not yet in the repository, the developer must add it, and the whole process must be monitored to avoid tag explosion.

Business Component

This section discusses some of the design considerations for business components. First, it clarifies some inter-tier relationships by illustrating how to think about the separation between the user workspace domain and the enterprise resource domain. Then it presents some design aspects for each tier, with the exclusion of the r-tier, which, because of the importance of persistence, is addressed within the section, "Persistence."

UWD-ERD

Chapter 4, "The Business Component," introduced the concepts of *user work-space domain* (UWD) and *enterprise resource domain* (ERD). This section further expands on related design principles and considerations. The UWD and ERD are logical domains of responsibility, and as such they can be seen as existing in any client/server structure and can even be seen in a stand-alone PC application that manages its own database. The two domains, and the two tiers in each domain, are highly useful design tools that assist significantly in the separation of concerns found in distributed systems. Interestingly, having two tiers in each domain is not a coincidence. At a certain level of abstraction, the UWD and the ERD are structurally mirrors of each other; each has a functional tier (e-tier and w-tier), and each has a "device" tier (the r-tier and the u-tier) responsible for mapping the functional tiers to the extra-functional world of computing systems.

The exact separation between the UWD and ERD responsibilities is an important design decision with development, performance, and scalability consequences. For example, an explicit design objective of the UWD-ERD separation is that the ERD can be built and tested independently from the UWD. Another is that a new UWD that accesses an existing ERD can be built without affecting the ERD.

The UWD-ERD concept is primarily aimed at the functional designer. Remembering that the domains are logical and not physical, Figure 12.8 shows their probable physical mapping in an Internet browser-based solution, while Figure 12.9 shows a traditional fat-client situation, where the UWD is located physically on a PC. In the following discussion, the fat-client case is used to illustrate design principles (which can easily be extended to the Internet browser case). The UWD, shown in Figure 12.9, can be rolled out to many users, in which case there will be a UWD on each user's PC. A UWD may extend over both a PC and a server system, for example, where some UWD persistence must be more secure than the PC can provide.

Requests into a given ERD from sources other than a UWD, such as from another ERD, or from the Internet in an e-commerce environment, can access

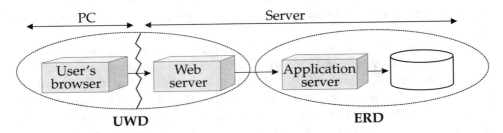

Figure 12.8   UWD-ERD split in a browser-based solution.

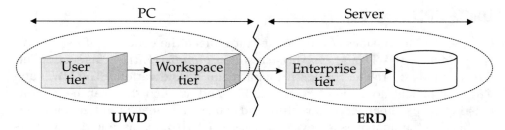

Figure 12.9   UWD-ERD split in a fat-client solution.

that ERD directly. That is, the ERD should be conceptually designed to be the same for any requester—UWD, another ERD, or an external application.

There are several important and general characteristics of the UWD-ERD separation: interactions between tiers, interactions between UWD and ERD, copying data, transactional behavior, and the relationship with the three-tier model.

Interactions between Tiers within the Same Domain

The interactions between the business component tiers within the same domain tend to be strict. For example, the user tier (u-tier) collaborates very strictly with the w-tier; on a fat client it may work with many small, frequent, and short interactions. Similarly, the e-tier may access the r-tier and the database with frequent small interactions.

Of course, the kind of collaboration will depend on the target deployment architecture. For example, the w-tier can be designed as a movable tier, in such a way that it can be deployed either co-located with the u-tier or remote from the u-tier. The best design of the w-tier takes the most probable deployment architecture into account—as long as it is known. If remote location is expected to be prevalent, the design should aim at diminishing the number of u-tier-to-w-tier interactions. If co-location is expected to be prevalent, minimizing interactions is less necessary, and, in addition, technologies that work only within a single machine or address space may profitably be used to implement communication between the tiers.

When physically on the same machine as the u-tier (for example, on a PC), the w-tier may be colocated in the same address space or in a separate address space. While the first solution is viable, it does not make the best use of the resources found on today's PCs. For example, if any one component in the UWD crashes, then it may easily also crash the address space, which means taking down the entire UWD, which, for that particular user, means that the entire system disappears. Although often built this way, a UWD so constrained is not nearly as resilient as one that can make use of several address spaces concurrently. Supporting this is something for the BCVM to address.

Interactions between the UWD and the ERD

The interaction between the UWD and ERD domains tends to be loose. Indeed, the prevalent assumption is that the two domains will not be co-located. Hence design tends to be done in such a way that there are few isolated invocations of the ERD, each one with a precise business meaning. Even if more sparse than the collaboration between the u-tier and the w-tier, the w-tier of a business component still has a well-defined collaboration with its own e-tier, as seen in various collaboration patterns in Chapter 9 and Chapter 11. The w-tier also has privileged visibility of the e-tier's interfaces within the same business component: It is often the only part of the system able to perform all the CRUD operations provided by the e-tier. This is reflected in the fact that, as discussed in Chapter 4, the visibility of operations in an EDC interface can be scoped to its own WDC or to sources external to the business component. In this sense, levels of collaboration can be identified as being strict between u-tier and w-tier, and between e-tier and r-tier; loose but extended between w-tier and e-tier, where the term "extended" refers to the visibility of a broader interface surface area; and loose and reduced between business components.

Copying Data

It is a useful general design rule that when data is copied from one place to another in a system, for example, from the ERD to the UWD, then it should be considered different data. An analogy that applies to copying data from the ERD to the UWD and also to the general case of copying from any DC to another is the *fax analogy*. When a fax of a contract, for example, is sent from one office to another, at the receiving end a totally autonomous entity is obtained: that is, a new sheet of paper representing the original contract. The received fax can be modified by scribbling on it, and these scribbles, if signed, may have legal implications. The received fax can even become the master copy of the contract, as far as the receiver is concerned. Of course, when the contract is sent back over the fax to the original sender, there must be a managed process to decide which copy is now the valid copy. If it is the newly received copy, then the original must be discarded and replaced with the new one. The contract identity (the fact that this is the contract number 151187 between John Smith and the Greener Houses company for building a house) is not affected because this identity is independent of the fact that the contract is copied. Similarly, when a business data type is returned from the ERD to the UWD due to an explicit request of the UWD or sent on an event notification, it becomes a different object. This conforms with traditional pass-by-value semantics. The copied data may even have a different name or a different implementation. Its data is not kept in sync with the original in the ERD, but rather the now-UWD-resident business data type acquires a life of its own.

In particular cases, data in the UWD may be required to be refreshed, either by some event (for example, interest registration or user action) or at intervals (policy-determined). This is the case for data that is passed not for a particular business transaction, but rather for local caching to improve performance. For example, in a supply chain management system for a company that has a very stable and relatively small product line, information about all products could be replicated on all PCs, with substantial performance benefits. Any change to the master data must be replicated into all copies of the data.

Transactional Behavior

For reasons of scalability, the UWD should implement the "transactional" model for requests to the ERD. That is, the user first prepares a set of information (for example, fills in an order form) and then, through an explicit action (such as pressing a "Commit" button), requests the UWD to submit the data as a transaction (request) to the ERD. Requests to the ERD made "behind the scenes" and not initiated by an explicit user action should in general be avoided because without careful (and usually sophisticated) design, they can result in apparently inexplicable delays at the user interface. However, one of the advantages of running the w-tier in a separate address space (or at least in a separate thread) is that the BCVM can provide carefully designed support for requests to be sent concurrently with user interaction, for example, to prefetch data that the user is likely to request and so improve perceived response times.

As discussed in Chapter 9, when the user prepares a set of information, the u-tier and the w-tier collaborate to collect all the relevant information for a particular transaction (see Figure 12.10), and when the business function has reached an appropriate point—the end of some user unit of work—the data is sent to the ERD. More complex user interface scenarios (for example, allocating stock while entering an order) can be treated as a set of separate transaction requests made to the ERD. On receipt by the ERD, each request is an ACID transaction as understood by the underlying resource manager. Unless read-only, the request causes a state change in the ERD from one consistent state to another (ensured by normal good design principles in the ERD.)

The ERD manages all enterprise-level considerations. Any database locking, and the style of such locking, is defined entirely within the ERD (but in such a way that it is transparent to the functional developer). While the UWD concentrates on a single user, the ERD needs to manage all the complexities of concurrent access, including locking, transactions, and security.

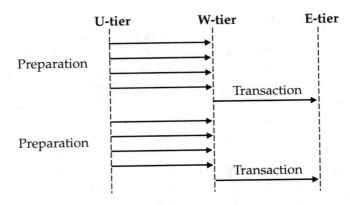

Figure 12.10 UWD coordinates transaction.

Relationship with the Three-Tier Model

The UWD-ERD model and its four tiers are an expansion of the three-tier model specifically developed to handle observed realities of distributed systems. It does not answer all questions, but it does answer all those addressed by the three-tier model, plus some more. The three tiers of the three-tier model are data services (corresponds roughly to the r-tier), business services (corresponds roughly to the e-tier), and application services. The latter is typically seen as an application on a PC. When the PC must support something more than the simplest user model, however, then there may be "business services" to be provided on the PC as well. In that case, there arises the question of where to split—and whether it's business services or application services that should be split. This is in general a crucial question, but the three-tier model provides no ready answer to it—indeed it is the three-tier model itself that generates the question. The four-tier model does, however, answer the question, and the answer is the u-tier/w-tier separation. As a superset of the three-tier model, the four-tier model provides a more useful framework for thinking about typical distributed business systems—although as always, good designers will use it for guidance only, not as something to which they must slavishly adhere. More information can be found in [Eeles 1998] and in [Sims 1994, 1997].

User Interface

This section is not a treatise on user interface modeling, human factors, technology, or programming. Rather it addresses the main user interface requirements as far as the business component approach is concerned.

The user interface is the first contact a user has with the business system, and as such it is an important part of it. If the user interface is poor, frustratingly difficult, and tedious to use, then no matter how good the rest of the system is, it will not deliver its full potential benefit. The better the user interface, the greater the benefit. Building a prototype user interface is simple, and there are a wealth of tools to use. Building a production user interface is more difficult. Building a business component-based user interface that provides for separate pluggability of each business component's u-tier, that can be plugged into a running system with no modification of other components (no re-link, no recompile, no redeployment), that provides for fast evolution at the same time as delivering a choice of user models, and that is simple for the functional developer, all that is another matter entirely. Although it can be done today, it requires investment in the BCVM aspects, as was briefly touched on in Chapter 8.

This section is in five parts. First, the state of today's user interfaces is established. Second, the overall mindset required for user interfaces in the context of distributed system is briefly illustrated, dispelling two prevalent myths in the process. Third, the design of individual user interface components is discussed in the context of the business component approach. Fourth, some of the characteristics of a component-based user interface, from an architectural point of view, are discussed assuming today's mature compiler-based technology, and finally run-time pluggable component-based user interfaces are illustrated, again in the context of business components. The intention in this section is to indicate directions rather than to provide a "how-to-do-it" manual.

User Interfaces Today

Before the advent of graphical user interfaces, it was relatively easy to develop a user interface. They were relatively dumb and were often driven by the application itself. Given the state of user interface technology, expectations in terms of user friendliness were relatively low by today's standards. Nowadays, developing a user interface is an art requiring a mixture of cognitive knowledge and sophisticated technologies. There is also the need to keep up-to-date with the wide array of new technologies that are constantly emerging and a corresponding need to understand which ones are product-strength and which are not.

One interesting recent development is that, with the whole field of computing evolving so quickly, the user often accepts compromises that would have been unacceptable only a few years ago. For example, only four years ago user interfaces were headed toward a standard behavior, with standard, predictable, and sophisticated controls and navigation, and with increasing ease-of use goals driving more technically complex user model implementations. Demands for fast response times were driving increased use of asynchronous operation in the UWD and greater interest in caching strategies, so that trivial user interactions were not blocked by network delays in accessing the ERD. Further, user models were developing that were appropriate both for beginners and power users.

Today, the Internet and the Web have caused this evolution to be put on hold at least. Web-based user interface technology today, although providing access to an incredible array of worldwide information and services, is, from a technical architecture point of view, fairly primitive. The Internet user accepts slow user interfaces as a fact of life because the low performance can always be blamed on the speed of the connection. Many technologies and techniques that made user interfaces more powerful are not yet widely available for browser-based interfaces. For example, how many Web-based user interfaces today allow for drag and drop in the same manner as yesterday's object-based interfaces? Further, user interfaces have tended to standardize on those that satisfy beginners and are in many ways a step backward in terms of usability. The user is in most cases happy to trade off the incredible accessibility of Web interfaces with low performance and relatively low user friendliness.

Mindset

The mindset for designing a good user interface for a distributed system is fundamentally different from that for a stand-alone system. Let us illustrate this by dispelling two myths:

1. *Myth:* It is possible to design a distributed system's user interface such that the user perceives his or her personal computing resource as the entire system—as if it were a stand-alone system. Part of this myth is the notion that the user interface can be designed independently from any transactional considerations. In reality, the user interface must imply a certain transactional model. This can be rephrased as the "Here and There" principle: In a distributed system, the difference between "my" machine (the user's—"here") and other machines (including servers—"there") cannot and should not be hidden. There are some things (data and resources) that are visible only to a given single user, and there are other things (data and resources) that are visible, through a user interface, to other users as well. For example, the data that a user is typing into some entry field is visible only to that user, whereas data in the enterprise's customer database is visible to many users. Hence the UWD must always understand when to talk from "here" (the UWD) to "there" (the ERD). Because ERD interfaces for scalable systems are one-shot and stateless in nature, the UWD is required to present "user units of work" to the user, which is done within the UWD, and when completed are sent to the ERD as a request that initiates a transaction. In this way, the user interface will explicitly present a "transactional" model to the user. Another implication of the here-and-there principle is that there are three possible "commits" or "saves" in more advanced user models: first, saving the status of what has been typed in a window over window close and re-open; second, saving a user unit of work in a partially completed state,

perhaps for the user to continue working on the next day; and third, making the results of the user unit of work visible to other users through a transactional request to the ERD.

2. *Myth:* It is possible to design a user-friendly user interface for a large-scale system simply by reflecting the database structure. This is the approach taken by a number of rapid application development tools, where the developer establishes the database structure and then to a large extent simply generates the user interface. Although it is an excellent approach for small or stand-alone applications, and with low user-friendliness requirements, this approach does not scale to the development context addressed in this book.

Discussion of the preceding two myths reflects perhaps two extreme approaches to the user interface. The first myth sees user interface design as a modeling activity that can be done independently of transactional and enterprise-level considerations: The user interface is designed as a stand-alone system, and the rest of the distributed system is supposed to adapt. The second sees user interface design as a direct reflection (by generation) of the structure of the database. As extremes, both of these approaches will fail in the context of large distributed systems.

The appropriate mindset for user-friendly, cost-effective user interfaces in this context is, of course, a healthy combination of factors. Assuming a well-architected component-based system, with a clean transactional model, the user interface should directly reflect and also influence this model and system partitioning. To some extent, the database model should be reflected in individual screens, but a direct link between the two should not be created. Rather, the user interface and the database should evolve at their own speed and with their own requirements.

User Interface Components

The components discussed in this section are neither business components nor distributed components; rather they are fine-grained GUI-related components. Such components are the first to have developed a component market—the VBX controls of several years ago, in the early and mid 1990s. This section discusses the extent to which such user interface components can be integrated into the business component approach as far as the u-tier is concerned.

Today, a variety of technologies are used to implement user interfaces, from JavaBeans through ActiveX to Web page scripting. Most allow for the development of individual controls as pluggable binary components. By "control" we mean the implementation of user interface artifacts such as a text entry box, list boxes, property sheets, icons, and so forth. Another name often used for this meaning of "control" is "widget." Thus we can define a *user interface component* as any user interface control that can be considered a build-time-pluggable binary with interfaces. Such user interface components range from simple entry fields up to trees and property sheets. An important question is how to fit these controls with the business component concept.

Let us address this question taking a simple entry field pattern as an example: the "id-description" pattern. In business systems, many entities are often identified in the system by a concise key (for example, a customer number or an item number), but for user friendliness they are often displayed along with a textual description on the user interface. For example, in Figure 12.11, the item is displayed with an item number, but also with an item description (and even an extended description in the example illustrated). An intelligent implementation of an entry field for item number would, as soon as the item number is entered, also load and display the associated description.

Because the main entities in the system, such as item information in a supply chain management system, need to appear on multiple screens, and because it is highly desirable not only that they appear consistently but also that their implementation cost is reduced as much as possible, it would be useful to have the ability to implement an entry field and its associated features as per the id-description pattern, once only and then reuse it across the system. In other words, it would be useful to implement the control as a reusable user interface component delivered with everything required to use that component across such distribution tiers as are appropriate.

In general, there are two relevant design approaches for such a user interface component: a black-box design and a white-box design. In the *black-box* design, illustrated in Figure 12.12, the control and anything required to implement the control are accessible only through the interface of the control itself, no matter how complicated the implementation is. This may be thought to be the preferred design from the point of view of the user of the control because it makes use easier: The user has to worry only about the interface to the control itself. Black-box controls can go so far as to include a specific server and database implementation, often designed for a PC, so that the database is on the PC. In this case, as might be the case with our example, the internal architecture of the control is quite at odds with the separations provided by the four tiers. Unless there is no other choice, controls that encapsulate all four tiers seamlessly should therefore be avoided.

In the *white-box* design illustrated in Figure 12.13, the user interface control is a component architected and structured such that appropriate parts are accessible by other parts of the system and, in turn, share other parts of the system. The figure illustrates a control, here called *efItem*, where "ef" stands for entry field, delivered in this example with the u-tier part and some corresponding w-tier language classes (1), that will be integrated (2) into the user interface and w-tier of the using component, for example, an *OrderManager* business component, and executed at run-time as part of this component. The item con-

Item A-10001		☒

General	Inventory	Manufacturing

Item Number: `A-10001`   Mode: `Revise`

Item Description: `External V.90 56K (Mac or PC)`

Extra Description: `                          `

Lot Control
○ Lot Controlled
● Not Lot Controlled

General
☒ Container Control   ☐ Single Issue
☒ Bypass WIP Tracking

Item Type: `        ▼`   Volume: `        `

Item Class: `        ▼`   Volume UOM: `        ▼`

Item Status: `        ▼`   ABC Code: `        ▼`

Stock U/M: `        ▼`   Cycle Count Frequency: `        `

New   Ok   Cancel

Figure 12.11   Item entry field.

trol, before being delivered to the *OrderManager* business component, has already been tested against the *eItem* EDC (3).

This approach obliges both the user of the control and its functional developer to be *architecture-aware*, hence theoretically making the usage more complex. In reality, however, a wholly black-box control creates so many issues that the white-box approach is the preferred approach. In the white-box

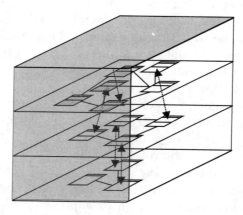

Figure 12.12   Black-box implementation of UI control.

OrderManager

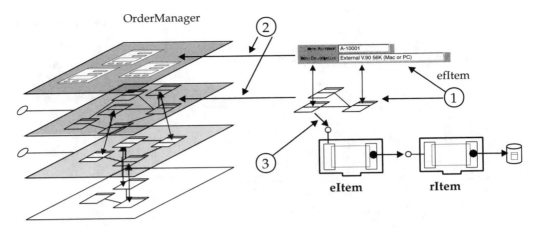

Figure 12.13   White-box implementation of UI control.

approach, the user interface component is simply aware of and perfectly integrated with the business component to which it belongs.

Component-Based User Interface

So what are the architectural characteristics of a user interface entirely built using the concepts illustrated in the previous subsection? This question is discussed here in the context of a class-based framework based on today's mature compiler-based technology, while the next section provides some additional considerations about the kind of user interface framework presented in Chapter 8.

A class-based UI framework, provided by the BCVM, can deliver a set of base capabilities as well as base controls. Such a framework would be built by technical designers and programmers using, for example, a current C++ or Java environment. This kind of approach is well grounded and mature, and as such it can be attractive as an implementation choice for the u-tier. A somewhat generalized example of this approach for a business component development is illustrated in Figure 12.14, which shows a fragment of a controls class hierarchy. The following elements can be seen:

- A set of user interface classes—whose names begin with "C" in the figure—that are owned and delivered by the BCVM. These classes could be the native controls provided by the commercially available class library provided with the C++ or Java development kit.

- A set of base classes, typically developed by GUI programming experts, which "wrap" the native controls to provide basic user interface-related function and consistency across the system. Examples shown in the figure are the class *EFBase* that implements the entry field concept, a set of

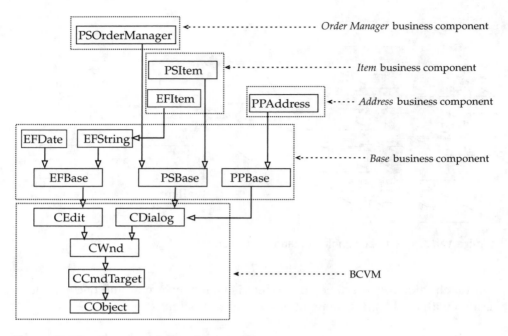

Figure 12.14 Class-based client framework.

more specific classes expanding the behavior of the *EFBase*, namely the *EFString* and *EFDate*, and the classes *PPBase* and *PSBase* that implement the property page and the property sheet concepts, respectively. *PSBase* could provide consistency across all property sheets in the system by, for example, providing specific default behavior for the "ok," "cancel," and "help" buttons.

- *PPAddress*. A property page belonging to the *Address* business component and implementing the UI behavior specific to *Address* u-tier. As illustrated in the scenario in Chapter 2, this property page may be used only in the property sheet of a component higher up in the hierarchy, in such a way that in practice there would never be a u-tier for *Address* at run-time.

- *PSItem*. A property sheet belonging to the Item business component and implementing the UI behavior specific to *Item* u-tier.

- *PSOrderManager*. A a property sheet providing the user interface for the *OrderManager* business component.

The property sheet *PSOrderManager* may represent the whole order-entry process, and as such it is the visualization of the coordination of all the business components on which the *OrderManager* business component depends. The various property pages of this property sheet may be built by any of the coordinated components, for example, *Address* provides a property page *PPAddress*. Each component may provide one or more controls, for example, the *Item* component provides a property sheet, which at run-time will be part of the u-tier of *Item*, and an entry field *EFItem*, for reuse at development-time by other components and that will be part of their u-tiers at run-time.

Such a client framework provides the ability to build the user interface out of progressively more complex controls, providing for high levels of reuse and abstraction. Once a GUI expert provides a *PPBase* or *PSBase* that is consistent with the project UI guidelines and that takes care of most of the default activities for the functional developer, these controls can be (relatively) easily used and even extended without requiring a GUI expert. This UI framework, with GUI elements organized and owned by individual business components, fits nicely within the overall component architecture.

Pluggable User Interface

Although the framework illustrated in the previous section may suit many requirements, and, once established, allows powerful component-based user interfaces to be built rapidly and cost-effectively, it does not provide for a pluggable user interface.

The section "User Interface Framework" in Chapter 8 provided an example of an architecture explicitly aimed at ease of use for the functional developer, and that also provided for pluggability at run-time. This framework relies heavily on tagged data to identify dynamically which data should be displayed by which control on a window or property page, and which property pages would be placed on which property sheets. In this way, the u-tier can be made largely generic, assisted by provision of standard interfaces for w-tier components, as described in the next section. It does much more than just that. To fully implement the business component requires a fully component-based approach for the u-tier. For many interesting user models, this goes significantly beyond merely using componentized controls. Rather the u-tier of each business component should itself be one or more components that can be autonomously developed and plugged in. Such an environment, to the best of the authors' knowledge, cannot be purchased on the market today, although the authors have been involved in the design and construction of such environments.

The kind of capability provided can be illustrated by the following example. Suppose that all four tiers of an *OrderManager* business component are already deployed. The item business component, however, has only the e-tier and r-tier deployed. This means that item data is displayed directly by the *OrderManager* component, perhaps as a property page delivered with the *OrderManager*'s u-tier. Of course, in development this property page would have belonged to the *Item* component—possibly the only artifact, at development time, of the *Item*'s u-tier. Now suppose that a w-tier and u-tier are added to a new version of the *Item* business component and are deployed. A new version of the *OrderManager* component would not technically need to be deployed. Rather, already in its code would be an invocation of the *Item*'s u-tier. Prior to deployment of the item's u-tier, this invocation would have failed, and the *OrderManager* component would revert to look for a property page physically within itself—the "borrowed" *Item* property page. When the *Item* u-tier is installed, this invocation would succeed. The net effect of this is a situation where a user interface can receive significant updates and changes with no change to already-deployed code.

One final comment of interest is that today's technology for user interface controls uses either a "push" or a "pull" model. In the push model, data to be displayed is pushed out to a control by invoking a "put" operation on the control. A pull model control pulls data to be displayed to itself by invoking a "get" operation on a data object within a u-tier, which can be seen as the control's own private cache. When the user enters data on the screen, then the control sends the data to this private cache by invoking a "put" operation on it. The cache may then publish an event to tell any interested parties that its data has changed. In general, the pull model is to be preferred. Indeed, there is a synergy here with the rest of the DAG as applied to the distribution tiers. This is shown in Figure 12.15. Each part of the system pulls data from the part to its right by invoking an operation on it. Each part may also subscribe to events published by a part to its right and so receive event notifications from it. This includes the GUI infrastructure (a combination of the GUI system infrastructure and the CEE GUI infrastructure shown in Figure 8.10 in Chapter 8). As a final note of interest, the pull model implements the essence of the Model-View-Controller pattern—especially the Model and View parts. But so do the u-tier and the w-tier. The u-tier is the "view," and the w-tier is the "model." More than that, the whole UWD can be seen as a "view" of the ERD "model."

Workspace Tier

The workspace tier supports a single-user model, which provides for many simplifications in design when compared to the e-tier. ERD design issues such as

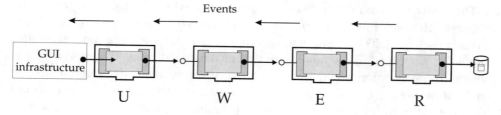

Figure 12.15   The DAG from UI to DB.

transaction management, locking, and enterprise security are not present. For some user models, however, issues such as concurrency, user unit of work management, and w-tier persistence must be faced. Although these issues are similar to issues in the ERD, they are less stringent in their requirements for high performance, scalability, and security.

Component technology can be used to implement the w-tier. This provides for a strong separation between the w-tier implementation and the u-tier, allowing benefits such as the ability to replace the u-tier (for example, change user interface technology or layout) with minimal impact on other parts of the system, the ability to develop, test, and deploy the w-tier autonomously, and the ability to change the implementation of the w-tier with minimal impact on the rest of the system. In addition, the natural provision of useful interfaces by w-tier components makes it relatively easy to integrate the PC-based parts of workflow products.

Using component implementation technology coupled with tagged data technology, the WDCs can be provided, in addition to other interfaces, with a small set of standard generic interfaces. For example, each DC might provide standard interfaces along the following general lines (using the instance-based style):

```
read(in TaggedData items, out TaggedData item_values);
update(in TaggedData item_values);
delete();
remove(in TaggedData contained_items);
validate(in TaggedData item_values);
```

The first parameter of the read operation contains the tags for the data items to be retrieved from the WDC. The second parameter returns those tags with their values. Other operations accept the tagged data provided and perform update, delete, remove (contained items), or validate functions on the target WDC as appropriate. When all WDCs support these operations, then a generic and configurable u-tier, such as that discussed in Chapter 8, can get and put data from a WDC without having to know about specific operation signatures. Without common signatures across all WDCs, then generic operations based on a configuration is made much more difficult to effect because a generic u-tier would have to be given the unique operation signatures of each WDC used. Further, interfaces such as these open up a number of interesting design possibilities, some, for example, to do with workflow integration, others to do with the technical and application architectures of the UWD, and yet others for user unit of work management. Standards applied to the tagged data used as parameters can also allow a WDC interface to manage collections in a generic way, so that a *Read(...)* might be for a given item in a collection, for the whole collection, or for an abbreviated list of the items in the collection, depending on how the first parameter is structured. In addition, a standard if minimal set of events published by all WDCs is useful. Such a set might include Changed, Created, and Deleted. Code implementing these functions tends to be much the same for most WDCs and can in many cases be generated.

When using component implementation technology to implement the w-tier, the general mindset of the w-tier designer is often of a set of smaller granularity components, often instance-based, participating in smaller, more frequent, and shorter interactions with the u-tiers. The components are usually state-based (as opposed, as we will see in the next section, to the EDCs that are usually stateless). On the other hand, the whole w-tier for a business component could also be conceived as a single type-based DC, usually with multiple interfaces, and it is even possible to forget about components altogether and implement the w-tier as one or more object-oriented applications (although this would make interactions with a generic u-tier more complicated). These three cases are illustrated in Figure 12.16. The object-oriented case usually implies that for a given business component the u-tier and the w-tier are actually linked together: This may have application architecture consequences, and such an approach is less resilient to change. And, of course, the w-tier could not be moved to a machine separate from the u-tier. The chief danger, however, is that, unless application architecture guidelines are very strictly enforced, the separation of concerns is easily lost during development—there can easily be "leaks" from the w-tier responsibilities to those of the u-tier and vice-versa, with impacts on speed of evolution and maintenance.

The component object model for a business component's w-tier often has, at least at analysis time, much in common with that of the e-tier, even if the two do not share the same implementation technology. After all, the two are mostly dealing with the same business concepts. If they are sharing the same implementation technology, the two tiers can be designed in such a way that they reuse as many classes as possible, not only for business data types but also for business language classes. The details of the w-tier object model, however, are

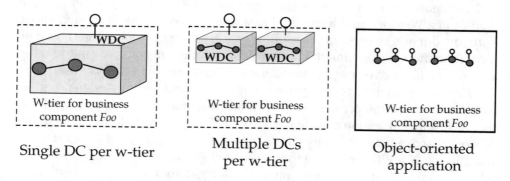

| Single DC per w-tier | Multiple DCs per w-tier | Object-oriented application |

Figure 12.16   Implementation alternatives.

different from those of the e-tier object model, the w-tier object model being based on the user model rather than on the enterprise model. Also, sharing the same implementation technology allows for a noticeable reduction of complexity: The functional developer has in this case a very simple and consistent programming model for both the e-tier and w-tier.

When using component implementation technology for its implementation, some of the functionality provided by a w-tier can also be usefully applied to the implementation of an "adapter" for access to the e-tier by requests other than those from the UWD. For example, suppose that an electronic sales order is received from outside the information system. Because no assumption can be made about the validity of the received data, and because the w-tier logic to validate external input (from the u-tier) is already implemented in the w-tier, the gateway could parse the order data and feed it to the server-resident w-tier code. When there is a need to differentiate, this particular application of w-tier responsibility is referred to as the gateway workspace tier (gw-tier).

Enterprise Tier

Various design aspects of the e-tier have been discussed elsewhere in this book, including Chapter 3. This section concentrates on one important principle: *Enterprise DCs should be designed and built as stateless components.* This is a well-known and generally understood principle.[1]

Before analyzing the principle itself, it is important to clarify the meaning of the term *stateless*, which is a useful term but also a source of many misunderstandings. A stateless component retains no information about a subject component that has invoked it, nor any memory of its state, after a particular invocation has completed. For example, in the case of load balancing, any subsequent request by the same or any other subject component can be handled by any copy of the target component running in a different address space for load-balancing reasons. Load balancing for ERD components or servers is the ability to balance the incoming message load by routing individual incoming messages to any of several identical servers in such a way that the load on each is roughly equal. In other words, the system should be able to *clone* a stateless target component several times, and a given subject component cannot rely on a particular clone keeping something in memory in order to complete a given business transaction.

This does not mean that the target component is stateless under all points of view. Any given target component can certainly be stateful from the following viewpoints:

- *Database state.* During any transaction or part thereof, any given component can write to the database. Under all points of view, the database can thus record "state"; indeed maintaining a consistent state across continuous changes is a prime purpose of a database. For example, creating an order on the database undoubtedly leads to the database having a new database state: The next time the client accesses the ERD, it can assume this order is there.

- *State for "component accounting" purposes.* A component can keep various kinds of data about its own functioning. For example, it may maintain an internal count of how many transactions it has executed, which can help in a self-analysis of state. The term "component accounting" covers all such self-analysis aspects.

- *Introspection state.* It may be useful for the component to be able to answer questions about its meta-information, such as identity, version, and provided interfaces. This can also be seen as a kind of state.

- *Static data.* There may be some business data, usually read-only data, that can be loaded when the component is activated. In effect, such components keep their data in memory for everybody to access—a kind of global variable but one scoped to the containing individual component. For example, at the initialization of a pricing component, a set of parameters that drive the calculation of prices for the whole system can be loaded in memory and retained there.

The use of stateless components drastically reduces the complexity of providing high reliability and run-time scalability. It becomes easy to clone the component any number of times, which directly facilitates implementation of load balancing. It allows for extremely reliable systems because any subject component is not tied to a specific instance of a target component, and hence the loss of a target component clone due to some failure will not disrupt the system because the remaining target component clones can handle any requests from any subject component. The principle of stateless server code is well known, and it was applied by online transaction processing (OLTP) systems long before component or object technologies arose.

Statelessness also facilitates development-time scalability because it provides for increased determinism and simpler testing. Modeless interfaces become easier to implement, and it is much easier to develop and test the whole system because each transaction can, to a large extent, be considered autonomous.

The "stateless" paradigm is less appropriate for the UWD components, for which interface design and subsequent implementation can take advantage of state-full design. The general mindset that should be applied is that UWD-resident components manage the state of the user unit of work (the UWD part of a business transaction) and use it as the basis for data sent on invocations of an ERD target component.

Persistence

Persistence is the single most important aspect of the category of systems addressed in this book. This section continues with the assumption made elsewhere that a relational database is used, which reflects today's reality for most large business systems.

Chapter 8 presented various categories of persistence. This section focuses mainly on the business data persistence in the ERD, and specifically on the challenge of dealing with business data persistence in component-based systems.[2] The section first analyzes the concepts of database componentization, including the important *island of data* concept. Second, it presents a persistence framework suitable for the ERD. Third, it discusses some considerations around object-oriented and relational modeling. Finally, it illustrates how data integrity should be managed in a component-based system.

Database Componentization

Database modeling and implementation play crucial roles in enterprise-level component-based development. Many CBD practitioners see the componentization of a given business space as being completed if the situation shown in Figure 12.17 is reached. That is, the business logic is componentized but there is one single integrated database. All components can, in a relatively unconstrained way, access all database tables. Many who approach component-based development from an object-oriented perspective adopt this mindset toward the database, so conforming with an architectural style that could be called the *integrated database* style. Of course, usually the database would follow appropriate data architecture, and it would be modularized in one way or the other. But this modularization is done independently of the functional logic componentization, and the data management architecture is seen as separate from the component architecture.

The integrated database style is traditional for large-scale systems in which architecture is separated into processing and data management perspectives. The problem with this approach is that it severely inhibits the ability of components to be autonomous. The database becomes an integration point and creates a large number of dependencies between components.

To achieve true component autonomy, everything directly related to the component should be part of the component itself. This is not really possible for the distributed component level of component granularity: For example, it makes no sense to include user interface aspects in an enterprise distributed component, and experience teaches that it is not appropriate to include persistence aspects in each distributed component. But such inclusion is perfectly accept-

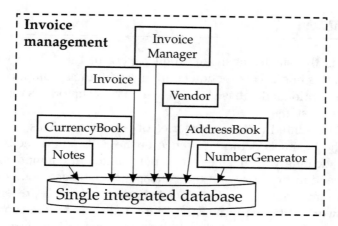

Figure 12.17   Components with integrated database.

able for business components and system-level components. The database must likewise be properly componentized, and persistent data should be appropriately assigned to each business component. This is probably the most controversial but powerful design principle in support of the autonomous development of business components, and it is referred to as the *componentized database* style. In this style, each business component contains an "island of data," as illustrated in Figure 12.18. We call this the *island of data principle*.

An island of data is totally contained within the business component and is a set of table definitions at design-time—corresponding to a component-specific schema—and the associated data at run-time. It is called an *island* because it has no direct link to any persistent data outside of the business component itself. Tables in an island of data can be thought of as *local* (to the component) tables. In a layered architecture (discussed in the section, "Persistence Framework"), each island of data has an associated resource tier (r-tier), possibly

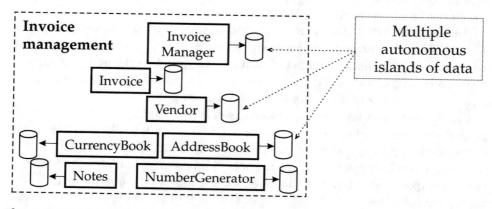

Figure 12.18   Components encapsulating their data.

implemented as a resource DC. The r-tier can be accessed only by the e-tier belonging to the same business component. Where a business component has more than one EDC in its e-tier, they usually have equal access rights to and visibility of the r-tier interfaces (see Figure 12.19).

Applying the islands of data principle, the whole database is partitioned into a set of islands, each of which is owned by a business component. Inside a business component, all the normal relational principles and techniques, such as normalization, query optimization, and referential integrity, are applied as usual. The only difference—and it's a big difference—is that the only way to access this data from outside the island is through the interfaces of the business component's EDCs, and not directly through an SQL interface or any other direct access mechanisms.

Each business component manages its own persistence. The user of the business component does not (need to) know whether, behind the interface, there is an RDBMS, a file system, some in-memory storage, or indeed whether all data returned through the interface is obtained from elsewhere, perhaps across the Internet.

Figure 12.18 shows a *logical* view of persistence, by which is meant a design-time or development-time view. The fact that logically the database is viewed as partitioned into multiple components does not mean that at run-time it must run on physically different databases. Given the current limitations of database technology, in most cases it is expected that at run-time Figure 12.18 will become as illustrated in Figure 12.20: All the islands of data are physically assigned to a single DBMS and resource manager.

The view of the persistence model as a set of islands of data is appropriate for addressing the "transactional part" of the system—that is, the ERD. Given the current level of component support provided by database-related tools such as report writers, there may be a need for some tool to see the database as a whole. This may well change with the maturity of database and component technology, but either way, the strength of the islands of data concept is unaffected.

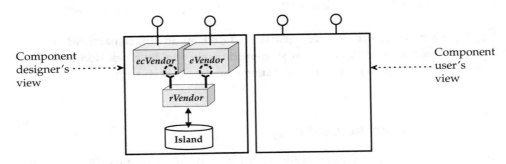

Figure 12.19   Accessing data through EDC interfaces.

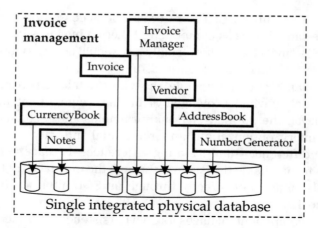

Figure 12.20 Physical view of Figure 12.18.

Thinking of the database in terms of islands of data pushes the componentization of a problem space a step further: Not only are the functional logic and user interface componentized and assigned to business components, but also the database model. This requires a new set of concepts and principles.

Granularity

Data that is frequently used together should logically belong to the same island of data, and hence to the same business component. The granularity of components is of critical importance: Experience shows that the appropriate granularity for an island of data and the appropriate granularity for business components are very close. A coarse granularity for the island of data allows most of the tables that are strictly related to be in the same island, leading the island of data concept to have a minimal impact on performance and scalability. Too fine a granularity would lead to a performance impact because the cost of accessing data across components may indeed be slightly higher than accessing the data directly in an integrated database. Granularity is key!

> **TIP** From experience, the average island of data for an EDC contains, when using a normalized relational model, approximately 5 to 20 tables. Numbers outside this range may indicate a possible modeling problem.

Inter-Component Navigation

The island of data principle dictates that the only way to access another component's data is through the interface of its e-tier distributed component(s).

Traditional database techniques should *not* be used across components. For example, joins between two tables belonging to different components should be banned, and the database should not be used to enforce referential integrity across components (see "Managing Data Integrity" later in this chapter).

Logical Foreign Keys

Tables that, if the database were integrated, would be linked through foreign keys are now linked only through the implementation of an interface. Tables in different islands of data are *never* linked using database foreign keys. In many cases, however, it makes sense, for example, for overall database consistency, to consider the columns that would otherwise be foreign keys as being logical foreign keys. A *logical foreign key* is a column (or a set of columns) in a table of an island of data that logically identifies a record in a different island of data. A logical foreign key, while not declared as foreign keys to the DBMS, can still be used as the information that effectively links tables of different business components through their interfaces.

For example, suppose that an order line record contains an *item_id* field that identifies the item ordered. The *item_id* field could also be the primary key of the *t_item* table (a table in the *Item* business component's island of data). In an integrated database style, the *item_id* field in the order line record would probably be declared as a foreign key. In a componentized database style, it is not declared as a foreign key, but the order line code in *eOrder* could use this field in invoking an *eItem* interface to retrieve information that would be read by *eItem* from the *t_item* table.

Using this approach there is the additional flexibility (if desired) of having different types for the foreign keys. Indeed, what is behind the interfaces is totally hidden from the accessing component. For example, the designer of the order line business language classes could have decided for some reason that the *item_id* field is of type string, while the *t_item* designer may have decided that it is of type numeric. This flexibility allows for smooth transitions in a system upgrade or in changes that would affect multiple tables in the database. This degree of freedom is further enhanced using XML (or any tagged data implementation technology) in the EDC interfaces. In this case, the type of each tag can be changed at the interface level, so giving an even higher degree of freedom.

Having said that, it is still advisable, certainly in a large-scale development, to maintain system-wide consistency of database types for logical foreign keys, unless there is a good reason to do otherwise. This rule enhances system integrity and consistency, and manageability of a project. In a large-scale project, this consistency rule may go so far as to be tool-supported, meaning that the concept of logical foreign key is added to the meta-model and type consistency is checked by the tools.

Normalized Islands of Data

Islands of data can be thought of as normalized, both in an intra-island sense—that is, any single island is normalized—and also in an inter-island sense, meaning that a given table should, as a default principle, not appear in two different islands. The latter consideration can be relaxed in complex situations, as was mentioned in the discussion about normalized components in Chapter 9. Another example of a situation in which the non-duplication rule can be broken is when a BC-level framework (see Chapter 11) is instantiated in more than one business component, and this framework contains predefined tables.

Of course, the reality of current relational technology must be taken in account. For example, because a physical database cannot have two tables with the same name, where a table is duplicated and it is known that the two islands of data will eventually belong to the same physical database, then the islands of data must follow appropriate naming conventions (perhaps managed and enforced by the development environment) to prevent duplicate names.

Cross-Reference Tables

To a large extent the assignment of tables to business components follows the same rules as the assignment of business language classes. It may not be initially obvious, though, how cross-reference tables should be assigned. A cross-reference table is a well-known relational database concept, and it is a table whose only purpose is to cross-reference one entity to a set of other entities. For example, suppose a manufacturing business has a number of facilities, each of which produces different items—in other words, they are in a *1:m* relationship. Given a facility entity and an item entity, then there could be a table *t_facility_item* in a *1:m* relationship with the table *t_items*. In assigning cross-reference tables to business components, the following heuristics can be used:

- One to many (*1:m*). A *1:m* cross-reference table should belong to one and only one business component, and it should normally be navigated in one direction only. The rule is this: *In the case of a cross-reference table linking together two entities in a* 1:m *relationship, the table is usually assigned to the component that is highest up in the DAG.*

- Many to many (*n:m*). In the case of *n:m* relationships, the cross-reference tables should belong to a "coordinator" component that is "above" (in the functional hierarchy) both of the components being cross-referenced. The rule is this: *In the case of a cross-reference table linking together two entities in an* n:m *relationship, the table is usually assigned to a coordinating component that manages the flow of information between the components containing the tables being cross-referenced.*

Both these guidelines apply where the two business entities that are linked by the cross-reference table(s) belong to different components. If they belong to the same component, then in most cases the cross-reference table will belong to that component as well.

Persistence Framework

Chapter 8 introduced a persistence framework appropriate for the UWD that was based to a large extent on externalization and internalization operations being made available by all DCs that wished to take part. As described, this framework assumed that a DC persisted either all of its state or none of it. ERD components usually do not load all the data that they could. For example, an operation on an order may need to read only order header data from the database, and not any order line detail. Although the persistence framework described in Chapter 8 might be extended to handle this kind of partial persistence, the mechanism may be less performant, for example, because it relies on several interactions for a single access to the r-tier.

This section discusses a persistence mechanism appropriate for the ERD with its stringent performance requirements: component-managed persistence. This term indicates an approach where persistence is driven directly from the internals of an EDC. If required, both framework-managed and component-managed persistence could be used within the same component instance. In both approaches, consistent with the overall philosophy of larger-grained components that are "responsible for their own fate," no persistence interfaces are made available for direct use by other components (unlike a number of persistence management approaches favored in purely object-oriented approaches). Rather, each operation describes a functional feature, such as *update_order (...)*, and it is up to the implementation of the operation to persist the data appropriately.

There are several ways to approach component-managed persistence. Each of these has advantages and disadvantages, and they are more or less appropriate for different contexts. They include the following:

Direct SQL access. The EDC implementation uses explicit or embedded SQL to access the database. In other words, the r-tier logic is mingled with e-tier logic. Although this is a very quick way to write applications, it does not support a reuse-based strategy well, it ties the business logic directly to the database, it threatens the proper separation of concerns, and it makes changes to the database potentially more expensive.

Layered access. In this case, the direct SQL access is embedded in a programmatic layer—the logical r-tier of the business component. A particular case of layering is the implementation of the r-tier as a separate DC—an

RDC. Through a combination of object-oriented frameworks internal to the DC and code generation, the objective of allowing the functional developer to ignore the r-tier persistence aspects can be achieved. In the EDC, rather than directly accessing the database, the functional developer accesses the r-tier through, for example, a set of persistence language classes (PLCs).

The trade-off between the two approaches is a matter of development costs, setup costs, and maintainability, as well as of run-time performance and scalability. Experience suggests that the first approach is faster to implement, requires minimal setup, can provide good performance, but proves expensive for development in the long run; for example, it is less maintainable. The second approach requires some initial investment in an appropriate framework, has some minimal performance impact due to the layering, but is able to scale at development-time to very large projects and proves more cost-effective in the long run. The following assumes layered access.

Figure 12.21 illustrates the separation of concerns in component-managed persistence using layered access. The persistence object model (POM) for a business component is known in the e-tier, and it is implemented using persistence language classes (PLCs). A given PLC type exists in only one business component, is owned by the e-tier of that business component, but can appear in more than one EDC in that e-tier. The mapping from POM to database (and back) is implemented in the r-tier, which also, of course, must know about the database schema (the persistence model implemented by tables in the RDBMS).

The interaction between the e-tier and the r-tier can be implemented by a PLC either internally or externally:

Internal. Each PLC includes in its implementation the persistence mechanism and access to the r-tier.

External. Each PLC is persisted by a mechanism external to itself. This is what was assumed in Chapter 3 where the PLC is described as a data-only class similar to a business data type. In this case, the persistence mechanism is implemented by a separate class that is associated with the PLC—the "PLC handler" class. This class has been given various names—PLC reference, PLC pointer—but the pattern has been the same, and it provides for a strong separation of concerns. That is, the responsibility for storing data is separated from the task of driving the r-tier for data access, update, and so forth. It is the PLC handler that provides a set of persistence interfaces and drives access to the r-tier. The PLC, on the other hand, has minimal business logic and an interface consisting mainly of "getter and setter" operations. Among other things, this allows for easier reuse of PLCs as business data types. The PLC handler class is the only part of an EDC that

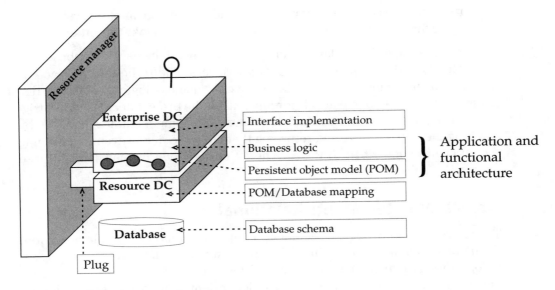

Figure 12.21 Persistence in a business component.

knows how to speak with the r-tier or that knows whether the r-tier is implemented as a DC.

To summarize, component-managed persistence using a layered approach, where business logic speaks only with PLCs and the mechanics for accessing the r-tier are hidden in the PLC handler classes and in the r-tier, is a very scalable approach for both run-time and development-time. It also has the interesting characteristic that, given appropriate specification and a few project-specific rules, the whole r-tier, all the PLCs, and all the PLC handler classes can be fully generated by the development environment.

The main design guidelines associated with the r-tier are as follows:

- The r-tier can be implemented using various technologies, and it does not necessarily have to be implemented as a distributed component. Depending on the precise EDC-to-RDC invocation technology, implementing as a distributed component may affect performance somewhat. On the other hand, the separation afforded by DC technology has many development-time and deployment-time advantages. For example, a new RDBMS can be introduced without needing to touch—no recompile, re-link, or re-deploy—the EDCs that use the r-tier.

- An r-tier can never directly call another r-tier, or any other tier of another component. This is due to the DAG principle. The only exception to this rule occurs where the r-tier is used to hide the fact that another system provides the data, in which case code on the r-tier will invoke this other system.

A final comment: In this layered approach, we avoid the use of database triggers. This is both to enhance portability (triggers tend to be different across database management vendors) and to avoid business logic from being dispersed in more than one place. If for any reason the project decides to use triggers, these are scoped to each individual business component, for example, by catching them in the r-tier and returning them to the e-tier as events (assuming the e-tier has subscribed to them). The e-tier may then further publish these events, if required.

Object-Oriented Meets Relational

The approach outlined so far includes an object-oriented EDC implementation, the database componentized into islands of data, and relational database technology for the persistence mechanism. This combination throws into prominence the challenge of mapping an object-oriented model into a relational model (the "POM/Database mapping" shown in Figure 12.21). Indeed, the problem of persistence for each individual business component now mostly consists of how to deal with this mapping.

For small systems, it is possible to simply and mechanically translate an object-oriented model into a relational model, as explained, for example, in [Jacobson 1995], but the question needs to be considered in more detail for larger systems. Indeed, there are several known challenges when interfacing OO and RDBMS, including relationships and identification:

Relationships. It is relatively simple to map a USES or a containment relationship. However, an object-oriented inheritance relationship can be translated in three different ways, and these lead to different query optimizations, different performance characteristics, and even different detailed semantics. Furthermore, even implementing all three of the possible ISA implementations in a relational database does not really capture all the semantics of the inheritance relationship.

Let us illustrate with an example. Figure 12.22 shows an example of a simple object-oriented inheritance hierarchy, where class A has an attribute—*number*—that serves as an identifier for instances.

Figure 12.23 shows the three implementations of this inheritance hierarchy in a relational database, where underlined columns are primary keys.

In Case 1, each class in the hierarchy is mapped to a separate table in the database. Each table has a separate primary key. Retrieving a complete instance of class B or class C from the database will require a join of table B or table C, respectively, with table A. Writing to the database requires

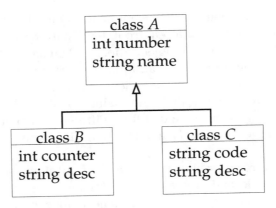

Figure 12.22 Object-oriented inheritance.

separate updates for each table involved in the hierarchy. In Case 2, each concrete class must be a leaf class of the hierarchy. If an intermediate class is expected to be concrete, then a "dummy" leaf class must be defined for this concrete class. For each concrete class, the developer must map all the attributes for classes in the hierarchy to columns in a table. Retrieving from the database requires a simple query for the class. In Case 3, all concrete classes are stored in the same table. Each row contains an additional (system-defined) attribute—a discriminator—that indicates the class type for the instance data stored in the row (shown as the string *class* in Figure 12.23). Also, each row in the table contains only data for the indicated class. Retrieving from the database requires the discriminator to be added to every query. Writing to the database also requires the discriminator to be provided.

Each case has different performance costs, evolution costs, and database size costs. A mature development environment should give the designer a choice of the desired strategy on a case-by-case basis.

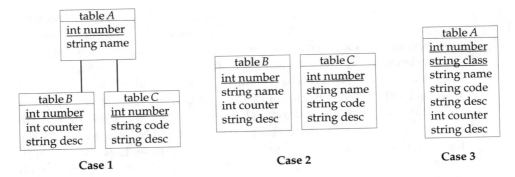

Figure 12.23 Relational inheritance.

Identification. The "identifier" concept in an OO world (that is, what identifies an instance) is very different from the "identifier" concept in the relational world. Basically, an object-oriented language class instance is identified by a pointer to its location in memory, not by the values in its data. It is quite acceptable in the object-oriented world for two different instances to have exactly the same values of data: The two instances would be equivalent but would still be different instances. On the other hand, a row in the database is uniquely identified by its primary key.

The examples of relationships and identification show how the mapping between an object model and a relational model is not necessarily automatic. One way or another, when mapping a persistence object model into a relational model (or vice versa), it is necessary to establish early on in the process the general philosophy for approaching the mapping problem. There are three possibilities:

1. Design the relational model, and then derive the persistence object model from it. In this case, the relational model can be relatively optimized, but this normally leads to some compromise with OO models because they are constrained to use concepts generated from a non-OO model. The resulting object-oriented model may turn out to be clumsy, ultimately impacting development performance. On the other hand, this approach leads to relatively scalable systems because it does allow for optimizing the data access.

2. Design the persistence object model, and then derive the relational model from it. This may lead to fewer compromises in object modeling: The object-oriented model is to a large extent done independently from the relational model, and mostly automatic mapping (following well-established rules) can create the relational model from the object-oriented model. This approach requires less work, less infrastructure, and less tool support. It is also less performant and less flexible, and it does not normally scale well.

3. Design the persistence object model and the relational model independently from each other, and then design a bridge between them. This permits maximum flexibility, and it implies few or no compromises either in OO modeling or in relational modeling. It is possible to have independent optimization of the two models while keeping them adequately consistent with each other. It also is the solution that requires the most development effort because an explicit mapping between the two models is more difficult to automate and requires more skill at all levels (in the other cases the mapping can be largely generated). This solution, however, leads to more scalable and higher-performance systems, and it is our preferred approach.

In a real-world persistence framework, there are many other aspects that need to be dealt with that we have not the space to cover in this brief exposition. A few questions that should be answered are these: Can a class map into several tables? Can several tables map into one class? Can wildcards be passed into an EDC interface? What is a precise strategy for null values?

Managing Data Integrity

A common question at this point is this: How is data integrity dealt with in the island of data approach? Because database capabilities are not used to navigate and manage any data-related aspects, including referential integrity, across islands of data, how can data be guaranteed to be consistent across the system? The answer is through *component-managed integrity*. It is desirable that a business component directly controls its own data integrity and also, indirectly, the data integrity of any components belonging to its own assembly, through their interfaces. By *directly* we mean by access to the database through the internals of the component; by *indirectly* we mean logically coordinating integrity but relying on the coordinated component to physically do what is necessary with its own island of data.

Within a given business component, if the component developer so desires, the usual database integrity checks can be used. But the system relies on higher-level components to ensure cross-component data integrity. This approach supports autonomy for components and provides for them to be combined and recombined in various ways. It also requires that higher-level components perform certain operations. Suppose a business component *A* depends on business components *B* and *C*, where *B* and *C* don't have direct dependencies on each other. Further suppose that all three provide a *delete* operation for a certain type of data, and that if a given business entity in *B* is deleted, then so should another in *C*. It is *A*'s responsibility to properly coordinate *B* and *C*. Should another component invoke *B*'s *delete* operation directly, then this will risk impacting system-wide data integrity.

An implication of this approach is that *components are delivered in collaborating assemblies*. A BC assembly can assume a certain type of predefined collaboration between its components that as a whole implements the desired assembly behavior and maintains data integrity across the assembly.

Summary

When designing a component-based system, an appropriate mindset is required to achieve the objectives of cost-effectively building high-performance and scalable systems. This mindset consists of a combination of concepts, principles, architecture, and development process. In a word, it is a whole approach, which can be characterized by a number of principles, including the following:

- Taking into account the real constraints of distribution
- Ensuring that components exchange information by value, and that, while the components themselves are never "passed," a way to reach them—a reference—is passed
- Designing so that network interactions are minimized
- Taking into account the levels of component granularity during design
- Applying discrete recursion
- Putting emphasis on the autonomy of coarse-grained components
- Strictly enforcing encapsulation

An important long-term asset for a component manufacturing organization, and one of the biggest issues in developing component-based systems, is the definition of component interfaces. An interface can be specified independently from the component implementing it, but in many cases it is simpler to assume that it is always associated with one component. A component can have multiple interfaces.

It is important to define what a well-formed and well-behaved component is. This includes the definition of the kinds of component interfaces required by the architecture, naming conventions, the interface design patterns that ensure consistency across different component's interfaces, and the expected behavior of the various interfaces.

Business data types are an important aspect of interfaces. A business data type should include the primary key for the business concept it represents, should be consistent with the database, should minimize nesting, and should conform to system-wide consistency rules.

The UWD and ERD are logical domains, and the exact separation between them is an important design decision with development, performance, and scalability consequences. Tiers within the same domain are connected strictly, while the interaction between the domains should be loose. The UWD conforms to the transactional behavior of the ERD. The distribution model, constituted by the two domains and the four tiers, is a superset of the traditional three-tier model and provides a more appropriate model for thinking about distributed systems.

As with everything else in a component-based system, the user interface is componentized. It is possible to build UI controls that take into account the overall component-based architecture. These controls can be part of a UI component-based functional framework that builds on a technical framework to make it easy to rapidly build user interfaces with the desired characteristics. At the same time, the business component ownership concept can be maintained, so that the user interface aspects of a given business component can be deployed and plugged in independently from the user interfaces of other business components.

The DCs in the enterprise tier should be built as stateless. Stateless means that an individual component does not retain its state between invocations. This principle leads to scalable, reliable, and deterministic systems. It also improves development-time performance.

Achieving all the objectives of a component-based approach requires adopting a componentized database style, in which each business component owns an island of data. A persistence framework appropriate for the ERD normally requires component-managed persistence, using layered access. In such an approach, data integrity is component-managed.

This completes the component modeling and design portion of Part Three. In the next chapter, we round off the book by discussing some of the main characteristics of the transition to component-based development.

Endnotes

1 See, for example, [Session 1997] and Stewart's article [1998].

2 Many excellent books exist on the general problem of persistence. One is [Date 1995].

Transitioning

Looking back over the previous chapters, we might well ask how an organization can take advantage of some or all of the business component approach. This concluding chapter indicates what might be done next, and it describes very briefly some of the main considerations in transitioning to the business component approach. Given the profound positive impact that the business component approach can make on all aspects of software manufacturing, transitioning to it from a non-component-based development approach is an attractive proposition. A successful transition, however, requires clarity of objectives and a well-founded plan. Assistance from those who have already traveled the transition road can help avoid a number of the surprises that await the unwary. This chapter describes some of the more important aspects of this transition. It does not pretend to provide a fully worked-out transition program, but it does identify several of the main considerations and is organized in two sections:

Concepts. Establishes a conceptual framework for a transition by presenting at a high level the five main elements that must be addressed by any organization desiring to achieve cost-effective software manufacturing.

Transition program. Discusses the prominent characteristics of a transition program, describes some of the main areas where assistance can be profitably applied, and provides examples of transition iterations. A transition program provides the framework for the transition and is highly desirable in adopting the business component approach.

For simplicity, the focus throughout the chapter is on software manufacturing aspects. This focus excludes the holistic view of the software supply chain, of which manufacturing is a part. For example, in a real transition, a software vendor would also need to transition its presales, sales, and postsales workforce, while an in-house IS organization may also have to transition software deployment and maintenance strategies, as well as some aspects of systems management.

Concepts

The main objective of transitioning, whether to component-based development or to some other approach, is to achieve cost-effective software manufacturing. Each organization will, of course, have its own effectiveness targets. A successful transition program requires a clear definition of the conceptual framework within which the transition will occur. A conceptual framework is the set of concepts that, in their various forms, present a cohesive vision for cost-effective manufacturing. It determines the aims and characteristics of the particular development philosophy adopted and establishes its main concepts and principles. The conceptual framework provided by the business component approach is (we believe) the best approach today for achieving the highest software manufacturing effectiveness.

The conceptual framework, with its concepts and its vision, informs and shapes the five main elements required for an organization to establish an efficient software manufacturing capability. These elements are methodology, best practices, architecture, software factory, and reuse program, as illustrated in Figure 13.1 where they are shown in a sequence. Organizations, however, approach transitioning from several different angles, and in reality the five elements are addressed iteratively and with some degree of concurrency. For example, an organization may decide to approach the instantiation of a methodology and the establishment of a technical architecture concurrently. The sequence shown generally reflects how each iteration is prioritized, and it has been used successfully by several organizations in prioritizing their transitions.

As can be seen in the figure, the five elements overlap to a large extent and represent a breakdown of the transitioning space that we happen to have found useful. Other practitioners may cut the same space differently. For example, many methodologists would argue that best practices are an integral part of methodology.

Methodology

The ability to cost-effectively manufacture software requires establishing a common methodology across the software manufacturing organization and

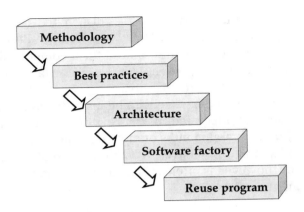

Figure 13.1   Elements of cost-effective software manufacturing.

even among the organizations participating in the production of a federation of systems. Use of a methodology involves a modeling language, a development process, and the associated modeling tools required to support them. Detailed guidelines on tool use, together with document and model templates, are also often provided by the methodology.

The *modeling language* establishes the main concepts, syntax, and semantics of the language and notation used to describe the problem space and develop the software. The most well-known modeling language today is UML [Booch 1999]. The *development process* defines the phases, activities, steps, and deliverables, describing the high-level and detailed approach to the development including workflows, roles, templates, and tasks.

The definition of a common methodology across the transitioning organization is a key aspect of any serious transition. Without this step, it is hard to establish a cost-effective development, or to attempt any serious reuse. It enables problems, solutions, and deliverables to be described in a common language that expresses shared concepts. Usually it is while establishing the methodological background that the important aspects of the business component approach itself are introduced to the transitioning organization.

Current COTS (commercial off-the-shelf) methodologies are generic in nature, given their need to be adaptable to multiple projects and constraints, and unfortunately they require some work to be adapted to the day-to-day needs of a large software manufacturing organization. Although they may provide guidance to a detailed level, generally they are not prescriptive at that level. For their day-to-day activities, however, developers require the definition of many minutiae such as how to version software artifacts, what specific names to give to them, and exactly what exit criteria for each phase and deliverable must be satisfied. In addition, COTS methodologies sometimes address only the early phases of the development lifecycle (requirements gathering, analysis, and design) but not, out of the box and in an integrated approach, aspects such as testing or how best to address distributed system aspects. Last but not least, to our knowledge no COTS methodology addresses the whole spectrum of end-to-end development required for a component-based distributed system in an integrated approach, from user interface modeling to database design to interoperability architecture.

Hence, any COTS methodology needs to be instantiated to the needs of the specific organization, as illustrated in Figure 13.2. A complete methodology instantiation may take several months or more depending on the organization's size, maturity, and strategic objectives. A small fraction of a complete methodology instantiation, however, is often sufficient to jump-start a transition and to achieve some early benefits.

Best Practices

Within the conceptual framework, and by extending the common methodology framework, organizations should implement the best practices appropriate for their application development objectives. By *best practices* we mean the software engineering practices that best support efficient software development manufacturing. In the business component approach, we adopt the classification and approach to best practices defined by the Capability Maturity Model (CMM) of the Software Engineering Institute (SEI),[1] with its five maturity levels of the CMM, as illustrated in Figure 13.3. Component development generally requires at least that an organization is at level 2, and preferably at or approaching level 3. Adoption of the business component approach as illustrated in this book is consistent with a level 3 organization.

Best practices are required across the whole development lifecycle, and they cover all aspects of large-scale development, from requirements gathering to verification, validation, and quality assurance, and from project management to process engineering. They include measurements and process optimization approaches. To a large extent, best practice can be defined as all the nontech-

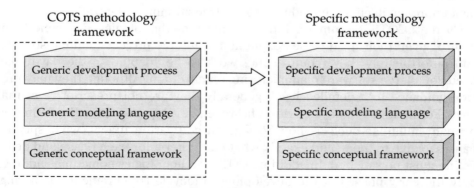

Figure 13.2 Methodology framework specific to organization.

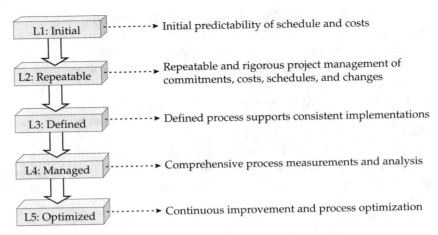

Figure 13.3   Maturity levels of software development organizations.

nology-specific aspects that are required to fill the gap between the instantiated methodology and real-life development. The difference between methodology and best practices is to a large extent arbitrary and perhaps only historical. At the time of writing, however, COTS methodologies typically do not explicitly address best practices in an integrated way. For example, a methodology rarely defines, out of the box, how to appropriately size and estimate a project. Or how to define a project plan that is consistent with the overall approach. Or which particular measures to apply to the process itself, or to establish the quality of the deliverables. Or the particular approach to software configuration management and version control.

At a high level, best practices are generic and not component-specific. At a detail level, most of them acquire new characteristics in a component-based development. For example, Chapter 10, "Project Management Architecture," showed how project management in the business component approach is totally component-centric, to the extent that all project plans, sizing, and estimating, and even software configuration management, are organized in terms of business components.

Architecture

Neither methodology nor best practices are concerned with the establishment of an architecture able to support large-scale development. The methodology usually points out when the architecture should be defined in the development process and how to describe it; best practices are concerned with the software engineering approaches required to efficiently manufacture software. Neither addresses specific architectural concerns.

Once the methodological framework and best practices have been defined (at least to satisfy the needs of the first transitioning iteration), it is time to put the architecture in place. Having said that, organizations with stringent budget and time constraints sometimes choose to prioritize architecture aspects, and in particular technical architecture aspects, before methodology.

The architecture aspect of a transition covers the definition of the architectural concepts *and* their instantiation for the specific organization. In the business component approach, this follows the four architectural viewpoints described in this book—the technical, application, project management, and functional architectures. Also covered are technical and architectural issues such as the kind of portability and interoperability framework required, the component execution infrastructure, and managing architectural training and mentoring.

Architectural transitioning is a concept that is much more recent than transitioning on methodology and best practices, and the techniques for architecture knowledge transfer are less well defined. The business component approach establishes a powerful framework for this transition.

Software Factory

The discussion so far has illustrated the concepts required to achieve the transitioning organization's development objectives, within the conceptual framework of the business component approach. Methodology, best practices, and architecture are the elements of the factory setup described in Part Two. Once the factory has been sufficiently established, the organization can concentrate, first, on producing software and running the software factory efficiently and, second, on bringing the organization to optimal productivity levels. This section addresses the first aspect (running the software factory), and the "Reuse Program" section addresses the second.

To run a software factory efficiently requires additional considerations, including organization, knowledge management, product deployment, and support considerations, which are not directly included in any of the aspects previously described. This section briefly illustrates the first two of these: organization and knowledge management. Each transitioning organization will define what they believe is important for efficiency. For example, an organization could define a rigorous internal issue tracking system. Another may decide that it is more important to establish rigorous processes to define when to buy and when to build components, and how to evaluate build or buy cost/benefits.

Organization

The organizational aspects are probably the most critical of any transition, having both human and cost implications. Each individual—and the whole organization—may be exposed to multiple concurrent learning curves, and even for a factory that is perfectly well set up, the human factor is still of primary importance.

An important characteristic of a successful organization is its ability not only to adopt the best approach to cost-effective software manufacturing, but also to be set up in such a way that it can continuously evolve and improve. Such an organization might be called a *learning organization.*

Dealing with organizational aspects also includes properly managing the hiring process, as well as retaining employees and managing careers. There is no point in starting a two-year-long transition program if after one year the key developers leave the organization. Indeed, professionals and their management and leadership are the most important assets of the organization, and given current employment dynamics (see Chapter 1, "Component-Based Development"), their retention must be properly addressed in a cost-effective software manufacturing organization.

Knowledge Management

The knowledge held within an organization is one of its key assets. An important part of large-scale software manufacturing is the explicit management of this knowledge. This includes document management and even apparently trivial aspects such as appropriately capturing ongoing project discussions. There are many different techniques in managing knowledge, and Web-based approaches have been found to be particularly successful.

A Web-based knowledge management system requires an intranet site, easily accessible by all members of the development team, and by which the whole team can (in a controlled way) participate in adding knowledge. The knowledge intranet grows organically, and it is structured according to the structure of the business component approach. For example, the development process and the various architectural viewpoints should directly correspond to a branch of the site. Of course, there is a need for various other navigational supports to make it useful so that information can be rapidly accessed. For example, the concept of *architectural monographs* (see Chapter 9, "Application Architecture") can be adopted—that is, collecting all the links and documents that pertain to a given subject and publishing them as a monograph.

An example of a monograph is an error-handling monograph. Error handling as a subject has aspects that concern the technical architecture (where services are provided, for example, by the CEE), the application architecture (such as conventions used to define errors), the functional architecture (functional errors required by the requirements), the project management architecture (for example, how errors are exported and imported across components), and the development process (the points in the development lifecycle where error-related deliverables are specified).

Table 13.1 indicates how a knowledge intranet might be organized, where

Table 13.1   Knowledge Management Organization

LEVEL 1	LEVEL 2	DESCRIPTION
Factory Setup	Methodology Best practices Technical architecture Application architecture …	Describes the concepts, methodology, and architectural framework
Components	Invoice Manager Invoice Vendor CurrencyBook …	Provides component deliverables for use by developers
Monographs	Error Handling Security Data Types …	Architectural monographs
Management	System Version 1.0 System Version 2.0	Stores all project plans, estimation, meeting minutes, and other artifacts required for day-to-day management of the main versions of software being produced
BCVM	XIDE CEE	Contains the deliverables, for example, a particular version of an internally developed XIDE or the user guide and detailed API guide.

"level 1" means a high-level link in a hyperlink tree and "level 2" indicates the next level down.

Reuse Program

Any serious approach to software manufacturing must be reuse-centric. The term "reuse-centric" means that the development process, best practices, architecture, and software factory all directly participate in supporting high levels of reuse. The distinction between *using* a software artifact and *reusing* it may appear arbitrary. In the business component approach, the simple fact of having established such things as an appropriate architecture and development process will encourage teams to use and reuse components, models, patterns, and other software artifacts produced by other teams. In this sense, reuse is an ever-present concern in the day-to-day life of a cost-effective organization, even if there is not an explicit reuse program in place. Indeed, the business component approach makes the boundary between normal development and reuse blend together more than for any other approach: All aspects of the business component approach encourage reuse even without an explicit reuse program.

The term *reuse* is introduced as an independent subject when it is time to optimize and bring the development to yet another level. At that point, it becomes important to explicitly target the setup of a reuse program in the organization. A *reuse program* in an advanced manufacturing shop is the set of principles and tools that are specifically and explicitly concerned with supporting reuse. A reuse program aims to ensure that software artifacts are developed with reuse as an explicit objective and that they are indeed reused by other developers. In normal cost-effective software manufacturing, reuse is an important side effect; in an explicit reuse program, it is the main aim.

With this distinction in mind, it is better to target a reuse program after having achieved at least the main milestones of a factory setup. For example, in general it doesn't make sense to propose for reuse a component developed for one project, unless the project that wants to reuse it shares many of the same factory setup characteristics, nor does it make sense to establish an explicit reuse team before having transitioned the organization to a common methodology. The prerequisites for reuse include a common modeling language, common architectural decisions, common semantics, and many other elements covered in the first four elements in Figure 13.1. At some point the organization will have made sufficient progress on the first four elements in a transition, and it may be ready to start optimizing the manufacturing operation through an explicit reuse program.

Not all organizations need such an explicit reuse program. An organization with fewer than 20 developers can be very efficient and still achieve high levels of reuse, especially if not spread out across multiple sites, without an explicit reuse program. An organization with 50 developers, producing a single software product line, and having succeeded in setting up the manufacturing as a software factory, may still not need an explicit reuse program: For example, an appropriate knowledge management infrastructure might be enough to allow every developer to find the appropriate documentation and components when needed. For these organizations, the focus should be on achieving the ability to develop quality software cost-effectively, rather than high levels of reuse: Reuse, of course, supports this objective, but it does not need to be an explicit organizational target. On the other hand, an organization addressing different projects, with different teams, possibly spread across multiple sites, may strongly benefit from having an explicit reuse program in addition to the factory setup. Such a program would focus on proactively informing and motivating teams who otherwise might never come into contact to search for software assets that they can reuse. Of course, this assumes an accessible asset repository, which is addressed in the next section.

Figure 13.4 illustrates, first, how there are many types of reuse and, second, how the benefits of reuse increase as an organization progressively approaches full realization of the full business component factory and component solutions. While the business component approach uses any trick available to reduce costs of development, it is mostly interested in the top three levels in the figure, that is, with component reuse, framework reuse, and solution reuse. This is what might be called *CBD reuse*. The first two levels in the figure, code reuse and pattern reuse, are *development reuse*.

In addition to the factory setup, an enterprise-wide reuse program requires the existence of an asset repository, a reuse process, and an appropriate organizational setup.

Asset Repository

The asset repository is a repository of software and other assets that can be reused by various people and in various situations, and that is also easily accessible to those who have not contributed to creating the asset. The objectives of the asset repository are to reduce development cost and to increase development productivity. Up to a certain productivity point, the knowledge management infrastructure, with its objective to capture the intellectual property of the organization or of the project, and to allow it to be shared across the organization, can provide a rudimentary asset repository and may be enough to satisfy the reuse needs of many organizations. For example, a Web-based knowledge management infrastructure could contain a pointer to the components and their documentation, organized according to a component diagram.

When a Web-based knowledge management infrastructure is insufficient and must be evolved into a repository that both stores knowledge and provides for

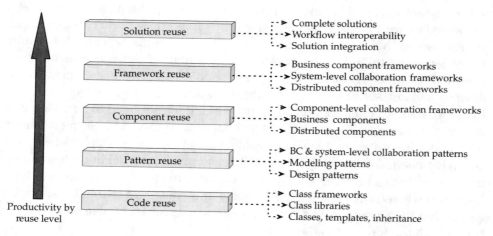

Figure 13.4 Reuse aspects.

reusable assets with the access requirements that implies, the following critical success factors should be addressed:

- Clear responsibilities for the management of the repository, as well as for the individual assets within it, must be defined.

- "Asset noise" must be avoided. A small repository with a few very reusable assets is better than a large repository, which becomes the dumping ground for anything anyone believes may one day be reused somewhere.

- Usability of the repository is key. Unless it is easy and convenient for a user to find what is needed, the repository will not be used. The asset repository must be easily accessible through a useful user interface— today usually using the organization's intranet.

- There must be clear incentives and practical reasons for a developer to use the assets in the repository. We are all human, and we all prefer to be part of the creative process rather than use something created by someone else's creative process. And technical developers are often more human than most.

The main measurement of success for an asset repository is whether people actually use the assets, and this should be measured and reported.

Reuse Process

Traditionally, reuse is approached in two phases: software manufacturing *for* reuse and software manufacturing *with* reuse. Software manufacturing for reuse consists of developing any software artifact explicitly for reuse. This requires that resources and budget must be assigned so that developers take the extra steps needed to ensure that the various software artifacts are of *reusable quality*. The reuse program may prescribe that these steps are executed by a specific reuse organization, rather than by the original producer of the software artifact. Software manufacturing with reuse implies that the organization defines the extra steps in the development process required to ensure that appropriate research and utilization of preexisting software artifacts is done.

To a large extent, this is a natural characteristic of a component-based development process, in which building components is manufacturing for reuse, and assembling is manufacturing with reuse. But when an organization decides to further optimize its development through a reuse program, reuse must become an overriding concern across the manufacturing process.

Reuse aspects are often shown, as illustrated in Figure 13.5, as an x-cycle— so named after the shape of the diagram. This representation extends the v-cycle of Figure 7.1 in Chapter 7, "Development Process," and shows how for each and every development phase in the topmost "V" of the cycle, there is a corresponding reuse phase in the lower half of the cycle. This consists of two aspects: harvesting delivered software artifacts for reuse by other teams and making sure that each phase reuses existing artifacts. No development phase should be started without first having researched the asset repository for appropriate reusable artifacts. This includes even the testing phases, in which particular care may be taken, on one hand, to appropriately test the artifacts to be reused and, on the other, to prepare for reuse and also reuse the testing deliverables, such as testing scripts and testing frameworks.

Reuse Organization

Reuse is not only a matter of technology, architecture, and development processes, but also, most importantly, it is an organizational issue. Two organizational aspects must be addressed: how to involve the development organization in reuse activities and how to set up the organization that will drive reuse, for example, design and administer the asset repository.

No matter how reusable artifacts are, and no matter how easy they are to find, if the organization or individuals are for any reason not willing to reuse,

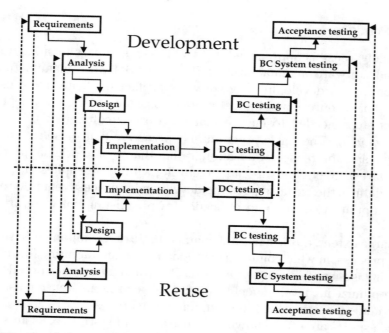

Figure 13.5 X-cycle for reuse.

then the program will fail. To a large extent, the industry favors quick solutions to software problems, and in practice there are very few incentives to widespread reuse. Such incentives must be put in place. A reuse program requires the direct support of senior management, as well as adequate involvement by all parts of the organization. An appropriate incentive system would, for example, reward the producer of a software artifact based on the number of times it is reused.

The organization also requires new roles, which include reuse program management and possibly reuse assurance (perhaps undertaken by one or more people responsible for taking existing software artifacts and bringing them to the level of quality required for reuse). Other roles are related to the asset repository, for example, asset repository management (responsible to the organization for the successful setup and use of the repository, and for its long-term evolution), asset repository administration (responsible for day to day operation of the repository), and asset repository development (provides for installation and technical evolution of the repository software itself, and also possibly for its development). These roles may not require full-time people, and several roles may be undertaken by the same person.

Transition Program

The previous section illustrated the main concepts required for a successful transition to a component-based development. This section describes the overall *characteristics* of a transition program, discusses the major aspects of *knowledge transfer* into the organization, and outlines the *iterations* through which a business component development may go. In this section, it is assumed that a business strategy has been defined, that the IS strategy is in line with the business goals, and that, for both technical and functional development, the IS strategy includes a move to component-based development. This would imply that the business benefits of components have been identified, and it is assumed that the organization now wishes to make a start on a transition to component-based development.

Characteristics

Any serious transition must be explicitly managed through a transition program. A *transition program* is the planned and managed set of activities required to bring an organization from a given level of development maturity with a given set of technologies to a target state of development maturity, usually with a new set of technologies. The program is defined within a given targeted conceptual framework and often requires the management of multiple organizational and individual learning curves. It is important to risk-manage the transition program in the same way as any other software project.

A transition program is likely to have at least some of the following characteristics.

Legacy Migration

A transition program is often coupled with an application migration of legacy systems toward new architectures, technologies, and approaches. While the transition program focuses on bringing the organization from one approach to development (possibly implicit and not well-documented) to another one (in our case, the business component approach), an application migration focuses on bringing the existing information system, or legacy system, to new architectures and technologies. The golden principle of any successful transition program is this:

Always apply the transition to a real-world development problem. The transition is never the final business objective; it is only a means to an end.

In other words, while a transition program aims at moving an organization from one set of development capabilities to another, it is completed only when the organization has not only acquired new capabilities, but has proved their use through successfully producing and deploying production-strength business components to end users.

The right point for a transition may be when an organization decides to migrate its legacy systems to a new technology. This will create the right focus required to make the transition successful. For example, the many organizations that have not yet embraced a distributed system approach will, over the next few years, have to expand their development to e-commerce. This is when many organizations will find it beneficial to move to component-based development.

Varying Time Scales

The transitioning process is highly specific to the transitioning organization. Depending on the size, maturity, budget, strategy, and needs of the development organization, it may involve a five-month effort focusing on a specific bounded and well-defined objective such as the production of a small number of enterprise components with little added on to the component implementation technology, or a set of strategic projects over several years. It is interesting that, on one hand, it has been rare for an organization to accept a transition plan that lasts this long, but, on the other hand, nonplanned transitions usually end up lasting several years and costing more.

Main Entry Points

Most organizations approach the transition to component-based development from one of two main entry points. The first entry point is a methodology deployment, where the organization has been convinced that the prime need is for a methodology, and external experts are often hired to assist in a methodology transition. The second entry point is more architectural in nature, and it may be approached either as the setup of an enterprise-wide architecture or from the more technical point of view of the deployment of a component implementation technology, such as CORBA or Enterprise Java Beans, which rapidly expands into a technical architecture deployment. While the second entry point has a much greater chance of achieving rapid benefits than the first, neither of these selective approaches leads to achieving the full benefits of CBD. All of the five elements described in the section "Concepts" should, at least to some degree, be addressed.

Knowledge Transfer

Any organization embarking on a transition to component-based development may well need assistance from transition experts in growing its internal knowledge base. This assistance is often provided by a consultancy organization, and this section assumes that this is the case. It discusses three important areas of knowledge transfer—initiation, training and mentoring, and joint development—in which such expert assistance can be profitably applied. These areas are usually applied to a number of iterations over time, for the different aspects of the maturity cycle, until the desired levels of software development efficiency are reached. There are, however, some prerequisites to this kind of assistance, and these are discussed first.

Prerequisites

A transition program works best when carried out within a predefined functional development strategy. This strategy should define the long-term goals, budget, constraints, and main milestones of the organization in terms of their functional development, in alignment with the organization's strategic business goals and vision. For example, the strategy could define which kinds of application need to be developed in which timeframes, and the level of efficiency the organization needs to achieve in developing these applications.

The strategy definition may require an assessment of the application development readiness of the organization, and it should also include an indication of overall development approach toward which the organization wants to transition. An initial high-level transition plan defining the budget, constraints, and main milestones of the transition itself should be defined. For example, the transition plan may define that 30 percent of the organization needs to have moved to a certified component-based development approach within 18 months.

Initiation

As its name implies, the initiation area mainly addresses the start of the transition program. The first aspect of any transition is the definition of the detailed transition plan. This is usually done within a given transitioning conceptual framework, for example, the five elements defined in the previous section. The detailed transition plan should define iterations of three to six months (and possibly, even shorter sub-iterations) with clear objectives and deliverables for each phase, and the benefits and success criteria of each iteration should be determined. The objectives of the program are validated as conforming with the strategic functional development goals and also with the overall business strategy.

In the process of formulating the detail plan, some important if often informal initial knowledge transfer can take place. This includes such things as the nature and characteristics of components, how component thinking informs the different architectures, and the main traits of component-based development. Concepts are communicated, and an initial meta-model (formal or informal) defining the main concepts may be started.

Training and Mentoring

Each iteration usually requires a set of training on different subjects, but training is rarely enough, and it needs to be supported by appropriate training camps, mentoring, and pilot projects. A *training camp* is an intense hands-on, instructor-led session or development, which can last from one week to three weeks depending on the topic. It permits the end user to actually apply new concepts in a learning-fostering environment. A training camp may be required for specific topics, such as requirements-gathering techniques, object-oriented analysis and design, or specific technologies such as programming languages and component implementation technologies. Training is usually followed up with *on-site mentoring*, which involves participation of subject experts such as senior architects and technical experts in the day-to-day work of the transitioning organization, typically on one or more pilot projects.

A *pilot project* usually differentiates itself from real development by the potential throw-away nature of the development: The objective of a pilot is risk management and managing the learning curve rather than achieving a real development deliverable at the end. While applying itself to a real-world problem, a transitioning organization should, if possible, choose a development project that is not on the critical path of IS strategic development. Typical criteria for a pilot project include the project being between three and six months long. In order to achieve this, and especially for iterations focused on methodology aspects, it must adopt some simplifying assumptions, for example, that during the pilot the database schema is unchanged, or to focus on functional modeling only, or to aim at a reduced set of features.

Joint Development

Knowledge transfer is significantly assisted when both the transitioning organization and the component experts work together on development. Such joint development usually evolves in two phases. In the first phase, the transitioning organization and the transitioning expert perform a joint development of one or more real functional applications, in which the transitioning expert typically leads the effort in such a way to continue the mentoring and knowledge transfer. Very often, these initial joint developments are used as proof to senior management of the benefits of the transition. Such developments usually target either the modeling aspects or an initial setup of a common technical infrastructure.

In the second phase, the transitioning organization and the transitioning expert partner in the development of one or more real functional applications, but this time it is the transitioning organization team taking the lead, while the transitioning expert works as an architectural and methodological reviewer, is on call to answer to specific challenges, and over time moves away from the fine details of the project. The transitioning organization continues its own development, using the transitioning expert only for specific consulting.

Iterations

The same iterative approach that often informs conventional software development thinking is also applied to the transition process. In this way, risks are better mastered and complexity reduced. Having established the longer-term transitioning strategy and its associated goals, a set of iterations and sub-iterations is defined, with well-defined objectives, exit criteria, and targeted benefits.

Two examples of such sets of iterations are shown in Tables 13.2 and 13.3. The first example, shown in Table 13.2, presents a typical sequence of iterations where the organization chooses to focus on a component factory setup, as a prerequisite for a full functional development. In this case, the initial iteration, composed of sub-iterations 1 to 4 in Table 13.2, is focused not so much on functional aspects, but on properly addressing the risks and learning curves of a factory setup. Each sub-iteration is expected to last three to five weeks on average and has a specific primary focus, following the factory setup aspects illustrated in Part Two of this book. Given this focus, each sub-iteration usually also ex-

Table 13.2   Component Factory Setup First

#	NAME	OBJECTIVE	COMMENT
1	Hello world	Initial set-up	Elementary proof-of-concept, with whatever tools and development environment are available. Setup is short, usually two to three weeks.
2	Technical architecture	Define, implement, and test the technical architecture aspects	Focuses on developing an elementary business component with a reduced number of operations and database tables.
3	Application architecture	Define, implement, and test the application architecture aspects (for example, test the whole error-handling framework)	Focuses on developing two simple but collaborating business components.
4	Project Management Architecture	Define, implement, and test the project management architecture aspects with the explicit objective of setting up and testing the collaboration between teams and concurrent development of business components	Focuses on developing two or three simple but collaborating business components, by two or more different teams.
5	Functional architecture	Initial functional prototype	The first iteration to focus primarily on functional development. From now on, all iterations are mainly focused on building the system.
6	Functional development	Completeness and correctness	Extension of function.
7	Functional development	Completeness and correctness	Extension of function.
8	Functional development	Completeness and correctness	Extension of function.
..	Training camp	Train new developers	An atypical iteration used purely to train new developers without disrupting the main development.

pands (where necessary) on aspects of the previous iteration. For example, an application architecture iteration can also further address and evolve the technical architecture (not shown in Table 13.2).

Table 13.3   Combined Transition

# #	NAME	OBJECTIVE	COMMENT
1 F	Hello functional world	Initial functional training	Training and mentoring on a simple functional problem. Could last two or three weeks.
T	Hello technical world	Initial technical set-up	Same as iteration 1 in Table 13.2.
2 F	Functional architecture version 1	Initial functional architecture definition; first component specification	The overall shape of the component-based system is defined, while at the same time allowing the organization to design in detail one or two components (as per "T" iterations in Chapter 7).
T	Technical architecture	Define, implement, and test the technical architecture aspects	Same as iteration 2 in Table 13.2.
3 F	Functional architecture version 2	Detailed component specification	A number of components are specified in detail.
T	Application architecture	Same as 3 in Table 13.2	Same as 3 in Table 13.2.
4 F	Functional architecture version 3	Additional detailed component specification	More components are specified in detail.
T	Project Management Architecture	Same as 4 in Table 13.2	Same as 4 in Table 13.2.
5	Functional architecture	Initial functional application	First iteration focusing principally on functional development. From now on, all iterations are mainly focused on building the system.
6	Functional development	Completeness and correctness	Extension of function.

Note that sub-iterations from 1 to 4 have no functional goal but are aimed principally at setting up for development, that is, at building or testing the component factory. This phase, required for large-scale development, can easily take 6 to 12 months or possibly more depending on the technologies and scope addressed.

The second example is where the intention is initially to build a component factory and also, in parallel, to address the functional architecture and develop a set of business components to be deployed operationally. In this case, factory setup and functional development are combined (done in parallel). Where the budget allows this approach to be taken (it requires more resources up-front), this is an efficient and lower-risk transition approach. The iterations might appear as shown in Table 13.3, where "F" indicates a functional iteration, and "T" indicates a technical iteration, in an extended meaning of the word "technical" covering all the factory setup aspects. The two aspects of the combined approach are targeted at different profiles in the organization: The functional iterations target functional analysts and functional developers, while the technical iterations allow technical developers to push forward with the factory setup.

The great advantage of this combined approach is that the organization is concurrently exposed to the two most important aspects of a CBD transition, the factory setup and the functional architecture. The two learning curves are managed in parallel, and at iteration number 5, the high-level functional specification having been completed, large-scale functional development can begin. Within any given iteration, each of the five elements in Figure 13.1 can be addressed to some degree. -

A full-blown transition from traditional development to CBD may last a couple of years, but in many cases can be managed such that benefits emerge all along the way. One reason for this length of time is that the transition is usually done concurrently with the on-going migration of the organization's information systems.

Summary

The main objective of a transition to the business component approach is to achieve cost-effective software manufacturing. The transition must address five elements—methodology, best practices, architecture, software factory, and reuse program. These elements are addressed within the conceptual framework of the business component approach.

The methodology element addresses not only the modeling language and development process, but also the set of modeling tools required to support them. It usually includes instantiating a generic methodology to the needs of the transitioning organization. Best practices fill the gap between the instantiated methodology and the day-to-day needs of an efficient software manufacturing organization, and usually include project management, change management, quality assurance, and related subjects.

Architecture concentrates on transitioning the architectural thinking of the organization and setting in place the architectural and infrastructural support required for component development. This is where decisions about such things as portability, interoperability, and similar concerns are addressed. It is also the element through which a specific component implementation technology is deployed.

The software factory is where software manufacturing is brought to efficient levels. Concerns addressed include organizational aspects, such as people management and the setup of a learning organization, knowledge management, and the processes supporting continuous improvement. Finally, the reuse program is where the transitioning organization addresses the need to optimize manufacturing. This is usually achieved through true component reuse, framework reuse, and solution reuse. The reuse program covers the setup of an asset repository, a reuse process, and a reuse organization. In the business component approach, an explicit reuse program is not always required.

For most organizations, moving to the full component-based development implied by the business component approach will need commitment to a properly resourced transition program. The good news is that such a program aims not only at setting up the business component factory for future high-productivity component-based software manufacturing, it also delivers the first business component systems. The transitioning process is iterative in nature. Three areas of knowledge transfer are initiation, training and mentoring, and joint development. Each iteration typically lasts between three and six months, with well-defined objectives and measurement of achieved benefits.

Endnote

1   For more information about the SEI, see www.sei.cmu.edu. A good description of the SEI Capability Maturity Model can be found in [Humphrey 1990].

Naming Conventions

Throughout the book, names such as *eVendor* are used in examples, and names such as "r-tier" and "EDC" are used for various kinds of software artifacts. The conventions used are as follows:

- Names for specific artifacts in the various examples are in italics, for example, a *Vendor* business component.

- Names for business components have no prefix and start with an upper-case letter, for example, *OrderManager*.

- Names for distributed components start with a lowercase prefix indicating the tier, for example *eOrderManager*. The set of lowercase prefixes used for various artifacts and names is shown in Table A.1. These prefixes can be combined.

- Uppercase prefixes are used with acronyms, for example, to distinguish among DCs according to which tier they implement, and are shown in Table A.2.

- Identifiers in pseudo-code examples follow the OMG's IDL Style Guide [OMG 1998b]. The guidelines for identifiers are briefly summarized in Table A.3.

Table A.1 Lowercase Prefixes

PREFIX	DESCRIPTION
bt	Business data type. For example, the identifier *btInvoice* is the "invoice" business data type.
d	Base data type. For example, *dCurrencyValue* is the currency value base data type; *dDecimal* is the decimal base data type.
e	The name is that of an enterprise tier artifact. For example, *eVendor* is the name of an artifact in the e-tier (enterprise tier).
i	The name of an interface. For example, *ieVendor* is the name of an interface to a *Vendor* enterprise-tier DC.
r	The name of an artifact in the r-tier (resource tier).
t	The name of an artifact used for testing. For example, *teVendor* is a testing DC for the *eVendor* EDC.
t_	The name of a table in an island of data; for example, "t_Customer" is the Customer table in the *Customer* business component's island of data.
u	The name of an artifact in the u-tier (user tier)
w	The name of an artifact in the w-tier (workspace tier)

Table A.2 Uppercase Prefixes

PREFIX	DESCRIPTION
U	User. For example, a UDC is a DC in the u-tier.
W	Workspace. For example, WDC is a DC in the w-tier.
E	Enterprise. For example, an EDC is a DC in the e-tier.
R	Resource. For example, an RDC is a DC in the r-tier.
P	Persistence or persistent. For example, a PLC is a Persistent Language Class.
T	Testing. For example, a TDC is a testing DC.
B	Pertaining to business. For example, a BLC is a Business Language Class.

Table A.3 Pseudo-code Identifiers

IDENTIFIER	DESCRIPTION
Interface, struct, enum, union, and exception names	Mixed case, beginning uppercase, no underscores; however, single-letter lowercase prefixes are allowed (this is a deviation from the OMG's style guide). For example: ieVendorCollection.
Operation, attribute, parameter, and structure member names	Lowercase with underscores. For example, get_address(…).
Enum values and constants	Uppercase with underscores. For example, **TAG_NAME**.

Glossary

Access point.   Any software artifact (or combination of software artifacts) that, at any moment in the development lifecycle of the component, from any architectural viewpoint, or at any distribution tier, is exported by the component. To an observer of the component, such an artifact provides an access point to the component, at which access point that artifact is available for import.

ACID.   Atomicity, Consistency, Isolation, Durability—the required properties of a transaction, described by Grey and Reuter as follows. "Atomicity: A transaction's changes to the state are atomic: either all happen or none happen. . . . Consistency: A transaction is a correct transformation of the state. The actions taken as a group do not violate any of the integrity constraints associated with the state. . . . Isolation: Even though transactions execute concurrently, it appears to each transaction, T, that others are executed either before T or after T, but not both. Durability: Once a transaction completes successfully (commits), its changes to the state survive failures." [Grey 1993, p. 6]

Address space.   The memory space supported by an operating system within which any memory address is either valid or invalid. Often called a process. Operating systems today support multiple address spaces concurrently. On Wintel systems, for example, when a program (a .exe file) is run, the operating system starts up a new process—that is, allocates a new address space—within which the program is run.

BC. Business component.

BCSM. Business component system model.

BCVM. Business component virtual machine.

BLC. Business language class.

Business component. The software implementation of an autonomous business concept or business process. It consists of all the software artifacts necessary to represent, implement, and deploy a given business concept as an autonomous, reusable element of a larger distributed information system.

Business component assembly. The closed set of business components on which a given business component depends.

Business component factory. An efficient software development capability able to cost-effectively and rapidly mass-produce, in a repeatable way, high-quality business components satisfying functional and extra-functional requirements.

Business component system. A composition of business components across one or more functional layers that constitutes a viable system.

Business component system model. A model representing the business components in a business component system, together with their interdependencies.

Business component virtual machine. The implementation of the technical architecture. It includes the set of development tools and run-time deliverables that enable business components to be built and run independently of underlying plumbing and software technology considerations.

CBD. Component-based development.

CEE. Component execution environment.

Closed layer. The term *closed layer* indicates a "separation layer" or "hiding layer."

Closured dependency list. A versioned dependency list that includes all indirect dependencies.

Component. A self-contained piece of software that can be independently deployed and plugged into an environment that provides a compatible socket. It has well-defined and network-addressable run-time interfaces, and it can cooperate out of the box with other components.

Component-based development. A software development approach where all aspects and phases of the development lifecycle, including requirements analysis, architecture, design, construction, testing, deployment, the supporting technical infrastructure, and the project management are based on components.

Component diagram. A graphical representation of the components in a system, implicitly representing the dependencies among them.

Component execution environment. The run-time technical infrastructure, services, and facilities required to provide the appropriate separation layer for distributed components and to enable business components to collaborate. A major objective of the component execution environment is to hide low-level technology issues from the functional developer.

Component implementation technology. A commercially-available component middleware technology and its associated connectivity capabilities. Examples are an implementation of the CORBA Components specification, EJB (Enterprise Java Beans), Microsoft's COM and DCOM, MOM (Message-Oriented Middleware) products, and transaction management products such as BEA's M3.

Component instance. The run-time instantiation of a distributed component (DC).

Component-level dependency list. A dependency list used to identify only the required components, and no other software artifacts.

Consistency set. A closured dependency list whose components are known to work with each other and thus constitute a consistent set.

CORBA. Common Object Request Broker Architecture.

CORBA IOR. CORBA Interoperable Object Reference—the name given to a network-addressable reference as defined by CORBA.

COTS. Commercial Off-The-Shelf. For example, "COTS software" is software available on the market and maintained by the supplier.

CRUD. Create, read, update, and delete. Used to indicate the typical maintenance-oriented interfaces for components.

CSL. Component specification language.

DBA. Database administrator.

DBMS. Database management system.

DC. Distributed component.

Dependency list. The dependency list of a component *Foo* identifies the set of all the components on which *Foo* depends, as well as the detailed software artifacts implementing each dependency. See also component-level dependency list, detailed dependency list, closured dependency list, and versioned dependency list.

Deploy. To ship, distribute, test operationally, and install. This term covers everything from release by development of a tested component to its live running on possibly multiple systems.

Detailed dependency list. A dependency list showing all required software artifacts.

Dimension. A dimension (as in "the five dimensions of the business component approach") is a specific combination of viewpoints, patterns, and concepts that is useful in thinking about the business component approach. The approach itself can be thought of as consisting of material, temporal, and conceptual aspects. Each of the five dimensions is a particular way of "viewing" (or better, thinking about) the business component approach.

Distributed component. A design pattern for an autonomous software artifact that can be deployed as a pluggable binary component into a runtime component execution environment. This design pattern is normally implemented using a commercially available component implementation technology. When a DC is implemented, the resulting software component is called a *distributed component implementation*. The term *DC* is normally used for both the design pattern and the implementation, unless the context requires a distinction to be made.

Distribution tier. See "tier."

Domain. (Used without qualification) An industry sector such as manufacturing, insurance, banking, telecommunications, etc.

EDC. Enterprise distributed component.

EJB. Enterprise Java Beans.

Enterprise component. A component used to resolve an enterprise-level problem.

Enterprise resource domain. The logical area of concern, as seen by the functional developer, that is responsible both for protecting the integrity of resources shared among a number of potentially concurrent requesters and for providing services to requesters. The scope of the ERD is that area capable of providing ACID transactions through an underlying resource manager such as a DBMS or a TPM. This is a logical domain, not a physical one, and from a business component viewpoint comprises its enterprise and resource tiers. Often the ERD is wholly physically located on a server system.

ERD. Enterprise resource domain.

ERP. Enterprise resource planning.

Extended interface. A collection of access points to a component.

External system release. A business component system version that is deployed or released to the end user. It is a consistent set of versioned business components assembled to the required level of proven quality and packaged together with a set of deliverables often not required for internal releases, such as user guides, install tools, and so forth.

FAA. Federation architecture and assembly, the manufacturing process for the federation.

FAQ. Frequently asked questions.

Functional. Relating to function that is directly relevant to business logic or data, as opposed to technical system infrastructure concerns or to application architecture concerns.

Functional designer. An IS professional whose main task is the design of applications, including placement of business function, algorithm definition, etc.

Functional developer. A general term applying to either or both functional design and functional programming.

Functional programmer. An IS professional whose main task is program code design and implementation of business function, application algorithms, and related activities.

GUI. Graphical user interface.

IDL. Interface definition language.

Intra-operability. A term used to indicate the interoperability problem within the boundaries of a single system.

IOR. See CORBA IOR.

Language class. A class in an object-oriented programming language.

Layer. See Closed Layer, Open Layer.

LC. Language class.

Modeless. A *modeless component* is a component whose functional operations can be meaningfully invoked in any sequence at any time. For example, many order-entry systems require that an order header is entered before any order line. This business rule is ingrained into the system: It is not possible, say, to enter an order line before creating the order header. In modeless order entry, order details can be entered in any sequence, so that an order line could be created whether or not the order header has been created.

Module. A physical file that is loadable into the run-time and capable of being executed. That is, a module consists of compiled and linked code (when written in a language that must be compiled and linked before being executed). An example of a module is a Windows DLL or EXE file.

NC. Network computer.

Network addressable. A software artifact that has an identified run-time address visible to other executables over the network.

OLTP. Online transaction processing.

OMG. Object Management Group.

OOPL. Object-oriented programming language.

Open layer. When used in the context of a business component, the term *open layer* indicates a "direction of dependency." For example, if the business component layers A, B, C are shown one on top of each other, this does not mean that B "hides" A from C, but that B depends on things in A but not on things in C. C may depend on things in A directly. Cf. *Closed layer*.

ORB. Object request broker.

PLC. Persistence language class.

Persistence language class. A data-only class used to contain data that is to be read/written from/to a persistent store.

Property page. A user-interface control with the look of a dialog box, but having a tab. Used within a property sheet.

Property sheet. A user-interface control containing one or more property pages.

Protocol.   The system of fixed rules and accepted behavior that governs the means of talking and interacting between information systems, that is, it governs the cohesive set of interactions that can cross the boundaries of an information system.

RCD.   Rapid component development, the manufacturing process for development of individual components.

RDBMS.   Relational database management system.

RDC.   Resource distributed component.

RSD.   Rapid system development, the manufacturing process for combined development of individual components and the system assembled out of these components.

SAA.   System architecture and assembly, the manufacturing process for architecture and assembly of a business component system.

Singleton.   A singleton instance is an instance of some component where the semantics of the component allow only a single instance to exist within a given scope. The given scope is that in which the component is unambiguously recognized. Thus where a server process is cloned across multiple processes and machines for load-balancing purposes, there may physically be multiple singleton instances of a given component in the system.

SLC.   System-level component.

Software component.   See component.

Tier.   A logical area of distributed system responsibility within a business component. Defined tiers are User, Workspace, Enterprise, and Resource.

TPM.   Transaction Processing Monitor.

Transaction.   Unless otherwise stated, "transaction" means an ACID transaction, such that the underlying transaction manager ensures either that all changes are committed or that no change is made.

UDC.   User distributed component.

UI.   User interface.

UML.   Unified modeling language.

User workspace domain.   (UWD) The logical area of concern, as seen by the functional developer, that is responsible for supporting a single human being through a presentation device, normally a GUI. This is a logical domain, not a physical one, and from a business component viewpoint comprises its user and workspace tiers. Often the UWD is physically located wholly on a PC.

UWD.   User workspace domain

Versioned dependency list.   A dependency list that shows the version numbers of all components in the list.

WDC.   Workspace distributed component.

WFM.   Workflow management.

XIDE.   Extended integrated development environment.

Bibliography

Abadi, Martin and Luca Cardelli. *A Theory of Objects*. New York, NY: Springer-Verlag, 1996.

Allen, Paul and Stuart Frost. *Component-Based evelopment for Enterprise Systems*. Cambridge, NY: Cambridge University Press, 1998.

Aranow, Eric. *Business Architecture as a Roadmap for Enterprise Distributed Computing*. Presentation to OMG, 1998. See www.reuse.com.

Becket, Samuel. *Waiting for Godot*. New York, NY: Grove Press, 1954.

Boehm, B. W. *Software Engineering Economics*. Upper Saddle River, NJ: Prentice-Hall, 1981.

Booch, Grady. *Object-Oriented Analysis and Design with Applications*. Reading, MA: Addison-Wesley, 1994

Booch, Grady; James Rumbaugh; and Ivar Jacobson. *The Unified Modeling Language User Guide*. Reading, MA: Addison-Wesley, 1999.

Computer Associates International, Inc. Platinum Aion Product Brochure. CAI 1999. See www.platinum.com/products/brochure/als/b_aion.htm

Coad, Peter; David North; and Mark Mayfield. *Object Models: Strategies, Patterns, and Applications*. Englewood Cliffs, NJ: Yourdon Press, Prentice-Hall, 1995.

Coleman, Derek; Patrick Arnold; and Stephanie Bodoff. *Object-Oriented Development*. Prentice Hall, 1993.

Cox, Brad J. and Andrew J. Novobilski. *Object-Oriented Programming: An Evolutionary Approach, Second Edition*. Reading, MA: Addison-Wesley, 1991.

Date, Chris J. *An Introduction to Database Systems*. Reading, MA: Addison-Wesley, 1995.

D'Souza, Desmond and Alan Cameron Wills. *Objects, Components, and Frameworks with UML: The Catalysis Approach*. Reading, MA: Addison-Wesley, 1998.

Eeles, Peter and Oliver Sims. *Building Business Objects*. New York, NY: John Wiley & Sons, 1998.

Esposito, Dino. "COM Objects with Scripting Languages." *Microsoft Developer Network (MSDN)*, http://msdn.microsoft.com/developer/news/devnews/novdec98/xmlscripts.htm, November 2, 1998.

Gamma, Erich; Richard Helm; Ralph Johnson; and John Vlissides. *Design Patterns: Elements of Reusable Object-Oriented Software*. Reading, MA: Addison-Wesley, 1995.

Grand, Mark. *Patterns in Java, Volume 1: A Catalog of Reusable Design Patterns Illustrated with UML*. New York, NY: John Wiley & Sons, 1998.

Grey, Jim and Andreas Reuter. *Transaction Processing: Concepts and Techniques.* San Francisco, CA: Morgan Kaufmann, 1993.

Hammer, Michael and James Champy. *Reengineering the Corporation: A Manifesto for Business Revolution.* New York, NY: HarperBusiness, 1993.

Harder, Theo and Andreas Reuter. "Principles of Transaction-Oriented Database Recovery." *ACM Comp Surv.* 15, No. 4 (December 1983)

Harold, Elliotte Rusty. *XML: Extensible Markup Language.* Foster City, CA: IDG Books Worldwide, 1998.

Hay, David C. *Data Model Patterns: Conventions of Thoughts.* New York, NY: Dorset House Publishing, 1996.

Henderson-Sellers, Brian and J. M. Edwards. *Book Two of Object-Oriented Knowledge: The Working Object: Object-Oriented Software Engineering: Methods and Management.* Upper Saddle River, NJ: Prentice-Hall, 1994.

Herzum, Peter and Oliver Sims. "The Business Component Approach." *Business Object Design and Implementation II : OOPSLA '96, OOPSLA '97, OOPSLA '98 Workshop Proceedings.* Eds. Dilip Patel, Jeff Sutherland, and Joaquin Miller. London, UK: Springer-Verlag, 1998.

Hollocker, Charles P. *Software Reviews and Audits Handbook.* John Wiley and Sons, 1990.

Humphrey, Watts S. *Managing the Software Process.* Reading, MA: Addison-Wesley, SEI Series in Software Engineering, 1990.

Humphrey, Watts S. *A Discipline for Software Engineering.* Reading, MA: Addison-Wesley, SEI Series in Software Engineering, 1995.

ISO 4217:1995. *Codes for the Representation of Currencies and Funds.* An ISO standard.

Jacobson, Ivar; Magnus Christerson; Patrik Jonsson; and Gunnar Overgaard. *Object-Oriented Software Engineering.* Reading, MA: Addison-Wesley, 1992.

Jones, Capers. *Applied Software Measurement: Assuring Productivity and Quality.* New York, NY: McGraw-Hill, 1991

Jones, Capers. *Assessment and Control of Software Risks.* Upper Saddle River, NJ: Prentice-Hall, 1994.

Kaner, Cem; Jack Falk; and Hung Quoc Nguyen. *Testing Computer Software.* 2nd ed., New York, NY: John Wiley & Sons, 1999

Mullender, Sape, ed. *Distributed Systems.* Reading, MA: ACM Press—Frontier Series, Addison-Wesley, 1993.

Myers, Glenford J. *Art of Software Testing.* New York, NY: John Wiley & Sons, 1979.

Object Management Group (OMG). "Business Object Facility." www.omg. org, document number: bom/971103 (SSA submission to the OMG Business Object RFP). 1997a.

Object Management Group (OMG). "UML Semantics version 1.1." www. omg.org, document number ad/97-08-04. 1997b.

Object Management Group (OMG). "Common Business Objects." White paper, www.omg.org, document number bom/97-12-04. 1997c.

Object Management Group (OMG). "CORBA Messaging—Joint Revised Submission." www.omg.org, document number: orbos/980505.

Object Management Group (OMG). "OMG IDL Style Guide." Document number: ab/98-06-03. 1998b.

Object Management Group (OMG). "Tagged Data Facility." www.omg.org, document number: orbos/98-12-06 (SSA submission to OMG's "Tagged Data" RFP). 1998d.

Object Management Group (OMG). "CORBA 2.2 Specification." www.omg.org, document number: formal/98-07-01. 1998e.

Object Management Group (OMG). "XMI SMIF Revised Submission." www.omg.org, document number: ad/98-10-07. 1999f.

Object Management Group (OMG). "CORBA Finance Currency Specification." www.omg.org, document number: formal/98-12-06. 1998g.

Object Management Group (OMG). "CORBA Components." www.omg.org, document number: orbos/99-07-01, 02 and 03 (joint submission to OMG's "Components" RFP). 1999a.

Object Management Group (OMG). "BODTF White Paper: Business Object Concepts." www.omg.org, document number: bom/99-01-01. 1999b.

Object Management Group (OMG). "Workflow Management Facility." www.omg.org, document number: bom/99-03-01. 1999c.

Orfali, Robert; Dan Harkey; and Jeri Edwards. *The Essential Distributed Objects Survival Guide*. New York, NY: John Wiley & Sons, 1996.

Orfali, Robert; Dan Harkey; and Jeri Edwards. *Client/Server Survival Guide*. 3rd ed. New York, John Wiley & Sons, 1999

Prins, Robert. *Developing Business Objects: A Framework Approach*. Maidenhead, England: McGraw-Hill, 1996.

Riemer, Karsten. *A Process-Driven, Event-Based Business Object Model*. Object Management Group (OMG), www.omg.org, document number: bom/98-11–02.

Rosen, Michael; David Curtis; Dan Foody. *Integrating CORBA and COM Applications*. New York, NY: John Wiley & Sons, 1998.

Schneider, Geri. *Applying Use Cases: A Practical Guide*. Reading, MA: Addison-Wesley, 1998.

Senge, Peter. *The Fifth Discipline: The Art and Practice of the Learning Organization*. New York, NY: Currency Doubleday, 1990.

Sessions, Roger. *Object Persistence: Beyond Object-Oriented Databases*. Upper Saddle River, NJ: Prentice-Hall, 1996.

Sessions, Roger. *COM and DCOM: Microsoft's Vision for Distributed Objects*. New York, NY: John Wiley & Sons, 1998.

Siegel, Jon. *CORBA Fundamentals and Programming*. New York, NY: John Wiley & Sons, 1996.

Sims, Oliver. *Business Objects*. New York, NY: McGraw-Hill 1994.

Sims, Oliver. "What a Difference a GUI Makes," *Object Expert*, September/October 1995: page 10.

Sims, Oliver. "The First Flush of GUI-ness—and Why It Shouldn't Last." *Object Expert*, November/December 1996: page 20.

Sims, Oliver. "Where to Split—The Fatal Question." *Object Expert* January/February 1997: page 58.

Sommerville, Ian. *Requirements Engineering*. New York, NY: John Wiley & Sons, 1997.

Sommerville, Ian and Pete Sawyer. *Software Engineering*, 3rd ed. (Later editions exist.) Reading, MA: Addison-Wesley, 1989.

Stroustrup, Bjarne. *The C++ Programming Language* (Later editions exist.) Reading, MA: Addison-Wesley, 1993.

Stroustrup, Bjarne. *The Design and Evolution of C++*. Reading, MA: Addison-Wesley, 1994.

Sun Microsystems. Preface to Sun JVM Specification at SunSite, Department of Computing, Imperial College, UK, http://sunsite.doc.ic.ac.uk/java-corner /vmspec/. 1999.

Szyperski, Clemens. *Component Software: Beyond Object-Oriented Programming*. Reading, MA: Addison-Wesley, 1998.

Whitgift, David. *Methods and Tools for Software Configuration Management*. New York, NY: John Wiley and Sons, 1991.

Wirfs-Brock, Rebecca; Brian Wilkerson; and Lauren Weiner. *Designing Object-Oriented Software*. Englewood Cliffs, New Jersey: Prentice Hall, 1990.

World Wide Web Consortium. *Extensible Markup Language (XML) 1.0-W3C Recommendation 10-February-1998*. www.w3.org/TR/REC-xml.html.

Workflow Management Coalition. *Workflow Reference Model*. Document TC00-1003 issue 1.1. 1995. www.wfmc.org.

Index

Page references followed by italic *t* indicate material in tables. Page references followed by italic *n* indicate material in footnotes, with the note number indicated.